LINES OF
SUCCESSION

HERALDRY OF THE ROYAL FAMILIES
OF EUROPE

TABLES BY
JIŘÍ LOUDA

TEXT BY
MICHAEL MACLAGAN

**BARNES
&NOBLE**
BOOKS
NEW YORK

*To my wife, Jára, for the countless silent evenings
and weekends during which this book was created*

Jiří Louda

This edition published by
Barnes & Noble, Inc., by arrangement with
Time Warner Books (UK)

2002 Barnes & Noble Books

This book is adapted from *Lines of Succession*, published in 1999

ISBN 0-7607-3287-6

Production by Omnipress, Eastbourne
Printed in Singapore

Time Warner Books UK
Brettenham House, Lancaster Place
London WC2E 7EN

The publishers would like to thank the following for providing the illustrations on the
pages listed below:

Ampliaciones Reproducciones, Mas, Barcelona 63 (Museo del Prado, Madrid); BBC
Hulton Picture Library, London 79, 108, 128; Bibliotèque Nationale, Paris 10;
Bibliotèque Royale, Albert I, Brussels 179; Bildarchiv Preussischer Kulturbesitz, Berlin
174 (Gemäldegalerie, Dresden); British Library, London 25, 185, 186; Caisse Nationale
des Monuments Historiques, Paris 8; Collection Viollet, Paris 175 (Gemäldegalerie,
Dresden); Danish Ministry of Foreign Affairs, Copenhagen 45; Det Nationalhistoriske
Museum, Frederiksborg 56; Giraudon, Paris 133 (Musée Condé, Chantilly);
Kunsthistorisches Museum, Vienna 142; Mansell Collection 100 (Museo del Prado), 114
top, 114 bottom, 197, 211; Musée de l'Armée, Paris 135; Ostereichische
Nationalbibliothek, Vienna 36; Popperfoto, London 32; Reproduced by gracious permis-
sion of Her Majesty the Queen 51, 168; Rijksmuseum, Amsterdam 73; Statens
Konstmuseer, Stockholm 207; Svenska Porträttarkivet Nationalmuseum, Stockholm 58

CONTENTS

FOREWORD

Genealogy is perhaps as old as the history of the human race itself. Ever since the hazy beginnings of organized human society the powerful have kept records of their ancestors. The Bible contains a fine collection of lineal descents of several outstanding personages, even of Jesus Christ himself, and although they are now hardly regarded as indisputable historical evidence, they certainly prove that genealogy has always stood in the forefront of interest for many people, being for some a time-honoured science and for others an exciting pastime.

As soon as heredity in the leadership of human tribes became a more or less established principle, it was obviously of the utmost importance for the aspiring leader to show that he was lineally descended from the former leaders and rulers. It is true that originally many nations adopted their rulers on the basis of an election, but even then it was customary to elect to the supreme post someone who was related, however remotely, to the previous prince. Both England in Saxon times and Bohemia under the Přemyslids are excellent examples. To prove this records had to be kept, and often falsified. When primogeniture became an accepted method of succession to the thrones and crowns, it was even more important to maintain records and charts showing all the branches and members of the reigning House, often together with a very intricate relationship to other princely Houses. That such charts and records were often twisted and abused so that they would suit an ambitious pretender was of course the result of his ardent desire or the sycophancy of his servants.

These sycophantic record-keepers and chroniclers were often busy tracing the descent of their sovereigns beyond any purely human origin in order to show them not only as rulers 'by the grace of God' but even as actual demi-gods. This can be seen in the old pedigrees of the ancient Saxon Kings of Wessex, where the chroniclers were trying to prove that the Kings were descended from the pagan storm-god Woden. It may seem surprising that people in the early days of Christianity were impressed by the doubtful fact that their pious sovereign had for his ultimate ancestor a member of the numerous family of heathen gods, but we should realize that the mind of the common people was still under the spell of heathen legends and customs for centuries after their conversion to Christianity.

What is probably less surprising is the fact that sovereigns prided themselves upon the most illustrious of their ancestors. It became a fashion to show that everybody whose brow was adorned (or burdened, whichever you prefer) by a crown descended from a famous, potent and ever victorious monarch such as Charlemagne. One of the Tables in this book shows the descent of all the present European sovereigns from William the Conqueror, who before the conquest of England called himself defiantly 'the Bastard'. Yet exactly the same Table would also show that the crowned heads of Europe descend from a forgotten tanner of Falaise whose daughter had the historical good luck to have been seduced by Robert the Devil, Duke of Normandy.

Many a haughty sovereign in past centuries tried hard to forget about his less illustrious ancestors, and yet if even a single one of them, no matter how low his style, had not lived, the haughty sovereign himself would never have been born to sway his mighty sceptre. Even today historians often discuss the Hanoverian heritage, to good or bad effect, in Queen Victoria's blood while no one seems to take into consideration the fact that she was just as much a descendant of the Counts of Erbach, and their moods and spirits, as she was of the rulers of Hanover.

Nevertheless, the study of genealogy is inseparable from the study of history. While not denying that economic, national and other deep reasons were the cause of many an important and basic change in the history of mankind, we must also accept that genealogical background can and must be sought as an explanation of many medieval and even later wars and other events. This has always been an easy excuse and reason for publishing genealogical books and Tables all over the world.

The present book ranks itself with a large number of genealogical works and yet it is not simply a repetition of what has already been collected and printed. There are several genealogical books in which fuller dates, and as far as possible all the branches of the European princely Houses, are given. A good example of this is, among others, a German handbook, Prince von Isenburg's *Stammtafeln*. Such absolutely complete genealogical Tables have, however, a very serious disadvantage; they are invariably and unavoidably so complicated that they lose much of their instructiveness. Moreover, not everybody wants the Tables encumbered with the names of dozens of children who died in their early infancy, or women who died unmarried without ever achieving anything spectacular, except having been born with a princely coronet. Furthermore, these books usually show all the respective Houses without too clear a stress on their succession in various countries. Yet, apart from deposed dynasties, princely Houses have never lived in a territorial vacuum; they were closely tied to a certain country. I have also tried to distinguish whether a death was a natural one or whether the person in question was accidentally killed, murdered, slain in a battle or even executed; there were times in practically all countries when natural death was almost an exception among the princes. Precisely this distinction is often omitted in other genealogical works.

On the other hand, there are genealogical Tables and books which are clear enough, but which in their information omit not only many dates and titles but also even names of members of collateral branches in spite of their eventual importance.

I have tried to take a middle path. The Tables are arranged according to the individual countries, the existing monarchies taking precedence, and not according to dynasties, although they are always clearly marked. Some of the former minor principalities in Germany and elsewhere have not been included: it can hardly be argued that for example, the Princes of Schwarzburg, although no doubt sovereigns, ever played a big role, either militarily or genealogically, in the history of Europe. However, all the former kingdoms of Europe are treated in sufficient detail, while for all German and Italian grand-duchies, and some duchies, at least a general survey is given.

For several practical reasons the eleventh century

has been taken as the earliest starting point. When necessary, the text gives an outline of the dynastic development prior to that dateline. The names given in the Tables are necessarily only a selection, but a much wider one than is usually found in historical handbooks. Omitted are those persons who played no important part in the history of Europe (i.e. most of the unmarried women) or persons who died very young without having been regarded as eventual heirs. Sometimes even women whose marriages were of no great importance or who remained without issue had to be excluded for lack of space or for the preservation of clarity. Children of married princesses are shown only when they played some role in the succession to the throne of the given country. The same ruling has been applied to natural children. The detailed Tables are preceded by Tables which give a general survey of practically all the male members of all the reigning Houses in each country, with an indication in which of the following Tables detailed information can be obtained. Lineal descent of the present sovereign or head of the House from the most remote ancestor is shown by a red line. Reigning sovereigns in each country are marked by a small crown next to their name (the actual crown used for this purpose having no other significance).

A word ought perhaps to be said about the spelling of names. The practice not only in Britain but in almost every other country is sadly confused. While some of the names are kept in their native form, such as the Carols of Rumania or Juans of Spain, others are 'translated' into English or the author's language. I have never in an English book read about a Johann or Karl in Germany, a Nikolai in Russia or a Georgios or Pavlos in Greece. In order to avoid what I have always felt to be a sort of discrimination, all the names in this book have been anglicized wherever it is possible. A compromise had, however, to be made for some names in some countries when the original name is too familiar to be dismissed – such as the Manuels in Portugal.

Apart from the usual type of genealogical Tables two other types are included. In one, a genealogical background is shown for various historical events, such as for the Wars of the Roses, the Union of Kalmar, or the Wars of the Spanish Succession. In the other, the descent from eight ancestors, called 'eight quarters' (i.e. three generations back), of some of the more outstanding or interesting princes is traced. This helps to show some of the little-known or even claimed forebears of the person in question.

In this the present book resembles other published works. There are, however, two features in which it differs considerably. Most people feel that genealogy and heraldry are two disciplines which are most closely related. Both the College of Arms in London and the Court of Lord Lyon in Edinburgh issue fine genealogies richly adorned and enlightened by coats-of-arms. Yet there has been no work to do the same for the whole of Europe, that is for the European reigning Houses. In this book I have considered heraldry to be an indispensable part of the genealogical Tables; the coats-of-arms illustrated here show the changes which went hand-in-hand with the various matrimonial alliances or territorial acquisitions or losses, or rise in rank.

Naturally it has not been possible to include the arms of all the persons listed in the Tables but only a relatively narrow selection. Nevertheless, the arms of almost all consorts of sovereigns have been illustrated, the arms of the sovereigns themselves being shown when they changed from the previously used form. I must, of course, warn the reader that in central Europe, and even elsewhere, several forms of arms were often in use by more than one person at the same time, in contrast with the one and only legal form used in Britain. In countries where differencing for cadets of the princely Houses is in practice, as wide a selection of the marks of cadency as possible has been made. It is in this sense that the book is a history of the regal heraldry of Europe.

The Tables with general surveys show two types of arms. On top, usually the original simple arms of the country or dynasty are reproduced, while below the latest form of the arms of the monarchy, with the proper crown and highest order of chivalry but without the supporters, is displayed. Supporters can, however, be seen in the line drawings at the chapter openings. The larger scale in which the arms accompanying the general survey Tables are drawn has enabled me to show the so-called 'greater' arms, with numerous quarterings (such as in Prussia, Naples etc.). Such complicated arms would be almost unreadable on the small shields in the detailed Tables, where a simpler form of arms is usually shown.

The other difference from any similar previous publication is the textual part. I have always felt that in spite of the fact that genealogical Tables speak for themselves, there are many facts which cannot find their way into the actual Tables and yet need to be mentioned and explained in one way or another. It can hardly be expected that by reading a haphazard historical book together with following a genealogical Table one would find all the explanations needed. In no history of Russia, for instance, can you find more than perhaps a mention of some of the several branches of the House of Rurik and their succession. A combination of genealogical Tables, illustrated with shields of arms and accompanied by a text which describes in words what the Tables leave untold, should fill a wide gap in literature of this sort.

Mr Michael Maclagan, CVO, Richmond Herald and Senior Fellow of Trinity College in Oxford, both an expert historian and a scholar in heraldry, who agreed to write such a text, has created a history book which makes fascinating reading in itself. I am very much indebted to him for his suggested corrections and amendments to my Tables. Without the close and friendly co-operation which has so happily existed between us I could hardly have hoped to see the book as it now is.

My gratitude goes, of course, to several people whose unselfish and untiring help enabled me to assemble all the material for such a vast enterprise. Years ago, Charles, Prince of Schwarzenberg, opened the treasures of both his library and knowledge to me, and most of the heraldry in these pages can really be traced to his friendly help. Nevertheless, when the actual work started, numerous question marks appeared, and if now few blank spaces remain in the following pages, it is due to the generous advice of the late M. Meurgey de Tupigny, President of the French Heraldic and Sigillographic Society, Mr G. Scheffer, Chamberlain and Herald of Sweden, M. Roger Harmignies, Mr Roger Pye of Oporto, expert in Portuguese heraldry, and many other scholars in different countries.

As for the section covering Britain, it is impossible not to mention the inexhaustible patience of the late Mr R.P. Graham-Vivian, MVO, MC, formerly Norroy and Ulster King of Arms, Mr J.P. Brooke-Little, CVO, the present Norroy and Ulster King of Arms, and the late Mr D. Pottinger, LVO, Islay Herald, who, in spite of their several and burdensome duties, have always found time to search for missing information and showed great interest in the progress of my work.

And last but not least, I am very much indebted to the skill of the publishers who have made it possible for such an extensive work to be produced at all, and I owe a special debt to Mr Martin Heller for his enthusiastic support throughout.

Finally, I should like to say that the study of history leads to the study of genealogy and heraldry and vice versa. When combined, none of these three is a dull affair. The medieval battlefields of Europe were – in spite of all the savage slaughtering – grand scenes of heraldic display where gaily coloured banners, shields of arms and surcoats worn over the armour proudly announced their owners' might. No princely marriage would ever have been complete without pompous heraldic pageantry, and when the people laid their princely leaders to their final rest, heraldry again played, and still plays, an important part in the funeral rites. If this book helps to show that history, by means of genealogy and heraldry, can be made an interesting and even thrilling study, I shall be happy that I have not been working in vain.

Chapter 1

INTRODUCTION TO HERALDRY

The practice of heraldry, as we understand it, arose in western Europe in the middle of the twelfth century. It comprises the use on a shield of patterns which are definable, recognizable and hereditary. There were probably two principal causes for this development. In the first place, helmets were covering more and more of the wearer's face making his identification in battle difficult. Secondly, increasing employment of documents called for a visual means of authentication; in an age when literacy was almost confined to the clergy, a seal was more use than a signature. To reproduce on the seal the same pattern as that on the shield was commonplace.

Most of our early evidence of heraldry comes from seals. Several English heraldic seals survive from around 1140. The arms of Savoy (Table 97) are found in 1149, those of the Count of Provence, which were the same as Aragon (Table 45), in 1150, those of Henry the Lion, Duke of Saxony (Table 85), in 1144. Many other early seals must have perished, but these examples demonstrate that heraldry was already an international manifestation. One exciting testimony from France is earlier and not sigillary: the famous enamel preserved at Le Mans appears to show the blazon of Geoffrey Plantagenet (d.1151) (Table 2). It is quite clear that the growth of heraldry answered a general need in the feudal societies of the twelfth century. It is also at least possible that its similarity in different countries was furthered by encounters on the organized crusades or in the Holy Land. Certainly warfare in the heat of Palestine encouraged the wearing of a linen covering or surcoat over the chainmail of the day; it was an easy and an obvious step to repeat on this the pattern from the shield; and from this is derived the English phrase 'coat-of-arms'.

To write thus about the beginnings of heraldry is not to deny that seals with some sort of device had been in use for centuries and that emblems, often of an animal kind, had been associated with units or peoples – the lion of the tribe of Judah, the eagle of the Roman legion or the crescent of Islam. It is also the case that very soon after heraldry started – and it could not be said to be established until numerous families had used a distinctive blazon for several generations – men began to invent coats-of-arms for people who had lived long before, for biblical characters, for kings and saints like Edward the Confessor (Table 63), or heroes of romance like Arthur, Charlemagne or Godfrey de Bouillon.

Certain basic laws were common to all countries. The hues available were divided into two main classes. The 'metals' were gold and silver, often, as in this volume, portrayed by yellow and white; and the 'colours' were red, blue, black, green and purple, of which the first three were by far the most often used. A third, and scarcer, class were 'furs' of which ermine (Table 64: Brittany) was the commonest. If the background of the shield, called the 'field', was of a metal, then the objects thereon, known as 'charges', must be of one of the colours and vice-versa. Either colour or metal could be placed on a fur. This rule was not unbreakable: it was deliberately flouted in devising a blazon for the Kingdom of Jerusalem (Table 90 and elsewhere) as a tribute to the sanctity of the city. Other breaches are recorded, not least in eastern Europe (Table 103: Narishkin or Razumovski, or 95: Douglas). An early convention allowed a background of mixed colour and metal to count as either (Table 2: Marshall). Not only individuals or families used coats-of-arms; they could be employed by countries, towns, bishoprics and, later on, by merchant companies, religious orders or any corporate body.

In England the upper classes spoke Norman-French at this time, and therefore the blazons were

The 12th-century enamel of Geoffrey of Anjou at Le Mans, one of the earliest pieces of heraldic evidence.

today: Moravia – 'Azure, an eagle displayed checky argent and gules, beaked, membered and crowned or', and Bourbon – 'Azure, semé of lys, a bend gules.' It will be seen that a 'bend' (French *bande*) is in fact a straight diagonal stripe; similarly an upright one is a 'pale' and transverse ones are 'bars'. In the other realms of western Europe, in Germany, France, Spain or Italy, the descriptions of heraldry are nearer to normal speech.

In many cases it is not known how a particular family acquired or chose its coat-of-arms; often it must have been a whim or accident. A certain number of basic geometric patterns clearly reflect strips of wood or leather affixed to the shield to strengthen it. Many others represent a play upon words. Easy examples are the blazons of Bowes-Lyon (Table 9) or of Castile and Leon (Table 47). Yet others may indicate regional or feudal fashions; there is a strong concentration of coats-of-arms with lions on barry fields or barry lions in the old province of Lotharingia (Limburg, Luxembourg, Hesse and so on); the 'tressure' with its fleurs-de-lys is commoner in Scotland than elsewhere (Table 13). In the animal world the eagle and the lion were regarded as the kings of birds and beasts, and were accordingly popular. The eagle grew in esteem as it became to be associated with empire, but was also used by quite humble families. From the start, the lion was portrayed in two basic postures: he was 'rampant' as he rose on one foot to strike, he was 'passant' when he ran across the shield from left to right, most often in a group of three (Table 1: England, Table 15: Denmark). In the Middle Ages the upright beast was simply called a lion; when he ran, he was a 'leopard'. It must be emphasized that, in describing the right and the left of a shield, one speaks as though wearing it, not from the viewpoint of the beholder. An early variant form was the lion with two tails (Table 2: Montfort).

DIVIDING THE SHIELD

Early in the story of heraldry, the problems posed by alliances, inheritance and large families began to make themselves felt. One pristine solution was dimidiation, that is to divide two shields vertically and unite half of each, but this could lead to bizarre results. Soon the simpler device of 'impalement' was evolved which represented the whole of each coat-of-arms on half a shield; the arms of the husband were normally represented on the right, or 'dexter' side. This was particularly the case in England and France, where bishops also used to 'impale' the arms of their diocese; but in Germany impalement often indicates the union of two lordships rather than a definite marriage, and

described in that tongue. As English developed into the national speech in the fourteenth and fifteenth centuries, the language of heraldry remained strongly infected with French terms and became increasingly esoteric. This tendency was fostered by the heralds in the sixteenth and seventeenth centuries, who were as anxious to have their own peculiar parlance, not easily comprehended by the layman, as the doctor, the lawyer or the parliamentary draftsman. As far as possible, this specialized terminology has been eschewed in the pages which follow; it has the advantage of being precise to the expert. As illustrations, two blazons follow for shields, as they would be described in England

bishops more often quarter their own arms with those of their See. In fact, the arrangements for 'marshalling' more than one coat-of-arms are apt to differ from country to country. It was, however, general practice that, when a ruler inherited two territories, as it might be one from his father and another through his mother, he divided his shield into four and placed his paternal blazon in the first and fourth quarters while that of his mother decorated the second and third. The earliest known illustration of this idea occurs in the combined arms of Castile and Leon on Table 47.

As a family began to build up dynastic power, it probably made many profitable alliances and acquisitions. A shield of four seconds was no longer enough. There is no limit to the number of divisions on a single shield; but in England it is normal to speak of 'quarterly of six', or eight, or sixty-eight, while on the Continent the nature of the divisions is specified. In England, also, representation of an heiress (that is, a woman without brothers) is common; in Scotland, and abroad, small attention was paid to her arms, unless she also brought land. In Germany, in particular, the extensive quartered coats tend to indicate a great aggregation of lordships (Table 84) with the actual family arms on a small shield in the middle, 'an escutcheon in pretence', or 'over all'. On the Continent, also, the terms 'sixteen quarterings', or 'thirty-two quarterings', had a specialized meaning. They did not signify that an individual represented that number of families or had acquired that number of fiefs, but that *all* his ancestors (male and female) for five or six generations backwards were of noble birth. Sets of eight shields, showing great-grandparents, are frequent in these Tables. The stern laws governing dynastic marriages in Germany and Austria (Chapter 22) made such a boast much more common than in England, where society was relatively fluid.

Naturally enough some form of control over the usages of a blazon became essential. This duty was assigned by a gradual process in the fourteenth and fifteenth centuries to the heralds, officers whose main functions hitherto had lain in the spheres of diplomacy and the tournament. Thus the general name 'heraldry' was born. One of their main duties was to avoid as far as possible the use by two different families of the same shield. In England a *cause célèbre* in the reign of Richard II concerned the rival claims of Scrope and Grosvenor to 'Azure, a bend or'. The fact that the Bohemian family of Count Thun of Hohenstein bore the same arms was as irrelevant as much of the other evidence offered. Rather more surprising is the fact that the important family of de Ligne in

Hainault and the rulers of Baden both bore 'Or, a bend gules' from the Middle Ages to today without exciting conflict.

Different countries found different solutions for the problems of the younger brother and the younger son, one charge, the 'label' (a narrow horizontal line across the top of the shield with three, four or five pendants dropping from it), was mostly confined to the shields of minor members of a family. It is relatively certain that it was originally a cord with tags which could be removed when necessary. In England (Table 3) and in Portugal (Table 93) labels became exceedingly elaborate. But other cadels of great families used a border (or 'bordure') and a small bend (or 'bendlet') as a mark of 'difference'. In France the bendlet was perhaps more popular than in England. Bastardy was sometimes signified by a bend from left to right, though this could be an innocent charge as in the Folkunga arms (Table 27). The French for a 'bend sinister' was *une barre*, which probably inspired the popular British myth of the '*bar* sinister', to mean illegitimacy.

ESSENTIAL DIFFERENCES

The heraldic connoisseur can often guess at the nationality of an unknown coat-of-arms, but may find his opinion no easier to explain than the difference between Claret and Burgundy. To indicate some possible characteristics is not to ignore the many common features in all realms or the incidence of migrants and 'rogues' in any grouping.

It is not easy to distinguish between the heraldry of France and England, which stemmed from a common root. French blazon did not pass through so marked a phase of complexity as did English in the sixteenth century, and never, perhaps, indulged in so lavish a display of quarterings. On the other hand the heraldry of the Bourbons was abruptly cut off by the Revolution, to be replaced by the orderly but artificial Napoleonic system (Chapter 16). Scotland boasts, it may be claimed, the most logical and systematic control of arms of any country and is still, heraldically, discrete from England. Great use is made of the bordure as a difference, often with many charges on it.

In the Iberian peninsula the shield itself is almost always drawn in a rather square shape. Hence it comes that a pattern of six charges will be arranged in three pairs (Table 92: Castro) and not in ranks of 3, 2 and 1 as is more usual. Considerable use is made of elaborate bordures (Table 47: Molina, Table 52: Moscoso) and also of letters (Table 95: Mendoça). The combination of two shields in one by a diagonal cross, or 'saltire',

(Table 46: Sicily, Urgel) is usually Spanish. An interesting Hispanic charge is the cauldron (Table 48 or 96: Guzman) which appears in many noble blazons. In the first instance, this was a mark of nobility denoting the ability to feed a contingent. The animals which appear from the pot are today usually blazoned as serpents, but may have begun life as the more palatable eel. Another most distinctive Spanish charge (Table 48) is the bending issuing from two lions' mouths.

The early heraldry of Germany shows a certain predilection for bold geometric patterns (Table 80: Hohenzollern). The popularity of the eagle led to the development of the 'bearing', or device, called a *kleestengel* (clover-stalk), on its breast, which could itself have an addition made to it; it was in origin probably only an artistic definition of the breastbone of the eagle.

A feature of Teutonic heraldry is the display of a large number of quarterings representing the fiefs held by the family; normally they were those which gave the right to one vote in the Diet of the Empire. On a smaller shield in the centre would be placed the arms of the family itself (often the same as its oldest or original estate) though there are exceptions. Among the quarterings is sometimes found one of plain red ('gules'); this is the 'Blut-Fahne' or 'Regalien' quartering (Table 87: Saxony) and was thought to indicate the ownership of royal prerogatives, personally bestowed by the emperor. It is a common artistic practice in Teutonic lands where there are lions disposed on both sides of the shield to make those on the 'dexter' or right, face inwards. This would not be done in France or Britain.

Italy was so fragmented that it is difficult to write cohesively of her heraldry. In Naples, Spanish influence not surprisingly made itself felt. The tree is perhaps more frequent than elsewhere; another highly typical charge is the mount, often triple, at the base of the shield, a feature which also occurs in the arms of Hungary 'modern'. Italian families often added a 'chief' (the top slice of the shield) of the Empire or Anjou to display Guelph or Ghibelline sympathies. In Poland a number of original and unusual charges appear, which have sometimes been derived from Scandinavian runes: crosses and arrows spring from horseshoes or from geometrical shapes (Table 100: Krasiński). Russian heraldry was not a natural growth, and shows signs of laboured invention: military emblems abound, as might be expected in an aristocracy which was originally one of service (Table 103: Apraxin or Razumovski).

The emphasis throughout these Tables is on the

The King of Arms for Brittany in an ermine tabard (the blazon of his duke) presents a roll of arms to the Duke of Bourbon sitting on a mantle of his own arms. MS of c.1460–5.

shield, for the shield with its blazon is the central feature of heraldry. None the less from the earliest days knights also used, especially in tournaments, a 'crest', a single object bound to their helmets with a wreath of twisted silk. As the pageantry of heraldry developed, differing coronets and helmets were introduced for the varying degrees of rank, and 'supporters' to uphold the shield became common. Below the shield might appear a motto or *cri de guerre*. The whole assembly of heraldic pride is known as an 'achievement' and for reigning Houses is often backed by a mangle or pavilion. Illustrations of such achievements appear at the head of many of the chapters which follow. The 'boast of heraldry' was indeed part of the 'pomp of power', but it is also a vivid and illuminating shorthand to dynastic history.

Chapter 2

ENGLAND: MEDIEVAL

'What! will the line stretch out to the crack of doom?'
Macbeth IV.I

England and Scotland have known many dynasties of rulers. Table 1 shows in outline the descent of the present Queen from Duncan, King of Scotland, and William the Conqueror of England, and the union of the two countries in the person of James I. The Scottish kings on the left are derived from characters who figure in Shakespeare's *Macbeth*; the rulers of England stem from William, Duke of Normandy, who won the Crown and the country at the decisive Battle of Hastings in 1066. Neither Duncan nor William has left direct male descendants but their blood has reached Queen Elizabeth II through a number of female links, links which brought other families – Stuart, Plantagenet, Tudor and so on – to the thrones of one or both realms.

The history of England goes back far beyond the reign of William I. South of Hadrian's Wall, the island had formed part of the Roman Empire, and then had been largely overrun by Teutonic invaders from northern Germany. These Anglo-Saxon barbarians had driven many of the original Celtic inhabitants towards the west and had seized control of the flatter, richer lands of south and east England, lands which throughout our history have been a temptation to raiders from the Continent. At first there were a number of separate Anglo-Saxon kingdoms, but from time to time outstanding rulers gained a brief supremacy; of such were Ethelbert of Kent, the first Christian king, at the end of the sixth century, or Offa of Mercia at the end of the eighth. The unity of England was accelerated by the need to resist a fresh series of invasions, by the Vikings who sailed from their Scandinavian homes to plunder, and later to settle, along the coasts of England and France.

Resistance to these invaders was led by Alfred, King of Wessex roughly the area south of the Thames – in fierce fighting at the end of the ninth century. For a hundred years his descendants were rulers of England. But troubled times came again at the beginning of the eleventh century; Danish and West Saxon kings both reigned, and there was no accepted system of succession. The death without children of the saintly but ineffectual Edward the Confessor left the way open for new contenders. At Hastings the Englishman Harold was defeated by the Duke of Normandy.

Since then England has been ruled by six families, not one of which could be called English by name. The Normans were succeeded by the Plantagenets who stemmed from Anjou, in central France. At the end of the Wars of the Roses the last Plantagenet king, Richard III, was overthrown by the Welshman, Henry Tudor. His family endured only for three generations; and Elizabeth I was followed by her Scottish cousin, James I and VI, in 1603. Thereafter England and Scotland shared the same ruler. Then, in 1714, George I, Elector of Hanover, arrived from Germany and the next five kings were of Teutonic stock. Queen Victoria married Prince Albert of Saxe-Coburg and Gotha, another German royal family; and our present Queen has married the Duke of Edinburgh who in male descent derives from the Danish dynasty (Table 109). Thus, the people of England early became used to the idea that the Crown could pass through a woman and that a queen could reign over them, ideas which have never been acceptable to (for example) the French.

The early history of Scotland is lost in mists of obscurity. The northern part of the country was inhabited by the Picts, whose origin is still debated. Much of the south was peopled by Celts, but to these were added Scandinavian and Anglo-Saxon settlers

TABLE 1

GREAT BRITAIN
General survey

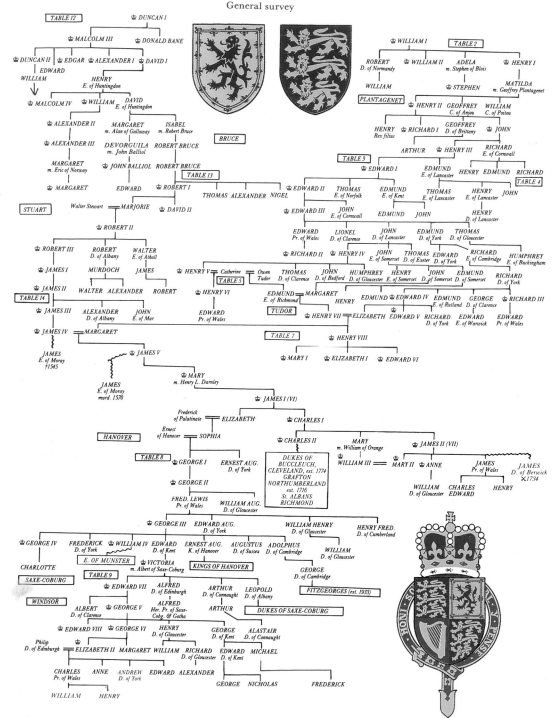

from the east and Irish from the west. It is one of the ironies of history that the very name 'Scot' is derived from a tribe originally settled in what today would be called Ulster.

At the head of Table 1 are the two shields of arms associated with Scotland and England; their story will be discussed in more detail later. They were not united until 1603, and even then were linked with the arms of France for another 200 years. It was also in 1603 that the harp, which symbolizes Ireland, was introduced into the royal arms, though the Kings of England had been Lords of Ireland since the twelfth century. Wales, which was conquered by Edward I of England, has never figured in the royal shield, though it appears in that of the Prince of Wales (Table 9). At the bottom of Table 1 are the arms of Queen Elizabeth II, encircled by the riband of the Garter, as they have been borne by every monarch since 1837. They are the arms of the country over which she reigns, rather than those of the Queen herself, and are flown wherever the Queen is in residence in England. In Scotland they appear in a different form; the upright lion of Scotland figures twice, in the first and fourth quarters, and the three running lions of England only feature once, in the second quarter.

THE NORMAN INVASION

In 1066 Duke William of Normandy conquered England. He claimed to be the heir to his cousin, Edward the Confessor, and regarded Harold as an usurper. In consequence there were two facets to his reign. He preserved much of what was best in former English government, including for example the shire system. But there was an almost complete change-over in the ownership of estates; the land-hungry followers of Duke William replaced the Anglo-Saxon or Danish proprietors. Two new features were at once apparent up and down the countryside, the mounted Norman knight and the Norman castle on its artificial hillock.

Who were these Normans? Their ducal family and most of their aristocracy were descended from Danes who settled near the mouth of the Seine under their leader Rollo in 911. It is probable that the stalwart resistance of Alfred deflected many Viking invaders from England to the less defended shores of France. In any case a substantial body of 'Northmen' soon gave their name to the district of Normandy, and rapidly acquired a polish of French chivalry and language.

William I made a stern and powerful king. He loved hunting and cleared part of Hampshire to make the New Forest. Rebellion in the north was savagely repressed, and the countryside devastated. Towards the end of his reign he carried out an exhaustive survey of his kingdom, village by village and county by county. The result, the Domesday Book, is an authoritative record which has no parallel to this day. When he died, he bequeathed Normandy to his firstborn, Robert, and England to his second son, William Rufus, so-called from his red face.

As has been seen in Chapter I, heraldry was unknown at this time. The shield shown for William I (Table 2) was not actually used by him in his lifetime; that displayed for his wife, Matilda of Flanders, was associated later with her kinsfolk. No coat-of-arms is known for Henry I. That shown for his son-in-law Geoffrey Plantagenet, is based on the beautiful enamel at Le Mans. Part of the shield is here hidden from the viewer, and it is uncertain whether the number of lions was intended to be six or seven; it is suggestive that one of Henry II's illegitimate children used six similar lions.

Henry I, a vigorous and able monarch, succeeded in winning both England and Normandy to his rule. He did not, however, succeed in persuading his subjects to accept his daughter as his heiress after his only legitimate son had been drowned. Matilda was haughty and her second husband, Geoffrey of Anjou, was not popular. On the death of Henry I, the barons of England chose Stephen as their king in preference to Matilda; but much of Stephen's reign was consumed in civil warfare between them. Matilda was at one point proclaimed queen, but she was never crowned; eventually it was agreed that her son should succeed at the death of Stephen. It is from this juncture that the Crown of England begins to pass by hereditary descent.

Henry II, son of Matilda and acknowledged heir of Stephen, had a long and splendid reign. In England he was keenly interested in justice; and his legal reforms effectively established a common law throughout the length and breadth of the land, with judges going on circuit as they do today. But he governed a much wider area than England. He naturally inherited Anjou; he had won back Normandy before he came to England; he became the Lord of Ireland; in addition he made a splendid match by marrying the heiress of the Duke of Aquitaine. With her extensive lands in his control, his realm had its northern frontier on the Tweed and the southern at the Pyrenees; but for all his territory in France – Normandy, Anjou and Aquitaine – he was a subject of the French king and not an independent ruler. This position led to many complications and caused the fortunes of England to be closely entangled with those of France for 400 years.

It is during the reign of Richard I, a romantic figure but a feckless and absentee king, that the well-known arms of England appear. Richard's first seal only shows part of the king's shield on which is a single upright ('rampant') lion; the whole shield may have exhibited two such lions. However, on his second great seal (1198) the whole shield is clearly visible, portraying three running lions with their heads turned towards the beholder; this has been the blazon of England from that day to this.

At Richard's death his younger brother John seized the throne, though some would have preferred their nephew Arthur. John almost certainly had Arthur murdered. He had considerable ability but lacked any capacity to make himself liked; towards the end of his reign a group of the nobility, exacerbated by their sovereign's caprice and by heavy taxation, compelled John to seal Magna Carta, the most famous charter of liberties in the history of the English people.

John's son, Henry III, continued to use the three leopards as his coat-of-arms. His younger brother, Richard, Earl of Cornwall, was a rich and ambitious man who sought in vain to secure effective election as Emperor of Germany. He devised his own shield (Table 2) of a red lion rampant within a black border dotted with gold discs (*bezants*, so called from the coinage of Byzantium). The lion may refer back to the first seal of Richard I; the gold discs (*poix*) allude to his French county of Poitou. As has been suggested, many early shields were linked with a play upon words of this character.

Like his father, Henry III failed to keep on good terms with his subjects. The opposition to him, at the end of his very long reign, was led by his brother-in-law, Simon de Montfort. His shield shows a lion with two tails; the popularity of the lion as a charge was already leading to ingenious variations. The struggle was protracted, and towards the end of it (1265) Simon de Montfort caused to be assembled what was perhaps the first English Parliament.

The reign of Edward I (Table 3) was important for several reasons; he was one of the most robust and forceful of English rulers. He carried to conclusion the conquest of Wales; and then gave to the Welsh, as he is said to have promised, a prince who could speak no English – his infant son Edward, the first Prince of Wales. He attempted, but in vain, to conquer Scotland. He waged long wars against the King of France, seeking to recover the full inheritance of Henry II, of which John and Henry III had lost considerable portions. The King and his advisers carried through a great volume of legislation, an achievement which, coupled with his arduous campaigning, has caused him to be called the English Justinian. Of more lasting significance were the steps taken under his guidance in the evolution of Parliament. Here he learned from the ideas of his uncle Simon.

Edward II married Isabel, the only daughter of Philip IV of France. The shield of the latter shows an example of dimidiation. Philip had three sons, but no grandsons, and thus Isabel could be regarded as his heiress (Table 62). As her son, Edward III proceeded to claim the throne of France itself; this was a more thorough and drastic step than any attempt to regain the lost provinces of his ancestors. In 1340 he symbolized this claim by uniting the arms of France with those of England. As a compliment to France, he placed the gold lilies in a blue field in the first (and fourth) quarters of his new shield and the leopards of England in the second and third. From this date until 1801 the rulers of England continued to style themselves Kings of France and show the French lilies somewhere on their shield.

THE HUNDRED YEARS' WAR

At first Edward III's war went well. A great naval victory at Sluys (1340) was followed by triumphs on land at Crécy (1346) and Poitiers (1356). He founded the Order of the Garter, the greatest surviving order of chivalry in the world. Its motto *Honi soit qui mal y pense* (Ashamed be he who thinks ill of it) may refer to the legendary Countess of Salisbury – though at this date ladies did not usually wear garters – but may with greater likelihood allude to his claims on the French Crown. At almost the same time, the pestilential Black Death spread disaster over Europe. The heavy mortality (probably more than a third of the population of England perished) contributed to social disorder and the Peasants' Revolt in the next reign (1381). The campaigns in France languished, and the King, grown senile, died in an atmosphere of unrest after his long and at times glorious reign.

The problem of distinguishing cadet members of the royal family can easily be seen on Table 3. The label and the bordure were the devices mainly employed in England. Down to and including Edward III the eldest sons of the ruler seem to have used a blue label of three points. Accordingly a white (or silver) label could be used for another son, as it was for Thomas of Brotherton, Earl of Norfolk. Edward the Black Prince, eldest son of Edward III, changed to a white label in 1340, presumably because a blue label would not have shown up well over the blue arms of France. Ever since then the eldest son has used a white label during the lifetime of the sovereign (see the shield of Prince Charles at the bottom of Table 9). The Black Prince, so-called from the colour of his armour, never came to the throne. His original shield, helmet and surcoat can still be seen over his tomb at Canterbury, splendid examples of fourteenth-century craftsmanship.

His next three brothers all used labels of various designs, but the youngest, Thomas, Duke of Gloucester, used a plain bordure. Other royal princes had used bordures before; the shield of John of Eltham on his effigy in Westminster Abbey is one of the master-

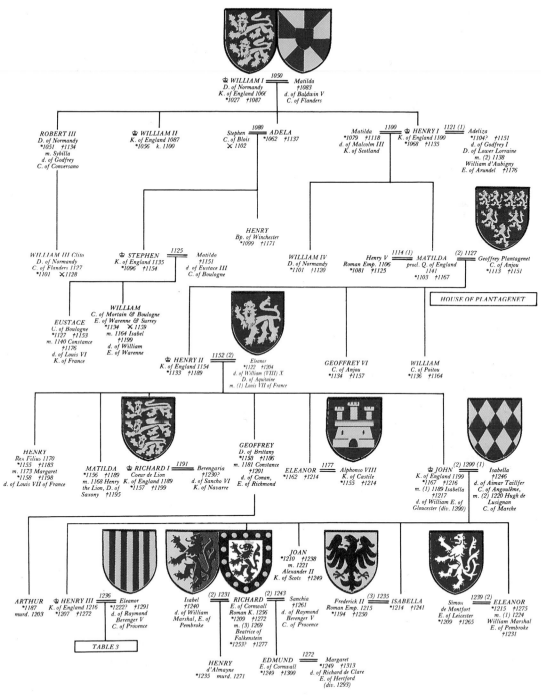

♚ WILLIAM I
D. of Normandy
K. of England 1066
*1027 †1087
═ 1050 ═
Matilda
†1083
d. of Baldwin V
C. of Flanders

ROBERT III
D. of Normandy
*1051 †1134
m. Sybilla
d. of Godfrey
C. of Conversano

♚ WILLIAM II
K. of England 1087
*1056 k. 1100

Stephen
C. of Blois
✕ 1102
═ 1080 ═
ADELA
*1062 †1137

Matilda
*1079 †1118
d. of Malcolm III
K. of Scotland

♚ HENRY I
K. of England 1100
*1068 †1135
═ 1100 ═
═ 1121 (1) ═
Adeliza
*1104? †1151
d. of Godfrey I
D. of Lower Lorraine
m. (2) 1138
William d'Aubigny
E. of Arundel †1176

HENRY
Bp. of Winchester
*1099 †1171

WILLIAM III Clito
D. of Normandy
C. of Flanders 1127
*1101 ✕1128

♚ STEPHEN
K. of England 1135
*1096 †1154
═ 1125 ═
Matilda
†1151
d. of Eustace III
C. of Boulogne

WILLIAM IV
D. of Normandy
*1101 †1120

Henry V
Roman Emp. 1106
*1081 †1125
═ 1114 (1) ═
MATILDA
procl. Q. of England
1141
*1103 †1167
═ (2) 1127 ═
Geoffrey Plantagenet
C. of Anjou
*1113 †1151

HOUSE OF PLANTAGENET

EUSTACE
C. of Boulogne
*1127 †1153
m. 1140 Constance
†1176
d. of Louis VI
K. of France

WILLIAM
C. of Mortain & Boulogne
E. of Warenne & Surrey
*1134 ✕ 1159
m. 1164 Isabel
†1199
d. of William
E. of Warenne

♚ HENRY II
K. of England 1154
*1133 †1189
═ 1152 (2) ═
Eleanor
*1122 †1204
d. of William (VIII) X
D. of Aquitaine
m. (1) Louis VII of France

GEOFFREY VI
C. of Anjou
*1134 †1157

WILLIAM
C. of Poitou
*1136 †1164

HENRY
Rex Filius 1170
*1155 †1183
m. 1173 Margaret
*1158 †1198
d. of Louis VII of France

MATILDA
*1156 †1189
m. 1168 Henry
the Lion, D. of
Saxony †1195

♚ RICHARD I
Coeur de Lion
K. of England 1189
*1157 †1199
═ 1191 ═
Berengaria
†1230?
d. of Sancho VI
K. of Navarre

GEOFFREY
D. of Brittany
*1158 †1196
m. 1181 Constance
†1201
d. of Conan,
E. of Richmond

ELEANOR
*1162 †1214
═ 1177 ═
Alphonso VIII
K. of Castile
*1155 †1214

♚ JOHN
K. of England 1199
*1167 †1216
m. (1) 1189 Isabella
†1217
d. of William E. of
Gloucester (div. 1200)
═ (2) 1200 (1) ═
Isabella
†1246
d. of Aimar Taillfer
C. of Angoulême,
m. (2) 1220 Hugh de
Lusignan
C. of Marche

JOAN
*1210 †1238
m. 1221
Alexander II
K. of Scots †1249

ARTHUR
*1187
murd. 1203

♚ HENRY III
K. of England 1216
*1207 †1272
═ 1236 ═
Eleanor
*1222? †1291
d. of Raymond
Berenger V
C. of Provence

Isabel
*1240
d. of William
Marshal, E. of
Pembroke
═ (2) 1231 ═
RICHARD
E. of Cornwall
Roman K. 1256
*1209 †1272
m. (3) 1269
Beatrice of
Falkenstein
*1253? †1277
═ (2) 1243 ═
Sanchia
†1261
d. of Raymond
Berenger V
C. of Provence

Frederick II
Roman Emp. 1215
*1194 †1250
═ (3) 1235 ═
ISABELLA
*1214 †1241

Simon
de Montfort
E. of Leicester
*1209 †1265
═ 1239 (2) ═
ELEANOR
*1215 †1275
m. (1) 1224
William Marshal
E. of Pembroke
†1231

TABLE 3

HENRY
d'Almayne
*1235 murd. 1271

EDMUND
E. of Cornwall
*1249 †1300
═ 1272 ═
Margaret
*1249 †1313
d. of Richard de Clare
E. of Hertford
(div. 1293)

TABLE 3

ENGLAND
Plantagenets and the Hundred Years' War

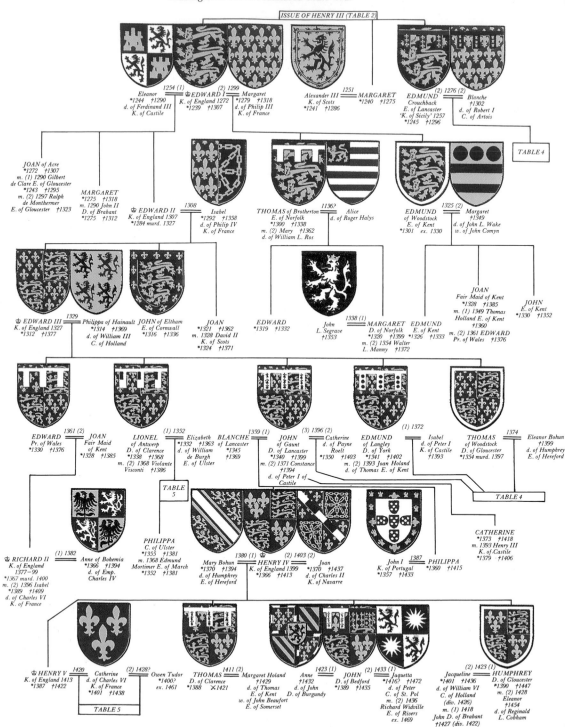

ISSUE OF HENRY III (TABLE 2)

Eleanor
*1244 †1290
d. of Ferdinand III
K. of Castile
1254 (1) ⚚ EDWARD I
K. of England 1272
*1239 †1307
1299 (2) Margaret
*1279 †1318
d. of Philip III
K. of France

Alexander III
K. of Scots
*1241 †1286
1251 MARGARET
*1240 †1275

EDMUND
Crouchback
E. of Lancaster
'K. of Sicily' 1257
*1245 †1296
1276 (2) Blanche
†1302
d. of Robert I
C. of Artois

TABLE 4

JOAN of Acre
*1272 †1307
m. (1) 1290 Gilbert
de Clare E. of Gloucester
*1243 †1295
m. (2) 1297 Ralph
de Monthermer
E. of Gloucester †1323

MARGARET
*1275 †1318
m. 1290 John II
D. of Brabant
*1275 †1312

⚚ EDWARD II
K. of England 1307
*1284 murd. 1327
1308 Isabel
*1292 †1358
d. of Philip IV
K. of France

THOMAS of Brotherton
E. of Norfolk
*1300 †1338
m. (2) Mary †1362
d. of William L. Ros
1136? Alice
d. of Roger Halys

EDMUND
of Woodstock
E. of Kent
*1301 ex. 1330
1325 (2) Margaret
†1349
d. of John L. Wake
w. of John Comyn

⚚ EDWARD III
K. of England 1327
*1312 †1377
1329 Philippa of Hainault
*1314 †1369
d. of William III
C. of Holland

JOHN of Eltham
E. of Cornwall
*1316 †1336

JOAN
*1321 †1362
m. 1328 David II
K. of Scots
*1324 †1371

EDWARD
*1319 †1332

John
L. Segrave
1338 (1) MARGARET
D. of Norfolk
*1320 †1399
m. (2) 1354 Walter
L. Manny †1372

EDMUND
E. of Kent
*1326 †1333

JOAN
Fair Maid of Kent
*1328 †1385
m. (1) 1349 Thomas
Holland E. of Kent
†1360
m. (2) 1361 EDWARD
Pr. of Wales †1376

JOHN
E. of Kent
*1330 †1352

EDWARD
Pr. of Wales
*1330 †1376
1361 (2) JOAN
Fair Maid
of Kent
*1328 †1385

LIONEL
of Antwerp
D. of Clarence
*1338 †1368
m. (2) 1368 Violante
Visconti †1386
(1) 1352 Elizabeth
*1332 †1363
d. of William
de Burgh
E. of Ulster

BLANCHE
of Lancaster
*1345 †1369
1359 (1) JOHN
of Gaunt
D. of Lancaster
*1340 †1399
m. (2) 1371 Constance
†1394
d. of Peter I of
Castile
(3) 1396 (2) Catherine
d. of Payne
Roelt
*1350 †1403

EDMUND
of Langley
D. of York
*1341 †1402
m. (2) 1393 Joan Holand
d. of Thomas E. of Kent
(1) 1372 Isabel
d. of Peter I
K. of Castile
†1393

THOMAS
of Woodstock
D. of Gloucester
*1354 murd. 1397
1374 Eleanor Bohun
†1399
d. of Humphrey
E. of Hereford

TABLE 5

TABLE 4

PHILIPPA
C. of Ulster
*1355 †1381
m. 1368 Edmund
Mortimer E. of March
*1352 †1381

(1) 1382 Anne of Bohemia
*1366 †1394
d. of Emp.
Charles IV
⚚ RICHARD II
K. of England
1377–99
*1367 murd. 1400
m. (2) 1396 Isabel
*1389 †1409
d. of Charles VI
K. of France

Mary Bohun
*1370 †1394
d. of Humphrey
E. of Hereford
1380 (1) HENRY IV
K. of England 1399
*1366 †1413
(2) 1403 (2) Joan
*1370 †1437
d. of Charles II
K. of Navarre

John I
K. of Portugal
*1357 †1433
1387 PHILIPPA
*1360 †1415

CATHERINE
*1373 †1418
m. 1393 Henry III
K. of Castile
*1379 †1406

⚚ HENRY V
K. of England 1413
*1387 †1422
1420 Catherine
d. of Charles VI
K. of France
*1401 †1438
(2) 1428? Owen Tudor
*1400?
ex. 1461

THOMAS
D. of Clarence
*1388 ×1421
1411 (2) Margaret Holand
†1429
d. of Thomas
E. of Kent
w. of John Beaufort
E. of Somerset

Anne
†1432
d. of John
D. of Burgundy
1423 (1) JOHN
D. of Bedford
*1389 †1435
1433 (2) Jaquetta
*1416? †1472
d. of Peter
C. of St. Pol
m. (2) 1436
Richard Widville
E. of Rivers
ex. 1469

Jacqueline
*1401 †1436
d. of William VI
C. of Holland
(div. 1426)
m. (1) 1418
John D. of Brabant
†1427 (div. 1422)
(2) 1423 (1) HUMPHREY
D. of Gloucester
*1390 †1447
m. (2) 1428
Eleanor
†1454
d. of Reginald
L. Cobham

TABLE 5

pieces of medieval art. Both a label and a bordure might be necessary, as in the case of Richard, Earl of Cambridge, younger son of the Duke of York (Table 4). It did not follow that a man would use the same arms all his life. John of Gaunt, in the latter part of his life, put forward a claim to the throne of Castile in right of his wife: he therefore abandoned his ermine label, and added the arms of Castile and Leon to his own. Richard II, son of the Black Prince, an artistic but on the whole unsuccessful monarch, had a more unusual whim; he impaled with his own arms the mythical blazon attributed to Edward the Confessor (who in fact lived and died before the age of heraldry), and allowed the same privilege to some of his kinsfolk, including Thomas Mowbray. Richard's composition can be seen on the Wilton Diptych in the National Gallery, London, and in Table 63. At the end of his reign, Richard, the reputed inventor of the handkerchief, showed signs of mental unbalance and tyranny. His cousin Henry invaded the country and was accepted as Henry IV.

This accession was, however, an act of violence. The descendants of Lionel of Clarence also had a claim; several of Edward III's sons had married wealthy English heiresses and established powerful families. Another future complication was caused by the private life of John of Gaunt. During the lifetime of his second wife he had several children by Catherine Roelt. Eventually he married her, but their offspring, who bore the name of Beaufort (Table 4), were not legitimate. They were later legitimized, but specifically not for the inheritance of the Crown. After their legitimation they bore the arms of England with a bordure of blue and white sections. Geoffrey Chaucer was a brother-in-law of Catherine Roelt. His greatest poem, the *Canterbury Tales*, written in the closing years of the fourteenth century, is a reminder that one of the results of the war against France was a gradual substitution of English for French as the language of the upper classes.

It will be noticed that where the arms of France appear in the lowest two ranks of Table 3, only three fleurs-de-lys are depicted. Henry IV, early in his reign, followed the example of Charles V (Table 63) in reducing the number shown; gradually other members of the English royal family copied him, so that the coat strewn with lilies (France ancient) disappeared.

Henry V re-opened the war with France, and won a sensational victory at Agincourt in 1415; the French nobility suffered hideous casualties from the English archers. Among the few English dead was Edward, Duke of York (Table 4). In 1420 Henry married the daughter of the French King and was proclaimed as his heir. The world seemed at his feet, but he died unexpectedly and prematurely of dysentery in 1422.

Henry's son was then less than one year old: minorities were always dangerous in the Middle Ages and that of Henry VI was no exception. Aristocratic factions began to compete for dominance. Prominent among them were the Beaufort descendants of John of Gaunt, and a group led by the Duke of Suffolk (his son's arms appear on Table 6). Gradually Richard, Duke of York, emerged as the most formidable critic of the Crown. He was himself descended from the fourth son of Edward III, but his mother, Anne Mortimer, had been the representative of Lionel, Duke of Clarence, the second son, a fact which gave him a better claim to the throne than the hapless Henry VI (Table 5). In 1454 Henry lost his reason and York was appointed Protector. However, in 1455 the King recovered his wits and York was expelled from office.

Gradually the situation deteriorated into civil war. After hesitation York bid for the Crown itself, but was slain before he could win it; it was his son who became Edward IV in 1461.

THE WARS OF THE ROSES

The struggles which are by custom called the Wars of the Roses were episodic and without principle, a contest of 'Outs' against 'Ins'. The Crown had not enough money or power; the aristocracy had too much. On the whole the wars had little effect on the life of the towns or the countryside, which were more conscious of lack of strong government and certain justice.

In 1471 Edward IV firmly defeated a coalition of his cousin Warwick, called the Kingmaker, and Margaret of Anjou, wife of Henry VI (Table 5); he reigned securely until his early death in 1483. But the battles, and the trials which followed them, did have a serious effect on the male descendants of Edward III; seven were killed and five more executed or murdered. After the death of Edward IV, his brother Richard seized the throne, prompted no doubt by ambition but also by fear of another minority. Allegedly, to safeguard his own position, he caused the death of his two nephews – the Princes in the Tower – a ruthless deed but in accord with the general spirit of a callous age. Two years later he was himself defeated and killed by Henry Tudor, Earl of Richmond, at Bosworth.

Nothing could be stronger evidence of the mortality among the Lancastrian party than the emergence of Henry VII; but he was the only adult male dimly connected with John of Gaunt or Henry V. It is true that his mother, Lady Margaret Beaufort, was the great-granddaughter of John of Gaunt; but the legitimation of the Beauforts expressly excluded any pretensions to the Crown. His father, Edmund Tudor, was the offspring of a curious alliance between Catherine of France and an obscure squire named Owen Tudor. It is usually accepted that they must have been married but no evidence survives of where, or when, the wedding took place. Henry VII proceeded to consolidate his position by marrying the eldest daughter of Edward IV. The red rose of Lancaster and the white rose of York were now symbolically united in the Tudor rose with petals of both colours.

None the less the Tudor rulers continued to be suspicious of anyone possessing Plantagenet blood, even by female descent. Table 6 demonstrates clearly the number of descendants of Edward III who perished, or nearly perished, on Tudor scaffolds. The last death shown, that of Thomas Howard in 1572, was for treason connected with Mary, Queen of Scots, but in the other eight cases Plantagenet ancestry was certainly a contributory cause. It was even alleged against the Earl of Surrey that he had used a coat-of-arms which laid stress on his kinship with Richard II and thus indicated his pretensions to the throne.

As can be seen the display of heraldry in this age was becoming more and more elaborate. In battle, men still used a simple shield – if they used one at all – for practical reasons. Richard Neville, the Kingmaker (Table 5), no doubt bore in action the simple blazon of his father, a white saltire on a red field, differenced with a label of blue and white, the colours of the bordure in his Beaufort mother's arms. But on his seal, in stained glass and elsewhere, he would add the proud quarterings of the families – Clare, Despencer, Montagu, Beauchamp and others – whose inherited lands made up his power and wealth.

The shields of two of the queens of this period illustrate this pattern of complexity. Margaret of Anjou (Table 5) was the daughter of King René who laid claim to the thrones of Hungary, Naples and Jerusalem, and to the Duchies of Lorraine and Bar. His six 'quarterings', including one for Anjou, make clear his pretensions; two of them call for comment. The third is for Jerusalem and seems to violate one of the basic laws of heraldry by having gold crosses on a silver field; this was a deliberate way of honouring the kingdom whose soil witnessed the life and death of Our Lord. The fifth section is for Bar and once again shows a play upon words, for the fish in it are barbels.

Elizabeth Widville (or Woodville) was the widow of a minor Lancastrian knight when she married the Yorkist King, Edward IV. Her mother was, however, a foreign lady of good birth. During her brief first marriage Elizabeth merely allied the simple arms of her father to those of her husband, John Grey. But when the attractive widow had captivated Edward

IV and become queen, this was not good enough. Accordingly the alien quarterings of her mother (to which she was not strictly entitled because her mother was in no sense an heiress) took pride of place and her paternal arms were relegated to the sixth quarter (Table 4). Study of the various royal differences will also suggest that certain marks were becoming associated with particular titles. Thus, Humphrey, Duke of Gloucester, echoed the silver bordure of his great-uncle Thomas, Duke of Gloucester (Table 3); this was possible since the latter died without a son. Similarly George, Duke of Clarence, younger brother of Edward IV (Table 4) employed the same label as Lionel, Duke of Clarence, the second son of Edward III.

More important things were happening in England in the fifteenth century than the disputes of factious nobles round an inane king (though Henry VI must be given credit for his foundation of Eton and his share in the soaring beauty of King's College, Cambridge). Gradually the influence of the Renaissance in Italy, with its humanist approach to art and letters, was reaching England. Magnificent, tall churches were being erected in the more prosperous parts of the country. Fortified castles were giving place to manor houses built for comfort rather than for defence. All our possessions in France, except Calais, had been lost before the accession of Edward IV, and England was thus freed of an inheritance which had become an entanglement. But of more consequence than all these was the return to England in 1476 of the artisan, William Caxton, who had learned his trade of printing abroad and now set up his press at Westminster. He was to introduce a revolution in communication more striking than the advent of television.

A revolution was also taking place in the practice of war. Gradually the use of fire-arms was increasing, both in the development of artillery and in weapons which could be operated by hand. The penetrating power of a bullet impelled by gunpowder was superior to that of the arrow, even if its accuracy was less. In consequence, the use of full body armour gradually diminished in the sixteenth century, and so did the wearing of a helmet which masked the owner's face. As a result the practical, military need for heraldry passed away, but it survived as a decorative facet of all the arts and can be found on textiles, on sculpture, on china, engraved on silver, and on book-stamps and book-plates.

Politically the end of the Yorkist dynasty and the coming of the Tudors was not very significant, least of all to those living at the time. But in the century and more of Tudor rule a great change took place; the Tudor sovereigns found a medieval kingdom, they left the beginnings of a modern one.

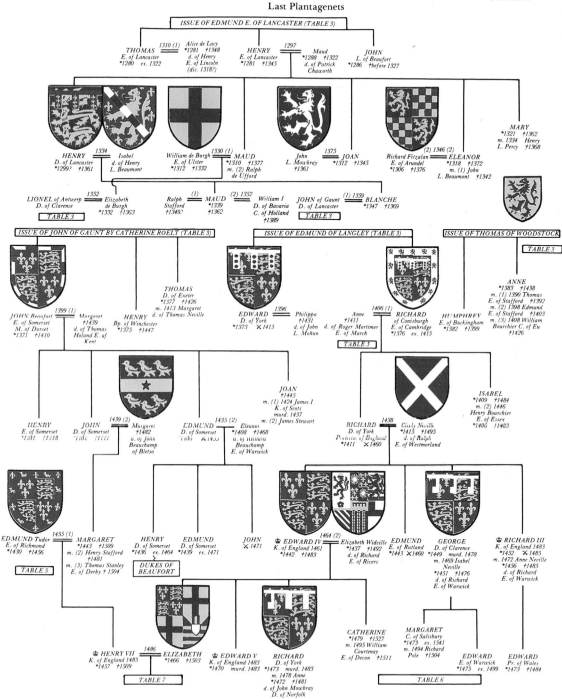

TABLE 5

ENGLAND
Wars of the Roses

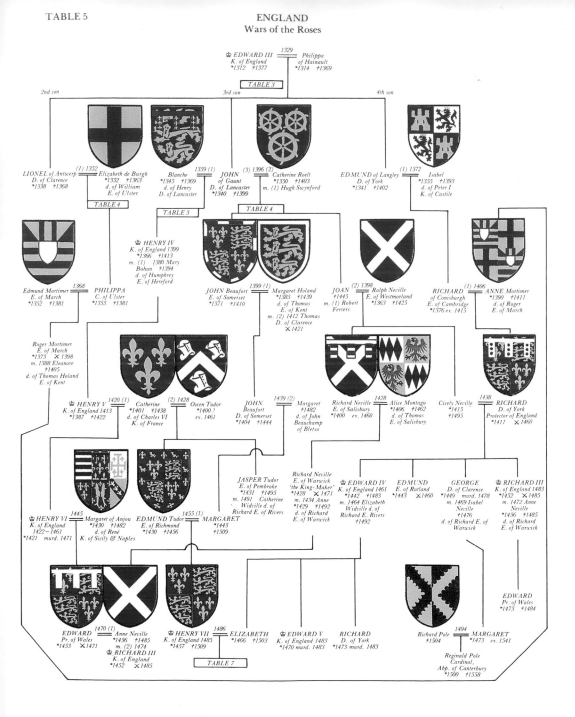

♚ EDWARD III
K. of England
*1312 †1377
1329
Philippa
of Hainault
*1314 †1369

TABLE 3

2nd son   3rd son   4th son

LIONEL of Antwerp
D. of Clarence
*1338 †1368
(1) 1352
Elizabeth de Burgh
*1332 †1363
d. of William
E. of Ulster

TABLE 4

Blanche
*1345 †1369
d. of Henry
D. of Lancaster
1359 (1)
JOHN
of Gaunt
D. of Lancaster
*1340 †1399
(3) 1396 (2)
Catherine Roelt
*1350 †1403
m. (1) Hugh Swynford

TABLE 3   TABLE 4

EDMUND of Langley
D. of York
*1341 †1402
(1) 1372
Isabel
*1355 †1393
d. of Peter I
K. of Castile

Edmund Mortimer
E. of March
*1352 †1381
1368
PHILIPPA
C. of Ulster
*1355 †1381

♚ HENRY IV
K. of England 1399
*1366 †1413
m. (1) 1380 Mary
Bohun †1394
d. of Humphrey
E. of Hereford

JOHN Beaufort
E. of Somerset
*1371 †1410
1399 (1)
Margaret Holand
*1385 †1439
d. of Thomas
E. of Kent
m. (2) 1412 Thomas
D. of Clarence
✕ 1421

JOAN
†1445
m. (1) Robert
Ferrers
(2) 1398
Ralph Neville
E. of Westmorland
*1363 †1425

RICHARD
of Conisburgh
E. of Cambridge
*1376 ex. 1415
(1) 1406
ANNE Mortimer
*1390 †1411
d. of Roger
E. of March

Roger Mortimer
E. of March
*1373 ✕ 1398
m. 1388 Eleanore
†1405
d. of Thomas Holand
E. of Kent

♚ HENRY V
K. of England 1413
*1387 †1422
1420 (1)
Catherine
d. of Charles VI
K. of France
(2) 1428
Owen Tudor
*1400 ?
ex. 1461

JOHN
Beaufort
D. of Somerset
*1404 †1444
1439 (2)
Margaret
†1482
d. of John
Beauchamp
of Bletso

Richard Neville
E. of Salisbury
*1400 ex. 1460
1428
Alice Montagu
*1406 †1462
d. of Thomas
E. of Salisbury

Cicely Neville
*1415 †1495
1438
RICHARD
D. of York
Protector of England
*1411 ✕ 1460

JASPER Tudor
E. of Pembroke
*1431 †1495
m. 1491 Catherine
Widville d. of
Richard E. of Rivers

Richard Neville
E. of Warwick
'the King-Maker'
*1428 ✕ 1471
m. 1434 Anne
*1429 †1492
d. of Richard
E. of Warwick

♚ EDWARD IV
K. of England 1461
*1442 †1483
m. 1464 Elizabeth
Widville d. of
Richard E. of Rivers
†1492

EDMUND
E. of Rutland
*1443 ✕ 1460

GEORGE
D. of Clarence
*1449 murd. 1478
m. 1469 Isabel
Neville
†1476
d. of Richard E. of
Warwick

♚ RICHARD III
K. of England 1483
*1452 ✕ 1485
m. 1472 Anne
Neville
*1456 †1485
d. of Richard
E. of Warwick

♚ HENRY VI
K. of England
1422–1461
*1421 murd. 1471
1445
Margaret of Anjou
*1430 †1482
d. of René
K. of Sicily & Naples

EDMUND Tudor
E. of Richmond
*1430 †1456
1455 (1)
MARGARET
*1443
†1509

EDWARD
Pr. of Wales
*1473 †1484

EDWARD
Pr. of Wales
*1453 ✕ 1471
1470 (1)
Anne Neville
*1456 †1485
m. (2) 1474
♚ RICHARD III
K. of England
*1452 ✕ 1485

♚ HENRY VII
K. of England 1485
*1457 †1509
1486
ELIZABETH
*1466 †1503

♚ EDWARD V
K. of England 1483
*1470 murd. 1483

RICHARD
D. of York
*1473 murd. 1483

Richard Pole
†1504
1494
MARGARET
*1473 ex. 1541

TABLE 7

Reginald Pole
Cardinal,
Abp. of Canterbury
*1500 †1558

Chapter 3

GREAT BRITAIN

At the end of the Battle of Bosworth (1485), after Richard III had died valiantly, sword in hand, the crown of England was found under a hawthorn bush and forthwith placed on the head of Henry VII. In a sense this acclamation was more valid than his tarnished descent from John of Gaunt or his later marriage. It remained to see how far Henry could make it good.

In the event the new King founded a great, though short-lived dynasty; his career was a remarkable achievement for the posthumous child of a thirteen-year-old widow with few expectations. His first aim was to establish his position at home and abroad. An early rising was defeated at Stoke in 1487 and the false pretender, Lambert Simnel, contemptuously dismissed to the royal kitchens; he claimed to be the Earl of Warwick, whom in truth Henry held in the Tower. A later insurgent, Perkin Warbeck, who had been accepted in Scotland as the Duke of York, son of Edward IV, was hanged after his defeat. And at the same time Henry put to death the real Earl of Warwick; thus perished unhappily the last descendant in male line of Geoffrey of Anjou, the sad and bloody sunset of the great Plantagenet family (Table 6). Henry VIII was more ruthless. At the beginning of his reign he beheaded the last Duke of Suffolk whose younger brother, doomed to exile, fell at the Battle of Pavia. In 1539 the Marquess of Exeter and Henry Pole, Lord Montagu, went to the block; and, more barbarously, the latter's mother was sent to the scaffold in 1541. The aged lady declined to lie down and the executioner had to attack her standing.

At the very end of his reign Henry VIII's fury blazed again. In 1521, on trumped-up charges, he had executed one of his greatest nobles, the Duke of Buckingham; now his suspicion fell on Buckingham's son-in-law and grandson, the Duke of Norfolk and the Earl of Surrey. The charge against Surrey was in part heraldic. It was alleged that he removed the silver label from the second quarter of his arms (which indicated his descent from Thomas of Brotherton, Table 3, younger son of Edward I) and thus displayed the pure blazon of England; furthermore, in virtue of his descent from the Mowbray family, to one of whom Richard II had accorded the privilege of the arms of Edward the Confessor, Lord Surrey had added the arms of the Confessor to his own. These heraldic actions were regarded as indicating a claim to the throne. Accordingly Surrey, a brave soldier and a talented poet, went to the block and only Henry's own death saved the aged Norfolk. Surrey's poetry included experiments in blank verse which foreshadowed the triumphs of Shakespeare and Milton in that metre.

Henry VII went cautiously in foreign affairs. He avoided trouble with France and sought peace with Scotland and an alliance with Spain. He married one daughter to the King of France and the other to the King of Scotland, an alliance from which stemmed the union of thrones in 1603. His elder son Arthur, Prince of Wales, was married to Katherine (usually called of Aragon) daughter of the King of Spain. Slowly and cautiously Henry VII moved towards stability and order. He preferred to punish by fine rather than by execution; he studiously fostered the royal revenues and encouraged commerce. John Cabot was allowed to sail under the English flag from Bristol to Newfoundland. When Henry died his fortune had reached the huge sum of £1,500,000; his subjects, looking back, could realize that the Wars of the Roses had ended at Stoke. Henry had proved himself a great king, prudent, parsimonious, peaceful, but above all successful.

Arthur had died in his father's lifetime, and his younger brother succeeded as Henry VIII, an equally outstanding ruler, but in different ways. The new

King began by marrying his brother's widow to preserve the Spanish alliance, an effort in diplomacy which produced unexpected consequences. The major event of his reign was the English Reformation, but this was political as well as religious, linked with the King's private life and the fate of his queens.

Henry was young, well-built, handsome and active, a good player of games, intelligent and ambitious to play his part in Europe. He spent his father's money freely on tournaments and displays, but also on ships and foreign expeditions. In 1513 his armies defeated France at the Battle of the Spurs, and Scotland, disastrously, at Flodden. Henry himself became increasingly concerned over the failure of his wife to produce a male heir and to safeguard the dynasty; only one daughter, Mary, born in 1516, had lived beyond birth. By about 1524 he was already in love with Anne Boleyn, but it was difficult to obtain permission for a divorce from the Pope. Failure to achieve this proved also to be failure for Cardinal Wolsey, the great minister on whom the King had relied in his early years. Wolsey fell from power in 1530, and in the next few years Henry broke away from the Papacy and in 1533 finally married Anne.

A Protestant reaction against orthodox Catholic religion and ritual was part of a European movement of ideas and revolt; but in England the rejection of the Pope's authority came in order to secure Henry's divorce. From the conversion in the seventh century, England had been part of the fabric of western Christendom owing loyalty to the Pope at Rome; now Henry declared himself supreme head of the Church of England. Gradually the liturgy was translated from Latin into English. By one of the ironies of history, the Pope had conferred on Henry only a few years before (1521) the title of Defender of the Faith, in reward for a tract composed by Henry against Luther. Unabashed, Henry continued to use the title; his successors followed him and it still appears on the English coinage today.

Queen Anne gave Henry one daughter, the future Queen Elizabeth; soon he began to look elsewhere in his search for a son. Anne was condemned on charges (probably fabricated) of adultery, and beheaded in 1536. In the same month the King married Jane Seymour; next year she produced the long-desired heir but died in doing so. She was the happiest of Henry's wives; his grief at her death kept him unmarried for two years.

To all his English wives he gave heraldic distinctions; two are shown at the head of Table 7. Anne Boleyn in youth used her father's simple coat with three bulls' heads (another punning coat: Table 10, top row); but this was not grand enough for Henry's Queen. A new shield of six proud quarterings was devised for her, stressing her devious descent from the Plantagenets through her Howard mother; by strict heraldic law, she was not entitled to one of them. Jane Seymour belonged to a more ancient family with lawful quarterings of their own. When she presented him with a son, the King added a new quartering (the first on her shield in Table 7) based on the lilies and leopards of the royal arms. The present Seymour family, descended from her brother, still use this augmentation.

On his death-bed Henry VIII probably still regarded himself as a Catholic who had quarrelled with the Pope. The forces of Protestantism had been growing, however, and took greater control in the short rule of his son, Edward VI. At Edward's death the Duke of Northumberland attempted to bring his daughter-in-law, Lady Jane Grey, to the throne. The coup enlisted no popular support and Mary, elder daughter of Henry VIII, became Queen. She was a resolute Catholic and married her cousin Philip II of Spain, who, though never crowned, was reckoned as King of England with her. The short reign saw a brief and violent Catholic reaction, including the burning of three Protestant bishops, but at Mary's death her half-sister succeeded without opposition.

Queen Elizabeth I was the third great Tudor sovereign. Her triumphs came slowly; had she died after, say, twenty years, she might have seemed less glorious. She achieved a religious settlement; England was firmly established in a Protestant and Episcopalian course, without yielding to extreme puritanism. The Queen dressed with great splendour, but conducted the national finances with prudence. Many of the great houses of England were rebuilt to entertain the royal retinue. Despite a number of suitors, she never married. Relations with Spain had worsened. In 1588 Drake and the English seamen defeated the great Armada which Philip II launched against England. Drake had already circumnavigated the globe in 1577 and had frequently plundered the Spanish colonies in the new world of America. Furthermore, the closing years of her long reign saw a ferment of literary activity which continued into the next century. Spenser, Marlowe, Raleigh, Sidney, Shakespeare and Bacon are only a few of the writers who were making their names known.

By the end of her life Elizabeth was indeed 'Gloriana' to many of her people; in fact her personal popularity, her combination of royal dignity and political circumspection, her proud if faded looks, concealed a series of problems which were to embarrass her successors. She was a true ruler of her realm and one of the most native-born in blood who ever held the throne. A glance at her ancestry in Table 10 reveals that six of her great-grandparents were English, one Welsh and one Irish. No other English or

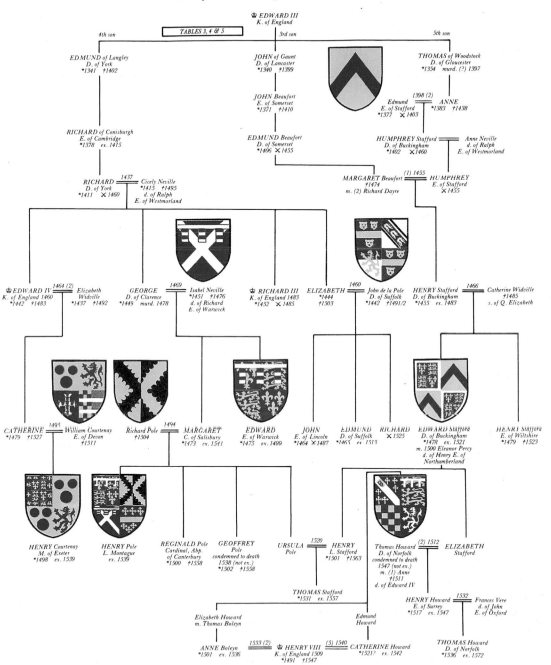

TABLE 7

ENGLAND
Tudors and Stuarts

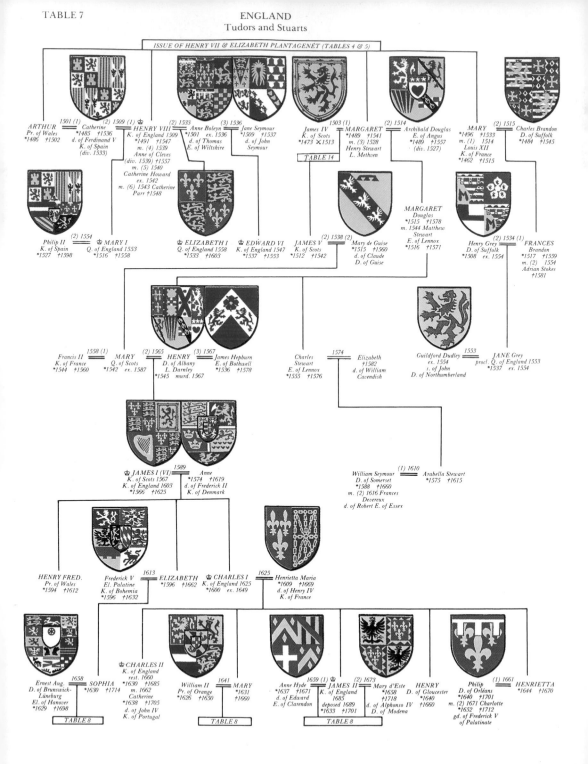

ISSUE OF HENRY VII & ELIZABETH PLANTAGENET (TABLES 4 & 5)

ARTHUR
Pr. of Wales
*1486 †1502

1501 (1)
Catherine
*1485 †1536
d. of Ferdinand V
K. of Spain
(div. 1533)

(2) 1509 (1) ♚ **HENRY VIII**
K. of England 1509
*1491 †1547
m. (4) 1539
Anne of Cleves
(div. 1539) †1557
m. (5) 1540
Catherine Howard
ex. 1542
m. (6) 1543 Catherine
Parr †1548

(2) 1533 Anne Boleyn
*1501 ex. 1536
d. of Thomas
E. of Wiltshire

(3) 1536 Jane Seymour
*1509 †1537
d. of John
Seymour

James IV
K. of Scots
*1473 ✕1513

1503 (1) **MARGARET**
*1489 †1541
m. (3) 1528
Henry Stewart
L. Methven

TABLE 14

(2) 1514 Archibald Douglas
E. of Angus
*1489 †1557
(div. 1527)

MARY
*1496 †1533
m. (1) 1514
Louis XII
K. of France
*1462 †1515

(2) 1515 Charles Brandon
D. of Suffolk
*1484 †1545

Philip II
K. of Spain
*1527 †1598

(2) 1554 ♚ **MARY I**
Q. of England 1553
*1516 †1558

♚ **ELIZABETH I**
Q. of England 1558
*1533 †1603

♚ **EDWARD VI**
K. of England 1547
*1537 †1553

JAMES V
K. of Scots
*1512 †1542

(2) 1538 (2) Mary de Guise
*1515 †1560
d. of Claude
D. of Guise

MARGARET
Douglas
*1515 †1578
m. 1544 Matthew
Stewart
E. of Lennox
*1516 †1571

Henry Grey
D. of Suffolk
*1508 ex. 1554

(2) 1534 (1) **FRANCES**
Brandon
*1517 †1559
m. (2) 1554
Adrian Stokes
†1581

Francis II
K. of France
*1544 †1560

1558 (1) **MARY**
Q. of Scots
*1542 ex. 1587

(2) 1565 **HENRY**
D. of Albany
L. Darnley
*1545 murd. 1567

(3) 1567 James Hepburn
E. of Bothwell
*1536 †1578

Charles
Stewart
E. of Lennox
*1555 †1576

1574 Elizabeth
†1582
d. of William
Cavendish

Guildford Dudley
ex. 1554
s. of John
D. of Northumberland

1553 **JANE Grey**
procl. Q. of England 1553
*1537 ex. 1554

♚ **JAMES I (VI)**
K. of Scots 1567
K. of England 1603
*1566 †1625

1589 Anne
*1574 †1619
d. of Frederick II
K. of Denmark

William Seymour
D. of Somerset
*1588 †1660
m. (2) 1616 Frances
Devereux
d. of Robert E. of Essex

(1) 1610 Arabella Stewart
*1575 †1615

HENRY FRED.
Pr. of Wales
*1594 †1612

Frederick V
El. Palatine
K. of Bohemia
*1596 †1632

1613 **ELIZABETH**
*1596 †1662

♚ **CHARLES I**
K. of England 1625
*1600 ex. 1649

1625 Henrietta Maria
*1609 †1669
d. of Henry IV
K. of France

Ernest Aug.
D. of Brunswick-
Lüneburg
El. of Hanover
*1629 †1698

1658 **SOPHIA**
*1630 †1714

TABLE 8

♚ **CHARLES II**
K. of England
rest. 1660
*1630 †1685
m. 1662
Catherine
*1638 †1705
d. of John IV
K. of Portugal

William II
Pr. of Orange
*1626 †1650

1641 **MARY**
*1631
†1660

TABLE 8

Anne Hyde
*1637 †1671
d. of Edward
E. of Clarendon

1659 (1) ♚ **JAMES II**
K. of England
1685
deposed 1689
*1633 †1701

(2) 1673 Mary d'Este
*1658
†1718
d. of Alphonso IV
D. of Modena

TABLE 8

HENRY
D. of Gloucester
*1640 †1660

Philip
D. of Orléans
*1640 †1701
m. (2) 1671 Charlotte
*1652 †1722
gd. of Frederick V
of Palatinate

(1) 1661 **HENRIETTA**
*1644 †1670

The funeral procession of Queen Elizabeth I in 1603. Her funeral bier is surrounded by the twelve banners of her forebears, beginning with that of Henry II (upper left) and ending with that of her father, Henry VIII (lower right).

British ruler can show a similar absence of alien blood.

Her nearest kinsman, James VI of Scotland (Tables 7 and 14), succeeded without controversy as James I of England, first of the Stuart kings. He was a Protestant, had already been King of Scotland for 36 years, and was an odd mixture of wisdom and conceit, of learning in theory and tactlessness in practice, which justified his nickname 'the wisest fool in Christendom'. It must be stressed that the union was at this stage only one of crowns, England and Scotland each preserved their own separate parliaments, peerages, judicatures and customs. This was recognized in the new arrangement of the royal arms. The claim to France was maintained (though the last piece of French soil, Calais, had been lost by Mary) and since it was attached to the Crown of England, the lilies and leopards were placed in the first and fourth quarters; Scotland filled the second, while the harp of Ireland appeared, for the first time, in the third.

One feature of government under the Tudors had been an increasing consultation with Parliament. This in turn had led the House of Commons to seek greater powers and privileges, to aim indeed at control of the Crown. The contest between Crown and Parliament was to be the main theme of the seventeenth century; two subjects which invited conflict were finance and religion. Elizabeth had been short of money at the end of her reign; James I was no better off. There was still a substantial Catholic minority in England; it was a desperate clique of them who tried to blow up Parliament by the hand of Guy Fawkes in 1605. On the other flank of the Church of England a more radical Puritan or Nonconformist movement was manifesting itself in the country and in Parliament.

Charles I, short, stubborn and godly, was not the monarch to find an answer to these problems. The first phase of his reign saw a series of disputes with the House of Commons; then for eleven years (1629-40) he tried to manage without summoning a Parliament and by reviving obsolete medieval taxes. In 1642 civil war broke out. In general the nobility, the Catholics, the west and the north were for the King. London, East Anglia, the merchant classes and the Puritans supported the Parliament. Sometimes brother fought against brother. A Huntingdonshire squire of Nonconformist opinions, Oliver Cromwell, became the outstanding general of the war. Finally, Charles fell into the hands of his enemies; after much debate he was tried and condemned to death by a special court. The King, who behaved with massive dignity, was beheaded on a cold January day in 1649 'by no known law and an unknown executioner'.

A by-product of the troubled times was the growth of emigration to America. About 25,000 had settled in New England by 1640; later in the century colonies were established as refuges for specific faiths, Pennsylvania for Quakers or Maryland for Catholics. The life of the early colonists was hard, but they cultivated alike the rich soil of the New World and a sturdy independence of thought in political fields.

For eleven years after Charles I's execution England was a Commonwealth under Oliver Cromwell as Lord Protector. The Crown was offered to this plain, blunt, dour, religious man, who bade his portraitist depict him warts and all, but he resolutely refused it. Various constitutional schemes were put forward, but none found universal favour. When he died there was but a brief hesitation before the restoration of the Stuarts with the crowning of Charles II in 1660.

THE RESTORATION

Charles II was a very different man from his father. Tall, good-looking, amusing, a lover of women and something of a cynic, he was determined not to face again the bitterness of exile. Under the able guidance of his Chancellor, Lord Clarendon, a settlement was reached. Absolute monarchy was a thing of the past – but so was republicanism. Henceforth taxation had to be approved by Parliament. After the austerities of the Commonwealth, the English, led by their King, embarked upon an age of licence, the world of Pepys' diaries. All was not pleasure; the fearful Plague broke out in 1665, and was followed the next year by the Great Fire of London, which gave extensive opportunities to Sir Christopher Wren, the greatest of English architects. Charles was childless and his brother James a Catholic, a circumstance which produced political unrest.

James II was less intelligent than his brother, more bigoted and more tactless. He had first married a daughter of his brother's great minister, Lord Clarendon; Anne Hyde was a loyal Protestant and brought up her two daughters in that faith. His second wife, Mary of Modena, appeared barren. James left his subjects in no doubt that he aimed to restore the Roman Catholic religion and popular anxiety was already considerable when the Queen finally produced a son. Hope of a peaceful Protestant succession vanished: seven prominent figures drawn from both Whig and Tory parties (as left and right had begun to be called) sent an appeal to William of Orange, nephew and son-in-law of the King.

With remarkable courage William collected a force and landed in Devon in 1688. James II lost heart and fled, petulantly flinging the Great Seal into the Thames, whence a fisherman very shortly recovered it. William III and Mary were proclaimed joint sovereigns in February 1689. They were offered their common crown by Parliament. It was now clear, if it had not been before, that Parliament could control the succession. This process was carried a stage further in 1701 when the Act of Settlement laid down that William should be followed by Anne (his wife's sister) and after her by the nearest available Protestant – at that date the Electress Sophia of Hanover (Table 7: bottom row). The real triumph of William and his friends was two-fold: the Glorious Revolution of 1688–9 was bloodless in England, and the settlement which sprang from it has stood the test of time. During his reign he imposed on the royal arms a small escutcheon of his family shield of Nassau (Table 8: top row).

Queen Anne made a more significant alteration. In 1707 was brought about the Union with Scotland, which gave the two realms a common Parliament of Great Britain as well as a common Crown. The people of Scotland prized their independence, but the blunt truth is that they were being kept back by lack of resources and a still primitive agriculture. If the benefits for Scotland were mainly economic, in the form of expanded commerce and intercourse with England, those for England were largely political. Queen Anne could not live for ever; and a Stuart restoration was more plausible north of the Tweed than south of it. In the years that followed, Scots were able to share with English in overseas expansion; from Canada to Calcutta their names will be found among the great administrators and on the humblest tombstones. To symbolize the Act of Union Anne altered the royal arms. The closer intimacy of England and Scotland was reflected by joining them in the first and fourth quarters while France was promoted to the second and Ireland held the third (Table 8). William III had involved England in war against the ambitions of Louis XIV; strife with France was to continue intermittently for more than a century, but the conflict in Anne's reign was made glorious by Blenheim and the other great victories of the Duke of Marlborough, the first prepotent Churchill.

THE HANOVERIANS

When Anne died in 1714, the Electress Sophia was a few weeks dead and the next Protestant heir was her son George Louis, the Elector of Hanover (Table 85); accordingly he became King George I of Great Britain. Fifty-seven living men, women and children had a better genealogical right but all adhered to the Catholic faith. George, stout and Teutonic, was already in late middle age; he was a soldier with a good grip of politics and more ability than has generally been credited to him. His paternal coat-of-arms was of Germanic complexity as can be seen from the shields of his father (Table 7: bottom row) or his wife, who was also his first cousin (Table 8: top row). Fortunately, not all his many quarterings were incorporated in the arms of Great Britain: it was enough to take the two lions of Brunswick, the white horse of Westphalia and the blue lion and red hearts of Lüneburg and place them in the fourth quarter. Above them on a smaller shield was the crown of Charlemagne which represented George's position as Arch-Treasurer of the Holy Roman Empire. The new King's ancestry can be seen on Table 10; of the eight forebears shown, only James I came from within Great Britain.

George I, quite rightly, suspected many of the Tories of sympathy with the exiled son of James II (the

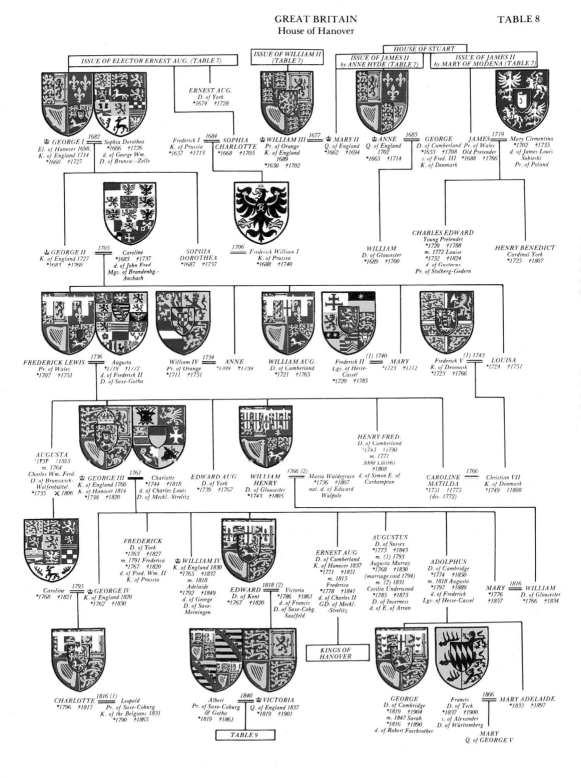

HOUSE OF STUART

ISSUE OF ELECTOR ERNEST AUG. (TABLE 7)

ISSUE OF WILLIAM II (TABLE 7)

ISSUE OF JAMES II by ANNE HYDE (TABLE 7)

ISSUE OF JAMES II by MARY OF MODENA (TABLE 7)

GEORGE I — 1682 — Sophia Dorothea
El. of Hanover 1698.
K. of England 1714
*1660 †1727
*1666 †1726
d. of George Wm.
D. of Brunsw.-Zelle

Frederick I
K. of Prussia
*1657 †1713

SOPHIA CHARLOTTE
*1668 †1705
— 1684

WILLIAM III — 1677 — **MARY II**
Pr. of Orange
K. of England 1689
*1650 †1702
Q. of England
*1662 †1694

ANNE — 1683 — GEORGE
Q. of England 1702
*1665 †1714
D. of Cumberland
*1653 †1708
s. of Fred. III
K. of Denmark

JAMES — 1719 — Mary Clementina
Pr. of Wales
Old Pretender
*1688 †1766
*1702 †1735
d. of James Louis
Sobieski
Pr. of Poland

GEORGE II — 1705 — Caroline
K. of England 1727
*1683 †1760
*1683 †1737
d. of John Fred
Mgv. of Brandenbg.-
Ansbach

SOPHIA DOROTHEA
*1687 †1757

Frederick William I — 1706
K. of Prussia
*1688 †1740

WILLIAM
D. of Gloucester
*1689 †1700

CHARLES EDWARD
Young Pretender
*1720 †1788
m. 1772 Louise
*1752 †1824
d. of Gustavus
Pr. of Stolberg-Gedern

HENRY BENEDICT
Cardinal York
*1725 †1807

FREDERICK LEWIS — 1736 — Augusta
Pr. of Wales
*1707 †1751
*1719 †1772
d. of Frederick II
D. of Saxe-Gotha

William IV — 1734
Pr. of Orange
*1711 †1751

ANNE
*1709 †1759

WILLIAM AUG.
D. of Cumberland
*1721 †1765

Frederick II — (1) 1740 — MARY
Lgv. of Hesse-
Cassel
*1720 †1785
*1723 †1772

Frederick V — (1) 1743 — LOUISA
K. of Denmark
*1723 †1766
*1724 †1751

AUGUSTA
*1737 †1813
m. 1764
Charles Wm. Ferd.
D. of Brunswick-
Wolfenbüttel
*1735 × 1806

GEORGE III — 1761 — Charlotte
K. of England 1760
K. of Hanover 1814
*1738 †1820
*1744 †1818
d. of Charles Louis
D. of Meckl. Strelitz

EDWARD AUG.
D. of York
*1739 †1767

WILLIAM HENRY
D. of Gloucester
*1743 †1805
— 1766 (2) — Maria Waldegrave
*1736 †1807
nat. d. of Edward
Walpole

HENRY FRED.
D. of Cumberland
*1745 †1790
m. 1771
Anne Luttrell
*1808
d. of Simon E. of
Carhampton

CAROLINE MATILDA — 1766 — Christian VII
*1751 †1775
(div. 1772)
K. of Denmark
*1749 †1808

Caroline — 1795 — **GEORGE IV**
*1768 †1821
K. of England 1820
*1762 †1830

FREDERICK
D. of York
*1763 †1827
m. 1791 Frederica
*1767 †1820
d. of Fred. Wm. II
K. of Prussia

WILLIAM IV
K. of England 1830
*1765 †1837
m. 1818
Adelaide
*1792 †1849
d. of George
D. of Saxe-
Meiningen

EDWARD
D. of Kent
*1767 †1820
— 1818 (2) — Victoria
*1786 †1861
d. of Francis
D. of Saxe-Cobg.
Saalfeld

ERNEST AUG
D. of Cumberland
K. of Hanover 1837
*1771 †1851
m. 1815
Frederica
*1778 †1841
d. of Charles II
GD. of Meckl.
-Strelitz

AUGUSTUS
D. of Sussex
*1773 †1843
m. (1) 1793
Augusta Murray
*1768 †1830
(marriage void 1794)
m. (2) 1831
Cecilia Underwood
*1785 †1873
D. of Inverness
d. of E. of Arran

ADOLPHUS
D. of Cambridge
*1774 †1850
m. 1818 Augusta
*1797 †1889
d. of Frederick
Lgv. of Hesse-Cassel

MARY — 1816 — WILLIAM
*1776 †1857
D. of Gloucester
*1766 †1834

CHARLOTTE — 1816 (1) — Leopold
*1796 †1817
Pr. of Saxe-Coburg
K. of the Belgians 1831
*1790 †1865

Albert — 1840 — **VICTORIA**
Pr. of Saxe-Coburg
& Gotha
*1819 †1861
Q. of England 1837
*1819 †1901

KINGS OF HANOVER

GEORGE
D. of Cambridge
*1819 †1904
m. 1847 Sarah
*1816 †1890
d. of Robert Fairbrother

Francis — 1866 — MARY ADELAIDE
D. of Teck
*1837 †1900
s. of Alexander
D. of Württemberg
*1833 †1897

MARY
Q. of GEORGE V

TABLE 9

TABLE 9

GREAT BRITAIN
House of Windsor

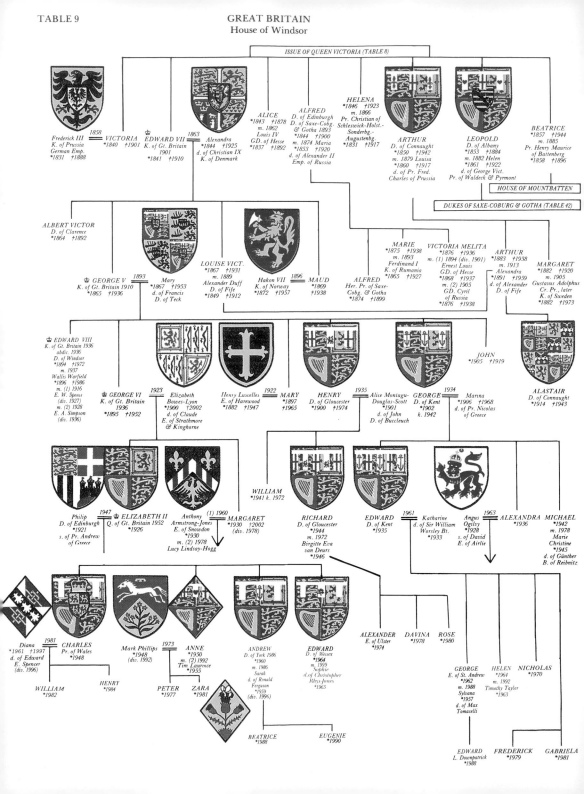

ISSUE OF QUEEN VICTORIA (TABLE 8)

Frederick III
K. of Prussia
German Emp.
*1831 †1888

— 1858 — VICTORIA
*1840 †1901

EDWARD VII
K. of Gt. Britain
1901
*1841 †1910

— 1863 — Alexandra
*1844 †1925
d. of Christian IX
K. of Denmark

ALICE
*1843 †1878
m. 1862
Louis IV
GD. of Hesse
*1837 †1892

ALFRED
D. of Edinburgh
& Saxe-Cobg.
& Gotha 1893
*1844 †1900
m. 1874 Maria
*1853 †1920
d. of Alexander II
Emp. of Russia

HELENA
*1846 †1923
m. 1866
Pr. Christian of
Schleswick-Holst.-
Sonderbg.-
Augustenbg.
*1831 †1917

ARTHUR
D. of Connaught
*1850 †1942
m. 1879 Louisa
*1860 †1917
d. of Pr. Fred.
Charles of Prussia

LEOPOLD
D. of Albany
*1853 †1884
m. 1882 Helen
*1861 †1922
d. of George Vict.
Pr. of Waldeck & Pyrmont

BEATRICE
*1857 †1944
m. 1885
Pr. Henry Maurice
of Battenberg
*1858 †1896

HOUSE OF MOUNTBATTEN

DUKES OF SAXE-COBURG & GOTHA (TABLE 42)

ALBERT VICTOR
D. of Clarence
*1864 †1892

GEORGE V
K. of Gt. Britain 1910
*1865 †1936

— 1893 — Mary
*1867 †1953
d. of Francis
D. of Teck

LOUISE VICT.
*1867 †1931
m. 1889
Alexander Duff
D. of Fife
*1849 †1912

Hakon VII
K. of Norway
*1872 †1957

— 1896 — MAUD
*1869 †1938

ALFRED
Her. Pr. of Saxe-
Cobg. & Gotha
*1874 †1899

MARIE
*1875 †1938
m. 1893
Ferdinand I
K. of Rumania
*1865 †1927

VICTORIA MELITA
*1876 †1936
m. (1) 1894 (div. 1901)
Ernest Louis
GD. of Hesse
*1868 †1937
m. (2) 1905
GD. Cyril
of Russia
*1876 †1938

ARTHUR
*1883 †1938
m. 1913
Alexandra
*1891 †1959
d. of Alexander
D. of Fife

MARGARET
*1882 †1920
m. 1905
Gustavus Adolphus
Cr. Pr., later
K. of Sweden
*1882 †1973

EDWARD VIII
K. of Gt. Britain 1936
abdic. 1936
D. of Windsor
*1894 †1972
m. 1937
Wallis Warfield
*1896 †1986
m. (1) 1916
E. W. Spenc
(div. 1927)
m. (2) 1928
E. A. Simpson
(div. 1936)

GEORGE VI
K. of Gt. Britain
1936
*1895 †1952

— 1923 — Elizabeth
Bowes-Lyon
*1900 †2002
d. of Claude
E. of Strathmore
& Kinghorne

Henry Lascelles
E. of Harewood
*1882 †1947

— 1922 — MARY
*1897 †1965

HENRY
D. of Gloucester
*1900 †1974

— 1935 — Alice Montagu-
Douglas-Scott
*1901 †2004
d. of John
D. of Buccleuch

GEORGE
D. of Kent
*1902
k. 1942

— 1934 — Marina
*1906 †1968
d. of Pr. Nicolas
of Greece

JOHN
*1905 †1919

ALASTAIR
D. of Connaught
*1914 †1943

Philip
D. of Edinburgh
*1921
s. of Pr. Andrew
of Greece

— 1947 — ELIZABETH II
Q. of Gt. Britain 1952
*1926

Anthony
Armstrong-Jones
E. of Snowdon
*1930
m. (2) 1978
Lucy Lindsay-Hogg

— (1) 1960 — MARGARET
*1930 †2002
(div. 1978)

WILLIAM
*1941 k. 1972

RICHARD
D. of Gloucester
*1944
m. 1972
Birgitte Eva
van Deurs
*1946

EDWARD
D. of Kent
*1935

— 1961 — Katharine
d. of Sir William
Worsley Bt.
*1933

Angus
Ogilvy
*1928
s. of David
E. of Airlie

— 1963 — ALEXANDRA
*1936

MICHAEL
*1942
m. 1978
Marie
Christine
*1945
d. of Günther
B. of Reibnitz

Diana
*1961 †1997
d. of Edward
E. Spencer
(div. 1996)

— 1981 — CHARLES
Pr. of Wales
*1948

Mark Phillips
*1948
(div. 1992)

— 1973 — ANNE
*1950
m. (2) 1992
Tim Laurence
*1955

ANDREW
D. of York 1986
*1960
m. 1986
Sarah
d. of Ronald
Ferguson
*1959
(div. 1996)

EDWARD
D. of Wessex
*1964
m. 1999
Sophie
d.of Christopher
Rhys Jones
*1965

ALEXANDER
E. of Ulster
*1974

DAVINA
*1978

ROSE
*1980

GEORGE
E. of St. Andrew
*1962
m. 1988
Sylvana
*1957
d. of Max
Tomaselli

HELEN
*1964
m. 1992
Timothy Taylor
*1963

NICHOLAS
*1970

WILLIAM
*1982

HENRY
*1984

PETER
*1977

ZARA
*1981

BEATRICE
*1988

EUGENIE
*1990

EDWARD
L. Downpatrick
*1988

FREDERICK
*1979

GABRIELA
*1981

Old Pretender) whose titular reign (1701–66) was longer even than that of Queen Victoria; he therefore relied on Whig ministers of whom the most distinguished was Sir Robert Walpole, a tough, coarse, Norfolk squire of immense political capacity. Under his guidance, and with the King often absent, the cabinet system and the leadership of the 'Prime' Minister began to evolve. The supporters of the Stuart dynasty – the Jacobites – made two vain attempts at restoration, in 1715 and 1745; the second was led by the glamorous figure of Prince Charles Edward (the Young Pretender) and came nearer to success.

George II spoke English, but not well. At the Battle of Dettingen (1743) he was the last British sovereign to lead his troops into battle. His own campaigns on the Continent were far less important than those being waged overseas at the end of his reign. During the Seven Years' War, the commanding genius of William Pitt, Earl of Chatham, directed the armies of Britain to victory in India and Canada and laid the foundations of the British Empire, a task which could not have been accomplished without mastery of the seas. In 1757 the Battle of Plassey marked the end of French rivalry in India; in 1759 British arms triumphed at Quebec in Canada, Minden in Germany and Quiberon Bay off Brittany. George II died at a glorious moment.

His son, Frederick, Prince of Wales, predeceased him. It will be noticed that the red escutcheon in the centre of his Hanover quartering is blank, because he never became the Treasurer of the Empire, and that he uses the conventional silver label of an eldest son. By that date it was established that sons of the sovereign had labels of three points, the younger sons marking one or more points with a sign of distinction (William, Duke of Cumberland, or George, Duke of Cambridge, on Table 8), while grandsons used a label of five points, again with appropriate differences (William Henry, Duke of Gloucester). The continuance of the practice can be observed on Table 9.

George III was much more English in his upbringing; his reign of sixty years – longer than that of Henry III – saw fantastic changes in his realms. It is impossible to outline more than the most significant. Saddest was the loss of the American colonies. Freed from all danger of French invasion, their independence became more manifest; their complaints were ill-handled at home; war broke out, and within a decade the Americans, under the talented leadership of George Washington, had gained their freedom. A more complex process transformed England, which in 1700 was still basically an agricultural nation, into an industrial people with rich resources in coal and iron. With the Industrial Revolution came a shift in population from south to north which is only being redressed in our own day.

A more political manoeuvre was the Act of Union with Ireland in 1800. By this measure the hitherto separate Irish Parliament was amalgamated with that of Great Britain; the United Kingdom was thus created. From 1801 a further change took place in the royal arms. The empty claim to France was at long last abandoned (partly perhaps because Napoleon was now in control there) after 461 years. England, now divorced from its link with Scotland, took the first and fourth quarters, Scotland the second and Ireland the third. Hanover, which was not represented at Westminster, was placed on a central escutcheon with above it the bonnet of an elector. In 1814 Hanover became a kingdom and the bonnet was replaced by a crown; the new shield is shown on Table 8 for George III. This promotion was one of the consequences of the great wars against Napoleon (Table 69). There are curious parallels between this grim conflict and the war against Hitler. In both, the United Kingdom stood awhile alone; in both, invasion of England was threatened but not achieved; in both, the enemy received a devastating blow amid the snows of Russia; in both, British armies ultimately invaded the homeland of the foe. When the Duke of Wellington finally triumphed at Waterloo (1815), George III was already old and senile.

Neither of his sons, George IV and William IV, produced an heir; accordingly in 1837 the throne passed to their niece, Queen Victoria. Hanover, however, was governed by the Salic Law, which forbade the accession of a female, and passed to another son of George III, Ernest, Duke of Cumberland (Table 86). As a result of this, the escutcheon of Hanover disappeared, and the royal arms of England assumed the form which they still exhibit today (Table 1, bottom, or Table 8: bottom row). Queen Victoria married her cousin, Albert of Saxe-Coburg and Gotha, who was given the style of Prince Consort and the arms shown at the base of Table 8; his family arms can be seen in the top rank of Table 11. Victoria was an essentially British queen, but it can be seen from Table 11 that her ancestors were almost exclusively Germanic.

Her reign, the longest in British history, was mainly one of peace and prosperity. At home Britain became the workshop of the world; overseas her dominions expanded, not least in Australia and New Zealand. To modern purses a striking feature of the period would be the general stability of prices; this was accompanied by a great growth in population. In the world of politics the rivalry of Liberals and Conservatives, replacing the old Whigs and Tories, saw such formidable figures as Peel and Palmerston, Disraeli and Gladstone locked in parliamentary battle. Bill by reform bill the suffrage was extended, though women did not obtain the vote until the present century. At

TABLE 10

ENGLAND
Ancestors of Elizabeth I and George I

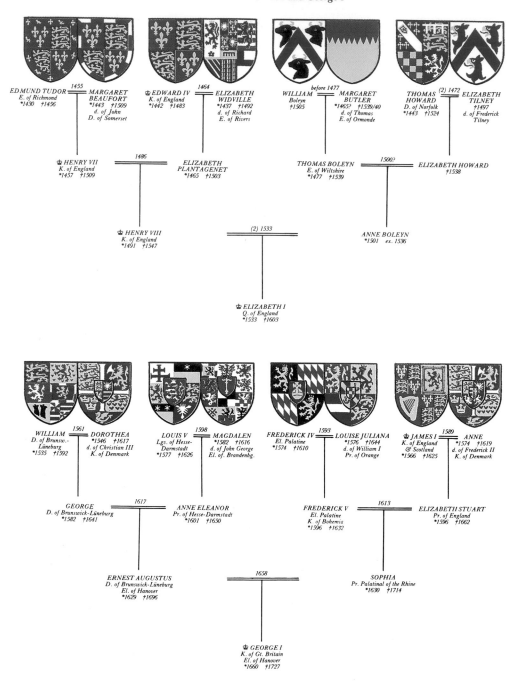

EDMUND TUDOR
E. of Richmond
*1430 †1456

— 1455 —

MARGARET BEAUFORT
*1443 †1509
d. of John
D. of Somerset

EDWARD IV
K. of England
*1442 †1483

— 1464 —

ELIZABETH WIDVILLE
*1437 †1492
d. of Richard
E. of Rivers

WILLIAM
Boleyn
†1505

— before 1477 —

MARGARET BUTLER
*1465? †1539/40
d. of Thomas
E. of Ormonde

THOMAS HOWARD
D. of Norfolk
*1443 †1524

— (2) 1472 —

ELIZABETH TILNEY
†1497
d. of Frederick
Tilney

HENRY VII
K. of England
*1457 †1509

— 1486 —

ELIZABETH PLANTAGENET
*1465 †1503

THOMAS BOLEYN
E. of Wiltshire
*1477 †1539

— 1500? —

ELIZABETH HOWARD
†1538

HENRY VIII
K. of England
*1491 †1547

— (2) 1533 —

ANNE BOLEYN
*1501 ex. 1536

ELIZABETH I
Q. of England
*1533 †1603

WILLIAM
D. of Brunsw.-
Lüneburg
*1535 †1592

— 1561 —

DOROTHEA
*1546 †1617
d. of Christian III
K. of Denmark

LOUIS V
Lgv. of Hesse-
Darmstadt
*1577 †1626

— 1598 —

MAGDALEN
*1582 †1616
d. of John George
El. of Brandenbg.

FREDERICK IV
El. Palatine
*1574 †1610

— 1593 —

LOUISE JULIANA
*1576 †1644
d. of William I
Pr. of Orange

JAMES I
K. of England
& Scotland
*1566 †1625

— 1589 —

ANNE
*1574 †1619
d. of Frederick II
K. of Denmark

GEORGE
D. of Brunswick-Lüneburg
*1582 †1641

— 1617 —

ANNE ELEANOR
Pr. of Hesse-Darmstadt
*1601 †1650

FREDERICK V
El. Palatine
K. of Bohemia
*1596 †1632

— 1613 —

ELIZABETH STUART
Pr. of England
*1596 †1662

ERNEST AUGUSTUS
D. of Brunswick-Lüneburg
El. of Hanover
*1629 †1696

— 1658 —

SOPHIA
Pr. Palatinal of the Rhine
*1630 †1714

GEORGE I
K. of Gt. Britain
El. of Hanover
*1660 †1727

FREDERICK   1736   AUGUSTA   CHARLES LOUIS   1735   ELIZABETH   ERNEST   1749   SOPHIA   HENRY XXIV   1754   CAROLINA
LEWIS   *1719 †1772   D. of Mecklenbg.-   *1713 †1761   FREDERICK   *1724 †1802   C. Reuss-   *1727 †1796
Pr. of Wales   d. of Frederick II   Strelitz   d. of Ernest Fred. I   D. of Saxe-Coburg   d. of Ferdinand   Ebersdorf   d. of George Augustus
*1707 †1751   D. of Saxe-Gotha   *1708 †1752   D. of Saxe-   & Saalfeld   D. of Brunswick-   *1724 †1779   C. of Erbach-
                                                                Hildburghausen   *1724 †1800   Wolfenbüttel   Schönberg

✠ GEORGE III   1761   CHARLOTTE   FRANCIS FREDERICK   1777   AUGUSTA CAROLINA
K. of Gt. Britain   Pr. of Mecklenburg-Strelitz   D. of Saxe-Cobg. & Saalfeld   C. of Reuss-Ebersdorf
K. of Hanover   *1744 †1818   *1750 †1806   *1757 †1831
*1738 †1820

EDWARD   1818 (2)   VICTORIA
D. of Kent   Pr. of Saxe-Coburg
*1767 †1820   & Saalfeld
                                                               *1786 †1861

✠ VICTORIA
Q. of Gt. Britain, Emp. of India
*1819 †1901

✠ EDWARD VII   1863   ALEXANDRA   FRANCIS   1866   MARY ADELAIDE   CLAUDE   1853   FRANCES DORA   CHARLES   (2)1859(1)   CAROLINA
K. of Gt. Britain   *1844 †1925   D. of Teck   *1833 †1897   BOWES-LYON   *1832 †1922   CAVENDISH   BURNABY
Emp. of India   d. of Christian IX   *1837 †1900   d. of Adolphus   E. of Strathmore   d. of Oswald Smith   -BENTINCK   *1833 †1918
*1841 †1910   K. of Denmark   D. of Cambridge   & Kinghorne   of Blendon Hall   *1817 †1865   d. of Edwin Burnaby
                                                                                 *1824 †1904   gs. of William   of Baggrave Hall
                                                                                                                         D. of Portland

✠ GEORGE V   1893   MARY   CLAUDE BOWES-LYON   1881   NINA
K. of Gt. Britain   Pr. of Teck   E. of Strathmore   CAVENDISH-BENTINCK
Emp. of India   *1867 †1953   & Kinghorne   *1862 †1938
*1865 †1936   *1855 †1944

✠ GEORGE VI   1923   ELIZABETH
K. of Gt. Britain   BOWES-LYON
Emp. of India   *1900 †2002
*1895 †1952

♛ ELIZABETH II
Q. of Gt. Britain
*1926

CHRISTIAN IX   1842   LOUISA   CONSTANTINE   1848   ALEXANDRA   ALEXANDER   1851   JULIA   LOUIS IV   1862   ALICE
K. of Denmark   *1817 †1898   NIKOLAEVICH   *1830 †1911   Pr. of Hesse   Pr. of Battenberg   GD. of Hesse   *1843 †1878
*1818 †1906   d. of William   GD. of Russia   d. of Joseph   *1823 †1888   *1825 †1895   *1837 †1892   d. of Victoria
                       Lgv. of Hesse-Kassel   *1827 †1892   D. of Saxe-Altenburg   d. of John Maurice   Q. of Gt. Britain
                                             s. of Emp. Nicolas I   C. of Hauke

GEORGE I   1867   OLGA   LOUIS   1884   VICTORIA
K. of the Hellenes   KONSTANTINOVNA   MOUNTBATTEN   Pr. of Hesse
*1845 †1913   GD. of Russia   M. of Milford Haven   *1863 †1950
                       *1851 †1926   *1854 †1921

ANDREW   1903   ALICE
Pr. of Greece & Denmark   MOUNTBATTEN
*1882 †1944   *1885 †1969

PHILIP
D. of Edinburgh
*1921

the end of her life the old Queen had done much to establish the role of a constitutional monarch, and had a memory and experience without parallel in Europe, not to mention her extensive kinship (Tables 56–7).

Her son Edward VII, genial and cosmopolitan, reigned only briefly in a splendid twilight of a now vanished age. To his son George V, straightforward and courageous, fell the crushing burden of leading his empire in the First World War (1914–18) and the troubled years which followed. The wealth and manpower of Britain had been sadly reduced by the war; unemployment rose; most of Ireland broke away from the United Kingdom. In all his tasks he was aided by his beloved wife, Queen Mary.

George V was followed by his eldest son, who had a brief reign. Even before he was crowned, he made known his desire to marry an American divorcée, Mrs Simpson. The sentiments of the country and the empire were resolutely opposed to the breach with tradition; at the end of 1936 he abdicated and was created Duke of Windsor.

George VI, like his father, had been trained as a sailor and had fought at Jutland. He had to lead his countrymen in the Second World War against the ambitions of Hitler, more sinister and more diseased than those of Louis XIV or Napoleon. Like many of his family in this century, George VI married outside the world of foreign princesses. As a consequence Table 11 reveals that the immediate ancestors of Queen Elizabeth II have more British blood than those of any sovereign since Elizabeth I. Similarly the arms of Lord Harewood, Angus Ogilvy and Lord Snowdon, of whom the first two belong to ancient families, have replaced the blazons of the Germanic princelings to whom the Hanoverian kings betrothed their daughters (Table 9).

The early death of King George VI brought the present Queen to the throne. Her husband, Prince Philip, Duke of Edinburgh, belongs to the royal

Queen Elizabeth II and Prince Philip on their wedding day in 1947, flanked by the then King George VI, the Queen Elizabeth and Mary the Queen mother.

family of Greece which is a branch of that of Denmark; his ancestors, as can be seen from Table 11, came mainly from Germany, but his mother was a Mountbatten and the prince had adopted that name before his marriage. The coat-of-arms devised for him refers in the four quarters to his Danish, Greek and Mountbatten ancestry and to the city of Edinburgh from which he takes his title. The arms of the royal issue exhibit some customary features. The Prince of Wales has a small escutcheon of the arms of Wales, surmounted by his coronet, in the centre of his shield. The blazons of Princess Anne and Lady Diana Spencer, now Princess of Wales, are shown upon lozenges, a custom for women which goes back at least to Tudor times. Even in heraldic display, the hopes of the future are mingled with the traditions of the past. For the sake of convenience, however, the practice has not been followed throughout this book.

Lady Diana's arms, used by her family since the end of the sixteenth century, are in fact a variant of the shield of the distinguished medieval family of Despencer. This is the first marriage of an heir to the throne to an Englishwoman since the future James II married Anne Hyde in 1659. Beside the lozenge of Princess Anne can be seen the blazon of her husband; this coat-of-arms was granted to the father of Captain Mark Phillips, who accordingly will use a label of three points during his father's lifetime. The Phillips arms reflect the family's equestrian interests. A second son, such as Angus Ogilvy, may similarly use a small crescent. Recent marriages of the royal family of the United Kingdom show a range of social standing and nationality which would have amazed, and certainly shocked, the Hanoverians of the eighteenth century with their rigid protocol.

Chapter 4

SCOTLAND

The earliest evidence of a cohesive northern kingdom is linked with the name of Kenneth MacAlpin and the period 843–50. He succeeded in uniting the four races which inhabited what today we call Scotland, the Picts in the north, the Celts in the South, the Angles in the southeast, and in the west the immigrants from Northern Ireland. It was to this group that Kenneth himself belonged, and their name, Scots, originally applied to the Irish, has come to be used for the northern Kingdom. The union of Scotland was made easier by attacks on the country from Scandinavia. Wide Norwegian settlement took place in the Orkneys, Shetlands and Western Isles and even in northeast Scotland. Orkney and Shetland did not finally become part of Scotland until 1468. The work of blending these various races, divided by mountains and seas, into a single nation was bound to be slow and laborious.

Kenneth MacAlpin died in 858. The Crown continued in his family but seldom directly from father to son; more normally a reigning King of Alba – as the realm was called – was succeeded by a brother or nephew. Gradually the kingship came to alternate between two branches of the descendants of Kenneth. This system avoided the peril of minorities, but substituted the temptation of anticipatory assassination. At the head of Table 12 is the name of Duncan I. He was murdered by Macbeth, a scion of the other line. Macbeth ruled for seventeen years before he was slain by Duncan's son, Malcolm III. This sort of thing had been going on for 200 years, but Shakespeare picked on a particular example to metamorphose into his powerful tragedy. Only with the descendants of David I does an hereditary descent begin to be visible.

Malcolm III married a remarkable woman, Margaret, who was a great-niece of the last Anglo-Saxon King, Edward the Confessor. Though saintly, she was a significant figure. Under her influence there was an infiltration of clergy and others from the south, while the splendour of her court encouraged commerce in wine and other luxuries and lessened the isolation of Scotland. Her son, David, profited by the disorders in England during the reign of Stephen and managed to occupy Carlisle and Newcastle, thus bringing his frontier down to the Roman wall: his authority even reached into parts of Lancashire. In 1149 the lands between Tweed and Tyne were ceded to him 'for ever'. While he reigned, a substantial number of Norman families came north and settled in Scotland, and others intermarried with Scottish neighbours. With their advent Scotland moved from tribalism into the feudal pattern of western Europe.

In Scotland the powerful King David I was succeeded by the youthful Malcolm IV; in England the weak Stephen was followed by the powerful Henry II, who in 1157 compelled Malcolm to give back the northern counties and in 1174 captured William the Lion and extorted an oath of feudal homage from him. However, Richard I sold back this superiority for 10,000 marks towards his crusade; Scotland was free again, and there was warm friendship between the two chivalrous Kings. All his life William hoped to regain Northumberland, but in vain. In 1237 his son, Alexander II, finally accepted by treaty the frontier of Cheviot and Tweed, which lasted till 1603 and is still marked today.

The well-known arms of Scotland are depicted on Table 12 by the name of William the Lion. He may well have used the lion which was his nickname; there is no positive evidence that it was enclosed within the decorative double line of fleurs-de-lys ('a double tressure flory counterflory'). But this blazon certainly appears on the seal (1215) of his son, Alexander II, and may well have been used by William also. Established tradition maintains that the fleurs-de-lys

TABLE 12

SCOTLAND
Kings until the accession of Robert Bruce

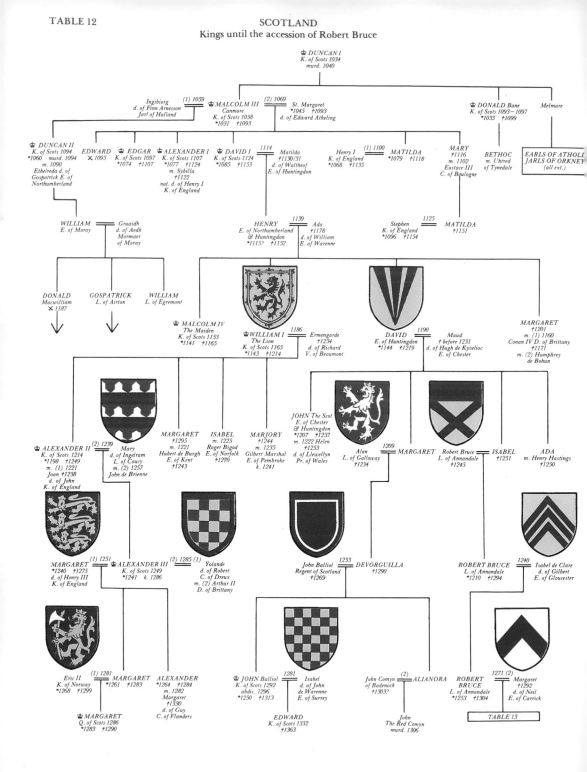

♔ DUNCAN I
K. of Scots 1034
murd. 1040

Ingibiorg (1) 1059 ♔ MALCOLM III (2) 1069 St. Margaret | ♔ DONALD Bane | Melmare
d. of Finn Arnesson | Canmore | *1045 †1093 | K. of Scots 1093–1097
Jarl of Halland | K. of Scots 1058 | d. of Edward Atheling | *1033 †1099
| *1031 †1093

♔ DUNCAN II | EDWARD | ♔ EDGAR | ♔ ALEXANDER I | ♔ DAVID I | 1114 Matilda | Henry I (1) 1100 MATILDA | MARY | BETHOC | EARLS OF ATHOLL
K. of Scots 1094 | ✗ 1093 | K. of Scots 1097 | K. of Scots 1107 | K. of Scots 1124 | d. of Waltheof | K. of England *1079 †1118 | †1116 | m. Uhtred | JARLS OF ORKNEY
*1060 murd. 1094 | | *1074 †1107 | *1077 †1124 | *1085 †1153 | E. of Huntingdon | *1068 †1135 | m. 1102 | of Tynedale | (all ext.)
m. 1090 | | | m. Sybilla | | †1130/31 | | Eustace III
Ethelreda d. of | | | †1122 | | | | C. of Boulogne
Gospatrick E. of | | | nat. d. of Henry I
Northumberland | | | K. of England

WILLIAM = Gruaidh | HENRY 1139 Ada | Stephen 1125 MATILDA
E. of Moray | d. of Aedk | E. of Northumberland | †1178 | K. of England | †1151
| Mormaer | & Huntingdon | d. of William | *1096 †1154
| of Moray | *1115? †1152 | E. of Warenne

DONALD | GOSPATRICK | WILLIAM | ♔ MALCOLM IV | ♔ WILLIAM I 1186 | DAVID 1190 Maud | MARGARET
Macuilliam | L. of Airton | L. of Egremont | The Maiden | The Lion | E. of Huntingdon | † before 1231 | †1201
✗ 1187 | | | K. of Scots 1153 | K. of Scots 1165 | *1144 †1219 | d. of Hugh de Kyvelioc | m. (1) 1160
| | | *1141 †1165 | *1143 †1214 | | E. of Chester | Conan IV D. of Brittany
| | | | Ermengarde | | | †1171
| | | | †1234 | | | m. (2) Humphrey
| | | | d. of Richard | | | de Bohun
| | | | V. of Beaumont

♔ ALEXANDER II (2) 1239 Mary | MARGARET | ISABEL | MARJORY | JOHN The Scot | Alan 1209 MARGARET | Robert Bruce = ISABEL | ADA
K. of Scots 1214 | d. of Ingelram | *1295 | m. 1225 | †1244 | E. of Chester | L. of Galloway | L. of Annandale | †1251 | m. Henry Hastings
*1198 †1249 | L. of Coucy | m. 1221 | Roger Bigod | m. 1235 | & Huntingdon | †1234 | †1245 | | †1250
m. (1) 1221 | m. (2) 1257 | Hubert de Burgh | E. of Norfolk | Gilbert Marshal | *1207 †1237
Joan †1238 | John de Brienne | E. of Kent | †1270 | E. of Pembroke | m. 1222 Helen
d. of John | | †1243 | | k. 1241 | †1253
K. of England | | | | | d. of Llewellyn
| | | | | Pr. of Wales

MARGARET (1) 1251 ♔ ALEXANDER III (2) 1285 (1) Yolande | John Balliol 1233 DEVORGUILLA | ROBERT BRUCE 1240 Isabel de Clare
*1240 †1275 | K. of Scots 1249 | d. of Robert | Regent of Scotland | †1290 | L. of Annandale | d. of Gilbert
d. of Henry III | *1241 k. 1286 | C. of Dreux | †1269 | | *1210 †1294 | E. of Gloucester
K. of England | | m. (2) Arthur II
| | D. of Brittany

Eric II (1) 1281 MARGARET | ALEXANDER | ♔ JOHN Balliol 1281 Isabel | John Comyn (2) ALIANORA | ROBERT 1271 (2) Margaret
K. of Norway | *1261 †1283 | *1264 †1284 | K. of Scots 1292 | d. of John | of Badenoch | BRUCE | †1292
*1268 †1299 | | m. 1282 | abdic. 1296 | de Warenne | †1303? | L. of Annandale | d. of Neil
| | Margaret | *1250 †1313 | E. of Surrey | | *1253 †1304 | E. of Carrick
| | †1330
| | d. of Guy
| | C. of Flanders

♔ MARGARET | EDWARD | John | TABLE 13
Q. of Scots 1286 | K. of Scots 1332 | The Red Comyn
*1283 †1290 | †1363 | murd. 1306

symbolize the 'auld' alliance between France and Scotland: legends that this amity went back to the time of Charlemagne can be dismissed. It may be that the tressure was initially a device for strengthening the shield, or that the king wished for a distinctive and decorative difference from other members of the nobility using lions of various colours. In any case we may say as did the poet Dunbar of the Scottish lion:

In field of gold he stude full myghtely
With floure-de-lucis sirculit lustely.

UNIFICATION

Alexander II died in 1249 leaving an infant son of the same name, whose minority was overseen by a body of regents. Unluckily Alexander III was killed in a riding accident in 1286 while still only 44. His son and daughter were dead, and his only descendant was a distant baby granddaughter, the Fair Maid of Norway. The nobles of Scotland recognized her as the heiress of the throne and appointed six guardians: their action shows how fully the idea of hereditary succession had become accepted. By 1290 it had also been agreed with Edward I of England that his eldest son should marry the infant princess and thus unite the two Kingdoms. Most unhappily little Margaret did not survive the voyage from Norway and died in Orkney later in the year.

The succession to the Scottish throne was now wide open. Thirteen candidates presented themselves, many the issue of illegitimate children of William the Lion. The most prominent were two descendants of David, Earl of Huntingdon, John Balliol and Robert Bruce, and also John Comyn who was descended from Bethoc, son of Donald Bane, and was brother-in-law of Balliol. The magnates of Scotland asked the help of Edward I; when he met them he made clear that he had come to give his decision as overlord of Scotland. This was an unwarrantable claim, for if Edward had truly believed himself the feudal Lord of Scotland, he ought to have assumed the wardship of the Fair Maid of Norway from the moment of Alexander III's death. None the less Edward was supported by a considerable army; the realm of Scotland, though protesting, was disorganized and the main competitors accepted his arbitration on his own terms.

In effect two of the claimants led the field. John Balliol was the son of an elder John Balliol, a northern English baron, and his wife Devorguilla, a great Scottish heiress (it was they who founded Balliol, one of the earliest Oxford colleges). Through his mother the younger Balliol was the senior descendant of David, Earl of Huntingdon. Robert Bruce derived from a younger daughter of Huntingdon but was a genera-tion nearer to him, a circumstance which counted for more in the Middle Ages than it would do today. At the end of 1292 Edward gave his verdict for Balliol, who became John I. Almost at once resistance in Scotland began to stiffen against Edward, regarded as a foreign tyrant, and Balliol, viewed as his puppet. The unification of the Scottish nation was undoubtedly advanced by Edward's aggression. In 1296 the hapless and spiritless King John abdicated and Edward took Scotland into his own hands.

For ten years Scotland had no king. At first, resistance crystallized round the heroic figure of Sir William Wallace; then Robert Bruce, Earl of Carrick, grandson of the competitor, took up the struggle. In 1306 he murdered John Comyn, the Red (son of the competitor, John the Black Comyn), a curious reversion to the dynastic rivalries of earlier centuries, and was crowned King of Scotland at Scone. Next year the aged Edward I died on his way to fight Bruce. The next King of England, Edward II, lacked both vigour and military capacity. Robert I (Table 13) was able to build up his forces and eventually to win a striking military triumph at Bannockburn in 1314; the English army was routed and many rich prisoners captured by the Scots while Edward fled southwards.

INDEPENDENCE

Before Bruce died in 1329, England had abandoned by treaty all claim to superiority over Scotland. Henceforward Scotland was free. David, King Robert's only son, was born late in life, and had a long minority; during this period Edward, son of John Balliol, landed with an army, contrived to be crowned but was soon driven out, only to be reinstated briefly by the forces of Edward III of England, to whom he proceeded to surrender the southern counties of Scotland. It was many years before the Scots recovered all that he had so improvidently given away. David II had been moved to France and soon after his return he was captured by the English at Neville's Cross (1346), and not released until 1357 when a heavy ransom was paid. The country had suffered severely from the constant wars, from the Black Death in 1349–50 (and again in 1361–2), and was now drastically taxed to free the King, who was only 46 when he died childless in 1371. During his reign we hear for the first time of the three estates of the Scottish Parliament – the prelates, the nobility and the burghs.

It had long been settled that Robert the Steward was heir to the throne. He belonged to a family, originally from Brittany, which had crossed to England where they became known as Fitzalan. A younger son, Walter, accompanied David I to Scotland and was appointed High Steward. Their coat-of-arms with its checkered fess may allude to the squared cloth spread in the Exchequer to aid counting; it is known from a seal dated 1190. Unluckily, Robert II came to the throne old and did not prove a vigorous king, nor did his son Robert III, who also became king at an advanced age. The nobility, strong in their own regions, began to usurp the power which ought to have belonged to the Crown. Ironically, after the death of Robert III in 1406, the problem of disorder and over-mighty subjects was complicated by a series of minorities resulting from violent deaths. James I was eleven, James II six, James III eight and James V and James VI each one year old at their accessions. Queen Mary was seven days old.

Scotland was normally allied to France; France and England were at war; there was intermittent fighting mingled with more serious campaigns. In the fifteenth century detachments of Scottish troops went to France and valiantly assisted the French in their battles with the English; indeed the French kings had a personal Scots Guard. Some Scottish nobles received French titles: Archibald Douglas, Earl of Douglas and Duke of Touraine (Table 13), is an example. His coat-of-arms with its red heart commemorates the mission of his ancestor, Sir James Douglas, who was charged to bear the heart of Robert Bruce to the Holy Land, but actually fell fighting the infidel in Spain. Another interesting shield is that of Sir John Lyon, son-in-law of Robert II: his original arms were simply a blue lion on a silver field, but he was granted on marriage the same tressure as appears in the royal arms. This blazon is still borne by his direct descendant, Elizabeth, the Queen Mother (Table 9).

For nearly fifty years Scottish history was dominated by the Dukes of Albany. Robert, brother of Robert III (who had been called John till he ascended the throne), was first regent in 1388 during the incapacity of his father and held the post for most of his brother's reign: his very title of Albany was derived from the old name for Scotland. In 1406 Robert III sent his infant son (James I to be) to France but he was captured by the English and kept prisoner till 1423 while the Albanys, father and son, continued as regents. James I was then in the prime of life and vigour; he passed a series of laws seeking to curb the disorders of the day and sought, though without success, to enlarge the Scottish Parliament rather on the lines of what he had seen in England. In private life he was musical and a writer of poetry; his murder in 1437 abruptly terminated the reign of one of the ablest Stuart kings. Disorder and lawlessness broke out again.

James II tried in the eleven years of his active reign to follow up the work of his father but was sadly slain by the explosion of one of his own guns at the

King James IV of Scotland (1473–1513) before an altar with the full achievement of Scotland. 16th-century MS.

siege of Roxburgh in 1460. Once again there was a minority; but when James III (Table 14) began to reign he proved a feckless ruler, interested in the arts but little concerned with government. The King continued to bicker with his nobility and was mysteriously murdered in 1488. It is fair to note that his reign saw widespread developments in architecture in Scotland and in general a higher standard of living. This was accompanied by inflation and debasement of the coinage; at this time four Scots pounds equalled one English.

James IV was a handsome, talented and industrious king. In his turn he attacked the problems of

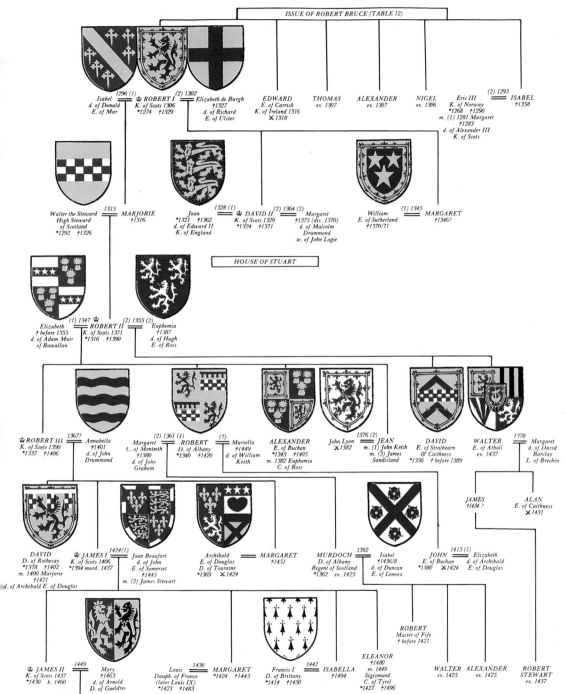

ISSUE OF ROBERT BRUCE (TABLE 12)

Isabel
d. of Donald
E. of Mar

1296 (1)

♚ ROBERT I
K. of Scots 1306
*1274 †1329

(2) 1302

Elizabeth de Burgh
†1327
d. of Richard
E. of Ulster

EDWARD
E. of Carrick
K. of Ireland 1316
✕ 1318

THOMAS
ex. 1307

ALEXANDER
ex. 1307

NIGEL
ex. 1306

Eric III
K. of Norway
*1268 †1290
m. (1) 1281 Margaret
†1283
d. of Alexander III
K. of Scots

(2) 1293

ISABEL
†1358

Walter the Steward
High Steward
of Scotland
*1292 †1326

1315

MARJORIE
†1316

Joan
*1321 †1362
d. of Edward II
K. of England

1328 (1)

♚ DAVID II
K. of Scots 1329
*1324 †1371

(2) 1364 (2)

Margaret
†1375 (div. 1370)
d. of Malcolm
Drummond
w. of John Logie

William
E. of Sutherland
†1370/71

(1) 1345

MARGARET
†1346?

HOUSE OF STUART

Elizabeth
† before 1355
d. of Adam Muir
of Rowallan

(1) 1347 ♚

ROBERT II
K. of Scots 1371
*1316 †1390

(2) 1355 (2)

Euphemia
†1387
d. of Hugh
E. of Ross

♚ ROBERT III
K. of Scots 1390
*1337 †1406

1367?

Annabella
†1401
d. of John
Drummond

Margaret
C. of Menteith
†1380
d. of John
Graham

(2) 1361 (2)

ROBERT
D. of Albany
*1340 †1420

(?)

Muriella
†1449
d. of William
Keith

ALEXANDER
E. of Buchan
*1343 †1405
m. 1382 Euphemia
C. of Ross

John Lyon
✕ 1382

1376 (2)

JEAN
m. (1) John Keith
m. (3) James
Sandisland

DAVID
E. of Strathearn
& Caithness
*1356 † before 1389

WALTER
E. of Atholl
ex. 1437

1378

Margaret
d. of David
Barclay
L. of Brechin

JAMES
†1434 ?

ALAN
E. of Caithness
✕ 1431

DAVID
D. of Rothesay
*1378 †1402
m. 1400 Marjorie
†1421
d. of Archibald E. of Douglas

♚ JAMES I
K. of Scots 1406
*1394 murd. 1437

1424(1)

Joan Beaufort
d. of John
E. of Somerset
†1445
m. (2) James Stewart

Archibald
E. of Douglas
D. of Touraine
*1369 ✕ 1424

MARGARET
†1451

MURDOCH
D. of Albany
Regent of Scotland
*1362 ex. 1425

1392

Isabel
†1456/8
d. of Duncan
E. of Lennox

JOHN
E. of Buchan
*1380 ✕ 1424

1413 (1)

Elizabeth
d. of Archibald
E. of Douglas

ROBERT
Master of Fife
† before 1421

♚ JAMES II
K. of Scots 1437
*1430 k. 1460

1449

Mary
†1463
d. of Arnold
D. of Gueldres

Louis
Dauph. of France
(later Louis IX)
*1423 †1483

1436

MARGARET
*1424 †1445

Francis I
D. of Brittany
*1414 †1450

1442

ISABELLA
†1494

ELEANOR
†1480
m. 1449
Sigismund
C. of Tyrol
*1427 †1496

WALTER
ex. 1425

ALEXANDER
ex. 1425

ROBERT
STEWART
ex. 1437

TABLE 14

TABLE 14

SCOTLAND
Stuart Kings until the accession to the English throne

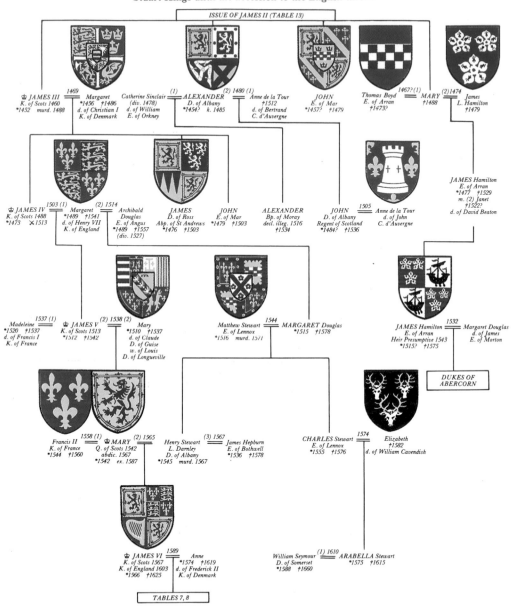

ISSUE OF JAMES II (TABLE 13)

♔ *JAMES III*
K. of Scots 1460
*1452 murd. 1488

1469 Margaret
*1456 †1486
d. of Christian I
K. of Denmark

Catherine Sinclair (1)
(div. 1478)
d. of William
E. of Orkney

ALEXANDER
D. of Albany
*1454? k. 1485

(2) 1480 (1) Anne de la Tour
†1512
d. of Bertrand
C. d'Auvergne

JOHN
E. of Mar
*1457? †1479

Thomas Boyd 1467?(1)
E. of Arran
†1473?

MARY (2)1474
†1488

James
L. Hamilton
†1479

♔ *JAMES IV*
K. of Scots 1488
*1473 ✕ 1513

1503 (1) Margaret
*1489 †1541
d. of Henry VII
K. of England

(2) 1514 Archibald
Douglas
E. of Angus
*1489 †1557
(div. 1527)

JAMES
D. of Ross
Abp. of St Andrews
*1476 †1503

JOHN
E. of Mar
*1479 †1503

ALEXANDER
Bp. of Moray
decl. illeg. 1516
†1534

JOHN
D. of Albany
Regent of Scotland
*1484? †1536

1505 Anne de la Tour
d. of John
C. d'Auvergne

JAMES Hamilton
E. of Arran
*1477 †1529
m. (2) Janet
†1522?
d. of David Beaton

Madeleine 1537 (1)
*1520 †1537
d. of Francis I
K. of France

♔ *JAMES V*
K. of Scots 1513
*1512 †1542

(2) 1538 (2) Mary
*1510 †1537
d. of Claude
D. of Guise
w. of Louis
D. of Longueville

Matthew Stewart
E. of Lennox
*1516 murd. 1571

1544 *MARGARET Douglas*
*1515 †1578

JAMES Hamilton
E. of Arran
Heir Presumptive 1543
*1515? †1575

1532 Margaret Douglas
d. of James
E. of Morton

DUKES OF
ABERCORN

Francis II 1558 (1)
K. of France
*1544 †1560

♔ *MARY* (2) 1565
Q. of Scots 1542
abdic. 1567
*1542 ex. 1587

Henry Stewart (3) 1567 James Hepburn
L. Darnley
D. of Albany
*1545 murd. 1567

E. of Bothwell
*1536 †1578

CHARLES Stewart
E. of Lennox
*1555 †1576

1574 Elizabeth
†1582
d. of William Cavendish

♔ *JAMES VI*
K. of Scots 1567
K. of England 1603
*1566 †1625

1589 Anne
*1574 †1619
d. of Frederick II
K. of Denmark

William Seymour (1) 1610 *ARABELLA Stewart*
D. of Somerset
*1588 †1660

*1575 †1615

TABLES 7, 8

the turbulent and powerful aristocracy, vigorously moving round the country and holding courts of law. Printing came to Scotland. Edinburgh was established as the royal capital, and the palace of Holyroodhouse erected. But his relations with the Tudors deteriorated, and in 1513 he advanced into England only to be defeated catastrophically at Flodden. The King was killed and the Scottish nobility suffered fearful losses.

The long minority of James V was marked by a new fear of England and a lack of enthusiasm for the old alliance with France, but when James at last came of age he sought two French brides in succession. He also courted the favour of the Pope and was able to found the College of Justice, Scotland's highest court, with money from the Church. But he foolishly invaded England in 1542; his army was defeated at Solway Moss, and James died on hearing the news, leaving his new-born daughter Mary as his only heir.

QUEEN OF SCOTS

Mary, Queen of Scots, is one of the romantic and tragic figures of history. Tall—over 1.8m (6ft)—and beautiful, with many talents, she lacked judgement and was faced with a political and religious situation which might have baffled an older and wiser sovereign. She had been sent to France at the age of six, had briefly married the French King and was a childless widow not yet nineteen when she returned to Scotland in 1561.

Much had changed in Scotland during her absence. In particular the waves of a Protestant Reformation had broken over the land and the new religion had been accepted by Parliament in 1560; the Mass was abolished and the authority of the Pope rejected. True, there was still a large Catholic party but it was to a kingdom pledged to the new religion that Mary, herself a devout Catholic, returned. She

can scarcely be blamed for her mistake in marrying her cousin Lord Darnley: he was tall and good-looking though also insolent and debauched. Furthermore, the union consolidated her claim on the throne of England (Table 14). Mary had already voiced this from France when Elizabeth ascended the throne, and had signified it by placing the arms of England on an escutcheon over the blazon of her husband and herself. Darnley was proclaimed as king (as had been Francis II of France). Unhappily Mary came to hate her husband, even before the birth of their only child, though it is far from certain that she was involved in his mysterious murder in January 1567. It is certain that her prompt marriage to Bothwell, who was implicated in the murder, outraged public opinion. Later in the year the hapless Queen was compelled to abdicate in favour of her infant son. A year later she fled over the border to take refuge with Elizabeth.

The English Queen was highly embarrassed. Mary was placed in captivity; but her name was involved in various plots, and in 1587 Elizabeth reluctantly consented to her execution. To the end her assumption of the English arms was a charge against her.

Not surprisingly the youthful James VI had a disturbed minority. As he grew older he feared domination by the Kirk, the reformed Church. As a measure of defence he fought long and successfully to keep some form of episcopal system. In external politics he moved closer to England; he married a Protestant princess from Denmark; he clearly had his eye firmly fixed on the English throne. His patience and powers of compromise were duly rewarded. In 1603, with 36 years of uneasy Scottish kingship behind him, he rode south to the richer land of England. He only once returned to Scotland.

James VI and I thus united the two Crowns on one head; but it was not until 1707 that the two realms were finally welded into the Kingdom of Great Britain.

Chapter 5

DENMARK

Of the three Scandinavian Kingdoms Denmark has always been the smallest and most fertile; in the Middle Ages it was also the most populous. In the eleventh century Canute the Great was briefly King of England and also ruler of Denmark, Norway and Sweden; he was the uncle of Sweyn Estridson who figures at the head of Tables 15 and 16.

The monarchy was elective, and no great attention was paid in the twelfth century to legitimacy of birth. It should also be remembered that almost throughout the Middle Ages the district of Scania, the southern tip of modern Sweden, was part of Denmark, which thus completely controlled the entrances to the Baltic. Waldemar I, the Great, brought some order after a period of violence and anarchy. He and both his sons carried on campaigns against the heathen Wends in Pomerania. Tradition relates that a red banner with a white cross descended from heaven (it was more plausibly a gift from the Pope) during an expedition of Waldemar II; this has become the national flag of Denmark and the insignia of the ancient Order of the Danebrog.

The attractive arms of Denmark first appear about 1190 in the reign of Canute VI. They consist of three running blue lions in a gold field dotted with red hearts. There were at first variations in the position of the lions' heads, which were at times crowned, and always in the number of hearts. Unluckily, the end of Waldemar II's reign was clouded by his capture and imprisonment and was followed by a period of instability.

Eric IV, nicknamed 'Ploughpenny' from putting a tax on ploughs, was murdered by his brother – a reversal of the biblical role of Abel. King Abel's wife was a daughter of the Count of Holstein. His curious and striking shield must have begun as an elaborate form of indented bordure; it came, however, to be regarded as a nettle leaf and even to be characteristic

of the prickly nature of the folk of Holstein, an area whose fortunes were constantly involved with those of Denmark. Eric V inherited an uncertain Crown; surrounded by potentially hostile kinsmen, he was protected by his mother, a dark, able queen renowned as a horsewoman. In 1282 he was compelled to grant an extensive charter of liberties which established a parliamentary assembly (*hof*) as a check on royal power. Eric VI and Christopher II were unsuccessful kings who wasted their resources on futile wars. For eight years after the death of Christopher there was no king in Denmark and the country was overrun by the Counts of Holstein. In 1340 Waldemar IV, called Atterdag from his reiteration that 'Tomorrow would be a new day', began a long and painful task of reconstruction. Under his patronage Copenhagen became the capital of Denmark, and after long struggles a commercial relationship with the wealthy and powerful Hanseatic towns of north Germany was achieved, though parts of Denmark had to be mortgaged to them, and they were given a say in the choice of the Danish king.

Waldemar Atterdag left no son; his two daughters had married the rulers of Mecklenburg and Norway. The people of Denmark chose the youthful Olaf of Norway as their king, a decision with which the Hanseatic towns concurred. His mother, Margaret, was his guardian and mentor. She was an outstanding woman, shrewd, pious and above all tactful, who made it her goal to unite the three northern Kingdoms (Table 18). When her son Olaf, already King of Norway and Denmark, died in 1387, she was constituted regent of both countries; next year a body of Swedish nobility appealed to her for help, and Queen Margaret defeated Albrecht of Sweden and became regent of that Kingdom also. She had already chosen her great-nephew Eric, son of the Duke of Pomerania, as the heir of Norway and in 1397 at

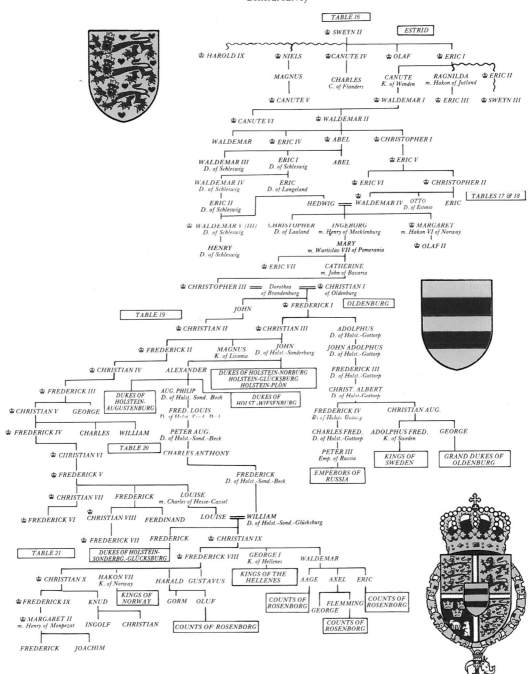

TABLE 16

DENMARK
House of Estrid

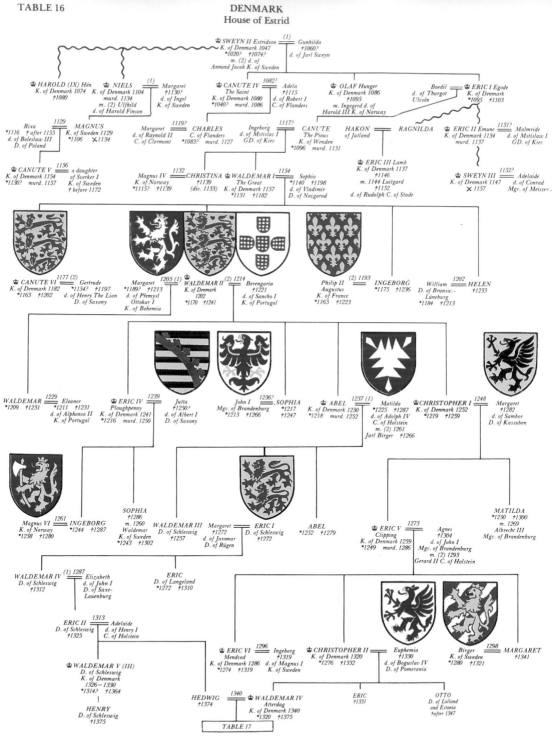

♔ SWEYN II Estridson (1) Gunhilda
K. of Denmark 1047 †1060?
*1020? †1074? d. of Jarl Sweyn
m. (2) d. of
Annund Jacob K. of Sweden

♔ HAROLD (IX) Hén ♔ NIELS (1) Margaret ♔ CANUTE IV 1082? Adela ♔ OLAF Hunger Boedil ♔ ERIC I Egode
K. of Denmark 1074 K. of Denmark 1104 †1130? The Saint †1115 K. of Denmark 1086 d. of Thurgot K. of Denmark
†1080 murd. 1134 d. of Ingel K. of Denmark 1080 d. of Robert I †1095 Ulvsön *1095 †1103
m. (2) Ulfhild K. of Sweden *1040? murd. 1086 C. of Flanders m. Ingegerd d. of
d. of Harold Finson Harold III K. of Norway

Rixa 1129 MAGNUS Margaret 1119? CHARLES Ingeborg 1117? CANUTE HAKON RAGNILDA ♔ ERIC II Emune 1131? Malmfride
*1116 † after 1155 K. of Sweden 1129 d. of Raynold II C. of Flanders d. of Mstislaw I The Pious of Jutland K. of Denmark 1134 d. of Mstislaw I
d. of Boleslaw III *1106 ✗1134 C. of Clermont *1083? murd. 1127 GD. of Kiev K. of Wenden murd. 1137 GD. of Kiev
D. of Poland *1096 murd. 1131

♔ CANUTE V 1156 a daughter Magnus IV 1132 CHRISTINA ♔ WALDEMAR I 1154 Sophia ♔ ERIC III Lamb ♔ SWEYN III 1152? Adelaide
K. of Denmark 1154 of Sverker I K. of Norway †1139 The Great *1140 †1198 K. of Denmark 1137 K. of Denmark 1147 d. of Conrad
*1130? murd. 1157 K. of Sweden *1115? †1139 (div. 1133) K. of Denmark 1157 d. of Vladimir †1146 ✗1157 Mgv. of Meissen
† before 1172 *1131 †1182 D. of Novgorod m. 1144 Luitgard
†1152
d. of Rudolph C. of Stade

♔ CANUTE VI 1177 (2) Gertrude Margaret 1205 (1) ♔ WALDEMAR II (2) 1214 Berengaria Philip II (2) 1193 INGEBORG William 1202 HELEN
K. of Denmark 1182 *1154? †1197 *1189? †1213 K. of Denmark †1221 Augustus *1175 †1236 D. of Brunsw.- †1233
*1163 †1202 d. of Henry The Lion d. of Přemysl 1202 d. of Sancho I K. of France Lüneburg
D. of Saxony Ottokar I *1170 †1241 K. of Portugal *1165 †1223 *1184 †1213
K. of Bohemia

WALDEMAR 1229 Eleanor ♔ ERIC IV 1239 Jutta John I 1236? SOPHIA ♔ ABEL 1237 (1) Matilda ♔ CHRISTOPHER I 1248 Margaret
*1209 †1231 *1211 †1231 Ploughpenny *1250? Mgv. of Brandenburg *1217 K. of Denmark 1250 *1225 †1287 K. of Denmark 1252 †1282
d. of Alphonso II K. of Denmark 1241 d. of Albert I *1213 †1266 †1247 *1218 murd. 1252 d. of Adolph IV *1219 †1259 d. of Sambor
K. of Portugal *1216 murd. 1250 D. of Saxony C. of Holstein D. of Kassuben
m. (2) 1261
Jarl Birger †1266

Magnus VI 1261 INGEBORG SOPHIA WALDEMAR III Margaret ERIC I ABEL ♔ ERIC V 1273 Agnes MATILDA
K. of Norway *1244 †1287 †1286 D. of Schleswig †1272 d. of Jaromar D. of Schleswig *1252 †1279 Clipping †1304 *1250 †1300
*1238 †1280 m. 1260 *1257 D. of Rügen †1272 K. of Denmark 1259 d. of John I m. 1269
Waldemar *1249 murd. 1286 Mgv. of Brandenburg Albrecht III
K. of Sweden m. (2) 1293 Mgv. of Brandenburg
*1243 †1302 Gerard II C. of Holstein

WALDEMAR IV (1) 1287 Elizabeth ERIC
D. of Schleswig d. of John I D. of Langeland
†1312 D. of Saxe- *1272 †1310
Lauenburg

ERIC II 1313 Adelaide ♔ ERIC VI 1296 Ingeborg ♔ CHRISTOPHER II Euphemia Birger 1298 MARGARET
D. of Schleswig d. of Henry I Mendved †1319 K. of Denmark 1320 †1330 K. of Sweden †1341
†1325 C. of Holstein K. of Denmark 1286 d. of Magnus I *1276 †1332 d. of Boguslav IV *1280 †1321
*1274 †1319 K. of Sweden D. of Pomerania

♔ WALDEMAR V (III) HEDWIG 1340 ♔ WALDEMAR IV ERIC OTTO
D. of Schleswig †1374 Atterdag †1331 D. of Lolland
K. of Denmark K. of Denmark 1340 and Estonia
1326–1330 *1320 †1375 †after 1347
*1314? †1364

HENRY TABLE 17
D. of Schleswig
†1375

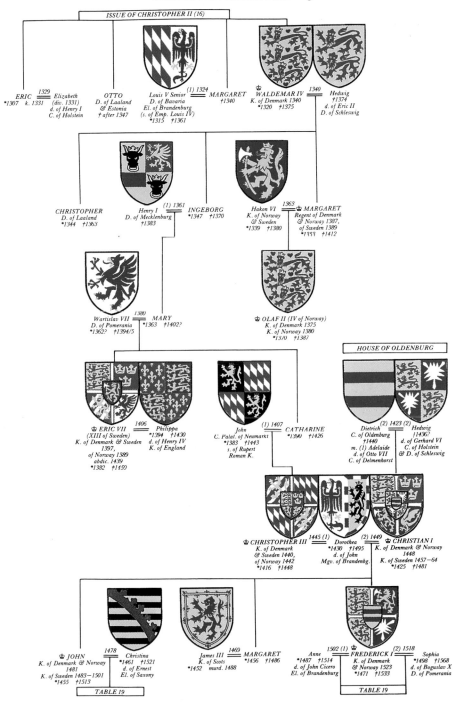

ISSUE OF CHRISTOPHER II (16)

ERIC ⚭ 1329 Elizabeth
*1307 k. 1331 (div. 1331)
d. of Henry I
C. of Holstein

OTTO
D. of Laaland
& Estonia
† after 1347

Louis V Senior ⚭ (1) 1324 MARGARET
D. of Bavaria †1340
El. of Brandenburg
(s. of Emp. Louis IV)
*1315 †1361

WALDEMAR IV ⚭ 1340 Hedwig
K. of Denmark 1340 †1374
*1320 †1375 d. of Eric II
D. of Schleswig

CHRISTOPHER
D. of Laaland
*1344 †1363

Henry I ⚭ (1) 1361 INGEBORG
D. of Mecklenburg *1347 †1370
†1383

Hakon VI ⚭ 1363 MARGARET
K. of Norway Regent of Denmark
& Sweden & Norway 1387,
*1339 †1380 of Sweden 1389
*1353 †1412

Wartislav VII ⚭ 1380 MARY
D. of Pomerania *1363 †1402?
*1362? †1394/5

♔ OLAF II (IV of Norway)
K. of Denmark 1375
K. of Norway 1380
*1370 †1387

HOUSE OF OLDENBURG

♔ ERIC VII ⚭ 1406 Philippa
(XIII of Sweden) *1394 †1430
K. of Denmark & Sweden d. of Henry IV
1397, K. of England
of Norway 1389
abdic. 1439
*1382 †1459

John ⚭ (1) 1407 CATHARINE
C. Palat. of Neumarkt *1390 †1426
*1383 †1443
s. of Rupert
Roman K.

Dietrich ⚭ (2) 1423 (2) Hedwig
C. of Oldenburg †1496?
†1440 d. of Gerhard VI
m. (1) Adelaide C. of Holstein
d. of Otto VII & D. of Schleswig
C. of Delmenhorst

♔ CHRISTOPHER III ⚭ 1445 (1) Dorothea ⚭ (2) 1449 ♔ CHRISTIAN I
K. of Denmark *1430 †1495 K. of Denmark & Norway
& Sweden 1440, d. of John 1448
of Norway 1442 Mgv. of Brandenbg. K. of Sweden 1457–64
*1416 †1448 *1425 †1481

♔ JOHN ⚭ 1478 Christina
K. of Denmark & Norway *1461 †1521
1481 d. of Ernest
K. of Sweden 1483–1501 El. of Saxony
*1455 †1513

James III ⚭ 1469 MARGARET
K. of Scots *1456 †1486
*1452 murd. 1488

Anne ⚭ 1502 (1) FREDERICK I ⚭ (2) 1518 Sophia
*1487 †1514 K. of Denmark *1498 †1568
d. of John Cicero & Norway 1523 d. of Boguslav X
El. of Brandenburg *1471 †1533 D. of Pomerania

TABLE 19

TABLE 19

TABLE 18

DENMARK, NORWAY AND SWEDEN
Union of Kalmar

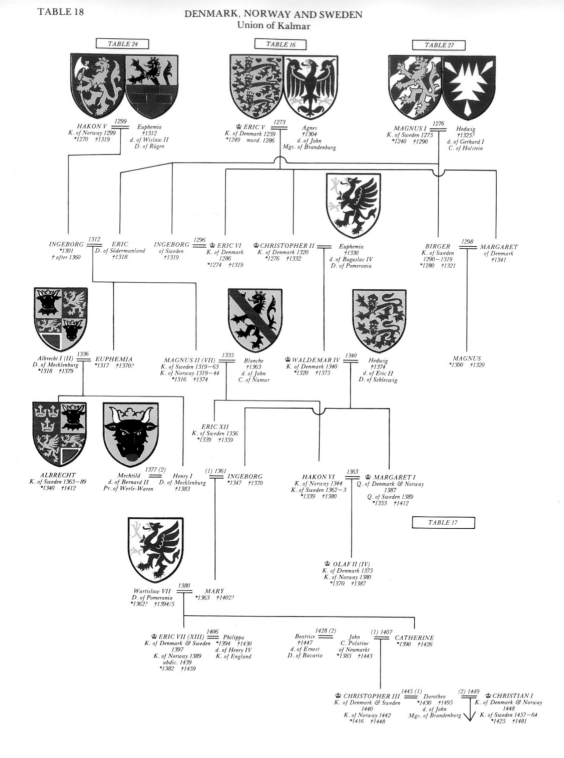

TABLE 24   TABLE 16   TABLE 27

HAKON V *1299*
K. of Norway 1299
*1270 †1319
═══ **Euphemia**
†1312
d. of Wislaw II
D. of Rügen

♚ **ERIC V** *1273*
K. of Denmark 1259
*1249 murd. 1286
═══ **Agnes**
†1304
d. of John
Mgv. of Brandenburg

MAGNUS I *1276*
K. of Sweden 1275
*1240 †1290
═══ **Hedwig**
†1325?
d. of Gerhard I
C. of Holstein

INGEBORG
*1301
† after 1360
═══ *1312* **ERIC**
D. of Södermanland
†1318

INGEBORG *1296*
of Sweden
†1319
═══ ♚ **ERIC VI**
K. of Denmark
1286
*1274 †1319

♚ **CHRISTOPHER II**
K. of Denmark 1320
*1276 †1332
═══ **Euphemia**
†1330
d. of Boguslav IV
D. of Pomerania

BIRGER
K. of Sweden
1290−1319
*1280 †1321
═══ *1298* **MARGARET**
of Denmark
†1341

Albrecht I (II)
D. of Mecklenburg
*1318 †1379
═══ *1336* **EUPHEMIA**
*1317 †1370?

MAGNUS II (VII) *1335*
K. of Sweden 1319−63
K. of Norway 1319−44
*1316 †1374
═══ **Blanche**
†1363
d. of John
C. of Namur

♚ **WALDEMAR IV** *1340*
K. of Denmark 1340
*1320 †1375
═══ **Hedwig**
†1374
d. of Eric II
D. of Schleswig

MAGNUS
*1300 †1320

ERIC XII
K. of Sweden 1356
*1339 †1359

ALBRECHT
K. of Sweden 1363−89
*1340 †1412

Mechtild *1377 (2)*
d. of Bernard II
Pr. of Werle-Waren
═══ **Henry I**
D. of Mecklenburg
†1383

(1) 1361 **INGEBORG**
*1347 †1370

HAKON VI *1363*
K. of Norway 1344
K. of Sweden 1362−3
*1339 †1380
═══ ♚ **MARGARET I**
Q. of Denmark & Norway
1387
Q. of Sweden 1389
*1353 †1412

TABLE 17

♚ **OLAF II (IV)**
K. of Denmark 1375
K. of Norway 1380
*1370 †1387

Wartislaw VII *1380*
D. of Pomerania
*1362? †1394/5
═══ **MARY**
*1363 †1402?

♚ **ERIC VII (XIII)** *1406*
K. of Denmark & Sweden
1397
K. of Norway 1389
abdic. 1439
*1382 †1459
═══ **Philippa**
*1394 †1430
d. of Henry IV
K. of England

Beatrice *1428 (2)*
†1447
d. of Ernest
D. of Bavaria
═══ **John**
C. Palatine
of Neumarkt
*1383 †1443
═══ *(1) 1407* **CATHERINE**
*1390 †1426

♚ **CHRISTOPHER III** *1445 (1)*
K. of Denmark & Sweden
1440
K. of Norway 1442
*1416 †1448
═══ **Dorothea**
*1430 †1495
d. of John
Mgv. of Brandenburg
═══ *(2) 1449* ♚ **CHRISTIAN I**
K. of Denmark & Norway
1448
K. of Sweden 1457−64
*1425 †1481

Kalmar she won recognition of Eric by Sweden and Denmark. The union which she so skilfully built up was one of Crowns rather than interests, but it survived uneasily until 1523.

Eric VII of Denmark (Eric XIII of Sweden) was less skilled in handling men than Queen Margaret; in 1439, after long and unrewarding conflict with Holstein and with the Hanseatic towns, he was compelled to abdicate in favour of his nephew, Duke Christopher of Bavaria (Table 17). Thereafter he became a pirate. By ill-fortune Christopher died childless at the age of 33. The Danish nobility promptly elected the young Count of Oldenburg, who claimed descent from Eric V and consolidated his position by marrying Christopher's widow. Christian I was accepted with less alacrity by Norway and only after some years by Sweden; from him all subsequent rulers of Denmark are descended. Christian's mother came of the family ruling Schleswig and Holstein, and now his uncle, the Duke, died childless. Christian was successful in taking his place and in 1460 issued a famous declaration that Schleswig and Holstein should always be united. The risk implicit in this promise was that Schleswig was a Danish province while Holstein was technically part of the Holy Roman Empire. Nor did the money he had to spend on this southward expansion endear him to his Swedish subjects who spoke of him as 'an empty purse'. In 1462 he founded the Order of the Elephant.

John and Christian II continued the endeavour to rule over all three Kingdoms, but in the face of discontent, mainly in Sweden. Christian II was a striking figure, enlightened in his attitude to his humbler subjects but capable of barbaric revenges; he broke with the Pope and began the Reformation in Denmark. By 1523, when the wayward Christian fled his realms, Sweden had been lost for ever and the Union of Kalmar was over. But for two centuries Norway and Denmark continued under the same Crown (Table 19).

Christian II was followed by his uncle, Frederick I, who bestowed the Duchy of Holstein-Gottorp (which he himself held previously) on his younger son Adolphus, from whom descended the Emperors of Russia (from Peter III), some later Kings of Sweden and the Grand-Dukes of Oldenburg. Christian III was an avowed Lutheran and completed the process of Reformation in Denmark, but he was a man of moderation and dealt justly with all his subjects. In 1550 however he placed on his coat-of-arms the three crowns of Sweden as a reminder of the claims under the Union of Kalmar which he had not forgotten. Frederick II was a patron of learning, as his father had been before him, and was on good terms with the famous astronomer Tycho Brahe. An

King Christian IV of Denmark (1577–1648), by Karel van Mander, 1640.

aggravation of bad relations between Danes and Swedes was the establishment of Magnus, the King's brother, as King of Livonia.

Christian IV had the longest reign in Danish history. Handsome and robust, he was a great builder and the first part of his rule saw a long period of peace and many triumphs of architecture such as Frederiksborg and Rosenborg castles. From 1625 to 1629 he was involved without much advantage in the Thirty Years' War in Germany, and then in 1643 Denmark was attacked by the now formidable forces of Sweden. The King resisted valiantly and lost an eye in a sea-battle, but the Treaty of Brömsebro (1645) really made clear that Denmark was only the second power in the north. Sweden acquired the provinces of Scania and Halland and reached her natural frontier.

Hitherto the King of Denmark had always been elected by the nobility and had been compelled to recognize this fact by the 'Capitulations' which they then granted. Frederick III was coerced into signing a capitulation strongly in favour of the aristocracy, who exercised great power through a Council of State. In 1657 war broke out with Sweden. The ensuing winter (1657-8) was one of the coldest in history and the Swedes crossed from the mainland to the islands of Denmark on ice. The Treaty of Roskilde (1658) ratified the changes which were taking place: Sweden consolidated her control of her sea coast and even acquired part of Norway for a short spell. The general discontent manifested itself in favour of the King. In 1660 a popular delegation offered Frederick the throne of Denmark as an hereditary kingdom; the power of the nobility was broken, and it also proved to be the last meeting of the Estates for two centuries. A law was drawn up giving expression to royal absolutism; this declaration applied also to Norway, but unhappily it proved impossible to establish it because of the now fragmentary Duchies of Schleswig-Holstein which had been further sub-divided among the sons and grandsons of Duke John of Holstein-Sonderburg (d. 1622). The rulers of Holstein-Gottorp (Table 15) were already pursuing a policy of their own.

Christian V, whose brother was husband of the English Queen Anne, was in turn involved in wars with Sweden which brought triumphs to the growing Danish navy. In 1679 peace was achieved and the two realms began to lose some of their ancient antagonism. Trade was fostered both with Iceland and the Faroes, which belonged to Denmark of old, and also with more recent colonies in the East and West Indies and in Africa (the castle at Accra in Ghana is Danish by origin). Administration fell more into middle-class hands, and a new code of laws was promulgated. During the reign of Frederick IV the Swedes made an unsuccessful attempt to conquer Norway, but the consequent peace again brought the northern Powers closer. Frederick tired of his first wife and married Anne Sophia morganatically (and bigamously) in 1712; only nine years later could the union become official. In 1728 a great fire devastated Copenhagen. Christian VI (Table 20), a pious narrow man, whose wife was much disliked, enjoyed an unusually peaceful reign; indeed Denmark played small part in the affairs of Europe throughout the mid-eighteenth century. Christian was busy and pedantic; his son Frederick was more worldly and more indolent, allowing a series of able ministers, including the elder Bernstorff, a Hanoverian by birth, to govern for him and to keep the country clear of the Seven Years' War. In 1743 Frederick V had been a candidate for the vacant throne of Sweden, but Russian diplomacy installed Adolphus Frederick of Holstein-Gottorp. As Table 23 demonstrates, the successful incumbent of the Swedish throne was a kinsman of Frederick V. The ancestry of the latter was almost wholly confined to north German alliances, with the exception of his uterine descent which stemmed from Franconia (Table 22).

Dissipation may have ended the life of Frederick V prematurely; it crippled that of Christian VII, who is thought to have been a victim of *dementia praecox*. In 1768 the young King fell under the influence of his doctor who advanced to become first minister and lover of the Queen, a sister of George III of England.

Struensee was a liberal at heart and issued many reforming edicts, but his social background and methods stimulated a palace revolution and he was executed in 1772. The younger Bernstorff slowly rose to power and encouraged a policy of understanding with Russia. The Gottorp section of Holstein, belonging to the Czar, was exchanged for the detached German Counties of Oldenburg and Delmenhorst, which in due course became an independent grand-duchy.

From 1784 the future Frederick VI was regent for his father, and with the aid of Bernstorff endeavoured to keep Denmark neutral in the convulsions which were overtaking Europe. Land reform was tackled and Denmark became the first nation to abolish and condemn the slave trade (1792). But neutrality has its perils; England in her desperate struggle against Napoleon felt compelled to eliminate the powerful Danish fleet. Nelson destroyed a part of it in 1801 and Canning mounted a more formidable attack in 1807 when Britain stood alone and the command of the sea was crucial. This arbitrary act drove Denmark into the arms of Bonaparte. By the peace treaty of 1814 she had to cede Norway to Sweden and Heligoland to Britain, and faced the future with a heavy debt and a capital in ruins.

Frederick VI, who had succeeded his mad father in 1808, was a liberal and popular ruler. Towards the end of his reign he introduced four diets, one for Jutland, one for the Islands, one each for Schleswig and Holstein; the last two also gained their own law courts. Unhappily, as the nineteenth century wore on, the sense of difference, the wide use of the German language and a long separatist tradition led to a movement for independence within the Duchies. Christian VIII, whose son was childless, announced that Schleswig was governed by the same rules of descent as Denmark, but voiced doubts about Holstein. Frederick VII on his accession in 1848, the year of revolutions, introduced a new constitution with a single assembly for all parts of the Kingdom. The Dukes of Holstein-Augustenburg proclaimed independence and called in the help of Prussia.

THE SCHLESWIG-HOLSTEIN QUESTION

After desultory campaigning, an international conference in London (1852) resolved that Duke Christian of Glücksburg should be recognized as Frederick's heir and should reign in Denmark and the Duchies. The nearest heir to Frederick VII was the Prince of Hesse-Cassel, but he obligingly resigned his claims in favour of his sister who was also Christian's wife. The last act of Frederick VII in 1863 was to promulgate a new constitution uniting Schleswig with Denmark and giving Holstein local government. On his death Christian IX succeeded

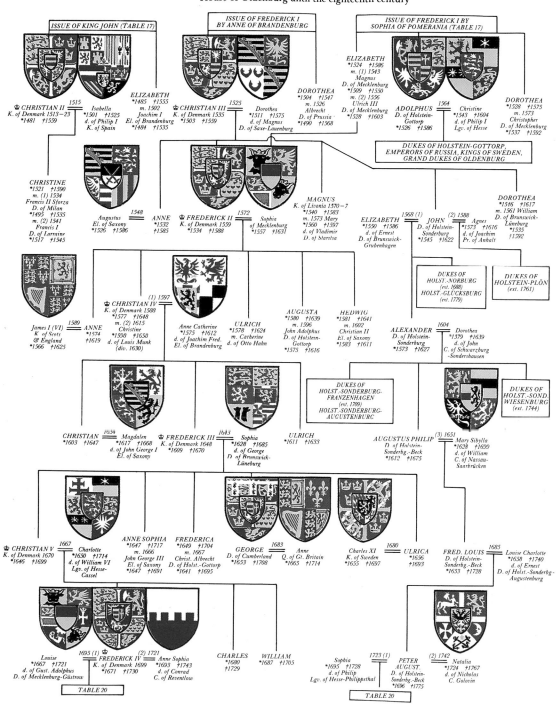

ISSUE OF KING JOHN (TABLE 17)

ISSUE OF FREDERICK I BY ANNE OF BRANDENBURG

ISSUE OF FREDERICK I BY SOPHIA OF POMERANIA (TABLE 17)

ELIZABETH
*1524 †1586
m. (1) 1543
Magnus
D. of Mecklenburg
*1509 †1550
m. (2) 1556
Ulrich III
D. of Mecklenburg
*1528 †1603

♔ CHRISTIAN II
K. of Denmark 1513–23
*1481 †1559
1515 Isabella
*1501 †1525
d. of Philip I
K. of Spain

ELIZABETH
*1485 †1555
m. 1502
Joachim I
El. of Brandenburg
*1484 †1535

♔ CHRISTIAN III
K. of Denmark 1535
*1503 †1559
1525 Dorothea
*1511 †1575
d. of Magnus
D. of Saxe-Lauenburg
*1490 †1568

DOROTHEA
*1504 †1547
m. 1526
Albrecht
D. of Prussia
*1490 †1568

ADOLPHUS
D. of Holstein-Gottorp
*1526 †1586
1564 Christine
*1543 †1604
d. of Philip I
Lgv. of Hesse

DOROTHEA
*1528 †1575
m. 1573
Christopher
D. of Mecklenburg
*1537 †1592

CHRISTINE
*1521 †1590
m. (1) 1534
Francis II Sforza
D. of Milan
*1495 †1535
m. (2) 1541
Francis I
D. of Lorraine
*1517 †1545

DUKES OF HOLSTEIN-GOTTORP,
EMPERORS OF RUSSIA, KINGS OF SWEDEN,
GRAND DUKES OF OLDENBURG

Augustus
El. of Saxony
*1526 †1586
1548 ANNE
*1532
†1585

♔ FREDERICK II
K. of Denmark 1559
*1534 †1588
1572 Sophia
of Mecklenburg
*1557 †1631

MAGNUS
K. of Livonia 1570–7
*1540 †1583
m. 1573 Mary
*1560 †1597
d. of Vladimir
D. of Staritsa

ELIZABETH
*1550 †1586
d. of Ernest
D. of Brunswick-Grubenhagen

JOHN
D. of Holstein-Sonderburg
*1545 †1622
1568 (1) ... (2) 1588
Agnes
*1573 †1616
d. of Joachim
Pr. of Anhalt

DOROTHEA
*1546 †1617
m. 1561 William
D. of Brunswick-Lüneburg
*1535 †1592

James I (VI)
K. of Scots
& England
*1566 †1625
1589 ANNE
*1574
†1619

♔ CHRISTIAN IV
K. of Denmark 1588
*1577 †1648
m. (2) 1615
Christine
*1598 †1650
d. of Louis Munk
(div. 1630)
(1) 1597

Anne Catherine
*1575 †1612
d. of Joachim Fred.
El. of Brandenburg

ULRICH
*1578 †1624
m. Catherine
d. of Otto Hahn

AUGUSTA
*1580 †1639
John Adolphus
D. of Holstein-Gottorp
*1575 †1616

HEDWIG
*1581 †1641
m. 1602
Christian II
El. of Saxony
*1583 †1611

ALEXANDER
D. of Holstein-Sonderburg
*1573 †1627
1604 Dorothea
*1579 †1639
d. of John
C. of Schwarzburg-Sondershausen

DUKES OF HOLST.-NORBURG
(ext. 1688)
HOLST.-GLÜCKSBURG
(ext. 1779)

DUKES OF HOLSTEIN-PLÖN
(ext. 1761)

DUKES OF HOLST.-SONDERBURG-FRANZENHAGEN
(ext. 1709)
HOLST.-SONDERBURG-AUGUSTENBURG

DUKES OF HOLST.-SOND.-WIESENBURG
(ext. 1744)

CHRISTIAN
*1603 †1647
1634 Magdalen
*1617 †1668
d. of John George I
El. of Saxony

♔ FREDERICK III
K. of Denmark 1648
*1609 †1670
1643 Sophia
*1628 †1685
d. of George
D. of Brunswick-Lüneburg

ULRICH
*1611 †1633

AUGUSTUS PHILIP
D. of Holstein-Sonderbg.-Beck
*1612 †1675
(3) 1651 Mary Sibylla
*1628 †1699
d. of William
C. of Nassau-Saarbrücken

♔ CHRISTIAN V
K. of Denmark 1670
*1646 †1699
1667 Charlotte
*1650 †1714
d. of William VI
Lgv. of Hesse-Cassel

ANNE SOPHIA
*1647 †1717
m. 1666
John George III
El. of Saxony
*1647 †1691

FREDERICA
*1649 †1704
m. 1667
Christ. Albrecht
D. of Holst.-Gottorp
*1641 †1695

GEORGE
D. of Cumberland
*1653 †1708
1683 Anne
Q. of Gt. Britain
*1665 †1714

Charles XI
K. of Sweden
*1655 †1697
1680 ULRICA
*1656
†1693

FRED. LOUIS
D. of Holstein-Sonderbg.-Beck
*1653 †1728
1685 Louise Charlotte
*1658 †1740
d. of Ernest
D. of Holst.-Sonderbg.-Augustenburg

Louise
*1667 †1721
d. of Gust. Adolphus
D. of Mecklenburg-Güstrow

♔ FREDERICK IV
K. of Denmark 1699
*1671 †1730
1695 (1) ... (2) 1721
Anne Sophia
*1693 †1743
d. of Conrad
C. of Reventlow

CHARLES
*1680
†1729

WILLIAM
*1687 †1705

Sophia
*1695 †1728
d. of Philip
Lgv. of Hesse-Philippsthal

PETER AUGUST.
D. of Holstein-Sonderbg.-Beck
*1696 †1775
1723 (1) ... (2) 1742
Natalia
*1724 †1767
d. of Nicholas
C. Golovin

TABLE 20

TABLE 20

TABLE 20

DENMARK AND NORWAY
House of Oldenburg in the eighteenth and nineteenth centuries

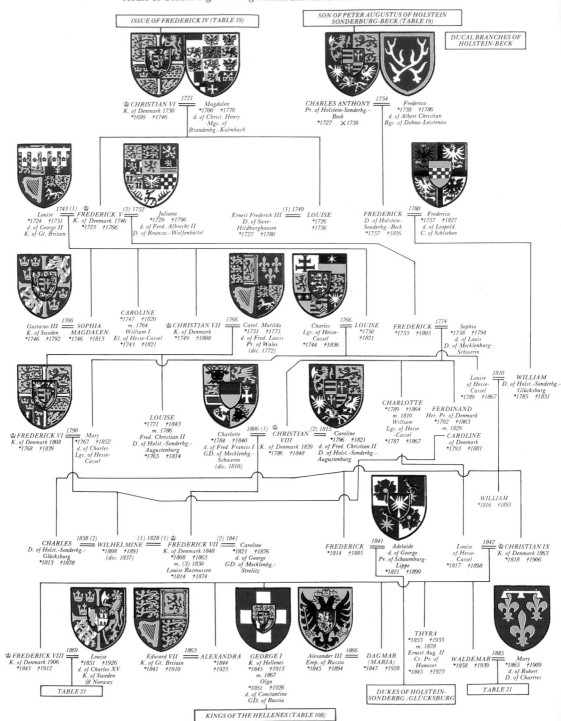

ISSUE OF FREDERICK IV (TABLE 19)

SON OF PETER AUGUSTUS OF HOLSTEIN
SONDERBURG-BECK (TABLE 19)

DUCAL BRANCHES OF
HOLSTEIN-BECK

♛ CHRISTIAN VI
K. of Denmark 1730
*1699 †1746
— 1721 —
Magdalen
*1700 †1770
d. of Christ. Henry
Mgv. of
Brandenbg.-Kulmbach

CHARLES ANTHONY
Pr. of Holstein-Sonderbg.-
Beck
*1727 ✕1759
— 1754 —
Frederica
*1738 †1786
d. of Albert Christian
Bgv. of Dohna-Leistenau

Louise
*1724 †1751
d. of George II
K. of Gt. Britain
— 1743 (1) —
FREDERICK V
K. of Denmark 1746
*1723 †1766
— (2) 1752 —
Juliana
*1729 †1796
d. of Ferd. Albrecht II
D. of Brunsw.-Wolfenbüttel

Ernest Frederick III
D. of Saxe-
Hildburghausen
*1727 †1780
— (1) 1749 —
LOUISE
*1726
†1756

FREDERICK
D. of Holstein-
Sonderbg.-Beck
*1757 †1816
— 1780 —
Frederica
*1757 †1827
d. of Leopold
C. of Schlieben

Gustavus III
K. of Sweden
*1746 †1792
— 1766 —
SOPHIA
MAGDALEN
*1746 †1813

CAROLINE
*1747 †1820
m. 1764
William I
El. of Hesse-Cassel
*1743 †1821

♛ CHRISTIAN VII
K. of Denmark
*1749 †1808
— 1766 —
Carol. Matilda
*1751 †1775
d. of Fred. Lewis
Pr. of Wales
(div. 1772)

Charles
Lgv. of Hesse-
Cassel
*1744 †1836
— 1766 —
LOUISE
*1750
†1821

FREDERICK
*1753 †1805
— 1774 —
Sophia
*1758 †1794
d. of Louis
D. of Mecklenburg-
Schwerin

Louise
of Hesse-Cassel
*1789 †1867
— 1810 —
WILLIAM
D. of Holst.-Sonderbg.-
Glücksburg
*1785 †1831

♛ FREDERICK VI
K. of Denmark 1808
*1768 †1839
— 1790 —
Mary
*1767 †1852
d. of Charles
Lgv. of Hesse-
Cassel

LOUISE
*1771 †1843
m. 1786
Fred. Christian II
D. of Holst.-Sonderbg.-
Augustenburg
*1765 †1814

Charlotte
*1784 †1840
d. of Fred. Francis I
GD. of Mecklenbg.-
Schwerin
(div. 1810)
— 1806 (1) —
CHRISTIAN
VIII
K. of Denmark 1839
*1786 †1848
— (2) 1815 —
Caroline
*1796 †1821
d. of Fred. Christian II
D. of Holst.-Sonderbg.-
Augustenburg

CHARLOTTE
*1789 †1864
m. 1810
William
Lgv. of Hesse
-Cassel
*1787 †1867

FERDINAND
Her. Pr. of Denmark
*1792 †1863
m. 1829
CAROLINE
of Denmark
*1793 †1881

WILLIAM
*1816 †1893

CHARLES
D. of Holst.-Sonderbg.-
Glücksburg
*1813 †1878
— 1838 (2) —
WILHELMINE
*1808 †1891
(div. 1837)
— (1) 1828 (1) —
♛ FREDERICK VII
K. of Denmark 1848
*1808 †1863
m. (3) 1850
Louise Rasmussen
*1814 †1874
— (2) 1841 —
Caroline
*1821 †1876
d. of George
GD. of Mecklenbg.-
Strelitz

FREDERICK
*1814 †1885
— 1841 —
Adelaide
d. of George
Pr. of Schaumburg-
Lippe
*1821 †1899

Louise
of Hesse-
Cassel
*1817 †1898
— 1842 —
♛ CHRISTIAN IX
K. of Denmark 1863
*1818 †1906

♛ FREDERICK VIII
K. of Denmark 1906
*1843 †1912
— 1869 —
Louise
*1851 †1926
d. of Charles XV
K. of Sweden
& Norway

Edward VII
K. of Gt. Britain
*1841 †1910
— 1863 —
ALEXANDRA
*1844
†1925

GEORGE I
K. of Hellenes
*1845 †1913
m. 1867
Olga
*1851 †1926
d. of Constantine
GD. of Russia

Alexander III
Emp. of Russia
*1845 †1894
— 1866 —
DAGMAR
(MARIA)
*1847 †1928

THYRA
*1853 †1933
m. 1878
Ernest Aug. II
Cr. Pr. of
Hanover
*1845 †1923

WALDEMAR
*1858 †1939
— 1885 —
Mary
*1865 †1909
d. of Robert
D. of Chartres

TABLE 21

DUKES OF HOLSTEIN-
SONDERBG.-GLÜCKSBURG

TABLE 21

KINGS OF THE HELLENES (TABLE 108)

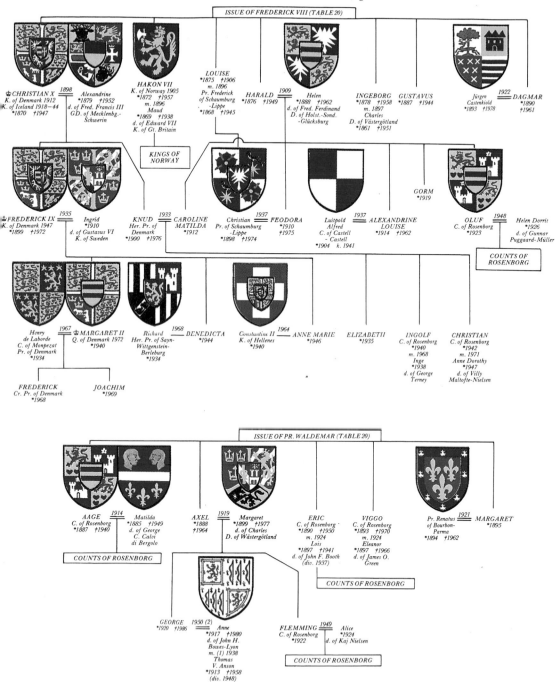

ISSUE OF FREDERICK VIII (TABLE 20)

CHRISTIAN X *1898* Alexandrine
K. of Denmark 1912 *1879 †1952
K. of Iceland 1918–44 d. of Fred. Francis III
*1870 †1947 GD. of Mecklenbg.-Schwerin

HAKON VII
K. of Norway 1905
*1872 †1957
m. 1896
Maud
*1869 †1938
d. of Edward VII
K. of Gt. Britain

LOUISE
*1875 †1906
m. 1896
Pr. Frederick
of Schaumburg
-Lippe
*1868 †1945

HARALD *1909*
*1876 †1949

Helen
*1888 †1962
d. of Fred. Ferdinand
D. of Holst.-Sond.
-Glücksburg

INGEBORG
*1878 †1958
m. 1897
Charles
D. of Västergötland
*1861 †1951

GUSTAVUS
*1887 †1944

Jürgen *1922* **DAGMAR**
Castenskiold *1890
*1893 †1978 †1961

KINGS OF
NORWAY

FREDERICK IX *1935* Ingrid
K. of Denmark 1947 *1910
*1899 †1972 d. of Gustavus VI
K. of Sweden

KNUD *1933* **CAROLINE
Her. Pr. of MATILDA**
Denmark *1912
*1900 †1976

Christian *1937* **FEODORA**
Pr. of Schaumburg *1910
-Lippe †1975
*1898 †1974

Luitpold *1937* **ALEXANDRINE
Alfred LOUISE**
C. of Castell *1914 †1962
-Castell
*1904 k. 1941

GORM
*1919

OLUF *1948* Helen Dorrit
C. of Rosenborg *1926
*1923 d. of Gunnar
Puggaard-Müller

COUNTS OF
ROSENBORG

Henry *1967* **MARGARET II**
de Laborde Q. of Denmark 1972
C. of Monpezat *1940
Pr. of Denmark
*1934

Richard *1968* **BENEDICTA**
Her. Pr. of Sayn- *1944
Wittgenstein-
Berleburg
*1934

Constantine II *1964* **ANNE
K. of Hellenes MARIE**
*1940 *1946

ELIZABETH
*1935

INGOLF
C. of Rosenborg
*1940
m. 1968
Inge
*1938
d. of George
Terney

CHRISTIAN
C. of Rosenborg
*1942
m. 1971
Anne Dorothy
*1947
d. of Villy
Maltofte-Nielsen

FREDERICK
Cr. Pr. of Denmark
*1968

JOACHIM
*1969

ISSUE OF PR. WALDEMAR (TABLE 20)

AAGE *1914* Matilda
C. of Rosenborg *1885 †1949
*1887 †1940 d. of George
C. Calvi
di Bergolo

AXEL *1919* Margaret
*1888 *1899 †1977
†1964 d. of Charles
D. of Wästergötland

ERIC
C. of Rosenborg
*1890 †1950
m. 1924
Lois
*1897 †1941
d. of John F. Booth
(div. 1937)

VIGGO
C. of Rosenborg
*1893 †1970
m. 1924
Eleanor
*1897 †1966
d. of James O.
Green

Pr. Renatus *1921* **MARGARET**
of Bourbon- *1895
Parma
*1894 †1962

COUNTS OF ROSENBORG

GEORGE *1950 (2)* Anne
*1920 †1986 *1917 †1980
d. of John H.
Bowes-Lyon
m. (1) 1938
Thomas
V. Anson
*1913 †1958
(div. 1948)

FLEMMING *1949* Alice
C. of Rosenborg *1924
*1922 d. of Kaj Nielsen

COUNTS OF ROSENBORG

TABLE 22

DENMARK
Ancestors of Frederick V, Christian IX and Margaret II

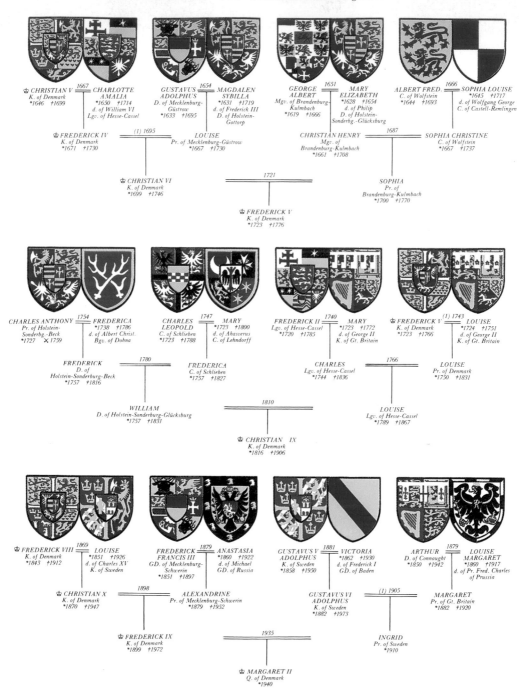

CHRISTIAN V ═══1667═══ **CHARLOTTE**
K. of Denmark   **AMALIA**
*1646 †1699   **1650 †1714*
     d. of William VI
     Lgv. of Hesse-Cassel

GUSTAVUS ═══1654═══ **MAGDALEN**
ADOLPHUS   **SYBILLA**
D. of Mecklenburg-   **1631 †1719*
Güstrow   *d. of Frederick III*
*1633 †1695   *D. of Holstein-*
     Gottorp

GEORGE ═══1651═══ **MARY**
ALBERT   **ELIZABETH**
Mgv. of Brandenburg-   **1628 †1654*
Kulmbach   *d. of Philip*
*1619 †1666   *D. of Holstein-*
     Sonderbg.-Glücksburg

ALBERT FRED. ═══1666═══ **SOPHIA LOUISE**
C. of Wolfstein   **1645 †1717*
*1644 †1693   *d. of Wolfgang George*
     C. of Castell-Remlingen

FREDERICK IV ───(1) 1695─── **LOUISE**
K. of Denmark   *Pr. of Mecklenburg-Güstrow*
*1671 †1730   **1667 †1730*

CHRISTIAN HENRY ───1687─── **SOPHIA CHRISTINE**
Mgv. of   *C. of Wolfstein*
Brandenburg-Kulmbach   **1667 †1737*
*1661 †1708

CHRISTIAN VI ─────1721─────
K. of Denmark
*1699 †1746

     SOPHIA
     Pr. of
     Brandenburg-Kulmbach
     *1700 †1770

FREDERICK V
K. of Denmark
*1723 †1776

CHARLES ANTHONY ═══1754═══ **FREDERICA**
Pr. of Holstein-   **1738 †1786*
Sonderburg.-Beck   *d. of Albert Christ.*
*1727 ✕1759   *Bgv. of Dohna*

CHARLES ═══1747═══ **MARY**
LEOPOLD   **1723 †1800*
C. of Schlieben   *d. of Ahasverus*
*1723 †1788   *C. of Lehndorff*

FREDERICK II ═══1740═══ **MARY**
Lgv. of Hesse-Cassel   **1723 †1772*
*1720 †1785   *d. of George II*
     K. of Gt. Britain

FREDERICK V ───(1) 1743─── **LOUISE**
K. of Denmark   **1724 †1751*
*1723 †1766   *d. of George II*
     K. of Gt. Britain

FREDERICK ───1780───
D. of
Holstein-Sonderburg-Beck
*1757 †1816

   FREDERICA
   C. of Schlieben
   *1757 †1827

CHARLES ───1766───
Lgv. of Hesse-Cassel
*1744 †1836

   LOUISE
   Pr. of Denmark
   *1750 †1831

WILLIAM ─────1810─────
D. of Holstein-Sonderburg-Glücksburg
*1757 †1831

     LOUISE
     Lgv. of Hesse-Cassel
     *1789 †1867

CHRISTIAN IX
K. of Denmark
*1816 †1906

FREDERICK VIII ═══1869═══ **LOUISE**
K. of Denmark   **1851 †1926*
*1843 †1912   *d. of Charles XV*
     K. of Sweden

FREDERICK ═══1879═══ **ANASTASIA**
FRANCIS III   **1860 †1922*
GD. of Mecklenburg-   *d. of Michael*
Schwerin   *GD. of Russia*
*1851 †1897

GUSTAVUS V ═══1881═══ **VICTORIA**
ADOLPHUS   **1862 †1930*
K. of Sweden   *d. of Frederick I*
*1858 †1950   *GD. of Baden*

ARTHUR ═══1879═══ **LOUISE**
D. of Connaught   **MARGARET**
*1850 †1942   **1860 †1917*
     d. of Pr. Fred. Charles
     of Prussia

CHRISTIAN X ───1898─── **ALEXANDRINE**
K. of Denmark   *Pr. of Mecklenburg-Schwerin*
*1870 †1947   **1879 †1952*

GUSTAVUS VI ───(1) 1905─── **MARGARET**
ADOLPHUS   *Pr. of Gt. Britain*
K. of Sweden   **1882 †1920*
*1882 †1973

FREDERICK IX ─────1935─────
K. of Denmark
*1899 †1972

     INGRID
     Pr. of Sweden
     *1910

MARGARET II
Q. of Denmark
*1940

(Table 20) but one of the Augustenburgs declared himself Duke of Schleswig-Holstein. The background to the Schleswig-Holstein question, confused by a long litter of unresolved treaties running back from the London agreement of 1852 to the pronouncement of 1460, was a nightmare to diplomats. Adroitly Bismarck organized an invasion by Prussian and Austrian troops; Denmark was swiftly defeated and savage terms imposed. Not only German-speaking Holstein (and the smaller adjacent Duchy of Lauenburg) but Danish Schleswig were handed over to joint rule by Prussia and Austria, which meant within a few years incorporation in Prussian Germany.

Christian IX was mainly of German descent (Table 22) for his Hanoverian forebears were scarcely British. His kingdom had been brutally reduced by two-fifths of its land area. His long reign was devoted to reconstruction, the development of agriculture and dairy-farming, and the growth of a parliamentary democracy. His second son became King of Greece and his daughter a beloved Queen of England. His grandson became King of Norway.

Christian X had to face the impact of the First World War, but his country, acting in concert with Norway and Sweden, managed to maintain neutrality. None the less changes occurred: in 1916 Denmark sold her West Indian islands to the United States for $25 million; in 1918 the status of Iceland, long a subject of debate, was temporarily settled by pronouncing it an independent state under the Danish Crown. In 1944 the island went on to complete freedom and republican government. The onslaught of the Second World War was more ruthless. Without warning the Nazi hordes overran Denmark in April 1940 and subjected an innocent countryside to the barbarities of German occupation.

Frederick IX, who reigned from 1947 to 1972, was

King Christian IX of Denmark (1816–1906) with his wife, Queen Louise, and family, by Laurits Tuxen, 1883.

known for his interest in music and the sea. His arms can be seen on Table 21. The four main quarters, separated by the cross of the Danebrog Order, display *1* Denmark, *2* Schleswig, *3* the Union of Kalmar, with the ram of the Faroes and the polar bear of Greenland (the crowned fish-tail of Iceland can still be seen on Table 11), and *4* the kingdoms of the Goths and Wends; thereon is a shield with Holstein, Stormania, Ditmarschen and Lauenburg with over all Oldenburg impaling Delmenhorst – a rich pageant of the history of this ancient Kingdom and its neighbours.

The laws of Denmark require approval by the Rigsdag (assembly) for royal marriages; those princes who make unequal marriages are given the title of Count of Rosenborg. Prince Aage (Table 21) was, for example, an officer of the French Foreign Legion. In 1953 the law of succession was altered to permit the daughters of King Frederick IX to inherit; accordingly in 1972 he was succeeded by Queen Margaret, his eldest daughter who had married in 1967 Henry, Count Laborde of Monpezat, a French diplomat, who is now styled Henry, Prince of Denmark.

The arms of Queen Margaret, which can be seen at the foot of Table 15, are simpler than those of her father, as the basic quarterings only have an escutcheon of Oldenburg superimposed. They are surrounded with the collar of the Order of the Elephant. The shield of her husband, Prince Henry, can be seen on Table 21, where he quarters his own family blazon with the basic arms of Denmark, the lions and the hearts. The ancestors of the Queen (Table 22) show a representative selection of the Protestant powers of Northern Europe – Denmark, England, Prussia and Sweden, together with Orthodox Russia.

Chapter 6

NORWAY

In medieval times Norway was the largest of the Scandinavian countries, but its terrain was wild, indented by many fjords and thinly populated. In the ninth and tenth centuries Viking raiders from Norway and Denmark spread havoc up and down the western seaboard of Europe. Settlements were made in Ireland, in Scotland and its islands, in England and in France; in the last-named the wild Northmen created the Duchy of Normandy.

Harold III (Hardrada), who heads Tables 23 and 24, was a tough, romantic figure who had fought bravely in the Byzantine Army, campaigned in Sicily, reigned in Norway and perished in an effort to conquer England. The Crown passed, and often bloodily, from one of his descendants to another, with small regard for matrimony. Magnus III reasserted Norwegian rule over the islands round Scotland, but after his death came a period of confusion. In 1152 Nicholas Breakspear, later the only English Pope, reorganized the Church. At the end of the twelfth century King Sverker achieved a measure of unity and discipline. Hakon IV asserted his authority over the clergy at home and over Iceland and Greenland overseas. His son, Magnus VI, Lawmender, ceded the Hebrides to Scotland and gave Norway her first code of laws (Table 24).

The crowned lion holding an axe which forms the shield of Norway first appears at the end of the twelfth century; it may be a version of the Scottish lion, for the two countries were closely linked, and might have been united if Princess Margaret, the Fair Maid of Norway, had lived. Down the centuries the haft of the axe has grown shorter.

Eric II, who married two Scots wives, fell into conflict with the Hanseatic towns, which gained a stranglehold over the rich cod-fishing industry of Norwegian ports. His brother Hakon V left an only daughter whose son, Magnus, united the Crowns of Sweden and Norway (Table 18). However, Magnus was unable to maintain his position; the Norwegians elected his younger son, Hakon VI, while the Swedes turned to his nephew Albrecht of Mecklenburg. King Hakon VI of Norway married the ablest woman of the north, the wise and talented Margaret of Denmark. Their little son was briefly King of Denmark and Norway, presaging the long union of the two countries. After the death of young Olaf IV (1387), his mother Margaret engineered the union of all three northern Kingdoms at Kalmar in 1397.

When the Danes elected Christian I in 1448, the Norwegians after hesitation followed suit. They were ill repaid when in 1468 he yielded Orkney and Shetland to the King of Scotland. While Sweden stirred in rebellion, Norway sank into submission to Denmark and made less progress than the other two realms; but like both of them she accepted the Lutheran faith at the time of the Reformation. In 1536 King Christian III declared that Norway was no longer strong or wealthy enough to maintain a separate kingdom and must be subjected to Denmark. The Norwegian Council was suppressed and the country ruled by a governor, but in fact Norway still preserved considerable independence. During the frequent wars between Sweden and Denmark, Norway with its long inland frontier was repeatedly invaded. In 1658, by the Treaty of Roskilde, Charles X of Sweden was actually ceded a large slice of central Norway around Trondheim, but two years later he was compelled to return this area to Denmark. In 1665 the King of Denmark gained the right of hereditary succession; since this applied to Norway also, it gave the latter enhanced status. But throughout the eighteenth century Norwegian interests were continuously subordinated to those of Denmark.

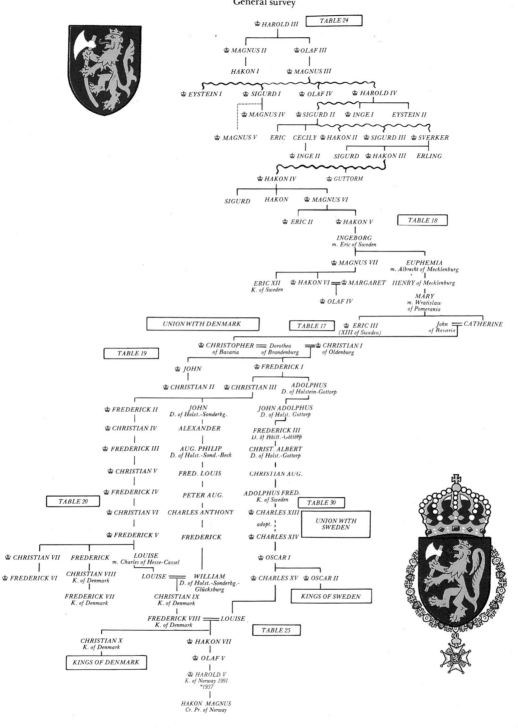

NORWAY — General survey

👑 HAROLD III — TABLE 24

👑 MAGNUS II — 👑 OLAF III

HAKON I — 👑 MAGNUS III

👑 EYSTEIN I — 👑 SIGURD I — 👑 OLAF IV — 👑 HAROLD IV

👑 MAGNUS IV — 👑 SIGURD II — 👑 INGE I — EYSTEIN II

👑 MAGNUS V — ERIC — CECILY — 👑 HAKON II — 👑 SIGURD III — 👑 SVERKER

👑 INGE II — SIGURD — 👑 HAKON III — ERLING

👑 HAKON IV — 👑 GUTTORM

SIGURD — HAKON — 👑 MAGNUS VI

👑 ERIC II — 👑 HAKON V — TABLE 18

INGEBORG
m. Eric of Sweden

👑 MAGNUS VII — EUPHEMIA
m. Albrecht of Mecklenburg

ERIC XII
K. of Sweden — 👑 HAKON VI = 👑 MARGARET — HENRY of Mecklenburg

👑 OLAF IV

MARY
m. Wratislaw
of Pomerania

UNION WITH DENMARK — TABLE 17 — 👑 ERIC III
(XIII of Sweden) — John = CATHERINE
of Bavaria

TABLE 19 — 👑 CHRISTOPHER = Dorothea = 👑 CHRISTIAN I
of Bavaria of Brandenburg of Oldenburg

👑 JOHN — 👑 FREDERICK I

👑 CHRISTIAN II — 👑 CHRISTIAN III — ADOLPHUS
D. of Holstein-Gottorp

👑 FREDERICK II — JOHN
D. of Holst.-Sonderbg. — JOHN ADOLPHUS
D. of Holst. Gottorp

👑 CHRISTIAN IV — ALEXANDER — FREDERICK III
D. of Holst.-Gottorp

👑 FREDERICK III — AUG. PHILIP
D. of Holst.-Sond.-Beck — CHRIST. ALBERT
D. of Holst.-Gottorp

👑 CHRISTIAN V — FRED. LOUIS — CHRISTIAN AUG.

👑 FREDERICK IV — PETER AUG. — ADOLPHUS FRED.
K. of Sweden — TABLE 30

TABLE 20 — 👑 CHRISTIAN VI — CHARLES ANTHONY — 👑 CHARLES XIII
adopt. — UNION WITH
SWEDEN

👑 FREDERICK V — FREDERICK — 👑 CHARLES XIV

👑 CHRISTIAN VII — FREDERICK — LOUISE
m. Charles of Hesse-Cassel — 👑 OSCAR I

👑 FREDERICK VI — CHRISTIAN VIII
K. of Denmark — LOUISE = WILLIAM
D. of Holst.-Sonderbg.-
Glücksburg — 👑 CHARLES XV — 👑 OSCAR II

FREDERICK VII
K. of Denmark — CHRISTIAN IX
K. of Denmark — KINGS OF SWEDEN

FREDERICK VIII = LOUISE
K. of Denmark — TABLE 25

CHRISTIAN X
K. of Denmark — 👑 HAKON VII

KINGS OF DENMARK — 👑 OLAF V

👑 HAROLD V
K. of Norway 1991
*1937

HAKON MAGNUS
Cr. Pr. of Norway

TABLE 24

NORWAY
Early Kings (House of Yngling)

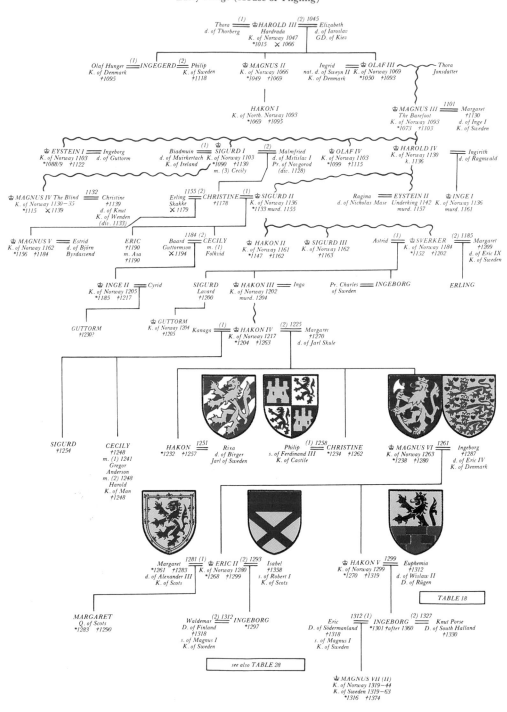

Thora *(1)* ✠ **HAROLD III** *(2)* 1045 Elizabeth
d. of Thorberg   Hardrada   d. of Iaroslav
K. of Norway 1047   GD. of Kiev
*1015 ✗ 1066

Olaf Hunger *(1)* **INGEGERD** *(2)* Philip   ✠ **MAGNUS II**   Ingrid ══ **OLAF III**   Thora
K. of Denmark   K. of Sweden   K. of Norway 1066   nat. d. of Sweyn II   K. of Norway 1069   Jonsdatter
†1095   †1118   *1049 †1069   K. of Denmark   *1050 †1093

HAKON I   ✠ **MAGNUS III** 1101 Margaret
K. of North. Norway 1093   The Barefoot †1130
*1069 †1095   K. of Norway 1093   d. of Inge I
     *1073 †1103   K. of Sweden

✠ **EYSTEIN I** ══ Ingeborg   Biadmuin ══ *(1)* **SIGURD I** *(2)* ══ Malmfried   **OLAF IV**   ✠ **HAROLD IV** ══ Ingirith
K. of Norway 1103   d. of Guttorm   d. of Muirkertach   K. of Norway 1103   d. of Mstislav I   K. of Norway 1103   K. of Norway 1130   d. of Ragnwald
*1088/9 †1122   K. of Ireland   *1090 †1130   Pr. of Novgorod   *1099 †1115   k. 1136
     m. (3) Cecily   (div. 1128)

✠ **MAGNUS IV** The Blind 1132 Christine   Erling ══ 1155 (2) **CHRISTINE** ══ (1) **SIGURD II**   Ragina ══ **EYSTEIN II**   ✠ **INGE I**
K. of Norway 1130–35   †1139   Skakke   †1178   K. of Norway 1136   d. of Nicholas Mase   Underking 1142   K. of Norway 1136
*1115 ✗ 1139   d. of Knut   ✗ 1179   *1133 murd. 1155   murd. 1157   murd. 1161
     K. of Wenden
     (div. 1133)

✠ **MAGNUS V** ══ Estrid   **ERIC**   Baard ══ 1184 (2) **CECILY**   ✠ **HAKON II**   ✠ **SIGURD III**   Astrid *(1)* ══ ✠ **SVERKER** *(2)* 1185 Margaret
K. of Norway 1162   d. of Björn   †1190   Guttormson   m. (1)   K. of Norway 1161   K. of Norway 1162   K. of Norway 1184   †1209
*1156 †1184   Byrdasvend   m. Asa   ✗ 1194   Folkvid   *1147 †1162   †1163   *1132 †1202   d. of Eric IX
     †1190   K. of Sweden

✠ **INGE II** ══ Cyrid   **SIGURD**   ✠ **HAKON III** ══ Inga   Pr. Charles ══ **INGEBORG**   **ERLING**
K. of Norway 1205   Lavard   K. of Norway 1202   of Sweden
*1185 †1217   †1200   murd. 1204

GUTTORM   ✠ **GUTTORM**
†1230?   K. of Norway 1204   Kanaga *(1)* ══ ✠ **HAKON IV** *(2)* 1225 Margaret
     †1205   K. of Norway 1217   †1270
       *1204 †1263   d. of Jarl Skule

SIGURD   **CECILY**   **HAKON** 1251 Rixa   Philip *(1)* 1258 **CHRISTINE**   ✠ **MAGNUS VI** 1261 Ingeborg
†1254   †1248   *1232 †1257   d. of Birger   s. of Ferdinand III   *1234 †1262   K. of Norway 1263   †1287
   m. (1) 1241   Jarl of Sweden   K. of Castile   *1238 †1280   d. of Eric IV
   Gregor   K. of Denmark
   Anderson
   m. (2) 1248
   Harold
   K. of Man
   †1248

     Margaret 1281 (1) ══ ✠ **ERIC II** (2) 1293 Isabel   ✠ **HAKON V** 1299 Euphemia
     *1261 †1283   K. of Norway 1280   †1358   K. of Norway 1299   †1312
     d. of Alexander III   *1268 †1299   s. of Robert I   *1270 †1319   d. of Wislaw II
     K. of Scots   K. of Scots   D. of Rügen

                                  | TABLE 18 |

MARGARET   Waldemar (2) 1312 **INGEBORG**   Eric 1312 (1) **INGEBORG** (2) 1327 Knut Porse
Q. of Scots   D. of Finland   *1297   D. of Södermanland   *1301 †after 1360   D. of South Halland
*1283 †1290   †1318   †1318   †1330
     s. of Magnus I   s. of Magnus I
     K. of Sweden   K. of Sweden

| see also TABLE 28 |

✠ **MAGNUS VII (II)**
K. of Norway 1319–44
K. of Sweden 1319–63
*1316 †1374

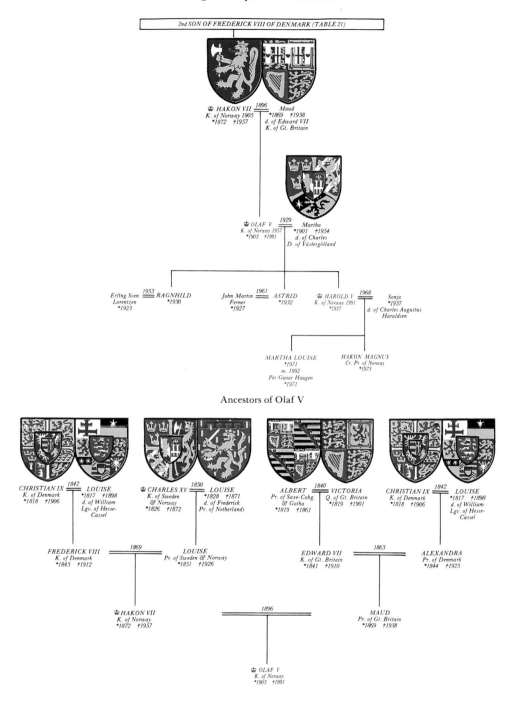

2nd SON OF FREDERICK VIII OF DENMARK (TABLE 21)

♔ HAKON VII ══1896══ Maud
K. of Norway 1905 *1869 †1938
*1872 †1957 d. of Edward VII
K. of Gt. Britain

♔ OLAF V ══1929══ Martha
K. of Norway 1957 *1901 †1954
*1903 †1991 d. of Charles
D. of Västergötland

Erling Sven ══1953══ RAGNHILD   John Martin ══1961══ ASTRID   ♔ HAROLD V ══1968══ Sonja
Lorentzen *1930   Ferner *1932   K. of Norway 1991 *1937
*1923   *1927   *1937 d. of Charles Augustus
                                                    Haraldsen

MARTHA LOUISE   HAKON MAGNUS
*1971   Cr. Pr. of Norway
m. 1992   *1973
Per Gunar Haugen
*1971

Ancestors of Olaf V

CHRISTIAN IX ══1842══ LOUISE   ♔ CHARLES XV ══1850══ LOUISE   ALBERT ══1840══ VICTORIA   CHRISTIAN IX ══1842══ LOUISE
K. of Denmark *1817 †1898   K. of Sweden *1828 †1871   Pr. of Saxe-Cobg. Q. of Gt. Britain   K. of Denmark *1817 †1898
*1818 †1906 d. of William   & Norway d. of Frederick   & Gotha *1819 †1901   *1818 †1906 d. of William
Lgv. of Hesse- *1826 †1872 Pr. of Netherlands   *1819 †1861   Lgv. of Hesse-
Cassel   Cassel

FREDERICK VIII ══1869══ LOUISE   EDWARD VII ══1863══ ALEXANDRA
K. of Denmark Pr. of Sweden & Norway   K. of Gt. Britain Pr. of Denmark
*1843 †1912 *1851 †1926   *1841 †1910 *1844 †1925

♔ HAKON VII ══════1896══════ MAUD
K. of Norway   Pr. of Gt. Britain
*1872 †1957   *1869 †1938

♔ OLAF V
K. of Norway
*1903 †1991

CHRISTIAN DER ERSTE KO DORTHEA GEBORN ZV
NIG ZV DENNEMARCKEN BRANDEN BVRGK VND KONIC
SCHWEDEN VND NORWE CHRISTOFFERS VON BEYRE
GEN HERTZOG ZV SCHLES GELASSENE WIT FRAW
WIG HOLSTEIN · K· FRIDER · K· FRIDERICHS MOTTER
ICHS DES ERSTEN VATTER ·

*King Christian I of Denmark, Sweden and Norway
(1425–81) and his wife, Dorothea of Brandenburg, with
their shields. Copy of a painting commissioned on his death.*

COMPLETE INDEPENDENCE

In 1814 Denmark, which had supported Napoleon,
was required to hand over Norway to Sweden.
The Norwegians resented this transfer and elected
their own king; in a lightning campaign they were
overcome by the Crown Prince of Sweden (Marshal
Bernadotte), who forthwith proffered generous
terms. Norway became a separate kingdom. The
union was one of Crowns only, but the people continued to long for complete freedom. Towards the
end of the nineteenth century the Norwegian Parliament (Storting) chafed increasingly at Swedish
dominance, demanded separate diplomatic
representation and ultimately the dissolution of the
union. A crisis developed in 1905; for a moment war
threatened, but the Swedish King and his government were tactful and ready to yield; in June Norway
became entirely independent.

The Crown of Norway was offered to Prince
Charles of Denmark (a younger son of Frederick
VIII) who took the name of Hakon VII; he was
already married to a daughter of Edward VII of
England (Table 25). During his long reign his
country had to face the two world wars. In the first,
like the other Scandinavian powers, Norway
remained neutral; in the second she was given no
choice. In April 1940 Norway was invaded by Germany; her stout resistance and an unprofitable intervention from Britain availed little against the weight
of attack. King Hakon left the country, not to return
until 1945.

His son King Olaf succeeded him in 1957 and his
arms can be seen on Table 23 encircled by the Order
of St Olaf, founded by Oscar I of Sweden and Norway in 1847. His ancestry (Table 25) shows a double
descent from Christian IX of Denmark, linked with
descent from the Kings of Sweden of the Bernadotte
family and from Queen Victoria. Both his daughters
have married commoners, for the Norwegian
monarchy is rooted more in democracy than in pomp
or protocol. In 1968 the Crown Prince followed their
example and married another commoner, Miss Sonja
Haraldsen.

Chapter 7

SWEDEN

Today Sweden is the most populous of the three Scandinavian Powers, but in the Middle Ages her situation was remote and backward. She had no access to the North Sea and till the seventeenth century the southernmost area of the peninsula (Scania) was part of Denmark. Sweden looked therefore towards the Baltic and the lands of Finland and Russia for commerce and expansion.

In the ninth century Swedish traders and warriors were already making their way across Russia to Constantinople and the rich routes of Asia; their main commodity was fur of various kinds. In Sweden itself the family of Stenkil (Tables 26 and 27) exercised an uneasy supremacy, but from 1134 onwards the descendants of Sverker and Eric IX occupied the throne in alternation. Later legend made a saint of Eric; in fact the first Swedish Archbishopric, at Uppsala, was founded in 1164. Eric X seems to have been the first ruler to have undergone a formal coronation. In the course of the twelfth century the position of 'Jarl', a single important nobleman, developed, and its holders were really more significant than the rival royal houses. Birger Jarl was leader of the army in campaigns against the eastern neighbours of Sweden – Finns and Estonians – which had a crusading character. The Jarl also encouraged the immigration of German merchants and the mining industry. After the death of Eric XI, the people elected Waldemar, son of Birger Jarl, and thus inaugurated a new dynasty which has been given the name of Folkunga.

The early heraldic history of the rulers of Sweden is complex. The seal of Eric X shows two crowned leopards, but not in the form of a coat-of-arms. His son Eric XI made use of the shield of his mother's family, the royal House of Denmark. Canute Johanson, the Tall, who deposed Eric in 1229, already had family arms which also served for the Kingdom (Table 27). Waldemar, who succeeded Eric XI, did not use the Folkunga arms, but continued to employ those of Denmark; on his private seal (*secretum*) he placed two crowns in pale. However, his successor Magnus I did adopt the blazon of his own family, a gold lion on a blue shield with three bends sinister of silver, but enriched the lion with a crown. Round the shield on his seal were three crowns, doubtless only an attribute of royalty.

Magnus I was a powerful ruler who consolidated his Kingdom and gave Sweden its first code of laws; to further his military ambitions he created a tax-free class of knights. But the reign of his son Birger was disfigured by bitter and confused struggles with his two brothers Eric and Waldemar; eventually Birger seized and murdered both after inviting them to dinner. In his turn Birger was driven into exile, and Magnus II, already heir to Norway, became ruler of both realms in 1319, while still a child (Table 28).

Magnus II was also a law-giver, and made an effort to extend Sweden's frontiers southwards by buying the province of Scania for 34,000 marks in 1333. Unhappily the sum was beyond his resources, and he lost the province again in 1360. He was castigated for his policies by Saint Bridget (Birgitta), when she could spare time from founding her order and correcting the Popes in Avignon. From 1356 to 1359 he was compelled to share his Kingdom with his son Eric XII; he had already been forced to give Norway to his younger son (1344). Finally, in 1363 the fractious but over-taxed nobility called in Magnus' nephew, Albrecht of Mecklenburg, who became King of Sweden. It was a sad end to the Folkunga dynasty.

The new ruler could scarcely continue to use the Folkunga blazon while Magnus still lived in exile. Accordingly he adopted a blue shield with three gold crowns which has since become the accepted coat-of-arms of Sweden. This is combined with the bull's head of Mecklenburg and quarterings for Rostock and Schwerin. Albrecht was a vigorous king but he favoured his German followers; in 1389 the nobles of Sweden appealed to the formidable figure of Queen Margaret, already Regent of Norway and Denmark. Her troops expelled Albrecht, and she became the effective ruler of all three Scandinavian realms. As has been seen in Chapter 5 she consolidated this union at Kalmar in 1397 in favour of her great-nephew the Duke of Pomerania, who thus became Eric XIII of Sweden and ruled in his own right from 1412, when the dynamic and dynastic Margaret died.

Revolts against the Danish dominance began as early as 1434. In the middle of the fifteenth century the leading figure was Charles Knutson who began as an official (Marshal) under the Danish Crown and then three times became King of Sweden. He was an ugly man and a tough politician with unusual powers of recovery; he placed his family arms of a boat in the centre of a shield with the arms of Sweden and Norway divided, on the Danish model, by a cross. This narrow cross has remained part of the Swedish royal arms.

After the death of Charles, Sweden was ruled by a series of regents. First came Sten Sture (1470–1503), then his namesake (but not kinsman) Svante Sture (1503–12) who was followed by his son Sten Sture the Younger (1512–20). None of them became king. Then, in 1520, Christian II of Denmark launched a successful attack on Sweden and was crowned. At the end of that year he executed 82 of the supporters of Sten Sture and even exhumed and burned the latter's corpse. Among the victims was Eric Vasa, a relation of Sten; his son Gustavus was a hostage in Denmark but escaped and began to raise a resistance movement. With some help from Lübeck and after many romantic escapes, he drove out the Danes and became regent and then king (1523).

Gustavus I, handsome with fair hair and long beard, was an outstanding ruler. He spoke brilliantly and with wit, he was not deterred by scruples and he combined industry and determination. In the course of his long reign he brought the Reformation to Sweden with the suppression of the monasteries in 1527. He established an hereditary monarchy in 1544, and instituted a national army. Above all he founded a dynasty of brilliant, if unstable, talent. Gustavus was a typical monarch of the sixteenth century, resolute in affairs of state, reformist in religion, the leader of a proud nation but autocratic in its management. In 1522 he was a hunted outlaw; he died in 1560 the father of princes and the hero of a free people, never again to know the Danish yoke. His family coat-of-arms was a canting one with a gold vase on the tripartite background; this he placed on an escutcheon over the three crowns and the traditional Folkunga arms, divided by a gold cross.

Eric XIV (Table 29), eldest son of Gustavus Vasa, was an able but unbalanced man. He extended Swedish rule on the east of the Baltic sea and used a new banner in naval warfare, a gold cross on a blue ground; in 1561 the people of Estonia invited him to be their king. But he fought a profitless war with Denmark, married the daughter of a lowborn soldier and began to put to death members of the nobility. In 1568 he was deposed in favour of his brother, John III. The new king was sympathetic to the Catholic faith and had married a Polish heiress; Sweden, however, remained loyal to the Reformation. John's son, Sigismund, a Catholic and already King of Poland, met sturdy resistance when he tried to reintroduce Romanism and was eventually deposed in favour of his uncle, Charles IX. This King was a firm Lutheran, and a reorganizer of the army; he was interested in extending the influence of Sweden in the Arctic and interfered successfully in the affairs of Russia. He founded the port of Gothenburg.

GUSTAVUS ADOLPHUS

The next King, Gustavus II Adolphus, was perhaps the greatest ruler in Swedish history. A brilliant leader and organizer of troops, an accomplished

King Gustavus I of Sweden (1496–1560), founder of the Vasa dynasty. A 17th-century painting by an unknown artist.

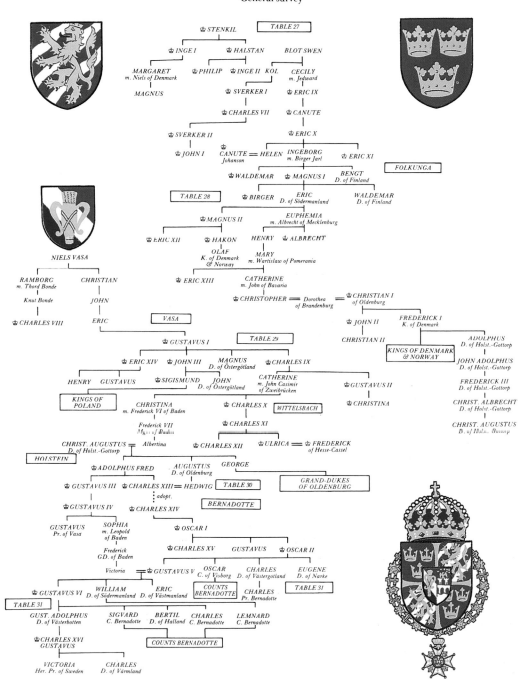

TABLE 27

👑 STENKIL

👑 INGE I   👑 HALSTAN   BLOT SWEN

MARGARET
m. Niels of Denmark

MAGNUS

👑 PHILIP   👑 INGE II   KOL   CECILY
m. Jedward

👑 SVERKER I   👑 ERIC IX

👑 CHARLES VII   👑 CANUTE

👑 SVERKER II   👑 ERIC X

👑 JOHN I   CANUTE = HELEN   INGEBORG   👑 ERIC XI
Johanson   *m. Birger Jarl*

👑 WALDEMAR   👑 MAGNUS I   BENGT
D. of Finland

FOLKUNGA

TABLE 28   👑 BIRGER   ERIC   WALDEMAR
D. of Södermanland   *D. of Finland*

👑 MAGNUS II   EUPHEMIA
m. Albrecht of Mecklenburg

👑 ERIC XII   👑 HAKON   HENRY   👑 ALBRECHT

OLAF
K. of Denmark
& Norway

MARY
m. Wartislaw of Pomerania

NIELS VASA

RAMBORG
m. Thord Bonde

CHRISTIAN

👑 ERIC XIII   CATHERINE
m. John of Bavaria

Knut Bonde

JOHN

👑 CHARLES VIII

ERIC

VASA

👑 CHRISTOPHER = Dorothea = 👑 CHRISTIAN I
of Brandenburg   *of Oldenburg*

👑 JOHN II   FREDERICK I
K. of Denmark

CHRISTIAN II

**KINGS OF DENMARK
& NORWAY**

ADOLPHUS
D. of Holst.-Gottorp

👑 GUSTAVUS I   **TABLE 29**

👑 ERIC XIV   👑 JOHN III   MAGNUS   👑 CHARLES IX
D. of Östergötland

JOHN ADOLPHUS
D. of Holst.-Gottorp

HENRY   GUSTAVUS   👑 SIGISMUND   JOHN
D. of Ostergötland

CATHERINE
*m. John Casimir
of Zweibrücken*

👑 GUSTAVUS II

FREDERICK III
D. of Holst.-Gottorp

**KINGS OF
POLAND**

CHRISTINA
m. Frederick VI of Baden

👑 CHARLES X   **WITTELSBACH**

👑 CHRISTINA

CHRIST. ALBRECHT
D. of Holst.-Gottorp

Frederick VII
Mgr. of Baden

👑 CHARLES XI

CHRIST. AUGUSTUS
D. of Holst.-Gottorp

CHRIST. AUGUSTUS = Albertina
D. of Holst.-Gottorp

👑 CHARLES XII   👑 ULRICA = 👑 FREDERICK
of Hesse-Cassel

HOLSTEIN

👑 ADOLPHUS FRED   AUGUSTUS   GEORGE
D. of Oldenburg

**GRAND-DUKES
OF OLDENBURG**

👑 GUSTAVUS III   👑 CHARLES XIII = HEDWIG   **TABLE 30**

⋮ *adopt.*

BERNADOTTE

👑 GUSTAVUS IV   👑 CHARLES XIV

GUSTAVUS
Pr. of Vasa

SOPHIA
*m. Leopold
of Baden*

👑 OSCAR I

Frederick
GD. of Baden

Victoria = 👑 GUSTAVUS V   👑 CHARLES XV   GUSTAVUS   👑 OSCAR II

OSCAR
C. of Visborg

CHARLES
D. of Vastergotland

EUGENE
D. of Narke

👑 GUSTAVUS VI   WILLIAM   ERIC
D. of Södermanland   *D. of Västmanland*

**COUNTS
BERNADOTTE**

CHARLES
Pr. Bernadotte

TABLE 31

TABLE 31

GUST. ADOLPHUS
D. of Västerbotten

SIGVARD
C. Bernadotte

BERTIL
D. of Halland

CHARLES
C. Bernadotte

LEMNARD
C. Bernadotte

👑 CHARLES XVI
GUSTAVUS

COUNTS BERNADOTTE

VICTORIA
Her. Pr. of Sweden

CHARLES
D. of Värmland

TABLE 27

SWEDEN
Early Kings and House of Folkunga

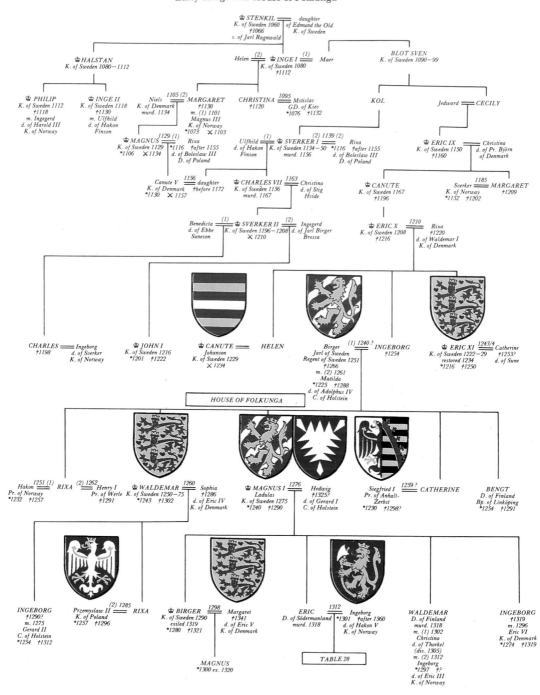

♚ STENKIL
K. of Sweden 1060
†1066
s. of Jarl Ragnwald
═══ daughter
of Edmund the Old
K. of Sweden

♚ HALSTAN
K. of Sweden 1080—1112

Helen (2) ♚ INGE I (1) Maer
K. of Sweden 1080
†1112

BLOT SVEN
K. of Sweden 1090—99

♚ PHILIP
K. of Sweden 1112
†1118
m. Ingegerd
d. of Harold III
K. of Norway

♚ INGE II
K. of Sweden 1118
†1130
m. Ulfhild
d. of Hakon
Finson

Niels
K. of Denmark
murd. 1134

1105 (2) MARGARET
†1130
m. (1) 1101
Magnus III
K. of Norway
*1073 ✗ 1103

CHRISTINA 1095 Mstislav
†1120 GD. of Kiev
*1076 †1132

KOL

Jedward ═══ CECILY

MAGNUS 1129 (1) Rixa
K. of Sweden 1129 *1116 †after 1155
*1106 ✗ 1134 d. of Boleslaw III
D. of Poland

Ulfhild (1) ♚ SVERKER I (2) 1139 (2) Rixa
d. of Hakon K. of Sweden 1134—50 *1116 †after 1155
Finson murd. 1156 d. of Boleslaw III
D. of Poland

♚ ERIC IX ═══ Christina
K. of Sweden 1150 d. of Pr. Björn
†1160 of Denmark

Canute V 1156 daughter
K. of Denmark †before 1172
*1130 ✗ 1157

♚ CHARLES VII 1163 Christina
K. of Sweden 1156 d. of Stig
murd. 1167 Hvide

♚ CANUTE
K. of Sweden 1167
†1196

1185 MARGARET
Sverker †1209
K. of Norway
*1152 †1202

Benedicta (1) ♚ SVERKER II (2) Ingegerd
d. of Ebbe K. of Sweden 1196—1208 d. of Jarl Birger
Suneson ✗ 1210 Brossa

♚ ERIC X 1210 Rixa
K. of Sweden 1208 †1220
†1216 d. of Waldemar I
K. of Denmark

CHARLES ═══ Ingeborg
†1198 d. of Sverker
K. of Norway

♚ JOHN I
K. of Sweden 1216
*1201 †1222

♚ CANUTE ═══ HELEN
Johanson
K. of Sweden 1229
✗ 1234

Birger (1) 1240 ? INGEBORG
Jarl of Sweden †1254
Regent of Sweden 1251
†1266
m. (2) 1261
Matilda
*1225 †1288
d. of Adolphus IV
C. of Holstein

♚ ERIC XI 1243/4 Catherine
K. of Sweden 1222—29 †1253?
restored 1234 d. of Sune
*1216 †1250

HOUSE OF FOLKUNGA

Hakon 1251 (1) RIXA (2) 1262 Henry I
Pr. of Norway Pr. of Werle
*1232 †1257 †1291

♚ WALDEMAR 1260 Sophia
K. of Sweden 1250—75 †1286
*1243 †1302 d. of Eric IV
K. of Denmark

♚ MAGNUS I 1276 Hedwig
Ladulas †1325?
K. of Sweden 1275 d. of Gerard I
*1240 †1290 C. of Holstein

Siegfried I 1259 ? CATHERINE
Pr. of Anhalt-
Zerbst
*1230 †1298?

BENGT
D. of Finland
Bp. of Linköping
*1254 †1291

INGEBORG
†1290?
m. 1275
Gerard II
C. of Holstein
*1254 †1312

Przemyslaw II (2) 1285 RIXA
K. of Poland
*1257 †1296

♚ BIRGER 1298 Margaret
K. of Sweden 1290 †1341
exiled 1319 d. of Eric V
*1280 †1321 K. of Denmark

ERIC 1312 Ingeborg
D. of Södermanland *1301 †after 1360
murd. 1318 d. of Hakon V
K. of Norway

WALDEMAR
D. of Finland
murd. 1318
m. (1) 1302
Christina
d. of Thorkel
(div. 1305)
m. (2) 1312
Ingeborg
*1297 †?
d. of Eric III
K. of Norway

INGEBORG
†1319
m. 1296
Eric VI
K. of Denmark
*1274 †1319

MAGNUS
*1300 ex. 1320

TABLE 28

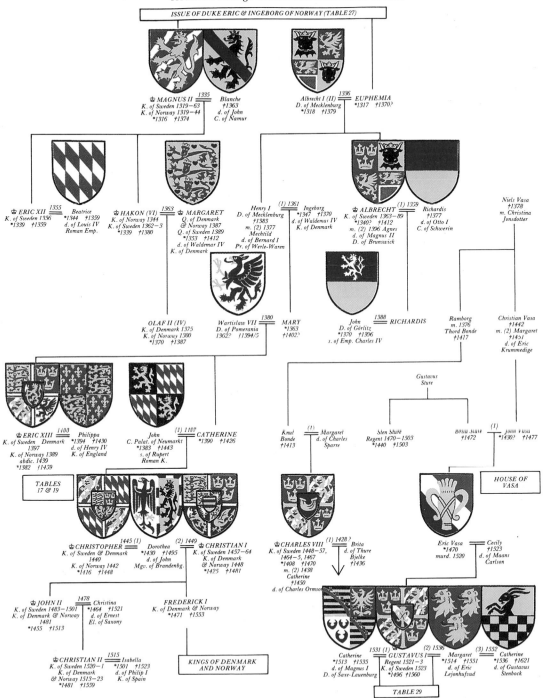

ISSUE OF DUKE ERIC & INGEBORG OF NORWAY (TABLE 27)

♔ **MAGNUS II** — 1335 — Blanche
K. of Sweden 1319–63
K. of Norway 1319–44
*1316 †1374
†1363
d. of John
C. of Namur

Albrecht I (II) — 1336 — **EUPHEMIA**
D. of Mecklenburg
*1318 †1379
*1317 †1370?

♔ **ERIC XII** — 1355 — Beatrice
K. of Sweden 1356
*1339 †1359
*1344 †1359
d. of Louis IV
Roman Emp.

♔ **HAKON (VI)** — 1363 — **MARGARET**
K. of Norway 1344
K. of Sweden 1362–3
*1339 †1380
Q. of Denmark
& Norway 1387
Q. of Sweden 1389
*1353 †1412
d. of Waldemar IV
K. of Denmark

Henry I — (1) 1361 — Ingeborg
D. of Mecklenburg
†1383
m. (2) 1377
Mechtild
d. of Bernard I
Pr. of Werle-Waren
*1347 †1370
d. of Waldemar IV
K. of Denmark

♔ **ALBRECHT** — (1) 1359 — Richardis
K. of Sweden 1363–89
*1340? †1412
m. (2) 1396 Agnes
d. of Magnus II
D. of Brunswick
†1377
d. of Otto I
C. of Schwerin

Niels Vasa
†1378
m. Christina
Jonsdotter

OLAF II (IV)
K. of Denmark 1375
K. of Norway 1300
*1370 †1387

Wartislaw VII — 1380 — **MARY**
D. of Pomerania
1362? †1394/5
*1363
†1402?

John — 1388 — **RICHARDIS**
D. of Görlitz
*1370 †1396
s. of Emp. Charles IV

Ramborg
m. 1376
Thord Bonde
†1417

Christian Vasa
†1442
m. (2) Margaret
†1451
d. of Eric
Krummedige

Gustavus
Sture

♔ **ERIC XIII** — 1406 — Philippa
K. of Sweden Denmark
1397
K. of Norway 1389
abdic. 1439
*1382 †1459
*1394 †1430
d. of Henry IV
K. of England

John — (1) 1407 — **CATHERINE**
C. Palat. of Neumarkt
*1383 †1443
s. of Rupert
Roman K.
*1390 †1426

Knut
Bonde
†1413

(1) Margaret
d. of Charles
Sparre

Sten Sture
Regent 1470–1503
*1440 †1503

Brita Sture
†1472

(1) John Vasa
*1430? †1477

TABLES
17 & 19

HOUSE OF
VASA

♔ **CHRISTOPHER** — 1445 (1) — Dorothea — (2) 1449 — **CHRISTIAN I**
K. of Sweden & Denmark
1440
K. of Norway 1442
*1416 †1448
*1430 †1495
d. of John
Mgv. of Brandenbg.
K. of Sweden 1457–64
K. of Denmark
& Norway 1448
*1425 †1481

♔ **CHARLES VIII** — (1) 1428? — Brita
K. of Sweden 1448–57,
1464–5, 1467
*1408 †1470
m. (2) 1438
Catherine
†1450
d. of Charles Ormsor
d. of Thure
Bjelke
†1436

Eric Vasa — Cecily
*1470
murd. 1520
†1523
d. of Maans
Carlson

♔ **JOHN II** — 1478 — Christina
K. of Sweden 1483–1501
K. of Denmark & Norway
1481
*1455 †1513
*1464 †1521
d. of Ernest
El. of Saxony

FREDERICK I
K. of Denmark & Norway
*1471 †1553

♔ **CHRISTIAN II** — 1515 — Isabella
K. of Sweden 1520–1
K. of Denmark
& Norway 1513–23
*1481 †1559
*1501 †1523
d. of Philip I
K. of Spain

KINGS OF DENMARK
AND NORWAY

Catherine
*1513 †1535
d. of Magnus I
D. of Saxe-Lauenburg

1531 (1) — **GUSTAVUS I** — (2) 1536 — Margaret
Regent 1521–3
K. of Sweden 1523
*1496 †1560
*1514 †1551
d. of Eric
Lejonhufvud

(3) 1552 — Catherine
*1536 †1621
d. of Gustavus
Stenbock

TABLE 29

TABLE 29

SWEDEN
House of Vasa

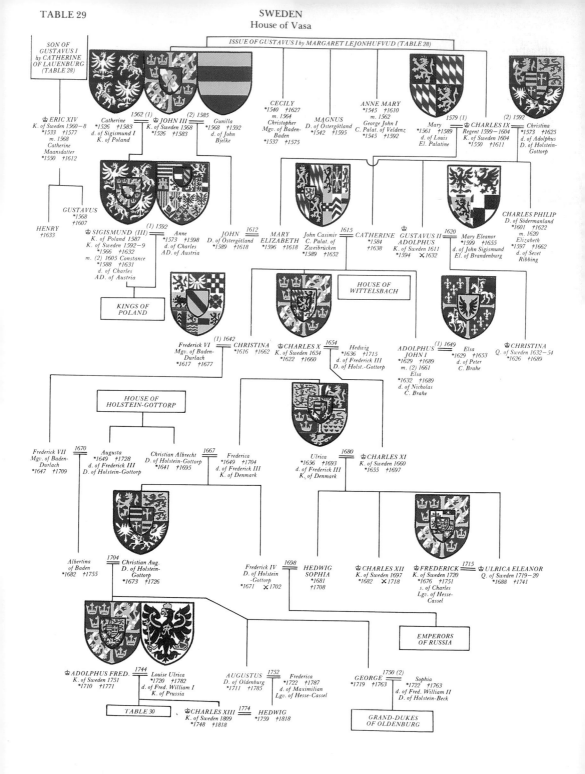

ISSUE OF GUSTAVUS I by MARGARET LEJONHUFVUD (TABLE 28)

SON OF
GUSTAVUS I
by CATHERINE
OF LAUENBURG
(TABLE 28)

✿ ERIC XIV
K. of Sweden 1560–8
*1533 †1577
m. 1568
Catherine
Maansdatter
*1550 †1612

Catherine
*1526 †1583
d. of Sigismund I
K. of Poland

1562 (1)
✿ JOHN III
K. of Sweden 1568
*1526 †1583

(2) 1585
Gunilla
*1568 †1592
d. of John
Bjelke

CECILY
*1540 †1627
m. 1564
Christopher
Mgv. of Baden-
Baden
*1537 †1575

MAGNUS
D. of Östergötland
*1542 †1595

ANNE MARY
*1545 †1610
m. 1562
George John I
C. Palat. of Veldenz
*1545 †1592

1579 (1)
Mary
*1561 †1589
d. of Louis
El. Palatine

✿ CHARLES IX
Regent 1599–1604
K. of Sweden 1604
*1550 †1611

(2) 1592
Christina
*1573 †1625
d. of Adolphus
D. of Holstein-
Gottorp

HENRY
†1633

GUSTAVUS
*1568
†1607

SIGISMUND (III)
K. of Poland 1587
K. of Sweden 1592–9
*1566 †1632
m. (2) 1605 Constance
*1588 †1631
d. of Charles
AD. of Austria

(1) 1592
Anne
*1573 †1598
d. of Charles
AD. of Austria

JOHN
D. of Östergötland
*1589 †1618

1612
MARY
ELIZABETH
*1596 †1618

John Casimir
C. Palat. of
Zweibrücken
*1589 †1652

1615
✿ CATHERINE
*1584
†1638

GUSTAVUS II
ADOLPHUS
K. of Sweden 1611
*1594 ✕1632

1620
Mary Eleanor
*1599 †1655
d. of John Sigismund
El. of Brandenburg

CHARLES PHILIP
D. of Södermanland
*1601 †1622
m. 1620
Elizabeth
*1597 †1662
d. of Sevet
Ribbing

KINGS OF
POLAND

HOUSE OF
WITTELSBACH

Frederick VI
Mgv. of Baden-
Durlach
*1617 †1677

(1) 1642
CHRISTINA
*1616 †1662

✿ CHARLES X
K. of Sweden 1654
*1622 †1660

1654
Hedwig
*1636 †1715
d. of Frederick III
D. of Holst.-Gottorp

ADOLPHUS
JOHN I
*1629 †1689
m. (2) 1661
Elsa
*1632 †1689
d. of Nicholas
C. Brahe

(1) 1649
Elsa
*1629 †1653
d. of Peter
C. Brahe

✿ CHRISTINA
Q. of Sweden 1632–54
*1626 †1689

HOUSE OF
HOLSTEIN-GOTTORP

Frederick VII
Mgv. of Baden-
Durlach
*1647 †1709

1670
Augusta
*1649 †1728
d. of Frederick III
D. of Holstein-Gottorp

Christian Albrecht
D. of Holstein-Gottorp
*1641 †1695

1667
Frederica
*1649 †1704
d. of Frederick III
K. of Denmark

Ulrica
*1656 †1693
d. of Frederick III
K. of Denmark

1680
✿ CHARLES XI
K. of Sweden 1660
*1655 †1697

Albertina
of Baden
*1682 †1755

1704
Christian Aug.
D. of Holstein-
Gottorp
*1673 †1726

Frederick IV
D. of Holstein
-Gottorp
*1671 ✕1702

1698
HEDWIG
SOPHIA
*1681
†1708

✿ CHARLES XII
K. of Sweden 1697
*1682 ✕1718

✿ FREDERICK
K. of Sweden 1720
*1676 †1751
s. of Charles
Lgv. of Hesse-
Cassel

1715
✿ ULRICA ELEANOR
Q. of Sweden 1719–20
*1688 †1741

EMPERORS
OF RUSSIA

✿ ADOLPHUS FRED.
K. of Sweden 1751
*1710 †1771

1744
Louise Ulrica
*1720 †1782
d. of Fred. William I
K. of Prussia

AUGUSTUS
D. of Oldenburg
*1711 †1785

1752
Frederica
*1722 †1787
d. of Maximilian
Lgv. of Hesse-Cassel

GEORGE
*1719 †1763

1750 (2)
Sophia
*1722 †1763
d. of Fred. William II
D. of Holstein-Beck

TABLE 30

1774
✿ CHARLES XIII
K. of Sweden 1809
*1748 †1818

HEDWIG
*1759 †1818

GRAND-DUKES
OF OLDENBURG

Queen Christina of Sweden (1626–89), by Sebastian Bourdon, 1653. She often wore mannish clothes.

linguist, a skilled diplomat, he was kingly in appearance and lustrous in performance. With equal enthusiasm he fought for Sweden and for the Protestant religion. His early campaigns brought him triumphs against Denmark and Russia. The control which he thus won of the east coast of the Baltic embroiled him in turn with Poland; through four campaigns he perfected the training of his army, strengthened by Scottish exiles, and his own powers of leadership. His troops were among the earliest to wear uniform dress. In 1630 he landed on the German shore of the Baltic and prepared to take part in the Thirty Years' War and to become the ally of France against the empire. At Breitenfeld (1631) he destroyed the imperial forces under the veteran Tilly, but in the following year he fell at Lützen on the field of victory. With him idealism vanished from the Thirty Years' War.

The policies of Gustavus Adolphus, who left only a young daughter called Christina, were carried on by his able and loyal minister Oxenstjerna. A noble himself, he ruled with the support of his peers and favoured their interests. The seventeenth century saw the building of great mansions in the country and the splendid Riddarhuset in Stockholm itself. Abroad, the pupils of Gustavus continued to win battles; in 1648 the Peace of Westphalia gave Sweden part of Pomerania and the area round Bremen, two strategic footholds on the mainland of Europe.

Queen Christina lived up to the remarkable tradition of her dynasty. Not beautiful, but highly intelligent and well-educated, she favoured peace and moved gradually towards a sympathy with the old religion. Resenting her sex, she often dressed as a man, swore freely and was outspoken and forthright in speech. Her court was the most cultivated of its age. But in 1654 she abdicated, embraced the Catholic faith and retired (with many of her finest paintings) to Rome. As her successor she had already established her cousin, Charles X, a soldier who at once embarked upon campaigns against Poland and Denmark. In the bitter winter of 1657–8 he achieved an epic march over the ice from the Danish mainland, across the islands to Copenhagen where negotiations at last gave Sweden the southern provinces and a sea-frontier. Indeed for two years he also held the Trondheim district of Norway.

Charles XI was a man of peace and devoted himself to the reconstruction of his country's finances and to welding the new southern provinces into a united Sweden. He increased the royal estates until they represented a third of the realm and reduced both the lands of the nobility and their political influence. By contrast, Charles XII was a creature of war, who inherited a prosperous, stable and now autocratic kingdom from his father in 1697. As can be seen from Table 32, his ancestry was predominantly from the Protestant families of Germany, though his great-grandmother linked him to the House of Vasa; in the ascending male line he was a Wittelsbach.

Russia, still deprived of access to the Baltic by Swedish possessions, and Poland both desired to humble their powerful neighbour. War broke out in 1700. Thin, tall, tough, seemingly inexperienced, Charles was like some northern meteor. At Narva he smashed the Russian army of Peter the Great, the prisoners taken outnumbered his own troops. He then devoted himself to a leisurely reduction of Poland and succeeded in dethroning King Augustus. Meanwhile Russia was rearming and reorganizing; Peter the Great had advanced to the Gulf of Finland and built St Petersburg (today known as Leningrad). In 1707 Charles XII moved into Russia; various disasters spoiled his plans to reach Moscow, and he suffered a severe defeat at Poltava in 1709 and had to retire into Turkey; he did not make his way back to Sweden until 1714. Undaunted, the taciturn genius, still popular with his troops, still believing that heaven was on his side, organized fresh armies and advanced into Norway (then united with Denmark). There he was killed, though it is still debated whether the bullet was fired by an enemy or a traitor. In 1721 Sweden was compelled to cede her most profitable Baltic provinces to Russia. It was the end of her period as a great power.

It was also the end of royal absolutism. Charles was succeeded by his sister Ulrica Eleanor who secured

TABLE 30

SWEDEN
Houses of Holstein-Gottorp and Bernadotte

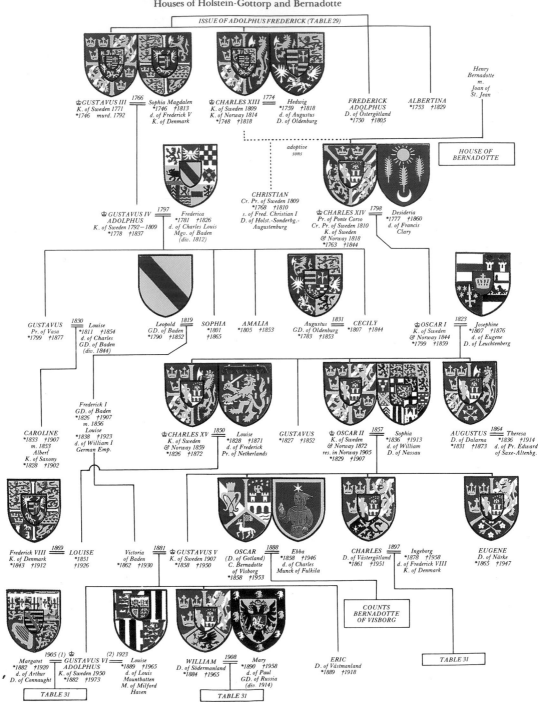

ISSUE OF ADOLPHUS FREDERICK (TABLE 29)

GUSTAVUS III | 1766 | Sophia Magdalen
K. of Sweden 1771 | | *1746 †1813
*1746 murd. 1792 | | d. of Frederick V
| | K. of Denmark

CHARLES XIII | 1774 | Hedwig
K. of Sweden 1809 | | *1759 †1818
K. of Norway 1814 | | d. of Augustus
*1748 †1818 | | D. of Oldenburg

FREDERICK ADOLPHUS
D. of Östergötland
*1750 †1805

ALBERTINA
*1753 †1829

Henry Bernadotte
m.
Joan of
St. Jean

adoptive sons

HOUSE OF BERNADOTTE

GUSTAVUS IV ADOLPHUS | 1797 | Frederica
K. of Sweden 1792—1809 | | *1781 †1826
*1778 †1837 | | d. of Charles Louis
| | Mgv. of Baden
| | (div. 1812)

CHRISTIAN
Cr. Pr. of Sweden 1809
*1768 †1810
s. of Fred. Christian I
D. of Holst.-Sonderbg.-
Augustenburg

CHARLES XIV | 1798 | Desideria
Pr. of Ponte Corvo | | *1777 †1860
Cr. Pr. of Sweden 1810 | | d. of Francis
K. of Sweden | | Clary
& Norway 1818 | |
*1763 †1844 | |

GUSTAVUS
Pr. of Vasa
*1799 †1877

Louise | 1830
*1811 †1854
d. of Charles
GD. of Baden
(div. 1844)

Leopold | 1819
GD. of Baden
*1790 †1852

SOPHIA
*1801 †1865

AMALIA
*1805 †1853

Augustus | 1831
GD. of Oldenburg
*1783 †1853

Cecily
*1807 †1844

OSCAR I | 1823 | Josephine
K. of Sweden | | *1807 †1876
& Norway 1844 | | d. of Eugene
*1799 †1859 | | D. of Leuchtenberg

CAROLINE
*1833 †1907
m. 1853
Albert
K. of Saxony
*1828 †1902

Frederick I
GD. of Baden
*1826 †1907
m. 1856
Louise
*1838 †1923
d. of William I
German Emp.

CHARLES XV | 1850 | Louise
K. of Sweden | | *1828 †1871
& Norway 1859 | | d. of Frederick
*1826 †1872 | | Pr. of Netherlands

GUSTAVUS
*1827 †1852

OSCAR II | 1857 | Sophia
K. of Sweden | | *1836 †1913
& Norway 1872 | | d. of William
res. in Norway 1905 | | D. of Nassau
*1829 †1907 | |

AUGUSTUS | 1864 | Theresa
D. of Dalarna | | *1836 †1914
*1831 †1873 | | d. of Pr. Edward
| | of Saxe-Altenbg.

Frederick VIII | 1869 | LOUISE
K. of Denmark | | *1851 †1926
*1843 †1912 | |

Victoria
of Baden
*1862 †1930

GUSTAVUS V | 1881
K. of Sweden 1907
*1858 †1950

OSCAR | 1888 | Ebba
(D. of Gotland) | | *1858 †1946
C. Bernadotte | | d. of Charles
of Visborg | | Munck of Fulkila
*1858 †1953 | |

CHARLES | 1897 | Ingeborg
D. of Västergötland | | *1878 †1958
*1861 †1951 | | d. of Frederick VIII
| | K. of Denmark

EUGENE
D. of Närke
*1865 †1947

COUNTS
BERNADOTTE
OF VISBORG

TABLE 31

Margaret | 1905 (1) | **GUSTAVUS VI** | (2) 1923 | Louise
*1882 †1920 | | **ADOLPHUS** | | *1889 †1965
d. of Arthur | | K. of Sweden 1950 | | d. of Louis
D. of Connaught | | *1882 †1973 | | Mountbatten
| | | | M. of Milford
| | | | Haven

WILLIAM | 1908 | Mary
D. of Södermanland | | *1890 †1958
*1884 †1965 | | d. of Paul
| | GD. of Russia
| | (div. 1914)

ERIC
D. of Västmanland
*1889 †1918

TABLE 31

TABLE 31

TABLE 31

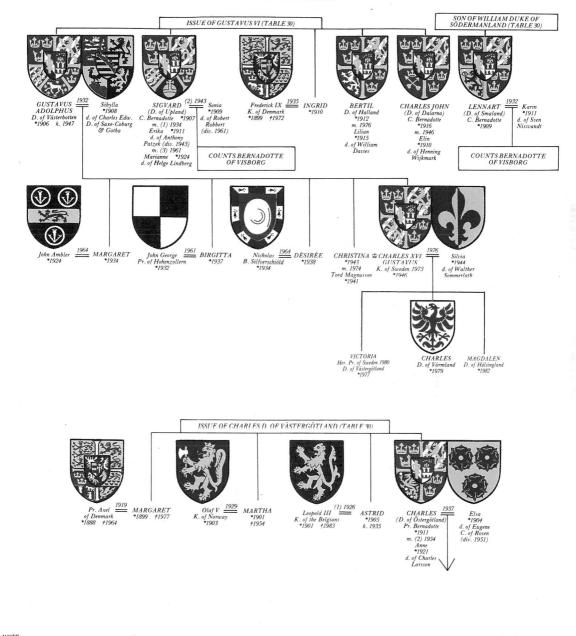

ISSUE OF GUSTAVUS VI (TABLE 30)

SON OF WILLIAM DUKE OF
SÖDERMANLAND (TABLE 30)

GUSTAVUS
ADOLPHUS
D. of Västerbotten
*1906 k. 1947
— 1932 —
Sibylla
*1908
d. of Charles Edw.
D. of Saxe-Coburg
& Gotha

SIGVARD
(D. of Upland)
C. Bernadotte *1907
m. (1) 1934
Erika *1911
d. of Anthony
Patzek (div. 1943)
m. (3) 1961
Marianne *1924
d. of Helge Lindberg
— (2) 1943 —
Sonia
*1909
d. of Robert
Robbert
(div. 1961)

COUNTS BERNADOTTE
OF VISBORG

Frederick IX
K. of Denmark
*1899 †1972
— 1935 —
INGRID
*1910

BERTIL
D. of Halland
*1912
m. 1976
Lilian
*1915
d. of William
Davies

CHARLES JOHN
(D. of Dalarna)
C. Bernadotte
*1916
m. 1946
Elin
*1910
d. of Henning
Wijkmark

LENNART
(D. of Smaland)
C. Bernadotte
*1909
— 1932 —
Karin
*1911
d. of Sven
Nissvandt

COUNTS BERNADOTTE
OF VISBORG

John Ambler
*1924
— 1964 —
MARGARET
*1934

John George
Pr. of Hohenzollern
*1932
— 1961 —
BIRGITTA
*1937

Nicholas
B. Silfverschiöld
*1934
— 1964 —
DÉSIRÉE
*1938

CHRISTINA
*1943
m. 1974
Tord Magnusson
*1941
⚭ CHARLES XVI
GUSTAVUS
K. of Sweden 1973
*1946
— 1976 —
Silvia
*1944
d. of Walther
Sommerlath

VICTORIA
Her. Pr. of Sweden 1980
D. of Västergötland
*1977

CHARLES
D. of Värmland
*1979

MAGDALEN
D. of Hälsingland
*1982

ISSUE OF CHARLES D. OF VÄSTERGÖTLAND (TABLE 30)

Pr. Axel
of Denmark
*1888 †1964
— 1919 —
MARGARET
*1899 †1977

Olaf V
K. of Norway
*1903
— 1929 —
MARTHA
*1901
†1954

Leopold III
K. of the Belgians
*1901 †1983
— (1) 1926 —
ASTRID
*1905
k. 1935

CHARLES
(D. of Östergötland)
Pr. Bernadotte
*1911
m. (2) 1954
Anne
*1921
d. of Charles
Larsson
— 1937 —
Elsa
*1904
d. of Eugene
C. of Rosen
(div. 1951)

NOTE
The arms as given for Charles, D. of Värmland, are those of Värmland, not his personal arms.

TABLE 32

SWEDEN
Ancestors of Charles XII, Gustavus VI and Charles XVI

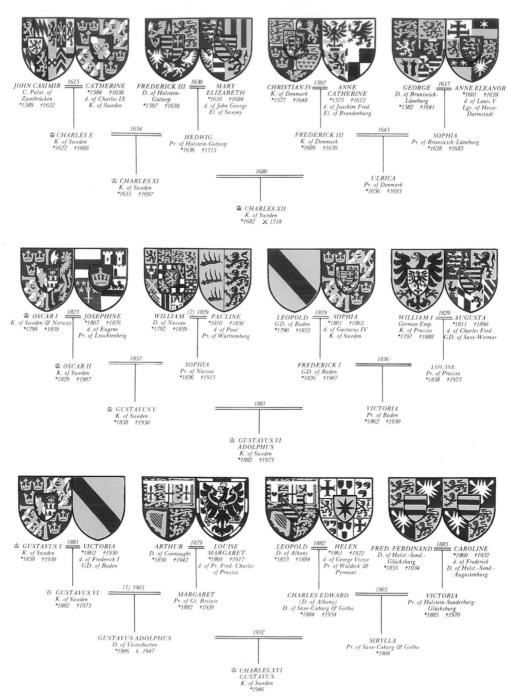

JOHN CASIMIR — 1615 — CATHERINE
C. Palat. of
Zweibrücken
*1589 †1652
*1584 †1638
d. of Charles IX
K. of Sweden

FREDERICK III — 1630 — MARY ELIZABETH
D. of Holstein-
Gottorp
*1597 †1659
*1610 †1684
d. of John George
El. of Saxony

CHRISTIAN IV — 1597 — ANNE CATHERINE
K. of Denmark
*1577 †1648
*1575 †1612
d. of Joachim Fred.
El. of Brandenburg

GEORGE — 1617 — ANNE ELEANOR
D. of Brunswick-
Lüneburg
*1582 †1641
*1601 †1659
d. of Louis V
Lgv. of Hesse-
Darmstadt

✠ CHARLES X — 1654
K. of Sweden
*1622 †1660

HEDWIG
Pr. of Holstein-Gottorp
*1636 †1715

FREDERICK III — 1643
K. of Denmark
*1609 †1670

SOPHIA
Pr. of Brunswick-Lüneburg
*1628 †1685

✠ CHARLES XI — 1680
K. of Sweden
*1655 †1697

ULRICA
Pr. of Denmark
*1656 †1693

✠ CHARLES XII
K. of Sweden
*1682 ✕ 1718

✠ OSCAR I — 1823 — JOSEPHINE
K. of Sweden & Norway
*1799 †1859
*1807 †1876
d. of Eugene
Pr. of Leuchtenberg

WILLIAM — (2) 1829 — PAULINE
D. of Nassau
*1792 †1839
*1810 †1856
d. of Paul
Pr. of Württemberg

LEOPOLD — 1819 — SOPHIA
GD. of Baden
*1790 †1852
*1801 †1865
d. of Gustavus IV
K. of Sweden

WILLIAM I — 1829 — AUGUSTA
German Emp.
K. of Prussia
*1797 †1888
*1811 †1890
d. of Charles Fred.
GD. of Saxe-Weimar

✠ OSCAR II — 1857
K. of Sweden
*1829 †1907

SOPHIA
Pr. of Nassau
*1836 †1913

FREDERICK I — 1856
GD. of Baden
*1826 †1907

LOUISE
Pr. of Prussia
*1838 †1923

✠ GUSTAVUS V — 1881
K. of Sweden
*1858 †1950

VICTORIA
Pr. of Baden
*1862 †1930

✠ GUSTAVUS VI ADOLPHUS
K. of Sweden
*1882 †1973

✠ GUSTAVUS V — 1881 — VICTORIA
K. of Sweden
*1858 †1950
*1862 †1930
d. of Frederick I
GD. of Baden

ARTHUR — 1879 — LOUISE MARGARET
D. of Connaught
*1850 †1942
*1860 †1917
d. of Pr. Fred. Charles
of Prussia

LEOPOLD — 1882 — HELEN
D. of Albany
*1853 †1884
*1861 †1922
d. of George Victor
Pr. of Waldeck &
Pyrmont

FRED. FERDINAND — 1885 — CAROLINE
D. of Holst.-Sond.-
Glücksburg
*1855 †1934
*1860 †1932
d. of Frederick
D. of Holst.-Sond.-
Augustenburg

✠ GUSTAVUS VI — (1) 1905
K. of Sweden
*1882 †1973

MARGARET
Pr. of Gt. Britain
*1882 †1920

CHARLES EDWARD — 1905
(D. of Albany)
D. of Saxe-Coburg & Gotha
*1884 †1954

VICTORIA
Pr. of Holstein-Sonderburg-
Glücksburg
*1885 †1970

GUSTAVUS ADOLPHUS — 1932
D. of Västerbotten
*1906 k. 1947

SIBYLLA
Pr. of Saxe-Coburg & Gotha
*1908

✠ CHARLES XVI GUSTAVUS
K. of Sweden
*1946

the election of her husband, Frederick of Hesse-Cassel, as king. Charles X, XI and XII had borne the arms of the Palatinate on an escutcheon; Frederick replaced this with the blazon of Hesse-Cassel. Frederick also established in 1748 the Order of the Seraphim (Table 26) whose origin tradition placed without much warrant in the Middle Ages. A new constitution was imposed on the Crown which set up four Estates (Nobles, Priests, Burgesses and Peasants) but left power mainly in the hands of the first-named. Two parties grew up, distinguished as 'Caps' (originally 'Nightcaps') and 'Hats'. In 1741 the Hats lost Finland to the Russians, but regained most of the province by accepting Adolphus Frederick of Holstein-Gottorp, a kinsman of the Empress Elizabeth of Russia, as Crown Prince. He proved to be an ineffectual sovereign, dominated and brow beaten by the nobility until the close of his life.

Gustavus III (Table 30) was less pliant; by a *coup d'état* in 1772 he re-established royal authority. Clever, but lacking formal education, theatrical, at times indolent, he was none the less successful in bringing about a large measure of financial reform. In 1792 he was assassinated at the opera, a dramatic end to a dramatic life. Gustavus IV was a febrile and wayward king who saw himself as a rival to Napoleon. His futile campaigns lost Finland and Pomerania, and he was forcibly dethroned in 1809; the old constitution was restored and, after an interval, Charles XIII, uncle of Gustavus, became king with limited powers. He was childless and debates were held about a possible heir.

The first choice of a successor was a Danish prince, Christian, then Commander-in-chief in Norway, but he died in 1810. An astonishing selection was then made, and Jean Baptiste Bernadotte, one of Napoleon's ablest Marshals, was offered the reversion of the Swedish throne. A big, handsome Gascon, of proven military talent, he became a successful and popular king. Almost from his arrival he had to rule, for Charles XIII, who had adopted him, was now senile. He never learned Swedish but his good looks and good sense won the hearts of his new countrymen. In 1814 he conquered Norway in a lightning campaign and four years later succeeded

his adoptive father as Charles XIV; his policy laid the foundation of the peace which Sweden has since enjoyed without a break.

His arms show the lions of Norway and the Folkunga combined with the three crowns of Sweden: on an escutcheon are the coats of Vasa and of Bernadotte – the latter a Napoleonic creation, since Charles XIV was the son of a small lawyer in Pau. His son, Oscar I, had been a liberal in youth but continued the main lines of his father's policy; domestic reforms, a campaign against drink, the advancement of agriculture and industry were the features of his reign. Charles XV was less vigorous, but put his confidence in good ministers who continued the pacific advance of the nation. True co-operation with Norway was still lacking, and many thousands of Swedes emigrated to the New World. During the reign of his brother, Oscar II, the separation of Norway from Sweden took place peacefully, partly thanks to the tact and moderation of the King. Gustavus V in his long reign led his country through two world wars without becoming involved in either. His son, Gustavus VI, was a distinguished archaeologist. It can be seen (Table 32) that his ancestry was mainly German; but through the Dukes of Baden he was descended from the former Swedish dynasty. Eugene, Prince of Leuchtenberg, was the son of the Empress Josephine by her first marriage.

The ancestry of his grandson King Charles XVI Gustavus (Table 32) shows a stronger infusion of British blood. In 1976 he married a commoner of German birth who has given birth to a daughter, born in 1977, and a son, Prince Charles Philip, born in 1979. At the time of his birth Prince Charles Philip was regarded as the heir to the throne, but the Swedish Parliament has since passed an Act of Succession which makes the eldest child of the monarch (irrespective of sex) heir to the throne. Accordingly on 1 January 1980, Princess Victoria replaced her younger brother as heir apparent. The various cadets of the royal family show versions of the arms of Sweden, Folkunga, Vasa and Bernadotte, usually with the arms of the province from which they take their title in base. Those who have made non-royal marriages are styled Counts of Visborg.

Chapter 8

NETHERLANDS AND LUXEMBURG

The early history of the Low Countries, which today in England are thought of as Holland, Belgium and Luxemburg, tells of a confusing welter of small states and varying allegiances. In the northern half of the Low Countries, men were already engaged in fishing and in the struggle against the sea, in maintenance of dykes and canals; in the southern section a powerful cloth trade developed with independent and wealthy cities such as Antwerp, Bruges and Ghent. At the end of the fourteenth century the invention of a better technique for salting herrings lent fresh impetus to the seaside towns. Town and country began to develop self-governing institutions and a tradition hostile to tyranny.

The first great unifying influence was the spread of the power of Burgundy, which began with the wedding of Philip the Good to Margaret, heiress of Flanders. Then in 1477 Charles the Bold died leaving an only daughter, Mary. The cities and counties summoned a congress which extracted from Duchess Mary a charter of liberties, including a proviso that she should not marry without the leave of the Estates (assemblies) of her provinces. In the event Mary married Maximilian of Hapsburg, who became emperor (Table 74); his son Philip married Joanna, the heiress of Castile and Aragon, thus linking the fortunes of the Netherlands with Spain. Their son, Charles V, rounded off the Hapsburg dominions in the Low Countries by adding northern lands which included the Duchy of Guelders and the Bishopric of Utrecht. At his abdication in 1556 he allotted Spain, America and the Netherlands to his son Philip II; his brother Ferdinand succeeded him in the Empire and the Hapsburg territories.

Charles was the last natural prince of the Low Countries, in the sense that his upbringing and language naturally conformed to the Burgundian tradition. Philip II, paperbound and assiduous in distant Spain, was never in touch with the problems of his northern lands, with their sturdy, burgher independence or with their sympathy with the reformed religion, of which Erasmus, the Dutch humanist, had been one of the prophets. It was at this juncture that the House of Nassau became embroiled with the fate of the Netherlands.

HOUSE OF NASSAU

The County of Nassau lies in Germany at the angle between the rivers Rhine and Main. In the second half of the thirteenth century the dynasty divided into two branches, the Walramian and the Ottonian (Table 33). To the former belonged Count Adolphus, who uneasily aspired from 1291 to 1298 to the position of emperor (Chapter 22): we are more concerned with the latter. The Counts of Nassau-Dillenburg showed the customary Teutonic tendency to subdivide and re-unite their estates, but Engelbert I made a fortunate marriage to Joanna, the heiress of Breda and other properties in Brabant. His grandson, Engelbert II, secured more estates in that region as a reward for his services to the Emperor Maximilian. In the next generation the family lands were again divided: Henry took Breda and the Flemish part, William, the less important German heritage (Table 34). Henry made a splendid alliance with the Princess of Orange, a tiny but independent sovereignty in the Rhône valley. His son René (Renatus) idly bequeathed the whole to his first cousin (although William had no Orange blood) and was then unexpectedly slain in battle.

Accordingly William the Silent resigned his German inheritance to a younger brother and prepared to take up his vast fortune in the Netherlands and elsewhere. He was good-looking, robust, charming and immensely accomplished: not taciturn, but a good listener and a skilful masker of his own

General survey of the House of Nassau

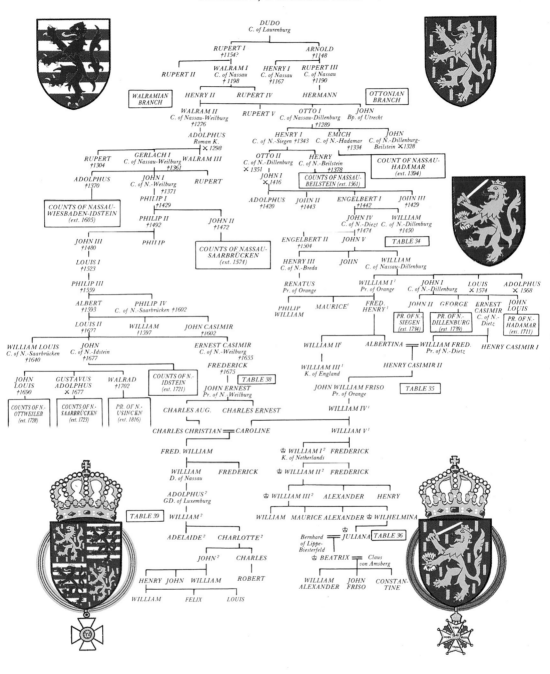

NOTE
[1] Stadholder
[2] Grand-Duke of Luxemburg

TABLE 34

NETHERLANDS
Stadholders from the House of Nassau-Orange

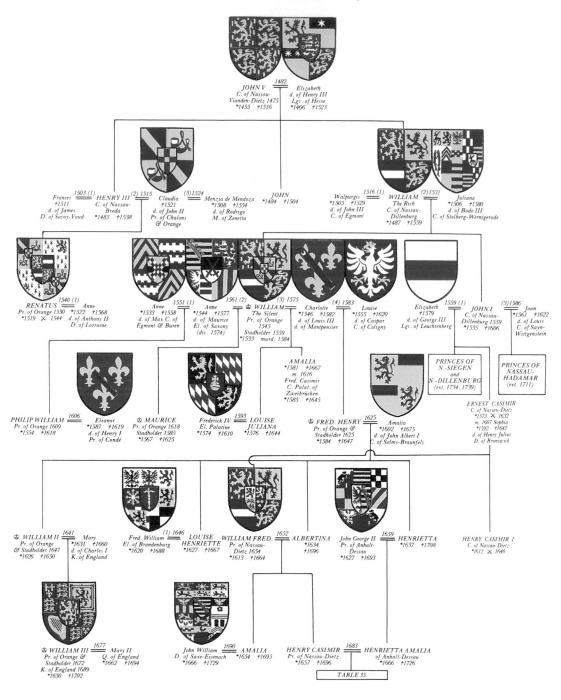

JOHN V
C. of Nassau-
Vianden-Dietz 1475
*1455 †1516

—1482—

Elizabeth
d. of Henry III
Lgv. of Hesse
*1466 †1523

Frances 1503 (1)
†1511
d. of James
D. of Savoy-Vaud

HENRY III (2)1515
C. of Nassau-
Breda
*1483 †1538

Claudia (3)1524
†1521
d. of John II
Pr. of Chalons
& Orange

Menzia de Mendoza
*1508 †1554
d. of Rodrigo
M. of Zenetta

JOHN
*1484 †1504

Walpurgis 1516 (1)
*1505 †1529
d. of John III
C. of Egmont

WILLIAM (2)1531
The Rich
C. of Nassau-
Dillenburg
*1487 †1559

Juliana
*1506 †1580
d. of Bodo III
C. of Stolberg-Wernigerode

RENATUS 1540 (1)
Pr. of Orange 1530
*1519 ✕ 1544

Anne
*1522 †1568
d. of Anthony II
D. of Lorraine

Anne 1551 (1)
*1533 †1558
d. of Max C. of
Egmont & Buren

Anne 1561 (2)
*1544 †1577
d. of Maurice
El. of Saxony
(div. 1574)

WILLIAM (3) 1575
The Silent
Pr. of Orange
1545
Stadholder 1559
*1533 murd. 1584

Charlotte (4) 1583
*1546 †1582
d. of Louis III
d. of Montpensier

Louise
*1555 †1620
d. of Caspar
C. of Coligny

Elizabeth 1559 (1)
†1579
d. of George III
Lgv. of Leuchtenberg

JOHN I
C. of Nassau-
Dillenburg 1559
*1535 †1606

Joan (3)1596
*1561 †1622
d. of Louis
C. of Sayn-
Wittgenstein

AMALIA
*1581 †1667
m. 1616
Fred. Casimir
C. Palat. of
Zweibrücken
*1585 †1645

**PRINCES OF
N.-SIEGEN
and
N.-DILLENBURG**
(ext. 1734, 1739)

**PRINCES OF
NASSAU-
HADAMAR**
(ext. 1711)

PHILIP WILLIAM 1606
Pr. of Orange 1609
*1554 †1618

Eleanor
*1587 †1619
d. of Henry I
Pr. of Condé

♔ MAURICE
Pr. of Orange 1618
Stadholder 1585
*1567 †1625

Frederick IV 1593
El. Palatine
*1574 †1610

**LOUISE
JULIANA**
*1576 †1644

♔ FRED. HENRY 1625
Pr. of Orange &
Stadholder 1625
*1584 †1647

Amalia
*1602 †1675
d. of John Albert I
C. of Solms-Braunfels

ERNEST CASIMIR
C. of Nassau-Dietz
*1573 ✕ 1632
m. 1607 Sophia
*1592 †1642
d. of Henry Julius
D. of Brunswick

♔ WILLIAM II 1641
Pr. of Orange
& Stadholder 1647
*1626 †1650

Mary
*1631 †1660
d. of Charles I
K. of England

Fred. William (1) 1646
El. of Brandenburg
*1620 †1688

**LOUISE
HENRIETTE**
*1627 †1667

WILLIAM FRED. 1652
Pr. of Nassau-
Dietz 1654
*1613 †1664

ALBERTINA
*1634
†1696

John George II 1659
Pr. of Anhalt-
Dessau
*1627 †1693

HENRIETTA
*1637 †1708

HENRY CASIMIR I
C. of Nassau-Dietz
*1612 ✕ 1640

♔ WILLIAM III 1677
Pr. of Orange &
Stadholder 1672
K. of England 1689
*1650 †1702

Mary II
Q. of England
*1662 †1694

John William 1690
D. of Saxe-Eisenach
*1666 †1729

AMALIA
*1654 †1695

HENRY CASIMIR 1683
Pr. of Nassau-Dietz
*1657 †1696

HENRIETTA AMALIA
of Anhalt-Dessau
*1666 †1726

TABLE 35

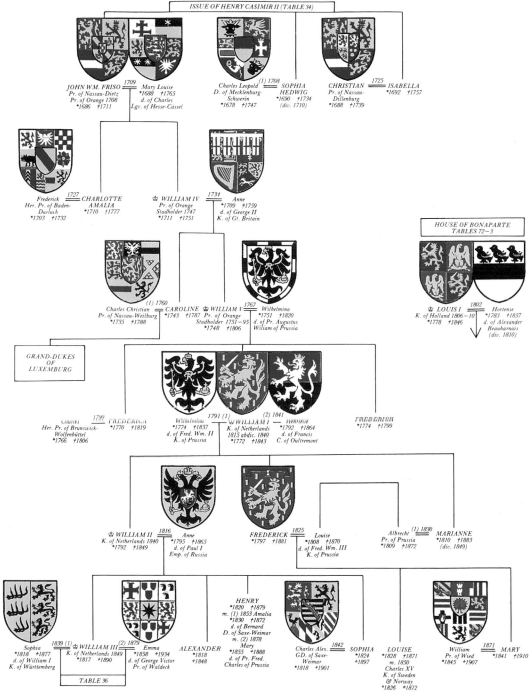

ISSUE OF HENRY CASIMIR II (TABLE 34)

JOHN WM. FRISO ══1709══ **Mary Louise**
Pr. of Nassau-Dietz   *1688 †1765
Pr. of Orange 1708   d. of Charles
*1686 †1711   Lgv. of Hesse-Cassel

Charles Leopold ══(1) 1708══ **SOPHIA**
D. of Mecklenburg-   **HEDWIG**
Schwerin   *1690 †1734
*1678 †1747   (div. 1710)

CHRISTIAN ══1725══ **ISABELLA**
Pr. of Nassau-   *1692 †1757
Dillenburg
*1688 †1739

Frederick ══1727══ **CHARLOTTE**
Her. Pr. of Baden-   **AMALIA**
Durlach   *1710 †1777
*1703 †1732

♔ **WILLIAM IV** ══1731══ **Anne**
Pr. of Orange   *1709 †1759
Stadholder 1747   d. of George II
*1711 †1751   K. of Gt. Britain

HOUSE OF BONAPARTE
TABLES 72–3

Charles Christian ══(1) 1760══ **CAROLINE** ♔ **WILLIAM V** ══1767══ **Wilhelmina**
Pr. of Nassau-Weilburg   *1743 †1787 Pr. of Orange   *1751 †1820
*1735 †1788   Stadholder 1751–95   d. of Pr. Augustus
        *1748 †1806   Wiliam of Prussia

♔ **LOUIS I** ══1802══ **Hortense**
K. of Holland 1806–10   *1783 †1837
*1778 †1846   d. of Alexander
        Beauharnais
        (div. 1810)

GRAND-DUKES
OF
LUXEMBURG

Charles ══1790══ **FREDERICA**
Her. Pr. of Brunswick-   *1770 †1819
Wolfenbüttel
*1766 †1806

Wilhelmina ══1791 (1)══ ♔ **WILLIAM I** ── (2) 1841 ── Henriette
*1774 †1837   K. of Netherlands   *1792 †1864
d. of Fred. Wm. II   1815 abdic. 1840   d. of Francis
K. of Prussia   *1772 †1843   C. of Oultremont

FREDERICH
*1774 †1799

♔ **WILLIAM II** ══1816══ **Anne**
K. of Netherlands 1840   *1795 †1865
*1792 †1849   d. of Paul I
        Emp. of Russia

FREDERICK ══1825══ **Louise**
*1797 †1881   *1808 †1870
        d. of Fred. Wm. III
        K. of Prussia

Albrecht ══(1) 1830══ **MARIANNE**
Pr. of Prussia   *1810 †1883
*1809 †1872   (div. 1849)

Sophia ══1839 (1)══ ♔ **WILLIAM III** ══(2) 1879══ **Emma**   **ALEXANDER**
*1818 †1877   K. of Netherlands 1849   *1858 †1934   *1818
d. of William I   *1817 †1890   d. of George Victor   †1848
K. of Württemberg   Pr. of Waldeck

TABLE 36

HENRY
*1820 †1879
m. (1) 1853 Amalia
*1830 †1872
d. of Bernard
D. of Saxe-Weimar
m. (2) 1878
Mary
*1855 †1888
d. of Pr. Fred.
Charles of Prussia

Charles Alex. ══1842══ **SOPHIA**
GD. of Saxe-   *1824
Weimar   †1897
*1818 †1901

LOUISE
*1828 †1871
m. 1850
Charles XV
K. of Sweden
& Norway
*1826 †1872

William ══1871══ **MARY**
Pr. of Wied   *1841 †1910
*1845 †1907

TABLE 36

NETHERLANDS
Queens in the twentieth century

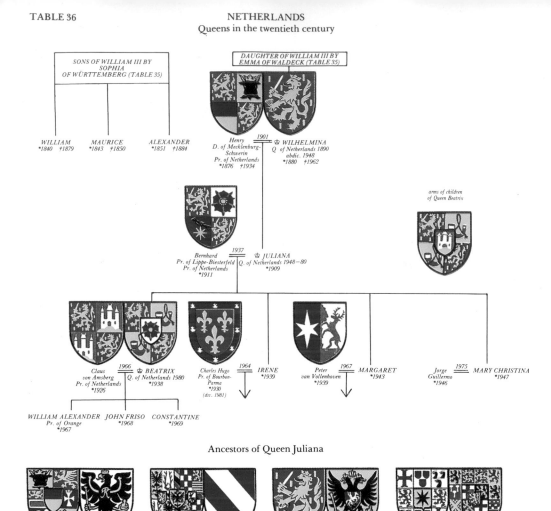

SONS OF WILLIAM III BY
SOPHIA
OF WÜRTTEMBERG (TABLE 35)

DAUGHTER OF WILLIAM III BY
EMMA OF WALDECK (TABLE 35)

WILLIAM
*1840 †1879

MAURICE
*1843 †1850

ALEXANDER
*1851 †1884

Henry
D. of Mecklenburg-
Schwerin
Pr. of Netherlands
*1876 †1934

1901

WILHELMINA
Q. of Netherlands 1890
abdic. 1948
*1880 †1962

arms of children
of Queen Beatrix

Bernhard
Pr. of Lippe-Biesterfeld
Pr. of Netherlands
*1911

1937

JULIANA
Q. of Netherlands 1948–80
*1909

Claus
von Amsberg
Pr. of Netherlands
*1926

1966

BEATRIX
Q. of Netherlands 1980
*1938

Charles Hugo
Pr. of Bourbon-
Parma
*1930
(div. 1981)

1964

IRENE
*1939

Peter
van Vollenhoven
*1939

1967

MARGARET
*1943

Jorge
Guillermo
*1946

1975

MARY CHRISTINA
*1947

WILLIAM ALEXANDER
Pr. of Orange
*1967

JOHN FRISO
*1968

CONSTANTINE
*1969

Ancestors of Queen Juliana

PAUL FREDERICK
GD. of Mecklenburg-
Schwerin
*1800 †1842

1822

ALEXANDRINE
*1803 †1892
d. of Fred. William III
K. of Prussia

Pr. ADOLPH
of Schwarzburg-
Rudolstadt
*1801 †1875

1847

MATILDA
*1826 †1914
d. of Otto Victor
Pr. of Schönburg-
Waldenburg

WILLIAM II
K. of Netherlands
*1792 †1849

1816

ANNE
*1795 †1865
d. of Paul I
Emp. of Russia

GEORGE VICTOR
Pr. of Waldeck
& Pyrmont
*1831 †1839

(1) 1853

HELENE
*1831 †1888
d. of William
D. of Nassau

FREDERICK
FRANCIS II
GD. of Mecklenburg-
Schwerin
*1823 †1883

(3) 1868

MARY
Pr. of Schwarzburg-
Rudolstadt
*1850 †1922

WILLIAM III
K. of Netherlands
*1817 †1890

(2) 1879

EMMA
Pr. of Waldeck & Pyrmont
*1858 †1934

HENRY
D. of Mecklenburg-Schwerin
Pr. of Netherlands
*1876 †1934

1901

WILHELMINA
Q. of Netherlands
*1880 †1962

JULIANA
Q. of Netherlands
*1909
abdic. 1980

NOTE
Arms shown for Queen Beatrix are those she used as a princess.

King Philip II of Spain (in hat) berating William the Silent in 1559, by Cornelis Kruseman, 1832.

By the time of his assassination by a squalid and fanatic devotee of Rome, his work was achieved; 'when he died the little children cried in the streets' – so runs a contemporary report.

The territorial and religious division thus engendered proved to be a lasting one. Protestant Holland, under the guidance of the House of Orange, became the United Provinces; the Catholic southern provinces continued under alien rule until the time of Napoleon, and approximate to the modern Belgium.

The original arms of the Nassau family (Table 33) showed a gold lion rampant on a blue field strewn with gold billets (originally blocks of wood). John V quartered this (Table 34) with the arms of Dietz; his wife brought him the County of Katzenellenbogen. So his son William used four quarterings, for Nassau, Katzenellenbogen, Vianen and Dietz. On these William the Silent imposed a smaller escutcheon with Chalon quartering Orange, and Geneva over all. After his death the civil governance of the United Provinces was in the hands of the great statesman, John of Oldenbarnevelt, but Maurice of Nassau took over the military side, reconstituted the army and rapidly became celebrated as the finest commander of his age. In 1609 the Twelve Years' Truce amounted to Spanish recognition of Dutch independence. Maurice held the position of Stadholder of Holland, the most important of the seven provinces, from 1587 and came to hold the same office in three other provinces. Philip William, eldest son of William the Silent, had been taken to Spain as a hostage; he remained a Catholic and a stranger to his family. On his death in 1618, the Principality of Orange and Chalon passed to Maurice.

The early years of the seventeenth century witnessed an astonishing advance in Dutch prosperity. Amsterdam became one of the commercial centres of Europe; an East India company was founded; and the ships and seamanship, which had contributed so effectively to resistance against Spain, became controllers of the carrying trade in European waters. In 1619 Batavia was founded in the East Indies, in 1625 New Amsterdam (now known as New York) in America. At home the reclamation of land from the sea continued. In the Netherlands themselves there was also a powerful school of painting: such names as Rembrandt, Vermeer and Frans Hals could be followed by a long list of lesser masters.

When Spain renewed the war in 1621, the House of Orange provided another talented general to drive them back. Maurice died soon after, but his half-brother, Prince Frederick Henry, successfully invaded the Spanish Netherlands and captured Maastricht. At the time of his death (1647) he would have liked to continue the war, but the peace party prevailed. The merchants had won their

emotions. At first he was a protégé and servant of Charles V, but as resistance to Philip II developed in the Low Countries he emerged as their natural and indomitable leader. He became a Calvinist, though he believed profoundly in tolerance, and lavished his enormous resources in the conflict against the repressive and bigoted government of Philip II. William's position was curious, for the power was vested in the Estates and he held only the office of stadholder, but his ability, diplomacy and resolution made him the founding father of the new republic. In 1579 the Union of Utrecht amalgamated the seven northern provinces, mainly those which had eschewed Catholicism, into a new European nation.

TABLE 37

NETHERLANDS
Ancestors of William III, Prince of Orange, and King William I

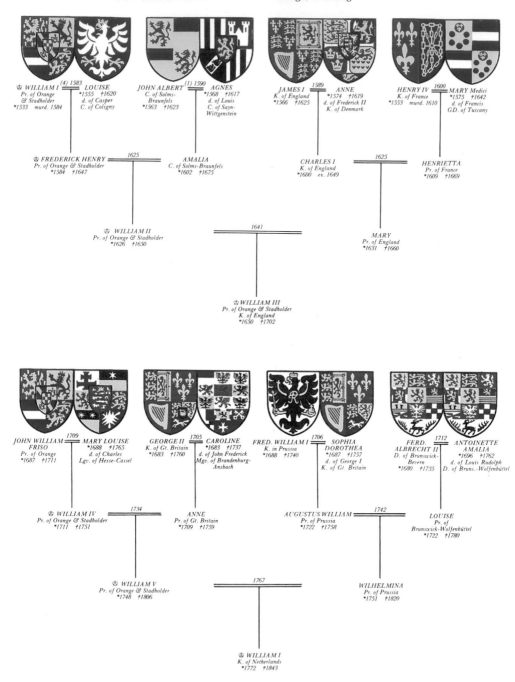

♔ WILLIAM I
Pr. of Orange
& Stadholder
*1533 murd. 1584

(4) 1583

LOUISE
*1555 †1620
d. of Casper
C. of Coligny

JOHN ALBERT
C. of Solms-
Braunfels
*1563 †1623

(1) 1590

AGNES
*1568 †1617
d. of Louis
C. of Sayn-
Wittgenstein

JAMES I
K. of England
*1566 †1625

1589

ANNE
*1574 †1619
d. of Frederick II
K. of Denmark

HENRY IV
K. of France
*1553 murd. 1610

1600

MARY Medici
*1575 †1642
d. of Francis
GD. of Tuscany

♔ FREDERICK HENRY
Pr. of Orange & Stadholder
*1584 †1647

1625

AMALIA
C. of Solms-Braunfels
*1602 †1675

CHARLES I
K. of England
*1600 ex. 1649

1625

HENRIETTA
Pr. of France
*1609 †1669

♔ WILLIAM II
Pr. of Orange & Stadholder
*1626 †1650

1641

MARY
Pr. of England
*1631 †1660

♔ WILLIAM III
Pr. of Orange & Stadholder
K. of England
*1650 †1702

JOHN WILLIAM
FRISO
Pr. of Orange
*1687 †1711

1709

MARY LOUISE
*1688 †1765
d. of Charles
Lgv. of Hesse-Cassel

GEORGE II
K. of Gt. Britain
*1683 †1760

1705

CAROLINE
*1683 †1737
d. of John Frederick
Mgv. of Brandenburg-
Ansbach

FRED. WILLIAM I
K. in Prussia
*1688 †1740

1706

SOPHIA
DOROTHEA
*1687 †1757
d. of George I
K. of Gt. Britain

FERD.
ALBRECHT II
D. of Brunswick-
Bevern
*1680 †1735

1712

ANTOINETTE
AMALIA
*1696 †1762
d. of Louis Rudolph
D. of Bruns.-Wolfenbüttel

♔ WILLIAM IV
Pr. of Orange & Stadholder
*1711 †1751

1734

ANNE
Pr. of Gt. Britain
*1709 †1759

AUGUSTUS WILLIAM
Pr. of Prussia
*1722 †1758

1742

LOUISE
Pr. of
Brunswick-Wolfenbüttel
*1722 †1780

♔ WILLIAM V
Pr. of Orange & Stadholder
*1748 †1806

1767

WILHELMINA
Pr. of Prussia
*1751 †1820

♔ WILLIAM I
K. of Netherlands
*1772 †1843

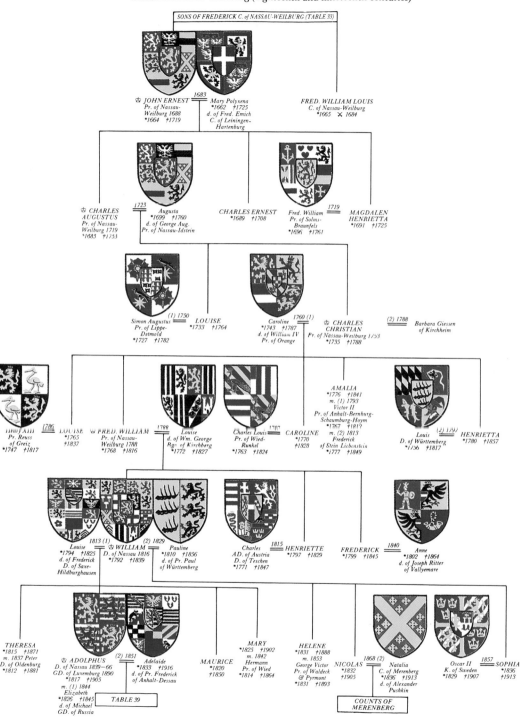

SONS OF FREDERICK C. of NASSAU-WEILBURG (TABLE 33)

✿ JOHN ERNEST
Pr. of Nassau-
Weilburg 1688
*1664 †1719

1683

Mary Polyxena
*1662 †1725
d. of Fred. Emich
C. of Leiningen-
Hartenburg

FRED. WILLIAM LOUIS
C. of Nassau-Weilburg
*1665 ✕ 1684

✿ CHARLES
AUGUSTUS
Pr. of Nassau-
Weilburg 1719
*1685 †1753

1723

Augusta
*1699 †1760
d. of George Aug.
Pr. of Nassau-Idstein

CHARLES ERNEST
*1689 †1708

Fred. William
Pr. of Solms-
Braunfels
*1696 †1761

1719

MAGDALEN
HENRIETTA
*1691 †1725

Simon Augustus
Pr. of Lippe-
Detmold
*1727 †1782

(1) 1750

LOUISE
*1733 †1764

Caroline
*1743 †1787
d. of William IV
Pr. of Orange

1760 (1)

✿ CHARLES
CHRISTIAN
Pr. of Nassau-Weilburg 1753
*1735 †1788

(2) 1788

Barbara Giessen
of Kirchheim

HENRY XIII
Pr. Reuss
of Greiz
*1747 †1817

1786

LOUISE
*1765
†1837

✿ FRED. WILLIAM
Pr. of Nassau-
Weilburg 1788
*1768 †1816

1788

Louise
d. of Wm. George
Rgt. of Kirchberg
*1772 †1827

Charles Louis
Pr. of Wied-
Runkel
*1763 †1824

1797

CAROLINE
*1770
†1828

AMALIA
*1776 †1841
m. (1) 1793
Victor II
Pr. of Anhalt-Bernburg-
Schaumburg-Hoym
*1767 †1812
m. (2) 1813
Frederick
of Stein Liebenstein
*1777 †1849

Louis
D. of Württemberg
*1756 †1817

(2) 1797

HENRIETTA
*1780 †1857

Louise
*1794 †1825
d. of Frederick
D. of Saxe-
Hildburghausen

1813 (1)

✿ WILLIAM
D. of Nassau 1816
*1792 †1839

(2) 1829

Pauline
*1810 †1856
d. of Pr. Paul
of Württemberg

Charles
A.D. of Austria
D. of Teschen
*1771 †1847

1815

HENRIETTE
*1797 †1829

FREDERICK
*1799 †1845

1840

Anne
*1802 †1864
d. of Joseph Ritter
of Vallyemare

THERESA
*1815 †1871
m. 1837 Peter
D. of Oldenburg
*1812 †1881

✿ ADOLPHUS
D. of Nassau 1839–66
GD. of Luxemburg 1890
*1817 †1905
m. (1) 1844
Elizabeth
*1826 †1845
d. of Michael
GD. of Russia

(2) 1851

Adelaide
*1833 †1916
d. of Pr. Frederick
of Anhalt-Dessau

TABLE 39

MAURICE
*1820
†1850

MARY
*1825 †1902
m. 1842
Hermann
Pr. of Wied
*1814 †1864

HELENE
*1831 †1888
m. 1853
George Victor
Pr. of Waldeck
& Pyrmont
*1831 †1893

NICOLAS
*1832
†1905

1868 (2)

Natalia
*1836 †1913
d. of Alexander
Pushkin

COUNTS OF
MERENBERG

Oscar II
K. of Sweden
*1829 †1907

1857

SOPHIA
*1836
†1913

TABLE 39

LUXEMBURG
Grand-Dukes in the twentieth century

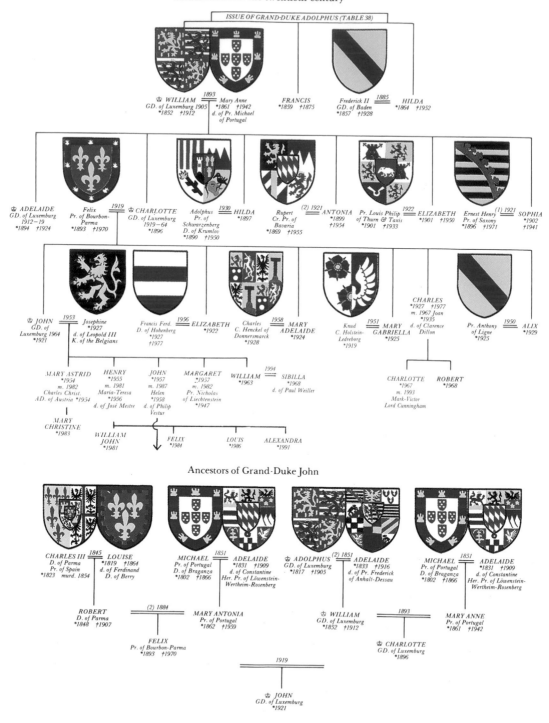

ISSUE OF GRAND-DUKE ADOLPHUS (TABLE 38)

♚ WILLIAM $\frac{1893}{}$ Mary Anne
GD. of Luxemburg 1905 *1861 †1942
*1852 †1912 d. of Pr. Michael
of Portugal

FRANCIS
*1859 †1875

Frederick II $\frac{1885}{}$ HILDA
GD. of Baden *1864 †1952
*1857 †1928

♚ ADELAIDE
GD. of Luxemburg
1912–19
*1894 †1924

Felix $\frac{1919}{}$ ♚ CHARLOTTE
Pr. of Bourbon- GD. of Luxemburg
Parma 1919–64
*1893 †1970 *1896

Adolphus $\frac{1930}{}$ HILDA
Pr. of *1897
Schwarzenberg
D. of Krumlov
*1890 †1950

Rupert $\frac{(2)\ 1921}{}$ ANTONIA
Cr. Pr. of *1899
Bavaria †1954
*1869 †1955

Pr. Louis Philip $\frac{1922}{}$ ELIZABETH
of Thurn & Taxis *1901 †1950
*1901 †1933

Ernest Henry $\frac{(1)\ 1921}{}$ SOPHIA
Pr. of Saxony *1902
*1896 †1971 †1941

♚ JOHN $\frac{1953}{}$ Josephine
GD. of *1927
Luxemburg 1964 d. of Leopold III
*1921 K. of the Belgians

Francis Ferd. $\frac{1956}{}$ ELIZABETH
D. of Hohenberg *1922
*1927 †1977

Charles $\frac{1958}{}$ MARY
C. Henckel of ADELAIDE
Donnersmarck *1924
*1928

Knud $\frac{1951}{}$ MARY
C. Holstein- GABRIELLA
Ledreborg *1925
*1919

CHARLES
*1927 †1977
m. 1967 Joan
$\frac{}{1935}$
d. of Clarence
Dillon

Pr. Anthony $\frac{1950}{}$ ALIX
of Ligne *1929
*1925

MARY ASTRID
*1954
m. 1982
Charles Christ.
AD. of Austria *1954

HENRY
*1955
m. 1981
Maria-Teresa
*1956
d. of José Mestre

JOHN
*1957
m. 1987
Helen
*1958
d. of Philip
Vestur

MARGARET
*1957
m. 1982
Pr. Nicholas
of Liechtenstein
*1947

WILLIAM $\frac{1994}{}$ SIBILLA
*1963 *1968
d. of Paul Weiller

CHARLOTTE
*1967
m. 1993
Mark-Victor
Lord Cunningham

ROBERT
*1968

MARY
CHRISTINE
*1983

WILLIAM
JOHN
*1981

FELIX
*1984

LOUIS
*1986

ALEXANDRA
*1991

Ancestors of Grand-Duke John

CHARLES III $\frac{1845}{}$ LOUISE
D. of Parma *1819 †1864
Pr. of Spain d. of Ferdinand
*1823 murd. 1854 D. of Berry

MICHAEL $\frac{1851}{}$ ADELAIDE
Pr. of Portugal *1831 †1909
D. of Braganza d. of Constantine
*1802 †1866 Her. Pr. of Löwenstein-
Wertheim-Rosenberg

♚ ADOLPHUS $\frac{(2)\ 1851}{}$ ADELAIDE
GD. of Luxemburg *1833 †1916
*1817 †1905 d. of Pr. Frederick
of Anhalt-Dessau

MICHAEL $\frac{1851}{}$ ADELAIDE
Pr. of Portugal *1831 †1909
D. of Braganza d. of Constantine
*1802 †1866 Her. Pr. of Löwenstein-
Wertheim-Rosenberg

ROBERT $\frac{(2)\ 1884}{}$
D. of Parma
*1848 †1907

MARY ANTONIA
Pr. of Portugal
*1862 †1959

♚ WILLIAM $\frac{1893}{}$
GD. of Luxemburg
*1852 †1912

MARY ANNE
Pr. of Portugal
*1861 †1942

FELIX
Pr. of Bourbon-Parma
*1893 †1970

♚ CHARLOTTE
GD. of Luxemburg
*1896

♚ JOHN $\frac{1919}{}$
GD. of Luxemburg
*1921

independence; they did not wish to intrude into the power politics of Europe. These ideas exacerbated the young and intelligent William II who saw himself as a future King of Holland. He carried out one coup against Amsterdam but died suddenly before the issue was truly joined. Alarmed by these events the State of Holland decided not to fill the office of stadholder; the principal power was exercised by the Grand Pensionary, John De Witt, for some twenty-two years. It was still an age of great prosperity and expansion at home and overseas; in 1652 Capetown was established and the foundations laid of Dutch South Africa. In Europe, however, France was replacing Spain as the main enemy by land, while England was emerging as a rival at sea. The arms used by the United Provinces in this period can be seen on Table 33. They comprised the lion of Nassau (but without the background of billets) crowned and holding a sword and a sheaf of seven arrows to symbolize the seven provinces.

In 1672 Louis XIV of France, buttressed by many allies, decided to invade the Netherlands, partly in order to facilitate his own ambitions on the Spanish Netherlands (Belgium of today). In the hour of crisis, the people turned once more to the House of Orange-Nassau. William III, young, inexperienced, and deliberately sheltered from public affairs, was appointed commander against the hosts of France with their distinguished Marshals, Turenne and Condé. His army was small and ill-trained. He resorted to the heroic remedy of breaching the dykes and flooding a defensive belt of country. At this difficult moment, the people rose against De Witt and demanded that William become stadholder like his forebears. By a narrow margin he succeeded in fending off the puissant French King, who it must be admitted – had not employed his vast resources with energy, speed or strategy. The war continued till 1678 but the Republic had been saved, and William III was able to consolidate his position. Four of the seven provinces, including Holland, made the stadholdership hereditary in the family of Nassau; William was supreme and dominant in foreign policy and military affairs. In this capacity he was able to organize in 1688 the bold and dramatic stroke by which he replaced his father-in-law as King of England and stood forth as a European statesman inspiring the coalition against Louis XIV.

After he was acknowledged king in 1689, William placed a simple shield of Nassau over the royal arms of Britain (Table 34). His ancestry was varied; with his Germanic forebears mingled the blood of the Stuarts and of the illustrious French Protestant family of Coligny (Table 37). Before his death he recognized his cousin John William Friso as his heir in the Netherlands. The principality and title of Orange passed to Frederick of Prussia, child of William's aunt Louise Henriette, but were ceded to France at the Peace of Utrecht in 1713; the Dutch estates thereof stayed with the Nassau family who also used the style of Prince of Orange. John William Friso (Table 35) was descended from John, younger brother of William the Silent, but his grandmother was an aunt of William III; he was a brave soldier but was unluckily drowned on a tempestuous night in 1711. The heir, William IV, was born posthumously. His reign saw a reassertion of oligarchic control, but in 1747 he was appointed stadholder of the whole country; he died a few years later leaving an infant son.

The eighteenth century saw a great decline in Dutch prosperity and wealth, though her commerce continued to be considerable. The United Provinces remained neutral in the Seven Years' War, but most unprofitably came to the aid of the American Colonies in 1776; their shipping suffered severely and Britain became a rival in the East Indies. William V, a slow man with little capacity for government, was widely censured, but in fact he would have preferred to help his British kinsfolk. At one point (1787) he was barred from the province of Holland and only restored thither by the Prussian bayonets of his brother-in-law. Soon after, the French Revolution broke out, and in 1795 French republican troops entered Holland, meeting little resistance and setting up the Batavian Republic. From 1806 to 1810 Louis Bonaparte was King of Holland, but in the latter year his brother incorporated the Netherlands into France.

In 1815, as a result of the Treaty of Vienna, William VI became King of the united Low Countries, as William I, King of the Netherlands. In that year he founded the Military Order of William, which surrounds his shield on Table 33. The new King added to the arms of Nassau a crown on the head of the lion, a sword in his right hand and a bunch of seven arrows in his left; the lion with sword and arrows (representing the seven states) had been the arms of the United Provinces. None the less the union was unreal; Belgium, Catholic and French or Flemish speaking, had by now little in common with the Calvinistic Dutch. In 1830 there was a rebellion; the Great Powers took charge, with England and France in the lead, and in 1839 a separate Belgian kingdom was established (Chapter 9). In the next year William I abdicated. His ancestry (Table 37) shows a strong predominance of varying branches of the House of Brunswick, whether in Germany or England. His son, William II, during his brief reign embarked on a programme of reform and transformed the Netherlands into a constitutional monarchy, whose most striking feature was that ministers could be appointed from outside the two chambers.

Under William III Holland grew in industrial prosperity and aspired to neutrality in international politics; as a consequence The Hague became the seat of the International Court of Justice. When he died, Luxemburg passed to his distant cousin while Holland was ruled by Queen Wilhelmina, whose long reign spanned the first half of the twentieth century. The Netherlands were successful in avoiding any commitment in the First World War and gave refuge to the Kaiser at its end: but the country was invaded by Hitler in May 1940. The Dutch were forced to capitulate; Rotterdam was savagely and wantonly bombed; the royal family fled overseas. Soon after her return, the venerable Queen Wilhelmina abdicated in favour of her daughter, Juliana (Table 36), whose ancestry exhibits a cross-section of the Protestant families of northern Europe. Since the War the Netherlands have lost their valuable colonies in the East Indies, but have nevertheless retained a high level of prosperity.

In her turn Queen Juliana had only daughters. The eldest married a German nobleman, Claus von Amsberg, who bears the title of Prince of the Netherlands. They have three sons, the first male heirs in three generations. The marriage of Princess Irene to a Catholic provoked some reaction in the predominantly Protestant Netherlands. In 1980 Queen Juliana followed her mother's example and abdicated in favour of her eldest daughter, who thus became Queen Beatrix.

LUXEMBURG

In the Middle Ages Luxemburg was a district in the Low Countries, slightly isolated by the great Bishopric of Liège and the hills of the Ardennes. Its rulers rose in the fourteenth century to be Emperors of Germany and Kings of Bohemia but their last descendant sold the Duchy to Burgundy. Thereafter its fortunes lay with the Spanish Netherlands, which in the eighteenth century passed to Austria. In 1815 it was attached to the new Kingdom of Holland (which united the Holland and Belgium of today) as a compensation to the Nassau family for the lands they lost east of the Rhine, and was declared to be a grand-duchy. In 1839 when the independence of Belgium was established, Luxemburg, somewhat reduced in size, remained a separate domain of the

King of Holland, who in 1841 founded the Order of the Oak Crown (Table 33).

William II (Table 35) gave the Grand-Duchy a liberal constitution. William III installed his brother Henry as his deputy with plenary powers. But in 1866, after the war between Prussia and Austria had dissolved the Germanic Confederation (of which Luxemburg was part), King William III conceived the idea of selling the province to France. Not surprisingly Prussia mistrusted this scheme, for the city of Luxemburg was deemed the strongest fortress in north Europe; and a conference of the major powers held in London (1867) guaranteed the sovereign independence of the Grand-Duchy.

When France and Prussia went to war in 1870 this freedom was precariously maintained. However, the death of William III in 1890 without male heirs posed a new problem since Luxemburg was under the Salic Law; accordingly the Grand-Duchy passed to Adolphus, Duke of Nassau, the senior male of the Walramian branch of the family, whose ancestors had been Princes of Nassau-Weilburg (Tables 33 and 38). His duchy had been annexed by Prussia in 1866.

Adolphus abandoned the complex quarterings of his former German fiefs and combined the lion of Nassau on its billety background with the ancient arms of Luxemburg, a red lion with two tails on a field of white and blue stripes. The Grand-Duke William (Table 39), who succeeded in 1905, strove to comply with the Salic Law, but finding himself the father of six daughters was constrained to modify the rules of succession. His eldest daughter Adelaide saw her territory invaded by the Germans in 1915, and abdicated in 1919 to enter a convent. Her sister Charlotte again saw Luxemburg's neutrality flouted by the German soldiery. Charlotte's son, Prince John, served in the British army during the war, in the course of which the Duchy saw heavy fighting when von Rundstedt counter-attacked in 1944–5, and reentered his state in 1945 with the Allied Forces. In 1964 his mother abdicated and he became grandduke in her stead; his ancestry (Table 39) shows a strong strain of Portuguese and Bourbon blood. An interesting morganatic marriage was made by Nicholas, younger step-brother of Grand-Duke Adolphus, with a daughter of the Russian poet Pushkin, himself half-negro. With the death of Grand-Duke William the numerous issue in tail male of the original twelfth-century Count of Nassau came to an end.

Chapter 9

BELGIUM

Something of the early history of Belgium has been described in the last chapter. There was little unity in the Low Countries between the break-up of the Carolingian Empire and the growth of the Burgundian dominions. In the division of his territories among the heirs of Charlemagne, Holland and Belgium (as known today) were part of the non-viable 'Middle Kingdom' set up for Lothair (Chapter 14: first section). The more stable powers of France and Germany both cast envious eyes on the lands between them, and have scarcely ceased to do so. The dramatic consolidation of territory, mainly south of the Scheldt, by the Dukes of Burgundy gave a new unity to the Belgic area, though the great Bishopric of Liège lay as a wedge between Luxemburg and the rest. The rich cultural evolution and commercial prosperity of the towns may be epitomized in the painting of van Eyck and his school and the towering churches and town halls of this epoch. The Burgundian territories passed to the Hapsburgs, and remained Catholic under their control while Protestant Holland battled to religious and political freedom. In 1713 the southern provinces were transferred from Spain to Austria.

The old map of Europe was in tatters at the end of the eighteenth century as a result of the French Revolution. Armies of fervent republicans invaded the Austrian Netherlands in 1792 and incorporated them in France. It was on Belgian soil that Napoleon was finally overthrown at Waterloo. In 1815 the two long-divided areas of the Netherlands were united into a single kingdom under William I of Orange-Nassau. The amalgamation did not work. William was a fussy and stubborn monarch; geography and politics might dictate the alliance, but tradition, religion, language and sentiment were hostile to it. In 1830 an uprising in Belgium enforced separation; the Great Powers met in London to regularize what had

taken place. At first the Crown was offered to the Duc de Nemours, son of Louis Philippe of France (Table 67), who refused. Ultimately the congress agreed to nominate Prince Leopold of Saxe-Coburg-Saalfeld. He had already been married to the only child of George IV, but the death in childbirth of Princess Charlotte robbed him of the throne of Britain; he now

Leopold I (1790–1865), King of the Belgians. He is wearing the insignia of the Golden Fleece.

BELGIUM
General survey

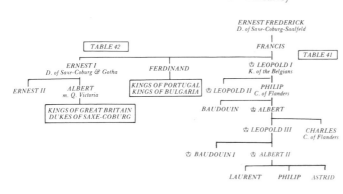

ERNEST FREDERICK
D. of Saxe-Coburg-Saalfeld

FRANCIS

- *ERNEST I* — *D. of Saxe-Coburg & Gotha* (TABLE 42)
  - *ERNEST II*
  - *ALBERT* — *m. Q. Victoria*
    - KINGS OF GREAT BRITAIN / DUKES OF SAXE-COBURG
- *FERDINAND*
  - KINGS OF PORTUGAL / KINGS OF BULGARIA
- ♔ *LEOPOLD I* — *K. of the Belgians* (TABLE 41)
  - ♔ *LEOPOLD II*
  - *PHILIP* — *C. of Flanders*
    - *BAUDOUIN*
    - ♔ *ALBERT*
      - ♔ *LEOPOLD III*
        - ♔ *BAUDOUIN I*
        - ♔ *ALBERT II*
          - *LAURENT*
          - *PHILIP*
          - *ASTRID*
      - *CHARLES* — *C. of Flanders*

Ancestors of Leopold I and Albert II

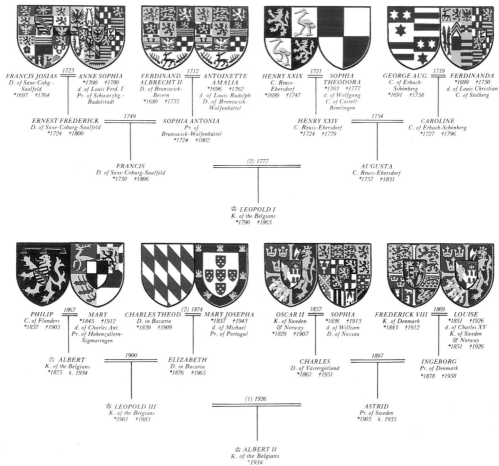

FRANCIS JOSIAS, *D. of Saxe-Cobg.-Saalfeld*, **1697 †1764* — 1723 — *ANNE SOPHIA*, **1700 †1780*, *d. of Louis Ferd. I Pr. of Schwarzbg.-Rudolstadt*

FERDINAND ALBRECHT II, *D. of Brunswick-Bevern*, **1680 †1735* — 1712 — *ANTOINETTE AMALIA*, **1696 †1762*, *d. of Louis Rudolph D. of Brunswick-Wolfenbüttel*

HENRY XXIX, *C. Reuss-Ebersdorf*, **1699 †1747* — 1721 — *SOPHIA THEODORA*, **1703 †1777*, *d. of Wolfgang C. of Castell-Remlingen*

GEORGE AUG., *C. of Erbach-Schönberg*, **1691 †1758* — 1719 — *FERDINANDA*, **1699 †1750*, *d. of Louis Christian C. of Stolberg*

ERNEST FREDERICK, *D. of Saxe-Coburg-Saalfeld*, **1724 †1800* — 1749 — *SOPHIA ANTONIA*, *Pr. of Brunswick-Wolfenbüttel*, **1724 †1802*

HENRY XXIV, *C. Reuss-Ebersdorf*, **1724 †1779* — 1754 — *CAROLINE*, *C. of Erbach-Schönberg*, **1727 †1796*

FRANCIS, *D. of Saxe-Coburg-Saalfeld*, **1750 †1806* — (2) 1777 — *AUGUSTA*, *C. Reuss-Ebersdorf*, **1757 †1831*

♔ *LEOPOLD I*
K. of the Belgians
**1790 †1865*

PHILIP, *C. of Flanders*, **1837 †1905* — 1867 — *MARY*, **1845 †1912*, *d. of Charles Ant. Pr. of Hohenzollern-Sigmaringen*

CHARLES THEOD., *D. in Bavaria*, **1839 †1909* — (2) 1874 — *MARY JOSEPHA*, **1857 †1943*, *d. of Michael Pr. of Portugal*

OSCAR II, *K. of Sweden & Norway*, **1829 †1907* — 1857 — *SOPHIA*, **1836 †1913*, *d. of William D. of Nassau*

FREDERICK VIII, *K. of Denmark*, **1843 †1912* — 1869 — *LOUISE*, **1851 †1926*, *d. of Charles XV K. of Sweden & Norway *1851 †1926*

♔ *ALBERT*, *K. of the Belgians*, **1875 k. 1934* — 1900 — *ELIZABETH*, *D. in Bavaria*, **1876 †1965*

CHARLES, *D. of Västergötland*, **1861 †1951* — 1897 — *INGEBORG*, *Pr. of Denmark*, **1878 †1958*

♔ *LEOPOLD III*, *K. of the Belgians*, **1901 †1983* — (1) 1926 — *ASTRID*, *Pr. of Sweden*, **1905 k. 1935*

♔ *ALBERT II*
K. of the Belgians
**1934*

1776 (1)
Sophia
*1760 †1776
d. of Ernest Frederick
D. of Saxe-Hildburghausen

FRANCIS
D. of Saxe-Coburg-
Saalfeld 1800
*1750 †1806

(2) 1777
Augusta
*1757 †1831
d. of Henry XXIV
C. Reuss-Ebersdorf

see also
TABLE 42

FERDINAND
*1785 †1851
m. 1816 Antonia
*1797 †1862
d. of Fr. Joseph
Pr. of Kohary

Louise
*1800 †1831
d. of Augustus
D. of Saxe-Gotha-Altenbg.
(div. 1826)

1817 (1)
ERNEST I
D. of Saxe-Coburg-
& Gotha 1826
*1784 †1844

(2) 1832
Mary
*1799 †1860
d. of Alexander
D. of Württemberg

Charles
Pr. of Leiningen
*1763 †1814

1803(1)
VICTORIA
*1786 †1861

(2)1818
Edward
D. of Kent
*1767 †1820

Charlotte
*1796 †1817
d. of George IV
K. of Gt. Britain

1816 (1)
LEOPOLD I
K. of the Belgians
1831
*1790 †1865

(2) 1832
Louise
*1812 †1850
d. of Louis Philippe
K. of the French

ALBERT
*1819 †1861

1840
VICTORIA
Q. of Gr. Britain
*1819 †1901

LEOPOLD II
K. of the Belgians
1865
*1835 †1909

1853
Mary Henrietta
*1836 †1902
d. of Joseph
AD. of Austria

PHILIP
C. of Flanders
*1837 †1905

1867
Mary
*1845 †1912
d. of Charles Anth.
Pr. of Hohenzollern-
Sigmaringen

Maximilian
AD. of Austria
Emp. of Mexico 1864
*1832 ex. 1867

1857
CHARLOTTE
*1840 †1927

LOUISE
*1858 †1924
m. 1875 (div. 1906)
Pr. Philip of Saxe-
Cobg. & Gotha
*1844 †1921

Rudolph
Cr. Pr. of Austria
*1858 suic. 1889

1881 (1)
STEPHANIE
*1864 †1945
m. (2) 1900
Elemér Pr. Lónyai
*1863 †1946

Victor
Pr. Napoleon
*1862 †1926

1910
CLEMENTINE
*1872 †1955

BAUDOUIN
*1869 †1891

HENRIETTE
*1870 †1948
m. 1896
Pr. Emanuel
of Orléans
D. of Vendôme
*1872 †1931

JOSEPHINE
*1872 †1958
m. 1894
Charles Anth.
Pr. of Hohenzollern
*1868 †1919

ALBERT I
K. of the Belgians
1909
*1875 k. 1934

1900
Elizabeth
d. of Charles Theod.
D. in Bavaria
*1876 †1965

Astrid
*1905 k. 1935
d. of Charles
D. of Västergötland

1926 (1)
LEOPOLD III
K. of the Belgians
1934–51
*1901 †1983

(2) 1941
Mary Lilian
Pr. of Réthy
*1916
d. of Henry Baels

CHARLES
C. of Flanders
Regent 1944–50
*1903 †1983

Humbert II
K. of Italy
*1904 †1983

1930
MARY JOSEPHA
*1906

John
GD. of Luxemburg
*1921

1953
JOSEPHINE
*1927

BAUDOUIN I
K. of the Belgians
1951
*1930
†1993

1960
Fabiola
*1928
d. of Gonzalo
Mora y Fernandez
M. of Casa Riera

ALBERT II
Pr. of Liège
K. of the Belgians
1993
*1934

1959
Paola
*1937
d. of Fulco
Pr. of
Ruffo di Calabria

ALEXANDER
*1942

MARY
CHRISTINA
*1951
m. (1) 1981
Paul Druker
*1938
(div. 1981)
m. (2) 1989
Jean Paul
Gourgue

MARY
ESMERALDA
*1956

PHILIP
D. of Brabant
*1960

ASTRID
*1962
m. 1984
Laurent
AD. of Austria
*1955

LAURENT
*1963

AMEDEO
*1986

MARIA-LAURA
*1988

JOACHIM
*1991

NOTE
The coat-of-arms given to King ALBERT II is
identical with the one he had owned as
Prince of Liège before his coronation.

TABLE 42   The House of Saxe-Coburg on the thrones of Europe

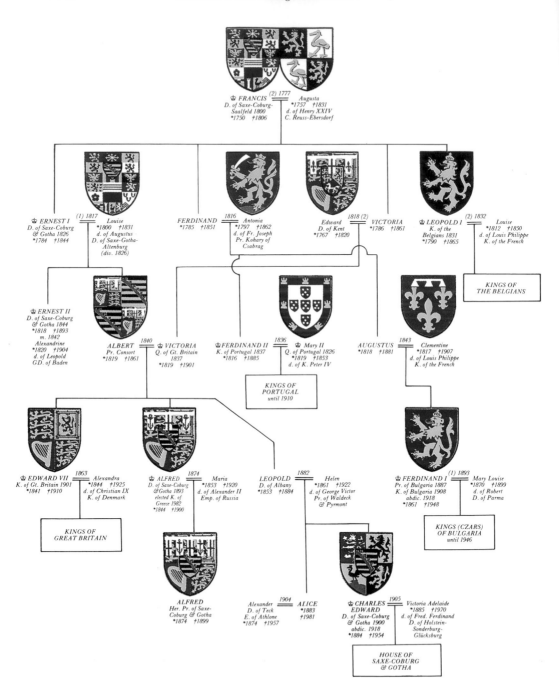

♔ FRANCIS (2) 1777 Augusta
D. of Saxe-Coburg- *1757 †1831
Saalfeld 1800 d. of Henry XXIV
*1750 †1806 C. Reuss-Ebersdorf

♔ ERNEST I (1) 1817 Louise
D. of Saxe-Coburg *1800 †1831
& Gotha 1826 d. of Augustus
*1784 †1844 D. of Saxe-Gotha-
Altenburg
(div. 1826)

FERDINAND 1816 Antonia
*1785 †1851 *1797 †1862
d. of Fr. Joseph
Pr. Kohary of
Csabrag

Edward 1818 (2) VICTORIA
D. of Kent *1786 †1861
*1767 †1820

♔ LEOPOLD I (2) 1832 Louise
K. of the *1812 †1850
Belgians 1831 d. of Louis Philippe
*1790 †1865 K. of the French

KINGS OF
THE BELGIANS

♔ ERNEST II
D. of Saxe-Coburg
& Gotha 1844
*1818 †1893
m. 1842
Alexandrine
*1820 †1904
d. of Leopold
GD. of Baden

ALBERT 1840 ♔ VICTORIA
Pr. Consort Q. of Gt. Britain
*1819 †1861 1837
*1819 †1901

♔ FERDINAND II 1836 ♔ Mary II
K. of Portugal 1837 Q. of Portugal 1826
*1816 †1885 *1819 †1853
d. of K. Peter IV

KINGS OF
PORTUGAL
until 1910

AUGUSTUS 1843 Clementine
*1818 †1881 *1817 †1907
d. of Louis Philippe
K. of the French

♔ EDWARD VII 1863 Alexandra
K. of Gt. Britain 1901 d. of Christian IX
*1841 †1910 K. of Denmark

KINGS OF
GREAT BRITAIN

♔ ALFRED 1874 Maria
D. of Saxe-Coburg *1853 †1920
& Gotha 1893 d. of Alexander II
elected K. of Emp. of Russia
Greece 1982
*1844 †1900

LEOPOLD 1882 Helen
D. of Albany *1861 †1922
*1853 †1884 d. of George Victor
Pr. of Waldeck
& Pyrmont

♔ FERDINAND I (1) 1893 Mary Louise
Pr. of Bulgaria 1887 *1870 †1899
K. of Bulgaria 1908 d. of Robert
abdic. 1918 D. of Parma
*1861 †1948

KINGS (CZARS)
OF BULGARIA
until 1946

ALFRED
Her. Pr. of Saxe-
Coburg & Gotha
*1874 †1899

Alexander 1904 ALICE
D. of Teck *1883
E. of Athlone †1981
*1874 †1957

♔ CHARLES 1905 Victoria Adelaide
EDWARD *1885 †1970
D. of Saxe-Coburg d. of Fred. Ferdinand
& Gotha 1900 D. of Holstein-
abdic. 1918 Sonderburg-
*1884 †1954 Glücksburg

HOUSE OF
SAXE-COBURG
& GOTHA

acquired that of Belgium and married a daughter of Louis Philippe (Table 41). Leopold I was of exclusively German ancestry, mainly from minor princely families (Table 40), but he proved an able, popular and resourceful ruler, combining tact with shrewd political sense. He was uncle to both Queen Victoria and the Prince Consort (Table 42) and lavished good advice upon them. The last difficulties with Holland were not resolved until 1839, when the neutrality of Belgium was guaranteed by treaty (the famous 'scrap of paper' of 1914), but, before he died, Leopold had firmly established Belgian freedom and nationality. He adopted as the arms of his realm the gold lion on black which was the ancient insignia of Brabant; this he combined with his personal arms (still including those of Princess Charlotte). In 1832 he founded the Order of Leopold (Table 40).

Leopold II is best known for his interest in colonial expansion. His initiative found a notorious opening in the Congo, where he became the ruler of an area 80 times that of Belgium, rich in rubber and ivory. But he was also concerned with the threat to his frontiers occasioned by the German occupation of Alsace and Lorraine in 1870. It fell to his nephew, Albert, to offer an heroic resistance to the Teutonic hordes which in 1914 ignored the treaty signed in 1839. King Albert's bravery and resolution won the admiration of his subjects; he and his wife were deeply loved. Not surprisingly, he ceased to use the German blazon of Saxony; as can be seen, his younger son and grandson have differenced the simple lion of Belgium with a bordure and label of gold respectively.

Leopold III married a charming Swedish princess who was killed in a car accident the year after his father died from a fall while climbing. Battered by these losses, he had to face the second aggression of the German nation. He chose to stay in his conquered country until deported to Germany in 1944, but his second, morganatic, marriage to a commoner and the bitter circumstances of the occupation reduced his prestige. When Belgium was liberated, his brother Charles, Count of Flanders, acted as regent until 1950 when a plebiscite invited Leopold to return; the latter, however, deemed it prudent to abdicate in 1951 in favour of his son, Baudouin. The young King had to face contentious problems, including linguistic discords between French and Flemish speakers and the loss into anarchy of the Congo (which had been annexed to Belgium in 1908). He and his brother have both sought their wives from the Mediterranean nobility, Baudouin from Spain and Albert from southern Italy. King Albert II. was elected after the deth of Baudouin I. The ancestry of the King, shows a wide spread from Catholic Portugal to the northern forebears of his mother, who was brought up a Lutheran.

THE HOUSE OF SAXE-COBURG

The ability and success of Leopold I and the illustrious marriage of his nephew Albert, the Prince Consort, constituted a good advertisement for the little dynasty of Saxe-Coburg (Table 42). Another nephew of Leopold of Belgium had made a distinguished alliance when he married Mary II, already Queen Regent of Portugal. Their descendants ruled in Portugal until the country became a republic in 1910 (Table 96). Meanwhile in 1878 an independent Bulgaria was set up by the Treaty of Berlin.

The first prince allotted to the new state was Alexander of Battenberg, a scion of the other great expanding family of this era. Alexander was deposed and exiled by a revolt in 1886; in his place the Bulgars chose Ferdinand of Saxe-Coburg, who reigned until 1918, promoting himself to King in 1908 but backing the wrong side in 1914. His grandson Simeon II was dethroned by the Communists in 1946. Thus at the accession of Edward VII of Great Britain in 1901, no less than four European realms were ruled by direct male descendants of Duke Francis of Saxe-Coburg-Saalfeld, a circumstance which would most certainly have astonished that rather obscure Saxon princeling.

Chapter 10

SPAIN: MEDIEVAL

The Iberian peninsula is one of the best defined geographical entities in Europe. The land mass, roughly rectangular, is bounded by sea on three sides: the fourth faces the Bay of Biscay and the formidable barrier of the Pyrenees. Yet the whole area has but seldom been united; nor have the Pyrenees always furnished the frontier which they seem so clearly to offer. Many races have occupied the peninsula and mixed their blood with the Celtic inhabitants who were conquered by Rome: Visigoths and Vandals have entered from the north, Arabs and Berbers from the south. In the seventh century AD almost the whole was occupied by a great wave of Islamic invaders, some of whom passed on to attack Gaul. Only in the bleak northwest and among the foothills of the Pyrenees did Christian societies survive. Charlemagne extended his dominions over the mountains to include Navarre at their western end and the Spanish March, down to Barcelona, at the east.

Meanwhile the whole of central and southern Spain constituted the prosperous and cultured Emirate of Cordova, ruled by the powerful Ommayad dynasty with every manifestation of civilized life. Christians were tolerated, the arts flourished and technical advances (such as the use of paper instead of animal skins) were fostered. At the beginning of the eleventh century, after the death in 1002 of the famous Almanzor, there was a sudden change. The political potency of Cordova collapsed and a period of civil war resulted. A great opportunity developed for the Christian kinglets who only a generation before were penned against the harsh Pyrenees and the chill Atlantic. At this epoch, the principal Christian states were, from west to east, Leon occupying the northwest corner and including the national shrine of St James at Santiago de Compostela, Castile centred round Burgos, Navarre

bestriding the Biscay end of the Pyrenees, Aragon, still small and crouched under the south flank of the mountains, and Barcelona, controlling the Mediterranean seaboard from that city north to Perpignan.

The epic of the reconquest, which dominates medieval Spain, may begin with Sancho III (1000–35), King of Navarre (Tables 43, 44 and 45), who conquered both Leon and Castile. A chance of Christian unity was forfeited when his realm was divided at his death. Garcias, his eldest son, took Navarre, Ferdinand received Castile, to which he soon added Leon on the death of his brother-in-law; Ramiro, an illegitimate brother, became the first King of Aragon. It was Ferdinand (Table 45) who launched the attack on the Moors; although he did defeat and kill his elder brother in 1054, his gaze was fixed to the south. The frontier of Castile was carried further inland, and most of the warring Moorish emirs paid tribute to him. Less sensational progress was made by Aragon and by the Count of Barcelona. It was, however, already becoming apparent that Navarre, dynastically the parent kingdom, was likely to lose in wealth and prestige by having almost no frontier with Islam and therefore less possibility of expansion.

Unhappily Ferdinand divided his kingdom between three sons; there was internecine warfare between them and their cousin Sancho IV of Navarre. In these futile struggles El Cid (Ruy Diaz de Bivar), the great Spanish hero of legend, made his name. In more sober history he seems also to have fought for the Moors or anyone who would pay him, ending up as an independent princeling in Valencia. In 1085 Alphonso VI of Castile captured the important city of Toledo, almost 300km (200 miles) south of Burgos, an indication of the scale of Castilian advance. His death was followed by a period of lamentable wars between the Christian states, including the

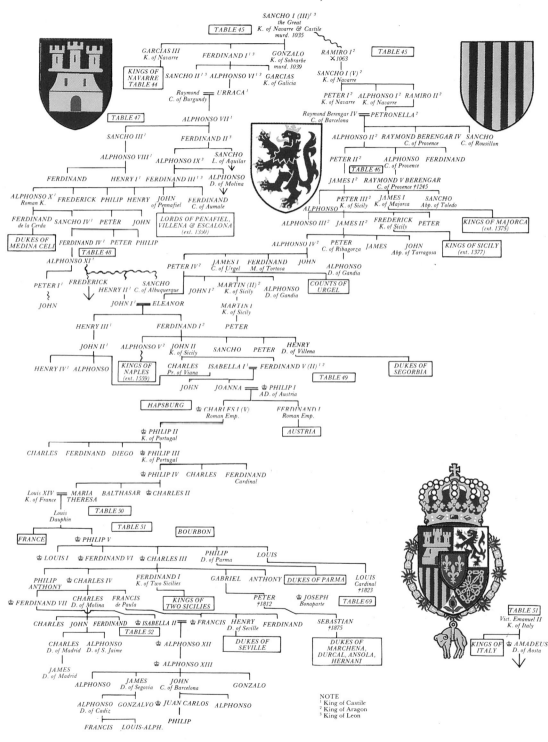

NOTE
[1] King of Castile
[2] King of Aragon
[3] King of Leon

TABLE 44

NAVARRE
General survey

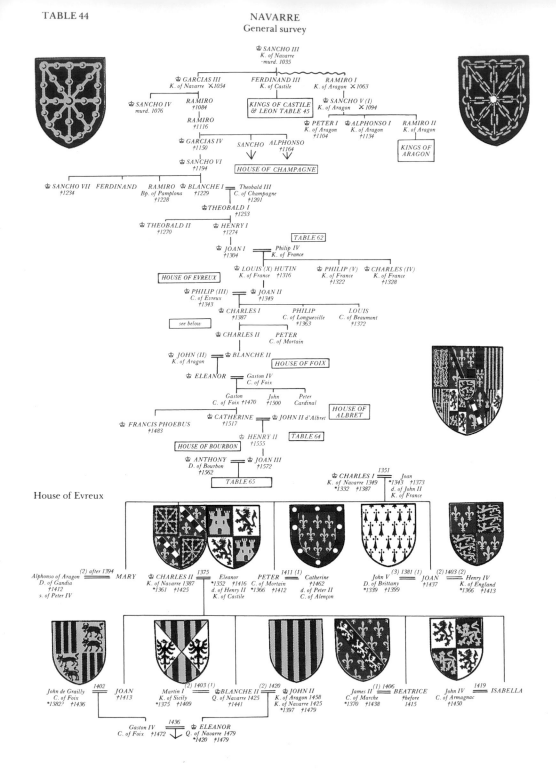

✪ SANCHO III
K. of Navarre
·murd. 1035

✪ GARCIAS III   FERDINAND III   RAMIRO I
K. of Navarre ✕1054   K. of Castile   K. of Aragon ✕1063

✪ SANCHO IV   RAMIRO   KINGS OF CASTILE   ✪ SANCHO V (I)
murd. 1076   †1084   & LEON TABLE 45   K. of Aragon ✕1094

RAMIRO †1116   PETER I   ALPHONSO I   RAMIRO II
K. of Aragon †1104   K. of Aragon †1134   K. of Aragon

✪ GARCIAS IV   SANCHO   ALPHONSO
†1150   †1164   KINGS OF ARAGON

✪ SANCHO VI   HOUSE OF CHAMPAGNE
†1194

✪ SANCHO VII   FERDINAND   RAMIRO   ✪ BLANCHE I ══ Theobald III
†1234   Bp. of Pamplona †1228   †1229   C. of Champagne †1201

✪ THEOBALD I
†1253

✪ THEOBALD II   ✪ HENRY I
†1270   †1274

TABLE 62

✪ JOAN I ═══ Philip IV
†1304   K. of France

✪ LOUIS (X) HUTIN   ✪ PHILIP (V)   ✪ CHARLES (IV)
K. of France †1316   K. of France †1322   K. of France †1328

HOUSE OF EVREUX

✪ PHILIP (III) ══ ✪ JOAN II
C. of Evreux †1343   †1349

✪ CHARLES I   PHILIP   LOUIS
†1387   C. of Longueville †1363   C. of Beaumont †1372

see below

✪ CHARLES II   PETER
C. of Mortain

✪ JOHN (II) ══ ✪ BLANCHE II
K. of Aragon   HOUSE OF FOIX

✪ ELEANOR ══ Gaston IV
C. of Foix

Gaston   John   Peter
C. of Foix †1470   †1500   Cardinal

HOUSE OF ALBRET

✪ FRANCIS PHOEBUS   ✪ CATHERINE ══ ✪ JOHN II d'Albret
†1483   †1517

✪ HENRY II   TABLE 64
†1555

HOUSE OF BOURBON

✪ ANTHONY ══ ✪ JOAN III
D. of Bourbon †1562   †1572

TABLE 65

House of Evreux

✪ CHARLES I   1351   Joan
K. of Navarre 1349   *1343 †1373
*1332 †1387   d. of John II
     K. of France

Alphonso of Aragon (2) after 1394 MARY   ✪ CHARLES II 1375 Eleanor   PETER 1411 (1) Catherine   John V (3) 1381 (1) ✪ JOAN 1403 (2) Henry IV
D. of Gandia ══   K. of Navarre 1387 ══ *1352 †1416   C. of Mortain ══ †1462   D. of Brittany ══ †1437 ══ K. of England
†1412   *1361 †1425   d. of Henry II   *1366 †1412   d. of Peter II   *1339 †1399   *1366 †1413
s. of Peter IV   K. of Castile   C. of Alençon

John de Grailly 1402 JOAN   Martin I (2) 1403 (1) ✪ BLANCHE II (2) 1420 ✪ JOHN II   James II (1) 1406 BEATRICE   John IV 1419 ISABELLA
C. of Foix ══ †1413   K. of Sicily ══ Q. of Navarre 1425 ══ K. of Aragon 1458   C. of Marche ══ †before   C. of Armagnac ══
*1382? †1436   *1375 †1409   †1441   K. of Navarre 1425   *1370 †1438   1415   †1450
                                  *1397 †1479

Gaston IV 1436 ✪ ELEANOR
C. of Foix †1472 ══ Q. of Navarre 1479
            *1420 †1479

new country of Portugal (Chapter 23) established by the husband of his illegitimate daughter, Theresa. Matters could have gone worse for Christendom if the revival of Moorish military might under the Berber dynasty of the Almoravides had not turned out to be so short-lived.

The attempt to unite northern Spain by the marriage of Urraca of Castile with Alphonso I of Aragon foundered on their incompatibility and the union was annulled on grounds of consanguinity. However, Alphonso enlarged Aragon by capturing Saragossa, which became his capital, and by severely defeating the Moors in 1120. He was abetted by the Count of Barcelona, who had also acquired by marriage the distant county of Provence.

Alphonso I of Aragon was childless and toyed with

King Alphonso VII of Castile and Leon (1105–57) rides to his coronation (1126) with shield and banner of those arms 14th-century MS.

the idea of bequeathing his realm to the Orders of the Temple and of St John. This concept did not commend itself to the nobility and they prevailed upon his younger brother, Ramiro II, to leave the monastery to which he had retired and to take a wife. This he dutifully did and, having engendered a daughter, Petronella, returned to his celibate cell. Her marriage to Raymond Berengar IV of Barcelona created an imposing power on the east coast of Spain. It was at this point that Navarre (which had been united with Aragon since 1076) broke away and chose Garcias IV (Table 44) as king.

Alphonso VII of Castile was a dominant king, who called himself emperor and led his forces far into the south, actually capturing Cordova but leaving the Muslim ruler as his vassal. At his death Castile and Leon were divided again between his two sons, and remained separate for three generations. In the second half of the twelfth century there was another Moorish revival under a second Berber dynasty from Africa, the Almohades. Alphonso VIII of Castile (Table 47), after a turbulent minority, had to face this attack and was beaten at Alarcos (1198); Toledo was besieged and with sorry particularism Leon and Navarre both invaded Castile in her hour of trouble. Before the end of his long reign the King had re-established his authority and married his talented daughter Berengaria to the unattractive King of Leon, Alphonso the Slobberer. In 1212 he led southwards a great host and inflicted a decisive defeat on the Almohades at Las Navas de Tolosa, a campaign which was proclaimed a crusade by Pope Innocent III. Considerable assistance was given by the three military Orders which combined the profession of arms (generally as cavalry) with the vows of a monk. That of Calatrava was founded in 1164, and quickly followed by those of Alcantara and Santiago (St James).

The coinage and seals of the Spanish kings give evidence of the development of their heraldry. The lion of Leon appears on the money of Alphonso VII, and the castle of Castile – both are obviously a play on words – on the money and seal of Alphonso VIII (Table 47). Ferdinand III finally united the two Kingdoms in 1230 and his great seal shows the arms of Castile and Leon quartered on his shield and separately on the trappings of his horse. This is probably the first example of 'quartering' known to heraldry. In Aragon the distinctive coat of four vertical red stripes on gold is to be seen on the seal of Alphonso II (Table 45). The earliest shields of the rulers of Navarre (Table 44) show an eagle, but one seal of Sancho VII exhibits an escarbuncle, that is a series of rays outwards from a central boss. Not till the seal of Theobald (1234–53) does the full pattern of escarbuncle and bordure of chains seem to appear.

The suggestion that the final coat-of-arms (Table 44: top right) is a play upon the words *una vara* (a chain) seems strained.

CASTILE

After the great victory of Las Navas, the Christian Powers were poised for further advance. The amalgamation of Castile and Leon under Ferdinand III (1230) created a power in the west to match that of Aragon in the east. At the same moment the throne of Navarre (Table 44) was inherited by the Counts of Champagne, whose interests lay more in France than in Spain. Alphonso II of Aragon (Table 45) had defined his complete independence from Castile; indeed he and Alphonso VIII had agreed in 1179 on their respective spheres of expansion. To Aragon fell Valencia and the Balearic Islands, but their conquest lay in the future. Alphonso II had seized Provence from his kinswoman there and bestowed it upon his second son. Peter II of Aragon was embroiled in the Albigensian crusade and perished at Muret in 1213; not until James I did expansion begin again. Through the mid-thirteenth century St Ferdinand III of Castile (Table 47: he was canonized in 1671) and James I of Aragon (Table 46) directed a series of campaigns against the now disorganized Islamic kingdoms. Ferdinand took Cordova in 1236 and Seville in 1248; James acquired the Balearics (1229-35) and Valencia in 1238, and assisted in the conquest of Murcia (1266), which the agreement of 1179 had allotted to Castile. Only the Kingdom of Granada remained to the Moors, defended by a ring of mountains and cultivating the delicacies of architecture exemplified in the Alhambra.

Alphonso X of Castile is called the Learned; he was indeed a poet and a lawgiver, but he wasted his resources competing for the Crown of Germany (Chapter 22) and failed to control his restless nobility. Ferdinand de la Cerda, the eldest son, died in Alphonso's lifetime; his splendid vesture and armorial sword-belt have been recovered from his grave at Burgos. Medieval opinion on succession was still apt to prefer a living son to a grandson; and Sancho IV successfully claimed the throne, thus disinheriting his nephews, the younger of whom was progenitor of the Dukes of Medina Celi. Their attractive shield (Table 47) combines their French ancestry with their paternal arms. No mistake could be greater than to think of Castile as a united kingdom. Particularism was still strong among the component provinces along the Biscayan coast, where men thought of themselves as belonging to Galicia or Leon or old Castile rather than the larger state. Equally, in the newly conquered lands was a welter of mixed populations, many Jews, Mozarabic Christians, converted Moors and adherents of Islam. The rich civilization of the south had already made notable contributions to European learning. Initially, the Kings of Castile exercised wide tolerance towards their subjects, but by the end of the fourteenth century a harsher attitude was arising.

The death of Alphonso the Learned introduced a period of disturbance. Sancho IV gained the throne at the expense of his nephews: his early demise left Ferdinand IV exposed to the rivalry of the Infante John and of the de la Cerda family, from which he was saved by the skill of his mother. But Ferdinand IV, a weak ruler, in turn died young, leaving a one-year-old son (Table 48). Once he came of age Alphonso XI devoted himself with some effect to restoring order. The rebellious nobility were brought to heel, privileges granted to the towns and the royal income augmented. The threat from Granada had been increased by the Sultan of Morocco, who seized Tarifa, near Gibraltar. Alphonso XI shattered the Moors at the battle of Salado (1340), and was besieging Gibraltar itself when he died of the Black Death. By the Ordinance of Alcala (1348) he did much to put into effect the laws made by Alphonso the Learned.

His private life did not match his political success, for he neglected his Portuguese Queen in favour of Leonora (Eleanor) Guzman. The cooking vessels (*calderas*) on her shield are an essentially Spanish charge and were once a mark of nobility (*rica hombría*). His death unleashed a frantic family struggle. Peter I, the Cruel, not lightly so named, was his only lawful son; Henry of Trastamara and his twin, Frederick, Grand-Master of the Order of Santiago, were supported by many of the nobility. The dead King's mistress was swiftly despatched, probably by the dead King's widow. Other acts of savagery followed: with his own hand Peter struck down a suppliant and exiled King of Granada, and two of his half-brothers were slain at his command. French aid placed Henry II on the throne, but he was evicted by Edward, the Black Prince, of England in alliance with Peter (1367); finally Peter was killed by Henry in a personal brawl.

Peter's private life was no more rewarding than that of his father. The spread of Islamic thought, which accepted polygamy, had encouraged in Spain a form of secondary marriage called *baragania*. Peter, wed to Blanche of Bourbon for political reasons, treated her abominably, was infatuated with Mary de Padilla and espoused her in this left-handed fashion; it was the marriage of her daughter to John of Gaunt which gave him, at least in his own eyes, a claim to Castile. The arms of Padilla show the unusual feature of three frying pans. The shield of Peter's bastard, John de Castella, shows a very Spanish feature, a bend *engolada*: that is, issuing from

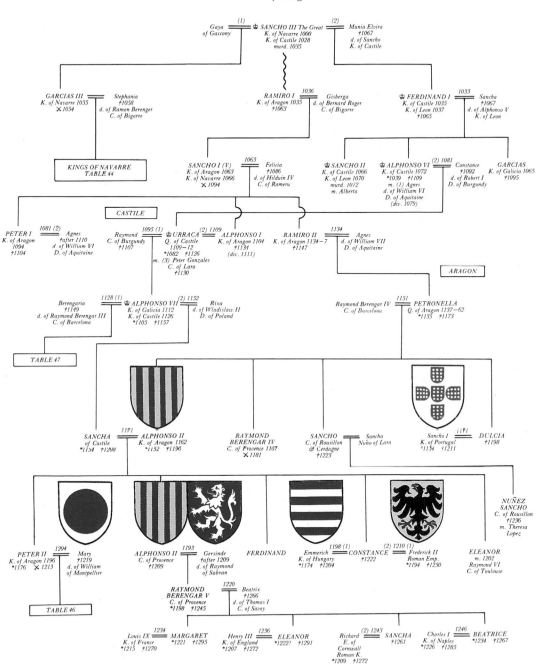

Gaya
of Gascony

(1) ♔ SANCHO III The Great
K. of Navarre 1000
K. of Castile 1028
murd. 1035

(2) Munia Elvira
†1067
d. of Sancho
K. of Castile

GARCIAS III
K. of Navarre 1035
✗ 1054

Stephania
†1058
d. of Ramon Berenger
C. of Bigorre

RAMIRO I
K. of Aragon 1035
†1063

1036 Gisberga
d. of Bernard Roger
C. of Bigorre

♔ FERDINAND I
K. of Castile 1035
K. of Leon 1037
†1065

1033 Sancha
†1067
d. of Alphonso V
K. of Leon

KINGS OF NAVARRE
TABLE 44

SANCHO I (V)
K. of Aragon 1063
K. of Navarre 1066
✗ 1094

1063 Felicia
†1086
d. of Hilduin IV
C. of Rameru

♔ SANCHO II
K. of Castile 1066
K. of Leon 1070
murd. 1072
m. Alberta

♔ ALPHONSO VI
K. of Castile 1072
*1039 †1109
m. (1) Agnes
d. of William VI
D. of Aquitaine
(div. 1079)

(2) 1081 Constance
†1092
d. of Robert I
D. of Burgundy

GARCIAS
K. of Galicia 1065
†1095

CASTILE

PETER I
K. of Aragon
1094
†1104

1081 (2) Agnes
†after 1110
d of William VI
D. of Aquitaine

Raymond
C. of Burgundy
†1107

1095 (1) ♔ URRACA
Q. of Castile
1109–12
*1082 †1126
m. (3) Peter Gonzales
C. of Lara
†1130

(2) 1109 ALPHONSO I
K. of Aragon 1104
†1134
(div. 1111)

RAMIRO II
K. of Aragon 1134–7
†1147

1134 Agnes
d. of William VII
D. of Aquitaine

ARAGON

Berengaria
†1149
d. of Raymond Berengar III
C. of Barcelona

1128 (1) ♔ ALPHONSO VII
K. of Galicia 1112
K. of Castile 1126
*1105 †1157

(2) 1152 Rixa
d. of Wladislaw II
D. of Poland

Raymond Berengar IV
C. of Barcelona

1151 PETRONELLA
Q. of Aragon 1137–62
*1135 †1173

TABLE 47

SANCHA
of Castile
*1154 †1208

1151 ALPHONSO II
K. of Aragon 1162
*1152 †1196

RAYMOND
BERENGAR IV
C. of Provence 1167
✗ 1181

SANCHO
C. of Rousillon
& Cerdagne
†1223

Sancha
Nuño de Lara

Sancho I
K. of Portugal
*1134 †1211

1151 DULCIA
†1198

PETER II
K. of Aragon 1196
*1176 ✗ 1213

1204 Mary
†1219
d. of William
of Montpellier

ALPHONSO II
C. of Provence
†1209

1193 Gersinde
†after 1209
d. of Raymond
of Sabran

FERDINAND

Emmerich
K. of Hungary
*1174 †1204

1198 (1) CONSTANCE
†1222

(2) 1210 (1) Frederick II
Roman Emp.
*1194 †1250

ELEANOR
m. 1202
Raymond VI
C. of Toulouse

NUÑEZ
SANCHO
C. of Rousillon
†1236
m. Theresa
Lopez

TABLE 46

RAYMOND
BERENGAR V
C. of Provence
*1198 †1245

1220 Beatrix
†1266
d. of Thomas I
C. of Savoy

Louis IX
K. of France
*1215 †1270

1234 MARGARET
*1221 †1295

Henry III
K. of England
*1207 †1272

1236 ELEANOR
*1222? †1291

Richard
E. of
Cornwall
Roman K.
*1209 †1272

(2) 1243 SANCHA
†1261

Charles I
K. of Naples
*1226 †1285

1246 BEATRICE
*1234 †1267

TABLE 46

ARAGON
End of the original dynasty

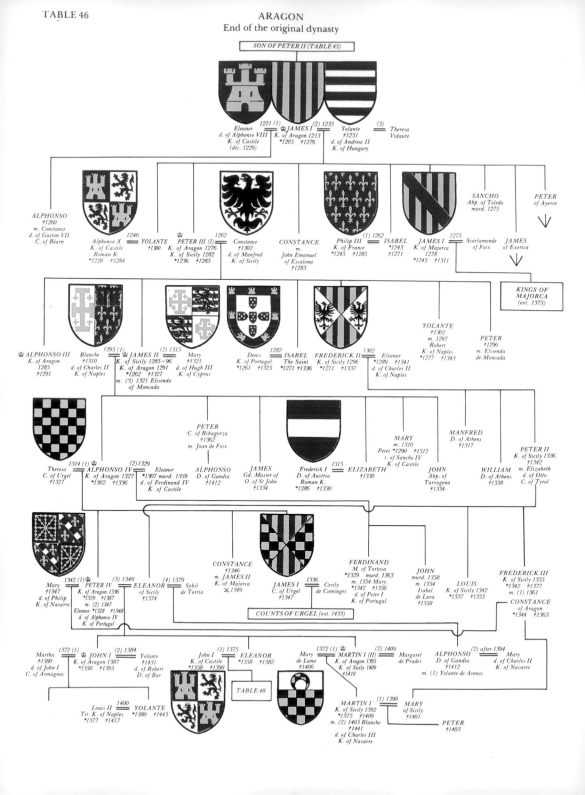

SON OF PETER II (TABLE 45)

Eleanor 1221 (1) JAMES I (2) 1235 Yolante (3) Theresa
d. of Alphonso VIII K. of Aragon 1213 †1251 Vidaure
K. of Castile *1205 †1276 d. of Andrew II
(div. 1229) K. of Hungary

ALPHONSO
†1260
m. Constance
d. of Gaston VII
C. of Béarn

Alphonso X 1246 YOLANTE PETER III (I) 1262 Constance CONSTANCE Philip III (1) 1262 ISABEL JAMES I 1275 Scarlamonde JAMES
K. of Castile †1300 K. of Aragon 1276 †1302 m. K. of France *1243 K. of Majorca of Foix of Exorica
Roman K. K. of Sicily 1282 d. of Manfred John Emanuel *1245 †1285 †1271 1278
*1220 †1284 *1236 †1285 K. of Sicily of Escalona *1243 †1311
†1283

SANCHO PETER
Abp. of Toledo of Ayerve
murd. 1275

JAMES
of Exorica

KINGS OF
MAJORCA
(ext. 1375)

ALPHONSO III Blanche 1295 (1) JAMES II (2) 1315 Mary Denis 1282 ISABEL FREDERICK II 1302 Eleanor YOLANTE PETER
K. of Aragon †1310 K. of Sicily 1285–96 †1321 K. of Portugal The Saint K. of Sicily 1296 *1289 †1341 †1302 †1296
1285 d. of Charles II K. of Aragon 1291 d. of Hugh III *1261 †1325 *1271 †1336 *1271 †1337 d. of Charles II m. 1297 m. Elisenda
†1291 K. of Naples *1262 †1327 K. of Cyprus K. of Naples Robert de Moncada
m. (3) 1321 Elisenda K. of Naples
of Moncada *1277 †1343

PETER
C. of Ribagorza
†1362
m. Joan de Foix

MARY MANFRED
m. 1310 D. of Athens
Peter *1290 †1312 †1317
s. of Sancho IV
K. of Castile

PETER II
K. of Sicily 1336
†1342
m. Elizabeth
d. of Otto
C. of Tyrol

Theresa 1314 (1) ALPHONSO IV (2) 1329 Eleanor ALPHONSO JAMES Frederick I 1315 ELIZABETH JOHN WILLIAM
C. of Urgel K. of Aragon 1327 *1307 murd. 1359 D. of Gandia Gd. Master of D. of Austria †1330 Abp. of D. of Athens
†1327 *1302 †1336 d. of Ferdinand IV †1412 O. of St John Roman K. Tarragona †1338
K. of Castile †1334 *1286 †1330 †1334

CONSTANCE FERDINAND JOHN LOUIS FREDERICK III
†1346 M. of Tortosa murd. 1358 K. of Sicily 1342 K. of Sicily 1355
m. JAMES II *1329 murd. 1363 m. 1354 †1337 †1355 *1342 †1377
K. of Majorca m. 1354 Mary Isabel m. (1) 1361
× 1349 *1342 †1362 de Lara
d. of Peter I †1358
K. of Portugal

Mary 1342 (1) PETER IV (3) 1349 ELEANOR (4) 1379 Sybil JAMES I 1336 Cecily
†1347 K. of Aragon 1336 of Sicily de Tortia C. of Urgel de Cominges
d. of Philip *1319 †1387 †1374 †1347
K. of Navarre m. (2) 1347
Eleanor *1328 †1348
d. of Alphonso IV
K. of Portugal

CONSTANCE
of Aragon
*1344 †1363

COUNTS OF URGEL (ext. 1433)

Martha 1372 (1) JOHN I (2) 1384 Yolante John I (1) 1375 ELEANOR Mary 1372 MARTIN I (II) (2) 1409 Margaret ALPHONSO (2) after 1394 Mary
†1380 K. of Aragon 1387 †1431 K. of Castile *1358 †1382 de Luna K. of Aragon 1395 de Prades D. of Gandia d. of Charles II
d. of John I *1350 †1395 d. of Robert *1358 †1390 †1406 K. of Sicily 1409 †1412 K. of Navarre
C. of Armagnac D. of Bar †1410 m. (1) Yolante de Arenos

Louis II 1400 YOLANTE
Tit. K. of Naples *1380 †1443
*1377 †1417

TABLE 48

MARTIN I (1) 1390 MARY
K. of Sicily 1392 of Sicily
*1375 †1409 †1401
m. (2) 1403 Blanche
†1441
d. of Charles III
K. of Navarre

PETER
†1403

two animal heads. Equally Hispanic is the dice-like arrangement of the six roundels of Castro.

Heraldic insignia were of course required for the brothers of Henry II. The House of Albuquerque used the lion of Leon (which began to be crowned again under Sancho IV) in a pointed base between two castles of Castile: this can be seen (Table 48) for the wife of Ferdinand I. The cognate family of Henriques, descended from Henry II's twin, surrounded the same blazon with a bordure charged with anchors (after his grandson became Admiral of Castile), such charged borders being another Spanish usage: this can be seen for the second wife of John II of Aragon. Henry II himself had a difficult reign: invasions from Portugal, Navarre and England had to be rebuffed. His contentious nobility were partially placated with his new titles, such as duke and marquess, but the epithet of 'Generous' was a poor return for the wastage of Crown lands.

ARAGON

The fortunes of Aragon had been more engaged in the Mediterranean than within Spain. The splendid harbours of her east coast bred generations of sailors who travelled to the related ports of Provence and also overseas to Sicily. Like Castile, this kingdom lacked basic unity; Aragon was an inland and Catalonia (or Barcelona) a maritime society, while Valencia shared the ambitions of both. It might be added that the speech of Catalonia (then as now) differed considerably from that of Aragon, and that an instinct for separatism was already well-established here. James I (Table 46), in his long reign, had extended the borders of Aragon southwards; he had also married his son, Peter III, to the daughter of Manfred, King of Sicily; less wisely perhaps he had bestowed upon his younger son, James, the Balearic Islands and his French fiefs of Roussillon and Montpellier. This imprudent disposition was not liquidated until 1344, by which date the ruthless Peter IV of Aragon had dispossessed his island cousins.

After the death of the Emperor Frederick II, his bastard Manfred had established himself as ruler of Sicily. Against him was embodied the implacable hostility of the Papacy, which conferred the Crown of Sicily on Charles of Anjou, the younger brother of St Louis IX of France and also the husband of the heiress of Provence. Charles' government was harsh, and at Eastertide 1282 the revolt broke out known as the Sicilian Vespers. Peter III of Aragon accepted the challenge and became King of Sicily; the south Italian mainland remained in the grasp of Charles of Anjou and his heirs. One decisive battle, at sea off Naples, was won in 1284 by the Catalan fleet under a Sicilian admiral. At his death, Peter bequeathed Aragon to his eldest son and Sicily to his second; the

early death of Alphonso III necessitated some rearrangement. James gave up Sicily, after reaching an agreement with the Papacy, and reigned in Aragon. The third brother became Frederick II of Sicily. In 1299 Frederick II won a great victory over the forces of Naples, and secured the title of King of Trinacria; he then married the daughter of Charles I of Anjou, King of Naples. These struggles had very greatly reduced the prosperity of his island kingdom. The settlement left unemployed the highly competent Catalan mercenaries who had fought for Frederick: moving eastwards by a bizarre set of circumstances, they seized and controlled the Duchy of Athens.

The branch of Aragon in Majorca differenced the family coat with a blue bend (Table 46). Frederick II of Sicily divided his coat saltire-wise with the black eagle of Sicily; a similar arrangement was adopted by James, Count of Urgel, with the black and gold chequers of that lordship. On the whole the administration of Aragon was more orderly than that of Castile. In both states an assembly grew up which was known as the 'Cortes'. In Aragon this body was composed of nobles, clerics and townsmen; they normally met separately for Aragon, Catalonia and Valencia, thus emphasizing the intense localism of Spain.

Peter IV was a tough monarch who added Majorca to his Kingdom and worked powerfully to assert his authority in his fourfold realm. His vigorous revenge won him the nickname of 'Peter of the Poniard', though he was more generally known as Peter the Ceremonious. He even secured the homage of the distant Catalan Duchy in Athens (1381). His two sons (John and Martin) reigned in turn after him; but at the end of his life Martin I succeeded his own son, another Martin, as King of Sicily. The death of Martin I, now childless, in 1410 raised a formidable succession problem, for the male line of Aragon had become extinct. It is to the credit of the Aragonese Cortes that the issue was peaceably solved in favour of Ferdinand (younger son of John I of Castile and his wife, Eleanor of Aragon) who inherited both Aragon and Sicily.

CASTILE AND ARAGON

When the illegitimate Henry II of Castile, who had attained the throne by stabbing his half-brother, Peter the Cruel, died in 1379, he had made his position secure. Castilian fleets had scoured the English Channel; her rivals at home had been disciplined. Unluckily both the next two kings, John I and Henry III (Table 48), died young after relatively brief reigns. John I attempted to claim the Crown of Portugal but sustained a crushing defeat in 1385. Under Henry III hostility to the Jews, accompanied by wanton massacres, began to appear. John II proved to be a feeble creature, dominated by his friend, Alphonso de Lara, Grand-Master of the Order of Santiago. His son, Henry IV, the Impotent, was if anything worse: it was widely rumoured that his daughter Joanna was not his child. In 1465 his half-brother Alphonso was briefly put forward as king; Castile had reached a low ebb in her fortunes when Henry IV died in 1474, leaving his sister Isabella as one possible recognized heiress and his daughter as another.

As has been seen, Ferdinand of Castile became King of Aragon and Sicily in 1412; he was scarcely established when he died. Alphonso V, his eldest son, was a highly successful king. It is true that he spent little time in his native land, but he married his younger brother, John, to the heiress of Navarre. Alphonso had been adopted as her heir by the lecherous (though childless) Joanna, Queen of Naples, and from 1435 he devoted his energies to establishing himself on the Italian mainland and reuniting the Two Sicilies. He was well-placed, for his tastes and patronage inclined him to the Renaissance and he was admirably suited to an Italian court. At his death (1458), he left Naples to his illegitimate son Ferdinand (Ferrante).

John II, brother of Alphonso V, had ruled Navarre in right of his wife since 1425 and had acted as regent in Aragon while Alphonso was busy in Naples; he had effectually disinherited his own son, the Prince of Viana, after the death of Blanche of Navarre. The mysterious death of Prince Charles brought forth a formidable Catalan revolt. John II's fortunes wavered a while but ultimately triumphed, for in 1469 he engineered the all-important marriage between Ferdinand, son of his second marriage and heir of Aragon, and Isabella, half-sister and heiress presumptive of Henry IV of Castile. The nobles of Castile, fearful of the enhanced strength of the monarchy, opposed the match, which actually took place in sordid and furtive circumstances in a private house in Valladolid. When Henry IV died in 1474, civil strife broke out forthwith in the best Castilian tradition. Portugal supported the claim of 'La Beltraneja' – as Joanna was nicknamed from her putative father – and might, under firmer leadership, have obtained part or all of Castile just as the New World was opened up; in 1479, however, Ferdinand and Isabella were accepted as the rulers of Aragon and Castile. Spain was united at last (Table 48).

NAVARRE

To write thus may seem to ignore the fate of Navarre. The death of Sancho VII in 1234 allowed the Kingdom to pass to Theobald of Champagne (Table 44). His two sons were more concerned with their French county than with the little Spanish Kingdom which straddled the Pyrenees. His granddaughter, Joan, married Philip IV of France. Although her eldest son, Louis X, had only a daughter who should have succeeded to Navarre, that province was retained by Philip V and Charles IV. On the death of the last-named, Navarre was relinquished to Joan II and her husband, the Count of Evreux, although Champagne was held by the French Crown. It may be noted that Joan and her issue had, by accepted standards, a better claim to the French Crown than Edward III of England. Such a claim was understood by Charles I, the Bad, one of the more intransigent subjects of John II of France. Able, eloquent and unscrupulous, Charles even began to negotiate with Edward III for a partition of France, However his misdeeds and his treachery belong more to the history of France than of Spain. By contrast, his son Charles II had a long and peaceful reign lacking alike in pretensions and incident.

At his death Navarre passed to his daughter Blanche, the wife of John II of Aragon; at her death it passed to her son, Charles of Viana (Table 48), but that slightly ineffectual Prince was dispossessed by his more vigorous father. John II arranged with the King of France that he should be followed in Navarre by his daughter Eleanor and Gaston IV of Foix (Table 44). In the event, Eleanor was succeeded by her grandson, Francis Phoebus, Count of Foix. His sister Catherine married John d'Albret, from whom Ferdinand of Aragon easily seized Spanish Navarre in 1512. Their granddaughter Joan III married Anthony of Bourbon and was mother of Henry IV who united French Navarre with the Crown of France. The arms of Anthony, King of Navarre (Table 44), show eight quarterings, namely: *1* Navarre, *2* Bourbon, *3* Albret, *4* Aragon, *5* Foix and Bearn, *6* Armagnac and Rodez, *7* Evreux and *8* Bigorre.

THE CATHOLIC KINGS

The long reigns of Ferdinand II of Aragon and his wife, Isabella the Catholic of Castile (Table 48), mark more than the union of the two great, crusading, Spanish Kingdoms. Indeed, for all that union, strong local feeling and patriotism, and separate languages like Catalan and Gallegan (the speech of Galicia) continued to flourish, and do so today. But the reigns of the two sovereigns mark a turning point in the history of Spain and her emergence as a world power. By 1479 both were secure upon their thrones. Three years later they embarked upon the capture of Granada, the last Moorish Kingdom. The campaign was deliberate, and Granada itself did not fall until 1492. Thus ended the long sojourn of Islam in Iberia; it is permissible to regret the extinction of this civilized little society with its tolerance, learning and airy architecture. At first the inhabitants were

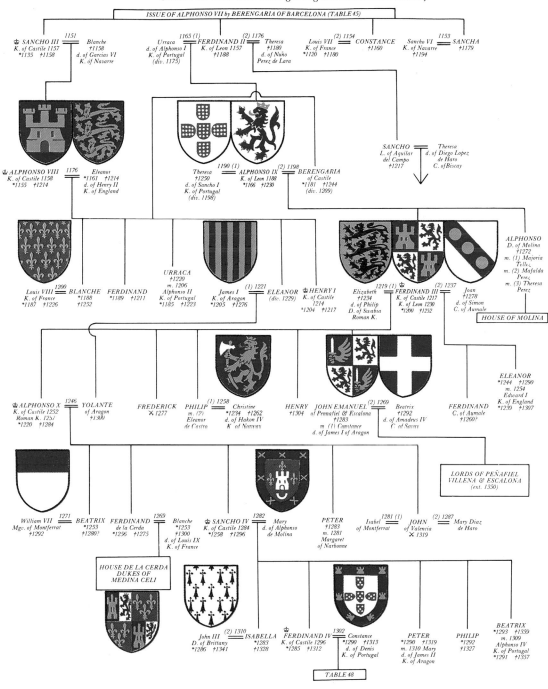

ISSUE OF ALPHONSO VII by BERENGARIA OF BARCELONA (TABLE 45)

✠ SANCHO III
K. of Castile 1157
*1135 †1158

1151
Blanche
†1158
d. of Garcias VI
K. of Navarre

1165 (1)
Urraca
d. of Alphonso I
K. of Portugal
(div. 1175)

FERDINAND II
K. of Leon 1157
†1188

(2) 1176
Theresa
†1180
d. of Nuño
Perez de Lara

Louis VII
K. of France
*1120 †1180

(2) 1154
CONSTANCE
†1160

Sancho VI
K. of Navarre
†1194

1153
SANCHA
†1179

SANCHO
L. of Aquilar
del Campo
†1217

Theresa
d. of Diego Lopez
de Haro
C. of Biscay

✠ ALPHONSO VIII
K. of Castile 1158
*1155 †1214

1176
Eleanor
*1161 †1214
d. of Henry II
K. of England

Theresa
†1250
d. of Sancho I
K. of Portugal
(div. 1198)

1190 (1)
ALPHONSO IX
K. of Leon 1188
*1166 †1230

(2) 1198
BERENGARIA
of Castile
*1181 †1244
(div. 1209)

ALPHONSO
D. of Molina
†1272
m. (1) Majoria
Tellez
m. (2) Mafalda
Perez
m. (3) Theresa
Perez

Louis VIII
K. of France
*1187 †1226

1200
BLANCHE
*1188
†1252

FERDINAND
*1189 †1211

URRACA
†1220
m. 1206
Alphonso II
K. of Portugal
*1185 †1223

James I
K. of Aragon
*1205 †1276

(1) 1221
ELEANOR
(div. 1229)

✠ HENRY I
K. of Castile
1214
*1204 †1217

Elizabeth
†1234
d. of Philip
D. of Swabia
Roman K.

1219 (1)
FERDINAND III
K. of Castile 1217
K. of Leon 1230
*1200 †1252

(2) 1237
Joan
†1278
d. of Simon
C. of Aumale

HOUSE OF MOLINA

ELEANOR
*1244 †1290
m. 1254
Edward I
K. of England
*1239 †1307

✠ ALPHONSO X
K. of Castile 1252
Roman K. 1257
*1220 †1284

1246
YOLANTE
of Aragon
†1300

FREDERICK
✕ 1277

PHILIP
m. (2)
Eleanor
de Castro

(1) 1258
Christine
*1234 †1262
d. of Hakon IV
K. of Norway

HENRY
†1304

JOHN EMANUEL
of Pennafiel & Escalona
†1283
m (1) Constance
d. of James I of Aragon

(2) 1269
Beatrix
†1292
d. of Amadeus IV
C. of Savoy

FERDINAND
C. of Aumale
†1260?

LORDS OF PEÑAFIEL
VILLENA & ESCALONA
(ext. 1350)

William VII
Mgv. of Montferrat
†1292

1271
BEATRIX
*1253
†1280?

FERDINAND
de la Cerda
*1253
†1275

1269
Blanche
*1253
†1300
d. of Louis IX
K. of France

✠ SANCHO IV
K. of Castile 1284
*1258 †1296

1282
Mary
d. of Alphonso
de Molina

PETER
†1283
m. 1281
Margaret
of Narbonne

Isabel
of Montferrat

1281 (1)
JOHN
of Valencia
✕ 1319

(2) 1287
Mary Diaz
de Haro

HOUSE DE LA CERDA
DUKES OF
MEDINA CELI

John III
D. of Brittany
*1286 †1341

(2) 1310
ISABELLA
*1283
†1328

✠ FERDINAND IV
K. of Castile 1296
*1285 †1312

1302
Constance
†1313
d. of Denis
K. of Portugal

PETER
*1290 †1319
m. 1310 Mary
d. of James II
K. of Aragon

PHILIP
*1292
†1327

BEATRIX
*1293 †1359
m. 1309
Alphonso IV
K. of Portugal
*1291 †1357

TABLE 48

TABLE 48

CASTILE
Union with Aragon

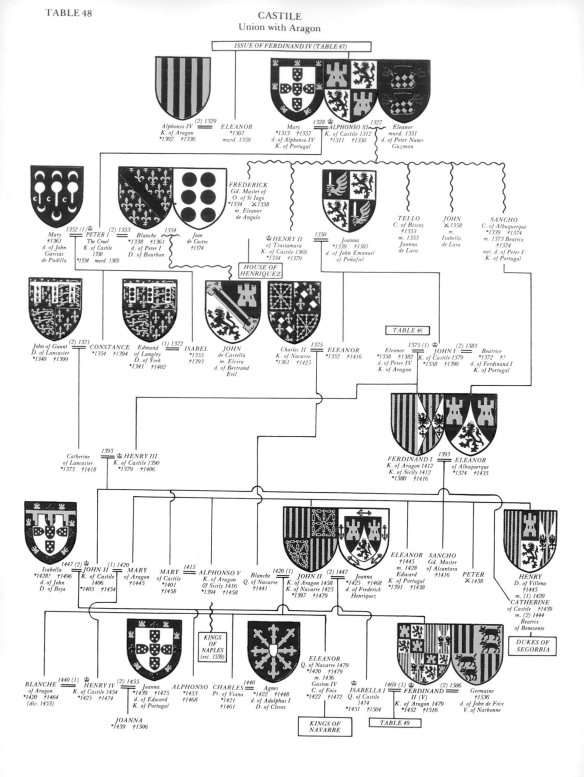

ISSUE OF FERDINAND IV (TABLE 47)

Alphonso IV (2) 1329 | *ELEANOR* | *Mary* 1328 *ALPHONSO XI* 1327 | *Eleanor*
K. of Aragon | *1307 | *1313 †1357 K. of Castile 1312 | murd. 1351
*1302 †1336 | murd. 1359 | d. of Alphonso IV *1311 †1350 | d. of Peter Nunes
| K. of Portugal | Guzman

FREDERICK Gd. Master of O. of St Iago *1334 ✕1358 m. Eleanor de Angulo

Joanna | *TELLO* | *JOHN* | *SANCHO*
*1339 †1381 | C. of Biscay | ✕1358 | C. of Albuquerque
d. of John Emanuel | †1353 | m. | *1339 †1374
of Peñafiel | m. 1353 | Isabella | m. 1373 Beatrix
| Joanna | de Lara | †1374
| de Lara | | nat. d. of Peter I
| | | K. of Portugal

Mary 1352 (1) **PETER I** (2) 1353 *Blanche* 1354 *Joan* | **HENRY II** 1350
*1361 | The Cruel | *1338 †1361 de Castro | of Trastamara
d. of John | K. of Castile | d. of Peter I | †1374 | K. of Castile 1369
Garcias | 1350 | D. of Bourbon | | *1334 †1379
de Padilla | murd. 1369 | | |
*1334 | | | |

HOUSE OF HENRIQUEZ

TABLE 46

John of Gaunt (2) 1371 **CONSTANCE** *Edmund* (1) 1372 *ISABEL* *JOHN* | *Charles II* 1375 *ELEANOR* | *Eleanor* 1375 (1) **JOHN I** (2) 1383 *Beatrice*
D. of Lancaster | *1354 †1394 of Langley | *1355 de Castella | K. of Navarre | *1352 †1416 | *1358 †1382 K. of Castile 1379 | *1372 †?
*1340 †1399 | | D. of York | †1393 m. Elvira | *1361 †1425 | | d. of Peter IV *1358 †1390 | d. of Ferdinand I
| | *1341 †1402 | d. of Bertrand | | | K. of Aragon | K. of Portugal
| | | Eril | | | |

Catherine 1393 **HENRY III** | **FERDINAND I** 1393 **ELEANOR**
of Lancaster | K. of Castile 1390 | K. of Aragon 1412 | of Albuquerque
*1373 †1418 | *1379 †1406 | K. of Sicily 1412 | *1374 †1435
| | *1380 †1416 |

Isabella 1447 (2) **JOHN II** (1) 1420 *MARY* | *MARY* 1415 *ALPHONSO V* | *Blanche* 1420 (1) **JOHN II** (2) 1447 *Joanna* | *ELEANOR* *SANCHO* *PETER* | **HENRY**
*1428? †1496 | K. of Castile | of Aragon | of Castile | K. of Aragon | Q. of Navarre | K. of Aragon 1458 | *1425 †1468 | †1445 Gd. Master ✕1438 | D. of Villena
d. of John | 1406 | †1445 | *1401 | & Sicily 1416 | †1441 | K. of Navarre 1425 | d. of Frederick | m. 1428 of Alcantara | †1445
D. of Beja | *1405 †1454 | | †1458 | *1394 †1458 | | *1397 †1479 | Henriquez | Edward †1416 | m. (1) 1420
| | | | | | | | K. of Portugal | CATHERINE
| | | | | | | | *1391 †1438 | of Castile †1439
| | | | | | | | | m. (2) 1444
| | | | | | | | | Beatrix
| | | | | | | | | of Benevente

KINGS OF NAPLES (ext. 1559)

DUKES OF SEGORBIA

BLANCHE 1440 (1) **HENRY IV** 1455 *Joanna* *ALPHONSO* | *CHARLES* 1440 *Agnes* | *ELEANOR* | **ISABELLA I** 1469 (1) **FERDINAND** (2) 1506 *Germaine*
of Aragon | K. of Castile 1454 | *1439 †1475 *1453 | Pr. of Viana | *1422 †1448 | Q. of Navarre 1479 | Q. of Castile | **II (V)** | *1536
*1420 †1464 | *1425 †1474 | d. of Edward †1468 | *1421 | d. of Adolphus I | *1420 †1479 | 1474 | K. of Aragon 1479 | d. of John de Foix
(div. 1453) | | K. of Portugal | | †1461 | D. of Cleves | m. 1436 | *1451 †1504 | *1452 †1516 | V. of Narbonne
					Gaston IV		
					C. of Foix		
					*1422 †1472		

JOANNA *1459 †1506

KINGS OF NAVARRE

TABLE 49

treated in a liberal manner, but soon a harsher climate prevailed.

Later in that year came an event of shattering importance. After much hesitation Isabella had conferred her patronage on the Genoese mariner, Christopher Columbus: on 12 October 1492, he landed in the Bahamas. Whether or not Irish monks and Viking adventurers had already made perilous voyages to America is immaterial, the discovery – and exploitation – of the New World dates from this moment. With a renowned and dramatic gesture the Spanish Pope, Alexander VI, drew a line of demarcation down the Atlantic dividing the spheres of interest of Spain and Portugal. Columbus was able to make a valuable staging point at the Canaries, which were then being added to the Spanish dominions. The adventures of the Spanish conquerors in Mexico and Peru cannot concern us here.

There was, however, a more sombre side to the rule of the Catholic sovereigns. In 1478 the Spanish Inquisition was established. In 1492 all Jews were abruptly expelled from Spain and a decade later the same fate overtook the resident Muslims. Any gain to fanaticism was savagely offset by the loss to commerce occasioned by the persecution of these diligent and skilful communities. To the credit of Ferdinand and Isabella is the restoration of order, especially in Castile, which was the leading partner in the union. Brigandage was suppressed; the military orders, now obsolete in aim, were taken over by the Crown; alienated royal lands were resumed. Of more doubtful long term value was the encouragement of sheep-farming at the expense of agriculture.

In 1496 a marriage was finally arranged between their daughter Joanna and the young, handsome and wealthy Philip the Fair, Duke of Burgundy. At the same time her eldest sister married the King of Portugal, and a little later her ill-fated younger sister Catherine married the son of the King of England (Table 49). The death in 1497 of John, the only son of Ferdinand and Isabella, altered the picture and Charles, the eldest son of Joanna, emerged as the heir of Spain, Burgundy and the Empire. The ancestry of the Emperor Charles V (Table 53) – Charles I in Spanish history – shows that five of his great-grandparents came from the peninsula: he was more Hispanic than anything else. His coat-of-arms (Table 49) shows in the upper half Castile and Leon, Aragon and Sicily with the pomegranate of Granada: in the lower, Austria, Burgundy ancient and modern and Brabant, with Flanders and Tyrol over all.

Joanna herself, lacking the love of her husband, drifted into insanity, and the inconstant Philip died before his father in 1506. Accordingly Ferdinand II of Aragon acted as regent for his mad daughter and infant grandson. His second marriage to Germaine de Foix (Table 48) even raised the possibility that he might beget a son to inherit Aragon and undo the union. His main preoccupation, an emphatic continuation of Aragonese interests in the western Mediterranean, was with war in Italy and the ejection of the French from Naples. In these sterile campaigns the Spanish infantry began to win its great reputation under the *Gran Capitan* Gonzalvo de Cordova. In addition, Ferdinand II, as has been seen, annexed Spanish Navarre and regained Rousillon from France. He even invaded North Africa; and it has been argued that the true overseas interests of Spain lay here rather than in Italy. The multiple inheritance of Charles V ensured however that Spain would be drawn fully into the complicated politics of central Europe and the Reformation. The comparative isolation of the Iberian peninsula was now at an end.

Chapter 11

SPAIN: HAPSBURG AND BOURBON

Two reigns spanned almost all of the sixteenth century for Spain, those of Charles I and Philip II. The two were very different men. Charles V (he is better known by his notation as Emperor than as King of Spain) was resolute in the hideous toil and travel required to maintain his scattered dominions, though in consequence each realm supposed it was being neglected for others. He was the inheritor of perhaps the largest European burden since Charlemagne. A competent captain with a dislike for bloodshed, an accomplished negotiator, too much perhaps of a centralizer, crippled latterly with gout, he laboured to overcome his twin enemies of heresy and debt. In 1506 he became heir to Burgundy and the Low Countries; in 1516 King of Spain; and in 1519, after profuse expenditure on the Electors, he was chosen King of the Romans, and called himself Emperor-Elect. His actual coronation took place at Bologna in 1530; he was the last Emperor to be crowned by a pope. He was in Spain from 1522 to 1529, but was not a popular sovereign. Not without reason his Spanish subjects suspected him of disbursing their own wealth (and also the untold sums which began to come in from the New World) on greedy German princelings and a seemingly endless war with France.

The great victory of his forces at Pavia (1525) secured his hold on Naples and Milan, but did not finish the conflict. In 1527 Spanish troops brutally sacked Rome. In Germany he was involved in heavy fighting against the Protestants and won an important battle at Mühlberg in 1547. In weariness, he joined the select company of Diocletian and a few others by voluntarily resigning great power (1556). His brother Ferdinand (Chapter 17) succeeded him in Austria and the Empire; his son Philip II followed him in Spain, Italy and the Netherlands (Table 49).

Philip II was intensely industrious, but he was also suspicious, sinister and secretive. Like a mole, he worried away, beset by detail, in the great palace-monastery of the Escorial, which he built north of Madrid. Disaster outweighed triumph in his reign. It is true that in 1580 he added Portugal, to which he had a claim through his mother and his first wife, to his dominions, and for sixty years one ruler was to govern the whole peninsula. But Philip II's second marriage to Mary Tudor of England was childless and frustrated: nor did it bring alliance with England. His efforts to stamp out heresy in the Low Countries led, after the bitterest strife and persecution, to the independence of the Netherlands. Later, his gigantic invasion plan for England, the Armada, came to nothing thanks to the brilliance of Drake and his colleagues, abetted by foul weather. He did, however, achieve peace with France in 1559, which he sealed by marrying a French wife, his third. Worst of all, the extravagance of the court and the misunderstanding of the economic consequences of the vast imports of gold and silver from the New World began a steady deterioration in the financial position of Spain. Rumour also accused Philip of having encompassed the deaths of his own eldest son (Charles) and his more glamorous (illegitimate) half-brother, Don John of Austria, the victor of Lepanto. The arms of Philip II show a small escutcheon of Portugal added to the blazon of his father (Table 49).

SIGLO DE ORO

The history of Spain in the next two reigns presents a curious contrast. Her political power, her influence abroad, her military repute, her general finance were all on the decline, but in the world of arts this was her golden century (*Siglo de Oro*). The names of Lope de Vega, Cervantes, creator of Don Quixote, and Calderon in Literature, or El Greco and Velazquez in painting, and the splendid achievements in architecture, lend a rare glory to the hundred years or so

House of Hapsburg

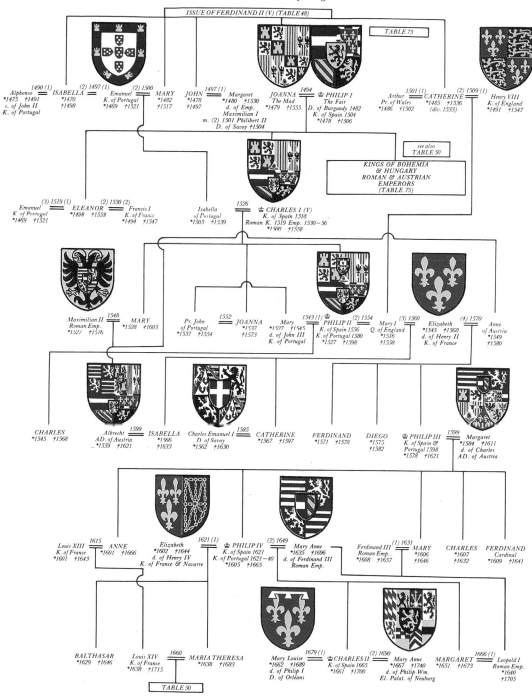

ISSUE OF FERDINAND II (V) (TABLE 48)

TABLE 73

1490 (1)
Alphonso
*1475 †1491
s. of John II
K. of Portugal

(2) 1497 (1)
ISABELLA
*1470
†1498

Emanuel
K. of Portugal
*1469 †1521

(2) 1500
MARY
*1482
†1517

1497 (1)
JOHN
*1478
†1497

Margaret
*1480 †1530
d. of Emp.
Maximilian I
m. (2) 1501 Philibert II
D. of Savoy

1494
JOANNA
The Mad
*1479 †1555

✠ PHILIP I
The Fair
D. of Burgundy 1482
K. of Spain 1504
*1478 †1506

1501 (1)
Arthur
Pr. of Wales
*1486 †1502

(2) 1509 (1)
CATHERINE
*1485 †1536
(div. 1533)

Henry VIII
K. of England
*1491 †1547

see also
TABLE 50

KINGS OF BOHEMIA
& HUNGARY
ROMAN & AUSTRIAN
EMPERORS
(TABLE 75)

(3) 1519 (1)
Emanuel
K. of Portugal
*1469 †1521

ELEANOR
*1498 †1558

(2) 1530 (2)
Francis I
K. of France
*1494 †1547

Isabella
of Portugal
*1503 †1539

1526
✠ CHARLES I (V)
K. of Spain 1516
Roman K. 1519 Emp. 1530—56
*1500 †1558

1548
Maximilian II
Roman Emp.
*1527 †1576

MARY
*1528 †1603

Pr. John
of Portugal
*1537 †1554

1552
JOANNA
*1537
†1573

Mary
*1527 †1545
d. of John III
K. of Portugal

1543 (1)
PHILIP II
K. of Spain 1556
K. of Portugal 1580
*1527 †1598

(2) 1554
Mary I
Q. of England
*1516
†1558

(3) 1560
Elizabeth
*1545 †1560
d. of Henry II
K. of France

(4) 1570
Anne
of Austria
*1549
†1580

CHARLES
*1545 †1568

1599
Albrecht
AD. of Austria
*1559 †1621

ISABELLA
*1566
†1633

Charles Emanuel I
D. of Savoy
*1562 †1630

1585
CATHERINE
*1567 †1597

FERDINAND
*1571 †1578

DIEGO
*1575
†1582

✠ PHILIP III
K. of Spain &
Portugal 1598
*1578 †1621

1599
Margaret
*1584 †1611
d. of Charles
AD. of Austria

1615
Louis XIII
K. of France
*1601 †1643

ANNE
*1601 †1666

Elizabeth
*1602 †1644
d. of Henry IV
K. of France & Navarre

1621 (1)
✠ PHILIP IV
K. of Spain 1621
K. of Portugal 1621—40
*1605 †1665

(2) 1649
Mary Anne
*1635 †1696
d. of Ferdinand III
Roman Emp.

(1) 1631
Ferdinand III
Roman Emp.
*1608 †1657

MARY
*1606
†1646

CHARLES
*1607
†1632

FERDINAND
Cardinal
*1609 †1641

BALTHASAR
*1629 †1646

Louis XIV
K. of France
*1638 †1715

1660
MARIA THERESA
*1638 †1683

TABLE 50

Mary Louise
*1662 †1689
d. of Philip I
D. of Orléans

1679 (1)
✠ CHARLES II
K. of Spain 1665
*1661 †1700

(2) 1690
Mary Anne
*1667 †1740
d. of Philip Wm.
El. Palat. of Neuburg

MARGARET
*1651 †1673

1666 (1)
Leopold I
Roman Emp.
*1640
†1705

TABLE 50

SPAIN
War of Succession (Houses of Hapsburg and Bourbon)

TABLES 49, 73

JOANNA
*1479 †1333
d. of Ferdinand II (V)
K. of Aragon & Castile

1496

♛ PHILIP I The Fair
K. of Spain 1504
*1478 †1506
s. of Emp. Maximilian I

SPAIN

AUSTRIA

♛ CHARLES I (V)
K. of Spain 1516–56
Roman K. 1519, Emp. 1530
*1500 †1558

FERDINAND I
K. of Bohemia & Hungary
1526
Roman K. 1531, Emp. 1558
*1503 †1564

♛ PHILIP II
K. of Spain 1556
*1527 †1598

(4) 1570

ANNE
of Austria
*1549 †1580

MARY
*1528 †1603

1548

MAXIMILIAN II
Roman Emp. 1564
*1527 †1576

CHARLES
D. of Styria
*1540 †1590

FRANCE

Henry IV
K. of France
*1553 murd. 1610

♛ PHILIP III
K. of Spain 1598
*1578 †1621

1599

MARGARET
of Austria
*1584 †1611

RUDOLPH II
Roman Emp. 1576
*1552 †1612

MATTHIAS
Roman Emp. 1612
*1557 †1619

FERDINAND II
Roman Emp. 1619
*1578 †1637

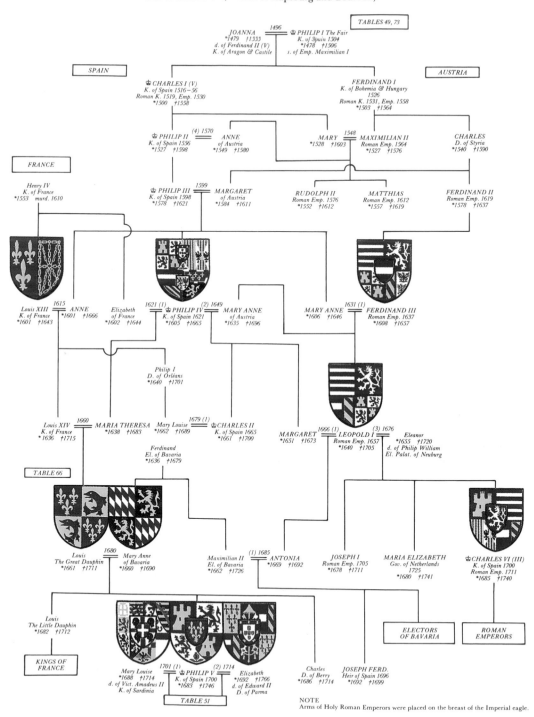

Louis XIII
K. of France
*1601 †1643

1615

ANNE
*1601 †1666

Elizabeth
of France
*1602 †1644

1621 (1)

♛ PHILIP IV
K. of Spain 1621
*1605 †1665

(2) 1649

MARY ANNE
of Austria
*1635 †1696

MARY ANNE
*1606 †1646

1631 (1)

FERDINAND III
Roman Emp. 1637
*1608 †1657

Philip I
D. of Orléans
*1640 †1701

Louis XIV
K. of France
*1636 †1715

1660

MARIA THERESA
*1638 †1683

Mary Louise
*1662 †1689

1679 (1)

♛ CHARLES II
K. of Spain 1665
*1661 †1700

MARGARET
*1651 †1673

1666 (1)

LEOPOLD I
Roman Emp. 1657
*1640 †1705

(3) 1676

Eleanor
*1655 †1720
d. of Philip William
El. Palat. of Neuburg

TABLE 66

Ferdinand
El. of Bavaria
*1636 †1679

Louis
The Great Dauphin
*1661 †1711

1680

Mary Anne
of Bavaria
*1660 †1690

Maximilian II
El. of Bavaria
*1662 †1726

(1) 1685

ANTONIA
*1669 †1692

JOSEPH I
Roman Emp. 1705
*1678 †1711

MARIA ELIZABETH
Gov. of Netherlands
1725
*1680 †1741

♛ CHARLES VI (III)
K. of Spain 1700
Roman Emp. 1711
*1685 †1740

Louis
The Little Dauphin
*1682 †1712

KINGS OF
FRANCE

ELECTORS
OF BAVARIA

ROMAN
EMPERORS

Mary Louise
*1688 †1714
d. of Vict. Amadeus II
K. of Sardinia

1701 (1)

♛ PHILIP V
K. of Spain 1700
*1683 †1746

(2) 1714

Elizabeth
*1692 †1766
d. of Edward II
D. of Parma

Charles
D. of Berry
*1686 †1714

JOSEPH FERD.
Heir of Spain 1696
*1692 †1699

TABLE 51

NOTE
Arms of Holy Roman Emperors were placed on the breast of the Imperial eagle.

before 1680. The reign of Philip III witnessed the expulsion of the Moriscos (Christianized Moors); power at this time was in the hands of the King's favourites. Philip IV allowed a free hand to his minister, the Count-Duke of Olivares. Portugal broke away in 1640, and the last years of his reign were disfigured by a series of provincial revolts. In 1659 he ceded Cerdagne and Rousillon to France.

Charles II, the last Hapsburg King of Spain, was an even more pathetic figure. Flimsy and epileptic, he was sadly inbred. Philip IV had married his Austrian niece; Philip III had wed another Austrian princess; so the now debilitated Hapsburg blood ran too profusely in the veins of Charles. He married twice but it was widely believed that fatherhood was beyond him; like vultures, the great European Powers brooded over the disposition of the corpse. For while the internal condition of Spain was distressing, her possessions still commanded envy. The wealth of the New World, the Belgian half of the Low Countries, Milan, Naples, Sicily and Sardinia were a strong lure to the contenders.

By the closing years of the seventeenth century three candidates were in the field (Table 50). Two great sovereigns were closely related to the sickly King (who was not weaned until he was four and had the use of fourteen wet-nurses). His half-sister had married her first cousin Louis XIV of France; his sister had been the wife of the Emperor Leopold I of Austria, whose mother was also a sister of Philip IV. Neither monarch dared claim the inheritance for himself; Louis XIV sponsored his grandson, Philip, Duke of Anjou, while Leopold put forward Charles, the younger son of his second marriage. In 1698 the diplomacy of William III of England engineered the First Partition Treaty, which gave the lion's share to a third candidate, Joseph Ferdinand of Bavaria, son of the Elector Maximilian and Antonia, daughter of the first marriage of the Emperor Leopold. Unluckily the Electoral Prince died in 1699 at the age of six. The ailing Charles II bequeathed all his dominions to Philip of Anjou and died in 1700: he stipulated that if the French prince did not accept the entire bequest, it should pass *en bloc* to the Archduke Charles.

THE BOURBON KINGS

Philip V became King of Spain in 1700 at the age of 17. As his ascending pedigree shows (Table 53), he had a strong strain of Hapsburg blood and a strong strain of Bourbon: the remaining quarter was divided between Savoy and Bavaria. The first 13 years of his reign were occupied with the War of the Spanish Succession. Spain did not play an active part, but at the peace she had to forfeit Gibraltar and Minorca to England and her possessions in Italy and the Low Countries to Austria. In the meantime the Archduke

Charles, who had claimed the Spanish throne in 1700, had become emperor. It may be noted in passing that Gibraltar was only in Spanish hands from 1462 to 1704 (242 years) and has already been in British possession for 277 years. The Catalans, who had supported Charles, were ruthlessly suppressed and their language banned from official use. Philip also renounced any claim to the throne of France: during the childless and delicate youth of Louis XV, this was an important proviso.

Philip V himself wearied of his throne, and in 1724 abdicated in favour of his son, Louis I (Table 51). The young King died later in the same year, and Philip resumed the throne until his own death in 1746, to be succeeded by his colourless second son, Ferdinand VI. In 1759 Charles III became king: he was born of the second marriage of Philip V to the vigorous and able Elizabeth Farnese, who became the heiress of Parma on the death of her uncle. She secured the province for Charles and indeed orientated the policy of Spain towards Italy with the aim of providing for her family. Charles went on to become King of Naples in 1734 and transmitted that throne to his younger son Ferdinand on inheriting Spain; Philip, younger brother of Charles III, became Duke of Parma in 1748. During the intervening years (1735–48) Parma was governed by the Hapsburgs from Vienna. The youngest brother, Louis, rose to be an archbishop and a cardinal before abandoning the church for matrimony.

Charles III was the most experienced and competent of the Bourbons; Spain became more prosperous under his rule, absolute as it was. Authority was asserted over the Church and the Jesuits were expelled (1767). Towards the end of his reign he joined France in assisting the American colonies in their successful revolt from Britain. At the peace of 1783 he recovered Minorca and Florida, though the long siege of Gibraltar was unsuccessful. His arms, in their simpler form, show Castile and Leon, with Granada in base, and over all France within a red border for Anjou (Table 51); his son and brother combined these with the blazons of their Italian dominions. The famous chivalric Order of the Golden Fleece had, of course, been founded in Burgundy, and had been maintained by the Hapsburg Kings of Spain. In 1700, at the death of Charles II, it was claimed by the Austrian Hapsburgs; in 1713 the archives were transferred to Vienna. But the Bourbon Kings of Spain also asserted their right to appoint; in 1748 agreement was reached that there should be two branches of the Order, one Austrian (Table 71) and one Spanish (Table 43).

The long, melancholy, prognathous faces of the Hapsburgs have been immortalized by Velazquez. The sorry countenances of the next two rulers and

their court were immortalized by Goya. Charles IV was of limited intelligence and dominated by his wife: complaisantly he accepted as his first minister her lover, Manuel Godoy, who was even permitted to marry an unimportant princess (herself the child of an Archbishop of Toledo). Outraged by the execution of Louis XVI, this gimcrack regime attacked France, which invaded and occupied Catalonia. Godoy negotiated a treaty with the French Republic and was rewarded with the slightly absurd title of 'Prince of the Peace'. Spain was now allied to France, in maintenance of the Bourbon tradition, and was to pay dearly for this when Napoleon came to power.

The events of 1808 read almost like the plot of a light opera. Charles IV abdicated in favour of his son Ferdinand VII at the behest of a mob, who found him wrapped up in a carpet; later in the year, Ferdinand was lured to Bayonne by Napoleon and there witnessed his father first resume the throne and then assign it to Joseph, the brother of Napoleon. Ferdinand was detained in France, but his supporters in Spain were not slow to rise against King Joseph Bonaparte; thus began the long struggle known in England as the Peninsular War but in Spain as the War of Independence; to Napoleon it was the Spanish ulcer. In 1808 Wellington first landed in Portugal; in 1813 he crossed the Bidassoa into France.

In 1814 Ferdinand VII returned to Spain. His reign was tyrannical and disastrous. The lessons of recent years had not been lost on the Spanish colonies in America: one by one they revolted, until only Cuba and Puerto Rico remained to Spain. For a brief period Ferdinand flirted with liberalism, but then turned to French bayonets to restore autocracy. Finally, he failed to provide a male heir; although he was four times married, twice to his own nieces, he engen-

King Charles IV of Spain (1747–1819) with wife and family, painted with unflattering realism by Francisco Goya in 1800.

dered only two daughters. It was not certain whether a queen could succeed, though of course the Bourbons had inherited through a woman; conservative opinion favoured the King's brother, Charles (Don Carlos). It may be observed that most Spanish titles of nobility can pass through a female.

Ferdinand had only taken his fourth wife Mary Christina in 1829: Isabella was born in 1830. The King died in 1833. The baby Queen was proclaimed, with her mother as regent, but the followers of Charles, Count of Molina, proclaimed him as king. A bitter civil war ensued, fought mainly in the northern provinces, and lasted for seven years. Mary Christina made a secret morganatic marriage with an ex-sergeant: a dukedom of Riansares might conceal his vulgar origins, but it was less easy to keep dark the Queen Mother's frequent pregnancies. Isabella was a wayward and ill-educated princess with whose morals rumour made free. The choice of her husband perplexed the chanceries of Europe for five years (1841–6) but Mary Christina finally married the Queen to Francis, Duke of Cadiz, who was Isabella's first cousin and her own nephew. He was a hypochondriacal and effeminate bigot. Few royal families have been so closely inbred as the Spanish Bourbons in the nineteenth century.

Meanwhile political power was seized in turn by a series of generals of whom Espartero, Narvaez and O'Donnell were the most noteworthy. The passing of years did nothing to improve Isabella's reputation, and in 1868 General Prim, who had made his name in Morocco, organized a revolution which drove the Queen into exile: she finally abdicated in 1870. For

SPAIN
House of Bourbon and the Carlist branch

TABLE 51

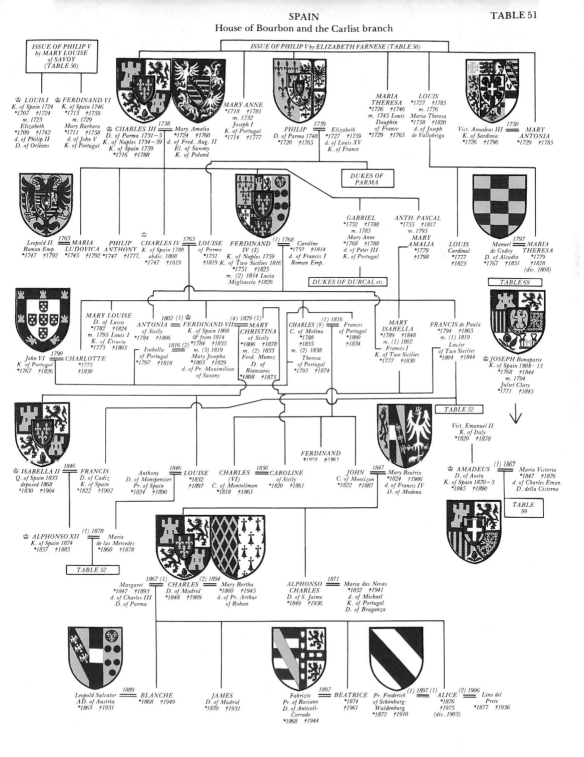

ISSUE OF PHILIP V
by MARY LOUISE
of SAVOY
(TABLE 50)

ISSUE OF PHILIP V by ELIZABETH FARNESE (TABLE 50)

♔ LOUIS I
K. of Spain 1724
*1707 †1742
m. 1723
d. of Philip II
D. of Orléans

♔ FERDINAND VI
K. of Spain 1746
*1713 †1759
m. 1729
Mary Barbara
*1711 †1758
d. of John V
K. of Portugal

1738
CHARLES III ⚓ Mary Amalia
D. of Parma 1731–5 *1724 †1760
K. of Naples 1734–59 d. of Fred. Aug. II
K. of Spain 1759 El. of Saxony
*1716 †1788 K. of Poland

MARY ANNE
*1718 †1781
m. 1732
Joseph I
K. of Portugal
*1714 †1777

1739
PHILIP ══ Elizabeth
D. of Parma 1748 *1727 †1759
*1720 †1765 d. of Louis XV
K. of France

MARIA
THERESA
*1726 †1746
m. 1745 Louis
Dauphin
of France
*1729 †1765

LOUIS
*1727 †1785
m. 1776
Maria Theresa
*1758 †1820
d. of Joseph
de Vallabriga

Vict. Amadeus III
K. of Sardinia
*1726 †1796

1750
══ MARY
ANTONIA
*1729 †1785

Leopold II
Roman Emp.
*1747 †1792

1765
MARIA
LUDOVICA
*1745 †1792

PHILIP
ANTHONY
*1747 †1777

♔
CHARLES IV
K. of Spain 1788
abdic. 1808
*1747 †1819

1765
══ LOUISE
of Parma
*1751 †1819

FERDINAND
IV (I)
K. of Naples 1759
K. of Two Sicilies 1816
*1751 †1825
m. (2) 1814 Lucia
Migliaccio †1826

(1) 1768
Caroline
*1752 †1814
d. of Francis I
Roman Emp.

DUKES OF
PARMA

GABRIEL
*1752 †1788
m. 1785
Mary Anne
*1768 †1788
d. of Peter III
K. of Portugal

ANTH. PASCAL
*1755 †1817
m. 1795
MARY
AMALIA
*1779
†1798

LOUIS
Cardinal
*1777
†1823

1797
Manuel ══ MARIA
de Godoy THERESA
D. of Alcudia *1779
*1767 †1851 †1828
(div. 1808)

TABLE 69

DUKES OF DURCAL etc.

MARY LOUISE
D. of Lucca
*1782 †1824
m. 1795 Louis I
K. of Etruria
*1773 †1803

1790
John VI ══ CHARLOTTE
K. of Portugal *1775
*1767 †1826 †1830

1802 (1) ♔
ANTONIA ══ FERDINAND VII
of Sicily K. of Spain 1808
*1784 †1806 & from 1814
*1784 †1833
Isabella m. (3) 1819
of Portugal Mary Josepha
*1797 †1818 *1803 †1829
d. of Pr. Maximilian
of Saxony

(4) 1829 (1)
══ MARY
CHRISTINA
of Sicily
*1806 †1878
m. (2) 1833
Ferd. Munoz
D. of
Riansares
*1808 †1873

CHARLES (V)
C. of Molina
*1788
†1855
m. (2) 1838
Theresa
of Portugal
*1793 †1874

(1) 1816
Frances
of Portugal
*1800
†1834

MARY
ISABELLA
*1789 †1848
m. (1) 1802
Francis I
K. of Two Sicilies
*1777 †1830

FRANCIS de Paula
*1794 †1865
m. (1) 1819
Louise
of Two Sicilies
*1804 †1844

TABLE 52

Vict. Emanuel II
K. of Italy
*1820 †1878

♔ JOSEPH Bonaparte
K. of Spain 1808–13
*1768 †1844
m. 1794
Juliet Clary
*1771 †1845

♔ ISABELLA II
Q. of Spain 1833
deposed 1868
*1830 †1904

1846
FRANCIS
D. of Cadiz
K. of Spain
*1822 †1902

Anthony
D. of Montpensier
Pr. of Spain
*1824 †1890

1846
LOUISE
*1832
†1897

CHARLES
(VI)
C. of Montelimon
*1818 †1861

1850
CAROLINE
of Sicily
*1820 †1861

JOHN
C. of Montizon
*1822 †1887

1847
══ Mary Beatrix
*1824 †1906
d. of Francis IV
D. of Modena

♔ AMADEUS
D. of Aosta
K. of Spain 1870–3
*1845 †1890

(1) 1867
Maria Victoria
*1847 †1876
d. of Charles Eman.
D. della Cisterna

TABLE
99

♔ ALPHONSO XII
K. of Spain 1874
*1857 †1885

(1) 1878
Maria
de las Mercedes
*1860 †1878

TABLE 52

Margaret
*1847 †1893
d. of Charles III
D. of Parma

1867 (1)
CHARLES
D. of Madrid
*1848 †1909

(2) 1894
══ Mary Bertha
*1860 †1945
d. of Pr. Arthur
of Rohan

1871
ALPHONSO ══ Maria das Nevas
CHARLES *1852 †1941
D. of S. Jaime d. of Michael
*1849 †1936 K. of Portugal
D. of Braganza

FERDINAND
†1924 †1961

Leopold Salvator
AD. of Austria
*1863 †1931

1889
══ BLANCHE
*1868 †1949

JAMES
D. of Madrid
*1870 †1931

Fabrizio
Pr. of Roviano
D. of Anticoli-
Corrado
*1868 †1944

1897
══ BEATRICE
*1874
†1961

Pr. Frederick
of Schönburg-
Waldenburg
*1872 †1910

(1) 1897 (1)
ALICE
*1876
†1975
(div. 1903)

(2) 1906
Lino del
Prete
*1877 †1956

TABLE 52

SPAIN
House of Bourbon since the Restoration in 1874

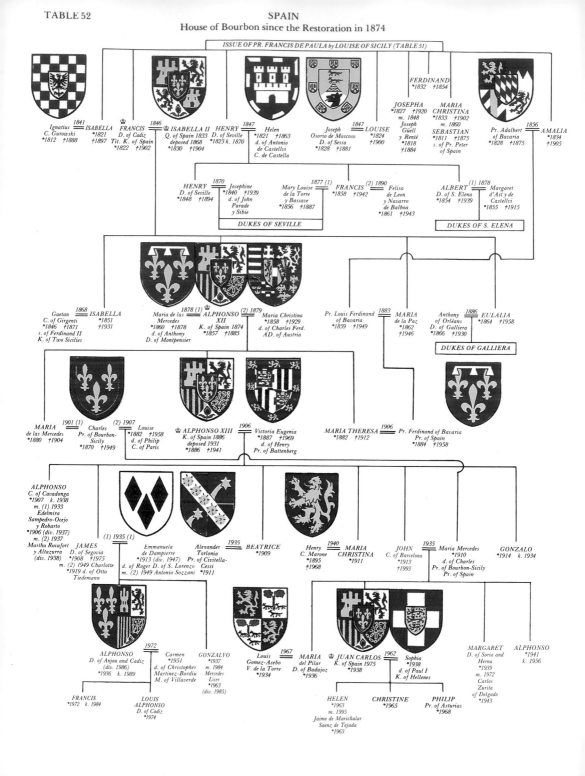

ISSUE OF PR. FRANCIS DE PAULA by LOUISE OF SICILY (TABLE 51)

Ignatius 1841 ISABELLA
C. Gurowski *1821
*1812 †1888 D. of Cadiz
*1822 †1902

FRANCIS 1846 ISABELLA II
Tit. K. of Spain Q. of Spain 1833
*1897 deposed 1868
*1830 †1904

HENRY 1847 Helen
D. of Seville *1821 †1863
*1823 k. 1870 d. of Antonio
de Castellvi
C. de Castella

Joseph 1847 LOUISE
Osorio de Moscoso *1824
D. of Sessa †1900
*1828 †1881

FERDINAND
*1832 †1854

JOSEPHA
*1827 †1920
m. 1848
Joseph
Güell
y Renté
*1818
†1884

MARIA
CHRISTINA
*1833 †1902
m. 1860
SEBASTIAN
*1811 †1875
s. of Pr. Peter
of Spain

Pr. Adalbert 1856 AMALIA
of Bavaria *1834
*1828 †1875 †1905

HENRY 1870 Josephine
D. of Seville *1840 †1939
*1848 †1894 d. of John
Parade
y Sibie

Mary Louise 1877 (1) FRANCIS (2) 1890 Felisa
de la Torre *1858 †1942 de Leon
y Bassave y Navarro
*1856 †1887 de Balboa
*1861 †1943

DUKES OF SEVILLE

ALBERT (1) 1878 Margaret
D. of S. Elena d'Ast y de
*1854 †1939 Castellvi
*1855 †1915

DUKES OF S. ELENA

Gaetan 1868 ISABELLA
C. of Girgenti *1851
*1846 †1871 †1931
s. of Ferdinand II
K. of Two Sicilies

Maria de las 1878 (1) ALPHONSO (2) 1879 Maria Christina
Mercedes XII *1858 †1929
*1860 †1878 K. of Spain 1874 d. of Charles Ferd.
d. of Anthony *1857 †1885 AD. of Austria
D. of Montpensier

Pr. Louis Ferdinand 1883 MARIA
of Bavaria de la Paz
*1859 †1949 *1862
†1946

Anthony 1886 EULALIA
of Orléans *1864 †1958
D. of Galliera
*1866 †1930

DUKES OF GALLIERA

MARIA 1901 (1) Charles (2) 1907 Louise
de las Mercedes Pr. of Bourbon- *1882 †1958
*1880 †1904 Sicily d. of Philip
*1870 †1949 C. of Paris

ALPHONSO XIII 1906 Victoria Eugenia
K. of Spain 1886 *1887 †1969
deposed 1931 d. of Henry
*1886 †1941 Pr. of Battenberg

MARIA THERESA 1906 Pr. Ferdinand of Bavaria
*1882 †1912 Pr. of Spain
*1884 †1958

ALPHONSO
C. of Cavadonga
*1907 k. 1938
m. (1) 1933
Edelmira
Sampedro-Ocejo
y Robarto
*1906 (div. 1937)
m. (2) 1937
Martha Rucafort
y Altazurra
(div. 1938)

JAMES
D. of Segovia
*1908 †1975
m. (2) 1949 Charlotte
*1919 d. of Otto
Tiedemann

(1) 1935 (1) Emmanuela
de Dampierre
*1913 (div. 1947)
d. of Roger D. of S. Lorenzo
m. (2) 1949 Antonio Sozzani

Alexander 1935 BEATRICE
Torlonia *1909
Pr. of Civitella-
Cessi
*1911

Henry 1940 MARIA
C. Marone CHRISTINA
*1895 *1911
†1968

JOHN 1935 Maria Mercedes
C. of Barcelona *1910
*1913 d. of Charles
†1993 Pr. of Bourbon-Sicily
Pr. of Spain

GONZALO
*1914 k. 1934

ALPHONSO
D. of Anjou and Cadiz
(div. 1986)
*1936 k. 1989

1972 Carmen
*1951
d. of Christopher
Martinez-Bordiu
M. of Villaverde

GONZALVO
*1937
m. 1984
Mercedes
Licer
*1963
(div. 1985)

Louis 1967 MARIA
Gomez-Acebo del Pilar
V. de la Torre D. of Badajoz
*1934 *1936

JUAN CARLOS 1962 Sophia
K. of Spain 1975 *1938
*1938 d. of Paul I
K. of Hellenes

MARGARET
D. of Soria and
Herna
*1939
m. 1972
Carlos
Zurita
of Delgado
*1943

ALPHONSO
*1941
k. 1956

FRANCIS
*1972 k. 1984

LOUIS
ALPHONSO
D. of Cadiz
*1974

HELEN
*1963
m. 1995
Jaime de Marichalar
Saenz de Tejada
*1963

CHRISTINE
*1965

PHILIP
Pr. of Asturias
*1968

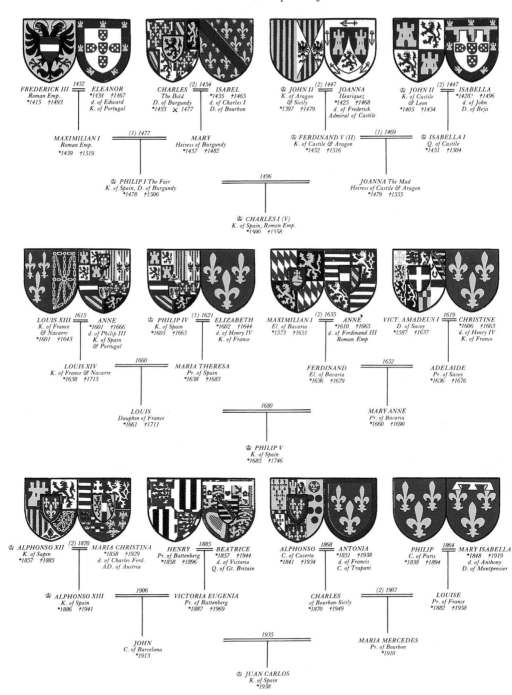

FREDERICK III
Roman Emp.
*1415 †1493

═ 1452

ELEANOR
d. of Edward
K. of Portugal
*1431 †1467

CHARLES
The Bold
D. of Burgundy
*1433 × 1477

═ (2) 1454

ISABEL
*1435 †1465
d. of Charles I
D. of Bourbon

♔ JOHN II
K. of Aragon
& Sicily
*1397 †1479

═ (2) 1447

JOANNA
Henriquez
*1425 †1468
d. of Frederick
Admiral of Castile

♔ JOHN II
K. of Castile
& Leon
*1405 †1454

═ (2) 1447

ISABELLA
*1428? †1496
d. of John
D. of Beja

MAXIMILIAN I
Roman Emp.
*1459 †1519

═ (1) 1477

MARY
Heiress of Burgundy
*1457 †1482

♔ FERDINAND V (II)
K. of Castile & Aragon
*1452 †1516

═ (1) 1469

♔ ISABELLA I
Q. of Castile
*1451 †1504

♔ PHILIP I The Fair
K. of Spain, D. of Burgundy
*1478 †1506

═ 1496

JOANNA The Mad
Heiress of Castile & Aragon
*1479 †1555

♔ CHARLES I (V)
K. of Spain, Roman Emp.
*1500 †1558

LOUIS XIII
K. of France
& Navarre
*1601 †1643

═ 1615

ANNE
*1601 †1666
d. of Philip III
K. of Spain
& Portugal

♔ PHILIP IV
K. of Spain
*1605 †1665

═ (1) 1621

ELIZABETH
*1602 †1644
d. of Henry IV
K. of France

MAXIMILIAN I
El. of Bavaria
*1573 †1651

═ (2) 1635

ANNE
*1610 †1665
d. of Ferdinand III
Roman Emp

VICT. AMADEUS I
D. of Savoy
*1587 †1637

═ 1619

CHRISTINE
*1606 †1663
d. of Henry IV
K. of France

LOUIS XIV
K. of France & Navarre
*1638 †1715

═ 1660

MARIA THERESA
Pr. of Spain
*1638 †1683

FERDINAND
El. of Bavaria
*1636 †1679

═ 1652

ADELAIDE
Pr. of Savoy
*1636 †1676

LOUIS
Dauphin of France
*1661 †1711

═ 1680

MARY ANNE
Pr. of Bavaria
*1660 †1690

♔ PHILIP V
K. of Spain
*1683 †1746

♔ ALPHONSO XII
K. of Sapin
*1857 †1885

═ (2) 1870

MARIA CHRISTINA
*1858 †1929
d. of Charles Ferd.
AD. of Austria

HENRY
Pr. of Battenberg
*1858 †1896

═ 1885

BEATRICE
*1857 †1944
d. of Victoria
Q. of Gt. Britain

ALPHONSO
C. of Caserta
*1841 †1934

═ 1868

ANTONIA
*1851 †1938
d. of Francis
C. of Trapani

PHILIP
C. of Paris
*1838 †1894

═ 1864

MARY ISABELLA
*1848 †1919
d. of Anthony
D. of Montpensier

♔ ALPHONSO XIII
K. of Spain
*1886 †1941

═ 1906

VICTORIA EUGENIA
Pr. of Battenberg
*1887 †1969

CHARLES
of Bourbon-Sicily
*1870 †1949

═ (2) 1907

LOUISE
Pr. of France
*1882 †1958

JOHN
C. of Barcelona
*1913

═ 1935

MARIA MERCEDES
Pr. of Bourbon
*1910

♔ JUAN CARLOS
K. of Spain
*1938

the best part of two years the Crown of Spain was hawked round Europe. The Duke of Montpensier was considered; then overtures were made to Prince Leopold of Hohenzollern-Sigmaringen, which helped to start the Franco-Prussian War; the King of Portugal and his Saxe-Coburg father were both discussed; at last the throne was accepted, late in 1870, by Amadeus of Savoy, Duke of Aosta and younger son of the first King of United Italy (Tables 51 and 99). His arms show the normal smaller shield of Spain, with his own differenced coat of Savoy over all. His reign was short and unhappy; opposition mounted, some in favour of Isabella's son, some advocating Charles, Duke of Madrid, grandson of the original Carlist claimant. In 1873 Amadeus abdicated and returned to Italy.

For a year there was an uneasy republic under four fleeting presidents. In the north the Carlists set up an independent state, centred on the Basque area of Navarre. At the very end of 1874 part of the army declared for Alphonso XII; the young King, then a cadet at Sandhurst, entered upon his short reign. He insisted on marrying his first cousin, a daughter of the Duke of Montpensier, but she died five months later. His second marriage was to an Austrian princess who provided him with two daughters. The King's rule was constitutional: a Conservative Government was followed by a Liberal one, and a more promising era for Spain seemed about to materialize. Unhappily the King developed consumption and died, genuinely mourned by his subjects, at the end of 1885. The Queen was pregnant and six months later had a son, Alphonso XIII, who was thus a king from the moment of his birth. In 1883 there had died the exiled Count of Chambord, the last male descendant of Louis XV. Alphonso XII thus became head of the House of Bourbon and the senior heir of Hugh Capet. Accordingly he adopted the undifferenced arms of France, which can be seen over the traditional shield of Spain on Table 52.

Under the regency of the Queen Mother the minority of Alphonso XIII was passed in parliamentary government. The end of the century saw a crisis in Cuba, where a revolution, which broke out in 1895, led finally to war with the United States and the loss of the island. In 1906 the King made a marriage of affection with Princess Victoria of Battenberg, who had been brought up in England as a Protestant. Though she became a Catholic, the King's choice was criticized on the score of religion and non-royal birth. The neutrality of Spain in the First World War brought considerable prosperity to the country. At the same time socialist movements were spreading and there was a resurgence of Catalan separatism. From 1923 to 1930 there was a dictatorship under General Primo de Rivera; it was followed

by massive manifestations of republicanism. In 1931 the King left Spain, partly with the aim of avoiding civil war, but he never abdicated. He died in 1941. The eldest son of Alphonso XIII resigned all his rights in 1933 on marrying a commoner; the second, who was born deaf and dumb, did the same although he has sometimes advanced claims to the thrones of both France and Spain.

The Second Republic had a brief and violent career. In 1936 a military rising in Morocco spread to Spain and the civil war began. Like the internal conflicts between the supporters of Queen Isabella and the Carlists in the nineteenth century, it was waged with extreme bitterness and brutality. But in this savage conflict alien powers were all too ready to interfere, whether from Fascist right or Communist left; the war ended in 1939 with victory for the right. From that date until his death in 1975 the ruler of Spain was a Gallegan soldier, General Francisco Franco, styled the *Caudillo*. This is no place to judge his regime. Against the indubitable woes of internal dictatorship may be set his success in not involving Spain in the Second World War, despite his obligations to the Axis.

General Franco declared that Spain was a monarchy and in 1969 chose as his successor the son of Juan, Count of Barcelona, the Bourbon claimant (Table 52). The Prince, Juan Carlos, was partly brought up in Spain, while his father maintained his exile in Portugal. After Franco's death, he was duly proclaimed and crowned as King of Spain in November 1975, but it was not until 1977 that the Count of Barcelona actually resigned his rights in his son's favour. King Juan Carlos is married to a Greek princess and their son bears the traditional title of Prince of the Asturias. He has courageously embarked upon a policy of transforming Spain into a parliamentary monarchy.

Many traditional problems such as the separatist ambitions of some areas survive all changes of constitution. The true Carlist branch came to an end with the death of Alphonso, Duke of San Jaime, in 1936 (Table 51). However, he designated as head of the Carlist movement Prince Xavier of Bourbon-Parma who was banned from Spain in 1968 (though his genealogical claims were remote) and died in 1977. His eldest son, Charles Hugo, is married to a Dutch princess (Table 36) and lives in Paris.

The King's formal arms can be seen at the foot of Table 43; they show the ancient Spanish quarterings of Castile, Leon, Aragon and Navarre, with Granada in base, ensigned with an escutcheon of France and surrounded by the Golden Fleece. For King Juan Carlos is the heir male of Hugh Capet, who ascended the French throne in 987, a line of direct descent not easily equalled.

Chapter 12

MONACO

The Principality of Monaco, a mere one and a half square kilometres in area, is a narrow strip along the shore of the Mediterranean. Today the Côte d'Azur is renowned as an international holiday resort; its early history was more violent and chequered. Fraxinetum, a famous nest of Saracen pirates who preyed on the shipping of those waters, was not extirpated until the end of the tenth century; the various steep promontories were a temptation to the castle-building and restless nobility. In the twelfth century the Emperor Frederick I (Barbarossa) gave the Republic of Genoa certain rights over the coastline near Nice. Among the leading families of Genoa was that of Grimaldi, and its scions began to interest themselves in the excellent harbour of Monaco and the rocky headland beside it.

In 1297 Francis Grimaldi (Table 54) seized Monaco and established himself there. By tradition he and his companions got into the castle by disguising themselves as friars; and two Franciscans with swords are still the supporters of the princely arms, which consist of a bold pattern of fifteen red diamonds on a white background. Charles I of Monaco (d. 1363) was an admiral in the service of France, and raided Southampton in 1339; he also fought at Crécy. He was, however, ejected from Monaco by the Genoese ruler Simone de Boccanegra, commemorated in the opera by Verdi. Rainier II recaptured the town; of his sons Ambrose was drowned and John became an Admiral of France. He laid down in his will that any heiress must marry another Grimaldi; this duly occurred when his grand-daughter, Claudine, was won by her cousin Lambert, Lord of Antibes, after a certain amount of competition. Gradually Monaco began to assert its independence. In 1489 the Dukes of Savoy recognized that the Lordship was free of other suzerains; in 1512 the King of France admitted that Lucien (k. 1523)

was entirely independent, in consequence of which Lucien began to mint his own coins.

In 1525 the Emperor Charles V in turn conceded independence and protection to Monaco, in favour of Augustine (who was also Bishop of Grasse), and paid a state visit a few years later. Honoré I fought during the siege of Malta and at the Battle of Lepanto against the Turks. Honoré II abandoned the protection of Spain for that of France; he was the first of the Grimaldi to give up the use of the surname in official documents and to style himself prince; in 1642 he was created Duke of Valentinois and a peer of France.

His descendants made a series of marriages which added to their wealth and their titles, if not to their happiness. Louis I (Table 55), who was finally recognized as sovereign prince by Louis XIV (his godfather) in 1688, married Charlotte de Gramont, who furnished Dumas with material for one of his novels. Their son Anthony espoused a member of the House of Lorraine, but she bore him only daughters. In 1715 James de Goyon de Matignon, the head of an ancient Breton family (the Goyon-Matignon alliance took place in about 1200) was prepared to give up his name and arms (which are shown on Table 54) to assume those of Grimaldi and marry the heiress Louise-Hyppolite. Archbishop Honoré ceded his rights to James, who at first incurred the wrath of Prince Anthony by combining the blazons of Matignon and Monaco. Louise died shortly after her father, and, after ruling for two years, James withdrew to the comforts of Paris. Their son Honoré III also acquired a wealthy wife, but she left him to live for half a lifetime with the Prince of Condé whom she eventually married after a liaison of 48 years. In 1793 the French Revolutionaries incorporated the little state in the *département* of Alpes Maritimes and for a while the Principality vanished.

Honoré IV was too ill to rule in person after the

TABLE 54

MONACO
General survey (House of Grimaldi)

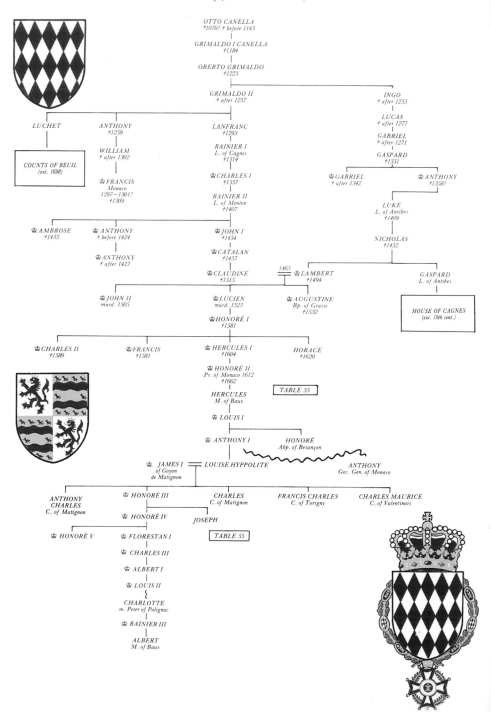

OTTO CANELLA
*1070? † before 1143

GRIMALDO I CANELLA
†1184

OBERTO GRIMALDO
†1223

GRIMALDO II
† after 1257

INGO
† after 1235

LUCHET

ANTHONY
†1259

LANFRANC
†1293

LUCAS
† after 1277

GABRIEL
† after 1271

WILLIAM
† after 1302

RAINIER I
L. of Cagnes
†1314

GASPARD
†1331

COUNTS OF BEUIL
(ext. 1698)

♛ FRANCIS
Monaco
1297–1301?
†1309

♛ CHARLES I
†1357

♛ GABRIEL
† after 1342

♛ ANTHONY
†1358?

RAINIER II
L. of Menton
†1407

LUKE
L. of Antibes
†1409

♛ AMBROSE
†1433

♛ ANTHONY
† before 1424

♛ JOHN I
†1454

NICHOLAS
†1452

♛ ANTHONY
† after 1427

♛ CATALAN
†1457

1465

♛ CLAUDINE
†1515

♛ LAMBERT
†1494

GASPARD
L. of Antibes

♛ JOHN II
murd. 1505

♛ LUCIEN
murd. 1523

♛ AUGUSTINE
Bp. of Grasse
†1532

HOUSE OF CAGNES
(ext. 19th cent.)

♛ HONORÉ I
†1581

♛ CHARLES II
†1589

♛ FRANCIS
†1581

♛ HERCULES I
†1604

HORACE
†1620

♛ HONORÉ II
Pr. of Monaco 1612
†1662

TABLE 55

HERCULES
M. of Baux

♛ LOUIS I

♛ ANTHONY I

HONORÉ
Abp. of Besançon

ANTHONY
Gov. Gen. of Monaco

♛ JAMES I
of Goyon
de Matignon

LOUISE HYPPOLITE

ANTHONY
CHARLES
C. of Matignon

♛ HONORÉ III

CHARLES
C. of Matignon

FRANCIS CHARLES
C. of Torigny

CHARLES MAURICE
C. of Valentinois

♛ HONORÉ IV

JOSEPH

♛ HONORÉ V

♛ FLORESTAN I

TABLE 55

♛ CHARLES III

♛ ALBERT I

♛ LOUIS II

CHARLOTTE
m. Peter of Polignac

♛ RAINIER III

ALBERT
M. of Baux

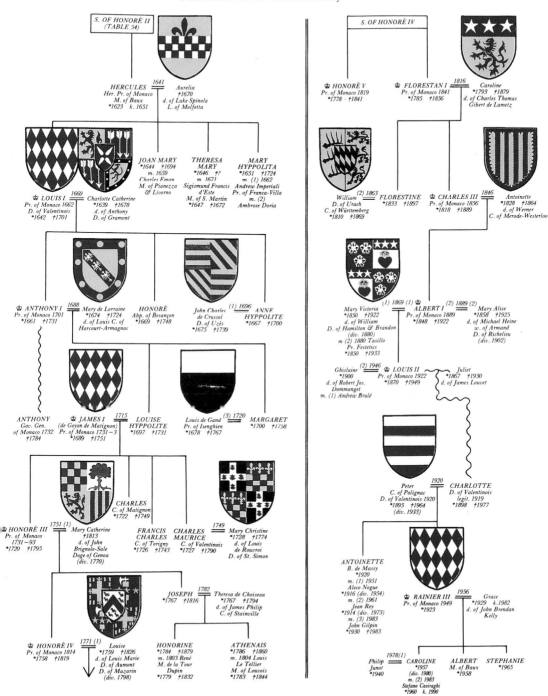

S. OF HONORÉ II
(TABLE 54)

HERCULES — 1641 — Aurelia
Her. Pr. of Monaco
M. of Baux
*1623 k. 1651
†1670
d. of Luke Spinola
L. of Molfetta

JOAN MARY
*1644 †1694
m. 1659
Charles Eman.
M. of Pianezza
& Livorno

THERESA MARY
*1646 †?
m 1671
Sigismund Francis
d'Este
M. of S. Martin
*1647 †1672

MARY HYPPOLITA
*1651 †1724
m. (1) 1662
Andrew Imperiali
Pr. of Franca-Villa
m. (2)
Ambrose Doria

♛ LOUIS I — 1660 — Charlotte Catherine
Pr. of Monaco 1662
D. of Valentinois
*1642 †1701
*1639 †1678
d. of Anthony
D. of Gramont

♛ ANTHONY I — 1688 — Mary de Lorraine
Pr. of Monaco 1701
*1661 †1731
*1674 †1724
d. of Louis C. of
Harcourt-Armagnac

HONORÉ
Abp. of Besançon
*1669 †1748

John Charles — (1) 1696 — ANNE
de Crussol   HYPPOLITE
D. of Uzès   *1667 †1700
*1675 †1739

ANTHONY
Gov. Gen.
of Monaco 1732
†1784

♛ JAMES I — 1715 — LOUISE
(de Goyon de Matignon)   HYPPOLITE
Pr. of Monaco 1731–3   *1697 †1731
*1689 †1751

Louis de Gand — (3) 1720 — MARGARET
Pr. of Isenghien   *1700 †1758
*1678 †1767

CHARLES
C. of Matignon
*1722 †1749

FRANCIS
CHARLES
C. of Torigny
*1726 †1743

CHARLES
MAURICE
C. of Valentinois
*1727 †1790

1749 — Mary Christine
d. of Louis
de Rouvroi
D. of St. Simon

♛ HONORÉ III — 1751 (1) — Mary Catherine
Pr. of Monaco   †1813
1731–93   d. of John
*1720 †1795   Brignole-Sale
                       Doge of Genoa
                       (div. 1770)

JOSEPH — 1782 — Theresa de Choiseau
*1767 †1816   *1767 †1794
                    d. of James Philip
                    C. of Stainville

♛ HONORÉ IV — 1771 (1) — Louise
Pr. of Monaco 1814   *1759 †1826
*1758 †1819   d. of Louis Marie
                        D. of Aumont
                        D. of Mazarin
                        (div. 1798)

HONORINE
*1784 †1879
m.1803 René
M. de la Tour
Dupin
*1779 †1832

ATHENAIS
*1786 †1860
m. 1804 Louis
Le Tellier
M. of Louvois
*1783 †1844

S. OF HONORÉ IV

♛ HONORÉ V
Pr. of Monaco 1819
*1778 · †1841

♛ FLORESTAN I — 1816 — Caroline
Pr. of Monaco 1841   *1793 †1879
*1785 †1856   d. of Charles Thomas
                       Gibert de Lametz

William — (2) 1863 — FLORESTINE
D. of Urach   *1833 †1897
C. of Württemberg
*1810 †1869

♛ CHARLES III — 1846 — Antoinette
Pr. of Monaco 1856   *1828 †1864
*1818 †1889   d. of Werner
                       C. of Merode-Westerloo

Mary Victoria — (1) 1869 (1) — ♛ ALBERT I — (2) 1889 (2) — Mary Alice
*1850 †1922   Pr. of Monaco 1889   *1858 †1925
d. of William   *1848 †1922   d. of Michael Heine
D. of Hamilton & Brandon   w. of Armand
(div. 1880)   D. of Richelieu
m (2) 1880 Tassilo   (div. 1902)
Pr. Festetics
*1850 †1933

Ghislaine — (2) 1946 — ♛ LOUIS II — Juliet
*1900   Pr. of Monaco 1922   *1867 †1930
d. of Robert Jos.   *1870 †1949   d. of James Louvet
Dommanget
m. (1) Andrew Brulé

Peter — 1920 — CHARLOTTE
C. of Polignac   D. of Valentinois
D. of Valentinois 1920   legit. 1919
*1895 †1964   *1898 †1977
(div. 1933)

ANTOINETTE
B. de Massy
*1920
m. (1) 1951
Aleco Nogue
*1916 (div. 1954)
m. (2) 1961
Jean Rey
*1914 (div. 1973)
m. (3) 1983
John Gilpin
*1930 †1983

♛ RAINIER III — 1956 — Grace
Pr. of Monaco 1949   *1929 k.1982
*1923   d. of John Brendan
                        Kelly

Philip — 1978(1) — CAROLINE
Junot   *1957
*1940   (div. 1980)
                  m. (2) 1983
                  Stefano Casiraghi
                  *1960 k. 1990

ALBERT
M. of Baux
*1958

STEPHANIE
*1965

Rainier III (b.1923), Prince of Monaco, broke with precedent by marrying the film star, Grace Kelly.

Empire. Returning to his father's domain in 1815, he met Napoleon just returned from Elba, but declined to exchange the reality of Monaco for the hazards of the Hundred Days. In 1816 he was compelled to do homage to the King of Sardinia for the outlying lands of Menton and Roquebrune.

In the early nineteenth century the tiny Principality was barren and impoverished. It was Charles III who took the sensational step of giving Louis Blanc in 1863 a concession to establish sea-bathing and a casino. Complaints from the French Government were met by a threat to abdicate in favour of his German nephew the Duke of Urach. He thus established the modern prosperity of his state and began the now traditional lure of Monte Carlo, though his dominions were diminished by the cession of Menton and Roquebrune to France in 1861. In 1858 he founded the Order of St Charles (Table 54).

Albert I, who followed Charles III, was a distinguished scholar in marine biology who built up an important aquarium in Monaco. His marriage with a daughter of the British Duke of Hamilton was unhappy; and his wife left him having borne one son. This son, Prince Louis, showed no inclination to marry at all, which became a source of disquiet to the French Government; the next heir was still the Duke of Urach, a subject of the German Emperor. Accordingly, in 1911 an illegitimate daughter, whom Louis had casually begotten in North Africa, was brought to Monaco and by stages declared legitimate, and made heiress to the Principality. She was created Duchess of Valentinois and married to a Frenchman, Count Peter of Polignac in 1920. The union was scarcely successful, but a son and a daughter were born and the dynasty ensured. Count Peter assumed the name and arms of Grimaldi.

Prince Louis II, though his appearance was Teutonic, joined the French Army in the First World War. His grandson, Prince Rainier, fought in the Second under General de Lattre de Tassigny. Towards the end of his life Prince Louis married an actress; meanwhile his daughter had already (1944) resigned her rights in favour of her son. Accordingly, on the death of Prince Louis, his grandson succeeded as Prince Rainier III. In 1956 he married the American actress, Grace Kelly, a romantic alliance of princely lineage and rare beauty, designed to perpetuate this small, enduring state into the uncertain future.

restoration of 1814, but he did make a profitable alliance; his wife brought him the Duchy of Mazarin – though she divorced him during the Revolution and re-married several times. Honoré V entered the service of Napoleon, was Grand Equerry to the Empress Josephine, and was created a Baron of the

Chapter 13

DYNASTIC RELATIONS

Such alliances as that between the Prince of Monaco and a glamorous actress of the international screen would have been quite impossible, for more reasons than one, only a short time ago. A long tradition has prevailed that the members of royal or reigning families marry only among their own class. When a new family, such as the Tudors in England or the Bonapartes in France, secured a throne, one of its first impulses was to marry into an established princely dynasty. In consequence the ruling Houses of Europe have always been closely related one to another. Marriages were arranged to cement old and enduring friendships, such as those between France and Scotland or between England and Portugal; but more often they were designed to ratify treaties or to end a period of hostility. The pages of history are spattered with sad examples of the illusion that a wedding between two rival kingdoms must bring peace in its wake. A parallel error was the belief that the loyalty of cadets of the royal House could be secured by the bestowal of large domains. York and Lancaster in England or Burgundy in France are illustrations of the failure of such plans.

The passage of time strengthened the convention that royalty only allied with royalty, and from the sixteenth century onwards marriages between crown and commoner became rarer and rarer. At the same time the impact of the Reformation and the subsequent wars of religion tended to divide the ruling princes of Europe into two groups, Catholic and Protestant, between which intermarriage was infrequent. Thus in the eighteenth and nineteenth centuries the sovereigns of England, Holland and the Scandinavian Powers normally sought their wives among themselves or among the Reformed dynasties of Germany. On the other hand the Bourbons, Hapsburgs and Savoyards of France, Spain, Austria and Italy wedded among their own numerous branches or with the Catholic Houses in Germany. The bar was in no sense complete, because one partner in the alliance (more usually the wife) could change religion to conform to the spouse's faith. Orthodox Russia in general sought marriages in Protestant Germany or Sweden.

Nowhere was the principle of dynastic purity taken more seriously than in Germany, where various reigning families laid down codes regulating possible marriages. To lend some status to weddings between non-equal persons, the morganatic marriage was evolved, whereby the issue were given a title, and a status below that of truly royal alliances. These refinements never prevailed in England; two German families, the Dukes of Teck and the Princes of Battenberg (later Mountbatten), morganatically descended from the Houses of Württemberg and Hesse respectively, married into the British dynasty in the reign of Queen Victoria.

Tables 56–7 show the close connection which existed between the kings of Europe in 1914. The important rulers were all intimately related to each other, and even the remoter Balkan rulers were linked to the historic dynasties. Thus, King George V of England was first cousin of his ally the Emperor of Russia, to whom he bore a striking resemblance. But he was also first cousin of Emperor William II of Germany, whom he was to defeat after four catastrophic years of war. Similarly, in southern, Catholic Europe, Victor Emanuel III of Italy was the second cousin of his enemy the Emperor Francis Joseph of Austria. Mere kinship was no protection against rising economic and national hostility.

COMMON ANCESTRY

Tables 58–9 illustrate how all the reigning sovereigns of the present day are descended from William the Conqueror. It may be added that the same descent

Relationship of European monarchs before and at the time of the First World War

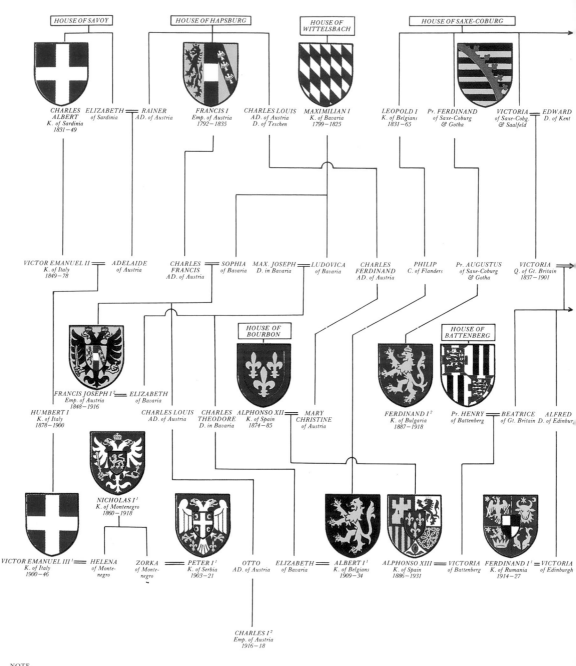

HOUSE OF SAVOY

HOUSE OF HAPSBURG

HOUSE OF WITTELSBACH

HOUSE OF SAXE-COBURG

CHARLES ALBERT
K. of Sardinia
1831–49

ELIZABETH
of Sardinia

RAINER
AD. of Austria

FRANCIS I
Emp. of Austria
1792–1835

CHARLES LOUIS
AD. of Austria
D. of Teschen

MAXIMILIAN I
K. of Bavaria
1799–1825

LEOPOLD I
K. of Belgians
1831–65

Pr. FERDINAND
of Saxe-Coburg
& Gotha

VICTORIA
of Saxe-Cobg.
& Saalfeld

EDWARD
D. of Kent

VICTOR EMANUEL II
K. of Italy
1849–78

ADELAIDE
of Austria

CHARLES FRANCIS
AD. of Austria

SOPHIA
of Bavaria

MAX. JOSEPH
D. in Bavaria

LUDOVICA
of Bavaria

CHARLES FERDINAND
AD. of Austria

PHILIP
C. of Flanders

Pr. AUGUSTUS
of Saxe-Coburg
& Gotha

VICTORIA
Q. of Gt. Britain
1837–1901

HOUSE OF BOURBON

HOUSE OF BATTENBERG

FRANCIS JOSEPH I
Emp. of Austria
1848–1916

ELIZABETH
of Bavaria

CHARLES LOUIS
AD. of Austria

CHARLES THEODORE
D. in Bavaria

ALPHONSO XII
K. of Spain
1874–85

MARY CHRISTINE
of Austria

FERDINAND I
K. of Bulgaria
1887–1918

Pr. HENRY
of Battenberg

BEATRICE
of Gt. Britain

ALFRED
D. of Edinbur.

HUMBERT I
K. of Italy
1878–1900

NICHOLAS I
K. of Montenegro
1860–1918

VICTOR EMANUEL III
K. of Italy
1900–46

HELENA
of Montenegro

ZORKA
of Montenegro

PETER I
K. of Serbia
1903–21

OTTO
AD. of Austria

ELIZABETH
of Bavaria

ALBERT I
K. of Belgians
1909–34

ALPHONSO XIII
K. of Spain
1886–1931

VICTORIA
of Battenberg

FERDINAND I
K. of Rumania
1914–27

VICTORIA
of Edinburgh

CHARLES I
Emp. of Austria
1916–18

NOTE
[1] Allied sovereign
[2] Sovereign of the Central Powers
All dates are those of regnal years.
The dynastic arms of a House are shown beneath its name.

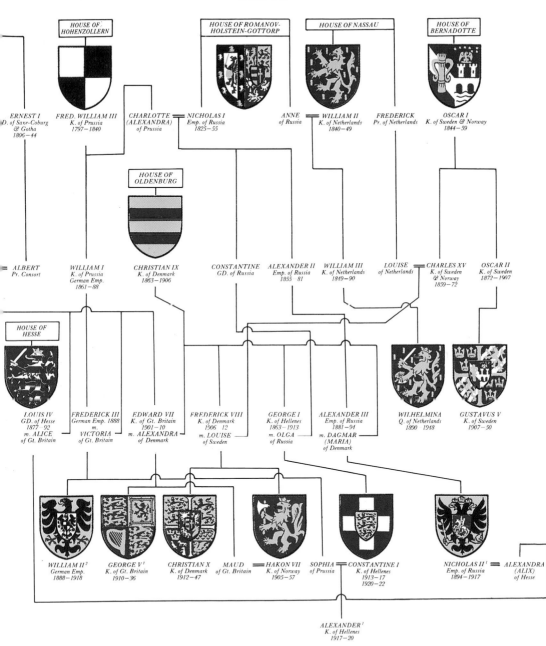

HOUSE OF HOHENZOLLERN

HOUSE OF ROMANOV-HOLSTEIN-GOTTORP

HOUSE OF NASSAU

HOUSE OF BERNADOTTE

ERNEST I
D. of Saxe-Coburg
& Gotha
1806–44

FRED. WILLIAM III
K. of Prussia
1797–1840

CHARLOTTE
(ALEXANDRA)
of Prussia
═ NICHOLAS I
Emp. of Russia
1825–55

ANNE
of Russia
═ WILLIAM II
K. of Netherlands
1840–49

FREDERICK
Pr. of Netherlands

OSCAR I
K. of Sweden & Norway
1844–59

HOUSE OF OLDENBURG

═ ALBERT
Pr. Consort

WILLIAM I
K. of Prussia
German Emp.
1861–88

CHRISTIAN IX
K. of Denmark
1863–1906

CONSTANTINE
GD. of Russia

ALEXANDER II
Emp. of Russia
1855–81

WILLIAM III
K. of Netherlands
1849–90

LOUISE
of Netherlands
═ CHARLES XV
K. of Sweden
& Norway
1859–72

OSCAR II
K. of Sweden
1872–1907

HOUSE OF HESSE

LOUIS IV
GD. of Hesse
1877–92
m. ALICE
of Gt. Britain

FREDERICK III
German Emp. 1888
m.
VICTORIA
of Gt. Britain

EDWARD VII
K. of Gt. Britain
1901–10
m. ALEXANDRA
of Denmark

FREDERICK VIII
K. of Denmark
1906–12
m. LOUISE
of Sweden

GEORGE I
K. of Hellenes
1863–1913
m. OLGA
of Russia

ALEXANDER III
Emp. of Russia
1881–94
m. DAGMAR
(MARIA)
of Denmark

WILHELMINA
Q. of Netherlands
1890–1948

GUSTAVUS V
K. of Sweden
1907–50

WILLIAM II[2]
German Emp.
1888–1918

GEORGE V[1]
K. of Gt. Britain
1910–36

CHRISTIAN X
K. of Denmark
1912–47

MAUD
of Gt. Britain
═ HAKON VII
K. of Norway
1905–57

SOPHIA
of Prussia
═ CONSTANTINE I
K. of Hellenes
1913–17
1920–22

NICHOLAS II[1]
Emp. of Russia
1894–1917
═ ALEXANDRA
(ALIX)
of Hesse

ALEXANDER[1]
K. of Hellenes
1917–20

Common descent of the present European sovereigns since William the Conqueror

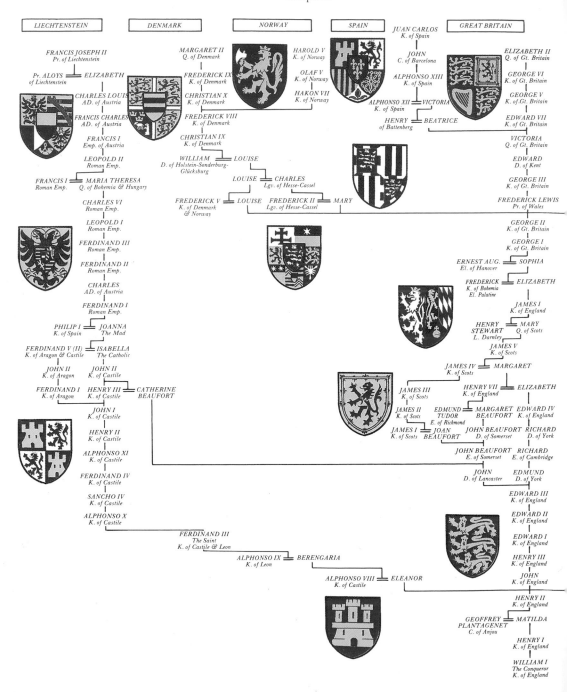

| LIECHTENSTEIN | DENMARK | NORWAY | SPAIN | | GREAT BRITAIN |

LIECHTENSTEIN

FRANCIS JOSEPH II
Pr. of Liechtenstein

Pr. ALOYS ═ ELIZABETH
of Liechtenstein

CHARLES LOUIS
AD. of Austria

FRANCIS CHARLES
AD. of Austria

FRANCIS I
Emp. of Austria

LEOPOLD II
Roman Emp.

FRANCIS I ═ MARIA THERESA
Roman Emp. *Q. of Bohemia & Hungary*

CHARLES VI
Roman Emp.

LEOPOLD I
Roman Emp.

FERDINAND III
Roman Emp.

FERDINAND II
Roman Emp.

CHARLES
AD. of Austria

FERDINAND I
Roman Emp.

PHILIP I ═ JOANNA
K. of Spain *The Mad*

FERDINAND V (II) ═ ISABELLA
K. of Aragon & Castile *The Catholic*

JOHN II   JOHN II
K. of Aragon *K. of Castile*

FERDINAND I   HENRY III ═ CATHERINE
K. of Aragon *K. of Castile* BEAUFORT

JOHN I
K. of Castile

HENRY II
K. of Castile

ALPHONSO XI
K. of Castile

FERDINAND IV
K. of Castile

SANCHO IV
K. of Castile

ALPHONSO X
K. of Castile

DENMARK

MARGARET II
Q. of Denmark

FREDERICK IX
K. of Denmark

CHRISTIAN X
K. of Denmark

FREDERICK VIII
K. of Denmark

CHRISTIAN IX
K. of Denmark

WILLIAM ═ LOUISE
D. of Holstein-Sonderburg-
Glücksburg

LOUISE ═ CHARLES
Lgv. of Hesse-Cassel

FREDERICK V ═ LOUISE   FREDERICK II ═ MARY
K. of Denmark   *Lgv. of Hesse-Cassel*
& Norway

NORWAY

HAROLD V
K. of Norway

OLAF V
K. of Norway

HAKON VII
K. of Norway

SPAIN

JUAN CARLOS
K. of Spain

JOHN
C. of Barcelona

ALPHONSO XIII
K. of Spain

ALPHONSO XII ═ VICTORIA
K. of Spain

HENRY ═ BEATRICE
of Battenberg

GREAT BRITAIN

ELIZABETH II
Q. of Gt. Britain

GEORGE VI
K. of Gt. Britain

GEORGE V
K. of Gt. Britain

EDWARD VII
K. of Gt. Britain

VICTORIA
Q. of Gt. Britain

EDWARD
D. of Kent

GEORGE III
K. of Gt. Britain

FREDERICK LEWIS
Pr. of Wales

GEORGE II
K. of Gt. Britain

GEORGE I
K. of Gt. Britain

ERNEST AUG. ═ SOPHIA
El. of Hanover

FREDERICK ═ ELIZABETH
K. of Bohemia
El. Palatine

JAMES I
K. of England

HENRY ═ MARY
STEWART *Q. of Scots*
L. Darnley

JAMES V
K. of Scots

JAMES IV ═ MARGARET
K. of Scots

JAMES III   HENRY VII ═ ELIZABETH
K. of Scots   *K. of England*

JAMES II   EDMUND ═ MARGARET   EDWARD IV
K. of Scots TUDOR   BEAUFORT   *K. of England*
         E. of Richmond

JAMES I ═ JOAN   JOHN BEAUFORT   RICHARD
K. of Scots BEAUFORT *D. of Somerset* *D. of York*

JOHN BEAUFORT   RICHARD
E. of Somerset *E. of Cambridge*

JOHN   EDMUND
D. of Lancaster *D. of York*

EDWARD III
K. of England

EDWARD II
K. of England

EDWARD I
K. of England

HENRY III
K. of England

JOHN
K. of England

HENRY II
K. of England

GEOFFREY ═ MATILDA
PLANTAGENET
C. of Anjou

HENRY I
K. of England

WILLIAM I
The Conqueror
K. of England

FERDINAND III
The Saint
K. of Castile & Leon

ALPHONSO IX ═ BERENGARIA
K. of Leon

ALPHONSO VIII ═ ELEANOR
K. of Castile

Common descent of the present European sovereigns since William the Conqueror

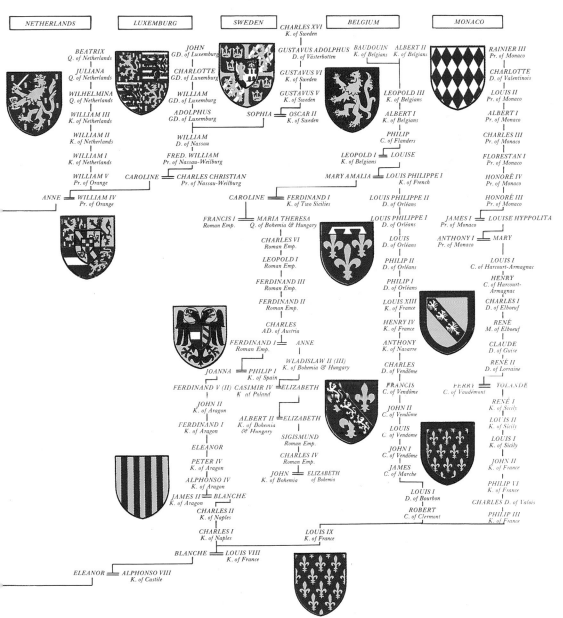

NETHERLANDS	LUXEMBURG	SWEDEN	BELGIUM	MONACO

CHARLES XVI
K. of Sweden

BEATRIX
Q. of Netherlands

JOHN
GD. of Luxemburg

GUSTAVUS ADOLPHUS
D. of Västerbotten

BAUDOUIN
K. of Belgians

ALBERT II
K. of Belgians

RAINIER III
Pr. of Monaco

JULIANA
Q. of Netherlands

CHARLOTTE
GD. of Luxemburg

GUSTAVUS VI
K. of Sweden

CHARLOTTE
D. of Valentinois

WILHELMINA
Q. of Netherlands

WILLIAM
GD. of Luxemburg

GUSTAVUS V
K. of Sweden

LEOPOLD III
K. of Belgians

LOUIS II
Pr. of Monaco

WILLIAM III
K. of Netherlands

ADOLPHUS
GD. of Luxemburg

SOPHIA ═ OSCAR II
K. of Sweden

ALBERT I
K. of Belgians

ALBERT I
Pr. of Monaco

WILLIAM II
K. of Netherlands

WILLIAM
D. of Nassau

PHILIP
C. of Flanders

CHARLES III
Pr. of Monaco

WILLIAM I
K. of Netherlands

FRED. WILLIAM
Pr. of Nassau-Weilburg

LEOPOLD I ═ LOUISE
K. of Belgians

FLORESTAN I
Pr. of Monaco

WILLIAM V
Pr. of Orange

CAROLINE ═ CHARLES CHRISTIAN
Pr. of Nassau-Weilburg

MARY AMALIA ═ LOUIS PHILIPPE I
K. of French

HONORÉ IV
Pr. of Monaco

ANNE ═ WILLIAM IV
Pr. of Orange

CAROLINE ═ FERDINAND I
D. of Two Sicilies

LOUIS PHILIPPE II
D. of Orléans

HONORÉ III
Pr. of Monaco

FRANCIS I ═ MARIA THERESA
Roman Emp.   Q. of Bohemia & Hungary

LOUIS PHILIPPE I
D. of Orléans

JAMES I ═ LOUISE HYPPOLITA
Pr. of Monaco

CHARLES VI
Roman Emp.

LOUIS
D. of Orléans

ANTHONY I ═ MARY
Pr. of Monaco

LEOPOLD I
Roman Emp.

PHILIP II
D. of Orléans

LOUIS I
C. of Harcourt-Armagnac

FERDINAND III
Roman Emp.

PHILIP I
D. of Orléans

HENRY
C. of Harcourt-Armagnac

FERDINAND II
Roman Emp.

LOUIS XIII
K. of France

CHARLES I
D. of Elboeuf

CHARLES
AD. of Austria

HENRY IV
K. of France

RENÉ
M. of Elboeuf

FERDINAND I ═ ANNE
Roman Emp.

ANTHONY
K. of Navarre

CLAUDE
D. of Guise

WLADISLAW II (III)
K. of Bohemia & Hungary

CHARLES
D. of Vendôme

RENÉ II
D. of Lorraine

JOANNA ═ PHILIP I
K. of Spain

FRANCIS
C. of Vendôme

FERRY ═ YOLANDE
C. of Vaudémont

FERDINAND V (II)
K. of Aragon

CASIMIR IV ═ ELIZABETH
K. of Poland

JOHN II
C. of Vendôme

RENÉ I
K. of Sicily

JOHN II
K. of Aragon

ALBERT II ═ ELIZABETH
K. of Bohemia & Hungary

LOUIS
C. of Vendôme

LOUIS II
K. of Sicily

FERDINAND I
K. of Aragon

SIGISMUND
Roman Emp.

JOHN I
C. of Vendôme

LOUIS I
K. of Sicily

ELEANOR

CHARLES IV
Roman Emp.

JAMES
C. of Marche

JOHN II
K. of France

PETER IV
K. of Aragon

JOHN ═ ELIZABETH
K. of Bohemia of Bohemia

PHILIP VI
K. of France

ALPHONSO IV
K. of Aragon

LOUIS I
D. of Bourbon

CHARLES D. of Valois

JAMES II ═ BLANCHE
K. of Aragon

ROBERT
C. of Clermont

PHILIP III
K. of France

CHARLES II
K. of Naples

CHARLES I
K. of Naples

LOUIS IX
K. of France

BLANCHE ═ LOUIS VIII
K. of France

ELEANOR ═ ALPHONSO VIII
K. of Castile

Count of Paris, for example, is descended no less than 108 times from Henry IV of France (Table 65) who lived only 370 years ago.

The fascinating links are those which bring into the heart of Europe a strain from elsewhere. Henry I of France, a contemporary of William the Conqueror, married a Russian princess and introduced into Capetian veins a rich and alien blood. But it is more than possible that the grandmother of Henry I's wife, Queen Anne, was a Byzantine princess who transmitted the genes of the Macedonian and, conceivably, the Isaurian dynasties. At the other end of Europe the progeny of Alphonso XI of Castile (Table 48) and his wife probably derived (through her) from an earlier union between a Spanish king and a Moorish princess from Seville. It has been asserted that her father was descended from the prophet Mahomed, but Islamic descents present many problems and are apt to give scanty information on wives. If, however, this is the case, the Queen of England and all the other sovereigns shown at the head of Tables 58–9 are very distant kinsmen of the Aga Khan or the Hashemite King of Jordan. And what is true of the rulers is also true of many of their subjects.

Historically it is not possible to carry back any European pedigree beyond the ill-documented period of political unrest and upheaval which we call the Dark Ages. But men and women marry and beget, however indifferently their issue is recorded. It can scarcely be doubted that in one realm or another there still exist descendants, probably numerous, of Alexander, Augustus, or even St Augustine.

Above: Queen Victoria with her royal kindred in 1894. On her right William II of Germany, on her left the widowed Empress Frederick, her daughter. The future Edward VII (in uniform) is two behind the Kaiser.
Right: Nicholas II of Russia (left) and his first cousin, George V of England in 1913 – a striking resemblance.

could also be shown for the pretenders to vacant thrones; nor is there anything surprising in this. Alternative descents could easily be traced; for example the Princes of Monaco could be deduced through the Stuarts and the Dukes of Hamilton. Each one of us alive today would have had more than 1,100,000,000 ancestors living in 1066, if there had been no intermarriage among them. At that date the total population of the world can scarcely have exceeded 200 millions. Statistically, most of the inhabitants of western Europe are probably descended from William the Conqueror; they are equally likely to be descended from the man who groomed his charger, given that the latter was reasonably philoprogenitive. In fact, almost all ancestries are affected by confinement to a particular region and a consequent frequency of repeated ancestors. More complete records make it easier to trace this reduplication in royal families; the

Chapter 14

FRANCE: MEDIEVAL

On Christmas Day, AD 800, the Emperor Charles the Great, also known as Charlemagne, was crowned by the Pope in Rome. His dominions included what today would be France and Germany, the Low Countries and northern Italy. By the custom of the time they were divided and redivided among his descendants. A particularly crucial partition was arranged in 843, by the Treaty of Verdun, between his three grandchildren, Lothair, Louis and Charles. Louis took Germany, and Charles took France; Lothair received a rich strip running between, including the Low Countries, Lorraine, Burgundy, Provence and north Italy. His inheritance was to be the battleground of Europe for a thousand years; but from the time of Louis and Charles we can trace the fortunes of a separate Germany and France, speaking different languages.

The Carolingian rulers of France were not robust kings, and from time to time one of the great nobles seized the Crown. This happened again in 987 when Hugh Capet became king, but with a difference; the direct male descendants of Hugh continued to occupy or claim the throne of France from that day to this. The remarkable continuity of the dynasty (Table 60) is a contrast to the number of families which have ruled the other important countries of Europe. Several branches of the Capetian family have died out, but the male succession has never been in danger and is well fortified today.

The early Kings of France in the eleventh century had relatively small estates between Paris and Orléans, and were surrounded by potent, feudal vassals, the Counts of Flanders and the Dukes of Normandy in the north, the Dukes of Burgundy and the Dukes of Aquitaine in the east and south. The last-named ruled over an extensive area south of the Loire where the Langue d'Oc, a language distinct from northern French, was spoken. But the Capetian kings could

generally count on the support of the Church and were fortunate in suffering only one minority in their early days; they derived authority from their coronation at Rheims and developed the practice of crowning the eldest son in his father's lifetime. Robert II, Henry I and Philip I all contrived to maintain their position and to make some show of authority, often by playing off one feudatory against another. In particular Robert II (there had been an earlier Robert, grandfather of Hugh Capet) gained the Duchy of Burgundy, though he then conferred it on his own s e c o n d son (Table 61); and Philip survived his minority without difficulty.

Louis VI, though stout, was an active warrior and fought steadily to increase the prestige of the monarchy. He consolidated his position in his own lands and received a striking tribute when Duke William X of Aquitaine bequeathed to him his daughter and heiress Eleanor, who was promptly married to the future Louis VII. It seemed as though the Kings of France might be on the way to real power. Eleanor, however, presented Louis with nothing but daughters and was suspected of infidelity; in 1152 Louis divorced her, and she promptly married Henry II, Duke of Normandy and soon to be King of England (Table 2) – the most powerful vassal of Louis – to whom she bore more sons than he could easily control. A great opportunity had miscarried, but Louis reacted well in face of the new threat. Henry was constantly reminded that the French monarch was his overlord for all lands south of the Channel, and Louis skilfully fomented the discords among Henry's unruly family.

The beautiful French coat-of-arms, a blue field strewn with golden fleurs-de-lys, first appears on the royal seal in the reign of Louis VIII, but there is good literary evidence for its use on banners by Philip II; the fleur-de-lys is almost certainly based on the lily,

TABLE 60

FRANCE
General survey

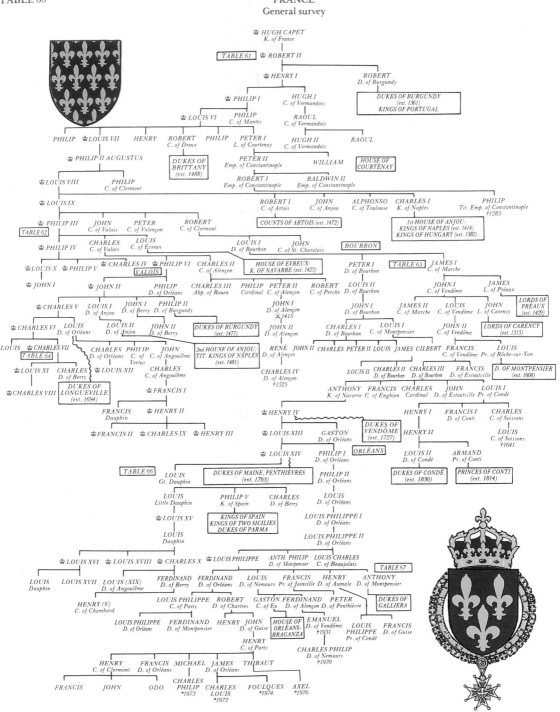

♔ HUGH CAPET
K. of France

TABLE 61 ♔ ROBERT II

♔ HENRY I

ROBERT
D. of Burgundy

DUKES OF BURGUNDY
(ext. 1361)
KINGS OF PORTUGAL

♔ PHILIP I

HUGH I
C. of Vermandois

PHILIP
C. of Mantes

RAOUL
C. of Vermandois

♔ LOUIS VI

PHILIP

PETER I
L. of Courtenay

HUGH II
C. of Vermandois

RAOUL

PHILIP ♔ LOUIS VII HENRY ROBERT
C. of Dreux

PHILIP

PETER II
Emp. of Constantinople

WILLIAM

HOUSE OF
COURTENAY

♔ PHILIP II AUGUSTUS

DUKES OF
BRITTANY
(ext. 1488)

ROBERT I
Emp. of Constantinople

BALDWIN II
Emp. of Constantinople

♔ LOUIS VIII PHILIP
C. of Clermont

♔ LOUIS IX

ROBERT I
C. of Artois

JOHN
C. of Anjou

ALPHONSO
C. of Toulouse

CHARLES I
K. of Naples

PHILIP
Tit. Emp. of Constantinople
†1283

♔ PHILIP III

TABLE 62

JOHN
C. of Valois

PETER
C. of Valençon

ROBERT
C. of Clermont

COUNTS OF ARTOIS (ext. 1472)

1st HOUSE OF ANJOU:
KINGS OF NAPLES (ext. 1414)
KINGS OF HUNGARY (ext. 1382)

♔ PHILIP IV

CHARLES
C. of Valois

LOUIS
C. of Evreux

LOUIS I
D. of Bourbon

JOHN
C. of St. Charolais

BOURBON

PETER I
D. of Bourbon

TABLE 65

JAMES I
C. of Marche

♔ LOUIS X ♔ PHILIP V ♔ CHARLES IV ♔ PHILIP VI

CHARLES II
C. of Alençon

HOUSE OF EVREUX:
K. OF NAVARRE (ext. 1425)

LOUIS II
D. of Bourbon

JOHN I
C. of Vendôme

JAMES
L. of Préaux

♔ JOHN I

VALOIS

PHILIP
D. of Orléans

CHARLES III
Abp. of Rouen

PHILIP
Cardinal

PETER II
C. of Alençon

ROBERT
C. of Perche

JOHN I
D. of Bourbon

JAMES II
C. of Marche

LOUIS
C. of Vendôme

JOHN
L. of Carency

LORDS OF
PRÉAUX
(ext. 1429)

♔ JOHN II

JOHN I
D. of Alençon
X 1415

CHARLES I
D. of Bourbon

LOUIS I
C. of Montpensier

JOHN II
C. of Vendôme

LORDS OF
CARENCY
(ext. 1515)

♔ CHARLES V

LOUIS I
D. of Anjou

JOHN I
D. of Berry

PHILIP II
D. of Burgundy

JOHN II
D. of Alençon

RENÉ
D. of Alençon

JOHN II

CHARLES
D. of Bourbon

PETER II
D. of Bourbon

LOUIS
C. of Vendôme

JAMES

GILBERT

FRANCIS
C. of Vendôme

LOUIS
Pr. of Rôche-sur-Yon

♔ CHARLES VI

LOUIS
D. of Orléans

LOUIS II
D. of Anjou

JOHN III
D. of Berry

DUKES OF BURGUNDY
(ext. 1477)

2nd HOUSE OF ANJOU:
TIT. KINGS OF NAPLES
(ext. 1481)

CHARLES IV
D. of Alençon
†1525

LOUIS II
D. of Bourbon

CHARLES II
D. of Bourbon

CHARLES III
D. of Bourbon

FRANCIS
D. of Estoutville

D. OF MONTPENSIER
(ext. 1608)

LOUIS ♔ CHARLES VII

TABLE 64

CHARLES
D. of Orléans

PHILIP
C. of
Vertus

JOHN
C. of Angoulême

ANTHONY
K. of Navarre

FRANCIS
C. of Enghien

CHARLES
Cardinal

JOHN
D. of Estoutville

LOUIS I
Pr. of Condé

♔ LOUIS XI

CHARLES
D. of Berry

♔ LOUIS XII

CHARLES
C. of Angoulême

DUKES OF
LONGUEVILLE
(ext. 1694)

♔ FRANCIS I

HENRY I

♔ HENRY IV

FRANCIS I
D. of Conti

CHARLES
C. of Soissons

♔ CHARLES VIII

FRANCIS
Dauphin

♔ HENRY II

HENRY I
D. of Condé

FRANCIS I
D. of Conti

LOUIS
C. of Soissons
†1641

♔ FRANCIS II ♔ CHARLES IX ♔ HENRY III

♔ LOUIS XIII

GASTON
D. of Orléans

DUKES OF
VENDÔME
(ext. 1727)

HENRY II

♔ LOUIS XIV

ORLÉANS

PHILIP I
D. of Orléans

LOUIS II
D. of Condé

ARMAND
Pr. of Conti

DUKES OF CONDÉ
(ext. 1830)

PRINCES OF CONTI
(ext. 1814)

TABLE 66

LOUIS
Gt. Dauphin

DUKES OF MAINE, PENTHIÈVRES
(ext. 1793)

PHILIP II
D. of Orléans

LOUIS
Little Dauphin

PHILIP V
K. of Spain

CHARLES
D. of Berry

LOUIS
D. of Orléans

♔ LOUIS XV

KINGS OF SPAIN
KINGS OF TWO SICILIES
DUKES OF PARMA

LOUIS PHILIPPE I
D. of Orléans

LOUIS
Dauphin

LOUIS PHILIPPE II
D. of Orléans

♔ LOUIS XVI ♔ LOUIS XVIII ♔ CHARLES X ♔ LOUIS PHILIPPE

ANTH. PHILIP
D. of Montpensier

LOUIS CHARLES
C. of Beaujolais

TABLE 67

LOUIS
Dauphin

LOUIS XVII

LOUIS (XIX)
D. of Angoulême

FERDINAND
D. of Berry

FERDINAND
D. of Orléans

LOUIS
D. of Nemours

FRANCIS
Pr. of Joinville

HENRY
D. of Aumale

ANTHONY
D. of Montpensier

DUKES OF
GALLIERA

HENRY (V)
C. of Chambord

LOUIS PHILIPPE
C. of Paris

ROBERT
D. of Chartres

GASTON
C. of Eu

FERDINAND
D. of Alençon

PETER
D. of Penthièvre

LOUIS PHILIPPE
D. of Orléans

FERDINAND
D. of Montpensier

HENRY
JOHN
D. of Guise

HOUSE OF
ORLÉANS-
BRAGANZA

EMANUEL
D. of Vendôme
†1931

LOUIS
PHILIPPE
Pr. of Condé

FRANCIS
D. of Guise

HENRY
C. of Paris

CHARLES PHILIP
D. of Nemours
†1970

HENRY
C. of Clermont

FRANCIS
D. of Orléans

MICHAEL

JAMES
D. of Orléans

THIBAUT

CHARLES
PHILIP
*1973

CHARLES
LOUIS
*1972

FOULQUES
*1974

AXEL
*1976

FRANCIS JOHN ODO

TABLE 61

FRANCE
Early Capetian Kings

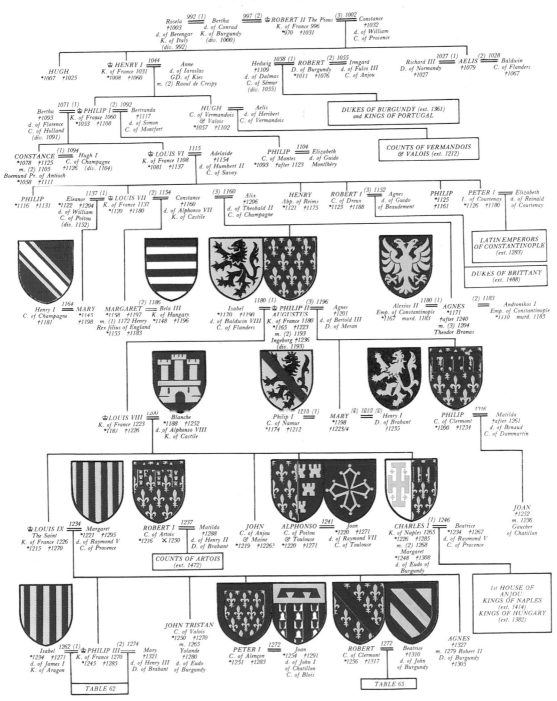

Rosela †1003 d. of Berengar K. of Italy (div. 992) — *992 (1)* — Bertha d. of Conrad K. of Burgundy (div. 1000) — ♔ ROBERT II The Pious K. of France 996 *970 †1031 — *997 (2)* — *(3) 1002* — Constance †1032 d. of William C. of Provence

HUGH *1007 †1025

♔ HENRY I K. of France 1031 *1008 †1060 — *1044* — Anne d. of Iaroslav GD. of Kiev m. (2) Raoul de Crespy

Hedwig †1109 d. of Dalmas C. of Sémur (div. 1055) — *1038 (1)* — ROBERT D. of Burgundy *1011 †1076 — *(2) 1055* — Irmgard d. of Fulco III C. of Anjou

Richard III D. of Normandy †1027 — *1027 (1)* — AELIS †1079 — *(2) 1028* — Baldwin C. of Flanders †1067

Bertha †1093 d. of Florence C. of Holland (div. 1091) — *1071 (1)* — ♔ PHILIP I K. of France 1060 *1053 †1108 — *(2) 1092* — Bertrada †1117 d. of Simon C. of Montfort

HUGH C. of Vermandois & Valois *1057 †1102 — Aelis d. of Heribert C. of Vermandois

DUKES OF BURGUNDY (ext. 1361) and KINGS OF PORTUGAL

CONSTANCE *1078 †1125 m. (2) 1105 Boemund Pr. of Antioch *1058 †1111 — *(1) 1094* — Hugh I C. of Champagne †1126 (div. 1104)

♔ LOUIS VI K. of France 1108 *1081 †1137 — *1115* — Adelaide †1154 d. of Humbert II C. of Savoy

PHILIP C. of Mantes *1093 †after 1123 — *1104* — Elizabeth d. of Guido Montlhéry

COUNTS OF VERMANDOIS & VALOIS (ext. 1212)

PHILIP *1116 †1131

Eleanor *1122 †1204 d. of William C. of Poitou (div. 1152) — *1137 (1)* — ♔ LOUIS VII K. of France 1137 *1120 †1180 — *(2) 1154* — Constance †1160 d. of Alphonso VII K. of Castile

Alix †1206 d. of Theobald II C. of Champagne — *(3) 1160*

HENRY Abp. of Reims *1121 †1175

ROBERT I C. of Dreux *1123 †1188 — *(3) 1152* — Agnes d. of Guido of Beaudement

PHILIP *1125 †1161

PETER I L. of Courtenay *1126 †1180 — Elizabeth d. of Reinald of Courtenay

LATIN EMPERORS OF CONSTANTINOPLE (ext. 1283)

DUKES OF BRITTANY (ext. 1488)

Henry I C. of Champagne †1181 — *1164* — MARY *1145 †1198

MARGARET *1158 †1197 m. (1) 1172 Rex filius of England *1155 †1183 — *(2) 1186* — Bela III K. of Hungary *1148 †1196

Isabel *1170 †1190 d. of Baldwin VIII C. of Flanders — *1180 (1)* — ♔ PHILIP II AUGUSTUS K. of France 1180 *1165 †1223 m. (2) 1193 Ingeborg †1236 (div. 1193) — *(3) 1196* — Agnes †1201 d. of Bertold III D. of Meran

Alexios II Emp. of Constantinople *1167 murd. 1183 — *1180 (1)* — AGNES *1171 †after 1240 m. (3) 1204 Theodor Branas — *(2) 1183* — Andronikos I Emp. of Constantinople *1110 murd. 1185

♔ LOUIS VIII K. of France 1223 *1187 †1226 — *1200* — Blanche *1188 †1252 d. of Alphonso VIII K. of Castile

Philip I C. of Namur *1174 †1212 — *1210 (1)* — MARY *1198 †1223/4 — *(2) 1210 (2)* — Henry I D. of Brabant †1235

PHILIP C. of Clermont *1200 †1234 — *1216* — Matilda †after 1261 d. of Renaud C. of Dammartin

JOAN †1252 m. 1236 Gaucher of Chatillon

♔ LOUIS IX The Saint K. of France 1226 *1215 †1270 — *1234* — Margaret *1221 †1295 d. of Raymond V C. of Provence

ROBERT I C. of Artois *1216 ✗ 1250 — *1237* — Matilda †1288 d. of Henry II D. of Brabant

COUNTS OF ARTOIS (ext. 1472)

JOHN C. of Anjou & Maine *1219 †1226?

ALPHONSO C. of Poitou & Toulouse *1220 †1271 — *1241* — Joan *1220 †1271 d. of Raymond VII C. of Toulouse

CHARLES I K. of Naples 1265 *1226 †1285 m. (2) 1268 Margaret *1248 †1308 d. of Eudo C. of Burgundy — *(1) 1246* — Beatrice *1234 †1267 d. of Raymond V C. of Provence

1st HOUSE OF ANJOU — KINGS OF NAPLES (ext. 1414) KINGS OF HUNGARY (ext. 1382)

Isabel *1234 †1271 d. of James I K. of Aragon — *1262 (1)* — ♔ PHILIP III K. of France 1270 *1245 †1285 — *(2) 1274* — Mary *1321 d. of Henry III D. of Brabant

JOHN TRISTAN C. of Valois *1250 †1270 m. 1265 Yolande †1280 d. of Eudo of Burgundy

PETER I C. of Alençon *1251 †1283 — *1272* — Joan *1254 †1291 d. of John I of Chatillon C. of Blois

ROBERT C. of Clermont *1256 †1317 — *1272* — Beatrice †1310 d. of John of Burgundy

AGNES †1327 m. 1279 Robert II D. of Burgundy †1305

TABLE 62

TABLE 65

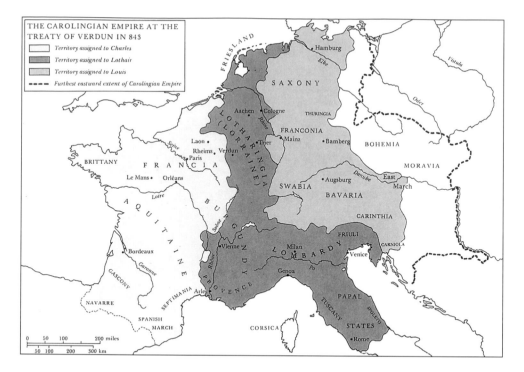

THE CAROLINGIAN EMPIRE AT THE
TREATY OF VERDUN IN 843
☐ *Territory assigned to Charles*
▨ *Territory assigned to Lothair*
▤ *Territory assigned to Louis*
━ ━ ━ *Furthest eastward extent of Carolingian Empire*

and lilies had been placed on the coinage of Louis VI
and VII. Later generations liked to think of the
flower as an emblem of the Virgin and of blue as her
colour; but it is doubtful if these sentiments prevailed
in the twelfth century. As in England the problem
arose of distinguishing cadet branches of the family;
Tables 61 and 62 reveal that the French made use of
the label and the bordure but also frequently employed the bend, or diagonal stripe. Examples of each
can be seen in the two lowest rows of Table 61;
Robert, Count of Artois (whose label reflects the
blazon of his mother), Peter, Count of Alençon, and
Robert, Count of Clermont. It will be seen that
Agnes, sister of Philip II, married the Emperor
Alexios II; the arms displayed for him are what western authorities thought he ought to use, for heraldry
in its western usage was not known in the Byzantine
Empire.

RISE OF CAPETIAN POWER

Philip Augustus was a great and successful King of
France. Talented, agile and unscrupulous, he was
able to detach large portions of the Angevin inheritance and to extend his domain in other direc-
tions: Normandy, Maine and Anjou were wrested

from John of England and he also acquired Artois
and Berry. These provinces were to provide titles for
generations of French princes. His son even invaded
England unsuccessfully at the end of the reign of
John, and during his short reign, as Louis VIII, conquered Poitou and lands in the south. Louis IX
(Saint Louis) survived the perils of minority, partly
thanks to his determined mother. He proved the pattern of medieval kingship. Austere but not weakly,
brave and just, he ruled France devotedly and also
spent much money and energy on crusades which
were less successful. We know a lot about him because
one of his admiring followers (Joinville) wrote a full
life of the holy monarch. His father had bestowed
large apanages on all his children and St Louis did
the same. One of his brothers, Charles, Duke of
Anjou, fared better still: first he married the heiress of
Raymond IV of Provence, which was not then part
of France, and secondly, at the request of the Pope,
he undertook the conquest of the Kingdom of Naples
and founded a dynasty there, which later briefly acquired Hungary also. These royal princes
could at first be controlled by the head of
the family, but later became a cause of trouble.
Robert, Count of Clermont, a son of St Louis, was the

[118]

ancestor of all the Kings of France from Henry IV onwards. It will be noticed that the arms of the wife of Louis IX (and that of Charles of Anjou), coming from Provence, and those of Isabel of Aragon, wife of Philip III, are the same, because they both belonged to branches of the same family.

One of the statesmanlike acts of St Louis was to renounce any claims south of the Pyrenees in favour of Aragon which equally gave up any claims on Languedoc. During the thirteenth century the potency of the German monarchy declined, and at the death of St Louis the Kingdom of France was the outstanding power in western Europe. This power was maintained by Philip III and Philip IV, who ruled with a series of professional advisers, well-read in law and devoted to the interests of the French monarchy. Their fortunes were linked with those of the Papacy. In 1271 Philip III inherited the wide estates of his childless uncle, Alphonse, Count of Poitou, whose arms include the blazon of his county; as an act of piety this rather colourless King bestowed upon the Pope the little County of Venaissin on the Rhône with Avignon as its chief town. His son Philip IV was a more sinister ruler, whose character is difficult to discern behind the acts of his ruthless and legalistic ministers. He became embroiled with Pope Boniface VIII, principally over the right of the lay rulers to tax the clergy of their own realms, and eventually sent agents to Italy who briefly seized the person of the Pontiff. The next Pope was a Frenchman and abandoned the turmoil of Rome for residence in Avignon.

King Philip IV made an important marriage with the heiress of Henry I, King of Navarre and also Count of Champagne (Table 69). Navarre was to pass, as has been seen, into other hands, but the Kings of France kept the rich and prosperous lands of Champagne; its chief city, Troyes, has given its name to troy weight. Philip also called, in 1302, the first meeting of the Three Estates – nobles, clergy and burgesses. In 1314 he completed his unscrupulous suppression of the Order of the Temple; the last Grand-Master was burned and is rumoured to have called upon the King to meet him hereafter. Within the year Philip was dead. He had enhanced the power of France, even if by doubtful means, and had gained some important towns on his eastern frontier, including Lyons. He also began in 1295 the long alliance with Scotland against England.

Philip IV left three sons who all succeeded to the throne, and who confronted France with the first succession problem since 987. Louis X died after a brief reign leaving a daughter and a pregnant wife; the latter gave birth to a son, John I, who lived only a few days. Promptly, Philip V, the next brother of Louis X, seized the throne. Some voices were raised in favour of his niece, Joanna, but an assembly in Paris declared that no female could inherit the throne of France. Accordingly, when Philip V died in 1322, leaving four daughters, he was naturally succeeded by his brother Charles IV, but the death of Charles IV six years later, also without sons, posed a more difficult problem.

His widow was pregnant, and Philip of Valois, the King's first cousin, was declared regent. When the Queen gave birth to a daughter, one thing was clear; Navarre would have to pass to Joanna, the senior heiress of Philip IV and his wife. But who should succeed to France? Edward III of England was male and a nephew of the late King; Philip of Valois was the nearest agnatic relation, that is by male descent. Not surprisingly the nobles who met in the capital decided in favour of their compatriot who became Philip VI, and inaugurated the House of Valois. Meanwhile Joanna married her cousin Philip, Count of Evreux, who reigned as Philip III of Navarre and whose descendants ruled there until 1425.

THE HUNDRED YEARS' WAR

Like many of his predecessors, Philip VI sought to extend his influence in Flanders. The towns of Flanders were already exceedingly prosperous centres of weaving and had a natural alliance with England which was a supplier of raw wool. Two parties in the area bore quasi-heraldic names; the mercantile upper classes, who had been linked with Philip IV against their Count, were called *leliaerts* from the lilies of France, while the lower ranks called themselves *clauwerts* (claw-men) in allusion to the lion in the arms of Flanders (Table 61, top row). By 1328 the reigning Count had allied himself to the *leliaerts* and called in the help of his overlord, Philip VI, against the workers. At the battle of Mount Cassel, the latter were massacred by the French cavalry, an event which may have given the French knights an inflated opinion of their military value. The Flemings, undaunted, turned again to England and besought Edward III to renew his claim to the Crown of France (Table 63).

As has been seen (Chapter 2) Edward responded to this challenge in 1340 by quartering the arms of France with his own as a symbol of his pretensions, and the long struggle of the Hundred Years' War began. On the one side Philip VI and his son John II, and on the other Edward III, were all very much children of their age and saw life and war in terms of chivalry. Not much strategy entered into their campaigns. In both Kingdoms the war meant increased taxation; at first it was more popular in England than in France, not least because it was fought on the soil of France with intermittent but destructive raids. The early pitched battles went in favour of England, and at Poitiers (1356), John II was captured. The

TABLE 62

FRANCE
Succession of the House of Valois

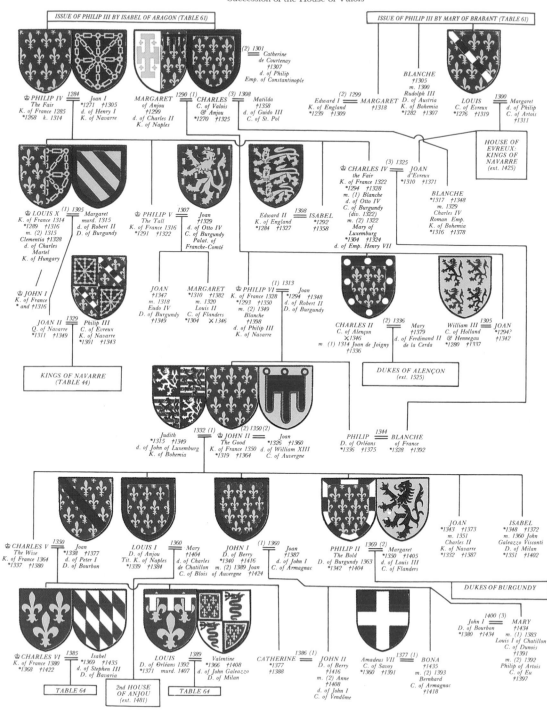

ISSUE OF PHILIP III BY ISABEL OF ARAGON (TABLE 61)

ISSUE OF PHILIP III BY MARY OF BRABANT (TABLE 61)

(2) 1301 Catherine
de Courtenay
†1307
d. of Philip
Emp. of Constantinople

♔ PHILIP IV
The Fair
K. of France 1285
*1268 k. 1314

1284 Joan I
*1271 †1305
d. of Henry I
K. of Navarre

MARGARET
of Anjou
†1299
d. of Charles II
K. of Naples

1290 (1) CHARLES
C. of Valois
& Anjou
*1270 †1325

(3) 1308 Matilda
†1358
d. of Guido III
C. of St. Pol

(2) 1299
Edward I — MARGARET
K. of England †1318
*1239 †1309

BLANCHE
†1305
m. 1300
Rudolph III
D. of Austria
K. of Bohemia
*1282 †1307

LOUIS
C. of Evreux
*1276 †1319

1300 Margaret
d. of Philip
C. of Artois
†1311

HOUSE OF
EVREUX:
KINGS OF
NAVARRE
(ext. 1425)

♔ LOUIS X
K. of France 1314
*1289 †1316
m. (2) 1315
Clementia †1328
d. of Charles
Martel
K. of Hungary

(1) 1305 Margaret
*1290 †1315
d. of Robert II
D. of Burgundy

♔ PHILIP V
The Tall
K. of France 1316
*1291 †1322

1307 Joan
†1329
d. of Otto IV
C. of Burgundy
Palat. of
Franche-Comté

Edward II — ISABEL
K. of England *1292
*1284 †1327 †1358

(3) 1325
♔ CHARLES IV — JOAN
the Fair d'Evreux
K. of France 1322 *1310 †1371
*1294 †1328
m. (1) Blanche
d. of Otto IV
C. of Burgundy
(div. 1322)
m. (2) 1322
Mary of
Luxemburg
*1304 †1324
d. of Emp. Henry VII

BLANCHE
*1317 †1348
m. 1329
Charles IV
Roman Emp.
K. of Bohemia
*1316 †1378

♔ JOHN I
K. of France
* and †1316

JOHN I
K. of France
* and †1316

JOAN II
Q. of Navarre
*1311 †1349

1329 Philip III
C. of Evreux
K. of Navarre
*1301 †1343

JOAN
†1347
m. 1318
Eudo IV
D. of Burgundy
†1349

MARGARET
*1310 †1382
m. 1320
Louis II
C. of Flanders
*1304 ✕1346

(1) 1313
♔ PHILIP VI — Joan
K. of France 1328 *1294 †1348
*1293 †1350 d. of Robert II
m. (2) 1349 D. of Burgundy
Blanche
*1398
d. of Philip III
K. of Navarre

CHARLES II
C. of Alençon
✕1346
m (1) 1314 Joan de Joigny
†1336

(2) 1336
Mary
†1379
d. of Ferdinand II
de la Cerda

William III
C. of Holland
& Hennegau
*1280 †1337

1305 JOAN
*1294?
†1342

KINGS OF NAVARRE
(TABLE 44)

DUKES OF ALENÇON
(ext. 1525)

Judith
*1315 †1349
d. of John of Luxemburg
K. of Bohemia

1332 (1) ♔ JOHN II — Joan
The Good *1326 †1360
K. of France 1350 d. of William XIII
*1319 †1364 C. of Auvergne

(2) 1350 (2)

PHILIP
D. of Orléans
*1336 †1375

1344 BLANCHE
of France
*1328 †1392

♔ CHARLES V
The Wise
K. of France 1364
*1337 †1380

1350 Joan
*1338 †1377
d. of Peter I
D. of Bourbon

LOUIS I
D. of Anjou
Tit. K. of Naples
*1339 †1384

1360 Mary
†1404
d. of Charles
de Chatillon
C. of Blois

JOHN I
D. of Berry
*1340 †1416
m. (2) 1389 Joan
d. of Auvergne
†1424

(1) 1360 Joan
†1387
d. of John I
C. of Armagnac

PHILIP II
The Bold
D. of Burgundy 1363
*1342 †1404

1369 (2) Margaret
*1350 †1405
d. of Louis III
C. of Flanders

JOAN
*1343 †1373
m. 1351
Charles II
K. of Navarre
*1332 †1387

ISABEL
*1348 †1372
m. 1360 John
Galeazzo Visconti
D. of Milan
*1351 †1402

DUKES OF BURGUNDY

♔ CHARLES VI
K. of France 1380
*1368 †1422

1385 Isabel
*1369 †1435
d. of Stephen III
D. of Bavaria

LOUIS
D. of Orléans 1392
*1371 murd. 1407

1389 Valentine
*1366 †1408
d. of John Galeazzo
D. of Milan

CATHERINE
*1377
†1388

1386 (1) JOHN II
D. of Berry
C. of Savoy
m. (2) Anne
†1408
d. of John I
C. of Vendôme

Amadeus VII
C. of Savoy
*1360 †1391

1377 (1) BONA
*1435
m. (2) 1393
Bernhard
C. of Armagnac
†1418

1400 (3)
John I — MARY
D. of Bourbon †1434
*1380 †1434 m. (1) 1383
Louis I of Chatillon
C. of Dunois
†1391
m. (2) 1392
Philip of Artois
C. of Eu
†1397

TABLE 64

2nd HOUSE
OF ANJOU
(ext. 1481)

TABLE 64

chivalry of France was quite unable to cope with the archers of England and suffered hideous losses in these battles. The condition of France was now sombre; her King was in prison and needing ransom, her treasury empty, her coinage debased and her fields devastated. There were risings of the miserable peasants known as *Jacquerie*. In 1360 peace was concluded between Edward III and the Dauphin of France; a large area of Aquitaine and also Calais was ceded to the English King absolutely while John II was to be ransomed for 3,000,000 gold crowns.

The future Charles V was the first French heir apparent to use the title of Dauphin. It was derived from the province of Dauphiné, between Savoy and Provence, whose ruler had sold it to Philip VI with the condition that the eldest son of the King of France should be so styled. One great chance fell in favour of John II. The first line of Dukes of Burgundy, descended from Robert II (Table 60), died out in the male line in 1361, and the Duchy of Burgundy, lying within France, therefore escheated to the French Crown. John II then bestowed it on his fourth son. The County of Burgundy (the later Franche-Comté), lying within the Empire of Germany, passed to the descendants of Philip V of France, but was reunited with the French province by the marriage of Philip the Bold. France was unable to raise the ransom required for John II; one of his hostages fled and with typical, if futile, chivalric spirit the King returned to London and died there.

Charles V was a very different man from his father. He was scholarly, he was not interested in battles but in law, he had a sense of order. Good fortune brought him a distinguished and successful Breton soldier, Bertrand du Guesclin, who was rewarded with the Constableship of France. Artillery was introduced into the reformed French army, pitched battles were avoided and the English conquests were gradually whittled away. With some art, the so-called Free Companies, which had been ravaging the soil of France, were lured into Spain, then, as often, the scene of civil war. Gradually the French gained command of the Channel and began to plunder the south coast harbours of England. When Charles V died in 1380, France was again in the ascendant; but triumph had not been achieved without heavy taxation. The salt-tax (*Gabelle*), first raised in 1341, had become permanent, and a crippling hearth tax had been introduced to pay the ransom (never in fact fully delivered) of King John II. If there were signs of revival, France had still not won back the position which she had held at the death of Philip IV. For this the long, savage war was a prime cause.

THE THREAT OF BURGUNDY

It will be seen that the coat-of-arms of Charles VI displays only three fleurs-de-lys (Table 69). The general view is that Charles V altered the blazon of France to this form in about 1365 and in honour of the Holy Trinity. In fact there had been a period of indecision and a pattern of only three fleurs-de-lys can be found as early as 1228 (on a seal of the town of Lens). Equally, Charles VI has the old arrangement, known briefly as 'France ancient', on his counter-seal, though he uses 'France modern' everywhere else. Some earlier writers associate the Trinity with the three petals of the fleur-de-lys. In any case the change must be associated with the reign of Charles V, and was echoed in the arms of his descendants. It is possible that the alteration was not unwelcome since it distinguished the current blazon of France from that usurped by England in 1340; but Henry IV of England adopted 'France modern' in his turn (Table 63).

Unhappily for France, the revival of her fortunes under Charles V was not maintained. Like his contemporary, Richard of England, Charles VI was a minor surrounded by powerful uncles with large estates. The Dukes of Anjou, Berry and Burgundy had no common purpose and little sense of what was needed for France. Nor had Louis, Duke of Bourbon,

King Charles VI of France (1368–1422) on an expedition, with shield and banner of France modern. 15th-century MS.

TABLE 63

FRANCE
The Hundred Years' War

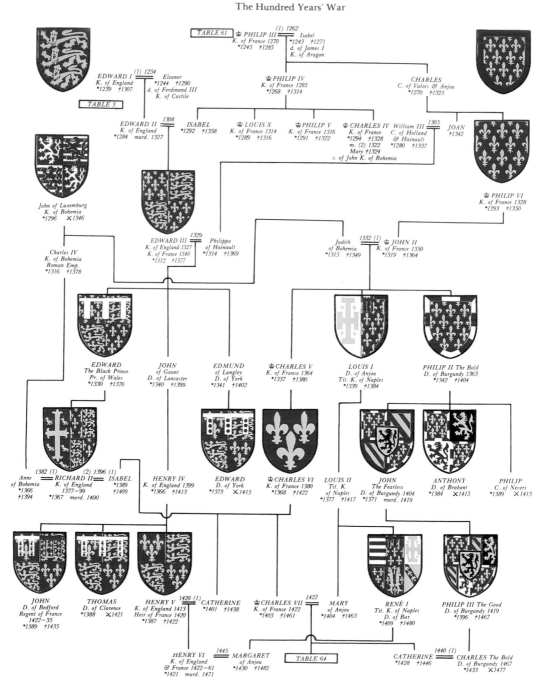

TABLE 61
♚ **PHILIP III** ══ Isabel
(1) 1262
K. of France 1270   *1243 †1271
*1245 †1285   d. of James I
K. of Aragon

EDWARD I ══ Eleanor
(1) 1254
K. of England   *1244 †1290
*1239 †1307   d. of Ferdinand III
K. of Castile

TABLE 3

♚ **PHILIP IV**
K. of France 1285
*1268 †1314

CHARLES
C. of Valois & Anjou
*1270 †1325

EDWARD II
1308
K. of England
*1284 murd. 1327

ISABEL
*1292 †1358

♚ **LOUIS X**
K. of France 1314
*1289 †1316

♚ **PHILIP V**
K. of France 1316
*1291 †1322

♚ **CHARLES IV**
K. of France
*1294 †1328
m. (2) 1322
Mary †1324
s. of John K. of Bohemia

William III ══
C. of Holland
& Hainault
*1280 †1337
1305

JOAN
†1342

John of Luxemburg
K. of Bohemia
*1296 ✕1346

♚ **PHILIP VI**
K. of France 1328
*1293 †1350

Charles IV
K. of Bohemia
Roman Emp.
*1316 †1378

EDWARD III ══ Philippa
1329
K. of England 1327   of Hainault
K. of France 1340   *1314 †1369
*1312 †1377

Judith
of Bohemia
*1315 †1349

♚ **JOHN II**
1332 (1)
K. of France 1350
*1319 †1364

EDWARD
The Black Prince
Pr. of Wales
*1330 †1376

JOHN
of Gaunt
D. of Lancaster
*1340 †1399

EDMUND
of Langley
D. of York
*1341 †1402

♚ **CHARLES V**
K. of France 1364
*1337 †1380

LOUIS I
D. of Anjou
Tit. K. of Naples
*1339 †1384

PHILIP II The Bold
D. of Burgundy 1363
*1342 †1404

Anne ══ **RICHARD II** ══ **ISABEL**
of Bohemia   K. of England   *1389
*1366   1377–99   †1409
†1394   *1367 murd. 1400
1382 (1)   (2) 1396 (1)

HENRY IV
K. of England 1399
*1366 †1413

EDWARD
D. of York
*1373 ✕1415

♚ **CHARLES VI**
K. of France 1380
*1368 †1422

LOUIS II
Tit. K.
of Naples
*1377 †1417

JOHN
The Fearless
D. of Burgundy 1404
*1371 murd. 1419

ANTHONY
D. of Brabant
*1384 ✕1415

PHILIP
C. of Nevers
*1389 ✕1415

JOHN
D. of Bedford
Regent of France
1422–35
*1389 †1435

THOMAS
D. of Clarence
*1388 ✕1421

HENRY V
K. of England 1413
Heir of France 1420
*1387 †1422

1420 (1)
CATHERINE
*1401 †1438

♚ **CHARLES VII**
K. of France 1422
*1403 †1461

1422
MARY
of Anjou
*1404 †1463

RENÉ I
Tit. K. of Naples
D. of Bar
*1409 †1480

PHILIP III The Good
D. of Burgundy 1419
*1396 †1467

HENRY VI
K. of England
& France 1422–61
*1421 murd. 1471

1445
MARGARET
of Anjou
*1430 †1482

TABLE 64

CATHERINE
*1428 †1446

1440 (1)
CHARLES The Bold
D. of Burgundy 1467
*1433 ✕1477

FRANCE
Houses of Valois-Orléans and Angoulême

TABLE 64

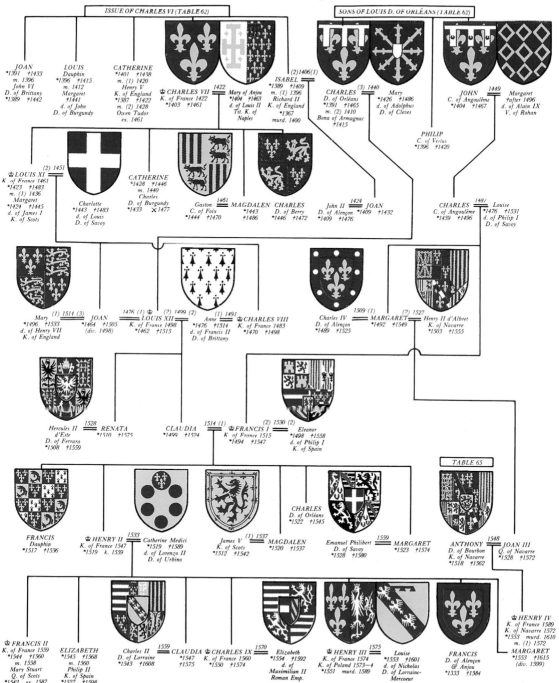

ISSUE OF CHARLES VI (TABLE 62)

SONS OF LOUIS D. OF ORLÉANS (TABLE 62)

JOAN
*1391 †1433
m. 1396
John VI
D. of Brittany
*1389 †1442

LOUIS
Dauphin
*1396 †1415
m. 1412
Margaret
†1441
d. of John
D. of Burgundy

CATHERINE
*1401 †1438
m. (1) 1420
Henry V
K. of England
*1387 †1422
m. (2) 1428
Owen Tudor
ex. 1461

♛ **CHARLES VII** — 1422 — Mary of Anjou
K. of France 1422 — *1404 †1463
*1403 †1461 — d. of Louis II
Tit. K. of
Naples

ISABEL (2)1406(1)
*1389 †1409
m. (1) 1396
Richard II
K. of England
*1367
murd. 1400

CHARLES (3) 1440 **Mary**
D. of Orléans — *1426 †1486
*1391 †1465 — d. of Adolphus
m. (2) 1410 — D. of Cleves
Bona of Armagnac
†1415

JOHN — 1449 — Margaret
C. of Angoulême — †after 1496
*1404 †1467 — d. of Alain IX
V. of Rohan

PHILIP
C. of Vertus
*1396 †1420

♛ **LOUIS XI** (2) 1451
K. of France 1461
*1423 †1483
m. (1) 1436
Margaret
*1424 †1445
d. of James I
K. of Scots

Charlotte
*1443 †1483
d. of Louis
D. of Savoy

CATHERINE
*1428 †1446
m. 1440
Charles
D. of Burgundy
*1433 × 1477

Gaston
C. of Foix
*1444 †1470

MAGDALEN — 1461
*1443
†1486

CHARLES
D. of Berry
*1446 †1472

John II — 1424 — **JOAN**
D. of Alençon — *1409 †1432
*1409 †1476

CHARLES — 1487 — Louise
C. of Angoulême — *1476 †1531
*1459 †1496 — d. of Philip I
D. of Savoy

Mary (1) 1511 (3) **JOAN**
*1496 †1533 — *1464 †1505
d. of Henry VII — (div. 1498)
K. of England

♛ **LOUIS XII** (2) 1499 (2) **Anne** (1) 1491 ♛ **CHARLES VIII**
K. of France 1498 — *1476 †1514 — K. of France 1483
*1462 †1515 — d. of Francis II — *1470 †1498
D. of Brittany

Charles IV 1509 (1) **MARGARET** (2) 1527 **Henry II d'Albret**
D. of Alençon — *1492 †1549 — K. of Navarre
*1489 †1525 — *1503 †1555

Hercules II 1528 **RENATA**
d'Este — *1510 †1575
D. of Ferrara
*1508 †1559

CLAUDIA
*1499 †1524

FRANCIS I 1514 (1) (2) 1530 (2) **Eleanor**
K. of France 1515 — *1498 †1558
*1494 †1547 — d. of Philip I
K. of Spain

TABLE 65

FRANCIS
Dauphin
*1517 †1536

♛ **HENRY II** 1533 **Catherine Medici**
K. of France 1547 — *1519 †1589
*1519 k. 1559 — d. of Lorenzo II
D. of Urbino

James V (1) 1537 **MAGDALEN**
K. of Scots — *1520 †1537
*1512 †1542

CHARLES
D. of Orléans
*1522 †1545

Emanuel Philibert 1559 **MARGARET**
D. of Savoy — *1523 †1574
*1528 †1580

ANTHONY 1548 **JOAN III**
D. of Bourbon — Q. of Navarre
K. of Navarre — *1528 †1572
*1518 †1562

♛ **FRANCIS II**
K. of France 1559
*1544 †1560
m. 1558
Mary Stuart
Q. of Scots
*1542 ex. 1587

ELIZABETH
*1545 †1568
m. 1560
Philip II
K. of Spain
*1527 †1598

Charles II 1559 **CLAUDIA** ♛ **CHARLES IX** 1570 **Elizabeth**
D. of Lorraine — *1547 †1575 — K. of France 1560 — *1554 †1592
*1543 †1608 — *1550 †1574 — d. of
Maximilian II
Roman Emp.

♛ **HENRY III** 1575 **Louise**
K. of France 1574 — *1553 †1601
K. of Poland 1573–4 — d. of Nicholas
*1551 murd. 1589 — D. of Lorraine-
Mercoeur

FRANCIS
D. of Alençon
& Anjou
*1555 †1584

♛ **HENRY IV**
K. of France 1589
K. of Navarre 1572
*1553 murd. 1610
m. (1) 1572

MARGARET
*1553 †1615
(div. 1599)

the King's maternal uncle, who shared the guardianship with Burgundy, any greater capacity for statesmanship (Table 62). The reimposition of the hearth tax brought widespread uprisings in 1382, possibly influenced by the Peasants' Revolt in England a year before. In 1388 the King, now 20, declared himself of age, but unfortunately in 1392 he had a mental collapse and was never again capable of a vigorous interest in affairs. Two of his uncles were in their way men of talent. Philip II, Duke of Burgundy, married the heiress of Flanders whose inheritance also included Franche-Comté, and was the founder of the remarkable fifteenth-century state of Burgundy. John, Duke of Berry, with his seat at Bourges, was a magnificent patron of the arts for whom splendid books were illuminated.

During the King's madness, his brother Louis, Duke of Orléans, became a rival of Burgundy. Orléans also married an heiress, the daughter of the Visconti Duke of Milan; he was a lover of literature and a profligate. The famous soldier, Dunois, was one of his bastards. Embittered relations between Orléans and John the Fearless, Duke of Burgundy (Table 63), led to the murder of Orléans in Paris by supporters of Burgundy. The stage was set for civil war. The new Duke of Orléans, Charles (Table 64), was an attractive, youthful figure, a poet of merit but doomed to spend his best years in an English prison. He had married Bona, the daughter of a tough southern French nobleman, Bernard, Count of Armagnac, who gave his name to the anti-Burgundian party and became Constable of France.

While France was sinking into internecine strife and disorder, a new and vigorous King had ascended the English throne. In 1415 Henry V invaded France; the French commanders forgot all that du Guesclin had taught them and were savagely defeated with heavy mortality at Agincourt. Among the captives were the Dukes of Orléans and Bourbon. Henry V set about the systematic reduction of northern France. In 1419 John the Fearless, Duke of Burgundy, was wantonly slain during an interview with the Dauphin, and in 1420 Henry V was able to negotiate the Treaty of Troyes whereby he married Catherine of France and was accepted as heir to the French throne.

Resistance to Henry V was still organized by the Dauphin and the Armagnacs south of the Loire; England was now linked to Burgundy. But speculation as to whether the great talents of Henry V could have enforced the Treaty of Troyes are otiose because of his unexpected and early death in 1422, a year which also saw the death of the hapless Charles VI, his father-in-law. The tide was partly turned in favour of France by the appearance in 1429 of the singular figure of Joan of Arc whose simple faith in the beastliness of the English led her to attempt their expulsion.

Later that year she successfully engineered the coronation of Charles VII at Rheims. In 1430 she was captured, and in 1431 burned for heresy; her treatment by the authorities of the Catholic Church (which canonized her 500 years later) was probably no better or worse than that of many other religious suspects. Charles VII, a weak and inconstant man, may be censured for making no effort to save her.

Nor did the tide of battle turn at once, but in 1435 a treaty was achieved between France and Burgundy; and England, now isolated, began to be preoccupied with domestic discord. The French forces were still ill-organized and often ill-led, but they paid some attention to the developing weapon of artillery. By 1453 the English had been driven out of Normandy and Gascony and only retained Calais. They did not, however, abate their claims; fresh invasion was a possibility and the rulers of England styled themselves Kings of France until 1801.

The end of his reign saw Charles VII a successful, though scarcely an estimable king. His servants were loyal, industrious, and drawn from the middle classes; the power of the nobility was tamed, though the threat of Burgundy remained. Charles never returned to Paris, which had been in English hands for much of his reign, and the Loire valley with its great châteaux set in a lovely landscape became the centre of the reunited Kingdom. His reign witnessed also an advantageous settlement with the Papacy and the beginnings of provincial *Parlements*; the *Parlement* of Paris had long been the chief law-court of the land.

WARS WITH ITALY

Louis XI, shabby, miserly, suspicious and unpompous, was none the less an important King of France. In 1465 he successfully broke a powerful aristocratic conspiracy, which included his younger brother, the Duke of Berry, and had some backing from the quasi-independent Dukes of Brittany and Burgundy, by giving the rebels good terms, which he gradually undermined in the years that followed. In 1469 he founded the Order of St Michael, whose collar surrounds his shield at the head of this chapter. His intelligence made clear to him that Burgundy was the real enemy of French development; it was lucky for him that Charles the Bold died without male heirs which made it easy for Louis to seize his French estates. An equally fortunate event was the extinction of the family of René of Anjou which gave the Crown the county of Maine, and the valuable fief of Provence across the Rhône. René of Anjou was an attractive figure. His proud blazon (Table 63) vaunts claims to the Kingdoms of Naples, Hungary and Jerusalem, but in truth he lived off his French estates in Provence and Lorraine. He was a writer in prose and verse, even a painter of a sort, and a patron of the arts interested in the work of both Italians and Flemings.

Charles VIII, delicate and romantic, was brought up by his sister Anne. By marrying the heiress of Brittany, he finally united that maritime and separatist province to the Crown. But he also began the sad series of profitless incursions into Italy which are a feature of the sixteenth century and which only added to the political distress of that turbulent peninsula. Reasserting the claim to Naples, which had been but feebly voiced by the second House of Anjou (Table 60), he invaded and swiftly conquered south Italy. His licentious army provoked a rapid reaction and he was as swiftly flung back into France, though with considerable booty. Dying childless, he was succeeded by his cousin Louis XII, the head of the House of Orléans, who had ambitions on Milan as the descendant of the Visconti (Table 62), and occasionally quartered their alarming, serpentine arms (sometimes alleged to refer to a monster slain by the founder of the family). For 12 years he held Milan (1500–12), Naples was won and lost, but he gained nothing permanent.

His cousin and heir, Francis I, was young, handsome and high-spirited, a generous lover of the arts. Again the lure of Italy was too much for him, but four successive wars against the Emperor Charles V, in one of which Francis himself was captured at Pavia (1525), brought little in the way of enduring success. He used a famous badge of a salamander amid flames which is widely displayed on his castles in the Loire valley, or at Fontainebleau. Francis I also began the palace of the Louvre in Paris, today one of the great museums of the world. The shield of his eldest son, Francis, who predeceased his father, has the arms of the Dauphin quartered with those of the heir of Brittany. His son Henry II carried on the struggle against Charles V. Calais was captured from the English, but in 1559 a moment of realism prevailed and he finally abandoned the Italian claims of France at the Treaty of Cateau-Cambrésis. Later in the same year he was accidentally killed in one of the tournaments which were so popular and lavish an entertainment. Henry married the Florentine, Catherine dei Medici. Her family originally bore six red roundels, but Louis XI had granted them the right of turning the uppermost into a roundel of France.

WARS OF RELIGION

The preoccupation of France with Italy was replaced by the equally disastrous wars of religion. Protestantism had grown in France in the reigns of Francis I and his son, and had been persecuted fairly savagely: none the less it spread over much of the country. By ill fortune none of the children of Henry II were strong rulers. Francis II was sickly and reigned but a

year; Charles IX was unbalanced and died young; Henry III, though valiant in youth, proved an effeminate king under the influence of men friends. All died childless. Much influence devolved upon Catherine the Queen Mother and also on the House of Lorraine and its junior branch the Dukes of Guise, to which the mother of Queen Mary Stuart belonged. Catherine dei Medici strove for peace and toleration, but often by paths so serpentine as to arouse suspicion.

The Guise faction led the Catholics; the reformers looked to the Kings of Navarre, heads of the House of Bourbon and (if the Valois died out, as became increasingly probable) heirs male of France. It would be tedious to trace the long and savage conflict in detail: both sides enlisted foreign aid. The future Henry III, while still Duke of Anjou, was suggested as a husband for Elizabeth of England; indeed on the strength of battles gained against the Huguenots (as the Protestants were termed) he was actually chosen King of Poland (1573–4). At one point (1561) the Third Estate even contemplated the complete nationalization of the Church. In 1570 an agreement was reached, of which one clause arranged for the marriage of the King's sister to Henry of Navarre. This wedding took place in Paris in August 1572. A week later, on the feast of St Bartholomew, a ghastly massacre of the Huguenots, who had flocked to Paris, was organized: several thousand were butchered by the Paris mob and the hirelings of the Guise faction. The Pope celebrated with a Mass, and Philip II of Spain smiled; happily Henry escaped.

The war broke out again; by now many moderate men, the *Politiques*, were moving towards the Protestant side. Power at the court was increasingly usurped by the Guises and the fanatical Catholic League, particularly strong in Paris. Eventually the unmanly Henry III was goaded into murdering the Duke of Guise and his brother the Cardinal. When the degenerate monarch was himself assassinated by a crackpot friar, opinion rallied on all sides to Henry of Navarre: his military talents were already clear, his shrewdness was evident and a long list of gallantries attested his virility. Henry IV was a realist and after fighting for some years to establish order, he announced his conversion to the Catholic faith. Only then was he able to enter Paris.

The middle years of this sombre century in French history were ennobled by a group of poets – the *Pléiade* – who, headed by Pierre de Ronsard, strove to improve the lyric verse of their language and who introduced the sonnet to France. Henry III also established the Order of the Holy Ghost, which replaced that of St Michael as the principal order of France; its insignia can be seen on Table 60 and at the head of the next chapter.

Chapter 15

FRANCE: MODERN

The accession of the Protestant Henry IV, already King of Navarre, to the throne of France in 1589 did not bring immediate peace. The bitter dissensions and the harsh doctrinal persecutions of the long religious wars were not to be dispelled overnight. Although Henry adopted the Catholic faith in 1593, he was not able to enter Paris until the following year. His conversion was one of policy rather than belief: 'Paris is well worth a Mass', he is reputed to have exclaimed. In 1598 by the Edict of Nantes he gave liberty of worship to the Protestants of France; and as the seventeenth century dawned France was gathering her powers and resources for the great role which lay ahead of her. The basic difference between Henry IV and the effete and shadowy Valois kings whom he followed, was Henry's concern for the ordinary folk of France. He worked, with his great minister and friend, the Duke of Sully, for prosperity as well as peace: agriculture was encouraged, roads built, commerce fostered, and above all the national debt was redeemed and taxation meanwhile actually reduced. When the knife of a deranged Catholic assassin ended Henry's life, the Kingdom was almost miraculously different from its condition 21 years earlier.

It can be seen that Henry IV was only a remote relation of Henry III, but both were descended from St Louis IX, and they became brothers-in-law. The throne of Navarre had passed, as has been explained, to the daughter of Louis X who married her cousin, the Count of Evreux (Table 62). Their male descendants gave out in 1425, and marriages were made with two local families, the Counts of Foix and the Lords of Albret. In 1512 Ferdinand of Aragon wrested from John d'Albret (see also Chapter 10) that part of Navarre which lay south of the Pyrenees, leaving him only lower Navarre. None the less Henry IV of France added the ancient arms of Navarre to those of France (Table 65); although it

has been suggested, the elaborate pattern of chains is probably not a pun on the Spanish words *una vara* – a chain. This shield was used occasionally by Louis XIII but abandoned by Louis XIV.

The first wife of Henry IV was barren, and he divorced her accordingly. For his second he chose Mary, daughter of the Grand-Duke of Tuscany and a cousin of Catherine dei Medici, wife of Henry II. It was part of an Italian policy aimed against Spain, in pursuit of which Henry IV also won from Savoy the two Duchies of Bresse and Bugey. His sudden death altered the situation. His widow became regent for the youthful Louis XIII, and arranged a Spanish wife for him. The moment of his majority (1614) saw the last summons of the Estates General (the Three Estates) until 1789. Once in power, Louis set himself to reduce the might of the nobility and to curb the separatism of the Huguenot communities in the southern half of the Kingdom, The latter was achieved by the Treaty of Montpellier (1622), a year which also saw the entry into the King's council of Cardinal Richelieu whose statesmanship dominated the remainder of the reign.

Richelieu was not concerned, as were Henry IV and Sully, with internal reforms and prosperity: his dominant concern was for the expansion and prestige of France. The branches of the Hapsburg family controlled the Low Countries (approximately the Belgium of today), the Empire of Germany, Spain and Portugal. The Cardinal endeavoured to extend the frontiers of France and thus react against the threat of encirclement. To do this he was prepared to ally himself with Catholics or non-Catholics as circumstances suggested; it was a naked display of power politics. By intervening in the Thirty Years' War in Germany (1635) he changed the character of that struggle from a religious to a dynastic contest. In 1648 France gained Alsace and some lands in

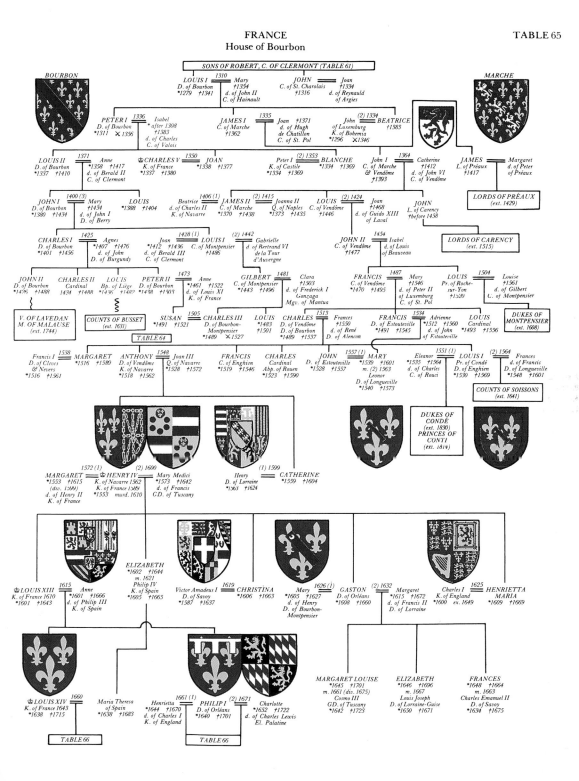

SONS OF ROBERT, C. OF CLERMONT (TABLE 61)

BOURBON

MARCHE

LOUIS I 1310 *Mary* | **JOHN** = *Joan*
D. of Bourbon †1354 | C. of St. Charolais †1334
*1279 †1341 d. of John II †1316 | d. of Reynauld
C. of Hainault | of Argies

PETER I 1336 *Isabel* | **JAMES I** 1335 *Joan* †1371 | **John** (2) 1334 **BEATRICE**
D. of Bourbon *after 1308 | C. of Marche d. of Hugh | of Luxemburg †1383
*1311 ✕1356 †1383 | †1362 de Chatillon | K. of Bohemia
d. of Charles | †1362 | *1296 ✕1346
C. of Valois

LOUIS II 1371 *Anne* †1358 †1417 | ✠**CHARLES V** 1350 **JOAN** | *Peter I* (2) 1353 **BLANCHE** | **John I** 1364 *Catherine* | **JAMES** = *Margaret*
D. of Bourbon d. of Berald II | K. of France *1338 †1377 | K. of Castile *1334 †1369 | C. of Marche †1412 | L. of Préaux d. of Peter
*1337 †1410 C. of Clermont | *1337 †1380 | *1334 †1369 | & Vendôme d. of John VI | †1417 of Préaux
| | | †1393 C. of Vendôme

LORDS OF PRÉAUX
(ext. 1429)

JOHN I 1400 (3) *Mary* †1434 | **LOUIS** | *Beatrice* | **JAMES II** (2) 1415 *Joanna II* | **LOUIS** (2) 1424 *Joan* | **JOHN**
D. of Bourbon d. of John I | *1388 †1404 | d. of Charles III C. of Marche Q. of Naples | C. of Vendôme †1468 | L. of Carency
*1380 †1434 of Berry | | K. of Navarre *1370 †1438 *1373 †1435 | †1446 d. of Guido XIII | †before 1458
| | of Laval

LORDS OF CARENCY
(ext. 1515)

CHARLES I 1425 *Agnes* | *Joan* 1428 (1) **LOUIS I** | (2) 1442 *Gabrielle* | **JOHN II** 1454 *Isabel*
D. of Bourbon *1407 †1476 | *1412 †1436 C. of Montpensier | d. of Bertrand VI | C. of Vendôme d. of Louis
*1401 †1456 d. of John | d. of Berald III †1486 | de la Tour | †1477 of Beauveau
D. of Burgundy | C. of Clermont | d'Auvergne

JOHN II **CHARLES II** **LOUIS** **PETER II** 1473 *Anne* | **GILBERT** 1481 *Clara* | **FRANCIS** 1487 *Mary* | **LOUIS** 1504 *Louise*
D. of Bourbon Cardinal Bp. of Liège D. of Bourbon *1461 †1522 | C. of Montpensier †1503 | C. of Vendôme †1546 | Pr. of Roche- *1561
*1426 †1488 1434 †1488 *1436 †1482 *1438 †1503 d. of Louis XI | *1443 †1496 d. of Frederick I | *1470 †1495 d. of Peter II | sur-Yon d. of Gilbert
K. of France | Gonzaga | C. of St. Pol | †1520 C. of Montpensier
| Mgv. of Mantua

V. OF LAVEDAN
M. OF MALAUSE
(ext. 1744)

COUNTS OF BUSSET
(ext. 1631)

SUSAN 1505 **CHARLES III** **LOUIS** **CHARLES** 1513 *Frances* | **FRANCIS** 1534 *Adrienne* | **LOUIS** | DUKES OF
*1491 †1521 D. of Bourbon- *1483 †1501 D. of Vendôme †1550 | D. of Estouteville *1512 †1560 | Cardinal MONTPENSIER
Montpensier D. of Bourbon d. of René | *1491 †1545 d. of John | *1493 †1556 (ext. 1608)
*1489 ✕1527 *1489 †1537 D. of Alençon | of Estouteville

TABLE 64

Francis I 1538 **MARGARET** **ANTHONY** 1548 *Joan III* | **FRANCIS** **CHARLES** **JOHN** 1557 (1) **MARY** | *Eleanor* 1551 (1) **LOUIS I** (2) 1564 *Frances*
D. of Cleves *1516 †1589 D. of Vendôme Q. of Navarre | C. of Enghien Cardinal D. of Estouteville *1539 †1601 | *1535 †1564 Pr. of Condé d. of Francis
& Nevers K. of Navarre *1528 †1572 | *1519 †1546 Abp. of Rouen *1528 †1557 m. (2) 1563 | d. of Charles D. of Enghien D. of Longueville
*1516 †1561 *1518 †1562 | *1523 †1590 Leonor | C. of Rouci *1530 †1569 *1548 †1601
| D. of Longueville

COUNTS OF SOISSONS
(ext. 1641)

DUKES OF
CONDÉ
(ext. 1830)
PRINCES OF
CONTI
(ext. 1814)

MARGARET 1572 (1) ✠**HENRY IV** (2) 1600 *Mary Medici* | *Henry* (1) 1599 **CATHERINE**
*1553 †1615 K. of Navarre 1562 *1573 †1642 | D. of Lorraine *1559 †1604
(div. 1599) K. of France 1589 d. of Francis | *1563 †1624
d. of Henry II *1553 murd. 1610 GD. of Tuscany
K. of France

✠**LOUIS XIII** 1615 *Anne* | *Victor Amadeus I* 1619 **CHRISTINA** | *Mary* 1626 (1) **GASTON** (2) 1632 *Margaret* | *Charles I* 1625 **HENRIETTA**
K. of France 1610 *1601 †1666 | D. of Savoy *1606 †1663 | *1605 †1627 D. of Orléans *1615 †1672 | K. of England **MARIA**
*1601 †1643 d. of Philip III | *1587 †1637 | d. of Henry *1608 †1660 d. of Francis II | *1600 ex. 1649 *1609 †1669
K. of Spain | D. of Bourbon- | D. of Lorraine
| Montpensier

ELIZABETH
*1602 †1644
m. 1621
Philip IV
K. of Spain
*1605 †1665

✠**LOUIS XIV** 1660 *Maria Theresa* | *Henrietta* 1661 (1) **PHILIP I** (2) 1671 *Charlotte* | **MARGARET LOUISE** **ELIZABETH** **FRANCES**
K. of France 1643 of Spain | *1644 †1670 D. of Orléans *1652 †1722 | *1645 †1701 *1646 †1696 *1648 †1664
*1638 †1715 *1638 †1683 | d. of Charles I *1640 †1701 d. of Charles Lewis | m. 1661 (div. 1675) m. 1667 m. 1663
| K. of England El. Palatine | Cosmo III Louis Joseph Charles Emanuel II
| GD. of Tuscany D. of Lorraine-Guise D. of Savoy
| *1642 †1723 *1650 †1671 *1634 †1675

TABLE 66

TABLE 66

Lorraine at the Treaty of Westphalia. Military success came slowly and only at the battle of Rocroy in 1643 did the Duke of Condé (Louis II: see Table 60) achieve supremacy over the famous Spanish infantry. Richelieu fostered French expansion abroad, especially in Canada (Quebec had been founded in 1608) and encouraged the navy and shipping. Numerous aristocratic conspiracies against him were answered by resolute decapitations of even the greatest nobles. He must stand high in any list of French statesmen.

LOUIS XIV

Louis XIV, the most remarkable of the Bourbons, was only four when his father died, and was to reign for the vast span of 72 years. Until 1661, his mother, Anne of Austria, was regent, relying on the Italian Cardinal Mazarin (a nominee of Richelieu) as her chief minister. Mazarin continued the policies of Richelieu and reaped his triumphs, in particular at the Treaty of Westphalia, which left Germany fragmented and brought French frontiers to the Rhine. But, like his mentor, Mazarin had little ability with finance: taxation continued to be oppressive, and not surprisingly reaction took place among the nobles and in the *Parlement* of Paris. Two rebellions, known as the first and second Frondes, broke out in 1648 and 1651–2, the second led by the Duke of Condé, but the

King Louis XIV of France (1638–1715), by H. Rigaud, 1701. He wore high heels to enhance his height.

adroit and unscrupulous Cardinal was successful in dividing or buying off his enemies, often with promises which he neither kept nor intended to keep. The young King had observed with horror how he was driven from his capital by a factious nobility, and resolved that their power should be broken for ever. In 1659 Mazarin ended the long war with Spain: France acquired Rousillon in the south and large extensions in Flanders and Hainault on her northern border. Furthermore Louis was married to the eldest daughter of the King of Spain.

From 1661 Louis XIV ruled himself. He took kingship very seriously, even wearing high heels to neutralize his shortness. Periwigged and dignified, he combined an air of authority with immense assiduity for business. He chose his servants well: Colbert was an exceedingly able financier, with a correct sense of the needs of his country's economy. If he had had some grasp of international economics, he would have been a genius: as it was, he promoted French expansion in new colonies and ordered the budget at home. On his successes Louis was able to build the most splendid court yet seen in Europe, centred on his new palace at Versailles. France became the arbiter of fashion for Europe. Corneille, Racine and Molière contributed the lustre of their verse. The proud nobility of France were entrapped in the ceremonial which hedged the King, neglecting their estates and divorced from any real power. If France could have eschewed European wars, she might have dominated the world overseas.

However, the ambitions of Louis were orthodox: he lusted to extend the boundaries of France. In the War of Devolution (1667–8) he acquired from Spain more territory on the northern frontier, including the strongest fortresses in the area. The only resistance came from the United Provinces (the modern Holland); in 1672 a combination of prestige and economic rivalry prompted Louis to attack them in their turn. But the Dutch put up a devoted and desperate resistance to the armies of France, even flooding their own low-flying fields in defence of their towns. Allies came to their aid, and by 1678 Louis was glad to make peace: he gained the province of Franche-Comté on the east and something of Lorraine, but he had in fact failed in his bid to become master of Europe. Moreover there had appeared an antagonist, William III, ruler in Holland and later King of England, who was passionately resolved to frustrate the ambitions of Louis.

In 1685 Louis committed a grave blunder in domestic policy. Growing pious with age, he revoked the Edict of Nantes; the Huguenots, rather than submit to the loss of their liberty, emigrated in large numbers to England, Holland and Brandenburg, taking with them their industry and technical skill.

Once again, from 1688 to 1697, Louis engaged, without allies, in war along his northern frontiers. His generals won victories but they could not overcome William III and his combinations. The ensuing peace brought France nothing.

Then, in 1700, the weak and childless King of Spain died. For a generation the Powers of Europe had been discussing the division of the scattered Spanish domains in the New World and the Old, and agreement had been reached. But the dying King in fact left all his lands to Philip of Anjou, grandson of Louis XIV. After hesitation Louis accepted the fateful legacy, to be confronted by a united and outraged Europe. In the War of the Spanish Succession which followed, Britain produced a consummate general, the Duke of Marlborough. By the Treaty of Utrecht, Philip of Anjou (Philip V of Spain) held Spain and the Indies; the Spanish territories in the Low Countries and Italy passed to Austria. It was laid down that the Crowns of France and Spain were never to be united. Two years later, in 1715, Louis XIV himself died. The last years of his reign had seen almost continual warfare against the odds and for small profit – except to the Bourbon dynasty, now established on both sides of the Pyrenees. England gained many advantages overseas, including the Rock of Gibraltar.

THE AGE OF REASON

The aged, but still glorious, ruler of France had seen son and grandson precede him to the tomb, and was succeeded by Louis XV, a child of five. The ancestry of Louis XIV – the Sun King – is set out on Table 68; it is ironical that more than half of his forbears belonged to one branch or another of the Hapsburgs against whom he waged so many wars; only on his grandfather's side had he much French blood. By contrast the grandparents of Louis XVI show a much wider spread, with a strong mixture of Polish and German families.

Philip II, Duke of Orléans (Table 66), was regent for the young King. Able but debauched, he was hostile to many of the ideas of Louis XIV, including his piety. Life in Paris became more gay and more dissolute, and Louis XV grew up in a tainted atmosphere, surrounded by an aristocracy mindful of days when it played an active part in public life. It was a period of lost opportunities for France. Her financial system, especially taxation with its medieval network of local variation and exemptions, mainly for the rich, called out for reform. Except during the ascendancy of Cardinal Fleury, the country was involved too long in profitless war. Louis XV lacked the capacity for autocratic rule but failed to give his confidence to any chief minister. Energy which might have profited France overseas was squandered on the battlefields of Europe. Intermittently from 1742 to 1763 France and England were at war. The struggle began with the death of Charles VI, the last male Hapsburg Emperor (1740). All Europe had sworn to accept his daughter as Empress: led by Frederick of Prussia her neighbours broke their oaths to attack the young Queen. England came to her aid; the war in Europe had many vicissitudes and fresh perjuries by Prussia, but it was on the sea and in their colonial settlements overseas that the rivalry of France and Great Britain was keenest. By 1763 France had lost her influence in India and Canada.

The prestige of France still stood high. Her manners were copied, her writers admired, her language became the speech of diplomacy. In literature a critical spirit was dominant; whether in the spry genius of Voltaire, the 34 volumes of Diderot's Encyclopedia, or the misty doctrines of Rousseau, whatever was established was analyzed and censured. The age of reason was replacing the age of faith.

The death of Louis XV in 1774 brought to the throne his grandson, the blameless, stupid and pathetic Louis XVI. His reign began with a triumph over England: aid given to the American colonists in revolt ensured the emergence and independence of the United States; but the victory did nothing to improve the tottering finances of French government or to glorify the image of monarchy. One of his abler ministers described France as 'a kingdom of separate states and countries ... where privilege has upset all equilibrium ... impossible to govern'. The country was not poor; but its assets were ill-distributed and ill-organized. In 1789 the States-General, as a desperate measure, were summoned for the first time since the opening years of Louis XIII's reign; to the surprise of the King they turned themselves into a single National Assembly and began constitution-making. On 14 July (the French national holiday since then) the Paris mob stormed the Bastille, in truth an obsolescent prison, in fiction the symbol of tyranny. Step by step the Revolution grew in scope, until in 1793 the Republic despatched the ex-King ('citizen Capet') to the guillotine. His little son, the titular Louis XVII, was alleged to have died in prison, but many contradictions and uncertainties surrounded his death.

REPUBLICAN FRANCE

The process by which the Republic of France became a Consulate, and the Consulate an Empire (Chapter 16) does not concern the exiled Bourbons. In 1814 the victorious allies installed the middle-aged Count of Provence, younger brother of Louis XVI, as King Louis XVIII. The Bourbons, according to their enemies, had learned nothing and forgotten nothing. The new King, gouty, childless and halt, had none

TABLE 66

FRANCE
End of the monarchy

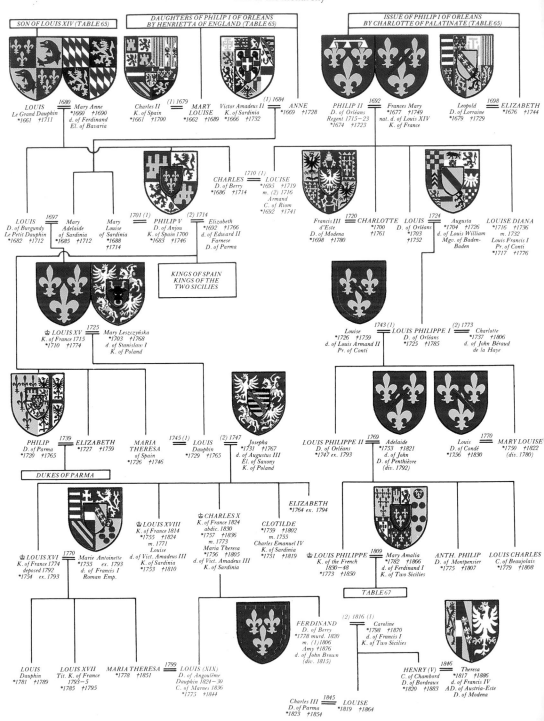

SON OF LOUIS XIV (TABLE 65)

DAUGHTERS OF PHILIP I OF ORLEANS BY HENRIETTA OF ENGLAND (TABLE 65)

ISSUE OF PHILIP I OF ORLEANS BY CHARLOTTE OF PALATINATE (TABLE 65)

LOUIS
Le Grand Dauphin
*1661 †1711

1680 **Mary Anne**
*1660 †1690
d. of Ferdinand
El. of Bavaria

Charles II
K. of Spain
*1661 †1700

(1) 1679 **MARY LOUISE**
*1662 †1689

Victor Amadeus II
K. of Sardinia
*1666 †1732

(1) 1684 **ANNE**
*1669 †1728

PHILIP II
D. of Orléans
Regent 1715–23
*1674 †1723

1692 **Frances Mary**
*1677 †1749
nat. d. of Louis XIV
K. of France

Leopold
D. of Lorraine
*1679 †1729

1698 **ELIZABETH**
*1676 †1744

CHARLES
D. of Berry
*1686 †1714

1710 (1) **LOUISE**
*1695 †1719
m. (2) 1716
Armand
C. of Riom
*1692 †1741

LOUIS
D. of Burgundy
Le Petit Dauphin
*1682 †1712

1697 **Mary Adelaide of Sardinia**
*1685 †1712

Mary Louise of Sardinia
*1688 †1714

1701 (1) **PHILIP V**
D. of Anjou
K. of Spain 1700
*1683 †1746

(2) 1714 **Elizabeth**
*1692 †1766
d. of Edward II
Farnese
D. of Parma

Francis III d'Este
D. of Modena
*1698 †1780

1720 **CHARLOTTE**
*1700 †1761

LOUIS
D. of Orléans
*1703 †1752

1724 **Augusta**
*1704 †1726
d. of Louis William
Mgv. of Baden-Baden

LOUISE DIANA
*1716 †1736
m. 1732
Louis Francis I
Pr. of Conti
*1717 †1776

KINGS OF SPAIN
KINGS OF THE TWO SICILIES

♔ **LOUIS XV**
K. of France 1715
*1710 †1774

1725 **Mary Leszczyńska**
*1703 †1768
d. of Stanislaw I
K. of Poland

Louise
*1726 †1759
d. of Louis Armand II
Pr. of Conti

1743 (1) **LOUIS PHILIPPE I**
D. of Orléans
*1725 †1785

(2) 1773 **Charlotte**
*1737 †1806
d. of John Béraud
de la Haye

PHILIP
D. of Parma
*1720 †1765

1739 **ELIZABETH**
*1727 †1759

MARIA THERESA
of Spain
*1726 †1746

1745 (1) **LOUIS**
Dauphin
*1729 †1765

(2) 1747 **Josepha**
*1731 †1767
d. of Augustus III
El. of Saxony
K. of Poland

LOUIS PHILIPPE II
D. of Orléans
*1747 ex. 1793

1769 **Adelaide**
*1753 †1821
d. of John
D. of Penthièvre
(div. 1792)

Louis
D. of Condé
*1756 †1830

1770 **MARY LOUISE**
*1750 †1822
(div. 1780)

DUKES OF PARMA

ELIZABETH
*1764 ex. 1794

♔ **LOUIS XVIII**
K. of France 1814
abdic. 1830
*1755 †1824
m. 1771
Louise
d. of Vict. Amadeus III
K. of Sardinia
*1753 †1810

♔ **CHARLES X**
K. of France 1824
abdic. 1830
*1757 †1836
m. 1773
Maria Theresa
*1756 †1805
d. of Vict. Amadeus III
K. of Sardinia

CLOTILDE
*1759 †1802
m. 1755
Charles Emanuel IV
K. of Sardinia
*1751 †1819

♔ **LOUIS XVI**
K. of France 1774
deposed 1792
*1754 ex. 1793

1770 **Marie Antoinette**
*1755 ex. 1793
d. of Francis I
Roman Emp.

♔ **LOUIS PHILIPPE**
K. of the French
1830–48
*1773 †1850

1809 **Mary Amalia**
*1782 †1866
d. of Ferdinand I
K. of Two Sicilies

ANTH. PHILIP
D. of Montpensier
*1775 †1807

LOUIS CHARLES
C. of Beaujolais
*1779 †1808

TABLE 67

LOUIS
Dauphin
*1781 †1789

LOUIS XVII
Tit. K. of France
1793–5
*1785 †1795

MARIA THERESA
*1778 †1851

1799 **LOUIS (XIX)**
D. of Angoulême
Dauphin 1824–30
C. of Marnes 1836
*1775 †1844

FERDINAND
D. of Berry
*1778 murd. 1820
m. (1)1806
Amy †1876
d. of John Brown
(div. 1815)

(2) 1816 (1) **Caroline**
*1798 †1870
d. of Francis I
K. of Two Sicilies

HENRY (V)
C. of Chambord
D. of Bordeaux
*1820 †1883

1846 **Theresa**
*1817 †1886
d. of Francis IV
AD. of Austria-Este
D. of Modena

Charles III
D. of Parma
*1823 †1854

1845 **LOUISE**
*1819 †1864

House of Orléans (nineteenth and twentieth centuries)

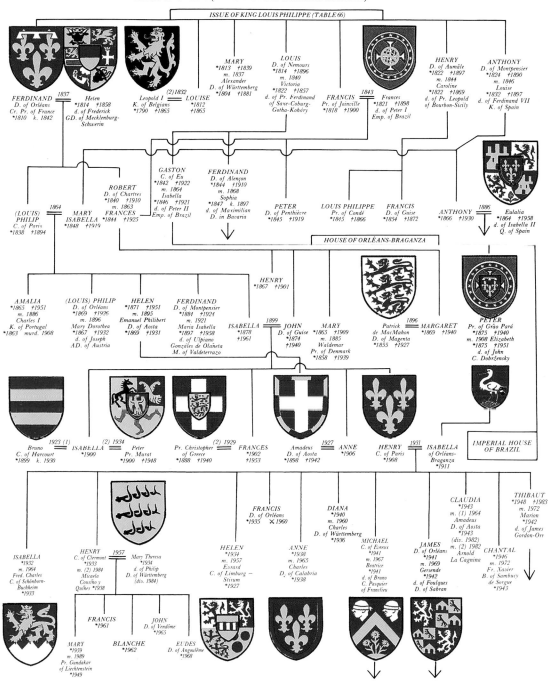

ISSUE OF KING LOUIS PHILIPPE (TABLE 66)

MARY
*1813 †1839
m. 1837
Alexander
D. of Württemberg
*1804 †1881

LOUIS
D. of Nemours
*1814 †1896
m. 1840
Victoria
d. of Pr. Ferdinand
of Saxe-Coburg-
Gotha-Koháry

HENRY
D. of Aumâle
*1822 †1897
m. 1844
Caroline
*1822 †1869
d. of Pr. Leopold
of Bourbon-Sicily

ANTHONY
D. of Montpensier
*1824 †1890
m. 1846
Louise
*1832 †1897
d. of Ferdinand VII
K. of Spain

FERDINAND   1837
D. of Orléans
Cr. Pr. of France
*1810 k. 1842

Helen
*1814 †1858
d. of Frederick
GD. of Mecklenburg-
Schwerin

Leopold I
K. of Belgians
*1790 †1865

(2)1832
LOUISE
*1812
†1865

FRANCIS   1843
Pr. of Joinville
*1818 †1900

Frances
*1821 †1898
d. of Peter I
Emp. of Brazil

GASTON
C. of Eu
*1842 †1922
m. 1864
Isabella
*1846 †1921
d. of Peter II
Emp. of Brazil

FERDINAND
D. of Alençon
*1844 †1910
m. 1868
Sophia
*1847 k. 1897
d. of Maximilian
D. in Bavaria

PETER
D. of Penthièvre
*1845 †1919

LOUIS PHILIPPE
Pr. of Condé
*1845 †1866

FRANCIS
D. of Guise
*1854 †1872

ANTHONY   1886
*1866 †1930

Eulalia
*1864 †1958
d. of Isabella II
Q. of Spain

ROBERT
D. of Chartres
*1840 †1910
m. 1863
FRANCES *1844 †1925

(LOUIS)
PHILIP
C. of Paris
*1838 †1894

1864

MARY
ISABELLA
*1848 †1919

HOUSE OF ORLÉANS-BRAGANZA

HENRY
*1867 †1901

AMALIA
*1865 †1951
m. 1886
Charles I
K. of Portugal
*1863 murd. 1908

(LOUIS) PHILIP
D. of Orléans
*1869 †1926
m. 1896
Mary Dorothea
*1867 †1932
d. of Joseph
AD. of Austria

HELEN
*1871 †1951
m. 1895
Emanuel Philibert
D. of Aosta
*1869 †1931

FERDINAND
D. of Montpensier
*1884 †1924
m. 1921
Maria Isabella
*1897 †1958
d. of Ulpiano
Gonzáles de Olañeta
M. of Valdeterrazo

ISABELLA
*1878
†1961

JOHN   1899
D. of Guise
*1874
†1940

MARY
*1865 †1909
m. 1885
Waldemar
Pr. of Denmark
*1858 †1939

Patrick   1896
de MacMahon
D. of Magenta
*1855 †1927

MARGARET
*1869 †1940

PETER
Pr. of Grão Pará
*1875 †1940
m. 1908 Elizabeth
*1875 †1951
d. of John
C. Dobřzensky

Bruno   1923 (1)
C. of Harcourt
*1899 k. 1930

ISABELLA   (2) 1934
*1900

Peter
Pr. Murat
*1900 †1948

Pr. Christopher   (2) 1929
of Greece
*1888 †1940

FRANCES
*1902
†1953

Amadeus   1927
D. of Aosta
*1898 †1942

ANNE
*1906

HENRY   1931
C. of Paris
*1908

ISABELLA
of Orléans-
Braganza
*1911

IMPERIAL HOUSE
OF BRAZIL

CLAUDIA
*1943
m. (1) 1964
Amadeus
D. of Aosta
*1943
(div. 1982)
m. (2) 1982
Arnold
La Cagnina

THIBAUT
*1948 †1983
m. 1972
Marion
*1942
d. of James
Gordon-Orr

FRANCIS
D. of Orléans
*1935 × 1960

DIANA
*1940
m. 1960
Charles
D. of Württemberg
*1936

MICHAEL
C. of Evreux
*1941
m. 1967
Beatrice
*1941
d. of Bruno
C. Pasquier
of Franclieu

JAMES
D. of Orléans
*1941
m. 1969
Gersende
*1942
d. of Foulques
D. of Sabran

CHANTAL
*1946
m. 1972
Fr. Xavier
B. of Sambucy
de Sorgue
*1943

ISABELLA
*1932
m. 1964
Fred. Charles
C. of Schönborn-
Buchheim
*1933

HENRY   1957
C. of Clermont
*1933
m. (2) 1984
Micaela
Cousiño y
Quiñes *1938

Mary Theresa
*1934
d. of Philip
D. of Württemberg
(div. 1984)

HELEN
*1934
m. 1957
Evrard
C. of Limburg –
Stirum
*1927

ANNE
*1938
m. 1965
Charles
D. of Calabria
*1938

FRANCIS
*1961

JOHN
D. of Vendôme
*1965

MARY
*1939
m. 1989
Pr. Gundakar
of Liechtenstein
*1949

BLANCHE
*1962

EUDES
D. of Angoulême
*1968

TABLE 68

FRANCE
Ancestors of Louis XIV, Louis XVI and Louis Philippe

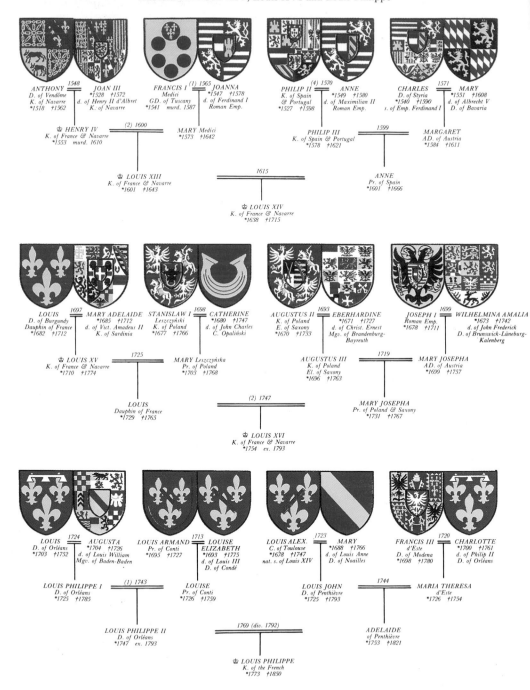

ANTHONY — 1548 — **JOAN III**
D. of Vendôme
K. of Navarre
*1518 †1562

JOAN III
*1528 †1572
d. of Henry II d'Albret
K. of Navarre

FRANCIS I (1) 1565 **JOANNA**
Medici
GD. of Tuscany
*1541 murd. 1587

JOANNA
*1547 †1578
d. of Ferdinand I
Roman Emp.

PHILIP II (4) 1570 **ANNE**
K. of Spain
& Portugal
*1527 †1598

ANNE
*1549 †1580
d. of Maximilian II
Roman Emp.

CHARLES 1571 **MARY**
D. of Styria
*1540 †1590
s. of Emp. Ferdinand I

MARY
*1551 †1608
d. of Albrecht V
D. of Bavaria

☼ **HENRY IV** (2) 1600
K. of France & Navarre
*1553 murd. 1610

MARY Medici
*1573 †1642

PHILIP III 1599
K. of Spain & Portugal
*1578 †1621

MARGARET
AD. of Austria
*1584 †1611

☼ **LOUIS XIII**
K. of France & Navarre
*1601 †1643

1615

ANNE
Pr. of Spain
*1601 †1666

☼ **LOUIS XIV**
K. of France & Navarre
*1638 †1715

LOUIS 1697 **MARY ADELAIDE**
D. of Burgundy
Dauphin of France
*1682 †1712

MARY ADELAIDE
*1685 †1712
d. of Vict. Amadeus II
K. of Sardinia

STANISLAW I 1698 **CATHERINE**
Leszczyński
K. of Poland
*1677 †1766

CATHERINE
*1680 †1747
d. of John Charles
C. Opaliński

AUGUSTUS II 1693 **EBERHARDINE**
K. of Poland
E. of Saxony
*1670 †1733

EBERHARDINE
*1671 †1727
d. of Christ. Ernest
Mgv. of Brandenburg-
Bayreuth

JOSEPH I 1699 **WILHELMINA AMALIA**
Roman Emp.
*1678 †1711

WILHELMINA AMALIA
*1673 †1742
d. of John Frederick
D. of Brunswick-Lüneburg-
Kalenberg

☼ **LOUIS XV** 1725
K. of France & Navarre
*1710 †1774

MARY Leszczyńska
Pr. of Poland
*1703 †1768

AUGUSTUS III 1719
K. of Poland
El. of Saxony
*1696 †1763

MARY JOSEPHA
AD. of Austria
*1699 †1757

LOUIS
Dauphin of France
*1729 †1765

(2) 1747

MARY JOSEPHA
Pr. of Poland & Saxony
*1731 †1767

☼ **LOUIS XVI**
K. of France & Navarre
*1754 ex. 1793

LOUIS 1724 **AUGUSTA**
D. of Orléans
*1703 †1752

AUGUSTA
*1704 †1726
d. of Louis William
Mgv. of Baden-Baden

LOUIS ARMAND 1713 **LOUISE ELIZABETH**
Pr. of Conti
*1695 †1727

LOUISE ELIZABETH
*1693 †1775
d. of Louis III
D. of Condé

LOUIS ALEX. 1723 **MARY**
C. of Toulouse
*1678 †1747
nat. s. of Louis XIV

MARY
*1688 †1766
d. of Louis Anne
D. of Noailles

FRANCIS III 1720 **CHARLOTTE**
d'Este
D. of Modena
*1698 †1780

CHARLOTTE
*1700 †1761
d. of Philip II
D. of Orléans

LOUIS PHILIPPE I (1) 1743
D. of Orléans
*1725 †1785

LOUISE
Pr. of Conti
*1726 †1759

LOUIS JOHN 1744
D. of Penthièvre
*1725 †1793

MARIA THERESA
d'Este
*1726 †1754

LOUIS PHILIPPE II
D. of Orléans
*1747 ex. 1793

1769 (div. 1792)

ADELAIDE
of Penthièvre
*1753 †1821

☼ **LOUIS PHILIPPE**
K. of the French
*1773 †1850

the less a modicum of good sense. True, he had to bolt from his capital for the Hundred Days which ended with Waterloo, but he contrived to avoid the grosser right-wing antics of some of the returned nobility while preserving a natural fear of radicalism. The murder of the Duke of Berry in 1820 compelled the old King to move towards the right; the process was accelerated by his brother Charles X, who was deliberately crowned at Rheims with all the old ceremony, and even 'touched' sufferers for the King's Evil (scrofula) which no English monarch had done since Anne. His finest action was the capture of Algiers and the foundation of the French dominion in North Africa. In 1830 a revolution in Paris easily dismissed the obstinate and obsolete monarch to exile, first in Scotland and then in Bohemia.

Many Frenchmen were still Republican, and others Bonapartist; others supported Louis Philippe, Duke of Orléans, who narrowly won the day. His father had attacked the court of Louis XVI, embraced the Revolution and adopted the name of Philippe Egalité, voted for the execution of the King, but was himself guillotined a few months later. The son, pear-shaped but well-educated, had a reputation for liberalism. He became King of the French, adopted the Napoleonic tricolor and modelled his constitutional monarchy on that of England. To fervent royalists the true king was the Count of Chambord (Henry V), grandson of Charles X. The July monarchy saw a sober, worthy but slightly dull pursuit of the middle path; in the wave of revolutions which swept Europe in 1848, the Orléans family quietly disappeared into bourgeois exile. France returned (Chapter 16) to her Bonapartist loyalty. It can be seen from Table 68 that Louis Philippe was in fact of mainly French (if royal French) ancestry.

When the Second Empire fell in 1870, the future constitution of France was once more in debate. France, defeated by Germany, had to endure the shattering loss of Alsace and Lorraine. The Count of Chambord, senior heir of Henry IV and Louis XVI, was a middle-aged and childless exile; his nearest heir was the Count of Paris who belonged to the Orléans line (Tables 66 and 67). The supporters of Orléans were prepared to accept 'Henry V' in confident expectation of the eventual succession. But the royalist claimant was unbending. Ready enough to resume the throne of his ancestors, he would not abandon the white banner of the Bourbons for the tricolor. To almost all Frenchmen the tricolor was the symbol not only of great glory won but also of the heritage of the Revolution. Chambord would not move and France has been a republic, whether the republic of Clemenceau, Laval or de Gaulle, ever since.

The death of 'Henry V' in 1883 meant that the senior heir of Hugh Capet was a Spanish Bourbon,

Louis Philippe (1773–1850), King of the French, with his five sons, by H. Vernet, 1846.

the Carlist claimant (see Table 51); with the death of his son in 1936, the representation passed to King Alphonso XIII. Both were descended from the second grandson of Louis XIV, but both were inhibited from claiming the throne of France by the Treaty of Utrecht (1713). Accordingly the Orleanist line, the heirs of Louis Philippe, have continued to make their stand as pretenders to the throne of France. Any claims to the French Crown by the heirs of Alphonso XIII must have been reduced by the accession of King Juan Carlos to the Crown of Spain in 1975.

A younger branch has inherited claims to the short-lived Empire of Brazil (Table 67) but Henry, Count of Paris, is the only serious, present-day competitor for the throne which Hugh Capet, his direct male progenitor, acquired almost a thousand years ago (987). His immediate ancestry is unusual, and complicated; like every human being, he has eight great-great-grandfathers and as many great-great-grandmothers, but among them Louis Philippe and his Queen each occur four times. The Count of Paris continued family tradition by marrying a cousin, but his consort's mother brought in an unaccustomed strain from the Slav domains of the old Austro-Hungarian Empire. His eldest son, another Henry, carries the title of Count of Clermont, originally held by that son of St Louis who founded the Bourbons. But of his later twin sons, the elder, Prince Michael, has made a marriage of non-dynastic character, with Beatrice Pasquier de Franclieu, while the union of the younger with Gersende de Sabran conforms to Capetian tradition and standards.

An alliance which cuts across the lines of history is that of the sister of the Count of Paris with Prince Peter Murat, who was both the descendant of Napoleon's brother-in-law and an officer in the British army in the Second World War.

Chapter 16

NAPOLEON

The family of Bonaparte appears to have originated in Florence, and passed over to Corsica in 1529 where they mainly devoted themselves to the law. The family could count itself as noble, and the original coat-of-arms is shown at the bottom of Table 69.

The French Revolution made possible a career for anybody of talent. The reign of terror was followed by the Directory, which had to seek artillery to maintain itself. General Bonaparte, when he rose to his first independent command, promptly quelled a Parisian riot. In 1796–7 he made his own revolution in the art of war by the brilliance and speed of his north Italian victories. In 1799 he became First Consul (the names of his two colleagues are not remembered) and in 1804 the Senate begged him to become emperor. The Pope was brought from Italy to consecrate Napoleon in Paris; visits to Aachen, the one-time capital of Charlemagne, and to Milan, where he assumed the Iron Crown of Lombardy, made it clear that the shadow of European dominion fell over the new monarch.

Military genius raised Napoleon to his throne but he had already given evidence of his omnivorous interest in government of all kinds. The Code Napoleon of 1804 is a masterpiece of legal clarity and sense, which is perhaps the most widespread legacy of the Napoleonic regime, though its conquests were also instrumental in extending the area which used the metric system (fully adopted in 1801). Nelson at Trafalgar (1805) denied the Emperor command of the sea, but his armies swept across Europe and he was able to redraw the political map on entirely new lines, often to the benefit of his own family. His elder brother Joseph was made King of Naples and then of Spain; the vacant throne of Naples went to his brother-in-law Marshal Murat, one of the most dazzling cavalry leaders of all time but politically incompetent. Louis Bonaparte became King of Holland

and Jerome King of an artificial German province of Westphalia.

The desire for a dynasty was dominant in Napoleon's mind. He had quarrelled with his ablest brother, Lucien, over the latter's second marriage (to a former mistress of no birth); Joseph had only daughters; Jerome had been coerced into divorcing his American wife. The Emperor's own wife, the beautiful Josephine Tascher de la Pagerie, was childless by him, though her daughter was married to Louis of Holland. In 1809 Napoleon divorced Josephine and extorted from the Emperor of Austria his daughter. The proud blood of Hapsburg-Lorraine was joined with that of the Corsican genius. Only one son graced the union, and his delighted father bestowed upon him the traditional style of King of Rome.

For his own arms Napoleon adopted a Roman eagle clutching a thunderbolt. After becoming emperor he instituted a new system of heraldry to match the new honours which he bestowed upon his marshals and his civil servants. His brothers combined the imperial eagle with the ancient blazon of the provinces over which they ruled. To his brother-in-law Joachim Murat of Naples he allowed a chief of the Empire. Each rank in the peerage also had a particular heraldic distinction. Thus every duke had a red chief sown with silver stars. In 1802 he founded the Legion of Honour, an order which was maintained by Louis XVIII and is still the principal decoration of France: the collar and badge surround his shield on Table 70.

Like so many conquerors Napoleon found it difficult to halt or withdraw. More than once he was offered terms which allowed France her so-called 'natural frontiers' – the Rhine, the Alps and the Pyrenees – but he refused them. His invasion of Russia in 1812, followed by the bitter retreat from

[134]

Moscow, marked a definite stage in his downfall. His new armies were shattered at Leipzig in 1813, and in 1814 he was compelled to abdicate. Exiled to Elba, he made a sensational but futile excursion which ended at Waterloo. From St Helena there was no physical return, but he cultivated a spiritual legend which served his nephew well. His son was borne off to Austria and given an Austrian title and Austrian arms. The Empress, allotted the Duchy of Parma, slid into adultery with a one-eyed general.

Napoleon ruled as an autocrat. Yet on three separate occasions, in 1800, 1802 and 1804, he sought the endorsement of the French people. He reigned as an Emperor, and yet he was the heir of the French Revolution. For example, in 1802 he made a Concordat with the Vatican, but the church as restored in France lacked all the privileges and splendour of the *ancien régime* and was almost an adjunct of the civil power. After royalist risings had taken place in France, he committed an arbitrary but effective act of violence against the old dynasty by kidnapping and executing the Duc d'Enghien, last of the Condé line of Bourbons. His personal interest in law reform and the aspects of civil government was detailed and indubitable; and both Goethe and Heine admired him. The creation of his own Empire caused the extinction of the centuries-old Holy Roman Empire (Chapter 22). One thing was certain: after his career Europe could never be the same again.

In France, the memory of Napoleon's greatness and glory outlived the recollection of his blunders and the carnage of his ceaseless campaigns. After the early death in Vienna of his son, King of Rome or Duke of Reichstadt, the leadership of the family was asserted by Louis Napoleon, son of the King of Holland (and grandson of Josephine). After the downfall of the July monarchy in 1848, he came forward as a candidate for the Presidency of the Second Republic. Such was now the repute of Bonapartism that this awkward, unimpressive little man, with no success to his name, was elected president by a vast majority. In 1852 he became emperor and, as a recognition of the Duke of Reichstadt, took the title of Napoleon III. The princesses of Europe fought shy of this new Prince, and he married for love a ravishingly beautiful Spanish countess.

Napoleon promised France peace, but he became involved in the Crimean War (allied with England against Russia), in campaigns against Austria in northern Italy (where the slaughter at Solferino in 1864 prompted the inauguration of the Red Cross), in an unprofitable expedition to Mexico and finally in conflict with Prussia. The Emperor lacked all trace of his uncle's grasp of warfare; Paris, which Napoleon III had done much to develop and beautify, was besieged and the Second Empire collapsed. His only

The Emperor Napoleon (1769–1821) wearing his coronation robes and the Legion of Honour, by Ingres, 1806.

child was killed with the British army in Zululand. Any legacy which remains to Bonapartism is now vested in the descendants of Jerome, King of Westphalia. Ironically, the heir, Prince Charles, has married a Bourbon princess, thus linking Bonapartism with the traditional rulers of France.

FRANCE
House of Bonaparte

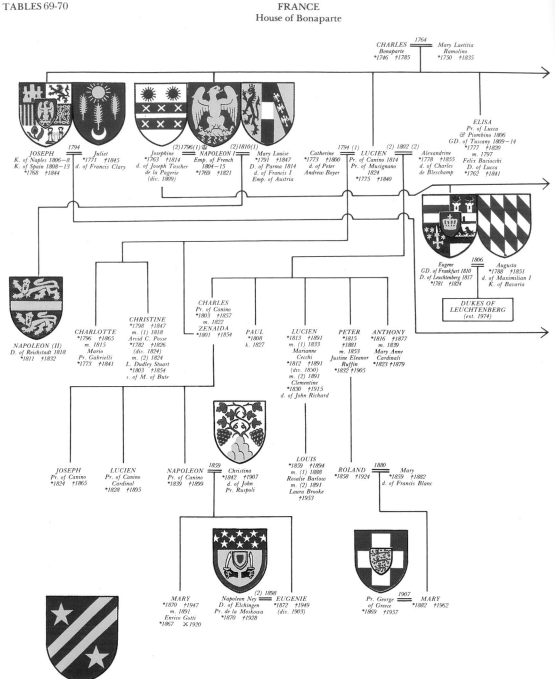

CHARLES *1764* Bonaparte
*1746 †1785

Mary Laetitia
Ramolino
*1750 †1835

ELISA
Pr. of Lucca
& Piombino 1806
GD. of Tuscany 1809–14
*1777 †1820
m. 1797
Felix Baciocchi
D. of Lucca
*1762 †1841

JOSEPH *1794*
K. of Naples 1806–8
K. of Spain 1808–13
*1768 †1844

Juliet
*1771 †1845
d. of Francis Clary

Josephine
*1763 †1814
d. of Joseph Tascher
de la Pagerie
(div. 1809)

(2)1796(1) NAPOLEON I (2)1810(1)
Emp. of French
1804–15
*1769 †1821

Mary Louise
*1791 †1847
D. of Parma 1814
d. of Francis I
Emp. of Austria

Catherine *1794 (1)*
*1773 †1800
d. of Peter
Andrew Boyer

(2) 1802 (2) LUCIEN
Pr. of Canino 1814
Pr. of Musignano
1824
*1775 †1840

Alexandrine
*1778 †1855
d. of Charles
de Bleschamp

Eugene *1806*
GD. of Frankfurt 1810
D. of Leuchtenberg 1817
*1781 †1824

Augusta
*1788 †1851
d. of Maximilian I
K. of Bavaria

DUKES OF
LEUCHTENBERG
(ext. 1974)

NAPOLEON (II)
D. of Reichstadt 1818
*1811 †1832

CHARLOTTE
*1796 †1865
m. 1815
Mario
Pr. Gabrielli
*1773 †1841

CHRISTINE
*1798 †1847
m. (1) 1818
Arvid C. Posse
*1782 †1826
(div. 1824)
m. (2) 1824
L. Dudley Stuart
*1803 †1854
s. of M. of Bute

CHARLES
Pr. of Canino
*1803 †1857
m. 1822
ZENAIDA
*1801 †1854

PAUL
*1808
k. 1827

LUCIEN
*1813 †1891
m. (1) 1833
Marianne
Cecchi
*1812 †1891
(div. 1850)
m. (2) 1891
Clementine
*1830 †1915
d. of John Richard

PETER
*1815
†1881
m. 1853
Justine Eleanor
Ruffin
*1832 †1905

ANTHONY
*1816 †1877
m. 1839
Mary Anne
Cardinali
*1823 †1879

JOSEPH
Pr. of Canino
*1824 †1865

LUCIEN
Pr. of Canino
Cardinal
*1828 †1895

NAPOLEON *1859*
Pr. of Canino
*1839 †1899

Christina
*1842 †1907
d. of John
Pr. Ruspoli

LOUIS
*1859 †1894
m. (1) 1888
Rosalie Barlow
m. (2) 1891
Laura Brooke
†1953

ROLAND *1880*
*1858 †1924

Mary
*1859 †1882
d. of Francis Blanc

MARY
*1870 †1947
m. 1891
Enrico Gotti
*1867 ✕1920

(2) 1898
Napoleon Ney
D. of Elchingen
Pr. de la Moskowa
*1870 †1928

EUGENIE
*1872 †1949
(div. 1903)

Pr. George
of Greece
*1869 †1957

1907

MARY
*1882 †1962

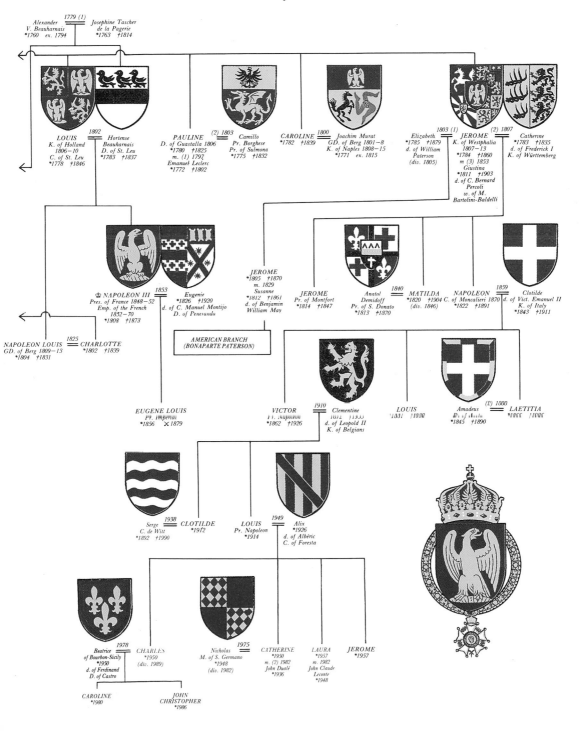

Alexander
V. Beauharnais
*1760 ex. 1794

1779 (1)

Josephine Tascher
de la Pagerie
*1763 †1814

LOUIS
K. of Holland
1806–10
C. of St. Leu
*1778 †1846

1802

Hortense
Beauharnais
D. of St. Leu
*1783 †1837

PAULINE
D. of Guastalla 1806
*1780 †1825
m. (1) 1797
Emanuel Leclerc
*1772 †1802

(2) 1803

Camillo
Pr. Borghese
Pr. of Sulmona
*1775 †1832

CAROLINE
*1782 †1839

1800

Joachim Murat
GD. of Berg 1801–8
K. of Naples 1808–15
*1771 ex. 1815

Elizabeth
*1785 †1879
d. of William
Paterson
(div. 1805)

1803 (1)

JEROME
K. of Westphalia
1807–13
*1784 †1860
m. (3) 1853
Giustina
*1811 †1903
d. of C. Bernard
Percoli
w. of M.
Bartolini-Baldelli

(2) 1807

Catherine
*1783 †1835
d. of Frederick I
K. of Württemberg

☩ NAPOLEON III
Pres. of France 1848–52
Emp. of the French
1852–70
*1808 †1873

1853

Eugenie
*1826 †1920
d. of C. Manuel Montijo
D. of Peneranda

JEROME
*1805 †1870
m. 1829
Susanne
*1812 †1861
d. of Benjamin
William May

JEROME
Pr. of Montfort
*1814 †1847

Anatol
Demidoff
Pr. of S. Donato
*1813 †1870

1840

MATILDA
*1820 †1904 C. of Moncalieri 1870
(div. 1846)

NAPOLEON
*1822 †1891

1859

Clotilde
d. of Vict. Emanuel II
K. of Italy
*1843 †1911

NAPOLEON LOUIS
GD. of Berg 1809–13
*1804 †1831

1825

CHARLOTTE
*1802 †1839

*AMERICAN BRANCH
(BONAPARTE PATERSON)*

EUGENE LOUIS
Pr. Imperial
*1856 ✗ 1879

VICTOR
Pr. Napoleon
*1862 †1926

1910

Clementine
1872 †1955
d. of Leopold II
K. of Belgians

LOUIS
*1851 †1890

Amadeus
Pr. of Spain
*1845 †1890

(2) 1000

LAETITIA
*1866 †1926

Serge
C. de Witt
*1892 †1990

1938

CLOTILDE
*1912

LOUIS
Pr. Napoleon
*1914

1949

Alix
*1926
d. of Albéric
C. of Foresta

Beatrice
of Bourbon-Sicily
*1950
d. of Ferdinand
D. of Castro

1978

CHARLES
*1950
(div. 1989)

Nicholas
M. of S. Germano
*1948
(div. 1982)

1975

CATHERINE
*1950
m. (2) 1982
John Dualé
*1936

LAURA
*1957
m. 1982
John Claude
Leconte
*1948

JEROME
*1957

CAROLINE
*1980

JOHN
CHRISTOPHER
*1986

Chapter 17

AUSTRIA: HAPSBURG

Bella gerant alii, tu felix Austria nube
(Let others make wars, you, fortunate Austria, marry)

The great historic name of Austria began as a frontier province of Germany. In the time of Charlemagne Bavaria had been a border state resisting the hosts of the Avars. Gradually German arms and the Christian religion spread eastwards and a group of marcher lordships developed beyond Bavaria; noteworthy among them (from north to south) were Austria, Styria, Carinthia and Carniola. In the tenth century a fresh and terrible menace assaulted Christian Europe, the Hungarians or Magyars, who swept across the Continent leaving a track of destruction. Otto I of Germany defeated them decisively at the battle of the Lechfeld near Augsburg in 955. The Magyars were driven back to the area which they have since occupied as Hungary, while Otto named a certain Burchard as ruler of Ostmark or eastern march. By the end of the century the holder of this position was known as a margrave, that is 'graf' or count of a border area or 'mark'.

In 976 Leopold I of Babenberg (the modern Bamberg) appears as Margrave of the Ostmark and his descendants continued to govern Austria under the Emperor until 1246. His great-grandson, Leopold III (Table 71), was a warm patron of the Church and benefactor of monasteries; he was proclaimed a saint in 1485, but had enjoyed a local reputation for sanctity long before formal canonization. His wife, Agnes, was the widow of Frederick of Hohenstaufen. This made his numerous sons half-brothers of the first Swabian Emperor, Conrad III. One of them, Leopold, became briefly Duke of Bavaria; his successor Henry 'Jasomirgott' (so-called from his favourite oath, 'So help me God') became the first Duke of Austria in 1156 by gift of the Emperor Frederick Barbarossa. In the course of the Second Crusade

Henry married a Byzantine princess. A third son, Otto, Bishop of Freising, was one of the most important German historians of the twelfth century; yet another was Archbishop of Salzburg.

Leopold V took part in the Third Crusade and was present at the capture of Acre (July 1190). Here he had a furious quarrel with Richard I of England, when the latter tore down the Austrian banner from a conquered tower. Duke Leopold had his revenge when he seized the English King who was seeking to travel home through Austria in disguise, handed him over to the Emperor and shared in the vast ransom extorted from Richard's domains. He extended his own importance by acquiring the Duchy of Styria (1192) as a legacy from its last duke.

Leopold VI was a prosperous ruler and acted as mediator between Empire and Papacy; by this time Vienna was one of the wealthiest cities of Germany. However, his son Frederick was involved in conflict with the Emperor Frederick II, was briefly deprived of his duchies and perished childless in battle against the Hungarians in 1246. It was the Babenberg family which had laid the solid basis of the Austrian state, had encouraged colonization of the land and established great monasteries in their dominions. The Duchy itself was a union of the two districts of Upper and Lower Austria: the arms of the latter can be seen on Table 71 with five eagles, and are sometimes styled Austria ancient. They have been overshadowed by the white bar on red of Austria modern, one of the historic blazons of European heraldry, and long linked with the Hapsburg dynasty, who virtually abandoned for it the use of their ancestral arms, a red lion on gold with a blue crown (Tables 71 and 72).

The extinction of the Babenberg dynasty almost coincided with the collapse of central authority in Germany following the death of Frederick II (1250). That Emperor had declared Austria and Styria to be escheated to the Crown, despite efforts by Hermann V of Baden, a nephew of the last Babenberg duke, to establish a claim to them. In 1251 Ottokar II, King of Bohemia, seized the duchies and proceeded to marry Margaret of Babenberg. He was a powerful and ambitious prince who aimed at dominating the German scene. In 1269 he extended his influence south of Austria by acquiring the Duchies of Carinthia and Carniola. It was a serious blow to his lofty aims when the Electors in 1273 chose Rudolph of Hapsburg to be King of the Romans (Chapter 22). In two campaigns (1276 and 1278) Ottokar was stripped of his conquests and finally slain.

THE HAPSBURGS

The family of the Counts of Hapsburg came originally from Alsace and had considerable property there and in what today is Switzerland: the actual castle of Hapsburg is in the Aargau. Rudolph was no longer young when chosen, but he was solid, respected, not too powerful, and had been a loyal adherent of the vanished Hohenstaufen dynasty. In 1282 he persuaded the Electors to sanction the grant of Austria and Styria to his sons Albrecht and Rudolph: here began the long connection between his descendants and Vienna.

Rudolph had hoped to obtain the succession of his younger son and namesake to Germany, but the boy died young: when Rudolph eventually died in 1291, the Electors regarded Albrecht of Austria as too powerful and chose Adolphus of Nassau, the 'Priests' King'. Seven years later they deposed him and did elect Albrecht of Austria, a tough and successful soldier but a less kindly and generous prince than his father. For a short time he secured Bohemia for his eldest son, presaging its future union with Austria, but in 1308 Albrecht was barbarously murdered by his nephew John the Parricide. For all Albrecht's power he had difficulty in maintaining control over some of the Alpine valleys; later legend has placed the story of William Tell in his reign. One of his sons, Leopold I (Table 73), was decisively defeated at Morgarten in 1315 by the Swiss peasantry, a blunt reminder to the feudal classes that their superiority in war could be challenged, and challenged effectively.

In 1314 there was a double election to the Empire, though more princes supported Louis of Bavaria than Frederick the Fair of Austria. Frederick and his brothers were beaten at the Battle of Mühldorf in 1322 and Frederick was made prisoner; his more capable brother Leopold directed Austria in his absence. Bit by bit the successive Hapsburg dukes built up their power. In 1363 they secured the Tyrol on the death of Count Meinhard V (Table 73). Rudolph IV gained the title of archduke in the same year. His shield shows the quarterings for Styria, Carinthia,

Hapsburg and Carniola with Austria over all. The arms of Styria were unusual and originally showed a mad bull, breathing flames, on a green field: this was a canting coat on the name 'Stier' or ox; later generations of heralds concluded that these fire-throwing exercises were more suited to a panther and sometimes altered the main charge to that monster. At this time an arrangement was made with the House of Luxemburg that if one family died out, the other would succeed to its possessions. Rudolph IV had high ambitions and even fabricated documents allegedly bestowing privileges on Austria by Julius Caesar: among the expert witnesses who condemned them was the poet Petrarch.

One of the basic factors in medieval German history was the slow adoption of the hereditary system and the passage of undiminished domains to the eldest son. In the fourteenth and fifteenth centuries the Hapsburgs were affected by the old Teutonic practice of subdivision of lands, which will be encountered in many other principalities. Thus Leopold III, youngest brother of Rudolph IV, became Duke of Styria, and his youngest son, Frederick, was Count of Tyrol. The full Hapsburg territories were not reunited until the time of Frederick V. But by that date a wider destiny was opening up before the Hapsburgs. The Electors to the Holy Roman Empire (Chapter 22) increasingly manifested a preference for emperors whose main power lay outside Germany. Sigismund of Hungary and Bohemia reigned from 1410 to 1437. His only child Elizabeth was married to Albrecht V, Duke of Austria, who in 1438 was elected to the vacant throne, as Albrecht II. His immediate demise makes his own reign unimportant save that it begins the long connection from 1438 to 1918 between the Hapsburgs and the Empire, a connection severed only for one short spell. On Albrecht's death the Electors turned to his cousin Frederick V who (with his brother Albrecht) was Duke of Styria, Carinthia and Carniola; his youth and good looks seemed to promise a vigorous reign.

Appearances were deceptive. Frederick III, as he became, was perhaps the most ineffectual of all the heirs of Charlemagne; his long reign saw scant political achievement though it offers certain landmarks. He was the last Emperor to be crowned in Rome; he was the first to show the famous Hapsburg jutting lower lip. An early difficulty arose when the widow of his predecessor gave birth to a posthumous son: Ladislas V was nominal King of Bohemia and Hungary and Duke of Austria for his brief life. By 1463 Frederick had reunited the family lands, except Tyrol, in his person and assumed the title of Archduke of Austria. If he was a bad monarch of Germany, he was a good Hapsburg. Ambitious schemes flitted across his mind, indulged by his hobbies of

TABLE 71

AUSTRIA
General survey

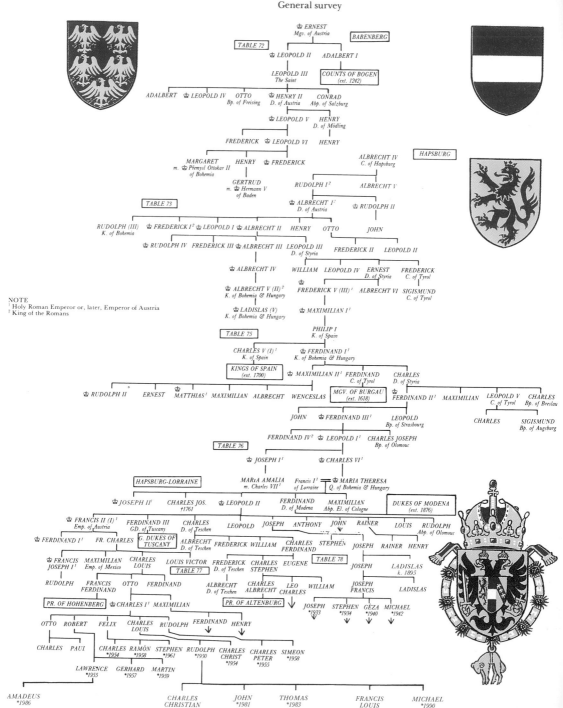

♔ ERNEST
Mgv. of Austria

BABENBERG

TABLE 72

♔ LEOPOLD II — ADALBERT I

LEOPOLD III
The Saint — COUNTS OF BOGEN
(ext. 1242)

ADALBERT — ♔ LEOPOLD IV — OTTO
Bp. of Freising — HENRY II
D. of Austria — CONRAD
Abp. of Salzburg

♔ LEOPOLD V — HENRY
D. of Mödling

FREDERICK — ♔ LEOPOLD VI — HENRY

MARGARET
m. ♔ Přemysl Ottokar II
of Bohemia — HENRY — ♔ FREDERICK — ALBRECHT IV
C. of Hapsburg

HAPSBURG

GERTRUD
m. ♔ Hermann V
of Baden — RUDOLPH I [2] — ALBRECHT V

TABLE 73 — ♔ ALBRECHT I [1,2]
D. of Austria — ♔ RUDOLPH II

RUDOLPH (III)
K. of Bohemia — ♔ FREDERICK I [2] — ♔ LEOPOLD I — ♔ ALBRECHT II — HENRY — OTTO — JOHN

♔ RUDOLPH IV — FREDERICK III — ♔ ALBRECHT III — LEOPOLD III
D. of Styria — FREDERICK II — LEOPOLD II

♔ ALBRECHT IV — WILLIAM — LEOPOLD IV — ERNEST
D. of Styria — FREDERICK
C. of Tyrol

♔ ALBRECHT V (II) [2]
K. of Bohemia & Hungary — ♔ FREDERICK V (III) [1] — ALBRECHT VI — SIGISMUND
C. of Tyrol

♔ LADISLAS (V)
K. of Bohemia & Hungary — ♔ MAXIMILIAN I [1]

TABLE 75 — PHILIP I
K. of Spain

♔ CHARLES V (I) [1]
K. of Spain — ♔ FERDINAND I [1]
K. of Bohemia & Hungary

KINGS OF SPAIN
(ext. 1700) — ♔ MAXIMILIAN II [1] — FERDINAND
C. of Tyrol — CHARLES
D. of Styria

♔ RUDOLPH II — ERNEST — MATTHIAS [1] — MAXIMILIAN — ALBRECHT — WENCESLAS — MGV. OF BURGAU
(ext. 1618) — FERDINAND II [1] — MAXIMILIAN — LEOPOLD V
C. of Tyrol — CHARLES
Bp. of Breslau

JOHN — ♔ FERDINAND III [1] — LEOPOLD
Bp. of Strasbourg — CHARLES — SIGISMUND
Bp. of Augsburg

FERDINAND IV [2] — ♔ LEOPOLD I — CHARLES JOSEPH
Bp. of Olomouc

TABLE 76 — ♔ JOSEPH I [1] — ♔ CHARLES VI [1]

HAPSBURG-LORRAINE — MARIA AMALIA
m. Charles VII — Francis I [1]
of Lorraine — ♔ MARIA THERESA
Q. of Bohemia & Hungary

♔ JOSEPH II [1] — CHARLES JOS.
†1761 — LEOPOLD II — FERDINAND
D. of Modena — MAXIMILIAN
Abp. El. of Cologne — DUKES OF MODENA
(ext. 1876)

♔ FRANCIS II (I) [1]
Emp. of Austria — FERDINAND III
GD. of Tuscany — CHARLES
D. of Teschen — LEOPOLD — JOSEPH — ANTHONY — JOHN — RAINER — LOUIS — RUDOLPH
Abp. of Olomouc

♔ FERDINAND I [1] — FR. CHARLES — G. DUKES OF
TUSCANY — ALBRECHT
D. of Teschen — FREDERICK — WILLIAM — CHARLES
FERDINAND — STEPHEN — JOSEPH — RAINER — HENRY

♔ FRANCIS
JOSEPH I [1] — MAXIMILIAN
Emp. of Mexico — CHARLES
LOUIS — LOUIS VICTOR — FREDERICK
D. of Teschen — CHARLES
STEPHEN — EUGENE — TABLE 78 — JOSEPH — LADISLAS
k. 1895

RUDOLPH — FRANCIS
FERDINAND — OTTO — FERDINAND — ALBRECHT
D. of Teschen — CHARLES
ALBRECHT — LEO
CHARLES — WILLIAM — JOSEPH
FRANCIS — LADISLAS

PR. OF HOHENBERG — ♔ CHARLES I [1] — MAXIMILIAN — PR. OF ALTENBURG — JOSEPH
*1933 — STEPHEN
*1934 — GÉZA
*1940 — MICHAEL
*1942

OTTO — ROBERT — FELIX — CHARLES
LOUIS — RUDOLPH — FERDINAND — HENRY

CHARLES — PAUL — CHARLES RAMÓN
*1954 — STEPHEN
*1958 — RUDOLPH
*1961 — CHARLES
CHRIST
*1954 — CHARLES
PETER
*1955 — SIMEON
*1958
*1930

LAWRENCE
*1955 — GERHARD
*1957 — MARTIN
*1959

AMADEUS
*1986 — CHARLES
CHRISTIAN
*1977 — JOHN
*1981 — THOMAS
*1983 — FRANCIS
LOUIS
*1988 — MICHAEL
*1990

NOTE
[1] Holy Roman Emperor or, later, Emperor of Austria
[2] King of the Romans

House of Babenberg and accession of the Hapsburgs

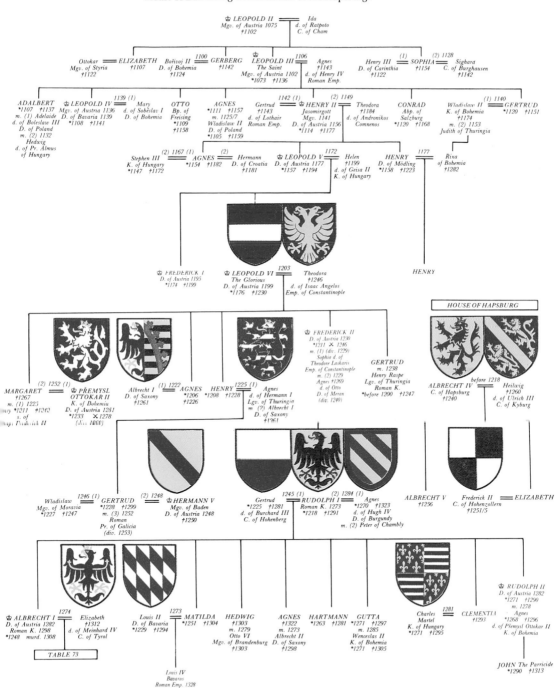

⚜ LEOPOLD II
Mgv. of Austria 1075
†1102
Ida
d. of Ratpoto
C. of Cham

Ottokar
Mgv. of Styria
†1122
= ELIZABETH
†1107
Boňvoj II
D. of Bohemia
†1124
GERBERG 1100
†1142
⚜ LEOPOLD III 1106
The Saint
Mgv. of Austria 1102
*1073 †1136
Agnes
†1143
d. of Henry IV
Roman Emp.
Henry III (1)
D. of Carinthia
†1122
SOPHIA (2) 1128
†1154
Sighara
C. of Burghausen
†1142

ADALBERT
*1107 †1137
d. of Boleslaw III
D. of Poland
m. (1) Adelaide
m. (2) 1132
Hedwig
d. of Pr. Almus
of Hungary
⚜ LEOPOLD IV 1139 (1)
Mgv. of Austria 1136
D. of Bavaria 1139
*1108 †1141
Mary
d. of Soběslav I
D. of Bohemia
OTTO
Bp. of
Freising
*1109
†1158
AGNES
*1111 †1157
m. 1125/7
Wladislaw II
D. of Poland
*1105 †1159
Gertrud
†1143
d. of Lothair
Roman Emp.
⚜ HENRY II (2) 1149
Jasomirgott
Mgv. 1141
D. of Austria 1156
*1114 †1177
Theodora
†1184
d. of Andronikos
Comnenos
CONRAD
Abp. of
Salzburg
*1120 †1168
Wladislaw II (1) 1140
K. of Bohemia
†1174
m. (2) 1153
Judith of Thuringia
GERTRUD
*1120 †1151

Stephen III
K. of Hungary
*1147 †1172
= AGNES 1167 (1)
*1154 †1182
(2) Hermann
D. of Croatia
†1181
⚜ LEOPOLD V 1172
D. of Austria 1177
*1157 †1194
Helen
†1199
d. of Geisa II
K. of Hungary
HENRY 1177
D. of Mödling
*1158 †1223
Rixa
of Bohemia
†1282

⚜ FREDERICK I
D. of Austria 1195
*1174 †1199
⚜ LEOPOLD VI 1203
The Glorious
D. of Austria 1199
*1176 †1230
Theodora
†1246
d. of Isaac Angelos
Emp. of Constantinople

HENRY

HOUSE OF HAPSBURG

⚜ FREDERICK II
D. of Austria 1230
*1211 × 1246
m. (1) (div. 1229)
Sophia d. of
Theodore Laskaris
Emp. of Constantinople
m. (2) 1229
Agnes †1269
d. of Otto
D. of Meran
(div. 1240)
GERTRUD
m. 1238
Henry Raspe
Lgv. of Thuringia
Roman K.
*before 1200 †1247
ALBRECHT IV
C. of Hapsburg
†1240
Heilwig before 1218
†1260
d. of Ulrich III
C. of Kyburg

MARGARET (2) 1252 (1)
m. (1) 1225
...ry †1211 †1242
s. of
...mp. Frederick II
⚜ PŘEMYSL
OTTOKAR II
K. of Bohemia
D. of Austria 1251
*1233 × 1278
(div. 1260)
Albrecht I (1) 1222
D. of Saxony
†1261
AGNES
*1206 †1226
HENRY 1225 (1)
*1208 †1228
Agnes
d. of Hermann I
Lgv. of Thuringia
m. (2) Albrecht I
D. of Saxony
†1261
ALBRECHT V
†1256
Frederick II
C. of Hohenzollern
†1251/5
= ELIZABETH

Wladislaw
Mgv. of Moravia
*1227 †1247
GERTRUD 1246 (1)
*1228 †1299
m. (3) 1252
Roman
Pr. of Galicia
(div. 1253)
⚜ HERMANN V (2) 1248
Mgv. of Baden
D. of Austria 1248
†1250
Gertrud
*1225 †1281
d. of Burchard III
C. of Hohenberg
⚜ RUDOLPH I 1245 (1)
Roman K. 1273
*1218 †1291
Agnes (2) 1284 (1)
*1270 †1323
d. of Hugh IV
D. of Burgundy
m. (2) Peter of Chambly

⚜ RUDOLPH II
D. of Austria 1271
*1271 †1290
Agnes
*1268 †1296
d. of Přemysl Ottokar II
K. of Bohemia

⚜ ALBRECHT I 1274
D. of Austria 1282
Roman K. 1298
*1248 murd. 1308
Elizabeth
†1312
d. of Meinhard IV
C. of Tyrol
Louis II
D. of Bavaria
*1229 †1294
MATILDA 1273
*1251 †1304
HEDWIG
†1301
m. 1279
Otto VI
Mgv. of Brandenburg
†1303
AGNES
*1322
m. 1273
Albrecht II
D. of Saxony
†1298
HARTMANN
*1263 †1281
GUTTA
*1271 †1297
m. 1285
Wenceslas II
K. of Bohemia
*1271 †1305
Charles 1281
Martel
K. of Hungary
*1271 †1295
CLEMENTIA
†1293

TABLE 73

Louis IV
Bavarus
Roman Emp. 1328

JOHN The Parricide
*1290 †1313

The Holy Roman Emperor Maximilian I (1459–1519) with his family, by B. Strigel, c. 1515. The characteristic Hapsburg jaw is very evident.

alchemy and the acquisition of gems. He invented, to adorn his possessions, the monogram AEIOU announcing with fortunate prophecy the sentiment *Austriae est imperare orbi universo* (it is for Austria to rule over all the world). Above all, in 1477 he arranged the marriage of his son to the heiress of Burgundy and much of the Netherlands. The election of that son, the vigorous and warlike Maximilian, as King of the Romans in 1486 may have been some consolation to Frederick III who had been evicted from his own capital by the King of Hungary. Finally, in 1490, Tyrol was secured by pensioning off the last Count (Table 73). At the least this sad, craven, dreaming Emperor bequeathed to a vigorous heir an inheritance of high potential.

MAXIMILIAN I AND CHARLES V

Maximilian I succeeded to the Empire without difficulty. He had been in real control of the family dominions for the last years of his father's long reign, and had been consolidating his power there. New influences were making themselves felt. To the southeast pressure from the Ottoman Turks was increasing; to the north and west the control of Germany was becoming more shadowy and elusive, while the invention of printing and the spread of the new learning over the Alps stimulated the intellectual ferment of the times. Two alliances arranged by Maximilian were to have great consequences, though in neither case were these predictable at the time. First, he married his son and daughter (Table 74) to the daughter and the son of Ferdinand of Aragon; secondly he betrothed his grandson and granddaughter to the two children of Wladislaw, King of Bohemia and Hungary. He himself was often short of money, which he had to seek from the Estates, or assemblies of his provinces, and was embroiled in war with France to establish his Burgundian inheritance.

Maximilian knew in his lifetime that the young Prince of Aragon, his son-in-law, was dead and without issue, and that his son Philip (also destined to an early death) was heir to Castile and Aragon in right of his wife, the mad Joanna. He was not to know that Louis of Bohemia would perish at Mohács in 1526, leaving his sister as heiress of Bohemia and Hungary. The great inheritance of the Hapsburgs was building up. Albrecht II had placed Austria alone on the breast of a one-headed eagle. Maximilian I impaled Austria with old Burgundy on a two-headed eagle after he became emperor (Table 73). His great-grandson Maximilian II (Table 74) has two superimposed escutcheons, the lower for Bohemia and Hungary and the upper for Austria and Burgundy.

Charles I of Austria is better known as the Emperor Charles V and on him descended the formidable burden of the Hapsburg territories. He followed one grandfather as King of Spain in 1516 and the other as Holy Roman Emperor in 1519. He was thus ruler of Spain, of Burgundy and the Netherlands, overlord of Germany and Archduke of Austria. The fortunate series of alliances by which this great dominion was achieved can be seen on Table 74. There also can be seen the heraldic display of his honours. Four quarters stand in turn for Castile and Leon, Aragon and Sicily, Austria and old Burgundy, Burgundy modern and Brabant; in the centre of the upper shield is the pomegranate of Granada and, on the escutcheon below it, Flanders and Tyrol. The load was too great. In 1521 Charles assigned the Austrian duchies to his brother Ferdinand with the title of Imperial Lieutenant.

The new Prince had been educated entirely in Spain, but he proceeded to celebrate the marriage with Anne of Bohemia, planned by his grandfather. After the death in battle of his brother-in-law, he became King of Bohemia and part of Hungary as well as ruler of Austria. Other Hapsburgs had reigned in these lands, but from now on the Danubian character of the Hapsburg monarchy is firmly established. So is its role as a protector of Europe from the Turks, for most of Hungary remained in Turkish hands after Mohács. Ferdinand had to contend also with the impact of the Reformation, which had serious repercussions in Bohemia and in Austria. He was a pious Catholic; he protected the Council of Trent and encouraged the brisk successes of the Jesuits in rescuing Austria from Protestant beliefs. In 1558, after his brother Charles had abdicated, Ferdinand finally became emperor, while Spain and the Low Countries passed to his nephew, Philip II. The latter inherited Portugal through his mother and married Mary of England. However Mary had no children: the march of the Hapsburgs was not destined to cross the channel.

Ferdinand I reverted to the practice of division. His eldest son Maximilian II became emperor and received Austria, Bohemia and Hungary; Ferdinand became Count of Tyrol and Charles, Duke of Styria. The younger sons (Table 75) bore elaborate shields reflecting their proud ancestry and also a large number of relatively unimportant lordships, such as the fief of Windeschenmark with its distinctive black hat. In all the provinces religious questions were paramount. Maximilian II was a kindly and tolerant man, but ineffectual in public life. His son Rudolph II, that rarity an unmarried emperor, was a shy and superstitious eccentric. Devoted to astrology and hating crowds, he lived mainly in Prague, which he greatly beautified, and whither he brought Kepler and Tycho Brahe. So remote and disastrous was his government that his brothers united against him, and in 1608 Matthias, who ultimately succeeded him, was named as his deputy. Another brother, Maximilian, was Grand-Master of the Teutonic Order, the black cross of which is superimposed on his quarterings.

Matthias was childless and took great care to pass on his dominions to his cousin Ferdinand. Ferdinand II was a zealous and passionate Catholic educated by Jesuits. Already he had persecuted the reformed religions in his Duchy of Styria. His second son, Leopold, was placed in the Church and at the age of eleven was in charge of two bishoprics and four abbeys to vindicate paternal piety. Unhappily Ferdinand's intransigent and arid virtue was of small service to his Empire. The celebrated 'Defenestration of Prague' had begun the Thirty Years' War, the worst disaster (before Hitler) in German history.

This conflict, which began as a religious uprising in Bohemia, was gradually enlarged until almost all the nations of western Europe played some part, not least France and Sweden. But the main theatre of war was always on German soil or in Bohemia itself; and it was the peasantry of these lands which bore the grimmest burden. The effects in devastation and suffering were fearful; furthermore the decline in imperial authority left Germany disunited and ineffective for two centuries. Ferdinand II himself had reunited the Austrian lands, but in 1625 he conferred the Tyrol upon his brother: final reunion did not take place until 1665. At his death in 1637, his good intentions had brought his domains to a sorry pass. His ancestry (Table 79) was strongly Hapsburg, for Ferdinand I was his grandfather on one side, his great-grandfather on the other; the least likely elements were provided by the blood of Spain and Foix. His industry was attested by the savage persecution of the Bohemian Protestants after the battle of the White Mountain.

To his son, Ferdinand III, fell the conduct of the later part of the Thirty Years' War, and the negotiation of peace. The greatest general on the Imperial side, Wallenstein (more properly Waldstein), was suspected of leniency and bluntly assassinated by some Irish hirelings. By 1635 the war had ceased to be mainly concerned with religion and was centred upon the political ambitions of Sweden and France; the possible profits for Austria were negligible. When the Peace of Westphalia was finally negotiated in 1648, the main gain to Ferdinand III was that the Crown of Bohemia was recognized as hereditary in the Hapsburg dynasty; on the other hand the ancient Alsatian estates of the Hapsburgs were ceded to France, and any hope of establishing a unified or central form of government in Germany was dead. The future of that country lay in the hands of a collection of princes, divided in religion and disparate in power. The future for the Hapsburg dynasty lay outside the traditional boundaries of the Empire. Ferdinand III, in his later years, was successful in securing the acceptance of his eldest son as King of Bohemia and King of the Romans, but Ferdinand IV predeceased his father, and the inheritance came in 1657 to Leopold I.

TABLE 73

AUSTRIA
House of Hapsburg in the fourteenth and fifteenth centuries

ISSUE OF ALBRECHT I (TABLE 77)

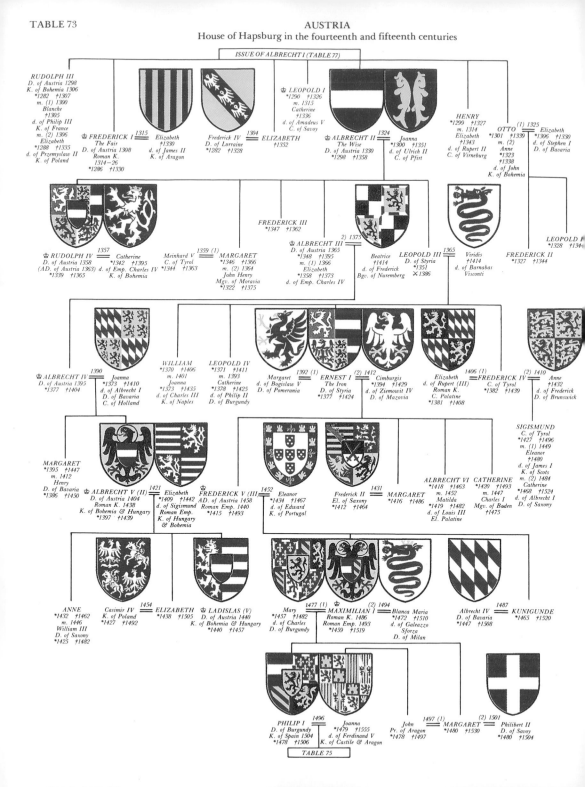

RUDOLPH III
D. of Austria 1298
K. of Bohemia 1306
*1282 †1307
m. (1) 1300
Blanche
d. of Philip III
K. of France
m. (2) 1306
Elizabeth
*1288 †1335
d. of Przemyslaw II
K. of Poland

FREDERICK I ══ 1315 ══ Elizabeth
The Fair   †1330
D. of Austria 1308   d. of James II
Roman K.   K. of Aragon
1314–26
*1286 †1330

Frederick IV ── 1304
D. of Lorraine
*1282 †1328

ELIZABETH
†1352

☩ **LEOPOLD I**
*1290 †1326
m. 1315
Catherine
d. of Amadeus V
C. of Savoy

☩ **ALBRECHT II** ══ 1324 ══ Joanna
The Wise   *1300 †1351
D. of Austria 1330   d. of Ulrich II
*1298 †1358   C. of Pfirt

HENRY
*1299 †1327
m. 1314
Elizabeth
d. of Rupert II
C. of Virneburg

OTTO (1) 1325
*1301 †1339
m. (2)
Anne
*1323
†1338
d. of John
K. of Bohemia

Elizabeth
*1306 †1330
d. of Stephen I
D. of Bavaria

FREDERICK III
*1347 †1362

ALBRECHT III
D. of Austria 1365
*1348 †1395
m. (1) 1366
Elizabeth
*1358 †1373
d. of Emp. Charles IV

2) 1375 ══ Beatrice
†1414
d. of Frederick
Bgv. of Nuremberg

LEOPOLD III ── 1365
D. of Styria
*1351
×1386

Viridis
†1414
d. of Barnabas
Visconti

LEOPOLD
*1328 †134

FREDERICK II
*1327 †1344

☩ **RUDOLPH IV** ── 1357 ── Catherine
D. of Austria 1358   *1342 †1395
(AD. of Austria 1363)   d. of Emp. Charles IV
*1339 †1365

Meinhard V ── 1359 (1) ── **MARGARET**
C. of Tyrol   *1346 †1366
*1344 †1363   m. (2) 1364
                  John Henry
                  Mgv. of Moravia
                  *1322 †1375

☩ **ALBRECHT IV** ── 1390 ── Joanna
D. of Austria 1395   *1373 †1410
*1377 †1404   d. of Albrecht I
                  D. of Bavaria
                  C. of Holland

WILLIAM
*1370 †1406
m. 1401
Joanna
*1373 †1435
d. of Charles III
K. of Naples

LEOPOLD IV
*1371 †1411
m. 1393
Catherine
*1378 †1425
d. of Philip II
D. of Burgundy

Margaret ── 1392 (1)
d. of Bogislaw V
D. of Pomerania

ERNEST I ── (2) 1412 ── Cimburgis
The Iron   *1394 †1429
D. of Styria   d. of Ziemowit IV
*1377 †1424   D. of Mazovia

Elizabeth
d. of Rupert (III)
Roman K.
C. Palatine
*1381 †1408

FREDERICK IV ── 1406 (1)
C. of Tyrol
*1382 †1439

── (2) 1410 ── Anne
*1432
d. of Frederick
D. of Brunswick

SIGISMUND
C. of Tyrol
*1427 †1496
m. (1) 1449
Eleanor
†1480
d. of James I
K. of Scots
m. (2) 1484
Catherine
*1468 †1524
d. of Albrecht I
D. of Saxony

MARGARET
*1395 †1447
m. 1412
Henry
D. of Bavaria
*1386 †1450

☩ **ALBRECHT V (II)** ── 1421 ── Elizabeth
D. of Austria 1404   *1409 †1442
Roman K. 1438   d. of Sigismund
K. of Bohemia & Hungary   Roman Emp.
*1397 †1439   K. of Hungary
                  & Bohemia

☩ **FREDERICK V (III)** ── 1452 ── Eleanor
AD. of Austria 1458   *1434 †1467
Roman Emp. 1440   d. of Edward
*1415 †1493   K. of Portugal

Frederick II ── 1431 ── **MARGARET**
                  *1416 †1486

ALBRECHT VI
*1418 †1463

CATHERINE
*1420 †1493
m. 1447
Charles I
Mgv. of Baden
†1475

m. 1452
Matilda
*1419 †1482
d. of Louis III
El. Palatine

ANNE
*1432 †1462
m. 1446
William III
D. of Saxony
*1425 †1482

Casimir IV ── 1454 ── **ELIZABETH**
K. of Poland   *1438 †1505
*1427 †1492

☩ **LADISLAS (V)**
D. of Austria 1440
K. of Bohemia & Hungary
*1440 †1457

Mary ── 1477 (1)
*1457 †1482
d. of Charles
D. of Burgundy

☩ **MAXIMILIAN I** ── (2) 1494 ── Blanca Maria
Roman K. 1486   *1472 †1510
Roman Emp. 1493   d. of Galeazzo
*1459 †1519   Sforza
                  D. of Milan

Albrecht IV ── 1487 ── **KUNIGUNDE**
D. of Bavaria   *1465 †1520
*1447 †1508

PHILIP I ── 1496 ── Joanna
D. of Burgundy   *1479 †1555
K. of Spain 1504   d. of Ferdinand V
*1478 †1506   K. of Castile & Aragon

John ── 1497 (1) ── **MARGARET** ── (2) 1501 ── Philibert II
Pr. of Aragon   *1480 †1530   D. of Savoy
*1478 †1497   *1480 †1504

TABLE 75

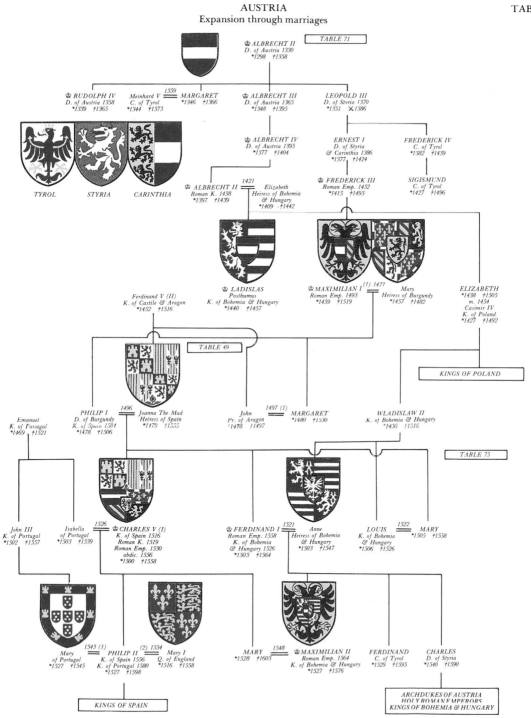

✠ ALBRECHT II
D. of Austria 1330
*1298 †1358

TABLE 71

✠ RUDOLPH IV
D. of Austria 1358
*1339 †1365

Meinhard V
C. of Tyrol
*1344 †1373

1359

MARGARET
*1346 †1366

✠ ALBRECHT III
D. of Austria 1365
*1348 †1395

LEOPOLD III
D. of Styria 1370
*1351 ✕1386

✠ ALBRECHT IV
D. of Austria 1395
*1377 †1404

ERNEST I
D. of Styria
& Carinthia 1386
*1377 †1424

FREDERICK IV
C. of Tyrol
*1382 †1439

TYROL   STYRIA   CARINTHIA

✠ ALBRECHT II
Roman K. 1438
*1397 †1439

1421

Elizabeth
Heiress of Bohemia
& Hungary
*1409 †1442

✠ FREDERICK III
Roman Emp. 1452
*1415 †1493

SIGISMUND
C. of Tyrol
*1427 †1496

Ferdinand V (II)
K. of Castile & Aragon
*1452 †1516

✠ LADISLAS
Posthumus
K. of Bohemia & Hungary
*1440 †1457

✠ MAXIMILIAN I
Roman Emp. 1493
*1459 †1519

(1) 1477

Mary
Heiress of Burgundy
*1457 †1482

ELIZABETH
*1438 †1505
m. 1454
Casimir IV
K. of Poland
*1427 †1492

TABLE 49

KINGS OF POLAND

Emanuel
K. of Portugal
*1469 †1521

PHILIP I
D. of Burgundy
K. of Spain 1501
*1478 †1506

1496

Joanna The Mad
Heiress of Spain
*1479 †1555

John
Pr. of Aragon
*1478 †1497

1497 (1)

MARGARET
*1480 †1530

WLADISLAW II
K. of Bohemia & Hungary
*1456 †1516

TABLE 75

John III
K. of Portugal
*1502 †1557

Isabella
of Portugal
*1503 †1539

1526

✠ CHARLES V (I)
K. of Spain 1516
Roman K. 1519
Roman Emp. 1530
abdic. 1556
*1500 †1558

✠ FERDINAND I
Roman Emp. 1558
K. of Bohemia
& Hungary 1526
*1503 †1564

1521

Anne
Heiress of Bohemia
& Hungary
*1503 †1547

LOUIS
K. of Bohemia
& Hungary
*1506 †1526

1522

MARY
*1505 †1558

Mary
of Portugal
*1527 †1545

1543 (1)

PHILIP II
K. of Spain 1556
K. of Portugal 1580
*1527 †1598

(2) 1554

Mary I
Q. of England
*1516 †1558

MARY
*1528 †1603

1548

✠ MAXIMILIAN II
Roman Emp. 1564
K. of Bohemia & Hungary
*1527 †1576

FERDINAND
C. of Tyrol
*1529 †1595

CHARLES
D. of Styria
*1540 †1590

KINGS OF SPAIN

ARCHDUKES OF AUSTRIA
HOLY ROMAN EMPERORS
KINGS OF BOHEMIA & HUNGARY

Chapter 18

AUSTRIA: MODERN

The long agony of the Thirty Years' War (1618–48) made clear the immediate destiny of the Hapsburgs. German unity had for the nonce become an impossibility, not to be achieved until the nineteenth century, and then under the banner of the Hohenzollerns. By the Treaty of Westphalia the Crown of Bohemia was acknowledged as the hereditary possession of the Hapsburgs. Over three hundred different states were recognized in Germany, many of them minute in land and resources; in general the worship of the inhabitants was dictated by the faith of the prince–*cujus regio ejus religio* was an oft-quoted maxim. Meanwhile the threat of the Turks continued to lour over Austria's eastern flank. It was perhaps fortunate for Europe that the Ottoman dynasty went through a period of weakness and instability just at this time.

Ferdinand, eldest son of Ferdinand III, had been elected King of Bohemia, but died in his father's lifetime. In 1657 Leopold I, the next brother, began his long reign. He was to add extensively to the Hapsburg domains, increasing their area by almost a half. The Emperor was an ugly, lonely man with a reserved and unwarlike disposition; in his features the family lip was almost a deformity. He was pious and a patron of learning, much under the influence of the Catholic Church. His second marriage brought him the Tyrol with the extinction of that branch of the Hapsburgs (Table 75); his first had been to his own niece, the Spanish Infanta. In 1664 his armies, with some help from France, defeated the Turks at St Gotthard and proved that Islam was vulnerable. But in 1683 the Sultan, now allied to France, set in motion a formidable attack on Austria, and reached the gates of Vienna. Leopold fled, but his brother-in-law, Charles of Lorraine, improvised a defence and the King of Poland, John Sobieski, came to his aid. In a desperate battle the Turks were routed and the city

saved; never again was the Ottoman Empire to be a threat to central Europe. The returned Emperor was ungrateful: 'How does one receive an elected king?' he sneered. 'With open arms,' replied the Duke of Lorraine, 'if he has saved one's capital'.

In 1686 Lorraine captured Buda and in the following year savagely defeated the Turks on the historic field of Mohács. The Hungarian Diet now resolved that their Crown should descend with the male line of the Hapsburg dynasty. By the Treaty of Karlowitz (1699) the Sultan ceded almost all Hungary and Croatia to the Emperor. One consequence of these triumphant campaigns, all led by foreign generals, was the establishment in 1680 of a regular, standing Austrian army.

But the Turkish problem was not Leopold's only anxiety. French aggression in western Germany threatened imperial interests, and in 1689 Austria joined an alliance with England and the Netherlands. Over international affairs at the end of the seventeenth century loomed the question of the childless, mad King of Spain (Charles II: Table 50). There was general agreement that the vast Spanish dominions must be broken up, but there were various claimants. By unanimity among the Great Powers Joseph Ferdinand of Bavaria, Leopold's grandson by his first marriage, was accepted as the main heir, but unluckily died in 1699. A second solution was elaborated which divided the Spanish inheritance between Philip of Anjou and Charles, younger son of Leopold, but in vain. The Austrian Hapsburgs aspired to the entire spoil and Leopold rejected the compromise, an act of ambition and folly. When Charles II of Spain died in 1700, he bequeathed all his lands to the French Duke of Anjou.

Most of the reign of Joseph I (Table 76) was taken up with the consequent War of the Spanish Succession; under Prince Eugene of Savoy the Emperor's

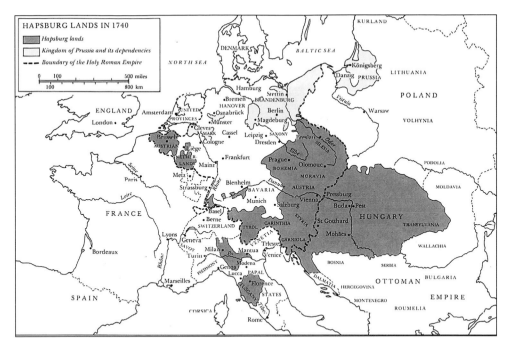

forces campaigned beside their English allies, led by Marlborough, at Blenheim and in the Low Countries. Joseph's death without sons brought his brother Charles VI to the imperial throne and, as a substantial ruler in his own right, he was clearly unacceptable to the Powers as an heir to Spain; by the Treaty of Rastatt (1714) Austria acquired the Spanish Netherlands (which Britain was resolved to withhold from France), Naples, Milan and Sardinia. The Austrian Empire thus became a considerable Italian power; its own future was, however, in serious hazard.

Joseph I begat only two girls; Charles VI devoted much of his reign and vast efforts to securing the succession of his own elder daughter, Maria Theresa, and to reversing the natural order of inheritance which would have favoured his nieces. The settlement designed to this end was known as the Pragmatic Sanction; one by one the constituent parts of the Empire acceded to it, and after them the various Great Powers of Europe. Not till 1735 did France and Spain agree to it at the Treaty of Vienna (which settled a brief and futile contest over the succession to Poland). This triumph of French diplomacy arranged also that Naples and Sicily should pass to Spain, and that Maria Theresa should marry Francis, Duke of Lorraine, who would give up his own duchy and receive that of Florence in its place.

MARIA THERESA

When Charles VI died in 1740, it might have been thought that his daughter's position was secure. But the presence of an inexperienced and youthful queen weighed more with some powers than the sanctity of treaties. Led by Prussia, Saxony, Spain and Bavaria all claimed portions of Maria Theresa's heritage. Charles of Bavaria was elected King of the Romans and then Emperor (1742) – the only non-Hapsburg to hold the imperial Crown since 1437; however, he died in 1745 and was replaced by Maria Theresa's husband, Francis. In 1741 a French statesman could declare that the House of Hapsburg was finished. Cardinal Fleury was wrong, and the Queen of Hungary (as Maria Theresa was styled at this time) made a remarkable recovery. Britain continued to be her ally and to subsidize her efforts; her Magyar subjects rallied with valour to her cause. The perfidious Frederick of Prussia, bribed with Silesia, turned, if only briefly, to her support. In 1748 she emerged from the War of the Austrian Succession, recognized, and with only minor losses in Italy. But the permanent Prussian seizure of Silesia, a wealthy province, left Austria with an antipathy to the Hohenzollerns; in the Seven Years' War (1756–63) the Empress was allied, though without much profit,

TABLE 75

AUSTRIA, BOHEMIA AND HUNGARY
Hapsburgs in the sixteenth and seventeenth centuries

ISSUE OF PHILIP I K. OF SPAIN (TABLE 73)

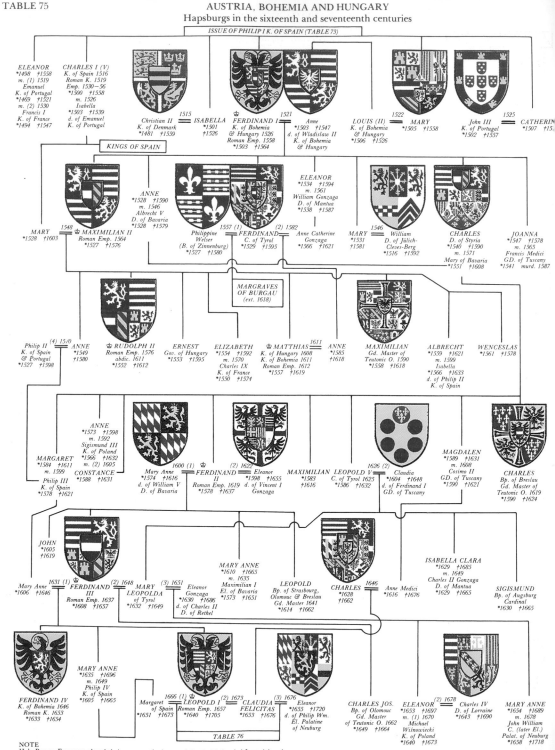

ELEANOR
*1498 †1558
m. (1) 1519
Emanuel
K. of Portugal
*1469 †1521
m. (2) 1530
Francis I
K. of France
*1494 †1547

CHARLES I (V)
K. of Spain 1516
Roman K. 1519
Emp. 1530–56
*1500 †1558
m. 1526
Isabella
*1503 †1539
d. of Emanuel
K. of Portugal

Christian II ═ **ISABELLA**
K. of Denmark   *1501
*1481 †1559   †1526

1515

FERDINAND I 1521 ═ **Anne**
K. of Bohemia   *1503 †1547
& Hungary 1526   d. of Wladislaw II
Roman Emp. 1558   K. of Bohemia
*1503 †1564   & Hungary

LOUIS (II)
K. of Bohemia
& Hungary
*1506 †1526

MARY 1522
*1505 †1558

John III
K. of Portugal
*1502 †1557

═ **CATHERIN** 1525
*1507 †15..

KINGS OF SPAIN

MARY 1548 ═ ♔ **MAXIMILIAN II**
*1528 †1603   Roman Emp. 1564
*1527 †1576

ANNE
*1528 †1590
m. 1546
Albrecht V
D. of Bavaria
*1528 †1579

**Philippine
Welser**
(B. of Zinnenburg)
*1527 †1580
═ **FERDINAND** 1557 (1)
C. of Tyrol   (2) 1582 ═ **Anne Catherine**
*1529 †1595   Gonzaga
            *1566 †1621

ELEANOR
*1534 †1594
m. 1561
William Gonzaga
D. of Mantua
*1538 †1587

MARY 1546 ═ **William**
*1531   D. of Jülich-
†1581   Cleves-Berg
         *1516 †1592

CHARLES
D. of Styria
*1540 †1590
m. 1571
Mary of Bavaria
*1551 †1608

JOANNA
*1547 †1578
m. 1565
Francis Medici
GD. of Tuscany
*1541 murd. 1587

*MARGRAVES
OF BURGAU
(ext. 1618)*

Philip II (4) 15/0 ═ **ANNE**
K. of Spain   *1549
& Portugal   †1580
*1527 †1598

♔ **RUDOLPH II**
Roman Emp. 1576
abdic. 1611
*1552 †1612

ERNEST
Gov. of Hungary
*1553 †1595

ELIZABETH
*1554 †1592
m. 1570
Charles IX
K. of France
*1550 †1574

♔ **MATTHIAS** 1611
K. of Hungary 1608
K. of Bohemia 1611
Roman Emp. 1612
*1557 †1619

ANNE
*1585
†1618

MAXIMILIAN
Gd. Master of
Teutonic O. 1590
*1558 †1618

ALBRECHT
*1559 †1621
m. 1599
Isabella
*1566 †1633
d. of Philip II
K. of Spain

WENCESLAS
*1561 †1578

ANNE
*1573 †1598
m. 1592
Sigismund III
K. of Poland
*1566 †1632
m. (2) 1605
CONSTANCE
*1588 †1631

MARGARET
*1584 †1611
m. 1599
Philip III
K. of Spain
*1578 †1621

Mary Anne 1600 (1) ♔ **FERDINAND**
d. of William V   (2) 1622 ═ **Eleanor**
D. of Bavaria   II   *1598 †1655
          Roman Emp. 1619   d. of Vincent I
          *1578 †1637   Gonzaga

MAXIMILIAN
*1583
†1616

LEOPOLD V (2) ═ **Claudia** 1626
C. of Tyrol 1625   *1604 †1648
*1586 †1632   d. of Ferdinand I
            GD. of Tuscany

MAGDALEN
*1589 †1631
m. 1608
Cosimo II
GD. of Tuscany
*1590 †1621

CHARLES
Bp. of Breslau
Gd. Master of
Teutonic O. 1619
*1590 †1624

JOHN
*1605
†1619

Mary Anne 1631 (1) **FERDINAND** (2) 1648 ═ **MARY**
*1606 †1646   III   LEOPOLDA
         Roman Emp. 1637   of Tyrol
         *1608 †1657   *1632 †1649

MARY ANNE
*1610 †1665
m. 1635
Maximilian I
El. of Bavaria
*1573 †1651

LEOPOLD
Bp. of Strasbourg,
Olomouc & Breslau
Gd. Master 1641
*1614 †1662

CHARLES 1646 ═ **Anne Medici**
*1628   *1616 †1676
†1662

ISABELLA CLARA
*1629 †1685
m. 1649
Charles II Gonzaga
D. of Mantua
*1629 †1665

SIGISMUND
Bp. of Augsburg
Cardinal
*1630 †1665

(3) 1651 **Eleanor
Gonzaga**
*1630 †1686
d. of Charles II
D. of Rethel

FERDINAND IV
K. of Bohemia 1646
Roman K. 1653
*1633 †1654

MARY ANNE
*1635 †1696
m. 1649
Philip IV
K. of Spain
*1605 †1665

**Margaret
of Spain**
*1651 †1673
═ 1666 (1) **LEOPOLD I** (2) 1673 ═ **CLAUDIA** (3) 1676
   Roman Emp. 1657   FELICITAS
   *1640 †1705   *1653 †1676

Eleanor
*1655 †1720
d. of Philip Wm.
El. Palatine
of Neuburg

CHARLES JOS.
Bp. of Olomouc
Gd. Master
of Teutonic O. 1662
*1649 †1664

ELEANOR (2) 1678 ═ **Charles IV**
*1653 †1697   D. of Lorraine
m. (1) 1670   *1643 †1690
Michael
Wiśniowiecki
K. of Poland
*1640 †1673

MARY ANNE
*1654 †1689
m. 1678
John William
C. (later El.)
Palat. of Neuburg
*1658 †1718

TABLE 76

NOTE
Holy Roman Emperors placed their arms on the breast of the double-headed Imperial eagle,
while Kings of the Romans (Roman K.) used the single-headed eagle.

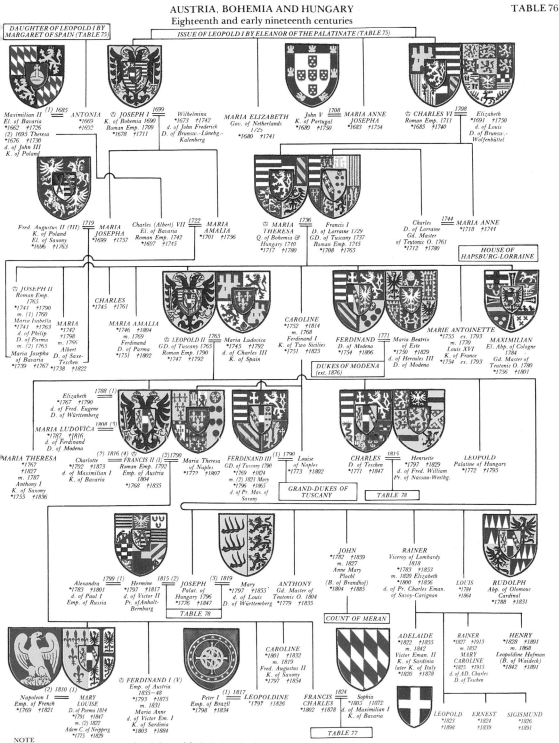

DAUGHTER OF LEOPOLD I BY MARGARET OF SPAIN (TABLE 75)

ISSUE OF LEOPOLD I BY ELEANOR OF THE PALATINATE (TABLE 75)

Maximilian II
El. of Bavaria
*1662 †1726
(1) 1685 (2) 1695 Theresa
*1676 †1730
d. of John III
K. of Poland

ANTONIA
*1669
†1692

JOSEPH I 1699
K. of Bohemia 1690
Roman Emp. 1709
*1678 †1711

Wilhelmina
*1673 †1742
d. of John Frederick
D. of Brunsw.-Lünebg.-
Kalenberg

MARIA ELIZABETH
Gov. of Netherlands
1725
*1680 †1741

John V 1708
K. of Portugal
*1689 †1750

MARIA ANNE
JOSEPHA
*1683 †1754

CHARLES VI 1708
Roman Emp. 1711
*1685 †1711

Elizabeth
*1691 †1750
d. of Louis
D. of Brunsw.-
Wolfenbüttel

Fred. Augustus II (III) 1719
K. of Poland
El. of Saxony
*1696 †1763

MARIA
JOSEPHA
*1699 †1757

Charles (Albert) VII 1722
El. of Bavaria
Roman Emp. 1742
*1697 †1745

MARIA
AMALIA
*1701 †1756

MARIA
THERESA
Q. of Bohemia &
Hungary 1710
*1717 †1780

Francis I 1736
D. of Lorraine 1729
GD. of Tuscany 1737
Roman Emp. 1745
*1708 †1765

Charles 1744
D. of Lorraine
Gd. Master
of Teutonic O. 1761
*1712 †1780

MARIA ANNE
*1718 †1744

HOUSE OF HAPSBURG-LORRAINE

JOSEPH II
Roman Emp.
1765
*1741 †1790
(1) 1760
Maria Isabella
*1741 †1763
d. of Philip
D. of Parma
(2) 1765
Maria Josepha
of Bavaria
*1739 †1767

CHARLES
*1745 †1761

MARIA
*1742
†1798
m. 1756
Albert
D. of Saxe-
Teschen
*1738 †1822

MARIA AMALIA
*1746 †1804
m. 1769
Ferdinand
D. of Parma
*1751 †1802

LEOPOLD II 1765
G.D. of Tuscany 1765
Roman Emp. 1790
*1747 †1792

Maria Ludovica
*1745 †1792
d. of Charles III
K. of Spain

CAROLINE
*1752 †1814
m. 1768
Ferdinand I
K. of Two Sicilies
*1751 †1825

FERDINAND 1771
D. of Modena
*1754 †1806

Maria Beatrix
of Este
*1750 †1829
d. of Hercules III
D. of Modena

MARIE ANTOINETTE
*1755 ex. 1793
m. 1770
Louis XVI
K. of France
*1754 ex. 1793

MAXIMILIAN
El. Abp. of Cologne
1784
Gd. Master of
Teutonic O. 1780
*1756 †1801

DUKES OF MODENA
(ext. 1876)

Elizabeth
*1767 †1790
d. of Fred. Eugene
D. of Württemberg

MARIA LUDOVICA 1808 (3)
*1787 †1816
d. of Ferdinand
D. of Modena

MARIA THERESA
*1767
†1827
m. 1787
Anthony I
K. of Saxony
*1755 †1836

Charlotte
*1792 †1873
d. of Maximilian I
K. of Bavaria

FRANCIS II (1) (2) 1790
Roman Emp. 1792
Emp. of Austria
1804
*1768 †1835

Maria Theresa
of Naples
*1772 †1807

FERDINAND III 1790
G.D. of Tuscany 1790
*1769 †1824
m. (2) 1821 Mary
*1796 †1865
d. of Pr. Max. of
Saxony

Louise
of Naples
*1773 †1802

CHARLES 1815
D. of Teschen
*1771 †1847

Henriette
*1797 †1829
d. of Fred. William
Pr. of Nassau-Weilbg.

LEOPOLD
Palatine of Hungary
*1772 †1795

GRAND-DUKES OF TUSCANY

TABLE 78

JOHN
*1782 †1859
m. 1827
Anne Mary
Plochl
(B. of Brandhof)
*1804 †1885

RAINER
Viceroy of Lombardy
1818
*1783 †1853
m. 1820 Elizabeth
*1800 †1856
d. of Pr. Charles Eman.
of Savoy-Carignan

LOUIS
*1784
†1864

RUDOLPH
Abp. of Olomouc
Cardinal
*1788 †1831

Alexandra 1799 (1)
*1783 †1801
d. of Paul I
Emp. of Russia

Hermine 1815 (2)
*1797 †1817
d. of Victor II
Pr. of Anhalt-
Bernburg

JOSEPH (3) 1819
Palat. of
Hungary 1796
*1776 †1847

Mary
*1797 †1855
d. of Louis
D. of Württemberg

ANTHONY
Gd. Master of
Teutonic O. 1804
*1779 †1835

COUNT OF MERAN

ADELAIDE
*1822 †1855
m. 1842
Victor Eman. II
K. of Sardinia
later K. of Italy
*1820 †1878

RAINER
*1827 †1913
m. 1852
MARY
CAROLINE
*1825 †1915
d. of AD. Charles
D. of Teschen

HENRY
*1828 †1891
m. 1868
Leopoldine Hofman
(B. of Waideck)
*1842 †1891

TABLE 78

Napoleon I (2) 1810 (1)
Emp. of French
*1769 †1821

MARY
LOUISE
D. of Parma 1814
*1791 †1847
m. (2) 1822
Adam C. of Neipperg
*1775 †1829

FERDINAND I (V)
Emp. of Austria
1835–48
*1793 †1875
m. 1831
Maria Anne
d. of Victor Em. I
K. of Sardinia
*1803 †1884

Peter I 1817
Emp. of Brazil
*1798 †1834

LEOPOLDINE
*1797 †1826

FRANCIS
CHARLES
*1802 †1878

Sophia 1824
*1805 †1072
d. of Maximilian I
K. of Bavaria

CAROLINE
*1801 †1832
m. 1819
Fred. Augustus II
K. of Saxony
*1797 †1854

LEOPOLD
*1823
†1898

ERNEST
*1824
†1839

SIGISMUND
*1826
†1891

TABLE 77

NOTE
Holy Roman Emperors placed their arms on the breast of the double-headed eagle,
which in the 17th century usually held in its claws a sword and a sceptre, and in the
18th century an orb instead of the sceptre.

TABLE 77

AUSTRIA, BOHEMIA AND HUNGARY
End of the monarchy

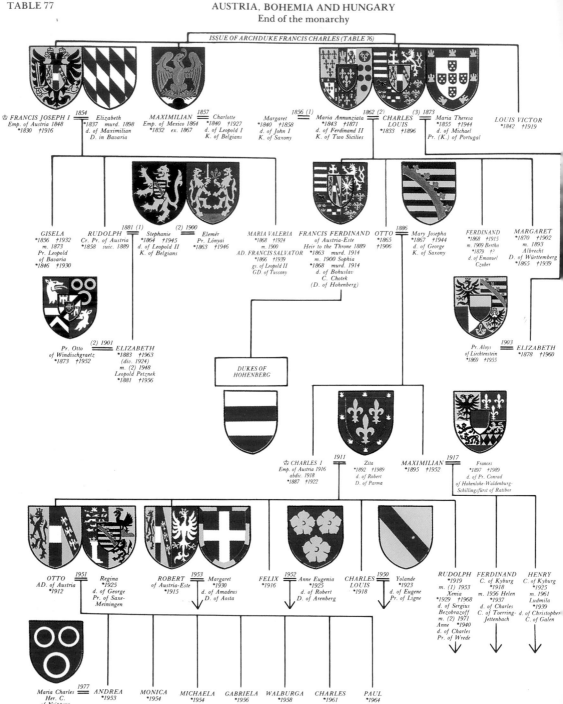

ISSUE OF ARCHDUKE FRANCIS CHARLES (TABLE 76)

☼ FRANCIS JOSEPH I
Emp. of Austria 1848
1830 †1916

1854

Elizabeth
1837 murd. 1898
d. of Maximilian
D. in Bavaria

MAXIMILIAN
Emp. of Mexico 1864
1832 ex. 1867

1857

Charlotte
1840 †1927
d. of Leopold I
K. of Belgians

Margaret
1840 †1858
d. of John I
K. of Saxony

1856 (1)

Maria Annunziata
1843 †1871
d. of Ferdinand II
K. of Two Sicilies

1862 (2)

CHARLES
LOUIS
1833 †1896

(3) 1873

Maria Theresa
1855 †1944
d. of Michael
Pr. (K.) of Portugal

LOUIS VICTOR
1842 †1919

GISELA
1856 †1932
m. 1873
Pr. Leopold
of Bavaria
1846 †1930

RUDOLPH
Cr. Pr. of Austria
1858 suic. 1889

1881 (1)

Stephanie
1864 †1945
d. of Leopold II
K. of Belgians

(2) 1900

Elemér
Pr. Lónyai
1863 †1946

MARIA VALERIA
1868 †1924
m. 1900
AD. FRANCIS SALVATOR
1866 †1939
gs. of Leopold II
GD. of Tuscany

FRANCIS FERDINAND
of Austria-Este
Heir to the Throne 1889
1863 murd. 1914
m. 1900 Sophia
1868 murd. 1914
d. of Bohuslav
C. Chotek
(D. of Hohenberg)

OTTO
1865
†1906

1886

Mary Josepha
1867 †1944
d. of George
K. of Saxony

FERDINAND
1868 †1915
m. 1905 Bertha
1879 †?
d. of Emanuel
Czuber

MARGARET
1870 †1902
m. 1893
Albrecht
D. of Württemberg
1865 †1939

Pr. Otto
of Windischgraetz
1873 †1952

(2) 1901

ELIZABETH
1883 †1963
(div. 1924)
m. (2) 1948
Leopold Petznek
1881 †1956

Pr. Aloys
of Liechtenstein
1869 †1955

1903

ELIZABETH
1878 †1960

DUKES OF
HOHENBERG

☼ CHARLES I
Emp. of Austria 1916
abdic. 1918
1887 †1922

1911

Zita
1892 †1989
d. of Robert
D. of Parma

MAXIMILIAN
1895 †1952

1917

Frances
1897 †1989
d. of Pr. Conrad
of Hohenlohe-Waldenburg-
Schillingsfurst of Ratibor

OTTO
AD. of Austria
1912

1951

Regina
1925
d. of George
Pr. of Saxe-
Meiningen

ROBERT
of Austria-Este
1915

1953

Margaret
1930
d. of Amadeus
D. of Aosta

FELIX
1916

1952

Anne Eugenia
1925
d. of Robert
D. of Arenberg

CHARLES
LOUIS
1918

1950

Yolande
1923
d. of Eugene
Pr. of Ligne

RUDOLPH
1919
m. (1) 1953
Xenia
1929 †1968
d. of Sergius
Bezobrazoff
m. (2) 1971
Anne *1940*
d. of Charles
Pr. of Wrede

FERDINAND
C. of Kyburg
1918
m. 1956 Helen
1937
d. of Charles
C. of Toerring-
Jettenbach

HENRY
C. of Kyburg
1925
m. 1961
Ludmila
1939
d. of Christopher
C. of Galen

Maria Charles
Her. C.
of Neipperg
1951

1977

ANDREA
1953

MONICA
1954

MICHAELA
1954

GABRIELA
1956

WALBURGA
1958

CHARLES
1961

PAUL
1964

with France against England and Prussia.

In 1765 Joseph II followed his father as Holy Roman Emperor, and shared the government with his mother. The decay of Poland prompted her powerful neighbours to plunder: in 1772 Austria shared in the first partition of Poland and acquired Galicia, a gain which could scarcely be justified on either historical or geographical grounds. But Maria Theresa, whose comely if unexciting features gaze down from so many state portraits in her dominions, was a great ruler in the domestic sphere also. Central organs of government were developed; noble and ecclesiastical privileges were reduced; she ended her reign with a larger revenue and a better established army than her mixed domains had known before. By her death in 1780 she had by courage and endurance transformed her challenged inheritance into an enlarged monarchy with a tincture of reform.

The ancestry of Maria Theresa (Table 79) shows a wide mixture of German blood; considering the degree of intermarriage among the Hapsburgs, the variety is noteworthy. She used several different arrangements of her arms; that shown on Table 76 displays four quarterings for Hungary, Austria and Burgundy, Moravia and Silesia, with the lion of Bohemia over all. The blazon of her husband, the Emperor Francis, shows the many pretensions of his House with the shield of his two Duchies of Lorraine and Tuscany in pretence.

Joseph II belonged to the group of late eighteenth-century sovereigns who are known as the enlightened despots. His ambitions and endeavours were shared by his younger brother Leopold, to whom the Grand-Duchy of Tuscany had been assigned as an apanage, and who strove with more flexibility and intelligence to modernize the antique system of the Medici grand-dukes. Joseph believed that a beneficent emperor could best achieve the happiness of his peoples. On the one hand he attacked and diminished the position of the Church; on the other his tendency to centralize provoked disquiet in his polyglot lands. Before the end of his reign he was compelled to modify many of his reforms, but education was widely encouraged and the sublime talent of Mozart adorned the Austria of his day.

The brief imperial reign of Leopold II served to tidy up some of the confusion left by Joseph. His shield (Table 76) shows the imperial two-headed eagle, to which in the eighteenth century a sword and orb were added in either claw, with a superimposed shield of Hungary, Bohemia, Burgundy and Bar, and over all Lorraine, Austria and Tuscany. His younger brother Ferdinand married the heiress of the Este Dukes of Modena, in north Italy, and founded a cadet branch which died out in 1876. Their coat-of-arms showed quarterings of the Empire and Ferrara (a version of France), with a central pale of the papal insignia surmounted by the family arms of Este, a white eagle, gold crowned, on a blue field.

NAPOLEONIC WARS

The Emperor Francis II had to face the wind of change engendered by the French Revolution, and the more positive gale of Napoleon thereafter. The first impact of the new climate was the execution of his aunt, Marie Antoinette, Queen of France, and the occupation of the Austrian Netherlands (Belgium) by the revolutionary armies. Poor compensation was achieved in 1795 when Austria annexed western Galicia from the third partition of Poland. During the campaigns of Bonaparte in Italy, boundaries were drawn and redrawn on many occasions; in Germany Francis lost the last vestiges of control or power. Accordingly, in August, 1804, he solemnly assumed the title of Emperor of Austria, thus matching the style of Emperor of the French asserted by Napoleon a few months earlier. His honorific availed him little when it came to war: at Austerlitz (1805) the parvenu French ruler overwhelmed the traditional Hapsburg dynast. Napoleon proceeded to redesign the map of Europe; in 1806 Francis II proclaimed the dissolution of the Holy Roman Empire. The long line of emperors, stemming (with some interruptions) from the coronation of Charles the Great in 800, thus sadly terminated a thousand years later in the limp hands of Francis. Four years later he was compelled to give his daughter in marriage to the Corsican upstart (Tables 69-70). The alliance was one of the earliest achievements of Metternich, the able minister who was to dominate Austrian politics for the next generation. In 1813 Napoleon was at last defeated at Leipzig by a coalition including imperial troops; the resulting peace congress met at Vienna in 1814, and – though rudely interrupted by the Hundred Days and Waterloo – set about reconstituting Europe.

From the furnace of this period a new Austria was forged. Belgium and western Galicia were lost, but virtually the whole of north Italy, including Venice, came under Hapsburg control. Modena was restored to the younger branch; Ferdinand, the Emperor's next brother, was reinstated in Tuscany; the Archduke Charles, who had commanded the Austrian armies with more skill than success, was Duke of Teschen (Těšín to the Czechs or Cieszyn to the Poles); two other brothers successively held rank as Palatine of Hungary and another as Viceroy of Lombardy: Anthony was Grand-Master of the Teutonic Order and Rudolph held the historic See of Olomouc (Olmütz). These Princes add the serpent of Milan and the winged lion of Venice together with the arms of Galicia to the older quarterings of Hungary and Bohemia: Rudolph places this blazon over the arms

[151]

TABLE 78

AUSTRIA
Collateral branches (nineteenth and twentieth centuries)

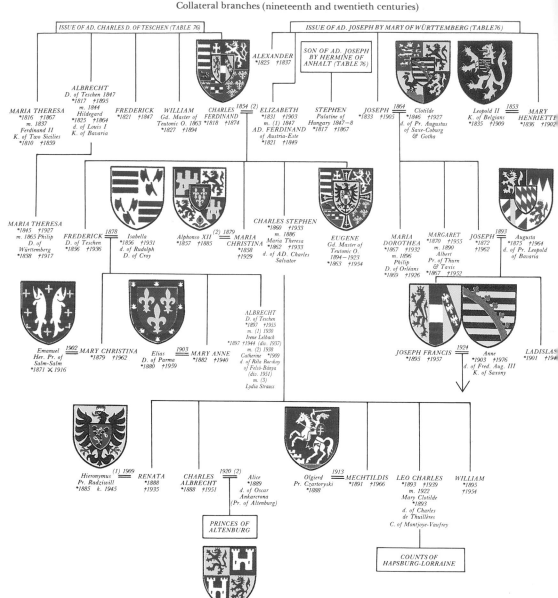

ISSUE OF AD. CHARLES D. OF TESCHEN (TABLE 76)

ISSUE OF AD. JOSEPH BY MARY OF WÜRTTEMBERG (TABLE 76)

ALEXANDER
*1825 †1837

SON OF AD. JOSEPH
BY HERMINE OF
ANHALT (TABLE 76)

MARIA THERESA
*1816 †1867
m. 1837
Ferdinand II
K. of Two Sicilies
*1810 †1859

ALBRECHT
D. of Teschen 1847
*1817 †1895
m. 1844
Hildegard
*1825 †1864
d. of Louis I
K. of Bavaria

FREDERICK
*1821 †1847

WILLIAM
Gd. Master of
Teutonic O. 1863
*1827 †1894

CHARLES 1854 (2)
FERDINAND
*1818 †1874
AD. FERDINAND
of Austria-Este
*1821 †1849

ELIZABETH
*1831 †1903
m. (1) 1847

STEPHEN
Palatine of
Hungary 1847–8
*1817 †1867

JOSEPH 1864
*1833 †1905

Clotilde
*1846 †1927
d. of Pr. Augustus
of Saxe-Coburg
& Gotha

Leopold II 1853
K. of Belgians
*1835 †1909

MARY
HENRIETTE
*1836 †1902

MARIA THERESA
*1845 †1927
m. 1865 Philip
D. of
Württemberg
*1838 †1917

FREDERICK 1878
D. of Teschen
*1856 †1936

Isabella
*1856 †1931
d. of Rudolph
D. of Croy

Alphonso XII
*1857 †1885

(2) 1879 MARIA
CHRISTINA
*1858
†1929

CHARLES STEPHEN
*1860 †1933
m. 1886
Maria Theresa
*1862 †1933
d. of AD. Charles
Salvator

EUGENE
Gd. Master of
Teutonic O.
1894–1923
*1863 †1954

MARIA
DOROTHEA
*1867 †1932
m. 1896
Philip
D. of Orléans
*1869 †1926

MARGARET
*1870 †1955
m. 1890
Albert
Pr. of Thurn
& Taxis
*1867 †1952

JOSEPH 1893
*1872
†1962

Augusta
*1875 †1964
d. of Pr. Leopold
of Bavaria

Emanuel 1902
Her. Pr. of
Salm-Salm
*1871 ✕ 1916

MARY CHRISTINA
*1879 †1962

Elias 1903
D. of Parma
*1880 †1959

MARY ANNE
*1882 †1940

ALBRECHT
D. of Teschen
*1897 †1955
m. (1) 1930
Irene Lelbach
*1897 †1944 (div. 1937)
m. (2) 1938
Catherine *1909
d. of Béla Borskay
of Felsö-Bánya
(div. 1951)
m. (3)
Lydia Strauss

JOSEPH FRANCIS 1924
*1895 †1957

Anne
*1903 †1976
d. of Fred. Aug. III
K. of Saxony

LADISLAS
*1901 †194

Hieronymus (1) 1909
Pr. Radziwill
*1885 k. 1945

RENATA
*1888
†1935

CHARLES 1920 (2)
ALBRECHT
*1888 †1951

Alice
*1889
d. of Oscar
Ankarcrona
(Pr. of Altenburg)

Olgierd 1913
Pr. Czartoryski
*1888

MECHTILDIS
*1891 †1966

LEO CHARLES
*1893 †1939
m. 1922
Mary Clotilde
*1893
d. of Charles
de Thuillères
C. of Montjoye-Vaufrey

WILLIAM
*1895
†1954

PRINCES OF
ALTENBURG

COUNTS OF
HAPSBURG-LORRAINE

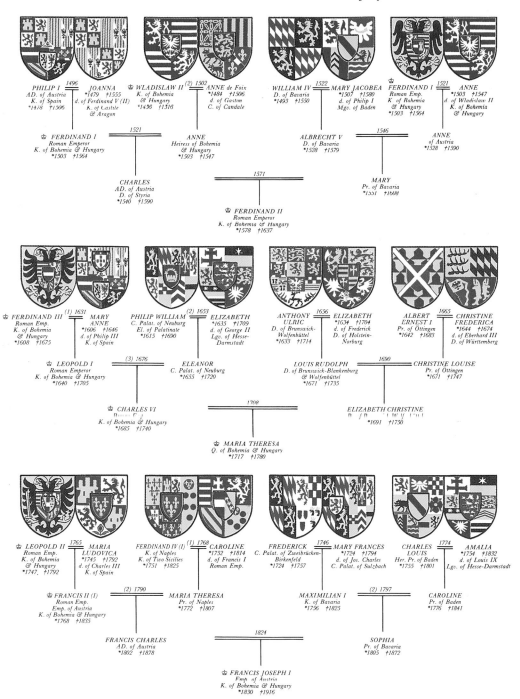

PHILIP I
AD. of Austria
K. of Spain
*1478 †1506

1496

JOANNA
*1479 †1555
d. of Ferdinand V (II)
K. of Castile
& Aragon

♚ WLADISLAW II
K. of Bohemia
& Hungary
*1456 †1516

(2) 1502

ANNE de Foix
*1484 †1506
d. of Gaston
C. of Candale

WILLIAM IV
D. of Bavaria
*1493 †1550

1522

MARY JACOBEA
*1507 †1580
d. of Philip I
Mgv. of Baden

FERDINAND I
Roman Emp.
K. of Bohemia
& Hungary
*1503 †1564

1521

ANNE
*1503 †1547
d. of Wladislaw II
K. of Bohemia
& Hungary

♚ FERDINAND I
Roman Emperor
K. of Bohemia & Hungary
*1503 †1564

1521

ANNE
Heiress of Bohemia
& Hungary
*1503 †1547

ALBRECHT V
D. of Bavaria
*1528 †1579

1546

ANNE
of Austria
*1528 †1590

CHARLES
AD. of Austria
D. of Styria
*1540 †1590

1571

MARY
Pr. of Bavaria
*1551 †1608

♚ FERDINAND II
Roman Emperor
K. of Bohemia & Hungary
*1578 †1637

♚ FERDINAND III
Roman Emp.
K. of Bohemia
& Hungary
*1608 †1675

(1) 1631

MARY
ANNE
*1606 †1646
d. of Philip III
K. of Spain

PHILIP WILLIAM
C. Palat. of Neuburg
El. of Palatinate
*1615 †1690

(2) 1653

ELIZABETH
*1635 †1709
d. of George II
Lgv. of Hesse-
Darmstadt

ANTHONY
ULRIC
D. of Brunswick-
Wolfenbüttel
*1633 †1714

1656

ELIZABETH
*1634 †1704
d. of Frederick
D. of Holstein-
Norburg

ALBERT
ERNEST I
Pr. of Öttingen
*1642 †1683

1665

CHRISTINE
FREDERICA
*1644 †1674
d. of Eberhard III
D. of Württemberg

♚ LEOPOLD I
Roman Emperor
K. of Bohemia & Hungary
*1640 †1705

(3) 1676

ELEANOR
C. Palat. of Neuburg
*1655 †1720

LOUIS RUDOLPH
D. of Brunswick-Blankenburg
& Wolfenbüttel
*1671 †1735

1690

CHRISTINE LOUISE
Pr. of Öttingen
*1671 †1747

♚ CHARLES VI
Roman Emp.
K. of Bohemia & Hungary
*1685 †1740

1708

ELIZABETH CHRISTINE
D. of Brunswick-Wolfenbüttel
*1691 †1750

♚ MARIA THERESA
Q. of Bohemia & Hungary
*1717 †1780

♚ LEOPOLD II
Roman Emp.
K. of Bohemia
& Hungary
*1747 †1792

1765

MARIA
LUDOVICA
*1745 †1792
d. of Charles III
K. of Spain

FERDINAND IV
K. of Naples
K. of Two Sicilies
*1751 †1825

(1) 1768

CAROLINE
*1752 †1814
d. of Francis I
Roman Emp.

FREDERICK
C. Palat. of Zweibrücken-
Birkenfeld
*1724 †1757

1746

MARY FRANCES
*1724 †1794
d. of Jos. Charles
C. Palat. of Sulzbach

CHARLES
LOUIS
Her. Pr. of Baden
*1755 †1801

1774

AMALIA
*1754 †1832
d. of Louis IX
Lgv. of Hesse-Darmstadt

♚ FRANCIS II (I)
Roman Emp.
Emp. of Austria
K. of Bohemia & Hungary
*1768 †1835

(2) 1790

MARIA THERESA
Pr. of Naples
*1772 †1807

MAXIMILIAN I
K. of Bavaria
*1756 †1825

(2) 1797

CAROLINE
Pr. of Baden
*1776 †1841

FRANCIS CHARLES
AD. of Austria
*1802 †1878

1824

SOPHIA
Pr. of Bavaria
*1805 †1872

♚ FRANCIS JOSEPH I
Emp. of Austria
K. of Bohemia & Hungary
*1830 †1916

of Olomouc. From Lombardy to Lemberg the Hapsburgs ruled over a solid block of prosperous territories. Good ports on the Adriatic were in fact worth more than distant harbours in the Low Countries.

The Holy Roman Empire was not restored; instead a German Confederation of 39 states was established, in which Austria strove to play the leading part. When Francis II reached the end of his long reign, he gave his son the advice, 'Rule, and change nothing.' His Empire had settled into a course of conservative stagnation. Ferdinand I was feeble-minded; it is rumoured that, having shot an eagle, he enquired why it had only one head. Discontent spread and reached a climax in 1848, the year of revolutions. Ferdinand abdicated; Metternich fled; the Archduke Francis Charles renounced the succession; his son, Francis Joseph (Table 77) began his long and often tragic reign. The pedigree of the young Emperor (Table 79) shows that his maternal ancestry derived from several German families, with a strong Wittelsbach infusion, while his paternal forebears were exclusively Hapsburg and Bourbon.

FRANCIS JOSEPH

The first years of Francis Joseph were devoted to the restoration of authority and the suppression of rebellion in Hungary. Thereafter the Emperor ruled in an increasingly autocratic manner; his absolutism was tinged with reform, and the general tenor of government was both more vigorous and more enlightened than under his uncle. He had, however, to contend with rising tides of nationalism in Italy, in Germany, in the Balkans and in his own dominions. His first losses were in Italy, where an alliance of the Savoyard Kings of Sardinia and Napoleon III transferred Lombardy to the former (1859); the Hapsburg Duke of Modena and Grand-Duke of Tuscany lost their territories a year later; the unification of Italy was under way. Within the Empire the various races, particularly the Magyars, were seeking a measure of independence. The Emperor oscillated between simple constitutionalism and some form of federalism. These manoeuvres were overshadowed by the involvement of Francis Joseph in a remote dispute over the Duchies of Schleswig and Holstein (Chapter 5), which culminated in a lightning attack by Prussia on Austria in 1866, and the Prussian victory at Sadowa. In consequence, Venetia had to be ceded to Italy and Austria was excluded from Germany, in whose affairs she had had a voice for over four hundred years.

The Emperor now settled for federalism. Through the *Ausgleich* (1867) the former Empire of Austria was transformed into the Dual Monarchy of Austria-Hungary. Broadly, the areas of Galicia, Bohemia and Austria constituted the first; Hungary, Transylvania and Croatia the second. The settlement, while flattering to the Magyars, left the Slav races unsatisfied; nevertheless it lasted 50 years.

Francis Joseph endured a series of personal disasters. His brother had been lured by Napoleon III into accepting the throne of Mexico. Adequate military support and sufficient local enthusiasm alike were lacking and Maximilian was ignominiously shot in 1867. In 1889 the Crown Prince Rudolph committed suicide in company with a girl not his wife; in 1898 the Empress Elizabeth, a wild and lovely horsewoman, was wantonly assassinated in Switzerland. In 1900 the Archduke Francis Ferdinand, the next heir to the throne, made a morganatic marriage with Countess Chotek which debarred his children from succession. In the Balkans the surge of Slavic nationalism was thrown back on itself by the Austrian annexation of Bosnia and Hercegovina in 1908. In the summer of 1914 the Archduke and his wife were assassinated at Sarajevo. Still the ageing Emperor toiled on until death relieved him in 1916. When he ascended the throne Metternich had just left office: when he quitted it, Woodrow Wilson was already President of the United States.

Francis Joseph was followed by his alrat-nephew Charles who abdicated in 1918. The peace terms of the Allies fragmented the Austrian Empire irretrievably and the long story of the Hapsburg and Hapsburg-Lorraine dynasties was ended. After the loss of the north Italian duchies, the Austrian archdukes used a shield which can be seen for Charles Louis (top of Table 77) or Charles Ferdinand (Table 78); it comprised quarterings for Hungary, Bohemia, Galicia and Austria ancient, with over all Hapsburg, Austria modern and Lorraine. Francis Ferdinand had been given the name of Este (after the extinction of the Dukes of Modena) and added their eagle to his escutcheon. This can be seen on Table 77. The Emperors themselves sometimes employed a highly elaborate device with the shields of their provinces spread over a two-headed eagle; more normally they used the simple pattern on Table 71 where the imperial eagle bears on its breast Hapsburg, Austria and Lorraine, and is surrounded by the ancient Burgundian Order of the Golden Fleece. Charles I died in Madeira in 1922, a remote grave for the last Hapsburg Emperor. His claims were inherited by his eldest son, the Archduke Otto, whose interests have been mainly academic. The younger brother, Robert, has been granted the name and arms of Este. Otto, however, has renounced all dynastic ambition and taken on West German citizenship; he is now a member of the European Parliament for Bavaria. Thus, by the ironies of history, the potential successor to the throne of Charlemagne sits as Herr von Hapsburg in a democratic assembly whose frontiers are not so very different from those of the ninth-century Emperor.

Chapter 19

BRANDENBURG, PRUSSIA AND GERMANY

The two Powers which have exercised the greatest influence on German history both grew out of frontier provinces. The growth of the Ostmark into Austria has been discussed in Chapter 17: the Mark of Brandenburg is the ancient core of Prussia and hence of the German Empire. Early medieval Germany was divided into five duchies, Lorraine, Franconia, Swabia, Bavaria and Saxony. On the eastern boundary of Saxony, which then covered the north German plain, developed the Mark of Brandenburg. In 1133 the title of Margrave of Brandenburg was conferred on Albrecht the Bear (Table 80) who was also briefly Duke of Saxony. His family is named Ascanian from the Latin name of their castle of Aschersleben; the elder branch ruled Brandenburg until its extinction in 1320, while the younger is still represented by the Princes of Anhalt. The successors of Albrecht the Bear steadily pushed eastwards, first across the Elbe and then across the Oder. New towns like Berlin and Frankfurt marked their progress. Otto II was invested with Pomerania; though not taken up, the claim remained.

After the death of Henry II in 1320, control of the Mark passed to the Wittelsbachs of Bavaria, who exercised it loosely, and from them to the Kings of Bohemia of the Luxemburg House. In 1351 the Emperor Charles IV finally attached the rank of Elector to the Margravate. In 1411 the Emperor Sigismund pawned the province to Frederick of Hohenzollern; he was unable to redeem it and in 1417 Frederick was solemnly installed as Elector and Margrave of Brandenburg. The province was impoverished; the peasants were mainly of Wendish stock, but the squires, or 'Junkers', were predominantly German.

BRANDENBURG

The castle of Zollern, later (1170) Hohenzollern, is in Swabia, not in fact far distant from the castle of Haps-burg. Counts of Zollern are known from the early twelfth century and one of them married the heiress of the Burgraves of Nuremberg. Their son, Frederick, who became Burgrave in 1192, founded the two branches of the Hohenzollern family: both used the dramatically simple shield of four white and black quarters (Table 80). Since the cadet branch became the more important, it may be simpler to deal with the elder first. The descendants of Frederick II acquired the Lordship of Sigmaringen in 1534, and became Princes of the Holy Roman Empire in 1576. There were two main branches, Hohenzollern-Sigmaringen and Hohenzollern-Hechingen, but the latter became extinct in 1869; both had already renounced their territories to Prussia in 1849. In 1866 Prince Charles of Hohenzollern-Sigmaringen became Prince (and later King) of Rumania; in 1870 the candidature of his elder brother Leopold for the throne of Spain was a proximate cause of the Franco-Prussian War which ended in 1871.

Conrad, the younger son, maintained the title over Nuremberg. Other Lordships were acquired, including Bayreuth (by marriage, 1234) and Ansbach (by purchase, 1331). Frederick V was a friend and supporter of the Emperor Charles IV, who made him a prince of the Empire in 1363; he divided his lands between his two sons. The younger Frederick, who received Nuremberg (which he later sold to the citizens thereof), was able to purchase the Margravate of Brandenburg and, after his elder brother's death, to reunite the Hohenzollern fiefs. The second great step up the ladder of power had been taken; and Frederick perceived with acumen that the future lay in the north rather than in Nuremberg and Swabia. His province was in disorder, but his resolve was firm: using the new weapon of artillery, he battered his nobility into submission. But for all his realism he was

TABLE 80

PRUSSIA AND BRANDENBURG
General survey

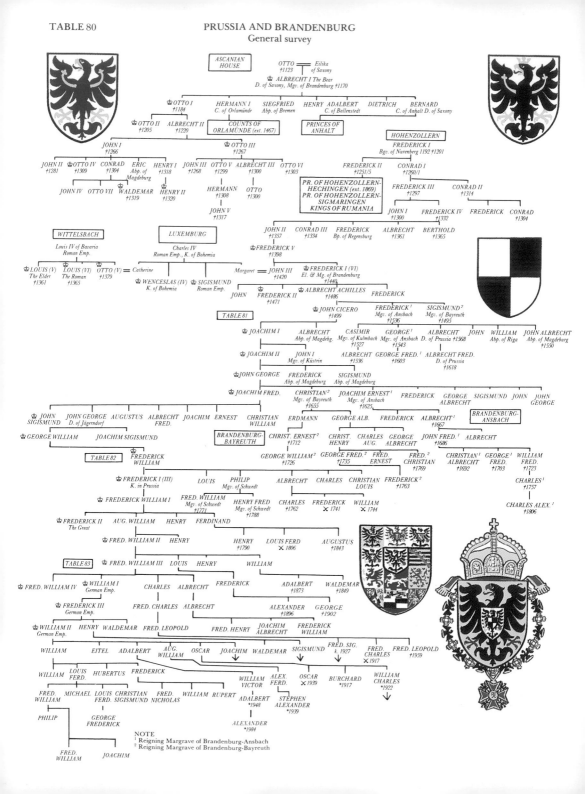

ASCANIAN HOUSE

OTTO †1123 = Eilika of Saxony

ALBRECHT I The Bear D. of Saxony, Mgv. of Brandenburg †1170

OTTO I †1184 — HERMANN I C. of Orlamünde — SIEGFRIED Abp. of Bremen — HENRY ADALBERT C. of Ballenstedt — DIETRICH — BERNARD C. of Anhalt D. of Saxony

OTTO II †1205 — ALBRECHT II †1220 — COUNTS OF ORLAMÜNDE (ext. 1467) — PRINCES OF ANHALT — HOHENZOLLERN FREDERICK I Bgv. of Nuremberg 1192 †1201

JOHN I †1266 — OTTO III †1267

JOHN II †1281 — OTTO IV †1309 — CONRAD †1304 — ERIC Abp. of Magdebg. — HENRY I †1318 — JOHN III †1268 — OTTO V †1299 — ALBRECHT III †1300 — OTTO VI †1303

FREDERICK II †1251/5 — CONRAD I †1260/1

PR. OF HOHENZOLLERN-HECHINGEN (ext. 1869) PR. OF HOHENZOLLERN-SIGMARINGEN KINGS OF RUMANIA

FREDERICK III †1297 — CONRAD II †1314

JOHN IV — OTTO VII — WALDEMAR †1319 — HENRY II †1320

HERMANN †1308 — OTTO †1300

JOHN V †1317

JOHN I †1300 — FREDERICK IV †1332 — FREDERICK — CONRAD †1304

JOHN II †1357 — CONRAD III †1334 — FREDERICK Bp. of Regensburg — ALBRECHT †1361 — BERTHOLD †1365

WITTELSBACH
Louis IV of Bavaria Roman Emp.

FREDERICK V †1398

LUXEMBURG
Charles IV Roman Emp., K. of Bohemia

LOUIS (V) The Elder †1361 — LOUIS (VI) The Roman †1365 — OTTO (V) = Catherine †1379

Margaret = JOHN III †1420 — FREDERICK I (VI) El. & Mg. of Brandenburg †1440

WENCESLAS (IV) K. of Bohemia — SIGISMUND Roman Emp.

JOHN — FREDERICK II †1471 — ALBRECHT ACHILLES †1486 — FREDERICK

TABLE 81

JOHN CICERO †1499 — FREDERICK¹ Mgv. of Ansbach †1536 — SIGISMUND² Mgv. of Bayreuth †1495

JOACHIM I — ALBRECHT Abp. of Magdebg. — CASIMIR Mgv. of Kulmbach †1527 — GEORGE¹ Mgv. of Ansbach †1543 — ALBRECHT D. of Prussia †1568 — JOHN — WILLIAM Abp. of Riga — JOHN ALBRECHT Abp. of Magdeburg †1550

JOACHIM II — JOHN I Mgv. of Küstrin — ALBRECHT †1536 — GEORGE FRED.¹ †1603 — ALBRECHT FRED. D. of Prussia †1618

JOHN GEORGE — FREDERICK Abp. of Magdeburg — SIGISMUND Abp. of Magdeburg

JOACHIM FRED. — CHRISTIAN² Mgv. of Bayreuth †1655 — JOACHIM ERNEST¹ Mgv. of Ansbach †1625 — FREDERICK — GEORGE ALBRECHT — SIGISMUND — JOHN GEORGE

JOHN SIGISMUND — JOHN GEORGE D. of Jägerndorf — AUGUSTUS — ALBRECHT FRED. — JOACHIM ERNEST — CHRISTIAN WILLIAM — ERDMANN — GEORGE ALB. — FREDERICK — ALBRECHT¹ †1667 — BRANDENBURG-ANSBACH

GEORGE WILLIAM — JOACHIM SIGISMUND

BRANDENBURG-BAYREUTH — CHRIST. ERNEST² †1712 — CHRIST. HENRY — CHARLES AUG. — GEORGE ALBRECHT — JOHN FRED.¹ †1686 — ALBRECHT

TABLE 82 — FREDERICK WILLIAM — CHRIST.ERNEST² †1712

GEORGE WILLIAM² †1726 — GEORGE FRED.² †1735 — FRED.² CHRISTIAN ERNEST †1769 — CHRISTIAN¹ ALBRECHT †1692 — GEORGE¹ FRED. †1703 — WILLIAM FRED. †1723

FREDERICK I (III) K. in Prussia — LOUIS — PHILIP Mgv. of Schwedt — ALBRECHT — CHARLES — CHRISTIAN LOUIS — FREDERICK² †1763 — CHARLES¹ †1757

FREDERICK WILLIAM I — FRED. WILLIAM Mgv. of Schwedt †1771 — HENRY FRED. Mgv. of Schwedt †1788 — CHARLES †1762 — FREDERICK ✕ 1741 — WILLIAM ✕ 1744 — CHARLES ALEX.¹ †1806

FREDERICK II The Great — AUG. WILLIAM — HENRY — FERDINAND

FRED. WILLIAM II — HENRY — HENRY †1790 — LOUIS FERD. ✕ 1806 — AUGUSTUS †1843

TABLE 83 — FRED. WILLIAM III — LOUIS — HENRY — WILLIAM

FRED. WILLIAM IV — WILLIAM I German Emp. — CHARLES — ALBRECHT — FREDERICK — ADALBERT †1873 — WALDEMAR †1849

FREDERICK III German Emp. — FRED. CHARLES — ALBRECHT — ALEXANDER †1886 — GEORGE †1902

WILLIAM II German Emp. — HENRY — WALDEMAR — FRED. LEOPOLD — FRED. HENRY — JOACHIM ALBRECHT — FREDERICK WILLIAM

WILLIAM — EITEL — ADALBERT — AUG. WILLIAM — OSCAR — JOACHIM — WALDEMAR — SIGISMUND — FRED. SIG. k. 1927 — FRED. CHARLES ✕ 1917 — FRED. LEOPOLD †1959

WILLIAM — LOUIS FERD. — HUBERTUS — FREDERICK — WILLIAM VICTOR — ALEX. FERD. — OSCAR ✕ 1939 — BURCHARD *1917 — WILLIAM CHARLES *1922

FRED. WILLIAM — MICHAEL — LOUIS FERD. — CHRISTIAN SIGISMUND — FRED. NICHOLAS — WILLIAM — RUPERT — ADALBERT *1948 — STEPHEN ALEXANDER *1939

PHILIP — GEORGE FREDERICK

ALEXANDER *1984

FRED. WILLIAM — JOACHIM

NOTE
¹ Reigning Margrave of Brandenburg-Ansbach
² Reigning Margrave of Brandenburg-Bayreuth

not proof against the German weakness: at his demise he shared his domains among his offspring. The death without issue of his two eldest sons brought the whole inheritance to Albrecht Achilles. In 1473 he ordained the *Dispositio Achillea* by which the Margravate of Brandenburg was to descend undivided in the male line, while Ansbach and Bayreuth could be allotted to younger sons, but not further divided. It was a momentous decision for the family's future greatness.

Accordingly his eldest son became Margrave while the Franconian fiefs went to the two younger sons. Successive Electors showed themselves men of ability and sense, and bit by bit built up their territories by diplomacy and purchase rather than by war. The shield of Joachim I (Table 81) shows quarterings for Brandenburg, Pomerania, Nuremberg and Hohenzollern, with the sceptre of the Grand-Chamberlain of the Empire over all. His brother Albrecht bears a wider range of quarterings and over all the shields of his three Sees, Halberstadt, Magdeburg and Mainz. The red eagle of Brandenburg can also be seen at the head of Table 80; the gold outline on the wings was originally a suggestion of anatomical structure, but developed into an addition, the *kleestengel* (cloverstalk), susceptible to variations and very typical of German heraldry. The Electors embraced the Lutheran faith, and Joachim II added three secularized bishoprics to his lands. But a greater prize was already in sight.

PRUSSIA

The Teutonic Order of Knights had been established at the end of the twelfth century to combat the infidel in the Holy Land. In 1229 a contingent was sent to fight the pagans in Prussia, and this became their only theatre of activity. The lands they conquered were controlled by great castles and towns like Königsberg. In 1511 the Order, after a period of decline, chose Albrecht of Hohenzollern-Ansbach (Table 80) as Grand-Master. Fourteen years later, the soldier-priest secularized the Order, married, and became Duke of Prussia under the King of Poland. His kinsmen were quick to see their chance. Duke Albrecht's son, Albrecht Frederick, proved to be an imbecile; and he sired only daughters. The Elector Joachim Frederick married one as his second wife, and his son, John Sigismund (Table 81) espoused the eldest. In 1618 the Duchy of Prussia passed to the latter. Nor was this all. The wife of the unhappy Duke Albrecht Frederick was a sister of the Duke of Cleves and Jülich, who died childless in 1609. His inheritance in the Rhineland was wealthy, and the claimants turned to the sword. The local struggle became part of the Thirty Years' War, and it was not until 1666 that Cleves, Mark and Ravenstein were finally allotted to Brandenburg as its share. Mean-

while Bayreuth and Ansbach, which had reverted to Elector Joachim Frederick, had been regranted to his younger brothers, Christian and Joachim Ernest. The shield of Elector George William, at the base of Table 81, now shows, beneath the imperial sceptre, quarterings for Prussia (a black eagle), Brandenburg (a red one), Berg, Cleves, Jülich, Nuremberg and Hohenzollern. George William himself was more interested in hunting than statecraft; he had great difficulty in making up his mind, and achieved only a policy of unrewarded neutrality until in 1631 he allied with his brother-in-law, Gustavus Adolphus of Sweden. In 1637 the last Duke of Pomerania died and the Elector claimed the Duchy as his right. Brandenburg was ravaged by war when he died in 1640.

His son was of different mettle. Not for nothing is Frederick William (Table 82) called the Great Elector. His long reign transformed his state and laid the foundations of future Prussian greatness. His resources were meagre, his realm devastated, but his supple diplomacy and dynamic powers of organization triumphed over these handicaps. At the Treaty of Westphalia he secured the eastern half of Pomerania (Sweden kept the west), the bishoprics of Halberstadt and Minden and the reversion of the larger diocese of Magdeburg. Already Brandenburg looked more powerful. In the wars between Sweden and Poland he adroitly changed sides and freed the Duchy of Prussia from any Polish suzerainty: the Elector was now its independent prince, though Prussia was still cut off by part of Poland from Brandenburg. The prestige of his forces was greatly enhanced by a victory over the hitherto invincible Swedes at Fehrbellin in 1679. Behind the complicated and unscrupulous foreign policy of the Elector lay a thorough reorganization of his realm. Berlin was mainly his creation and he was interested in science. But above all he welded Prussia and Brandenburg into an efficient and militarist instrument of absolute monarchy. The Prussian army was henceforward a factor in European politics.

In 1701, with the consent of the Emperor, Frederick III, son of the Great Elector, took the title of King *in* Prussia. This was permissible because that province lay outside the boundaries of the Holy Roman Empire, but it had also to be recognized that much of West Prussia was still in Polish hands. He crowned himself, with no priestly aid, at Königsberg; and on the same day founded the Order of the Black Eagle, whose collar can be seen on Table 80. Furthermore, he placed his initials FR on the breast of the Prussian eagle on his shield (Table 82). Despite his participation in the War of the Spanish Succession against Louis XIV his gains were negligible save for the general recognition of his kingship. The arms of his half-brother Philip show the black eagle of Prussia and the red of Brandenburg in a black and white border.

Frederick William I was a boorish and beery figure. For 27 years he ruled his Kingdom with routine military efficiency, lavishing attention on an army which was seldom launched into battle, and for which he collected outsize men with the zeal of a circus-proprietor. This army was increased from under 40,000 to over 80,000 men, but was only maintained at this figure by the use of mercenaries, merciless conscription and iron discipline. On his deathbed, hearing the words 'Naked I came into this world, and naked I shall leave it,' the King muttered, 'No, no, I shall have my uniform'. He had added Stettin and most of western Pomerania to his territory, but Sweden clung to Stralsund and the isle of Rügen.

FREDERICK THE GREAT

Frederick II, the Great, is one of the dazzling figures of history. His talents and success are indisputable; his behaviour at times was odious. Much may be attributed to his bitter youth under a drill-sergeant father, when he had to learn French or the flute by subterfuge. The German tongue he grew to loathe. Cynic, atheist, follower of Voltaire, he was without scruple and without a real friend. His first action was shamelessly to attack Maria Theresa of Austria and to seize the rich province of Silesia; in his first battle he fled, though his troops triumphed. With brutal self-interest he then switched sides: by the Treaty of Berlin (1742) he legitimized his conquest and augmented Brandenburg with Silesia. At this juncture his title was altered to King *of* Prussia. Many of his later campaigns were waged to defend this conquest, particularly the Seven Years' War (1756–63) in which he was allied with Britain against France and Austria; Britain laid the foundation of her overseas Empire at the expense of France. On the Continent Frederick II was hard pushed to preserve Prussia, and his victories against odds at Rosbach and Leuthen (1757) are clear evidence of his military brilliance. In 1759 he was again almost defeated; the highly trained army of his father was no more, and his country was ravaged by the Russians. With poison ready for suicide, the King fought on and his reputation hindered his adversaries from pressing home their attacks. A change of sovereign in Russia removed one foe; and when peace came in 1763, Frederick had just contrived to preserve Silesia and the prestige of Prussia. He was ably assisted by his brother Henry, a highly competent commander.

The ensuing years were devoted to refashioning the material resources of Prussia. Agriculture and trade were fostered: a new army constituted. The next coup came in 1772, when, in alliance with Russia, he coerced Austria into the first partition of Poland. West Prussia fell to Frederick's share, and his two principal provinces were no longer separated. Prussia was now beyond all question a major European Power: Frederick II had more than doubled her area and far more than doubled the size of her army. A master of war and movement, a diplomat devoid of any principle save the aggrandizement of Prussia, the little King in the faded blue coat had triumphed from the very edge of ruin. His ancestry (Table 84) shows a predominance of Hanover-Brunswick blood, and a quarter descent from Bavaria. It is tempting to connect Frederick II's affection for the French language with his French forebear, Eleanor d'Olbreuse.

PRUSSIA AND NAPOLEON

The marriage of Frederick II was childless as it was loveless; his successor was his nephew Frederick William II. Faced with the impact of the French Revolution, he made peace with the Republicans and turned his attention to further subdivision of the hapless Polish Kingdom. In 1793 Russia and Prussia cold-bloodedly helped themselves to vast areas of northern Poland; two years later Prussia acquired a further sizeable block of territory including Warsaw. Poland had been obliterated. Frederick William II added to the arms of Prussia the sceptre and orb of royalty. Frederick William III saw no point in attacking Napoleon; when Napoleon attacked him, he was without friends. At Jena in 1806 the French Emperor annihilated the old Prussian army and its reputation, a few weeks after Francis of Austria had jettisoned the ghostly title of Holy Roman Emperor. Bonaparte entered Berlin and desecrated the tomb of Frederick the Great, dead a mere twenty years. It was the nadir of the Prussian fortunes.

The Treaty of Tilsit (1807) deprived Prussia of all provinces west of the river Elbe and of all she had gained from the partitions of Poland; in the circumstances the terms were not ungenerous. Frederick William III, though more virtuous than his father, was a sovereign of limited imagination and powers; fortunately for his dynasty he was able to recruit an able group of ministers, mainly from outside his own realms. Scharnhorst and Gneisenau set about military reform of the army; Humboldt tackled education; over and above all Stein began the general reorganization of the administration. Serfdom was abolished (1807); centralization was diminished; teaching was modernized. Meanwhile a new army was being created with Blücher as its commander, and proved its worth at the battles of Leipzig (1813) and Waterloo (1815).

The Treaty of Vienna constitutes another milestone in the growth of Prussia. It is true she did not recover all the lands she had filched from Poland, but the compensation elsewhere was more than adequate. Most important was the acquisition of a

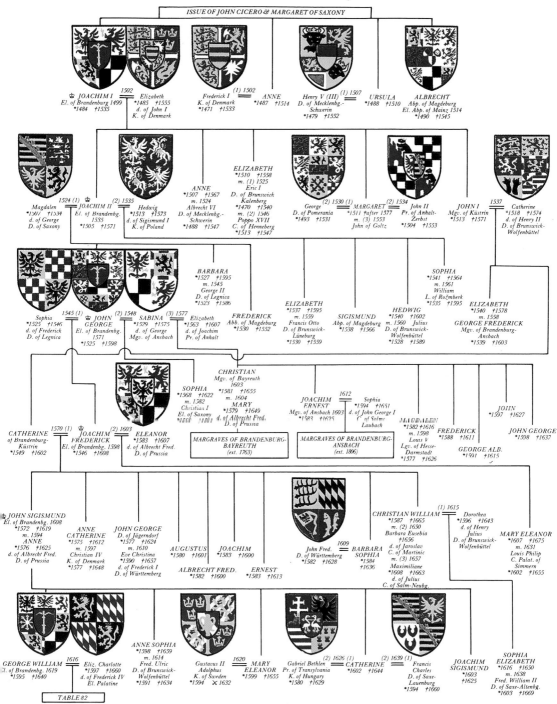

ISSUE OF JOHN CICERO & MARGARET OF SAXONY

♚ JOACHIM I ══1502══ Elizabeth
El. of Brandenburg 1499 · *1485 †1555
*1484 †1535 · d. of John I
K. of Denmark

Frederick I ══(1) 1502══ ANNE
K. of Denmark · *1487 †1514
*1471 †1533

Henry V (III) ══(1) 1507══ URSULA
D. of Mecklenbg.- · *1488 †1510
Schwerin
*1479 †1552

ALBRECHT
Abp. of Magdeburg
El. Abp. of Mainz 1514
*1490 †1545

Magdalen ══1524 (1)══ ♚ JOACHIM II ══(2) 1535══ Hedwig
*1307 †1534 · El. of Brandenbg. · *1513 †1573
d. of George · 1535 · d. of Sigismund I
D. of Saxony · *1505 †1571 · K. of Poland

ANNE
*1507 †1567
m. 1524
Albrecht VI
D. of Mecklenbg.-
Schwerin
*1488 †1547

ELIZABETH
*1510 †1558
m. (1) 1525
Eric I
D. of Brunswick-
Kalenberg
*1470 †1540
m. (2) 1546
Poppo XVII
C. of Henneberg
*1513 †1547

George ══(2) 1530 (1)══ MARGARET ══(2) 1534══ John II
D. of Pomerania · *1511 †after 1577 · Pr. of Anhalt-
*1493 †1531 · m. (3) 1553 · Zerbst
John of Goltz · *1504 †1553

JOHN I ══1537══ Catherine
Mgv. of Küstrin · *1518 †1574
*1513 †1571 · d. of Henry II
D. of Brunswick-
Wolfenbüttel

BARBARA
*1527 †1595
m. 1545
George II
D. of Legnica
*1523 †1586

SOPHIA
*1541 †1564
m. 1561
William
L. of Rožmberk
*1535 †1595

Sophia ══1545 (1)══ JOHN ══(2) 1548══ SABINA ══(3) 1577══ Elizabeth
*1525 †1546 · GEORGE · *1529 †1575 · *1563 †1607
d. of Frederick · El. of Brandenbg. · d. of George · d. of Joachim
D. of Legnica · 1571 · Mgv. of Ansbach · Pr. of Anhalt
*1525 †1598

FREDERICK
Abb. of Magdeburg
*1530 †1552

ELIZABETH
*1537 †1595
m. 1559
Francis Otto
D. of Brunswick-
Lüneburg
*1530 †1559

SIGISMUND
Abp. of Magdeburg
*1538 †1566

HEDWIG
*1540 †1602
m. 1560
Julius
D. of Brunswick-
Wolfenbüttel
*1528 †1589

ELIZABETH
*1540 †1578
m. 1558
GEORGE FREDERICK
Mgv. of Brandenburg-
Ansbach
*1539 †1603

CHRISTIAN
Mgv. of Bayreuth
1603
*1581 †1655

SOPHIA
*1568 †1622
m. 1582
Christian I
El. of Saxony
*1560 †1591

MARY
*1579 †1649
d. of Albrecht Fred.
D. of Prussia

JOACHIM ══1612══ Sophia
ERNEST · *1594 †1651
Mgv. of Ansbach 1603 · C. of Solms-
*1583 †1625 · Laubach

MAGDALEN
*1582 †1616
m. 1598
Louis V
Lgv. of Hesse-
Darmstadt
*1577 †1626

JOHN
*1597 †1627

FREDERICK
*1588 †1611

JOHN GEORGE
*1598 †1637

GEORGE ALB.
*1591 †1615

CATHERINE ══1570 (1)══ ♚ JOACHIM ══(2) 1603══ ELEANOR
of Brandenburg- · FREDERICK · *1583 †1607
Küstrin · El. of Brandenbg. 1598 · d. of Albrecht Fred.
*1549 †1602 · *1546 †1608 · D. of Prussia

MARGRAVES OF BRANDENBURG-
BAYREUTH
(ext. 1763)

MARGRAVES OF BRANDENBURG-
ANSBACH
(ext. 1806)

♚ JOHN SIGISMUND
El. of Brandenbg. 1608
*1572 †1619
m. 1594
ANNE
*1576 †1625
d. of Albrecht Fred.
D. of Prussia

ANNE
CATHERINE
*1575 †1612
m. 1597
Christian IV
K. of Denmark
*1577 †1648

JOHN GEORGE
D. of Jägerndorf
*1577 †1624
m. 1610
Eve Christina
*1590 †1657
d. of Frederick I
D. of Württemberg

AUGUSTUS
*1580 †1601

JOACHIM
*1583 †1600

ALBRECHT FRED.
*1582 †1600

ERNEST
*1583 †1613

John Fred. ══1609══ BARBARA
D. of Württemberg · SOPHIA
*1582 †1628 · *1584
†1636

CHRISTIAN WILLIAM ══(1) 1615══ Dorothea
*1587 †1665 · *1596 †1643
m. (2) 1650 · d. of Henry
Barbara Eusebia · Julius
†1656 · D. of Brunswick-
d. of Jaroslav · Wolfenbüttel
C. of Martinic
m. (3) 1657
Maximiliane
*1608 †1663
d. of Julius
C. of Salm-Neubg.

MARY ELEANOR
*1607 †1675
m. 1631
Louis Philip
C. Palat. of
Simmern
*1602 †1655

GEORGE WILLIAM ══1616══ Eliz. Charlotte
El. of Brandenbg. 1619 · *1597 †1660
*1595 †1640 · d. of Frederick IV
El. Palatine

ANNE SOPHIA
*1598 †1659
m. 1614
Fred. Ulric
D. of Brunswick-
Wolfenbüttel
*1591 †1634

Gustavus II ══1620══ MARY
Adolphus · ELEANOR
K. of Sweden · *1599 †1655
*1594 × 1632

Gabriel Bethlen ══(2) 1626 (1)══ CATHERINE ══(2) 1639 (1)══ Francis
Pr. of Transylvania · *1602 †1644 · Charles
K. of Hungary · D. of Saxe-
*1580 †1629 · Lauenburg
*1594 †1660

JOACHIM
SIGISMUND
*1603
†1625

SOPHIA
ELIZABETH
*1616 †1650
m. 1638
Fred. William II
D. of Saxe-Altenbg.
*1603 †1669

TABLE 82

TABLE 82

PRUSSIA
First Kings

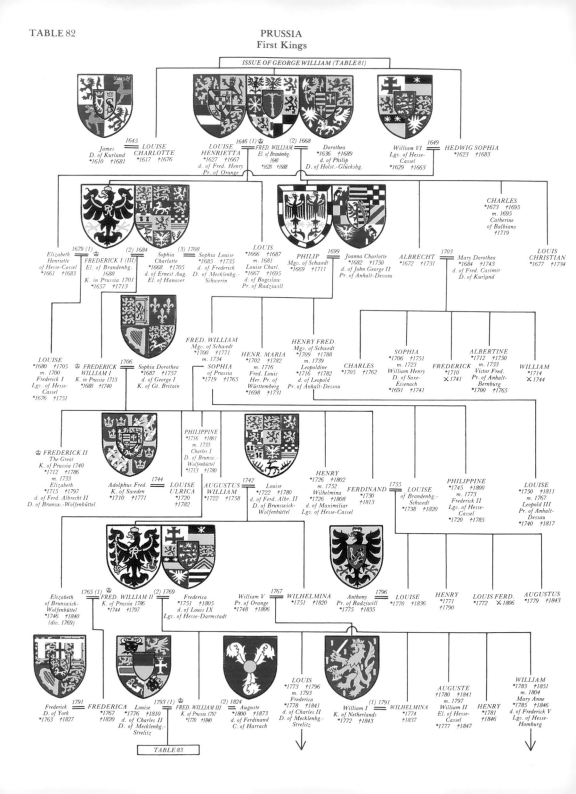

ISSUE OF GEORGE WILLIAM (TABLE 81)

James
D. of Kurland
*1610 †1681

1645
**LOUISE
CHARLOTTE**
*1617 †1676

**LOUISE
HENRIETTA**
*1627 †1667
d. of Fred. Henry
Pr. of Orange

1646 (1)
FRED. WILLIAM
El. of Brandenbg.
1640
*1620 †1688

(2) 1668
Dorothea
*1636 †1689
d. of Philip
D. of Holst.-Glücksbg.

William VI
Lgv. of Hesse-
Cassel
*1629 †1663

1649
HEDWIG SOPHIA
*1623 †1683

CHARLES
*1673 †1695
m. 1695
Catherine
of Balbiano
†1719

**Elizabeth
Henriette**
of Hesse-Cassel
*1661 †1683

1679 (1)
FREDERICK I (III)
El. of Brandenbg.
1688
K. in Prussia 1701
*1657 †1713

(2) 1684
**Sophia
Charlotte**
*1668 †1705
d. of Ernest Aug.
El. of Hanover

(3) 1708
Sophia Louise
*1685 †1735
d. of Frederick
D. of Mecklenbg.-
Schwerin

LOUIS
*1666 †1687
m. 1681
Louise Charl.
*1667 †1695
d. of Bogislav
Pr. of Radziwill

PHILIP
Mgv. of Schwedt
*1669 †1711

1699
Joanna Charlotte
*1682 †1750
d. of John George II
Pr. of Anhalt-Dessau

ALBRECHT
*1672 †1731

1703
Mary Dorothea
*1684 †1743
d. of Fred. Casimir
D. of Kurland

**LOUIS
CHRISTIAN**
*1677 †1734

LOUISE
*1680 †1705
m. 1700
Frederick I
Lgv. of Hesse-
Cassel
*1676 †1751

**FREDERICK
WILLIAM I**
K. in Prussia 1713
*1688 †1740

1706
Sophia Dorothea
*1687 †1757
d. of George I
K. of Gt. Britain

FRED. WILLIAM
Mgv. of Schwedt
*1700 †1771
m. 1734

SOPHIA
of Prussia
*1719 †1765

HENR. MARIA
*1702 †1782
m. 1716
Fred. Louis
Her. Pr. of
Württemberg
*1698 †1731

HENRY FRED.
Mgv. of Schwedt
*1709 †1788
m. 1739
Leopoldine
*1716 †1782
d. of Leopold
Pr. of Anhalt-Dessau

CHARLES
*1705 †1762

SOPHIA
*1706 †1751
m. 1723
William Henry
D. of Saxe-
Eisenach
*1691 †1741

FREDERICK
*1710 ✕1741

ALBERTINE
*1712 †1750
m. 1733
Victor Fred.
Pr. of Anhalt-
Bernburg
*1700 †1765

WILLIAM
*1714
✕1744

FREDERICK II
The Great
K. of Prussia 1740
*1712 †1786
m. 1733
Elizabeth
*1715 †1797
d. of Ferd. Albrecht II
D. of Brunsw.-Wolfenbüttel

Adolphus Fred.
K. of Sweden
*1710 †1771

1744
**LOUISE
ULRICA**
*1720
†1782

**AUGUSTUS
WILLIAM**
*1722 †1758

1742
Louise
*1722 †1780
d. of Ferd. Albr. II
D. of Brunswick-
Wolfenbüttel

HENRY
*1726 †1802
m. 1752
Wilhelmina
*1726 †1808
d. of Maximilian
Lgv. of Hesse-Cassel

FERDINAND
*1730
†1813

1755
LOUISE
of Brandenbg.-
Schwedt
*1738 †1820

PHILIPPINE
*1745 †1800
m. 1773
Frederick II
Lgv. of Hesse-
Cassel
*1720 †1785

LOUISE
*1750 †1811
m. 1767
Leopold III
Pr. of Anhalt-
Dessau
*1740 †1817

PHILIPPINE
*1716 †1801
m. 1733
Charles I
D. of Brunsw.-
Wolfenbüttel
*1713 †1780

Elizabeth
of Brunswick-
Wolfenbüttel
*1746 †1840
(div. 1769)

1765 (1)
FRED. WILLIAM II
K. of Prussia 1786
*1744 †1797

(2) 1769
Frederica
*1751 †1805
d. of Louis IX
Lgv. of Hesse-Darmstadt

William V
Pr. of Orange
*1748 †1806

1767
WILHELMINA
*1751 †1820

1796
Anthony
Pr. of Radziwill
*1775 †1835

LOUISE
*1770 †1836

HENRY
*1771
†1790

LOUIS FERD.
*1772 ✕1806

AUGUSTUS
*1779 †1843

Frederick
D. of York
*1763 †1827

1791
FREDERICA
*1767
†1820

Louise
*1776 †1810
d. of Charles II
D. of Mecklenbg.-
Strelitz

1793 (1)
FRED. WILLIAM III
K. of Prussia 1797
*1770 †1840

(2) 1824
Auguste
*1800 †1873
d. of Ferdinand
C. of Harrach

LOUIS
*1773 †1796
Frederica
*1778 †1841
d. of Charles II
D. of Mecklenbg.-
Strelitz

William I
K. of Netherlands
*1772 †1843

(1) 1791
WILHELMINA
*1774
†1837

AUGUSTE
†1780 †1841
m. 1797
William II
El. of Hesse-
Cassel
*1777 †1847

HENRY
*1781
†1846

WILLIAM
*1783 †1851
m. 1804
Mary Anne
*1785 †1846
d. of Frederick V
Lgv. of Hesse-
Homburg

TABLE 83

solid and prosperous block of territory in the Rhine valley and Westphalia. At long last the remainder of the Cleves inheritance became part of Prussia, and with it cities of the importance of Cologne, Aachen, Bonn, Trier and Coblenz. These provinces were detached from Prussia, but they formed a noteworthy extension and brought the east German Protestant state into contact with the Catholic lands bordering France and Belgium; moreover they included the Ruhr valley which was to develop in industrial importance all through the nineteenth century. Nearer home Prussia received the last Swedish fragment of Pomerania and the northern portion of Saxony. The last-named was in some sense compensation for the cession of Ansbach and Bayreuth to Bavaria: the cadet branches in control of them had died out in 1806 and 1769 respectively (Table 80). Hardenberg, the minister of Frederick William III at Vienna, tried without success to obtain Alsace and Lorraine, which were allowed to Bourbon France.

The resistance to Napoleon in the last years of his rule had partaken of a German nationalist character. Any hopes that a united Germany might arise from the peace settlement were disappointed. The fantastic confusion of the vanished Holy Roman Empire was replaced by a modified muddle of thirty-five independent principalities and four free cities. Among these, Catholic Austria in the south and Protestant Prussia in the north were pre-eminent: both depended for much of their power on eastern provinces, which were excluded from the new Germanic Confederation, an area not greatly different from the old Empire. Other monarchs such as the King of Denmark or the ruler of the United Kingdom had seats within the Diet in respect of Schleswig Holstein or Hanover. No longer were there any independent bishoprics. Austria, thanks to the influence of Metternich, was to preside.

PRUSSIAN HEGEMONY

In 1818 Prussia abolished the many tariff duties within her boundaries; ten years later several small principalities joined her; in 1833 a German Customs Union (*Zollverein*) was formed including all but a few states. Prussia was advertising herself as an alternative to Austria for the leadership of Germany. The long reign of Frederick William III came to an end in 1840; he was a decent, pious man, well served by his ministers who had raised Prussia from the disaster of 1806 to new greatness. His second wife has the slightly unusual Harrach coat-of-arms, with three silver feathers spreading out from a golden ball.

Frederick William IV (Table 83) had enjoyed some reputation as a liberal, but his reign offered scant profit to constitutionalists. The first Prussian Parliament, which he summoned in 1847, was little

to his taste. In 1848, the year of revolutions, German nationalism expressed itself in many areas. Metternich was unseated at Vienna. At Frankfurt-am-Main, the traditional crowning place of the old German emperors, a spontaneous Parliament was assembled without any princely prompting. Its task was formidable, since it operated by enthusiasm rather than from authority; its debates were lengthy, but ultimately it offered the Crown of a united Germany to Frederick William. The Prussian refused it with contempt: only a diadem proffered by the princes would have been acceptable to him, and he strove in the following years to unite them under his leadership only to be smartly rebuffed by Austria. In 1857 his mind gave way; his brother William had been regent for four years before ascending the throne in 1861.

One of his first actions was to modernize the Prussian army, a task ably performed by von Moltke and von Roon. In 1862 he appointed Bismarck his chief minister; the post was his until 1890. The great ministers who advised Frederick William III mainly came from other parts of Germany: the assistants of William I were native-born Prussians. Bismarck, a man gigantic in stature and in powers, hard-drinking, a heavy smoker, a resolute and industrious statesman unhampered by moral considerations, was the architect of the next phase of Prussian power and also of German unity. Often he had to carry with him the more cautious King, whom he had found on the point of abdication.

His first opportunity came with the death of King Frederick VII of Denmark (1863) and the problem of the Duchies of Schleswig and Holstein (Chapter 5). The two fiefs attracted Bismarck because of the possibility of extending Prussia to the North Sea. With masterly skill he persuaded a reluctant Austria to join him in attacking Denmark: the battle was one-sided and the hapless Danes were compelled to cede the Duchies to Austria and Prussia. Condominium was awkward, and in 1865 it was arranged that Austria should have Holstein, and Prussia Schleswig and the harbour of Kiel. Bismarck then secured the friendship of France and Italy and proceeded to turn on Austria. The brevity of the campaign has earned it the name of the Seven Weeks' War. In July 1866 the Austrian Army was routed at Sadowa (near Königgratz, by which name the battle is also known). By the ensuing Treaty of Prague, Prussia annexed both Schleswig and Holstein, and also Hanover, Hesse-Cassel, Nassau and the city of Frankfurt. These latter additions linked Prussia to her Rhineland provinces by land. By another clause the Austrian Empire was definitely excluded from German affairs. Sixty-five thousand square kilometres of land and five million new subjects had been added to Prussia at trifling cost. Austria only suffered the loss of Venice to Italy, for the far-sighted Bismarck desired her ultimate friendship. In 1867 the North German Confederation was established, in which twenty-two hitherto independent unities accepted Prussian dominion. It can have caused no surprise that Bismarck became the first Chancellor.

His ambitions did not rest there: his next target was France. In 1870 the vacant throne of Spain was offered to Prince Leopold of Hohenzollern-Sigmaringen, an infinitely remote kinsman of William I (Table 80), though it is true Leopold's father had briefly been Prussian Prime Minister. The French Government objected to this candidature, which was withdrawn; but in the resulting discussions Bismarck, partly by editing a telegram, provoked the French to war. In a bare two months of fighting, the main French army was annihilated by the efficiency and newer weapons of Prussia; the prestige of French arms and the ancient magic of the Napoleonic name availed nothing. German unity was now assured. Bavaria and Württemberg agreed to it, with certain reservations; in January, 1871, William of Prussia became German Emperor (*Kaiser in Deutschland*) in the great Hall of Mirrors at Versailles. It was precisely 170 years since Frederick I had assumed the Crown of Prussia at Königsberg. The provinces of Alsace and Lorraine were annexed to Prussia.

The arms of the Emperor William I can be seen at the head of Table 83 or, surrounded by the collar of the Black Eagle, on Table 80. The traditional black eagle on gold of Germany forms the base: thereon is an escutcheon of Prussia bearing a smaller escutcheon of Hohenzollern. The heir apparent of the day differenced this shield with a red border (shown above Crown Prince William 1882–1951); younger sons, like Prince Henry (1862–1929), enclosed the eagle of Prussia within a black and white border (Table 83). For public display a more elaborate blazon was produced which can be seen on Table 80. In the centre, on an escutcheon, is the black eagle of Prussia; round it are grouped the provinces whose seizure or acquisition were steps in the rise to power of the Hohenzollerns. They may best be described by rows: first row – Silesia, Brandenburg (charged with the sceptre of the chamberlainship of the Empire) and the Duchy of the Lower Rhine (the Prussian eagle suitably charged): second row – Grand-Duchy of Posen (also a variant of the Prussian eagle), (Prussia), Saxony: third row – Pomerania, Westphalia, Lüneburg: fourth row – Holstein, Schleswig and Lauenburg, Nuremberg and Hohenzollern, Thuringia, Nassau and Ruppin. In base the red section indicates regalian rights.

One of the advantages of the Prussian monarchy had been the longevity of its sovereigns. William I was no exception. When he died his eldest son was already stricken with cancer and reigned but ninety-nine days. The Emperor Frederick III was a fine and liberal character, married to the eldest daughter of Queen Victoria (Table 83). The Emperor William II was young, more volatile and flamboyant; early in his reign he dismissed Bismarck. The Iron Chancellor had ended his rule with twenty years of peace, which had witnessed an alliance with Austria-Hungary, an industrial revolution in Germany, entry into the expansionist field of colonialism and strong naval development. In Africa and at sea rivalry with England grew more bitter. Meanwhile France allied with Russia, a contingency always feared by Bismarck, and England drew closer to France.

The Prussian defeat of Austria in 1866 had turned the attention of the Hapsburg Empire more strongly towards the Balkans. It was here that the immediate cause of the First World War occurred, when the Archduke Francis Ferdinand was assassinated at Sarajevo on 28 June 1914. The ultimatum issued by Austria to Serbia was unpardonably severe. It was meant to provoke war and in this provocation Austria was backed by Germany. Previous conflicts may have led to the aggrandizement of dynasties: that of 1914–18 led to their wholesale downfall. All three empires of central and eastern Europe perished. In the cataclysm of 1918 William II abdicated, first as Emperor and – a few days later – as King of Prussia, and fled to Holland. The Crown Prince William renounced his rights in turn. The elder son of the Crown Prince abjured any dynastic rights on his non-royal marriage in 1933; the succession to the throne rests today in Prince Louis Ferdinand, the second son. Of his children, the two elder sons have made non-royal marriages and by traditional standards the hopes of the dynasty are pinned on the younger Louis Ferdinand (Table 84). The arms of the latter's wife are also quarterly but in red and white, contrasted with the basic white and black of Hohenzollern. Another heraldic curiosity (Table 83, bottom) shows the arms of Wellington linked in wedlock with Prussia in the person of Lord Douro.

The ancestry of the Emperor William II, set out on Table 84, shows a predominance of Saxon blood, partly because his mother was the child of cousins. Otherwise, given that the Russian rulers came from Holstein in male line and those of Britain from Hanover, his ascendance appears purely Teutonic.

In 1918 Germany became a republic, shorn of Alsace and Lorraine which returned to France, and of large areas round Posen and Danzig, which were awarded to a reconstituted state of Poland. The difficult career of the Weimar Republic and the sorry circumstances in which a powerful nation fell victim to the oratorial wiles of an Austrian mountebank do not directly concern the Hohenzollern dynasty.

ISSUE OF FREDERICK WILLIAM III (TABLE 82)

ALEXANDRINE
*1803 †1892
m. 1822
Paul Frederick
GD. of Mecklenbg.-
Schwerin
*1800 †1842

CHARLES
*1801 †1883
m. 1827
Mary
*1808
†1877
d. of Charles
Frederick
Pr. of
Netherlands
*1797 †1881

LOUISE
*1808 †1870
m. 1825
Frederick
Pr. of
Netherlands
GD. of Saxe-
Weimar

Marianne
*1810 †1883
d. of William I
K. of Netherlands
(div. 1849)

ALBRECHT 1830 (1)
*1809 †1872

(2) 1853
Rosalie
C. of Hohenau
*1820 †1879
d. of William
von Rauch

COUNTS OF
HOHENAU

FRED. WILLIAM IV 1823
K. of Prussia 1840
*1795 †1861

Elizabeth
*1801 †1873
d. of Maximilian I
K. of Bavaria

WILLIAM I 1829
K. of Prussia 1861
German Emp. 1871
*1797 †1888

Augusta
*1811 †1890
d. of Charles Fred.
GD. of Saxe-Weimar

Nicholas I 1817
Emp. of Russia
*1796 †1855

CHARLOTTE
*1798
†1860

LOUISE
*1808 †1870
m. 1825
Frederick
Pr. of
Netherlands
*1797 †1881

FREDERICK III 1858
German Emp. 1888
K. of Prussia
*1831 †1888

Victoria
*1840 †1901
d. of Victoria
Q. of Gt. Britain

Frederick I 1856
GD. of Baden
*1826 †1907

LOUISE
*1838
†1923

Mary
*1837 †1906
d. of Leopold
D. of Anhalt

FRED. CHARLES
*1828 †1885
m. 1854

Fred. William (2) 1833
Lgv. of Hesse-
Cassel
*1820 †1884

ANNE
*1836
†1918

CHARLOTTE
*1831 †1855
m. 1850
George II
D. of Saxe-
Meiningen
*1826 †1914

ALBRECHT 1873
*1837 †1906

Mary
*1854 †1898
d. of Ernest I
D. of Saxe-Altenbg.

ALEXANDRINE
*1842 †1906
m. 1865
William
D. of Mecklenburg-
Schwerin
*1827 †1879

WALDEMAR
*1868 †1879

Fred. Charles
Lgv. of Hesse-Cassel
*1868 †1940
m. 1893
MARGARET
*1872 †1954

ELIZABETH
*1857 †1895
m. 1878
Fred. Augustus
GD. of Oldenbg.
*1852 †1931

LOUISE
*1860 †1917
m. 1879
Arthur
D. of Connaught
*1850 †1942

FRED. HENRY
*1874 †1940

JOACHIM
ALBRECHT
*1876 †1939

FRED. WILLIAM
*1880 †1925
m. 1910 Agatha
*1888 †1960
d. of Victor
D. of Ratibor

FRED. LEOPOLD
*1865 †1931
m. 1889
Louise Sophia
*1866 †1952
d. of Frederick
D. of Schlesw.-Holst.-
Sonderbg.-Augustenbg.

WILLIAM II (1) 1881
German Emp. 1888–1918
*1859 †1941
m. (2) 1922 Hermine
*1887 †1947
d. of Henry XXII
Pr. Reuss

Augusta Victoria
*1858 †1921
d. of Frederick
D. of Schlesw.-Holst.-
Sonderbg.-Augustenbg.

HENRY 1888
*1862
†1929

Irene
*1866 †1953
d. of Louis IV
GD. of Hesse

Constantine I 1889
K. of Hellenes
*1868 †1923

SOPHIA
*1870
†1932

WILLIAM 1905
Cr. Pr. of Germany
& of Prussia
*1882 †1951

Cecily
*1886 †1954
d. of Fred. Francis III
GD. of Mecklenbg.-
Schwerin

EITEL 1906 (1)
FREDERICK
*1883 †1942

Sophia Charl.
of Oldenburg
*1879 †1964
(div. 1926)

ADALBERT
*1884 †1948
m. 1914
Adelaide
*1891 †1971
d. of Pr. Frederick
of Saxe-Meiningen

AUG. WILLIAM
*1887 †1949
m. 1908
Alexandra
*1887 †1957
d. of Fred. Ferd.
D. of Holst.-Sond.-
Glücksburg
(div. 1920)

OSCAR
*1888
†1958

Ina 1914
*1888 †1973
d. of Charles
C. of Bassewitz

JOACHIM
*1890 †1920
m. 1916
Augusta
*1890
d. of Edward
D. of Anhalt

VICTORIA LOUISE
*1892 †1980
m. 1913
Ernest Aug.
D. of Brunswick-
Lüneburg
*1887 †1953

WALDEMAR
*1889 †1945
m. 1919
Calixta
*1895
d. of Pr. William
of Lippe

SIGISMUND
*1896
m. 1919
Charlotte Agnes
*1899
d. of Ernest II
D. of Saxe-Altenbg.

WILLIAM 1933
*1906 ×1940

Dorothea
*1907
d. of Alexander
von Salviati

LOUIS 1938
FERDINAND
Pr. of Prussia
*1907
†1994

Kira
*1909 †1967
d. of Kiril
Wladimirowich
GD. of Russia

HUBERTUS
*1909 †1950
m. (1) 1941
Mary Anne
B. of Humboldt-Dachroeden
*1916 (div. 1943)
m. (2) 1943
Magdalen
*1920
d. of Henry XXXVI
Pr. Reuss

FREDERICK 1945 (1)
*1911 †1966

Brigid Guinness
*1920
d. of Rupert
E. of Iveagh

WILLIAM
VICTOR
*1919

Mary Antoinette 1944
*1920
d. of Frederick
C. Hoyos

TABLE 84

Dinnies 1958 (1)
von der Osten
*1929
(div. 1972)

FELICITAS
*1934
m. (2) 1972
Jörg von
Nostitz-Wallwitz
*1937

Peter 1960
Liebes
*1926
†1967

CHRISTA
*1936

FRED. NICHOLAS
*1946
m. 1980
Victoria
*1952
d. of Stormont
L. Mancroft

WILLIAM
*1948
m. 1979
Alexandra
d. of Frant.
Blaha
*1947

Philip 1976
Achache
*1948

VICTORIA
*1952

RUPERT
*1955
m. 1982
Ziba
Rastegar
*1954

Arthur
Wellesley
M. Douro
*1945

ANTONIA 1977
*1955

TABLE 84

PRUSSIA
Main line in the twentieth century

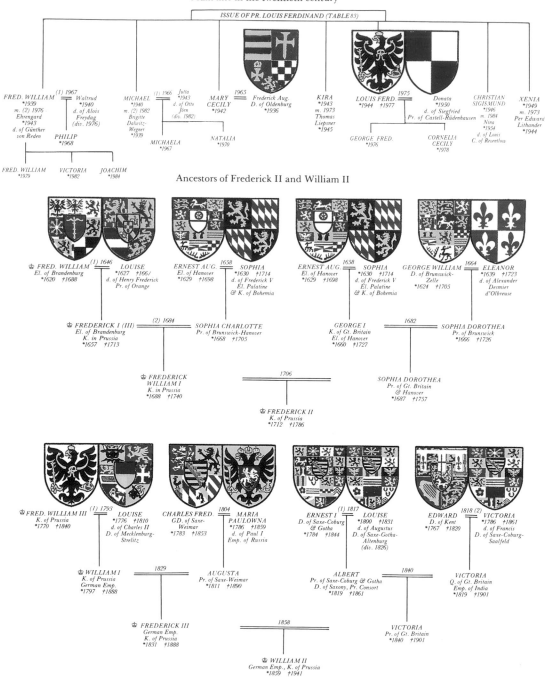

ISSUE OF PR. LOUIS FERDINAND (TABLE 83)

FRED. WILLIAM *1939 m. (2) 1976 Ehrengard *1943 d. of Günther von Reden — (1) 1967 Waltrud *1940 d. of Alois Freydag (div. 1976)

PHILIP *1968

FRED. WILLIAM *1979 VICTORIA *1982 JOACHIM *1984

MICHAEL *1940 m. (2) 1982 Brigitte Dalwitz-Wegner *1939 — (1) 1966 Jutta *1943 d. of Otto Jörn (div. 1982)

MICHAELA *1967

MARY CECILY *1942 = 1965 Frederick Aug. D. of Oldenburg *1936

NATALIA *1970

KIRA *1943 m. 1973 Thomas Liepsner *1945

LOUIS FERD. *1944 †1977 = 1975 Donata *1950 d. of Siegfried Pr. of Castell-Rüdenhausen

GEORGE FRED. *1976 CORNELIA CECILY *1978

CHRISTIAN SIGISMUND *1946 m. 1984 Nina *1954 d. of Louis C. of Reventlow

XENIA *1949 m. 1973 Per Edward Lithander *1944

Ancestors of Frederick II and William II

♔ FRED. WILLIAM El. of Brandenburg *1620 †1688 — (1) 1646 LOUISE *1627 †1667 d. of Henry Frederick Pr. of Orange

ERNEST AUG. El. of Hanover *1629 †1698 — 1658 SOPHIA *1630 †1714 d. of Frederick V El. Palatine & K. of Bohemia

ERNEST AUG. El. of Hanover *1629 †1698 — 1658 SOPHIA *1630 †1714 d. of Frederick V El. Palatine & K. of Bohemia

GEORGE WILLIAM D. of Brunswick-Zelle *1624 †1705 — 1664 ELEANOR *1639 †1723 d. of Alexander Desmier d'Olbreuse

♔ FREDERICK I (III) El. of Brandenburg K. in Prussia *1657 †1713 — (2) 1684 SOPHIA CHARLOTTE Pr. of Brunswick-Hanover *1668 †1705

GEORGE I K. of Gt. Britain El. of Hanover *1660 †1727 — 1682 SOPHIA DOROTHEA Pr. of Brunswick *1666 †1726

♔ FREDERICK WILLIAM I K. in Prussia *1688 †1740

1706

SOPHIA DOROTHEA Pr. of Gt. Britain & Hanover *1687 †1757

♔ FREDERICK II K. of Prussia *1712 †1786

♔ FRED. WILLIAM III K. of Prussia *1770 †1840 — (1) 1793 LOUISE *1776 †1810 d. of Charles II D. of Mecklenburg-Strelitz

CHARLES FRED. GD. of Saxe-Weimar *1783 †1853 — 1804 MARIA PAULOWNA *1786 †1859 d. of Paul I Emp. of Russia

ERNEST I D. of Saxe-Coburg & Gotha *1784 †1844 — (1) 1817 LOUISE *1800 †1831 d. of Augustus D. of Saxe-Gotha-Altenburg (div. 1826)

EDWARD D. of Kent *1767 †1820 — 1818 (2) VICTORIA *1786 †1861 d. of Francis D. of Saxe-Coburg-Saalfeld

♔ WILLIAM I K. of Prussia German Emp. *1797 †1888 — 1829 AUGUSTA Pr. of Saxe-Weimar *1811 †1890

ALBERT Pr. of Saxe-Coburg & Gotha D. of Saxony, Pr. Consort *1819 †1861 — 1840 VICTORIA Q. of Gt. Britain Emp. of India *1819 †1901

♔ FREDERICK III German Emp. K. of Prussia *1831 †1888

1858

VICTORIA Pr. of Gt. Britain *1840 †1901

♔ WILLIAM II German Emp., K. of Prussia *1859 †1941

Chapter 20

BRUNSWICK AND HANOVER

Sometimes a family falls from prominence and after many centuries rises again. Such was the case with the Dukes of Brunswick. A series of fortunate marriages brought Henry the Proud and Henry the Lion to a dominant position among the German princes. The former (Table 85) espoused Gertrude, daughter of the Emperor Lothair and granddaughter of Gertrude, heiress of the original Lords of Brunswick, who were called Bruno and gave the place its name. But although alliances within Germany brought importance to one line of the family, it was in fact of Italian origin, stemming from the little town of Este, near Padua. A younger branch remaining in the south eventually became Dukes of Modena.

In 1180 Henry the Lion fell from power and was stripped of his Duchies of Bavaria and Saxony. However, he was allowed to keep his family lands of Brunswick and Lüneburg. Henry was married to Matilda, the eldest daughter of Henry II of England. It has been suggested that the two gold lions, or leopards, on the red shield of Brunswick might be connected with the arms of England which were then evolving; the blue lion rampant surrounded by hearts for Lüneburg was related to the arms of Denmark, its northern neighbour. Otto IV was brought up in England and according to one chronicler enjoyed the earldom of York; on returning to Germany he became emperor in 1208, but his alliance with his uncle John of England brought him to complete disaster in 1214, at Bouvines, one of the truly decisive battles of the Middle Ages.

By its frequency the baptismal name Welf, or in its Italian form Guelph, was transferred to the dynasty as a whole and even to its political cause. Thus followers of later emperors or would-be emperors, who like Otto IV were opposed to the Hohenstaufen tradition or who enjoyed the support of the Papacy, styled themselves Guelphs. Their opponents were known as Ghibellines from an Italian version of the Staufen fortress of Waiblingen, near Stuttgart (Chapter 22).

The Emperor Frederick II, anxious to win the Guelphs to his side, created Otto I, the Child, Duke of Brunswick and Lüneburg in 1235. Before his death Otto added Hanover to his territories; all subsequent members of the dynasty are descended from him. The Teutonic principle of subdivision began to operate here also. Albrecht I divided his possessions with his younger brother in 1267, and his three sons later partitioned their father's Duchy of Brunswick. The first line of Dukes of Lüneburg died out in 1369, and after a considerable contest the sons of Magnus II, Duke of Brunswick, vindicated their right to succeed. Any reunion was short-lived. In 1428 Bernhard I made a fresh redistribution. His own descendants became Dukes of Brunswick-Lüneburg; those of his brother were Dukes of Brunswick-Wolfenbüttel, to which in 1463 they added Göttingen, on the death of Otto the One-Eyed.

Another significant division occurred in 1569 among the children of Duke Ernest I after a period of discord among them. Henry, Duke of Dannenburg, and William, Duke of Lüneburg, established two lines which existed separately until 1884. In 1635 these two families divided the estates of the Wolfenbüttel branch. The elder line was now known as Brunswick-Wolfenbüttel; its first duke, Augustus (d. 1666), was a celebrated bibliophile, but most of his race were renowned as soldiers. Charles I hired his troops to Britain to fight in the War of American Independence. His brother Ferdinand served under both Frederick the Great and George II of England, but devoted his later years to the study of freemasonry. Charles II also served in the Prussian army and later commanded against the French Republic at Valmy; he was mortally wounded at

TABLE 85

BRUNSWICK AND HANOVER
General survey (House of Guelph)

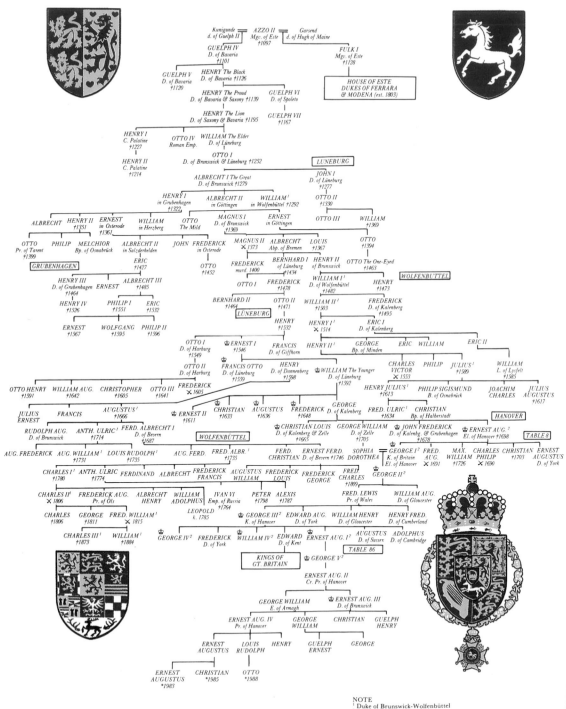

TABLE 86

HANOVER
Kings since the separation from Great Britain

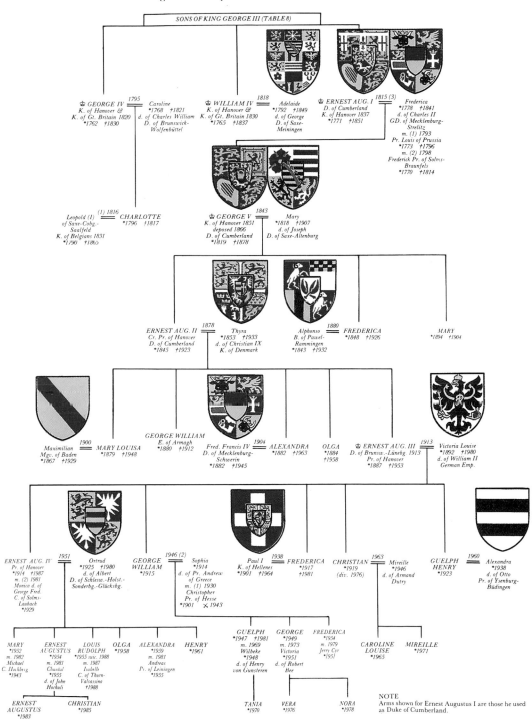

SONS OF KING GEORGE III (TABLE 8)

♔ GEORGE IV — 1795 — Caroline
K. of Hanover &
K. of Gt. Britain 1820
*1762 †1830
*1768 †1821
d. of Charles William
D. of Brunswick-Wolfenbüttel

♔ WILLIAM IV — 1818 — Adelaide
K. of Hanover &
K. of Gt. Britain 1830
*1765 †1837
*1792 †1849
d. of George
D. of Saxe-Meiningen

♔ ERNEST AUG. I — 1815 (3) — Frederica
D. of Cumberland
K. of Hanover 1837
*1771 †1851
*1778 †1841
d. of Charles II
GD. of Mecklenburg-Strelitz
m. (1) 1793
Pr. Louis of Prussia
*1773 †1796
m. (2) 1798
Frederick Pr. of Solms-Braunfels
*1770 †1814

Leopold (I) — (1) 1816 — CHARLOTTE
of Saxe-Cobg.-Saalfeld
K. of Belgians 1831
*1790 †1865
*1796 †1817

♔ GEORGE V — 1843 — Mary
K. of Hanover 1851
deposed 1866
D. of Cumberland
*1819 †1878
*1818 †1907
d. of Joseph
D. of Saxe-Altenburg

ERNEST AUG. II — 1878 — Thyra
Cr. Pr. of Hanover
D. of Cumberland
*1845 †1923
*1853 †1933
d. of Christian IX
K. of Denmark

Alphonso — 1880 — FREDERICA
B. of Pawel-Rammingen
*1843 †1932
*1848 †1926

MARY
*1894 †1904

Maximilian — 1900 — MARY LOUISA
Mgv. of Baden
*1867 †1929
*1879 †1948

GEORGE WILLIAM
E. of Armagh
*1880 †1912

Fred. Francis IV — 1904 — ALEXANDRA
D. of Mecklenburg-Schwerin
*1882 †1945
*1882 †1963

OLGA
*1884 †1958

♔ ERNEST AUG. III — 1913 — Victoria Louise
D. of Brunsw.-Lünebg. 1913
Pr. of Hanover
*1887 †1953
*1892 †1980
d. of William II
German Emp.

ERNEST AUG. IV — 1951 — Ortrud
Pr. of Hanover
*1914 †1987
m. (2) 1981
Monica d. of
George Fred.
C. of Solms-Laubach
*1929
*1925 †1980
d. of Albert
D. of Schlesw.-Holst.-Sonderbg.-Glücksbg.

GEORGE WILLIAM — 1946 (2) — Sophia
*1915
*1914
d. of Pr. Andrew
of Greece
m. (1) 1930
Christopher
Pr. of Hesse
*1901 ✕ 1943

Paul I — 1938 — FREDERICA
K. of Hellenes
*1901 †1964
*1917 †1981

CHRISTIAN — 1963 — Mireille
*1919
(div. 1976)
*1946
d. of Armand
Dutry

GUELPH
HENRY
*1923

1960 — Alexandra
*1938
d. of Otto
Pr. of Ysenburg-Büdingen

MARY
*1952
m. 1982
Michael
C. Hochberg
*1943

ERNEST
AUGUSTUS
*1954
m. 1981
Chantal
*1955
d. of John
Hochuli

LOUIS
RUDOLPH
*1955 suic. 1988
m. 1987
Isabell
C. of Thurn-Valsassina
*1988

OLGA
*1958

ALEXANDRA
*1959
m. 1981
Andreas
Pr. of Leiningen
*1955

HENRY
*1961

GUELPH
*1947 †1981
m. 1969
Wilbeke
d. of Henry
von Gunsteren

GEORGE
*1949
m. 1973
Victoria
*1951
d. of Robert
Bee

FREDERICA
*1954
m. 1979
Jerry Cyr
*1951

CAROLINE
LOUISE
*1965

MIREILLE
*1971

ERNEST
AUGUSTUS
*1983

CHRISTIAN
*1985

TANIA
*1970

VERA
*1976

NORA
*1978

NOTE
Arms shown for Ernest Augustus I are those he used
as Duke of Cumberland.

The marriage of the future King George IV of England (1762–1830) with Princess Caroline of Brunswick, which ended in divorce, by Henry Singleton, c. 1810.

Auerstädt. His son Frederick William was killed at Quatre Bras. Charles III was exceedingly unpopular and was deposed in 1830. Neither he nor his brother William married, and the death of the latter brought the elder line to an end. In theory the Duchy should have passed to the Kings of Hanover, but George V was strongly anti-Prussian and Prussia engineered a succession of regents until 1913.

The arms of Brunswick-Wolfenbüttel at the base of Table 85 show twelve quarterings for a variety of lordships:*1* Lüneburg, *2* Brunswick, *3* Eberstein, *4* Homburg, *5* Diepholz (with 8), *6* Lauterberg, *7* Hoja and Bruckhausen, *8* see 5, *9* Hohenstein, *10* Regenstein, *11* Klettenberg, *12* Blankenburg. The tenth and twelfth quarterings, both of an antler, are sometimes drawn together.

The younger line, of Brunswick-Lüneburg, fared rather better. The seven sons of William the Younger with rare self-denial made an agreement in 1610 that one only of their number should continue the family. The lucky prince was George. At the extinction in 1634 of the first Wolfenbüttel branch, George secured the Duchy of Kalenberg. The youngest son of Duke George, Ernest Augustus, was at first installed as Bishop of Osnabrück, but his ambitions ran higher than the Church. His marriage to Sophia, the daughter of Frederick, Count Palatine and briefly King of Bohemia, linked him with the Stuarts. Gradually he built together the inheritances of his brothers; Zelle he secured by marrying his son George to his niece Sophia Dorothea, a disastrous match (page 174). In 1692 the Emperor Leopold created him an elector, with the title of Hanover.

In 1714 George, Elector of Hanover, became King of Great Britain (Table 8); for over one hundred years the fortunes of Brunswick were linked to England. In 1814 George III became King of Hanover. His blazon can be seen on Table 85: the arms of the United Kingdom are surmounted with the three-fold escutcheon of Brunswick, Lüneburg and Hanover, with over all the crown of Charlemagne witnessing to the electoral dignity. Round the shield is the collar of the Guelphic Order, founded in 1815.

The death of William IV (1837) separated the two thrones; since Victoria, as a woman, could not succeed to Hanover, that Crown passed to her uncle, Ernest Augustus, Duke of Cumberland (Table 86). Autocratic and reactionary, he almost lost his throne in 1848, but saved himself by granting a constitution. George V was, unhappily, blind, but no more liberal than his father. Moved by dislike of Prussia, he joined with Austria in 1866, only to lose his Kingdom to the Hohenzollerns later in that year. His son, Ernest Augustus II, was deprived of his dukedom of Cumberland in 1917 and abdicated from the Duchy of Brunswick in 1918; it was scant compensation that Ernest Augustus III (married to a Prussian princess) had in 1913 claimed the Wolfenbüttel Duchy.

In 1955–6 Ernest Augustus IV, the heir to the Duchies of Brunswick, established his claim to be a British subject by a series of complicated legal actions which went to the House of Lords.

Chapter 21

SAXONY

Saxony is one of those geographical terms, like Burgundy, which have changed their significance down the centuries. Originally it meant a large area of northwest Germany stretching most of the way from the Elbe to the Rhine. At the end of the eighth century the wild and heathen denizens of this area, some of whom had migrated to England in the Dark Ages, were conquered by Charlemagne, converted to Christianity and incorporated in the Carolingian Empire. One of their leaders was a certain Wittekind, from whom the House of Wettin liked (without much evidence) to boast descent. Thereafter Saxony was one of the great duchies of the German kingdom.

Saxony was originally held by the descendants of Hermann Billung, but they died out in 1106. In 1137 the Emperor Lothair (who had been Duke of Saxony) gave the Duchy to Henry the Proud (Table 85), his son-in-law, but the next German ruler, Conrad III, transferred the Duchy to Albrecht the Bear (Table 87) whose mother belonged to the Billung family. In 1142 the Duchy was restored to Henry the Lion, son of Henry the Proud, who was also Duke of Bavaria, and thus the greatest feudatory of the German Crown. In 1180 Henry the Lion was broken by Frederick Barbarossa, but his fall was as much due to the jealousy of the other princes. Virtually all his lands were regranted to other nobles. The main gainers were the Ascanian House (Tables 80 and 87) and the family of Wittelsbach. From this moment the term Saxony began to lose its wider sense and to concentrate upon the upper valley of the Elbe, south of its junction with the Saale.

The title of Duke of Saxony was conferred upon Bernard, son of Albrecht the Bear, but his territory was far less extensive than that of Henry the Lion and was in any case subdivided among his children and grandchildren. The Princes of Anhalt still preserve

his blood today. The younger branch rose more rapidly. John founded the Duchy of Saxe Lauenburg which endured until 1689; his brother Albrecht became Duke of Saxe-Wittenberg in 1260. Albrecht's grandson Rudolph II was granted the title of Elector of Saxony in 1356 by the Golden Bull of Eger. However, this dignity ended with his nephew Albrecht III in 1422. From time to time the elder branch of Saxe-Lauenburg claimed the electoral rank, but with no success.

HOUSE OF WETTIN

The family of Wettin, which was to play so large a part in the history of Saxony, sought to trace its descent from Wittekind, but is first found reliably in a certain Dietrich, Count of Hassegau, who died about 982. His descendant Thimo built the castle of Wettin which gave the dynasty its name; and Thimo's son, Conrad, became Margrave of Meissen in 1127 or so, and was also granted part of Lusatia by the Emperor Lothair. Conrad's grandson, Dietrich, greatly improved his position by marrying the heiress of the Landgrave of Thuringia. Thus, at the extinction of the Ascanian Dukes of Saxony, the Wettin family had built up a considerable position in that part of Germany.

In 1423 the Emperor Sigismund awarded the Duchy of Saxe-Wittenberg with the rank of elector to Frederick I, the Warlike, Margrave of Meissen (Table 87). The style of 'Elector of Saxony' now became usual for him and his descendants. Any possibility that Saxony might develop into a cohesive and powerful state was dispelled by the customary tendency to fragmentation and civil war. Frederick II and William fought bitterly over their father's lands; a more far-reaching division was made in 1485 between the two sons of the former. Ernest and Albert had in fact reigned jointly over Meissen from 1464

TABLE 87

SAXONY
General survey

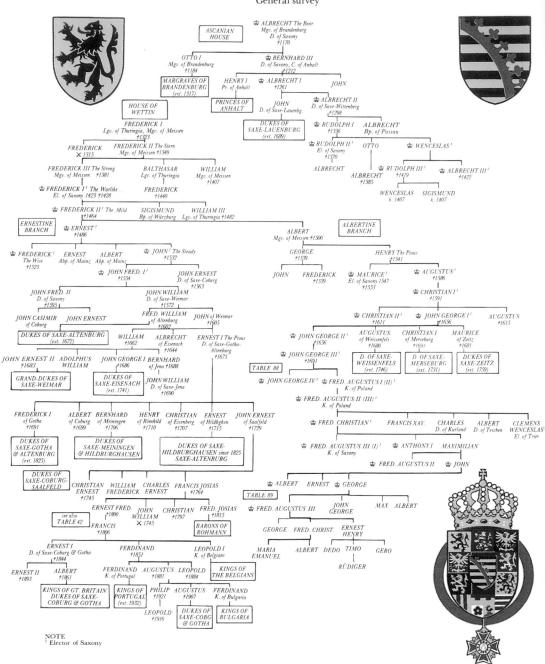

♔ ALBRECHT *The Bear*
Mgv. of Brandenburg
D. of Saxony
†1170

ASCANIAN HOUSE

OTTO I
Mgv. of Brandenburg
†1184

♔ BERNHARD III
D. of Saxony, C. of Anhalt
†1212

MARGRAVES OF BRANDENBURG
(ext. 1317)

HENRY I
Pr. of Anhalt

♔ ALBRECHT I
†1261

JOHN

HOUSE OF WETTIN

PRINCES OF ANHALT

JOHN
D. of Saxe-Lauenbg.

♔ ALBRECHT II
D. of Saxe-Wittenberg
†1298

FREDERICK I
Lgv. of Thuringia, Mgv. of Meissen
†1323

DUKES OF SAXE-LAUENBURG
(ext. 1689)

♔ RUDOLPH I
†1356

ALBRECHT
Bp. of Passau

FREDERICK
✕ 1315

FREDERICK II *The Stern*
Mgv. of Meissen †1349

♔ RUDOLPH II
El. of Saxony
†1370

OTTO

♔ WENCESLAS

FREDERICK III *The Strong*
Mgv. of Meissen †1381

BALTHASAR
Lgv. of Thuringia

WILLIAM
Mgv. of Meissen
†1407

ALBRECHT

ALBRECHT
†1385

♔ RUDOLPH III
†1419

♔ ALBRECHT III
†1422

♔ FREDERICK I *The Warlike*
El. of Saxony 1423 †1428

FREDERICK
†1440

WENCESLAS
k. 1407

SIGISMUND
k. 1407

♔ FREDERICK II *The Mild*
†1464

SIGISMUND
Bp. of Würzburg

WILLIAM III
Lgv. of Thuringia †1482

ERNESTINE BRANCH

♔ ERNEST
†1486

ALBERT
Mgv. of Meissen †1500

ALBERTINE BRANCH

♔ FREDERICK
The Wise
†1525

ERNEST
Abp. of Mainz

ALBERT
Abp. of Mainz

♔ JOHN *The Steady*
†1532

GEORGE
†1539

HENRY *The Pious*
†1541

♔ JOHN FRED. I
†1554

JOHN ERNEST
D. of Saxe-Coburg
†1563

JOHN

FREDERICK
†1539

♔ MAURICE
El. of Saxony 1547
†1553

♔ AUGUSTUS
†1586

JOHN FRED. II
D. of Saxony
†1595

JOHN WILLIAM
D. of Saxe-Weimar
†1572

♔ CHRISTIAN I
†1591

JOHN CASIMIR
of Coburg

JOHN ERNEST

FRED. WILLIAM
of Altenburg
†1602

JOHN of Weimar
†1605

♔ CHRISTIAN II
†1611

♔ JOHN GEORGE I
†1656

AUGUSTUS
†1615

DUKES OF SAXE-ALTENBURG
(ext. 1672)

WILLIAM
†1662

ALBRECHT
of Eisenach
†1644

ERNEST I *The Pious*
D. of Saxe-Gotha-
Altenburg
†1675

♔ JOHN GEORGE II
†1656

AUGUSTUS
of Weissenfels
†1680

CHRISTIAN I
of Merseburg
†1691

MAURICE
of Zeitz
†1681

JOHN ERNEST II
WILLIAM

ADOLPHUS
WILLIAM

JOHN GEORGE I
†1686

BERNHARD
of Jena †1688

♔ JOHN GEORGE III
†1691

D. OF SAXE-WEISSENFELS
(ext. 1746)

D. OF SAXE-MERSEBURG
(ext. 1731)

DUKES OF SAXE-ZEITZ
(ext. 1759)

GRAND-DUKES OF SAXE-WEIMAR

DUKES OF SAXE-EISENACH
(ext. 1741)

JOHN WILLIAM
D. of Saxe-Jena
†1690

TABLE 88

♔ JOHN GEORGE IV
†1694

♔ FRED. AUGUSTUS I (II)
K. of Poland

♔ FRED. AUGUSTUS II (III)
K. of Poland

FREDERICK I
of Gotha
†1691

ALBERT
of Coburg
†1699

BERNHARD
of Meiningen
†1706

HENRY
of Römhild
†1710

CHRISTIAN
of Eisenberg
†1707

ERNEST
of Hildbghsn.
†1715

JOHN ERNEST
of Saalfeld
†1729

♔ FRED. CHRISTIAN
†1763

FRANCIS XAV.

CHARLES
D. of Kurland

ALBERT
D. of Teschen

CLEMENS
WENCESLAS
El. of Trier

DUKES OF SAXE-GOTHA & ALTENBURG
(ext. 1825)

DUKES OF SAXE-MEININGEN & HILDBURGHAUSEN

DUKES OF SAXE-HILDBURGHAUSEN since 1825 SAXE-ALTENBURG

♔ FRED. AUGUSTUS III (I)
K. of Saxony

♔ ANTHONY I

MAXIMILIAN

DUKES OF SAXE-COBURG-SAALFELD

CHRISTIAN
ERNEST
†1745

WILLIAM
FREDERICK

CHARLES
ERNEST

FRANCIS JOSIAS
†1764

♔ FRED. AUGUSTUS II

♔ JOHN

♔ ALBERT

ERNEST

♔ GEORGE

ERNEST FRED.
†1800

JOHN
WILLIAM

CHRISTIAN
†1797

FRED. JOSIAS
†1815

♔ FRED. AUGUSTUS III

JOHN
GEORGE

MAX

ALBERT

see also
TABLE 42

FRANCIS
†1806

✕ 1745

BARONS OF ROHMANN

GEORGE

FRED. CHRIST.

ERNEST
HENRY

ERNEST I
D. of Saxe-Coburg & Gotha
†1844

FERDINAND
†1851

LEOPOLD I
K. of Belgians

MARIA
EMANUEL

ALBERT

DEDO

TIMO

GERO

RÜDIGER

ERNEST II
†1893

ALBERT
†1861

FERDINAND
K. of Portugal

AUGUSTUS
†1881

LEOPOLD
†1884

KINGS OF THE BELGIANS

KINGS OF GT. BRITAIN DUKES OF SAXE-COBURG & GOTHA

KINGS OF PORTUGAL
(ext. 1932)

PHILIP
†1921

AUGUSTUS
†1907

FERDINAND
K. of Bulgaria

LEOPOLD
†1916

DUKES OF SAXE-COBG & GOTHA

KINGS OF BULGARIA

NOTE
[1] Elector of Saxony

TABLE 89

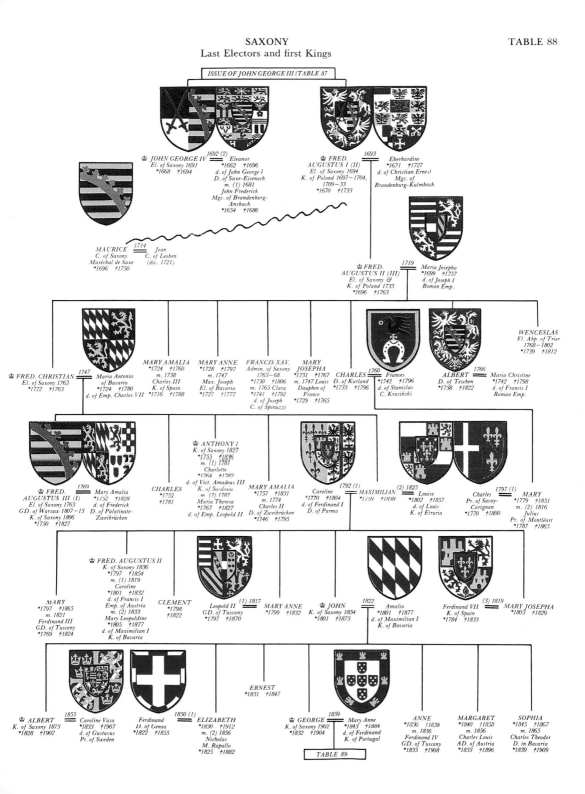

ISSUE OF JOHN GEORGE III (TABLE 87)

♔ **JOHN GEORGE IV** ══ 1692 (2) Eleanor
El. of Saxony 1691 *1662 †1696
*1668 †1694 d. of John George I
D. of Saxe-Eisenach
m. (1) 1681
John Frederick
Mgv. of Brandenburg-
Ansbach
*1654 †1686

♔ **FRED.** ══ 1693 Eberhardine
AUGUSTUS I (II) *1671 †1727
El. of Saxony 1694 d. of Christian Ernest
K. of Poland 1697–1704, Mgv. of
1709–33 Brandenburg-Kulmbach
*1670 †1733

MAURICE ══ 1714 Joan
C. of Saxony C. of Leoben
Maréchal de Saxe (div. 1721)
*1696 †1750

♔ **FRED.** ══ 1719 Maria Josepha
AUGUSTUS II (III) *1699 †1757
El. of Saxony & d. of Joseph I
K. of Poland 1733 Roman Emp.
*1696 †1763

♔ **FRED. CHRISTIAN** ══ 1747 Maria Antonia
El. of Saxony 1763 of Bavaria
*1722 †1763 *1724 †1780
d. of Emp. Charles VII

MARY AMALIA
*1724 †1760
m. 1738
Charles III
K. of Spain
*1716 †1788

MARY ANNE
*1728 †1797
m. 1747
Max. Joseph
El. of Bavaria
*1727 †1777

FRANCIS XAV.
Admin. of Saxony
1763–68
*1730 †1806
m. 1765 Clara
*1741 †1792
d. of Joseph
C. of Spinuzzi

MARY
JOSEPHA
*1731 †1767
m. 1747 Louis
Dauphin of
France
*1729 †1765

CHARLES ══ 1760 Frances
D. of Kurland *1742 †1796
*1733 †1796 d. of Stanislas
C. Krasiński

ALBERT ══ 1766 Maria Christine
D. of Teschen *1742 †1798
*1738 †1822 d. of Francis I
Roman Emp.

WENCESLAS
El. Abp. of Trier
1768–1802
*1739 †1812

♔ **FRED.** ══ 1769 Mary Amalia
AUGUSTUS III (I) *1752 †1828
El. of Saxony 1763 d. of Frederick
GD. of Warsaw 1807–13 D. of Palatinate-
K. of Saxony 1806 Zweibrücken
*1750 †1827

CHARLES
*1752
†1781

♔ **ANTHONY I**
K. of Saxony 1827
*1755 †1836
m. (1) 1781
Charlotte
*1764 †1782
d. of Vict. Amadeus III
K. of Sardinia
m. (2) 1787
Maria Theresa
*1767 †1827
d. of Emp. Leopold II

MARY AMALIA
*1757 †1831
m. 1774
Charles II
D. of Zweibrücken
*1746 †1795

Caroline ══ 1792 (1) **MAXIMILIAN** ══ (2) 1825 Louise
*1770 †1804 *1759 †1838 *1802 †1857
d. of Ferdinand I d. of Louis
D. of Parma K. of Etruria

Charles ══ 1797 (1) **MARY**
Pr. of Savoy- *1779 †1851
Carignan m. (2) 1816
*1770 †1800 Julius
Pr. of Montléart
*1787 †1865

♔ **FRED. AUGUSTUS II**
K. of Saxony 1836
*1797 †1854
m. (1) 1819
Caroline
*1801 †1832
d. of Francis I
Emp. of Austria
m. (2) 1833
Mary Leopoldine
*1805 †1877
d. of Maximilian I
K. of Bavaria

CLEMENT
*1798
†1822

Leopold II ══ (1) 1817 **MARY ANNE**
GD. of Tuscany *1799 †1832
*1797 †1870

♔ **JOHN** ══ 1822 Amalia
K. of Saxony 1854 *1801 †1877
*1801 †1873 d. of Maximilian I
K. of Bavaria

Ferdinand VII ══ (3) 1819 **MARY JOSEPHA**
K. of Spain *1803 †1829
*1784 †1833

MARY
*1797 †1865
m. 1821
Ferdinand III
GD. of Tuscany
*1769 †1824

ERNEST
*1831 †1847

♔ **ALBERT** ══ 1853 Caroline Vasa
K. of Saxony 1873 *1833 †1907
*1828 †1902 d. of Gustavus
Pr. of Sweden

Ferdinand ══ 1850 (1) **ELIZABETH**
D. of Genoa *1830 †1912
*1822 †1855 m. (2) 1856
Nicholas
M. Rapallo
*1825 †1882

♔ **GEORGE** ══ 1859 Mary Anne
K. of Saxony 1902 *1843 †1884
*1832 †1904 d. of Ferdinand
K. of Portugal

TABLE 89

ANNE
*1836 †1859
m. 1856
Ferdinand IV
GD. of Tuscany
*1835 †1908

MARGARET
*1840 †1858
m. 1856
Charles Louis
AD. of Austria
*1833 †1896

SOPHIA
*1845 †1867
m. 1865
Charles Theodor
D. in Bavaria
*1839 †1909

until the decease in 1482 of their uncle, William III of Thuringia. In 1485 they executed a treaty of partition at Leipzig, which divided for ever the House of Wettin and its lands into two branches, called after them Ernestine and Albertine. Both lines continued to use the same basic arms, of which the essentials are the black lion rampant on gold of Meissen and the distinctive blazon of Saxony, which has a crancelin, or wreath of rue, over a black and gold barry background. Tradition, which is unlikely to be authentic, relates that the Emperor Barbarossa took a chaplet of rue from his own head and draped it across the shield of Duke Bernard of Ascania, which had hitherto consisted of black and gold bars only.

ERNESTINE SAXONY

Ernest, the elder brother, retained the Electorate and took Wittenberg, Thuringia and the provinces of Vogtland. Albert received the Margravate of Meissen; in the event his line was to achieve more success than the elder branch, but its story must wait. Towards the end of the rule of Elector Ernest there was born in his dominions a peasant who was to change the world. Martin Luther, though not of outstanding talents, was to launch the Reformation: it was on the door of the castle church at Wittenberg, capital of electoral Saxony, that he nailed in 1517 his famous ninety-five theses. This is no place to develop the story of the great Protestant movement, but it must be recorded that, much as Luther owed to the University of Wittenberg, his debt was even greater to the protection and patronage which he received from the Elector Frederick the Wise. In a very real sense Wittenberg was the cradle of the great Lutheran faith and of the tremendous movement which rippled outwards from the little town. Frederick loved peace, his home and his bible; his reward was to see his land devastated by the bitter 'Peasants' War'. His brother John the Steady and his nephew John Frederick I were both staunch supporters of the reformers. The latter was captured by the Emperor Charles V at Mühlberg (1547) and compelled to sign away his electoral rank to his cousin Maurice (of the Albertine line); with the title went many of his estates. The Ernestine branch was never again of high consequence in Germany.

Its fate was the usual one of subdivision, amalgamation and further partition. The existing lines all stem from Duke John of Saxe-Weimar, who died in 1605. Two main branches descend from him and are still extant today, those of Weimar and Gotha. In the former the principle of primogeniture was established in 1725 and the separate Duchies of Saxe-Weimar, Saxe-Eisenach and Saxe-Jena were united; in 1815 the rulers became grand-dukes. Charles Augustus, who reigned at Weimar from 1775 to 1828, was an enlightened and conspicuous patron of the arts; Goethe and Schiller both entered his service, and the rebirth of German literature virtually took place at his tiny court.

The Dukes of Saxe-Gotha were even more a prey to fractions. At the end of the seventeenth century there were minuscule duchies each with its own capital and court at Gotha, Coburg, Meiningen, Eisenberg, Römhild, Hildburghausen and Saalfeld. In 1826 there was a massive rearrangement of lands of the *Nexus Gothanus* which produced Dukes of Saxe-Meiningen and Hildburghausen, Saxe-Altenburg and Saxe-Coburg and Gotha.

By a series of felicitous marriages the third and most junior of these principalities has contrived to supply kings to Great Britain, Portugal, Bulgaria and Belgium (Table 42 and Chapter 9). The succession to the Duchy passed in 1893 to the heirs of the Prince Consort, husband of Queen Victoria.

Their second son Alfred, Duke of Edinburgh, was duke until his death in 1900 and was followed by his nephew Charles Edward (Table 42) who was deprived of his British dukedom of Albany in 1917.

ALBERTINE SAXONY

The Albertine line was less resolutely wedded to the Reformation than the Ernestine line. Margrave George (d. 1539) was a zealous Catholic, but his brother Henry was a Protestant. Maurice, the next heir, though a Lutheran, put policy and ambition before faith. With more adroitness than consistency he first allied with the Emperor (Charles V) and then attacked him. As has been noted, in 1547 he was given the electoral rank and some of the estates of his Ernestine cousin; but the booty was not enough and Maurice returned to the Protestant side. His brother, Augustus, was more devoted to the arts of peace. Coal-mining, introduced by Maurice, was encouraged, agriculture and commerce fostered. It seemed as if a prosperous future might lie before Saxony, but this was not to be.

The Elector John George I was married to a niece of the last Duke of Cleves and Jülich. While he had sufficient wisdom to refuse the Crown of Bohemia, he was none the less deeply involved in the Thirty Years' War, of which Saxony was one of the major battlefields. It is true that he acquired Lusatia from the Emperor in 1635, but his own homeland was devastated in the fighting and his alliance with the Catholic Empire allowed the leadership of reformed Germany to pass to Brandenburg. The last act of this rather ineffectual Prince was to bequeath independent duchies to his three younger sons, thus further weakening the impoverished Electorate of Saxony. Fortunately all three died out by 1759, and their states returned to the main line one by one.

Royal House since the end of the monarchy

TABLE 89

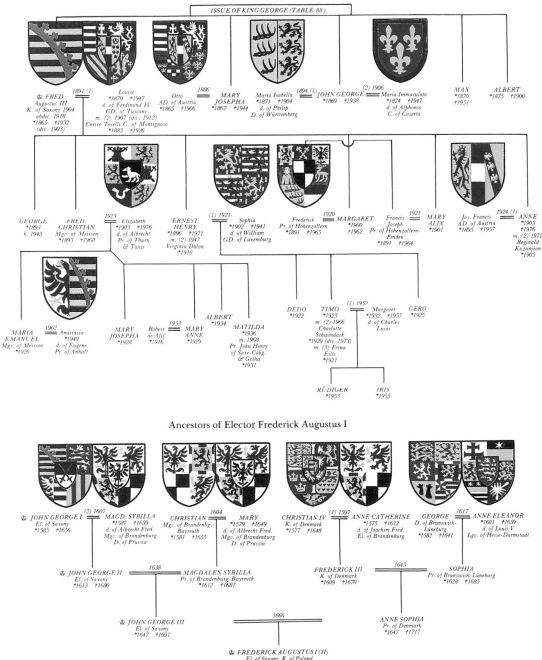

ISSUE OF KING GEORGE (TABLE 88)

♔ FRED.
Augustus III
K. of Saxony 1904
abdic. 1918
*1865 †1932
(div. 1903)

Louise   1891 (1)
*1870 †1947
d. of Ferdinand IV
GD. of Tuscany
m. (2) 1907 (div. 1912)
Enrico Toselli C. of Montignoso
*1883 †1926

Otto   1886
AD. of Austria
*1865 †1906

MARY
JOSEPHA
*1867 †1944

Maria Isabella   1894 (1)
*1871 †1904
d. of Philip
D. of Württemberg

JOHN GEORGE
*1869 †1938

Maria Immaculata   (2) 1906
*1874 †1947
d. of Alphonso
C. of Caserta

MAX
*1870
†1951

ALBERT
*1875 †1900

GEORGE
*1893
k. 1943

FRED.
CHRISTIAN
Mgv. of Meissen
*1893 †1968

Elizabeth   1923
*1903 †1976
d. of Albrecht
Pr. of Thurn
& Taxis

ERNEST
HENRY
*1896 †1971
m. (2) 1947
Virginia Dulon
*1910

Sophia   (1) 1921
*1902 †1941
d. of William
GD. of Luxemburg

Frederick   1920
Pr. of Hohenzollern
*1891 †1965

MARGARET
*1900
†1962

Francis   1921
Joseph
Pr. of Hohenzollern-
Emden
*1891 †1964

MARY
ALIX
*1901

Jos. Francis
AD. of Austria
*1895 †1957

ANNE   1924 (1)
*1903
†1976
m. (2) 1972
Reginald
Kazanjian
*1905

MARIA
EMANUEL
Mgv. of Meissen
*1926

Anastasia   1962
*1940
d. of Eugene
Pr. of Anhalt

MARY
JOSEPHA
*1928

Robert
de Afif
*1916

MARY   1953
ANNE
*1929

ALBERT
*1934

MATILDA
*1936
m. 1968
Pr. John Henry
of Saxe-Cobg.
& Gotha
*1931

DEDO
*1922

TIMO
*1923
Charlotte
Schwindack
*1929 (div. 1973)
m. (3) Erina
Eilts
*1921

Margaret   (1) 1952
*1932 †1957
d. of Charles
Lucas
m. (2) 1966

GERO
*1925

RÜDIGER
*1953

IRIS
*1955

Ancestors of Elector Frederick Augustus I

♔ JOHN GEORGE I   (2) 1607
El. of Saxony
*1585 †1656

MAGD. SYBILLA
*1587 †1659
d. of Albrecht Fred.
Mgv. of Brandenburg
D. of Prussia

CHRISTIAN   1604
Mgv. of Brandenbg.-
Bayreuth
*1581 †1655

MARY
*1579 †1649
d. of Albrecht Fred.
Mgv. of Brandenburg
D. of Prussia

CHRISTIAN IV   (1) 1597
K. of Denmark
*1577 †1648

ANNE CATHERINE
*1575 †1612
d. of Joachim Fred.
El. of Brandenburg

GEORGE   1617
D. of Brunswick-
Lüneburg
*1582 †1641

ANNE ELEANOR
*1601 †1659
d. of Louis V
Lgv. of Hesse-Darmstadt

♔ JOHN GEORGE II   1638
El. of Saxony
*1613 †1680

MAGDALEN SYBILLA
Pr. of Brandenburg-Bayreuth
*1612 †1687

FREDERICK III   1643
K. of Denmark
*1609 †1670

SOPHIA
Pr. of Brunswick-Lüneburg
*1628 †1685

♔ JOHN GEORGE III
El. of Saxony
*1647 †1691

1666

ANNE SOPHIA
Pr. of Denmark
*1647 †1717

♔ FREDERICK AUGUSTUS I (II)
El. of Saxony, K. of Poland
*1670 †1733

Augustus the Strong (1670–1733), Elector of Saxony and King of Poland, with Frederick William I, King in Prussia, by Louis de Silvestre, c. 1730.

At the beginning of the eighteenth century the fortunes of Saxony took a new and disastrous turn. John George IV (Table 88) was the fourth consecutive Elector to bear this name. His arms show the crancelin of Saxony impaled with the crossed swords of the Marshalcy of the Empire which went with the Saxon Electorate. From this shield were derived the crossed swords on Dresden porcelain, which began to be made at this time; the manufacture of hard-paste china began at Meissen in about 1710. Frederick Augustus succeeded his brother in 1694 and embarked on larger ambitions. His ancestry (on Table 89) shows that in fact he was half of Brandenburg descent, mingled with other German strains. The more elaborate blazon of Saxony given for John George I shows the shield of the Marshalcy over quarterings for Saxony, Thuringia, Magdeburg

and Landsberg. In 1696 John Sobieski, King of Poland, died and Augustus the Strong, as he is sometimes known, put himself forward for election. In order to fortify his claims he announced his conversion to Catholicism. He was crowned at Cracow in 1697 but had considerable difficulty in establishing his position, which indeed he had to abandon between 1704 and 1709. His preoccupation with Poland left Saxony again at the mercy of warring armies.

Augustus begot by his mistress, Aurora von Königsmarck, the famous Maréchal de Saxe, one of the greatest soldiers of the age. Her family, blazing comet-like across Europe at this time, merits a brief digression. The grandfather was a Swedish general in the Thirty Years' War; her uncle directed the artillery which in 1687 blew up the Parthenon; one brother (Charles) arranged the murder of the richest English commoner of the day in Pall Mall, another disappeared mysteriously in Hanover under suspicion of being the lover of Sophia Dorothea of Zelle, wife of the future George I of England (Table 85).

Augustus the Strong was possibly meditating a partition of Poland when he died in 1733. Frederick Augustus II, his son and heir, had been brought up a Catholic and was married to a Hapsburg (Table 88). Moreover he was a very different man from his father; portly and indolent, little attracted by public business, he was inclined to leave great affairs to his ministers and devote his own attention to hunting. For most of his reign, Count von Brühl ruled in Saxony and the Czartoryski family in Poland. During the Seven Years' War (1756–63) the Elector-King withdrew to Poland, and Saxony itself was devastated by the various campaigns. When both Frederick Augustus II and his son, Frederick Christian, died in succession in 1763, Saxony was in a sorry condition. Leipzig had, however, been enriched by the glorious genius of the composer J.S. Bach.

Frederick Augustus III was more conscious of the interests of Saxony than his predecessors; he devoted himself to the reconstruction of the Electorate, possibly aware that Frederick the Great of Prussia coveted his domain. His mother had been Bavarian, and in 1777 he advanced claims to her inheritance. The indecisive manoeuvrings of the War of the Bavarian Succession left him richer by four million thalers, which he was able to use in buying back Saxon land alienated by his grandfather. In 1791, with great good sense, he declined the Crown of Poland. In 1806 he attached himself to Napoleon and assumed the title of King of Saxony. As a reward he was given in 1807 the Grand-Duchy of Warsaw, which the French Emperor had created from among his conquests. In the same year he founded the Order of the Crown of Rue: this surrounds the shield at the bottom of Table 87. Frederick Augustus I is usually numbered as the first King of Saxony. The last great battle of Napoleon's main reign was on Saxon soil at Leipzig (1813) and King Frederick Augustus was captured by the Allies. Prussia was anxious to absorb Saxony, but this desire was opposed at the Congress of Vienna by Britain and Austria. Eventually, Saxony emerged as a separate kingdom, but she had to cede a large northern area to her voracious neighbour.

In 1830 there were risings in Leipzig and Dresden which resulted in the appointment of Frederick Augustus II as co-ruler with his uncle (his father, Maximilian, had renounced the succession). Further revolts in 1848 were quelled by Prussian arms. King John was a scholarly man, who had translated the works of the poet Dante into German, but his reign saw Saxony increasingly drawn into the orbit of Prussia, which governed her foreign affairs and exercised control over her army. The history of the state was uneventful between 1870 and 1914, save for a steady rise in popular support for socialism. The short reign of King George (1902–4) witnessed a sensational scandal when his daughter-in-law, Louise of Tuscany, eloped with the Frenchman hired to teach her children; the errant Princess was given the title of Countess of Montignoso.

Frederick Augustus III (Table 89) was a field-marshal in the German army. In 1918, like other rulers in that country, he was compelled to abdicate, and Saxony became a mere province of the German Republic. His eldest son, another George, renounced all his royal rights in 1923 and became a Jesuit priest; he perished mysteriously by drowning during the Nazi regime. The second son, Prince Frederick Christian, who used the title Margrave of Meissen, died in 1968 and the heir to the throne of Saxony is his child, Maria Emanuel. His marriage to a Princess of Anhalt links the Wettin House of Saxony with the Ascanian dynasty which held the province before them (Table 87). As a result of World War II his realm is now a component part of East Germany.

The full blazon of the Kings of Saxony can be seen on Table 87, surrounded by the Order of the Crown of Rue. There are twelve main quarterings, in rows

The Maréchal de Saxe, illegitimate son of Augustus the Strong who entered the French service, by J. E. Liotard, c. 1750. He carries the baton of a Marshal of France.

of three: *1* Meissen, *2* Thuringia, *3* Palatinate of Thuringia; *4* Palatinate of Saxony, *5* and *8* red with an escutcheon of Saxony over all, *6* Lordship of Pleissen; *7* Vogtland, *8* see *5*, *9* County of Orlamünde; *10* Landsberg, *11* divided into three, above Upper Lusatia and below Altenburg (a rose) and Henneberg (a cock or hen), *12* Eisenberg.

Chapter 22

HOLY ROMAN EMPIRE

The ghost of Charlemagne haunts a wide span of medieval history. This is not the place to discuss exactly what his coronation by Pope Leo III in Rome on Christmas Day 800 signified to the participants. It is enough that a new emperor appeared in the west in contrast to the dynamic continuity of the Byzantine Empire in the eastern Mediterranean, which continued the state established by Augustus down to 1453.

The Empire of Charlemagne comprised what we now call France and West Germany as well as the Low Countries, Switzerland, northern Italy and part of Spain. This burden was beyond the capacity of his successors; but in any case the Frankish or Germanic tradition was for division between the surviving sons of a parent. As has been seen (Chapter 14: first section), the Treaty of Verdun in 843 arranged a partition into three which later events have made memorable. Germany fell to the share of Louis: but none of his three sons had legitimate issue, though one bastard grandson, Arnulf, became ruler of Germany. Meanwhile the style of emperor had passed to ever more limp and shadowy figures among the descendants of the great and vigorous Charlemagne. His triumph had been a personal one; nor indeed was the idea of empire consonant with the practice of subdivision of estates.

In 919 a new dynasty came to power in Germany with Henry the Fowler, Duke of Saxony. His son Otto I, the Great (936–73), was a capable and vigorous ruler who brought Germany to order and finally quashed the Hungarian menace. In 962 he invaded Italy, entered Rome and was crowned emperor in St Peter's. He then proceeded to depose Pope John XII, who was scarcely an ornament to his high position. There can be no question that contemporaries looked back to the coronation of Charlemagne, but it is really from the sacring of Otto

that the story of the Holy Roman Empire begins: from this moment there is a series of rulers, under various titles and of differing powers, until the resignation of Francis II in 1806 (Table 76). But the successors of Otto I never had suzerainty over France or Spain, while their power in Italy steadily declined down the centuries. Otto I normally styled himself 'Imperator Augustus': it was probably his son, Otto II, who added the epithet 'Roman', as a weapon in his dispute with the Byzantine Emperor Basil II. The adjective 'Holy' was introduced by Barbarossa in 1157. Otto III, whose mother was a Greek princess, had lofty ideas of re-establishing the Roman Empire of classical times with a Christian tincture, but his early death (1002) put an end to them. His immediate successors were more concerned with being efficient rulers of Germany, though they journeyed to Rome to be crowned.

Henry III (Table 90), powerful and pious, was the second Emperor of the Salian House, which had succeeded the Saxon by the choice of the nobles. In 1046 he invaded Italy, purified the Papacy by deposing three rival Popes and installed a German Bishop of Rome (Clement II), who was devoted to the principles of reform which had developed in Burgundy and the Rhineland and are loosely known as the Cluniac movement. His early death was doubly unfortunate, for it exposed his son to a turbulent minority and to the growing ecclesiastical pressure of the reformed Papacy: from this sprang the destructive Investiture Contest. Henry IV was at one moment threatened by an anti-king, Rudolph of Swabia; more important, royal control of Germany was seriously weakened by civil war.

On the death of Henry V the Salian family became extinct; he had been married to Matilda, only daughter of Henry I of England, but it is idle to speculate what would have happened if they had

TABLE 90

HOLY ROMAN EMPIRE
General survey (until Frederick III)

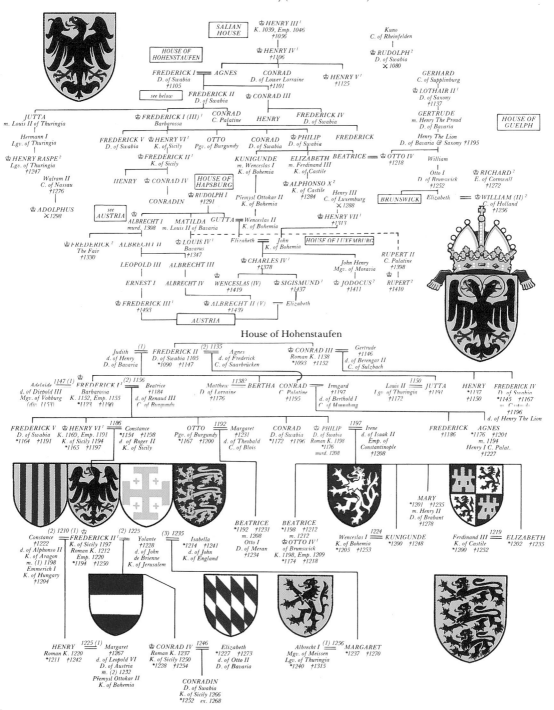

House of Hohenstaufen

AUSTRIA

OTE
Holy Roman Emperor
Rival King

procreated. The German princes, no doubt partly as a protest against the hereditary principle, eschewed Frederick of Hohenstaufen and elected Lothair II, Duke of Saxony. Perhaps for similar reasons, on Lothair's death they avoided his son-in-law, the richest noble in Germany, and selected in 1138 Conrad III of Hohenstaufen who had already been put forward as an anti-king. His reign was unsuccessful (as was his participation in the Second Crusade of 1147); the feud between Guelph (or Welf) and Hohenstaufen (or Ghibelline) was growing; Conrad never achieved the journey to Rome to be crowned emperor, but lived and died as King of the Romans, the title by now given (somewhat anomalously) to the ruler of Germany before his coronation by the Pope as emperor.

For once united in desire for a robust king, the German princes turned to Frederick 'Barbarossa' (Table 90 : lower half). Tall, handsome, auburn-bearded, he was a good soldier and well-educated; deservedly he has become a hero of German tradition. His long reign was devoted to the restoration of royal power in Germany after a century of strife and to an endeavour, only partially successful, to reassert imperial power in northern Italy where the great cities had made good their independence. In 1180 he broke the power of his most puissant subject, Henry the Lion, Duke of Saxony and Bavaria, partly because of the meagre help Henry had afforded him in Italy. From the redistribution of Henry's lands sprang many of the later German princely families (Chapter 2 1 : Saxony). At the end of his life the venerable Emperor departed on the Third Crusade and was drowned in Cilicia on his way to the Holy Land. By the time of his death the eagle was the recognized insignia of the Empire; it first appeared as the top of a sceptre on the seal of Henry III. The early arms of the sovereigns of Germany are thus those shown at the top of Table 90, or at the head of this chapter.

Henry VI had made a marriage which proved to be sensational; his wife Constance was, in the event, sole heiress of the wealthy and cosmopolitan Kingdom of Sicily (which included southern Italy), founded in the late eleventh century by Norman adventurers of the de Hauteville family. In his brief and dazzling reign this frail figure planned a consolidated Germano-Italian kingdom, an attack against Constantinople and, perhaps, a Europe paying homage to an august emperor of a new model. It was he who extorted submission from the captive Richard I of England. He himself had been elected King of the Romans in his father's lifetime, the first employment of this title for an heir-apparent. He now bribed the German princes into doing the same for his infant heir, Frederick II, and by lavish concessions of

privileges sought their agreement to an hereditary kingdom of Germany. Then at the age of 31 he died abruptly with his exalted dreams unfulfilled.

The picture changed with startling rapidity. In Germany, the Duke of Swabia, brother of the dead Emperor, became king, but his right was bitterly contested by Otto IV of Saxony (great-grandson of Lothair and son of Henry the Lion) and Philip was never crowned emperor. Much of the work of the Hohenstaufen was undone in the ensuing civil war, and lay and ecclesiastical princes rejoiced in the opportunity to acquire privileges, lands and immunities. In Italy Pope Innocent III consolidated the position of the Papacy.

In 1220 Frederick II was crowned as emperor. He is one of the most remarkable figures of the Middle Ages. Short and unimposing, he was a patron of science and of poetry, a practical experimenter in both fields and author of a splendid book on falconry. In politics he was ambitious, in warfare skilful, in love active. His three wives came from the first families of Europe, but it was in fact a cherished bastard who carried on his regime in Sicily. In right of his second wife he was King of Jerusalem and, while excommunicate by the Pope, he organized a successful crusade. But for all his brilliant talent, his positive achievement was slender and his death was followed by a disastrous period for the Holy Roman Empire.

THE EMPIRE IN DISPUTE

After the death of Conrad IV, the anti-king William, Count of Holland, held the field for a while until he fell in an obscure battle. The doctrine of election had advanced swiftly; it was now recognized that only seven of the great princes had a right to participate. These were the three great ecclesiastical prelates of the Rhineland, the Archbishops of Mainz, Trier and Cologne, who were respectively Arch-Chancellors of Germany, Gaul and Italy, and four lay dynasts, the King of Bohemia (Imperial Cupbearer), the Count Palatine of the Rhine (Imperial Seneschal), the Duke of Saxony (Imperial Marshal: Table 87) and the Margrave of Brandenburg (Imperial Chamberlain: Table 80). In the earliest days there was some doubt about the relative claims of Bavaria and Bohemia, especially as the latter was somewhat outside Germany, but opinion swung against having two members of the Wittelsbach family. It must also be allowed that it was political influence rather than their courtly titles which marked out these particular princes. The death of Conradin, Duke of Swabia, brought the Hohenstaufen line to an end after a remarkable series of sovereigns. Three black lions on gold (Table 90) were the arms associated with the province and the dynasty.

In 1257 two candidates were advanced for election,

*The Emperor Charles IV (1316–78) with the seven
Electors – three archbishops and four laymen. MS c. 1370.*

and each secured some of the seven votes; both were
rich and neither was a German. Richard, Earl of
Cornwall, was a brother of Henry III of England,
though also a brother-in-law of Frederick II, while
Alphonso X, the cultivated ruler of Castile, was a
grandson of Philip of Swabia. Alphonso first used a
nimbus round the single head of the eagle on his seal;
a two-headed eagle was already becoming known as
a symbol of empire, but it did not gain general acceptance until the time of the Emperor Sigismund. His
arms are shown in the middle of Table 90 with the
imperial crown; one of the earliest appearances of a
bicephalous eagle is in the mid-thirteenth-century
manuscript of the great English chronicler, Matthew
Paris of St Albans. The origin of the two-headed eagle
is still obscure. That it came from the East is tolerably
certain, but the Byzantine emperors and their subjects knew nothing of heraldry in the Western sense.
Only where their lands marched with heraldic neighbours was there some requirement for blazonry; then
either the cross between the four 'B's or the two-
headed eagle, which itself perhaps evolved from textiles, were called into play.

Neither Richard nor Alphonso were ever effective
rulers of Germany, and on the death of the former the
Electors made a new start. Still suspicious of a strong,
local candidate, they chose an able but relatively
obscure Swabian Count, Rudolph of Hapsburg
(Table 71 and 90). He proved a competent ruler,
but his interests were confined to Germany. His successor was Adolphus of Nassau, another nobleman
not of the first rank, and for two centuries the Crown
oscillated between the dynasties of Hapsburg, Wittelsbach and Luxemburg. Not surprisingly the emperors were constrained to play family politics and to
use their reigns to enhance their kindred; a striking
example is Rudolph of Hapsburg's acquisition of
Austria for his sons (Chapter 17). Between the death
of Frederick II (1250) and 1452, only Henry VII,
Louis IV, Charles IV, Sigismund and Frederick III
made the journey to Rome to receive the Imperial
Crown. Thereafter the practice almost ceased and
the title of 'Holy Roman Empire of the German
people', which appeared in the reign of Frederick III,
illustrated the new emphasis.

THE HAPSBURGS

In 1356 the Emperor Charles IV defined the
processes of election and the number of electors in
close detail in his famous Golden Bull; it is noteworthy that no mention is made of papal approval.
From 1437 the Hapsburg family provided an
unbroken series of rulers and the history of the

Empire is bound up with that of Austria, save for the brief reign (1742–5) of Charles Albrecht of Bavaria. But the character of the Empire continued to alter. The Reformation struck a deadly blow at any surviving idea of widespread dominion; henceforward Germany was fragmented in religion as well as in politics. The Thirty Years' War all but destroyed the authority of the Austrian Emperor within the bounds of Germany. And yet the Empire continued to exist, and furnished a ghostly semblance of unity for men of Teutonic speech. In the seventeenth century the number of the electors was increased; first, in 1648, a second electorate was allowed to the Wittelsbachs, and then in 1692 Leopold I awarded a ninth to Brunswick-Lüneburg. But if the number of actual electors was small, that of the princes was much larger. In the middle of the seventeenth century there were 43 lay principalities and 33 ecclesiastical with a vote in the Diet; this number tended to grow rather than diminish as the Emperor rewarded good service. The rise of Liechtenstein may be taken as an example.

Many of the German princes had tiny domains and most of the large states were intermittently subjected to division. The total number of independent states, towns, bishoprics and abbeys, not all of which by any means had a direct vote in the Diet, was reckoned at 365 in 1715. Some imperial knights held land directly of the Emperor but owned little more than a couple of villages. This society was rigidly and severely stratified. Reigning Houses gave their children only to each other in marriage: noble family allied with noble family or knight with knight. Many religious houses and orders of chivalry were only open to those who could prove their *seize-quartiers*, that is show that all their great-great-grandparents were of noble birth. From time to time genuine affection would break through the schemes of planned alliances, and numerous morganatic marriages bear witness to this. Such a wedding was one in which the parties were truly married, but the wife did not enjoy the full status of her husband, nor did the children, though spared the stigma of illegitimacy, inherit his titles or estates. The issue of two such unions have played

some part in British life in the last hundred years, the families of Teck and Mountbatten or Battenberg. It may be noted in passing that English law makes no provision whatsoever for such alliances (which are indeed mainly found in the Empire and Spain), a circumstance of some importance in 1936.

According to Goethe the Great Hall in Frankfurt (since 1424 the repository of the imperial insignia), decorated with portraits of the emperors, had but one space left when Francis II succeeded in 1792. The tempestuous career of Napoleon shook down the venerable, but by now decrepit, fabric of the Holy Roman Empire. His conquests swept across Germany and led to radical reorganization. In 1803 the rank of elector was conferred by Bonaparte on the rulers of Hesse-Cassel, Baden and Württemberg and on the Archbishop of Salzburg. All the ecclesiastical princes of Germany disappeared and their lands were annexed to secular states. In 1806 Francis abandoned the title of Holy Roman Emperor. In 1810 the traditional Hapsburg Emperor gave his daughter in marriage to the self-made Corsican ruler; it was with a deliberate sense of history that the Emperor Napoleon called his son the King of Rome.

In the resulting rearrangements in 1814–15 the map of Germany was greatly simplified. Over sixty princes, hitherto independent, lost their sovereignty, in particular those whose territory was entirely encircled by more powerful neighbours. They formed a new class of 'mediatized' princes; although they had forfeited independence and jurisdiction, their daughters were still eligible for marriage into reigning families. Thus in Table 89, the wife of Prince Frederick Christian of Saxony is the daughter of a 'mediatized' prince, Albrecht of Thurn and Taxis. The creation of a united Germany under the King of Prussia in 1870–71 still further reduced the number of semi-independent rulers; but the short-lived Empire of the Hohenzollerns had little to do with the now defunct Holy Roman Empire, which spanned the millenium between Charlemagne and Francis II, even if in its latest phase it was, according to Voltaire, neither holy nor Roman nor an empire.

Chapter 23

PORTUGAL

The story of Portugal as a separate state only begins at the end of the eleventh century. Before this point the territory north of the Douro was part of Leon, while the land south of that river was in Moorish hands. In 1093 King Alphonso VI of Castile married his illegitimate daughter Theresa to a French nobleman, Henry of Burgundy, and granted him a fief round Oporto. From the Latin name of this harbour, Portus Cale, the area came to be known as the County of Portugal. Henry began to aim at independence, which was achieved by his son, Alphonso I (Table 92), who started to call himself king in 1139 and was recognized as such by Castile in 1143. After unsuccessful and unworthy efforts to expand his kingdom northwards into Galicia, Alphonso turned his attention southwards. In 1147, with the assistance of a body of English and Flemish crusaders sailing to the Holy Land, he captured Lisbon. In 1179 the Pope also approved his royal title; his long reign was the formative period in the history of Portugal. Alphonso's new territories were scantily populated and he made use of religious orders, especially the Cistercians.

Succeeding Kings of Portugal continued the work of colonization and gradually extended their boundaries down to Cape St Vincent. Sancho I is remembered as a builder of towns; the first meeting of the *Cortes* (or assembly) is recorded under Alphonso II. Alphonso III gained Portugal her modern territorial limits. He had spent some time in France where his first wife gave him a title to the County of Boulogne. But he returned to Portugal to dethrone his brother, Sancho II, who had made an unpopular marriage. Ironically Alphonso III proceeded to marry a daughter of the King of Castile while his first wife was alive.

During his reign the arms of Portugal crystallized into their present form. It has been conjectured that they may originally have been a blue cross studded with silver nails. The seal of Alphonso I seems to show 12 small shields, each containing dots, arranged in a cruciform pattern. Sancho I has five shields crosswise, but with two on their sides; from then on there are considerable variations, and only gradually do all the shields become upright. In early examples the number of dots also varies. Alphonso III added a red border with gold castles, based no doubt on the arms of Castile, the dynasty to which his wife and his mother belonged. Later usage limited the number of castles to seven. Equally, later tradition, seeking meaning for heraldry, imagined that the five shields alluded to five Moorish kings defeated by Alphonso I and that the five discs referred to the five wounds of Christ. In popular speech these little shields (or escutcheons) with their five discs (or roundels) are known as 'quinas'.

King Denis is a noteworthy figure in the story of Portugal. He had been associated in the kingship by his father and made ruler of the Algarve, the southernmost area of the Kingdom. During his reign he added two tiny pieces of Castile to his country; he founded the Order of Christ (1319) to replace the disbanded Templars; he encouraged maritime trade and the growth of a fleet; he was a considerable poet and his works mark a stage in the evolution of the Portuguese language; to his own countrymen he is the 'Farmer king' because of his encouragement of agriculture. His wife, Isabel of Aragon, was a pious and charitable queen, later canonized; like many medieval rulers of Portugal her talented husband left several bastards. The oldest university in Portugal was founded in his reign at Lisbon in 1290, but transferred to Coimbra in 1308.

Alphonso IV was known as 'the Brave' from his courage in a great battle, fought in alliance with Castile, against the Moors at the river Salado in 1340. He

TABLE 91

PORTUGAL
General survey

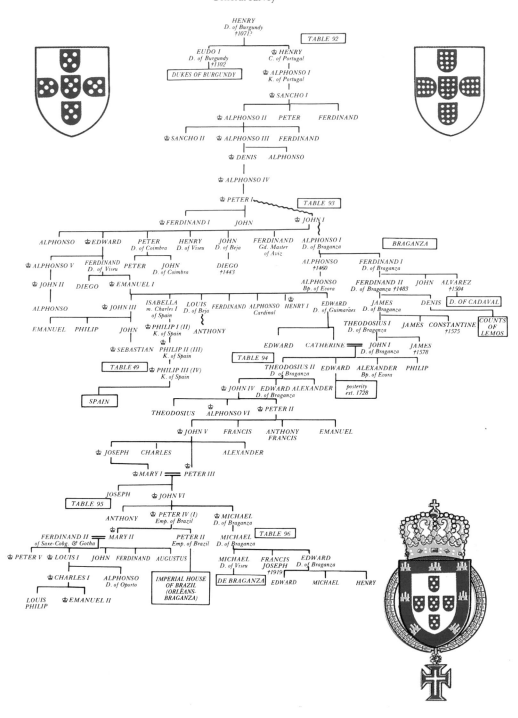

HENRY
D. of Burgundy
†1071?

TABLE 92

EUDO I
D. of Burgundy
†1102

✠ **HENRY**
C. of Portugal

DUKES OF BURGUNDY

✠ **ALPHONSO I**
K. of Portugal

✠ **SANCHO I**

✠ **ALPHONSO II** — PETER — FERDINAND

✠ **SANCHO II** — ✠ **ALPHONSO III** — FERDINAND

✠ **DENIS** — ALPHONSO

✠ **ALPHONSO IV**

✠ **PETER I**

TABLE 93

✠ **FERDINAND I** — JOHN — ✠ **JOHN I**

ALPHONSO — ✠ EDWARD — PETER D. of Coimbra — HENRY D. of Viseu — JOHN D. of Beja — FERDINAND Gd. Master of Aviz — ALPHONSO I D. of Braganza

BRAGANZA

✠ ALPHONSO V — FERDINAND D. of Viseu — PETER — JOHN D. of Coimbra — DIEGO †1443 — ALPHONSO †1460 — FERDINAND I D. of Braganza

✠ JOHN II — DIEGO — ✠ EMANUEL I — ALPHONSO Bp. of Evora — FERDINAND II D. of Braganza †1483 — JOHN — ALVAREZ †1504

ALPHONSO — ✠ JOHN III — ISABELLA m. Charles I of Spain — LOUIS D. of Beja — FERDINAND — ALPHONSO Cardinal — ✠ HENRY I — EDWARD D. of Guimarães — JAMES D. of Braganza — DENIS — D. OF CADAVAL

EMANUEL — PHILIP — JOHN — ✠ PHILIP I (II) K. of Spain — ANTHONY — THEODOSIUS I D. of Braganza — JAMES — CONSTANTINE †1575 — COUNTS OF LEMOS

✠ SEBASTIAN — PHILIP II (III) K. of Spain — EDWARD — CATHERINE ═ JOHN I D. of Braganza — JAMES †1578

TABLE 94

TABLE 49 — ✠ PHILIP III (IV) K. of Spain — THEODOSIUS II D. of Braganza — EDWARD — ALEXANDER Bp. of Evora — PHILIP

SPAIN — ✠ JOHN IV EDWARD ALEXANDER D. of Braganza — posterity ext. 1728

THEODOSIUS — ✠ ALPHONSO VI — ✠ PETER II

✠ JOHN V — FRANCIS — ANTHONY FRANCIS — EMANUEL

✠ JOSEPH — CHARLES — ALEXANDER

✠ MARY I ═══ PETER III

JOSEPH — ✠ JOHN VI

TABLE 95

ANTHONY — ✠ PETER IV (I) Emp. of Brazil — ✠ MICHAEL D. of Braganza

FERDINAND II of Saxe-Cobg. & Gotha ═ MARY II — PETER II Emp. of Brazil — MICHAEL D. of Braganza

TABLE 96

✠ PETER V — ✠ LOUIS I — JOHN — FERDINAND — AUGUSTUS — MICHAEL D. of Viseu — FRANCIS JOSEPH †1919 — EDWARD D. of Braganza

DE BRAGANZA — EDWARD — MICHAEL — HENRY

✠ CHARLES I — ALPHONSO D. of Oporto — IMPERIAL HOUSE OF BRAZIL (ORLÉANS-BRAGANZA)

LOUIS PHILIP — ✠ EMANUEL II

TABLE 92

PORTUGAL
Early Kings (House of Burgundy)

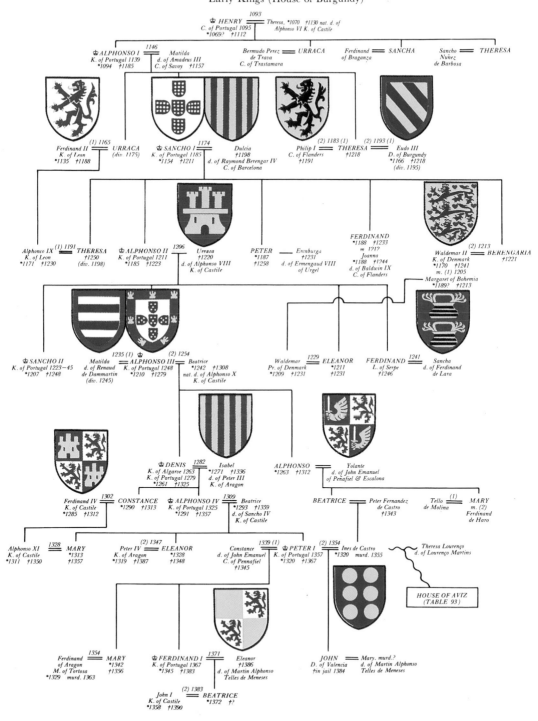

HENRY C. of Portugal 1095 *1069? †1112 — 1093 — Theresa, *1070 †1130 nat. d. of Alphonso VI K. of Castile

ALPHONSO I K. of Portugal 1139 *1094 †1185 — 1146 — Matilda d. of Amadeus III C. of Savoy †1157

Bermudo Perez de Trava C. of Trastamara = **URRACA**

Ferdinand of Braganza = **SANCHA**

Sancho Nunez de Barbosa = **THERESA**

Ferdinand II K. of Leon *1135 †1188 = (1) 1165 **URRACA** (div. 1175)

SANCHO I K. of Portugal 1185 *1154 †1211 — 1174 — Dulcia †1198 d. of Raymond Berengar IV C. of Barcelona

Philip I C. of Flanders †1191 = (2) 1183 (1) **THERESA** †1218 (2) 1193 (1) = Eudo III D. of Burgundy *1166 †1218 (div. 1195)

Alphonso IX K. of Leon *1171 †1230 = (1) 1191 **THERESA** †1250 (div. 1198)

ALPHONSO II K. of Portugal 1211 *1185 †1223 — 1206 — Urraca †1220 d. of Alphonso VIII K. of Castile

PETER *1187 †1258 = Erenburga †1231 d. of Ermengaud VIII of Urgel

FERDINAND *1188 †1233 m. 1212 Joanna *1188 †1244 d. of Baldwin IX C. of Flanders

Waldemar II K. of Denmark *1170 †1241 m. (1) 1205 Margaret of Bohemia *1189? †1213 = (2) 1213 **BERENGARIA** †1221

SANCHO II K. of Portugal 1223–45 *1207 †1248

Matilda d. of Renaud de Dammartin (div. 1245) = 1235 (1) **ALPHONSO III** K. of Portugal 1248 *1210 †1279 (2) 1254 = Beatrice *1242 †1308 nat. d. of Alphonso X K. of Castile

Waldemar Pr. of Denmark *1209 †1231 — 1229 — **ELEANOR** *1211 †1231

FERDINAND L. of Serpe †1246 — 1241 — Sancha d. of Ferdinand de Lara

Ferdinand IV K. of Castile *1285 †1312 = 1302 **CONSTANCE** *1290 †1313

DENIS K. of Algarve 1263 K. of Portugal 1279 *1261 †1325 — 1282 — Isabel *1271 †1336 d. of Peter III K. of Aragon

ALPHONSO IV K. of Portugal 1325 *1291 †1357 — 1309 — Beatrice *1293 †1359 d. of Sancho IV K. of Castile

ALPHONSO *1263 †1312 = Yolante d. of John Emanuel of Peñafiel & Escalona

BEATRICE = Peter Fernandez de Castro †1343

Trello de Molina — (1) — **MARY** m. (2) Ferdinand de Haro

Alphonso XI K. of Castile *1311 †1350 = 1328 **MARY** *1313 †1357

Peter IV K. of Aragon *1319 †1387 = (2) 1347 **ELEANOR** *1328 †1348

Constance d. of John Emanuel C. of Pennafiel †1345 = 1339 (1) **PETER I** K. of Portugal 1357 *1320 †1367 (2) 1354 = Ines de Castro *1320 murd. 1355

Theresa Lourenço d. of Lourenço Martins

HOUSE OF AVIZ (TABLE 93)

Ferdinand of Aragon M. of Tortosa *1329 murd. 1363 — 1354 — **MARY** *1342 †1356

FERDINAND I K. of Portugal 1367 *1345 †1383 — 1371 — Eleanor †1386 d. of Martin Alphonso Telles de Meneses

JOHN D. of Valencia †in jail 1384 = Mary. murd.? d. of Martin Alphonso Telles de Meneses

John I K. of Castile *1358 †1390 = (2) 1383 **BEATRICE** *1372 †?

TABLE 93

PORTUGAL
House of Aviz

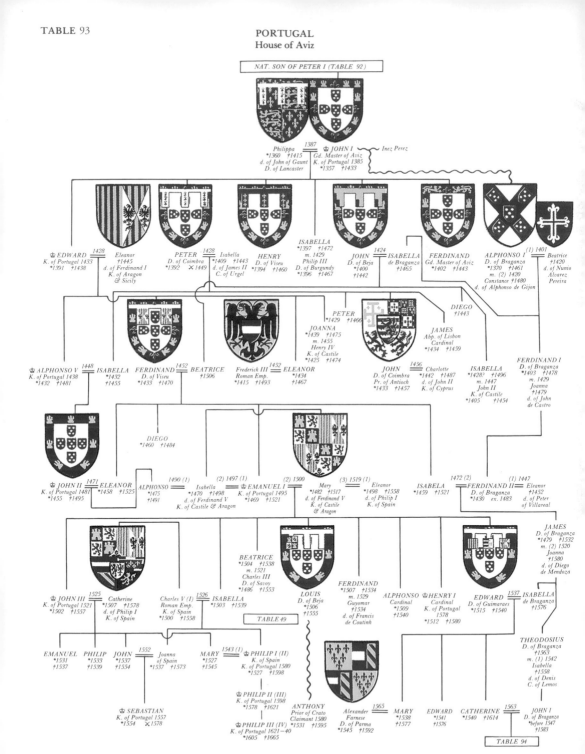

NAT. SON OF PETER I (TABLE 92)

Philippa ═══ 1387 ═══ ☩ JOHN I ～～ Inez Perez
*1360 †1415   Gd. Master of Aviz
d. of John of Gaunt   K. of Portugal 1385
D. of Lancaster   *1357 †1433

☙ EDWARD — 1428 — Eleanor   PETER — 1428 — Isabella   HENRY   ISABELLA   JOHN — 1424 — ISABELLA   FERDINAND   ALPHONSO I — (1) 1401 — Beatrice
K. of Portugal 1433   †1445   D. of Coimbra   *1409 †1443   D. of Viseu   *1397 †1472   D. of Beja   de Braganza   Gd. Master of Aviz   D. of Braganza   †1420
*1391 †1438   d. of Ferdinand I   *1392 ✗ 1449   d. of James II   *1394 †1460   m. 1429   *1400   †1465   *1402 †1443   *1370 †1461   d. of Nunio
   K. of Aragon   C. of Urgel   Philip III   †1442   m. (2) 1420   Alvarez
   & Sicily   D. of Burgundy   Constance †1480   Pereira
   *1396 †1467   d. of Alphonso de Gijon

PETER   DIEGO
*1429 †1466   †1443

JOANNA   JAMES
*1439 †1475   Abp. of Lisbon
m. 1455   Cardinal
Henry IV   *1434 †1459
K. of Castile
*1425 †1474

ALPHONSO V — 1448 — ISABELLA   FERDINAND — 1452 — BEATRICE   Frederick III — 1452 — ELEANOR   JOHN — 1456 — Charlotte   ISABELLA   FERDINAND I
K. of Portugal 1438   *1432   D. of Viseu   †1506   Roman Emp.   *1434   D. of Coimbra   *1442 †1487   *1428? †1496   *1403 †1478
*1432 †1481   †1455   *1433 †1470   *1415 †1493   †1467   Pr. of Antioch   d. of John II   m. 1447   m. 1429
   *1433 †1457   K. of Cyprus   John II   Joanna
   K. of Castile   †1479
   *1405 †1454   d. of John
   de Castro

DIEGO
*1460 †1484

☩ JOHN II — 1471 — ELEANOR   ALPHONSO ═ 1490 (1)   (2) 1497 (1) ═ Isabella ═ EMANUEL I ═ (2) 1500 ═ Mary   (3) 1519 (1) ═ Eleanor   ISABELA   FERDINAND II — 1472 (2)   (1) 1447 ═ Eleanor
K. of Portugal 1481   *1458 †1525   *1475   *1470 †1498   K. of Portugal 1495   *1482 †1517   *1498 †1558   *1459 †1521   D. of Braganza   *1452
*1455 †1495   †1491   d. of Ferdinand V   *1469 †1521   d. of Ferdinand V   d. of Philip I   *1430 ex. 1483   d. of Peter
   K. of Castile & Aragon   K. of Castile   K. of Spain   of Villareal
   & Aragon

JAMES
D. of Braganza
*1479 †1532
m. (2) 1520
Joanna
†1580
d. of Diego
de Mendoza

BEATRICE   FERDINAND   ALPHONSO   ☩ HENRY I   EDWARD — 1537 — ISABELLA
*1504 †1538   *1507 †1534   Cardinal   Cardinal   D. of Guimaraes   de Braganza
m. 1521   m. 1529   *1509   K. of Portugal   *1515 †1540   †1576
Charles III   Guyomar   †1540   1578
D. of Savoy   †1534   *1512 †1580
*1486 †1553   d. of Francis
   de Coutinh

☩ JOHN III — 1525 — Catherine   Charles V (I) — 1526 — ISABELLA   LOUIS
K. of Portugal 1521   *1507 †1578   Roman Emp.   *1503 †1539   D. of Beja
*1502 †1557   d. of Philip I   K. of Spain   *1506
   K. of Spain   *1500 †1558   †1555

TABLE 49

THEODOSIUS
D. of Braganza
†1563
m. (1) 1542
Isabella
*1558
d. of Denis
C. of Lemos

EMANUEL   PHILIP   JOHN — 1552 — Joanna   MARY ═ 1543 (1) ═ ☩ PHILIP I (II)
*1531   *1533   *1537   of Spain   *1527   K. of Portugal 1580
†1537   †1539   †1554   *1537 †1573   †1545   *1527 †1598

☩ PHILIP II (III)
K. of Portugal 1598
*1578 †1621   ANTHONY
   Prior of Crato   Alexander ═ 1565 ═ MARY   EDWARD   CATHERINE ═ 1563 ═ JOHN I
   Claimant 1580   Farnese   *1538   *1541   *1540 †1614   D. of Braganza
☩ SEBASTIAN   *1531 †1595   D. of Parma   †1577   †1576   before 1547
K. of Portugal 1557   ☩ PHILIP III (IV)   *1545 †1592   †1583
*1554 ✗ 1578   K. of Portugal 1621–40
   *1605 †1665   TABLE 94

Pedigree of the Kings of Portugal from an early 16th–century MS. It rises from Alphonso III (1210–79) and his second wife Beatrice and shows his son Denis (1261–1325) and grandson Alphonso IV (1291–1357) with other children and many versions of the arms of Portugal.

codified the laws of Portugal. The King deeply disapproved of the infatuation of his heir, Peter, for Ines de Castro, a Galician lady-in-waiting of Peter's legal wife. In 1355 he was persuaded to agree to her murder, which was followed by a brief and bitter civil war. When Peter succeeded in 1357 he announced that he had been married to Ines and (at least in the account given by the sixteenth-century poet Camoens

in *The Lusiads*) disinterred her corpse, to which his nobles were constrained to pay allegiance. To emphasize her status he constructed the two lovely tombs for himself and his beloved which are one of the glories of the great abbey of Alcobaça. His short reign was devoted to the spread of inflexible justice, including floggings administered by the King himself.

Ferdinand I was a weak and wayward king. He coveted the throne of Castile during the dispute between Peter the Cruel and Henry of Trastamara. In 1373 he negotiated an alliance with England. Portuguese gratitude to England already went back to the capture of Lisbon in 1147: since 1373 the two countries have never been at war, a rare example of diplomatic constancy. He fell in love with Eleanor Telles de Meneses, although she had a husband, and eventually married her: the Queen was exceedingly unpopular, produced only a daughter and took a lover. After numerous proposals the Infanta Beatrice was married to John I of Castile, and Ferdinand promised them the succession.

The people of Portugal resented the idea of Castilian rule and put forward John (Table 93), illegitimate son of Peter I. In 1385 he was accepted as king and, with some English help, he inflicted, in the same year, a severe defeat on the Castilians at Aljubarrota: nearby, in thanksgiving, he founded the splendid abbey of Batalha (Battle), whose style shows some English influences. John I had been Grand-Master of the Order of Aviz before he became king. Accordingly, he added to his shield the fleurs-de-lys ends of the green cross which was the badge of the Order (Table 93). This distinction was maintained by his descendants down to John II who resumed the traditional form — though it should be emphasised that there were many variations in the number of castles on the border or roundels on the 'quinas' or escutcheons. Moreover, John I married a daughter of John of Gaunt; and it seems a fair assumption that the Portuguese derived from the English the elaborate labels which begin to be used as differences for the younger princes (or 'Infants' as they were formally known in Spain and Portugal). A less common distinction was that of Ferdinand, Grand-Master of Aviz, who changed some of the castles on the border to lions of England. Ferdinand, Duke of Viseu (d. 1470), is unusual in having only two pendants to his label. Alphonso, Duke of Braganza, progenitor of a future line of kings, placed the five 'quinas' on a red saltire. Two coats-of-arms, rather typical of Iberian heraldry, can be seen on Table 92: the cooking pots with emergent snakes of de Lara (which can be compared with Guzman on Table 48), and the dice-like arrangement of the roundels of de Castro which in northern Europe would normally be arranged 3, 2 and 1.

EXPANSION OF PORTUGAL

During the fifteenth century Portuguese sailors made an epic contribution to the exploration of the world. The guiding spirit of these voyages of discovery was Henry the Navigator, Duke of Viseu and the son of John I, who had a castle at Sagre (in the extreme south) and a burning desire to extend Christian geography. Senegal was reached in 1445; and before the death of Prince Henry, Cape Verde had been doubled and the slave trade had begun. Alphonso V was more concerned with direct conquest in Morocco, but John II was keenly interested in the search for a route to India. Under his patronage Bartholomew Diaz reached the Cape of Good Hope, and he planned the celebrated voyage of Vasco da Gama, who actually attained an Indian port in 1498. In 1519–22 the ship of Ferdinand Magellan circumnavigated the world, though its captain perished on the journey. Meanwhile a powerful trading empire had been established in India, with its capital at Goa. Westward, the discovery of Brazil was made in 1500; the definition of interests in the new world between Spain and Portugal made by Pope Alexander VI in 1494 left this land in the Portuguese sphere.

Alphonso V had been involved in the succession to Castile, which he tried to secure for his son, the future John II. His defeat at Toro by Ferdinand of Aragon in 1476 checked this scheme, though Alphonso continued to dream of its realization as he grew older, portly, bearded and bald. John II was a more practical monarch. Heavily built, red-faced and red-haired, he set about reorganizing his Kingdom and fostering discovery. His dangerously powerful subject (and brother-in-law), Ferdinand of Braganza, was beheaded in 1483. At home the supremacy of the Crown was established by numerous executions among the aristocracy; abroad, the navies of Portugal traversed the globe.

King Emanuel, often known as Manuel the Fortunate, had perhaps the most glorious reign in Portuguese history. He has lent his name to the vigorous and vivid 'Manueline' style, which distinguishes the architecture of the period with its exuberant, and often maritime, decoration. Not without justice did King Emanuel assume the title of 'Lord of the conquest, navigation and commerce of India, Ethiopia, Arabia and Persia'. In East Africa or Burma, and around the coasts of India, mouldering fortresses recall this great age of Portuguese dominance of the oceans. The King himself was thin, diligent and abstemious, fond of music, but conscious of his royalty. He used as a badge an armillary sphere, which later appeared in the arms of Brazil (Table 95) and is seen all over Portugal. A generation later (1572) this golden age was celebrated by Camoens in

King John I of Portugal (1357–1433) entertains John of Gaunt. Late 15th-century MS.

his famous poem, *The Lusiads*.

In fact the situation was difficult. The flood of wealth led to a catastrophic fall in prices, particularly of imports like pepper and spices. The population of the country, long engaged in wars against the Moors or Castile, was inadequate for the stupendous tasks which drained manpower to the unhealthy East. A liberal importation of African slaves led to intermarriage and permanently affected the make-up of the people. From his three marriages Emanuel begat nine sons; he can scarcely have supposed that within sixty years his dynasty would be extinct and his country in Spanish hands.

John III arranged a double marriage with the Emperor Charles V, but was forced to provide his sister with a huge dowry. He was of moderate ability only, and came under the influence of the Church in his later years. His third son, Prince John, was a frail creature, perhaps reflecting the concentration of inbred Portuguese and Castilian blood in his veins, and died young. The next King, Sebastian, the grandson of John III, was also frail, but combined this with excessive piety and reluctance to marry. Forgotten crusading ideas fired his imagination, and he was killed conducting an incompetent campaign in Morocco. He was succeeded by his venerable great-uncle, and sometime guardian, the Cardinal-Prince Henry, Archbishop of Lisbon. The new monarch announced his wish to marry, but the Pope was as slow to dispense him as were his subjects incredulous of the value of his intention. The question of succession was clearly of paramount importance. Louis, Duke of Beja, had left an illegitimate son, Anthony, Prior of Crato; John, Duke of Braganza was married to a daughter of the Duke of Guimarães; Philip II of Spain was both nephew and son-in-law of John III (Table 93). In the event the King of Spain obtained the throne in 1580 with only a modest display of force. For

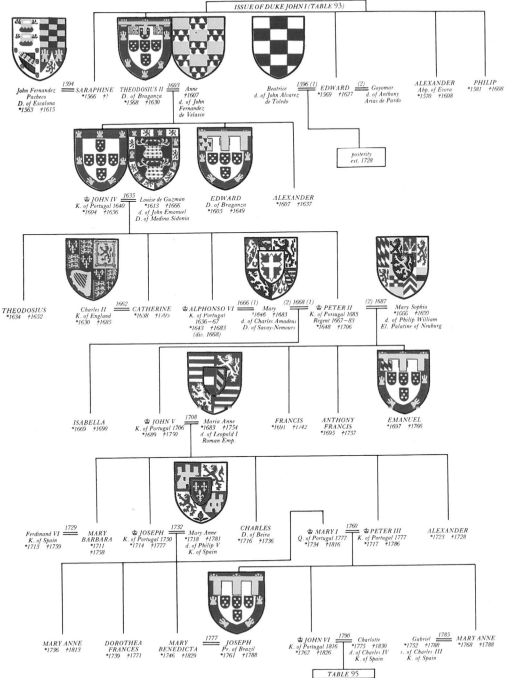

ISSUE OF DUKE JOHN I (TABLE 93)

John Fernandez
Pacheco
D. of Escalona
*1563 †1615

1594
═══ SARAPHINE
*1566 †?

THEODOSIUS II
D. of Braganza
*1568 †1630

1603
═══ Anne
†1607
d. of John
Fernandez
de Velasco

Beatrice
d. of John Alvarez
de Toledo

1596 (1)
═══ EDWARD
*1569 †1627

(2) ═══ Goyomar
d. of Anthony
Arias de Pardo

ALEXANDER
Abp. of Evora
*1570 †1608

PHILIP
*1581 †1608

posterity
ext. 1728

♔ JOHN IV
K. of Portugal 1640
*1604 †1656

1635
═══ Louise de Guzman
*1613 †1666
d. of John Emanuel
D. of Medina Sidonia

EDWARD
D. of Braganza
*1605 †1649

ALEXANDER
*1607 †1637

THEODOSIUS
*1634 †1652

Charles II
K. of England
*1630 †1685

1662
═══ CATHERINE
*1638 †1705

♔ ALPHONSO VI
K. of Portugal
1656–67
*1643 †1683
(div. 1668)

1666 (1)
═══ Mary
*1646 †1683
d. of Charles Amadeus
D. of Savoy-Nemours

(2) 1668 (1)
═══ ♔ PETER II
K. of Portugal 1683
Regent 1667–83
*1648 †1706

(2) 1687
═══ Mary Sophia
*1666 †1699
d. of Philip William
El. Palatine of Neuburg

ISABELLA
*1669 †1690

♔ JOHN V
K. of Portugal 1706
*1689 †1750

1708
═══ Maria Anne
*1683 †1754
d. of Leopold I
Roman Emp.

FRANCIS
*1691 †1742

ANTHONY
FRANCIS
*1695 †1757

EMANUEL
*1697 †1766

Ferdinand VI
K. of Spain
*1713 †1759

1729
═══ MARY
BARBARA
*1711
†1758

♔ JOSEPH
K. of Portugal 1750
*1714 †1777

1732
═══ Mary Anne
*1718 †1781
d. of Philip V
K. of Spain

CHARLES
D. of Beira
*1716 †1736

♔ MARY I
Q. of Portugal 1777
*1734 †1816

1760
═══ ♔ PETER III
K. of Portugal 1777
*1717 †1786

ALEXANDER
*1723 †1728

MARY ANNE
*1736 †1813

DOROTHEA
FRANCES
*1739 †1771

MARY
BENEDICTA
*1746 †1829

1777
═══ JOSEPH
Pr. of Brazil
*1761 †1788

♔ JOHN VI
K. of Portugal 1816
*1767 †1826

1790
═══ Charlotte
*1775 †1830
d. of Charles IV
K. of Spain

Gabriel
*1752 †1788
s. of Charles III
K. of Spain

1785
═══ MARY ANNE
*1768 †1788

TABLE 95

TABLE 95

PORTUGAL
House of Coburg-Braganza

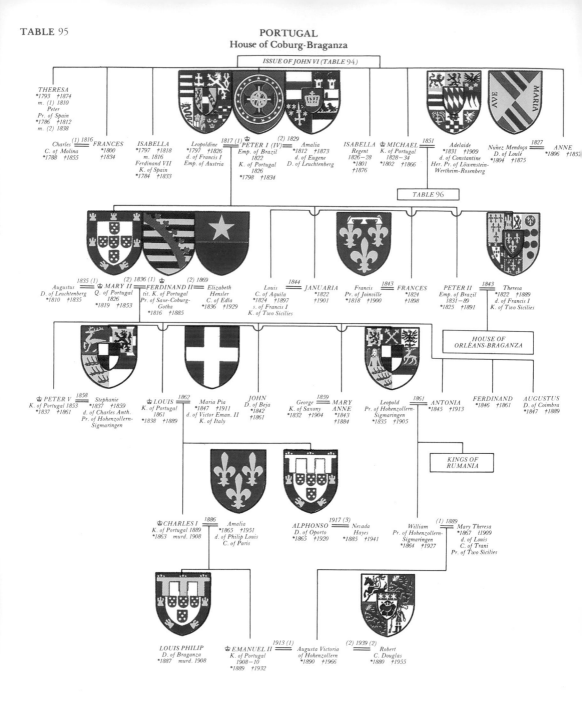

ISSUE OF JOHN VI (TABLE 94)

THERESA
*1793 †1874
m. (1) 1810
Peter
Pr. of Spain
*1786 †1812
m. (2) 1838

Charles (1) 1816 FRANCES
C. of Molina *1800
*1788 †1855 †1834

ISABELLA
*1797 †1818
m. 1816
Ferdinand VII
K. of Spain
*1784 †1833

Leopoldine 1817 (1) PETER I (IV) (2) 1829 Amalia
*1797 †1826 Emp. of Brazil *1812 †1873
d. of Francis I 1822 d. of Eugene
Emp. of Austria K. of Portugal D. of Leuchtenberg
1826
*1798 †1834

ISABELLA ♔ MICHAEL 1851 Adelaide
Regent K. of Portugal *1831 †1909
1826-28 1828-34 d. of Constantine
*1801 *1802 †1866 Her. Pr. of Löwenstein-
†1876 Wertheim-Rosenberg

Nuñez Mendoça 1827 ANNE
D. of Loulé *1806 †1857
*1804 †1875

TABLE 96

Augustus 1835 (1) MARY II (2) 1836 (1) FERDINAND II (2) 1869 Elizabeth
D. of Leuchtenberg Q. of Portugal tit. K. of Portugal Hensler
*1810 †1835 1826 Pr. of Saxe-Coburg- C. of Edla
*1819 †1853 Gotha *1836 †1929
*1816 †1885

Louis 1844 JANUARIA Francis 1843 FRANCES PETER II 1843 Theresa
C. of Aquila *1822 Pr. of Joinville *1824 Emp. of Brazil *1822 †1889
*1824 †1897 †1901 *1818 †1900 †1898 1831-89 d. of Francis I
s. of Francis I *1825 †1891 K. of Two Sicilies
K. of Two Sicilies

HOUSE OF
ORLÉANS-BRAGANZA

♔ PETER V 1858 Stephanie ♔ LOUIS 1862 Maria Pia JOHN George 1859 MARY Leopold 1861 ANTONIA FERDINAND AUGUSTUS
K. of Portugal 1853 *1837 †1859 K. of Portugal *1847 †1911 D. of Beja K. of Saxony ANNE Pr. of Hohenzollern- *1845 †1913 *1846 †1861 D. of Coimbra
*1837 †1861 d. of Charles Anth. 1861 d. of Victor Eman. II *1842 *1832 †1904 *1843 Sigmaringen *1847 †1889
Pr. of Hohenzollern- *1838 †1889 K. of Italy †1861 †1884 *1835 †1905
Sigmaringen

KINGS OF
RUMANIA

CHARLES I 1886 Amalia ALPHONSO 1917 (3) Nevada William (1) 1889 Mary Theresa
K. of Portugal 1889 *1865 †1951 D. of Oporto Hayes Pr. of Hohenzollern- *1867 †1909
*1863 murd. 1908 d. of Philip Louis *1865 †1920 *1885 †1941 Sigmaringen d. of Louis
C. of Paris *1864 †1927 C. of Trani
Pr. of Two Sicilies

LOUIS PHILIP EMANUEL II 1913 (1) Augusta Victoria (2) 1939 (2) Robert
D. of Braganza K. of Portugal of Hohenzollern C. Douglas
*1887 murd. 1908 1908-10 *1890 †1966 *1880 †1955
*1889 †1932

ISSUE OF MICHAEL (TABLE 95)

MARIA
DAS NEVAS
*1852 †1941
m. 1871
Alphonso
Pr. of Spain
D. of S. Jaime
*1849 †1936

Elizabeth
*1860 †1881
d. of Maximilian
Her. Pr. of Thurn
& Taxis

1877 (1) MICHAEL
D. of Braganza
*1853 †1927

(2) 1893 Theresa
*1870 †1935
d. of Charles
Pr. of Löwenstein-
Wertheim-Rosenberg

Charles Louis
A.D. of Austria
*1833 †1896

(3) 1873 MARIA
THERESA
*1855 †1944

MARIA
JOSEPHA
*1857 †1943
m. 1874
Charles Theodore
D. in Bavaria
*1839 †1909

Wiliam
GD. of Luxemburg
*1852 †1912

1893 MARY
ANNE
*1861
†1942

Robert
D. of Parma
*1848 †1907

(2) 1884 MARIA ANTONIA
*1862 †1959

MICHAEL
D. of Viseu
*1878 †1923

1909 (1) ANITA
*1886 †1977
d. of William
Stewart

MARIA THERESA
*1881 †1945
m. 1900
Pr. Charles Louis
of Thurn & Taxis
*1863 †1942

DE BRAGANZA

Francis Joseph
Pr. of Thurn & Taxis
*1893 †1971

1920 ELIZABETH
*1894
†1970

Pr. Charles Aug.
of Thurn & Taxis
*1898 †1982

1921 MARY
ANNE
*1899
†1971

EDWARD
D. of Braganza
*1907 †1976

1942 Mary Frances
*1914 †1968
d. of Peter
Pr. of Grão Pará

Nicholas
van Uden
*1921

1945 MARY
ADELAIDE
*1912

Isabel
Heredia
*1967

1995 EDWARD
D. of Braganza
*1945

MICHAEL
*1946

HENRY
*1949

Ancestors of John V and Charles I

THEODOSIUS II
D. of Braganza
*1568 †1630

1603 ANNE
†1607
d. of John
Fernandez
de Velasco

JOHN EMANUEL
de Guzman
D. of Medina Sidonia
*1579 †1638

JOANNA
d. of Francis
de Sandoval
D. of Lerma

WOLFGANG
WILLIAM
C. Palat. of Neuburg
*1578 †1653

(1) 1613 MAGDALEN
*1587 †1628
d. of William V
D. of Bavaria

GEORGE II
Lgv. of Hesse-
Darmstadt
*1605 †1661

1627 SOPHIA ELEANOR
*1609 †1671
d. of John George I
El. of Saxony

JOHN IV
K. of Portugal
*1604 †1656

1633 LOUISE FRANCISCA
*1613 †1666

PHILIP WILLIAM
El. Palatine
*1615 †1690

(2) 1653 ELIZABETH AMALIA
Pr. of Hesse-Darmstadt
*1635 †1709

PETER II
K. of Portugal
*1648 †1706

(2) 1687 MARY SOPHIA
Pr. Palatinal
*1666 †1699

JOHN V
K. of Portugal
*1689 †1750

Pr. FERDINAND
of Saxe-Cobg. & Gotha
D. of Saxony
*1785 †1851

1816 ANTONIA
*1797 †1862
d. of Francis Joseph
Pr. Kohary of Csabrag

PETER I (IV)
Emp. of Brazil
K. of Portugal
*1798 †1834

(1) 1817 LEOPOLDINE
*1797 †1826
d. of Francis I
Emp. of Austria

CHARLES
ALBERT
K. of Sardinia
*1798 †1849

1817 THERESA
*1801 †1855
d. of Ferdinand III
GD. of Tuscany

RAINER
A.D. of Austria
*1783 †1853

1820 ELIZABETH
*1800 †1856
d. of Charles Emanuel
Pr. of Savoy Carignan

FERDINAND II
tit. K. of Portugal
*1816 †1885

(1) 1836 (2) MARY II
Q. of Portugal
*1819 †1853

VICTOR EMANUEL II
K. of Italy
*1820 †1878

(1) 1842 ADELAIDE
A.D. of Austria
*1822 †1855

LOUIS I
K. of Portugal
*1838 †1889

1862 MARIA PIA
Pr. of Italy
*1847 †1911

CHARLES I
K. of Portugal
*1863 murd. 1908

many years his hapless people believed that Sebastian was not truly dead and would one day reappear.

The 60 years of Spanish rule were a period of gloom for Portugal. Three successive Philips neglected the interests of the country in favour of Spain. The harbours of Portugal were used for the Armada; more disastrously the agile seamen of England and the Netherlands began to challenge Portuguese supremacy in the East. Taxation was heavy; positions were given to Spaniards; the traditional privileges of Portugal were ignored. In 1640 an energetic body of conspirators seized their chance; the Spanish garrison was expelled and John, Duke of Braganza (Table 94), was proclaimed king as John IV. He was promptly recognized by France and less swiftly by England and Holland; Spanish efforts at reconquest were firmly repulsed, though Spain did not accept the inevitable until 1668. The status of the new dynasty was enhanced by the marriage of the Infanta Catherine to Charles II of England: her dowry included the valuable port of Bombay.

Alphonso VI was detested by his wife, who staged a revolution which deposed him and then procured a divorce in order to marry his brother Peter II; the latter ruled as regent until 1683 and then as king. In 1703 the famous treaty was negotiated which gave the wine of Oporto (port) preference in Britain. John V combined piety and extravagance; the vast palace and monastery at Mafra was a thank-offering for the birth of his son. His pedigree (Table 96) shows an equal balance between Iberian and German ancestry; his grandmother was descended from the luckless commander of the Armada. In 1755 Lisbon was destroyed by a terrible earthquake. For almost all the reign of King Joseph power was exercised by the capable but dictatorial Marquess of Pombal. He rebuilt the capital, encouraged trade and industry and fostered education. His patron unluckily had only daughters. The eldest was married to her uncle who became King-Consort (Peter III) and reigned with his niece-wife; after his death she became insane and the realm was ruled by her second son, John.

The policy of France, after the revolution, was hostile to Portugal; Napoleon demanded that she should close her ports to her ancient ally, Britain. In 1808 John fled to Brazil, while the French planned to subdivide his country. During the following years the British army under Wellington gradually drove the French out of the peninsula. While in Brazil, John proclaimed the province an independent kingdom; in 1816 he at last succeeded his old, mad mother. It was with reluctance that John VI returned to Portugal where he was compelled to accept the liberal constitution of 1822. In the same year the Brazilians, seeking total freedom from Portugal, proclaimed his son Peter to be Emperor of Brazil (Table 95).

On the death of John VI, Peter of Brazil designated his daughter, Mary, as Queen of Portugal, intending that she should marry her uncle, Michael, who was in exile. The latter in 1828 proclaimed himself absolute king and rejected the constitution prepared by Peter. In 1831 Peter abdicated in Brazil in favour of his son Peter II (who ruled until 1889 when Brazil became a republic) and returned to Europe to take up the cause of his daughter. In 1832 civil war broke out, but in 1834 the cause of Queen Mary triumphed and she was recognized as sovereign of Portugal. Later that year Peter IV died of tuberculosis. The first marriage of the young Queen lasted only a few months, but she then espoused Ferdinand of Saxe-Coburg and Gotha (Table 42).

The country had been sadly impoverished by 40 years of battle and invasion, and continued to be plagued by political upheavals and spasms of civil war. The Queen died in childbirth, and her eldest son of typhoid; Louis, her second son, reigned until 1889 constitutionally but without any outstanding achievements. His father was considered as a candidate for the Spanish throne in 1868. King Charles had to face a series of financial crises and a mounting tide of republicanism. His ancestry (Table 96) shows a fair spread of families, with Hapsburg the strongest element. In 1908, he and his eldest son were assassinated in Lisbon; the Infante Emanuel was wounded. Two years later a revolution forced Emanuel II to flee and Portugal became a republic.

For 20 years the new regime was turbulent and incompetent, but the prudent government of Dr Salazar wrought a remarkable change in his country's fortunes between 1932 and 1968. The undoubted economic benefits of his rule were to some extent counterbalanced by an increasingly totalitarian outlook. Since his death there have been a series of revolutions, and democracy in Portugal cannot yet be regarded as firmly established.

King Emanuel retired to England and devoted himself to scholarly research on Portuguese bibliography. His death without issue left the descendants of King Michael as undisputed pretenders to the throne (Table 96). Michael, Duke of Braganza (d. 1927), and his elder son both resigned their royal rights in 1920. In 1950 the younger son Edward, Duke of Braganza, was allowed to return to Portugal where he died in 1976. His eldest son, also Edward, is today the claimant to the Portuguese throne. It may be remarked that he is directly derived in the male line from Hugh Capet, founder of the French royal family, through the Houses of Burgundy, Aviz and Braganza, though the descent is broken by two illegitimacies (Table 91). His arms can be seen at the base of that Table surrounded by the simple chain of the Order of Christ.

Chapter 24

SAVOY, SARDINIA AND ITALY

As late as 1849 it was possible for Prince Metternich, the Austrian statesman, to declare that Italy was a geographical expression (*ein geographisches Begriff*). By this he meant that the seemingly well-defined peninsula, with its long seaboard and the Alps to the north, enjoyed no historical cohesion or social bond of interest. Within a very few years political unity was in fact achieved under the auspices of the House of Savoy; for the first time since the collapse of the west Roman Empire, Italy was under a single ruler. The next three chapters survey some of this complex history. It should be emphasized that in the Middle Ages some of the great Italian cities, most notably Venice, established republics which are at best scantily represented in a volume devoted to royalty, and that Rome continued to be the seat of a secular power passing in relatively steady succession from one pope to the next. It is, however, with the Counts of Savoy that the story must begin.

SAVOY

The earliest known scion of the family is Humbert I, with the White Hands, in the middle of the eleventh century (Table 97). The territorial strength of the County lay in the nebulous domain of Burgundy and stretched from the river Rhône to the lake of Geneva. Gradually the influence of the counts began to reach over the Alps into the Lombard plain; the history of Savoy, in brief, is a shift of emphasis from the French to the Italian side of the valuable Alpine routes which its rulers controlled, namely the Mont Cenis and the two St Bernard passes. The reigning Kings of Italy in this century descend in direct male line from these early counts, a remarkable example of dynastic continuity. Humbert's son, Count Otto, married the heiress of an important area on the Italian foothills of the Alps (hence later called 'Piedmont').

Some generations later, Count Thomas I is a sig-

nificant figure in the rise of the dynasty. He supported the Ghibelline (Hohenstaufen) emperors and was created Imperial Vicar, a position which he used to extend his lands on both sides of the Alps. Towards France he gained Bugey and Vaud, and to the east Carignan and other lordships. His influence reached down to the great ports of Savona and Genoa. One of his daughters wed the Count of Provence (Table 45), and their four daughters all married kings, including Henry III of England, who invited his wife's kinsmen to England. Boniface became Archbishop of Canterbury and Peter, Earl of Richmond, built a great palace on the strand of the Thames which has furnished the name of Savoy to that area of London. It is probable that Thomas I was already using the simple arms of Savoy — a silver cross on red; it is certainly found on the seal of his son Peter. At least by later tradition, the earlier counts had used a black eagle on a gold field: as they developed in power, the idea also grew up that they were descended from the German rulers of Saxony. Thomas I conferred Piedmont on his son Thomas II, whose grandson Philip married a Villehardouin heiress and thus acquired the title of Prince of Achaia.

It looked as though the state might suffer from fragmentation, but in the event Amadeus V firmly established his suzerainty both over the County of Piedmont and over his younger brother, Louis, Count of Vaud. Of his two sons, the elder was extravagant and the younger financially cautious. His grandson, Amadeus VI, the Green Count, was an amateur of crusading, chivalry and tournaments, at which he and the spectators wore green liveries. His crusading activities were altruistic in an age when the idealism of the movement had become tarnished. In about 1362 he founded the Order of the Annunciation, one of the most distinguished European orders of chivalry. The badge has always been worn from a

TABLE 97

ITALY AND SARDINIA
General survey (House of Savoy)

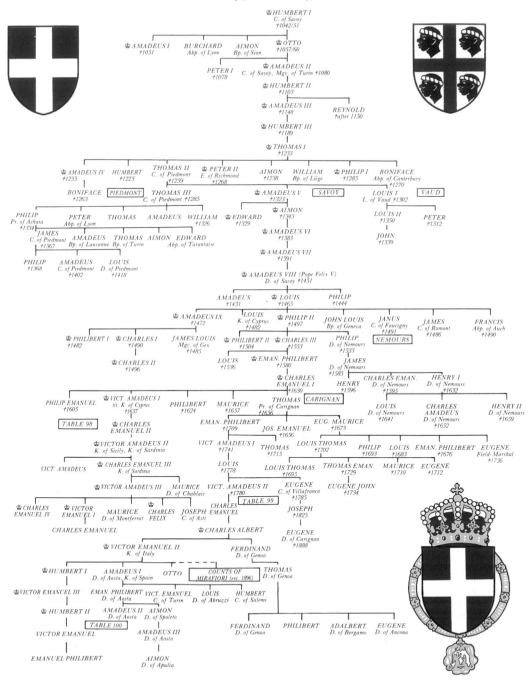

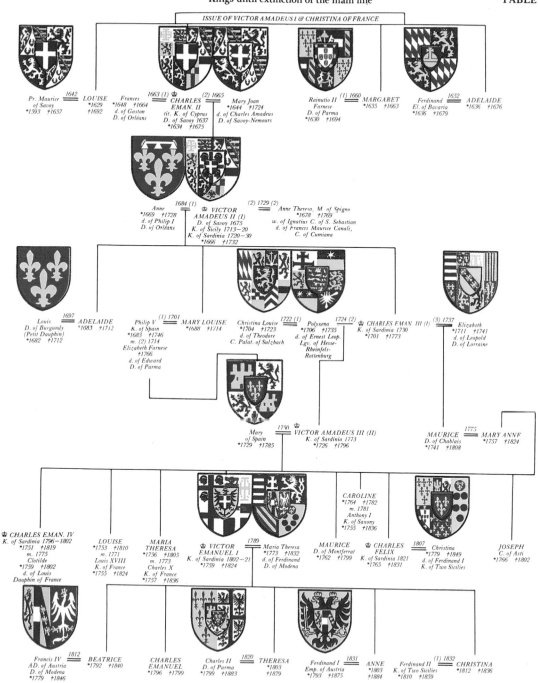

ISSUE OF VICTOR AMADEUS I & CHRISTINA OF FRANCE

Pr. Maurice —1642— LOUISE   Frances   1663 (1) CHARLES   (2) 1665 Mary Joan   Rainutio II (1) 1660 MARGARET   Ferdinand —1652— ADELAIDE
of Savoy   *1629   *1648 †1664   EMAN. II   *1644 †1724   Farnese   *1635 †1663   El. of Bavaria   *1636 †1676
*1593 †1657   †1692   d. of Gaston   tit. K. of Cyprus   d. of Charles Amadeus   D. of Parma   *1636 †1679
             D. of Orléans   D. of Savoy 1637   D. of Savoy-Nemours   *1630 †1694
                *1634 †1675

Anne —1684 (1)— VICTOR   (2) 1729 (2) Anne Theresa, M. of Spigno
*1669 †1728   AMADEUS II (1)   *1678 †1769
d. of Philip I   D. of Savoy 1675   w. of Ignatius C. of S. Sebastian
D. of Orléans   K. of Sicily 1713-20   d. of Francis Maurice Canali,
          K. of Sardinia 1720-30   C. of Cumiana
          *1666 †1732

Louis —1697— ADELAIDE   Philip V (1) 1701 MARY LOUISE   Christina Louise 1722 (1) Polyxena 1724 (2) CHARLES EMAN III (1) (3) 1737 Elizabeth
D. of Burgundy   *1685 †1712   K. of Spain   *1688 †1714   *1704 †1723   *1706 †1735   K. of Sardinia 1730   *1711 †1741
(Petit Dauphin)   *1683 †1746   d. of Theodore   d. of Ernest Leop.   *1701 †1773   d. of Leopold
*1682 †1712   m. (2) 1714   C. Palat. of Sulzbach   Lgv. of Hesse-   D. of Lorraine
          Elizabeth Farnese   Rheinfels-
          †1766   Rottenburg
          d. of Edward
          D. of Parma

Mary —1750— VICTOR AMADEUS III (II)   MAURICE —1775— MARY ANN
of Spain   K. of Sardinia 1773   D. of Chablais   *1757 †1824
*1729 †1785   *1726 †1796   *1741 †1808

CHARLES EMAN. IV   LOUISE   MARIA   VICTOR —1789— Maria Theresa   MAURICE   CHARLES 1807 Christina   JOSEPH
K. of Sardinia 1796-1802   *1753 †1810   THERESA   EMANUEL I   *1773 †1832   D. of Montferrat   FELIX   *1779 †1849   C. of Asti
*1751 †1819   m. 1771   *1756 †1805   K. of Sardinia 1802-21   d. of Ferdinand   *1762 †1799   K. of Sardinia 1821   d. of Ferdinand I   *1766 †1802
m. 1775   Louis XVIII   m. 1773   *1759 †1824   D. of Modena   *1765 †1831   K. of Two Sicilies
Clotilde   K. of France   Charles X   CAROLINE
*1759 †1802   *1755 †1824   K. of France   *1764 †1782
d. of Louis   *1757 †1836   m. 1781
Dauphin of France   Anthony I
                                    K. of Saxony
                                    *1755 †1836

Francis IV —1812— BEATRICE   CHARLES   Charles II —1820— THERESA   Ferdinand I —1831— ANNE   Ferdinand II (1) 1832 CHRISTINA
A.D. of Austria   *1792 †1840   EMANUEL   D. of Parma   *1803   Emp. of Austria   *1803   K. of Two Sicilies   *1812 †1836
D. of Modena   *1796 †1799   *1799 †1883   †1879   *1793 †1875   †1884   *1810 †1859
*1779 †1846

collar (Table 97 : base) and not from a ribbon. In 1388 Amadeus VII acquired Nice, on the Mediterranean. Amadeus VIII enjoyed a remarkable career. He reigned from 1391 to 1434 with signal success, extending his domains in Italy and receiving in 1416 the title of duke from the Emperor. On the extinction of the Counts of Piedmont in 1418 he added their lands to his own. But in 1434, after promulgating a famous code of laws for his people, he retired to a hermitage by the side of the lake of Geneva. In 1439, though still a layman, he was elected pope (as Felix V) by the remnants of the Council of Basel: he was never recognized by the whole Church and abdicated as pope in 1449 to receive a cardinal's hat.

Duke Louis married Anne of Lusignan, daughter of John I of Cyprus, acquiring thereby a claim to the thrones of Cyprus and Jerusalem; his son Louis married her younger sister. A series of brief reigns and minorities checked the progress of the Duchy. Philibert II was commemorated by his widow in the wonderful church of Brou, near Bourg-en-Bresse. His brother Charles III reigned longer but without much good fortune. Adherence to the Emperor Charles V led to frequent invasions by French forces. Geneva and Vaud were lost to Switzerland. At his death his duchy was in French occupation and his only son had entered the imperial service. The future of the Duchy seemed dim. Happily, Emanuel Philibert was a soldier of talent and a statesman of resource. He won the great victory of St Quentin (1557) for the Empire over France, a battle which effectually marked the end of a century of French intervention in Italy. The consequent Treaty of Cateau Cambrésis gave him possession of most of his father's duchy; it was no doubt hoped that Savoy might become a useful buffer state between France and the Hapsburgs. His rule was autocratic but crowned with success. Gradually he recovered the fortresses which had been assigned to the Great Powers. He gained Tende from the French by exchange for a small fief nearer France; he built up a useful army; he altogether refashioned the destiny of Savoy, but did so perhaps as a state looking towards the Lombard plain.

Charles Emanuel I continued the process and acquired in 1601 the important enclave of Saluzzo, for which he ceded Bresse and Bugey to France. Two of his sons founded branches which were to carry on the dynasty, Victor Amadeus as Duke of Savoy and Thomas as Prince of Carignan. A line of cousins had become Dukes of Nemours, but their activities were principally in France. Victor Amadeus was married to a daughter of Henry IV of France, who acted as regent for her infant son, Charles Emanuel II (Table 98); despite the efforts of both, Savoy continued to suffer in the Franco-Spanish conflicts of the seventeenth century. Matters changed under Victor

Amadeus II, partly because the Carignan branch had produced one of the ablest generals of the age, the celebrated Prince Eugene of Savoy (d. 1736). The Duke changed sides adroitly and in 1706 Prince Eugene, who had entered the imperial service, defeated the French severely outside Turin. At the Treaty of Utrecht (1713), Savoy was well-treated; she gained Montferrat on her eastern boundary and was also allotted the island of Sicily from which her ruler took the title of king. In 1720, however, the Powers arranged an exchange of islands and Victor Amadeus II became King of Sardinia.

His pedigree (Table 100) shows a mild preponderance of French blood, allowing the Houses of Lorraine and Savoy-Nemours to come under that heading; only Savoy and Medici can be reckoned Italian. The arms of Sardinia were a cross between four Moors' heads (Table 97) and they were incorporated with those of Savoy by Victor Amadeus II (Table 98). The elaborate arms of Savoy, as used by Charles Emanuel II, show four main quarterings. The first has itself four quarters for Jerusalem, Lusignan, Armenia and Cyprus (this last hidden), which represent the Cypriot marriage of Duke Louis; the second has a triple coat for Saxony, and reflects the spurious belief that the Savoyards sprang from Saxon stock; in the third, Chablais and Aosta, and in the fourth, Geneva and Montferrat are impaled. Over all is the plain cross of Savoy. Victor Amadeus II, as well as interposing Sardinia between the main shield and Savoy, added at the base of the shield the eagle allegedly borne by the earliest counts. This eagle can be seen again on the blazon of Victor Emanuel I. The Dukes of Savoy-Nemours differenced the cross of Savoy with an indented bordure (Table 100).

UNION OF ITALY

The island of Sardinia had suffered a confused history. It had been part of the Byzantine Empire, governed by native princelings, invaded by Saracens and disputed between the rising commercial powers of Genoa and Pisa. In 1175 the Emperor divided the island between them. The Emperor Frederick II (Chapter 22) tried to make it a kingdom for his handsome bastard Enzio; Pope Boniface VIII awarded the island to Aragon, though the Spaniards had to fight long and hard to establish their rule. In the division of spoils at the close of the War of the Spanish Succession it was allotted to Austria, and then, in exchange for Sicily, in 1720 it came to Savoy.

Charles Emanuel III was another competent soldier, who played his part in the wars of the eighteenth century, adding morsel after morsel to the dominions of Savoy. But Victor Amadeus III, his son, was a less robust character, who sought to oppose the French Revolution and saw his country overrun by

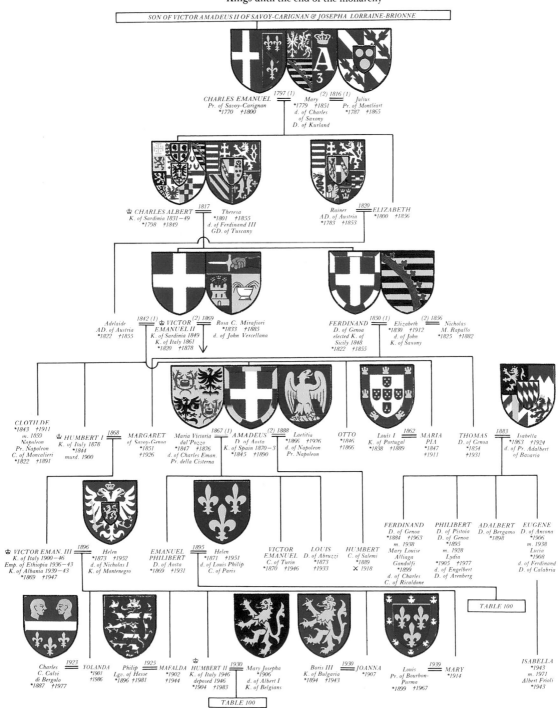

SON OF VICTOR AMADEUS II OF SAVOY-CARIGNAN & JOSEPHA LORRAINE-BRIONNE

1797 (1)   (2) 1816 (1)
CHARLES EMANUEL   Mary   Julius
Pr. of Savoy-Carignan   *1779 †1851   Pr. of Montléart
*1770 †1800   d. of Charles   *1787 †1865
                        of Saxony
                        D. of Kurland

1817
♔ **CHARLES ALBERT**   Theresa   Rainer   1820   **ELIZABETH**
K. of Sardinia 1831–49   *1801 †1855   AD. of Austria   *1800 †1856
*1798 †1849   d. of Ferdinand III *1783 †1853
                         GD. of Tuscany

Adelaide   1842 (1)   (2) 1869   Rosa C. Mirafiori   **FERDINAND**   1850 (1)   Elizabeth   (2) 1856   Nicholas
AD. of Austria ♔ **VICTOR**   *1833 †1885   D. of Genoa   *1830 †1912   M. Rapallo
*1822 †1855   **EMANUEL II**   d. of John Vercellana   elected K. of   d. of John   *1825 †1882
               K. of Sardinia 1849   Sicily 1848   K. of Saxony
               K. of Italy 1861   *1822 †1855
               *1820 †1878

CLOTILDE   Maria Victoria   1867 (1)   (2) 1888   Laetitia   OTTO   Louis I   1862   MARIA   THOMAS   1883   Isabella
*1843 †1911   ♔ **HUMBERT I**   1868   MARGARET   dal'Pozzo   **AMADEUS**   *1866 †1996   *1846   K. of Portugal   PIA   D. of Genoa   *1863 †1924
m. 1059   K. of Italy 1878   of Savoy-Genoa *1847 †1876 D. of Aosta   d. of Napoleon †1866   *1838 †1889   *1847   *1854   d. of Pr. Adalbert
Napoleon   *1844   *1851   d. of Charles Eman. K. of Spain 1870–3   Pr. Napoleon   †1911   †1931   of Bavaria
Pr. Napoleon   murd. 1900   †1926   Pr. della Cisterna *1845 †1890
C. of Moncalieri
*1822 †1891

                                                                                                           FERDINAND   PHILIBERT   ADALBERT   EUGENE
                                                                                                           D. of Genoa   D. of Pistoia D. of Bergamo D. of Ancona
                                                                                                           *1884 †1963   D. of Genoa   *1898   *1906
                                                                                                           m. 1938   *1895   m. 1938
♔ **VICTOR EMAN. III**   1896   Helen   EMANUEL   1895   Helen   VICTOR   LOUIS   HUMBERT   Mary Louise   m. 1928   Lucia
K. of Italy 1900–46   *1873 †1952   PHILIBERT   *1871 †1951   EMANUEL   D. of Abruzzi C. of Salemi   Alliaga   Lydia   *1908
Emp. of Ethiopia 1936–43   d. of Nicholas I D. of Aosta   d. of Louis Philip C. of Turin   *1873   *1889   Gandolfi   *1905 †1977   d. of Ferdinand
K. of Albania 1939–43   K. of Montenegro *1869 †1931   C. of Paris   *1870 †1946 †1933   ✕ 1918   *1899   d. of Engelbert D. of Calabria
*1869 †1947   d. of Charles D. of Arenberg
                                                                                                                       C. of Ricaldone

                                                                                                                                                    TABLE 100

Charles   1923   YOLANDA   Philip   1925   MAFALDA   **HUMBERT II**   1930   Mary Josepha   Boris III   1930   JOANNA   Louis   1939   MARY   ISABELLA
C. Calvi   *1901   Lgv. of Hesse   *1902   K. of Italy 1946   *1906   K. of Bulgaria   *1907   Pr. of Bourbon-   *1914   *1943
di Bergolo   †1986   *1896 †1981   †1944   deposed 1946   d. of Albert I   *1894 †1943   Parma   m. 1971
*1887 †1977   *1904 †1983   K. of Belgians   *1899 †1967   Albert Frioli
                                                                                                                                                                          *1943

TABLE 100

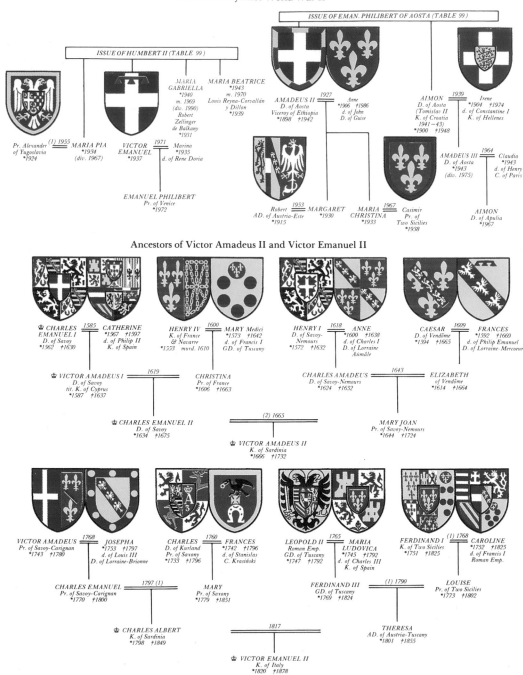

TABLE 100

ITALY
House of Savoy since World War II

ISSUE OF EMAN. PHILIBERT OF AOSTA (TABLE 99)

ISSUE OF HUMBERT II (TABLE 99)

MARIA
GABRIELLA
*1940
m. 1969
(div. 1990)
Robert
Zellinger
de Balkany
*1931

MARIA BEATRICE
*1943
m. 1970
Louis Reyna-Corvallán
y Dillon
*1939

AMADEUS II ═══ Anne
D. of Aosta   1927 *1906 †1986
Viceroy of Ethiopia   d. of John
*1898 †1942   D. of Guise

AIMON ═══ Irene
D. of Aosta 1939 *1904 †1974
(Tomislav II   d. of Constantine I
K. of Croatia   K. of Hellenes
1941–43)
*1900 †1948

Pr. Alexander (1) 1955 MARIA PIA
of Yugoslavia   *1934
*1924   (div. 1967)

VICTOR ═══ Marina
EMANUEL 1971 *1935
*1937   d. of Rene Doria

AMADEUS III ═══ Claudia
D. of Aosta   1964 *1943
*1943   d. of Henry
(div. 1975)   C. of Paris

EMANUEL PHILIBERT
Pr. of Venice
*1972

Robert ═══ MARGARET   MARIA ═══ Casimir   AIMON
AD. of Austria-Este 1953 *1930 CHRISTINA 1967 Pr. of   D. of Apulia
*1915   *1933   Two Sicilies *1967
*1938

Ancestors of Victor Amadeus II and Victor Emanuel II

♛ CHARLES ═══ CATHERINE
EMANUEL I 1585 *1567 †1597
D. of Savoy   d. of Philip II
*1562 †1630   K. of Spain

HENRY IV ═══ MARY Medici
K. of France 1600 *1573 †1642
& Navarre   d. of Francis I
*1553 murd. 1610 GD. of Tuscany

HENRY I ═══ ANNE
D. of Savoy- 1618 *1600 †1638
Nemours   d. of Charles I
*1572 †1632   D. of Lorraine
Aumâle

CAESAR ═══ FRANCES
D. of Vendôme 1609 *1592 †1669
*1594 †1665   d. of Philip Emanuel
D. of Lorraine-Mercoeur

♛ VICTOR AMADEUS I ═══ CHRISTINA
D. of Savoy   1619 Pr. of France
tit. K. of Cyprus   *1606 †1663
*1587 †1637

CHARLES AMADEUS ═══ ELIZABETH
D. of Savoy-Nemours 1643 of Vendôme
*1624 †1652   *1614 †1664

♛ CHARLES EMANUEL II
D. of Savoy
*1634 †1675

MARY JOAN
Pr. of Savoy-Nemours
*1644 †1724

(2) 1665

♛ VICTOR AMADEUS II
K. of Sardinia
*1666 †1732

VICTOR AMADEUS ═══ JOSEPHA
Pr. of Savoy-Carignan 1768 *1753 †1797
*1743 †1780   d. of Louis III
D. of Lorraine-Brionne

CHARLES ═══ FRANCES
D. of Kurland 1760 *1742 †1796
Pr. of Saxony   d. of Stanislas
*1733 †1796   C. Krasiński

LEOPOLD II ═══ MARIA
Roman Emp. 1765 LUDOVICA
GD. of Tuscany   *1745 †1792
*1747 †1792   d. of Charles III
K. of Spain

FERDINAND I ═══ CAROLINE
K. of Two Sicilies (1) 1768 *1752 †1825
*1751 †1825   d. of Francis I
Roman Emp.

CHARLES EMANUEL ═══ MARY
Pr. of Savoy-Carignan 1797 (1) Pr. of Saxony
*1770 †1800   *1779 †1851

FERDINAND III ═══ LOUISE
GD. of Tuscany (1) 1790 Pr. of Two Sicilies
*1769 †1824   *1773 †1802

♛ CHARLES ALBERT
K. of Sardinia
*1798 †1849

1817

THERESA
AD. of Austria-Tuscany
*1801 †1855

♛ VICTOR EMANUEL II
K. of Italy
*1820 †1878

French armies. Three of his sons reigned after him, two of them abdicating in favour of a brother; the Treaty of Vienna (1815) increased the kingdom of Victor Emanuel by adding Genoa, whose red cross on white figures in his arms. The death without issue of Charles Felix in 1831 marked the end of the main branch of Savoy. The Crown of Sardinia now passed to Charles Albert of Savoy-Carignan, Count of Soissons (Table 99). It may be added that Victor Emanuel I inherited in 1807 (through his great-grandmother Anne of Orléans) the Jacobite claim to the throne of England: at his death this passed to his eldest daughter and the Dukes of Modena, and thence to the Kings of Bavaria.

The convulsive changes in established boundaries, which were the aftermath of the Napoleonic campaigns, left a legacy of unrest in Italy. Despite the restoration of Hapsburg and Bourbon, despite the extinction of the ancient Republic of Venice, men began to dream again of Italian freedom and unity. Some of these dreamers believed that their only hope lay with the House of Savoy, an Italian dynasty with a well-trained army; others, like Joseph Mazzini who founded the Association of Italian Youth in 1831, were republican at heart; yet others had visions of a liberal pope. Charles Albert, the first king of the new line, was a cautious and slow-moving man. His elaborate arms (Table 99) show quarterings for Cyprus and Jerusalem, for the alleged Saxon descent, for Aosta, Genoa, Chablais and Piedmont and fourthly for Geneva and Montferrat. Two superimposed escutcheons stand for Sardinia and for Savoy ancient and modern; the eagle below and the cross above. Rightly, he doubted if his army was a match for the Austrian hosts, so firmly dominating the Lombard plain. In the year of the revolutions, risings broke out all over Italy. Almost hesitantly he led his troops against Austria, to be defeated at Custozza (1848) and Novara (1849). In the latter year he abdicated and died.

Victor Emanuel II, his son, was destined to be more fortunate. His ancestry (Table 100) shows a wide variety of strains: on the maternal side Bourbon and Hapsburg dominate, but his paternal forebears display a cadet branch of Lorraine and the wilder heraldic fancies of Kurland. The rapid triumph of Savoy was mainly due to the brilliant statesmanship of Cavour and to the refusal of Pope Pius IX to advance the unity of Italy. The virtuosity of Cavour lay in attracting the support of both France and Britain for the cause of Italian freedom. With calculated daring he aligned Savoy beside both in the Crimean War against Russia. In 1858 he made an agreement with Napoleon III to yield Nice and French Savoy; now he awaited any attack by Austria, and to his satisfaction one came in 1859. At Magenta and Sol-

Charles Albert of Savoy (1798–1849), King of Sardinia and ancestor of the Kings of Italy, by H. Vernet, 1834.

ferino, two sanguinary battles which contributed a violent colour and the foundation of the Red Cross movement to the sum of civilization, France and Savoy shattered the Hapsburg armies. Yet at the hour of triumph Napoleon made a peace with Austria which gave Lombardy only, not Venetia, to his ally. Cavour briefly resigned, but risings in Parma, Modena and Florence in favour of Savoy changed the picture. Cavour accepted their incorporation in the Kingdom of Sardinia, and honoured his earlier pledge by ceding to France both Nice and that part of Savoy which was the cradle of the dynasty. An effective kingdom of North Italy was now established.

It was at this juncture, and indubitably with the connivance of Cavour, that Garibaldi and his thousand red-shirted followers sailed for Sicily. In the summer of 1860 they liberated that island and crossed to the mainland to attack Naples. By the end of a fantastic year, all Italy except the environs of Rome and the provinces of Venice had demanded union with the Kingdom of Sardinia. The rise of Prussia did the rest: Austria ceded Venetia in 1866, the Papacy could no longer command French support after 1870. Florence became the capital of Italy in 1866; Rome replaced it in 1871. But the Papacy did not acquiesce and the Pontiff became the 'prisoner of the Vatican' in protest at the loss of his temporalities: Catholic clergy were forbidden to participate in the government of the new Kingdom. As King of Italy Victor Emanuel II assumed the plain and simple arms of

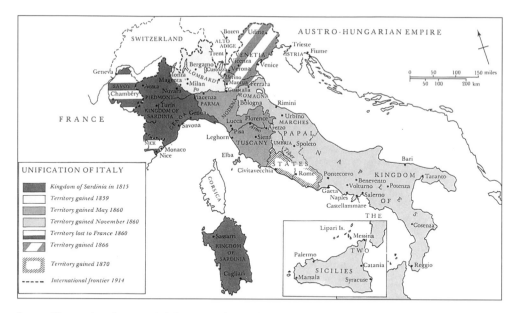

UNIFICATION OF ITALY

	Kingdom of Sardinia in 1815
	Territory gained 1859
	Territory gained May 1860
	Territory gained November 1860
	Territory lost to France 1860
	Territory gained 1866
	Territory gained 1870
	International frontier 1914

Savoy. His son, Amadeus, was briefly King of Spain (Chapter 11).

Hideous problems confronted the new monarchy. There were wide differences between the north and south; the country was overpopulated; its finances were precarious; its neighbour France was hostile. In 1882 Italy joined Germany and Austria in the Triple Alliance. An early venture in colonialism led to a disastrous defeat at Adowa in Ethiopia (1896); none the less colonies were achieved in Eritrea and Somaliland. In 1911 war with Turkey added Libya, Cyrenaica and the Dodecanese. When war broke out in 1914, Italy held back, and eventually joined England, France and Russia. Her armies were routed by an Austrian force at Caporetto and had to be rescued by the troops of her allies. At Versailles Italy was disappointed by her reception and her rewards; in particular she gained less than she had hoped in Dalmatia and in Turkey.

Victor Emanuel III had succeeded his father, Humbert I, the victim of an anarchist assassin, as long ago as 1900. He now found himself the ruler of a tired and disillusioned people. When in 1922 the ex-socialist Mussolini marched on Rome at the head of his blackshirt band, the tiny King entrusted him with the government of Italy. Within a few years a shadowy democracy was transformed into blunt dictatorship, and the word Fascist began its career as a term of abuse. None the less, many Italians supported the Duce. He achieved a reconciliation with the Papacy

(1929) which instituted the minuscule Vatican state; he gave a battered, and still young nation a sense of pride; he brought many overt signs of efficiency where these had been lacking. But a punctual railway service does not entirely compensate for gross bullying, a sombre curtailment of liberty and an outrageous foreign policy. In 1935 Ethiopia and in 1939 Albania were wantonly attacked and occupied; these tinsel titles were added to the more honourable styles of Victor Emmanuel III.

The increasing involvement of Fascism with Nazi Germany forced on Italy an unprofitable participation in the Second World War, which yielded a sorry tale of military disaster. In 1946 the old King abdicated in favour of his son, but the reign of the latter lasted only two months before Italy became a republic. King Humbert II never actually abdicated before his death in 1983.

The cadet members of the family, such as the Dukes of Aosta or Genoa (Table 99), differenced the basic arms of Savoy with a parti-coloured border. Amadeus II, Duke of Aosta (Table 100), was Viceroy of Ethiopia and died in captivity after losing a stern but honourable campaign. The Crown Prince (Table 100) bears the title of Duke of Naples; but hitherto the heir to the rulers of Savoy has for generations been known as the Prince of Piedmont. The arms of Count Calvi di Bergolo, the ex-king's brother-in-law, with their two hairless heads, are a play upon the Italian word calvo (bald).

Chapter 25

RUSSIA

The existence of Russia as a Great Power is of very recent date compared to most of the dynasties and realms which have already been discussed. The vast area of flattish land between the Crimea and the White Sea has an involved, if not long, history, and only came under one ruler as late as the eighteenth century. Much of this great space was settled by Slav peoples, though with a liberal mixture of Bulgars, Alans, Huns, and others, by the end of the tenth century. More than a hundred years before, a dynasty of 'Rus' under the semi-historical Rurik had settled at Novgorod, on Lake Volkhov. There is fairly wide agreement now that these Rus – who gave their name to the country – were Scandinavian adventurers, akin to the Varangians who penetrated to Constantinople. Igor, the son of Rurik, moved to Kiev.

A landmark in their history came in 988. Vladimir, Prince of Kiev, was dissatisfied with the religion of his forebears: he made careful enquiry into the faiths of the Arabs, the Jews, the Romans and the Christians of Constantinople. The splendour of the Byzantine liturgy enthralled him, and by a momentous decision he opted for the Orthodox Church. Given his somewhat lax sexual habits, his later canonization must be regarded as fortunate. From one of his many sons, Yaroslav I (Table 101), stem most of the later rulers of Russia. Little idea of unity prevailed among the princelings of this era, though the possession of Kiev gave a certain seniority. Vladimir Monomakh and Rostislav I were notable rulers of Kiev, but there were a great number of other lesser areas controlled by agnates of the House of Rurik who transferred to more important localities as they became vacant. Andrew I, Grand-Duke of Vladimir (Table 102), sacked Kiev and shifted the centre of gravity northwards to his own province, east of Moscow. Novgorod, an important commercial centre, Smolensk,

Halich (later Galicia), Ryazan and Chernigov were among the other more important lordships.

In the first half of the thirteenth century came the Tartar invasions which cut a great swathe across the south of Russia. Kiev was ravaged in 1240; two years later Batu Khan made his capital on the Volga: his successors were known as the Commanders of the Golden Horde, and levied tribute from the miscellaneous rulers of the House of Rurik, each of whom had to journey to Sarai to receive investiture. Only to the westward could Russia gain glory. Alexander Nevski, Prince of Novgorod (d. 1263), won two sensational battles, the first against the Swedes (1240) and the second on the frozen surface of Lake Peipus against the Teutonic knights. His youngest son, Daniel, founded the principality of Moscow, here, in 1325, the first Russian Metropolitan was to fix his see.

RISE OF MOSCOW

From this moment Moscow was of ever-increasing importance. Yuri (George) III contrived the murder of his cousin Michael (1318) and obtained from the Tartars the senior title of Grand-Duke (or Grand Prince) of Vladimir. His younger brother Ivan Kalita (of the Purse) became Grand Prince in 1328, but preferred to reign from Moscow and collect revenue from the other princes. Dimitri IV won a great battle against the Horde on the Don, and was thereafter known as Donskoi. The blow was not decisive, for the Golden Horde revived; but at this date the growing power of Lithuania on the west was a more serious threat to Russia, particularly after the union with Poland in 1386.

Basil I, Dimitri's son, married a Lithuanian princess; it is in his reign that a mounted figure first appears as the arms of the rulers of Moscow, which may easily be based on the arms of his wife. His grandson, Ivan

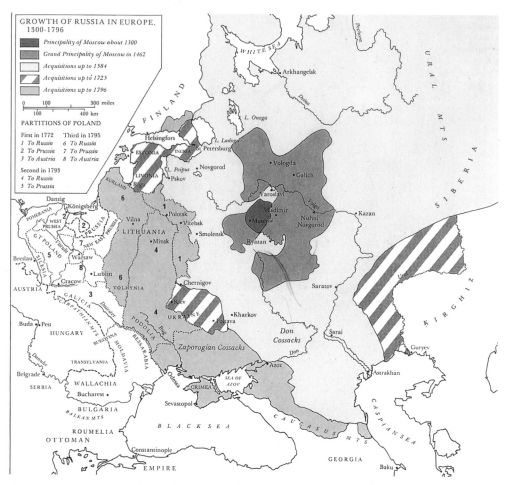

III, married a Byzantine princess; the horseman is now seen destroying a monster. Later generations were to associate this cavalier with St George and the dragon; but it is quite possible it is an importation from Constantinople of a much older iconographic motif of the emperor, as champion of Christianity, striking down evil.

Ivan III was a hunchback of evil appearance but he was the founder of Moscow's greatness. In 1478 he absorbed Novgorod; he extended his boundaries until they touched the Arctic and the Urals; he rejected the suzerainty of the Golden Horde; he adopted the title of gospodar or czar, a style hitherto applied by Slavs to the Emperor of the East. It is at this moment that the two-headed eagle begins to appear

as a Russian emblem. No doubt his marriage contributed to all this; if Constantinople had been the second Rome, a growing tradition was henceforward to claim Moscow as the third.

Basil III continued the work of his father, though his acquisitions of Pskov and Ryazan were less extensive. His court began to assume elements of grandeur; the nobility (the boyars) were consulted less than in former times when the prince had only been the first among equals. Since his first wife was childless, Basil secured a divorce which outraged the stricter ecclesiastics. From his second union came Ivan IV, known as the Terrible (Table 103), who was only three when his father died.

For a while the boyars reacted violently to the

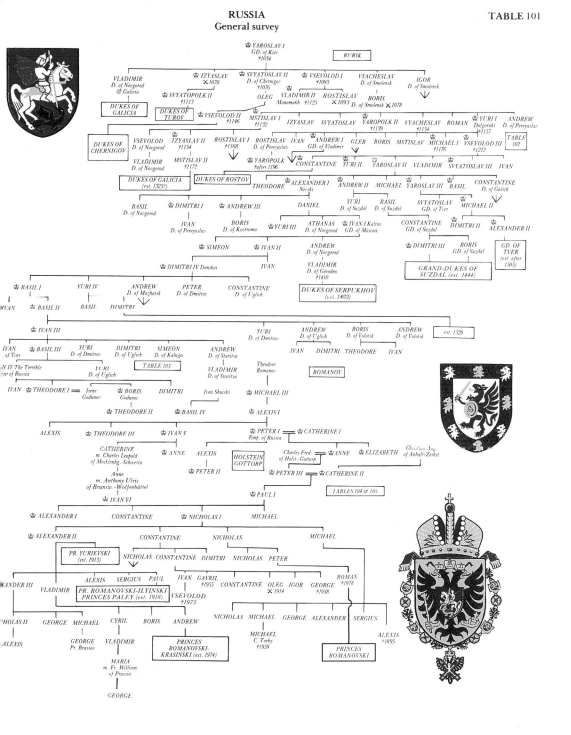

disappearance of authority. When Ivan came of age, he was formally crowned as czar – the first coronation in Russian history – and took up the family policy. Great areas in the Volga basin were annexed, including Kazan and Astrakhan. But the death of his first wife, who belonged to the Romanov family, and a serious illness seem to have warped his never stable character. He began a reign of terror and recruited a special corps of armed officials to carry out his savage decrees, the dreaded *Oprichnina* whose badge was a dog's head and a broom on their saddles. In 1581 he murdered his eldest son in a spasm of fury. It was in his reign that ships from England, seeking the Northwest Passage, first reached Russian ports. The Czar died, regretted by none, in 1584. His first marriage had been happy; but after the mysterious death of his third wife, he moved from one unsatisfactory alliance to another, despite the Orthodox custom only allowing three wives. He even solicited by proxy the hand of an English noblewoman, Lady Mary Hastings.

Theodore (Feodor) I suffered from rickets and an extreme addiction to religion. He came under the influence of his brother-in-law, Boris Godunov, who established the patriarchate of Moscow. He is also credited with establishing serfdom, but in fact he merely confirmed a long existing process, attaching the peasant to the soil. On Theodore's death Boris seemed the obvious successor, but his reign was unhappy and he could not control his fellow boyars. Moreover, rumours began to circulate that Dimitri, the half-brother of Theodore, who apparently perished in a brawl in 1591, was not dead. His reign is commemorated in the eponymous opera by Moussorgsky. When Boris died in 1605 his son Theodore II was soon killed and a false Dimitri (conceivably a natural son of Ivan IV) reigned for some months. But in 1606 he was overthrown in favour of Prince Basil Shuiski, a cadet of the House of Rurik, of insignificant appearance and small ability. The advent of another Dimitri drove Basil IV to abdicate; the principal sponsor of the pretender was Wladislaw, son of Sigismund III of Poland. From 1610 to 1612 the Poles controlled Moscow, but eventually a popular rising drove them out. In 1613 a national assembly was collected at the capital, and after some deliberation it chose Michael Romanov to be czar. The title czar is no more and no less than a Slavic form of the Latin *Caesar*.

THE HOUSE OF ROMANOV

The young ruler found his realm in sorry disarray. He made peace with Sweden and Poland and restored internal order; in the process the serfs were tied more closely to the estates of their owners. As an indication of his desire for firmer government, Michael III adopted the Byzantine title of autocrat. From 1618 until 1633 he shared the task of government with his father, Theodore, who had been forced into a monastery by Boris Godunov, and now, under his religious name of Philaret, was Patriarch of Moscow. Alexis I was unanimously elected on the death of Michael, and proved a sensible and normal ruler. His reign witnessed an influx of western advisers to give technical help and a great codification of the laws. Against this must be set a series of popular disorders, of which the most serious were a rising in 1670–71 in the Volga basin and a great schism in the Orthodox Church which led to the excommunication of the 'Old Believers'. After a war with Poland, Alexis added to his domains in 1667 a large part of Little Russia (or Ukraine), including the historic city of Kiev.

Before his death Alexis proclaimed his eldest surviving son, Theodore, as his heir, but the boy was puny and died aged twenty. After a brief crisis, Ivan V and his half-brother, Peter, were proclaimed joint sovereigns, with their sister Sophia as regent. Peter was exiled to a village, until at seventeen he staged a coup which disposed of the Regent and Ivan V. The new Czar was remarkable physically, for he was nearly 2.5m (8ft) and of enormous strength. He was scantily educated, delighted in carpentry and manual work, and possessed a dynamic will. Peter cared little for luxury but passionately believed in his country and its destiny, while lacking any talents for winning popularity. In 1697, after the death of his brother, he embarked on an unprecedented journey to western Europe, mainly to Holland and England, in order to inform himself about the civilization which Russia sorely needed.

For all his bouts of intoxication and his cruelty, his achievement was as titanic as his stature. Within the country he attacked the reactionary features of domestic life; the universal beard was prohibited, the seclusion of women and the wealth of the clergy diminished, even the alphabet was shorn of eight letters. He also had the foresight to begin the imperial collection of Russian archaeological remains. In every sphere the higher standards and techniques of Europe were introduced into a country still oriental in much of its lineage and habits. A minor reform was the appearance of a system of heraldry, though it was more personal than hereditary. Fuller organization only came under the Emperor Paul I (1796–1801). From the time of Ivan IV, the horseman arms of the Grand-Duchy of Moscow had been placed on a two-headed (Byzantine) eagle with a crown between the heads. Michael III increased the crowns to three, and Alexis I added an orb and sceptre to the eagle. But the blazons shown for his wife, and the wives of his sons (Table 103), were only granted to their respective families in the reign of Peter the Great. The personal

RUSSIA
Grand-Dukes of Vladimir and Moscow (House of Rurik)

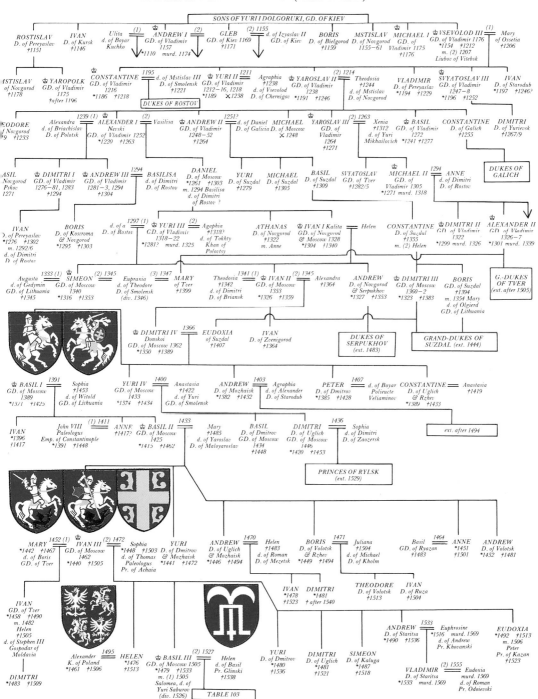

SONS OF YURI I DOLGORUKI, GD. OF KIEV

| ROSTISLAV D. of Pereyaslav †1151 | IVAN D. of Kursk †1146 | Ulita d. of Boyar Kuchko | (1) ♛ ANDREW I GD. of Vladimir 1157 *1110 murd. 1174 | (2) | GLEB GD. of Kiev 1169 †1171 | (2) 1155 | d. of Izyaslav II GD. of Kiev | BORIS D. of Bielgorod †1159 | MSTISLAV D. of Novgorod 1155–61 | MICHAEL I GD. of Vladimir 1175 †1176 | ♛ VSEVOLOD III GD. of Vladimir 1176 *1154 †1212 m. (2) 1207 Liubov of Vitebsk | (1) Mary of Ossetia †1206 |

| MSTISLAV of Novgorod †1178 | ♛ YAROPOLK GD. of Vladimir 1175 †after 1196 | CONSTANTINE GD. of Vladimir 1216 *1186 †1218 | 1195 d. of Mstislav III D. of Smolensk †1221 | ♛ YURI II GD. of Vladimir 1212–16, 1218 *1189 ✕1238 | 1211 Agraphia †1238 d. of Vsevolod D. of Chernigov | ♛ YAROSLAV II GD. of Vladimir 1238 *1191 †1246 | (2) 1214 Theodosia †1244 d. of Mstislav D. of Novgorod | VLADIMIR D. of Pereyaslav *1194 †1229 | SVYATOSLAV III GD. of Vladimir 1247–8 *1196 †1252 | IVAN D. of Starodub *1197 †1246? |

| ☐EODORE f Novgorod 9 †1233 | Alexandra d. of Briachislav D. of Polotsk | 1239 (1) ♛ ALEXANDER I Nevski GD. of Vladimir 1252 *1220 †1263 | (2) Vasilisa | ♛ ANDREW II GD. of Vladimir 1248–52 †1264 | 1251? d. of Daniel D. of Galicia | MICHAEL D. of Moscow ✕ 1248 | YAROSLAV III GD. of Vladimir 1264 †1271 | (2) 1263 Xenia †1312 d. of Yuri Mikhailovich | ♛ BASIL GD. of Vladimir 1272 †1241 †1277 | CONSTANTINE D. of Galich †1255 | DIMITRI D. of Yurievsk †1267/9 |

| ☐ASIL Pskov 1271 | ♛ DIMITRI I GD. of Vladimir 1276–81, 1283 †1294 | ♛ ANDREW III GD. of Vladimir 1281–3, 1294 †1304 | BASILISA d. of Dimitri D. of Rostov | DANIEL D. of Moscow *1261 †1303 m. 1294 Basilisa d. of Dimitri of Rostov ? | YURI D. of Suzdal †1279 | MICHAEL D. of Suzdal †1305 | BASIL D. of Suzdal †1309 | SVYATOSLAV GD. of Tver *1282/5 | MICHAEL II GD. of Vladimir 1305 *1271 murd. 1318 | 1294 ANNE d. of Dimitri D. of Rostov | DUKES OF GALICH |

| IVAN D. of Pereyaslav *1276 †1302 m. 1292/6 d. of Dimitri D. of Rostov | BORIS D. of Kostroma & Novgorod *1295 †1303 | d. of a D. of Rostov | 1297 (1) ♛ YURI III GD. of Vladimir 1318–22 *1281? murd. 1325 | (2) Agraphia †1319? d. of Tokhty Khan of Polovtsy | ATHANAS D. of Novgorod †1322 | ♛ IVAN I Kalita GD. of Vladimir & Moscow 1328 *1304 †1340 m. Anne | Helen | CONSTANTINE D. of Suzdal †1355 m. (2) Helen | ♛ DIMITRI II GD. of Vladimir 1322 *1299 murd. 1326 | ALEXANDER II GD. of Vladimir 1326–7 *1301 murd. 1339 |

| Augusta d. of Gedymin GD. of Lithuania †1345 | 1333 (1) ♛ SIMEON GD. of Moscow 1340 *1316 †1353 | (2) 1345 Eupraxia d. of Theodore D. of Smolensk (div. 1346) | (3) 1347 MARY of Tver †1399 | Theodosia †1342 d. of Dimitri D. of Briansk | 1341 (1) ♛ IVAN II GD. of Moscow 1353 *1326 †1359 | (2) 1345 Alexandra †1364 | ANDREW D. of Novgorod & Serpukhov *1327 †1353 | ♛ DIMITRI III GD. of Moscow 1360–2 *1323 †1383 | BORIS D. of Suzdal *1394 m. 1354 Mary d. of Olgierd GD. of Lithuania | G.-DUKES OF TVER (ext. after 1505) |

| ♛ DIMITRI IV Donskoi GD. of Moscow 1362 *1350 †1389 | 1366 EUDOXIA of Suzdal †1407 | IVAN D. of Zvenigorod †1364 | DUKES OF SERPUKHOV (ext. 1483) | GRAND-DUKES OF SUZDAL (ext. 1444) |

| ♛ BASIL I GD. of Moscow 1389 *13/1 †1425 | 1391 Sophia †1453 d. of Witold GD. of Lithuania | YURI IV GD. of Moscow 1433 *1374 †1434 | 1400 Anastasia †1422 d. of Yuri GD. of Smolensk | ANDREW D. of Mozhaisk *1382 †1432 | 1403 Agraphia d. of Alexander D. of Starodub | PETER D. of Dmitrov *1385 †1428 | 1407 d. of Boyar Polieucte Veliaminov | CONSTANTINE D. of Uglich & Rzhev *1389 †1433 | Anastasia †1419 |

| IVAN *1396 †1417 | John VIII Paleologus Emp. of Constantinople *1391 †1448 | (1) 1411 ANNE *1417? | ♛ BASIL II GD. of Moscow 1425 *1415 †1462 | 1433 Mary †1485 d. of Yaroslav D. of Maloyaroslav | BASIL D. of Dmitrov GD. of Moscow 1434 †1448 | DIMITRI D. of Uglich GD. of Moscow 1446 *1420 †1453 | 1436 Sophia d. of Dimitri D. of Zaozersk | ext. after 1494 |

PRINCES OF RYLSK (ext. 1529)

| MARY *1442 †1467 d. of Boris GD. of Tver | 1452 (1) ♛ IVAN III GD. of Moscow 1462 *1440 †1505 | (2) 1472 Sophia *1448 †1503 d. of Thomas Paleologus Pr. of Achaia | YURI D. of Dmitrov & Mozhaisk *1441 †1472 | ANDREW D. of Uglich & Mozhaisk *1446 †1494 | 1470 Helen †1483 d. of Roman D. of Mezetsk | BORIS D. of Volotsk & Rzhev *1449 †1494 | 1471 Juliana †1504 d. of Michael D. of Kholm | Basil GD. of Ryazan †1483 | 1464 ANNE *1451 †1501 | ANDREW D. of Volotsk *1452 †1481 |

| IVAN *1478 †1523 | DIMITRI *1481 † after 1540 | THEODORE D. of Volotsk †1513 | IVAN D. of Ruza †1504 |

| IVAN GD. of Tver *1458 †1490 m. 1482 Helen †1505 d. of Stephen III Gospodar of Moldavia | Alexander K. of Poland *1461 †1506 | 1495 HELEN *1476 †1513 | (2) 1527 ♛ BASIL III GD. of Moscow 1505 *1479 †1533 m. (1) 1505 Salomea, d. of Yuri Saburov (div. 1526) | Helen d. of Basil Pr. Glinski †1538 | YURI D. of Dmitrov *1480 †1536 | DIMITRI D. of Uglich *1481 †1521 | SIMEON D. of Kaluga *1487 †1518 | ANDREW D. of Staritsa *1490 †1536 | 1533 Euphrosine *1516 murd. 1569 d. of Andrew Pr. Khovanski | EUDOXIA *1492 †1513 m. 1506 Peter Pr. of Kazan †1523 |

| DIMITRI *1483 †1309 | | | | | | | VLADIMIR D. of Staritsa *1533 murd. 1569 | (2) 1555 Eudoxia murd. 1569 d. of Roman Pr. Odoievski |

TABLE 103

TABLE 103

RUSSIA
Accession of the House of Romanov

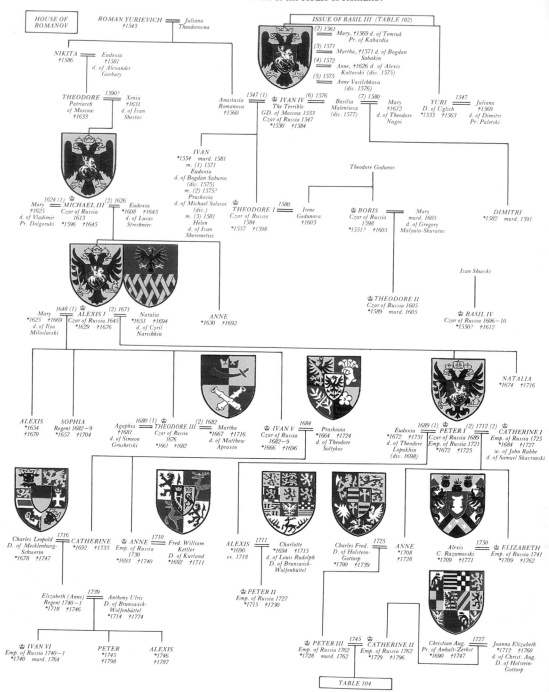

HOUSE OF
ROMANOV

ROMAN YURIEVICH ⚊ Juliana
†1543   Theodorovna

ISSUE OF BASIL III (TABLE 102)

NIKITA ⚊ Eudoxia
†1586   †1581
d. of Alexander
Gorbaty

(2) 1561 Mary, †1569 d. of Temruk
          Pr. of Kabardia

(3) 1571 Martha, †1571 d. of Bogdan
          Sobakin

(4) 1572 Anne, †1626 d. of Alexis
          Koltovski (div. 1575)

(5) 1575 Anne Vasilchkova
          (div. 1576)

THEODORE   1590? Xenia
Patriarch   ⚊   †1631
of Moscow   d. of Ivan
†1633   Shestov

Anastasia   1547 (1) IVAN IV (6) 1576
Romanova   ⚊   The Terrible
†1560   GD. of Moscow 1533
                        Czar of Russia 1547
                        *1530 †1584

Basilia   (7) 1580 Mary   YURI   1547 Juliana
Malentieva ⚊   †1612   D. of Uglich ⚊   †1569
(div. 1577)   d. of Theodore *1533 †1563 d. of Dimitri
                        Nagoi   Pr. Paletski

IVAN
*1554 murd. 1581
m. (1) 1571
Eudoxia
d. of Bogdan Saburov
(div. 1575)
m. (2) 1575?
Praskovia
d. of Michael Solovoi
(div.)
m. (3) 1581
Helen
d. of Ivan
Sheremetiev

Theodore Godunov

THEODORE I   1580 Irene
Czar of Russia ⚊   Godunova
1584   †1603
*1557 †1598

♚ BORIS   Mary
Czar of Russia ⚊ murd. 1605
1598   d. of Gregory
*1551? †1605 Malyuta-Skuratov

DIMITRI
*1582 murd. 1591

Mary   1624 (1) ♚ MICHAEL III (2) 1626 Eudoxia
†1625   ⚊   Czar of Russia ⚊   *1608 †1645
d. of Vladimir   1613   d. of Lucas
Pr. Dolgoruki   *1596 †1645   Streshniev

Ivan Shuiski

♚ THEODORE II
Czar of Russia 1605
*1589 murd. 1605

Mary   1648 (1) ♚ ALEXIS I (2) 1671 Natalia   ANNE
†1625   ⚊   Czar of Russia 1645 ⚊ *1651 †1694 *1630 †1692
d. of Ilya   *1629 †1676   d. of Cyril
Miloslavski   Narishkin

♚ BASIL IV
Czar of Russia 1606—10
*1550? †1612

NATALIA
*1674 †1716

ALEXIS   SOPHIA   Agaphia   1680 (1) ♚ THEODORE III (2) 1682 Martha   ♚ IVAN V   Praskovia   Eudoxia   1689 (1) ♚ PETER I (2) 1712 (2) ♚ CATHERINE I
*1654   Regent 1682—9 †1681   ⚊   Czar of Russia ⚊ *1667 †1716 Czar of Russia ⚊ *1664 †1724 *1672 †1731 ⚊   Czar of Russia 1689 ⚊   Emp. of Russia 1725
†1670   *1657 †1704   d. of Simeon   1676   d. of Matthew 1682—9   d. of Theodore d. of Theodore   Emp. of Russia 1721   *1684 †1727
                          Grushetski   *1661 †1682   Apraxin   *1666 †1696   Soltykov   Lopukhin   *1672 †1725   w. of John Rabbe
                                                                                                            (div. 1698)   d. of Samuel Skavronski

Charles Leopold 1716   ♚ ANNE   1710   ALEXIS   1711 Charlotte   Charles Fred. 1725 ANNE   Alexis   1750 ♚ ELIZABETH
D. of Mecklenburg- ⚊ CATHERINE Emp. of Russia ⚊ Fred. William *1690   ⚊   *1694 †1715   D. of Holstein- ⚊   *1708   C. Razumowski ⚊   Emp. of Russia 1741
Schwerin   *1692 †1733   1730   Kettler   ex. 1718   d. of Louis Rudolph Gottorp   †1728   *1709 †1771   *1709 †1762
*1678 †1747   *1693 †1740 D. of Kurland   D. of Brunswick- *1700 †1739
                                            *1692 †1711   Wolfenbüttel

♚ PETER II
Emp. of Russia 1727
*1715 †1730

Elizabeth (Anne) 1739 Anthony Ulric
Regent 1740—1   ⚊   D. of Brunswick-
*1718 †1746   Wolfenbüttel
                        *1714 †1774

♚ IVAN VI   PETER   ALEXIS
Emp. of Russia 1740—1 *1745   *1746
*1740 murd. 1764   †1798   †1787

♚ PETER III   1745 ♚ CATHERINE II   Christian Aug.   1727 Joanna Elizabeth
Emp. of Russia 1762 ⚊ Emp. of Russia 1762 Pr. of Anhalt-Zerbst ⚊ *1712 †1760
*1728 murd. 1762   *1729 †1796   *1690 †1747   d. of Christ. Aug.
                                                             D. of Holstein-
                                                             Gottorp

TABLE 104

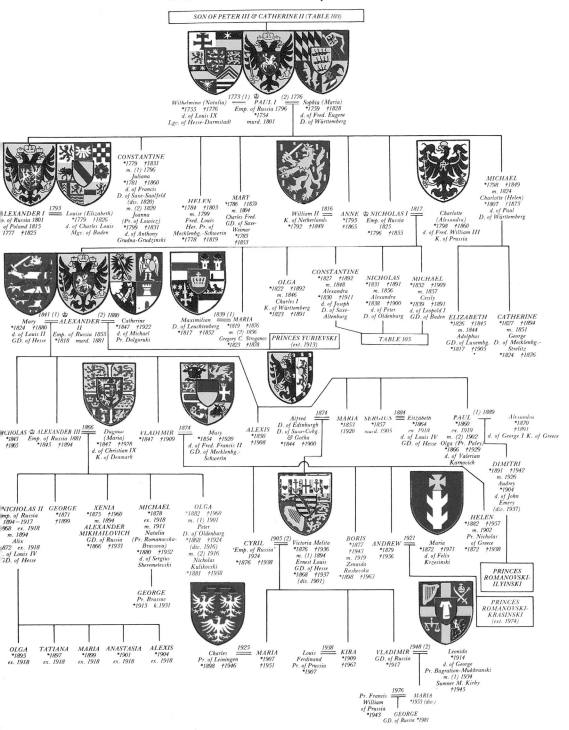

SON OF PETER III & CATHERINE II (TABLE 103)

1773 (1) ⚭ (2) 1776
Wilhelmina (Natalia) ══ PAUL I ══ Sophia (Maria)
*1755 †1776   Emp. of Russia 1796   *1759 †1828
d. of Louis IX   *1754   d. of Fred. Eugene
Lgv. of Hesse-Darmstadt murd. 1801   D. of Württemberg

CONSTANTINE
*1779 †1831
m. (1) 1796
Juliana
*1781 †1860
d. of Francis
D. of Saxe-Saalfeld
(div. 1820)
m. (2) 1820
Joanna
(Pr. of Lowicz)
*1799 †1831
d. of Anthony
Grudna-Grudzinski

MICHAEL
*1798 †1849
m. 1824
Charlotte (Helen)
*1807 †1873
d. of Paul
D. of Württemberg

ALEXANDER I ══ 1793 Louise (Elizabeth)
. of Russia 1801   *1779 †1826
of Poland 1815   d. of Charles Louis
1777 †1825   Mgv. of Baden

HELEN
*1784 †1803
m. 1799
Fred. Louis
Her. Pr. of
Mecklenbg.-Schwerin
*1778 †1819

MARY
*1786 †1859
m. 1804
Charles Fred.
GD. of Saxe-
Weimar
*1783
†1853

William II ══ 1816 ANNE ⚭ NICHOLAS I ══ 1817 Charlotte
K. of Netherlands   *1795   Emp. of Russia   (Alexandra)
*1792 †1849   †1865   1825   *1798 †1860
                  *1796 †1855   d. of Fred. William III
                              K. of Prussia

OLGA
*1822 †1892
m. 1846
m. 1848
Charles I
K. of Württemberg
*1823 †1891

CONSTANTINE
*1827 †1892
m. 1848
Alexandra
*1830 †1911
d. of Joseph
D. of Saxe-
Altenburg

NICHOLAS
*1831 †1891
m. 1856
Alexandra
*1838 †1900
d. of Peter
D. of Oldenburg

MICHAEL
*1832 †1909
m. 1857
Cecily
*1839 †1891
d. of Leopold I
GD. of Baden

ELIZABETH
*1826 †1845
m. 1844
Adolphus
GD. of Luxemb.
*1817 †1905

CATHERINE
*1827 †1894
m. 1851
George
D. of Mecklenbg.-
Strelitz
*1824 †1876

Mary ══ 1841 (1) ALEXANDER ══ (2) 1880 Catherine
*1824 †1880   II   *1847 †1922
d. of Louis II   Emp. of Russia 1855   d. of Michael
GD. of Hesse   *1818 murd. 1881   Pr. Dolgoruki

Maximilian ══ 1839 (1) MARIA
D. of Leuchtenberg   *1819 †1876
*1817 †1852   m. 1856
                  Gregory C. Stroganov
                  *1823 †1878

PRINCES YURIEVSKI
(ext. 1913)

TABLE 105

NICHOLAS ⚭ ALEXANDER III ══ 1866 Dagmar (Maria)
*1843   Emp. of Russia 1881   *1847 †1928
†1865   *1845 †1894   d. of Christian IX
                        K. of Denmark

VLADIMIR ══ 1874 Mary
*1847 †1909   *1854 †1920
            d. of Fred. Francis II
            GD. of Mecklenbg.-
            Schwerin

ALEXIS
*1850
†1908

Alfred ══ 1874 MARIA
D. of Edinburgh   *1853
D. of Sux.-Cobg.   †1920
& Gotha
*1844 †1900

SERGIUS ══ 1884 Elizabeth
*1857   *1864
murd. 1905   ex. 1918
            d. of Louis IV
            GD. of Hesse

PAUL ══ (1) 1889 Alexandra
*1860   *1870
ex. 1919   †1891
m. (2) 1902   d. of George I K. of Greece
Olga (Pr. Paley)
*1866 †1929
d. of Valerian
Karnovich

DIMITRI
*1891 †1942
m. 1926
Audrey
*1904
d. of John
Emery
(div. 1937)

HELEN
*1882 †1957
m. 1902
Pr. Nicholas
of Greece
*1872 †1938

NICHOLAS II ⚭ GEORGE
mp. of Russia   *1871
1894–1917   †1899
m. 1894
Alix
872 ex. 1918
. of Louis IV
GD. of Hesse

XENIA
*1875 †1960
m. 1894
ALEXANDER
MIKHAILOVICH
GD. of Russia
*1866 †1933

MICHAEL
*1878
ex. 1918
m. 1911
Natalia
(Pr. Romanovska-
Brassova)
*1880 †1952
d. of Sergius
Sheremetevski

OLGA
*1882 †1960
m. (1) 1901
Peter
D. of Oldenburg
*1868 †1924
(div. 1916)
m. (2) 1916
Nicholas
Kulikovski
*1881 †1958

CYRIL ══ 1905 (2) Victoria Melita
'Emp. of Russia'   *1876 †1936
1924   m. (1) 1894
*1876 †1938   Ernest Louis
                GD. of Hesse
                *1868 †1937
                (div. 1901)

BORIS
*1877
†1943
m. 1919
Zenaida
Rashevska
*1898 †1963

ANDREW ══ 1921 Maria
*1879   *1872 †1971
†1956   d. of Felix
            Krzesinski

PRINCES
ROMANOVSKI-
ILYINSKI

GEORGE
Pr. Brassov
*1913 k.1931

PRINCES
ROMANOVSKI-
KRASINSKI
(ext. 1974)

OLGA   TATIANA   MARIA   ANASTASIA   ALEXIS
*1895   *1897   *1899   *1901   *1904
ex. 1918   ex. 1918   ex. 1918   ex. 1918   ex. 1918

Charles ══ 1925 MARIA
Pr. of Leiningen   *1907
*1898 †1946   †1951

Louis ══ 1938 KIRA
Ferdinand   *1909
Pr. of Prussia   †1967
*1907

VLADIMIR ══ 1948 (2) Leonida
GD. of Russia   *1914
*1917   d. of George
                Pr. Bagration-Mukhranski
                m. (1) 1934
                Sumner M. Kirby
                †1945

Pr. Francis ══ 1976 MARIA
William   *1953 (div.)
of Prussia
*1943

GEORGE
GD. of Russia *1981

arms of the Romanov family can be seen on Table 101 and show a griffin with sword and shield within a black border charged with gold and silver lions' heads. In 1698 Peter founded the Order of St Andrew, whose insignia surround the Russian eagle (Table 101). In 1721 he adopted the western title of emperor in addition to that of czar. It may be doubted whether the average boyar regarded a blazon as compensation for his beard.

His travels had impressed on Peter the need for an outlet to the sea. In 1709 his army destroyed that of Charles XII at Poltava and broke the myth of Swedish invincibility; but already in 1703 the Emperor had founded his new capital of St Petersburg. Not only did this barren site amid the lakes and pine forests burgeon into a romantically beautiful city, it was a symbol of Peter's westward vision. By the time of his death, this truly remarkable man had provided Russia with a civil administration, an army, a navy and a sea on which his fleet could sail. The ancestry of Peter the Great, which is displayed on Table 106, reveals that he was of pure Russian stock. This is in marked contrast to the ascending pedigrees of most of his descendants, where German blood tends to predominate.

Peter had taken powers to nominate his own successor, but did not exercise them. In consequence he was followed arbitrarily by his widow, his grandson, his niece and his daughter. None of them proved an outstanding ruler; too much influence came to rest in the hands of the Guard regiments, which often determined the succession. Peter himself had condemned to a cruel death his only son, for participating in a conspiracy; he had also divorced his first wife. Catherine I, the daughter of a Lithuanian peasant, became the mistress of two of Peter's generals and was passed on to their sovereign who eventually married her. At the end of his life only she could control his formidable outbursts of rage; as a ruler she was brief, frivolous and extravagant. At her demise the claims of Peter II could no longer be overlooked, but the hapless prince died of smallpox on what should have been his wedding day. A group of nobles now offered the Crown to Anne, Duchess of Kurland, daughter of Ivan V, on condition that she accepted the governance of a Grand Council and moved the capital back to Moscow. Anne accepted the condition, but annulled it as soon as she was firmly on the throne. She was an autocratic and unpleasant sovereign, resenting her long, dull years at Kurland; so frail had been her father that doubts were widely expressed as to her share of Romanov blood. The port of Azov on the Black Sea was captured during her reign.

Anne did appoint an heir, her great-nephew Ivan VI, whose major handicap was his age of two months. The prospect of a regency by his mother alarmed many, including the surviving daughter of Peter the Great. Elizabeth, though not born in wedlock, was an obvious rival to Ivan VI and was likely to be sent to a nunnery. Throwing herself on the mercy of the Preobrazhenski Guards (named from the village of her father's exile), she was swiftly raised to the throne in 1741. Her German cousins were all imprisoned, some of them for very long periods. Indeed it was under Elizabeth that French became to a large extent the court language of Russia.

The Empress was pretty, with a good figure, and a great taste for music and dancing. After other liaisons she made a morganatic marriage with Count Alexis Razumovski. As her heir she called to Russia the only remaining descendant of Peter the Great, the orphan child of her sister, had him converted to the Orthodox faith, and styled him Grand-Duke Peter. He was then married to his second cousin Sophie of Anhalt-Zerbst, who at her Orthodox baptism was named Catherine. Peter was short, ill-educated and said to look like a monkey; his intellect was limited, his morals loose and his main passion was the drilling of soldiers. Catherine was good-looking, well-read and an excellent judge of men; she never pretended to care for Peter, and some uncertainty hangs over the origin of her son Paul, born after nine years of wedlock.

CATHERINE THE GREAT

Peter III cherished a childlike adulation of Frederick the Great of Prussia; his first act was to throw away the Russian position in the Seven Years' War – its first European conflict – by offering Prussia an easy peace. He then freed the nobility of their duty to perform service under the Crown. Only six months after his accession another revolution of the palace guards proclaimed Catherine Empress and Peter deposed; he perished a few weeks later in custody, after a drunken brawl. Thus began the extraordinary reign of this obscure German princess, which lasted 34 years. In a sense she was haunted, if not by the fate of her husband, at least by the insecurity of her position. Her son was alive; so was Ivan VI in his fortress; she was enchained by her debt to the guards and to the gentry who officered them. Thus she could not give full play to her lively intelligence and liberal views; she ranks among the enlightened despots of her generation, but in Russia the stress was as much on despotism as on enlightenment. She was sensual but frugal; her acknowledged lovers were mostly of a large stature, and were not few in number.

Great territorial accessions marked her reign through the annexation of the Crimea (1783) and the partitions of Poland. South Russia was reorganized by Prince Potemkin, one of her favourites. A Black Sea fleet was formed: the port of

Sevastopol was founded. Meanwhile the administration of the Empire was refashioned; the ten provinces of Peter I were broken down to 50 provincial governments. In her old age the Empress, perhaps forgetful of her own accession, was profoundly shocked by the decapitation of Louis XVI of France. In all, she was probably not an originator, but a talented controller of the course of events.

Paul I (Table 104) had waited a long time in the wings; his brief appearance was dramatic. His wayward fancy fastened upon Napoleon much the same admiration as his father had bestowed upon Frederick. Many of his mother's acts were reversed; but in 1797 he prudently established succession by primogeniture. In 1798 he was elected Grand-Master of the Order of St John by some knights evicted from Malta. But his behaviour was unstable and capricious, his cruelty all too apparent. In 1801 a number of conspirators entered the palace, perhaps seeking only his abdication, and strangled him.

Alexander I at once cancelled many of his father's more oppressive edicts, such as the bans on foreign travel and foreign books. He had been educated under the direction of his grandmother and was sympathetic to reform. The political horizon abroad was dominated by the rise of Napoleon, but at home the new Emperor embarked on a considerable programme of education and also tried to check the sale of serfs. In 1805 he was defeated by Napoleon at Austerlitz, and again in 1807 at Eylau and Friedland; he then came to terms with Napoleon at Tilsit. At the same time he completed the conquest of Finland from Sweden, and shortly afterwards won Bessarabia from the Turks; to gratify the Finns he adopted the title of Grand-Duke of Finland. Meanwhile his relations with France deteriorated; in 1812 Napoleon launched his great attack on Russia. The eminent general Kutuzov held Napoleon at Borodino, but was obliged to abandon Moscow, which Napoleon occupied for a mere month. The horrors of the French retreat through an early winter are notorious. In 1813 Russia and Prussia defeated Bonaparte at Leipzig. The negotiations at Vienna were briefly interrupted by the Hundred Days and Waterloo, but then continued to remodel Europe.

Alexander saw himself as the saviour of Europe; he went on to envisage a league of Austria, Prussia and Russia, the three Powers which dominated eastern Europe. This 'Holy Alliance' soon proved to be reactionary and to be dominated by Metternich, the principal statesman of the Hapsburg Empire; against it was set the liberalism of the West in Europe and America associated with the name of Canning. The domestic policy of Alexander, after Waterloo, made few concessions to reform but did encourage some commercial revival after the wreckage of the wars.

Catherine the Great of Russia (1729–96) with her husband Peter III, whom she deposed, and her child, the future Paul I, by R. Mathieu, 1756.

On the whole he became more autocratic as he grew older; but his subjects, who had travelled in the West, were increasingly interested in the problems of liberty and began to form secret societies.

On the death of Alexander I his next brother, Constantine, because he had made a morganatic marriage, renounced the succession. The Crown passed to Nicholas I, not without a period of confusion; he had been trained as a soldier, and was regarded as a natural conservative. Not much was done to dispel this image. A rebellion in Poland was harshly suppressed in 1831, and the very use of the Polish

TABLE 105

RUSSIA
The Imperial House and the Revolution

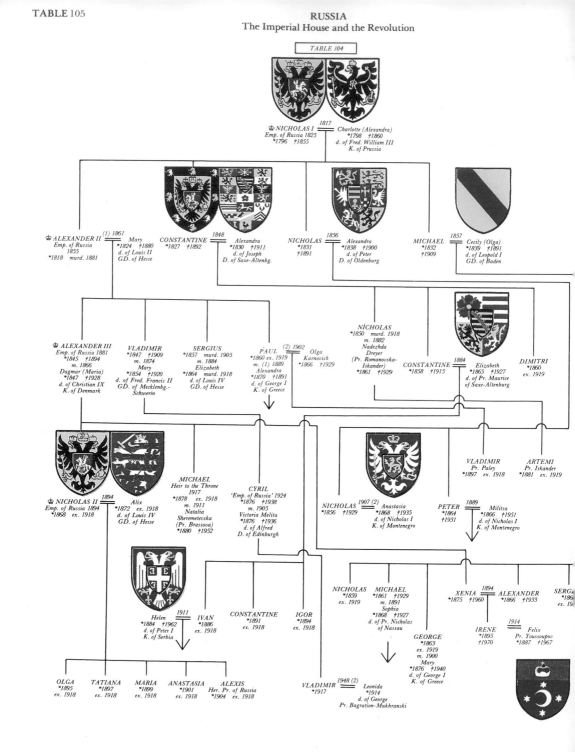

TABLE 104

♔ NICHOLAS I ═══ Charlotte (Alexandra)
Emp. of Russia 1825 *1798 †1860
*1796 †1855 d. of Fred. William III
K. of Prussia
1817

♔ ALEXANDER II ═══ Mary
Emp. of Russia *1824 †1880
1855 d. of Louis II
*1818 murd. 1881 GD. of Hesse
(1) 1861

CONSTANTINE ═══ Alexandra
*1827 †1892 *1830 †1911
d. of Joseph
D. of Saxe-Altenbg.
1848

NICHOLAS ═══ Alexandra
*1831 *1838 †1900
†1891 d. of Peter
D. of Oldenburg
1856

MICHAEL ═══ Cecily (Olga)
*1832 *1839 †1891
†1909 d. of Leopold I
GD. of Baden
1857

♔ ALEXANDER III ═══ Mary
Emp. of Russia 1881 Dagmar (Maria)
*1845 †1894 *1847 †1928
m. 1866 d. of Christian IX
K. of Denmark

VLADIMIR ═══ Mary
*1847 †1909 *1854 †1920
m. 1874 d. of Fred. Francis II
GD. of Mecklenbg.-
Schwerin

SERGIUS ═══ Elizabeth
*1857 murd. 1905 *1864 murd. 1918
m. 1884 d. of Louis IV
Elizabeth GD. of Hesse

PAUL ═══ Olga
*1860 ex. 1919 Karnovich
m. (1) 1889 *1866 †1929
Alexandra
*1870 †1891
d. of George I
K. of Greece
(2) 1902

NICHOLAS ═══ Elizabeth
*1850 murd. 1918 *1865 †1927
m. 1882 d. of Pr. Maurice
Nadezhda of Saxe-Altenburg
Dreyer
(Pr. Romanovska-
Iskander)
*1861 †1929

CONSTANTINE
*1858 †1915
1884

DIMITRI
*1860
ex. 1919

♔ NICHOLAS II ═══ Alix
Emp. of Russia 1894 *1872 ex. 1918
*1868 ex. 1918 d. of Louis IV
GD. of Hesse
1894

MICHAEL
Heir to the Throne
1917
*1878 ex. 1918
m. 1911
Natalia
Sheremetevska
(Pr. Brassova)
*1880 †1952

CYRIL
'Emp. of Russia' 1924
*1876 †1938
m. 1905
Victoria Melita
*1876 †1936
d. of Alfred
D. of Edinburgh

NICHOLAS ═══ Anastasia
*1856 †1929 *1868 †1935
d. of Nicholas I
K. of Montenegro
1907 (2)

PETER ═══ Militsa
*1864 *1866 †1951
†1931 d. of Nicholas I
K. of Montenegro
1889

VLADIMIR
Pr. Paley
*1897 ex. 1918

ARTEMI
Pr. Iskander
*1881 ex. 1919

Helen ═══ IVAN
*1884 †1962 *1896
d. of Peter I ex. 1918
K. of Serbia
1911

CONSTANTINE
*1891
ex. 1918

IGOR
*1894
ex. 1918

NICHOLAS
*1859
ex. 1919

MICHAEL ═══ Sophia
*1861 †1929 *1868 †1927
m. 1891 d. of Pr. Nicholas
of Nassau

XENIA ═══ ALEXANDER
*1875 †1960 *1866 †1933
1894

SERG
*186
ex. 19

GEORGE ═══ Mary
*1863 *1876 †1940
ex. 1919 d. of George I
m. 1900 K. of Greece

IRENE ═══ Felix
*1895 Pr. Youssoupov
†1970 *1887 †1967
1914

OLGA
*1895
ex. 1918

TATIANA
*1897
ex. 1918

MARIA
*1899
ex. 1918

ANASTASIA
*1901
ex. 1918

ALEXIS
Her. Pr. of Russia
*1904 ex. 1918

VLADIMIR ═══ Leonida
*1917 *1914
d. of George
Pr. Bagration-Mukhranski
1948 (2)

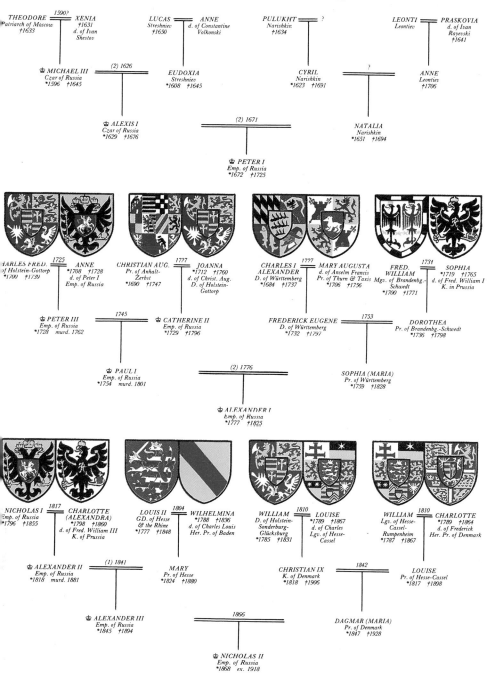

THEODORE
Patriarch of Moscow
†1633

— 1590? —

XENIA
†1631
d. of Ivan
Shestov

LUCAS
Streshniev
†1650

ANNE
d. of Constantine
Volkonski

PULUKHT
Narishkin
†1634

?

LEONTI
Leontiev

PRASKOVIA
d. of Ivan
Rayevski
†1641

♔ MICHAEL III
Czar of Russia
*1596 †1645

— (2) 1626 —

EUDOXIA
Streshniev
*1608 †1645

CYRIL
Narishkin
*1623 †1691

?

ANNE
Leontiev
†1706

♔ ALEXIS I
Czar of Russia
*1629 †1676

— (2) 1671 —

NATALIA
Narishkin
*1651 †1694

♔ PETER I
Emp. of Russia
*1672 †1725

CHARLES FRED.
of Holstein-Gottorp
*1700 †1739

— 1725 —

ANNE
*1708 †1728
d. of Peter I
Emp. of Russia

CHRISTIAN AUG.
Pr. of Anhalt-
Zerbst
*1690 †1747

— 1727 —

JOANNA
*1712 †1760
d. of Christ. Aug.
D. of Holstein-
Gottorp

CHARLES I
ALEXANDER
D. of Württemberg
*1684 †1737

— 1727 —

MARY AUGUSTA
d. of Anselm Francis
Pr. of Thurn & Taxis
*1706 †1756

FRED.
WILLIAM
Mgv. of Brandenbg.-
Schwedt
*1700 †1771

— 1731 —

SOPHIA
*1719 †1765
d. of Fred. William I
K. in Prussia

♔ PETER III
Emp. of Russia
*1728 murd. 1762

— 1745 —

♔ CATHERINE II
Emp. of Russia
*1729 †1796

FREDERICK EUGENE
D. of Württemberg
*1732 †1797

— 1753 —

DOROTHEA
Pr. of Brandenbg.-Schwedt
*1736 †1798

♔ PAUL I
Emp. of Russia
*1754 murd. 1801

— (2) 1776 —

SOPHIA (MARIA)
Pr. of Württemberg
*1759 †1828

♔ ALEXANDER I
Emp. of Russia
*1777 †1825

NICHOLAS I
Emp. of Russia
*1796 †1855

— 1817 —

CHARLOTTE
(ALEXANDRA)
*1798 †1860
d. of Fred. William III
K. of Prussia

LOUIS II
G.D. of Hesse
& the Rhine
*1777 †1848

— 1804 —

WILHELMINA
*1788 †1836
d. of Charles Louis
Her. Pr. of Baden

WILLIAM
D. of Holstein-
Sonderburg-
Glücksburg
*1785 †1831

— 1810 —

LOUISE
*1789 †1867
d. of Charles
Lgv. of Hesse-
Cassel

WILLIAM
Lgv. of Hesse-
Cassel-
Rumpenheim
*1787 †1867

— 1810 —

CHARLOTTE
*1789 †1864
d. of Frederick
Her. Pr. of Denmark

♔ ALEXANDER II
Emp. of Russia
*1818 murd. 1881

— (1) 1841 —

MARY
Pr. of Hesse
*1824 †1880

CHRISTIAN IX
K. of Denmark
*1818 †1906

— 1842 —

LOUISE
Pr. of Hesse-Cassel
*1817 †1898

♔ ALEXANDER III
Emp. of Russia
*1845 †1894

— 1866 —

DAGMAR (MARIA)
Pr. of Denmark
*1847 †1928

♔ NICHOLAS II
Emp. of Russia
*1868 ex. 1918

language was forbidden. In 1848 he showed his hand more clearly by sending a Russian army into Hungary to put down the insurrection there against the Hapsburgs. His armies made steady progress in the Caucasus; his diplomacy sought to dominate the Ottoman Empire and make Russia protector of the Balkans. In this field he encountered the rival aims of Britain and France. The Crimean War, one of the most futile struggles known to history, had begun before his death. The ancestry of Nicholas I, and equally of his elder brother Alexander I (Table 106), shows scant traces of Russian blood. Thanks to the policy of exogamic marriages, introduced by Peter the Great, the predominant strains are German, with Holstein and Prussia most evident. Alexander I was actually crowned as King of Poland and bore the blazons of Moscow and Poland over the Russian eagle (Table 104). His successors were less sympathetic to the Poles.

Alexander II, the eldest son of Nicholas I, came to the throne without difficulty. His first aim was to stop the war; he then announced his sympathy with the serfs. A considerable measure of emancipation was introduced in 1861, and was followed by large-scale legal reforms three years later. The press was liberated in St Petersburg; the universities were allowed a measure of freedom; regular budgets were introduced. On the other hand, a rising in Poland in 1863 was brutally repressed; the extensive secret police was ubiquitous; the ugly weapons of assassination and the sombre name of nihilism became part of Russian public life at all levels. The rich springs of Russian literature, associated with names like Turgenev, Dostoyevsky and Tolstoy, bubbled forth in his reign, but scarcely in his favour. Russian ambitions in the Balkans reached a high water mark in 1878 at the Treaty of San Stefano only to be cast down by the Treaty of Berlin. In 1881 Alexander II was killed by a bomb explosion.

Alexander III was a reactionary. His policy was one of nationalism, orthodoxy and autocracy. Minorities, who did not speak Russian or subscribe to the doctrines of the Eastern Church, were persecuted, including the Jews. At the beginning of his reign he supported the League of the Three Emperors (Germany, Austria and Russia), but gradually he came to suspect Germany and move towards France, with whom a military alliance was concluded in 1894. Huge areas of Asia were added to his dominions.

NICHOLAS II

Nicholas II was a simple, honest character who bore a striking facial resemblance to his first cousin, George V of England (their mothers were sisters). Pious, devoted to his wife, innocent of political sense, he was sadly ill-equipped to face the crises of his reign.

He believed in autocracy, but was reluctant to impose it. In 1904–5 Russia was catastrophically defeated in the Far East by Japan. In 1905, after a series of riots, which included the fragmentation by bomb of the Grand-Duke Sergius, a Duma, or parliamentary assembly, was granted by the Czar. It was a body with strictly limited powers, but it was gradually gaining experience until 1914, despite a mutual mistrust between Duma and government.

The savage ultimatum launched by Austria on Serbia, after the wanton murder of Francis Ferdinand in his own province of Bosnia, drew Russia to the defence of the tiny Kingdom in the Balkans, where for a century she had been posing as the protector of the Slavs. The massive and irreversible process of Russian mobilization was set on foot. Inexorably the Powers were plunged into war, for which Holy Russia was ill-trained and ill-equipped. The lack of incisive quality in the Czar became more apparent; in his anxiety for his late-born, much-loved, haemophiliac son, he leaned upon the strange gifts of the near-charlatan Rasputin. Revolution broke out in 1917; Nicholas abdicated in favour of his brother, but Michael declined the doubtful Crown unless offered by a popular assembly. It was the last act of Imperial Russia. In October the Bolsheviks seized power. Almost the first action of the new regime was to bring the war to an end.

For the doom-burdened dynasty of Romanov the end was drastic. The Czar and his family (Table 104) were taken to Yekaterinburg (Ural Mountains), and despite rumours to the contrary, it seems likely that they were all executed there in July 1918. Table 105 shows the ruthlessness with which their kinsfolk were eliminated by the Soviets, who were admittedly under pressure from military invasions in support of the fallen family. The ancestry of the weak but virtuous Nicholas II (Table 106) shows a spread of Germanic families; three lines of Hesse are represented and two of Denmark, to which his paternal line also pertained. Younger members of the family used the eagle of Russia, within a border derived from the original arms of Romanov (see Grand-Duke Constantine on Table 105). It should be noted that in 1856 the mounted horseman in the ancestral arms of the Czars of Moscow was turned to face the right (instead of looking left, contrary to western heraldic usage).

Today there is no emperor and autocrat of all the Russias. The claimant is the Grand-Duke Vladimir, first cousin of the last Czar. He has made an interesting marriage with a member of the ancient family of Bagration, sometime rulers of Georgia, which was annexed to Russia by Alexander I. The harp in the arms of Bagration (Table 104) asserts their descent from King David.

Chapter 26

GREECE

The name of Greece conjures up pictures of the Athens of Pericles and the splendour of the Acropolis, the heroic resistance to Persia or the tragedies of the Peloponnesian war. But the Hellas of that age was never united and preferred, on the whole, democratic forms of government to crowned monarchies. After the classical age the Greek peninsula was in turn part of the Macedonian, Roman and Byzantine empires; it enjoyed neither independence nor importance. At the end of the sixth century the Balkans were ravaged by Slav invaders. In the middle of the fifteenth century they became part of the Turkish (Ottoman) Empire and they thus remained until about a hundred and fifty years ago. But through all these vicissitudes the people of Greece clung to three things: their language, the Christian (Orthodox) religion and the memory of their glorious past.

One of the by-products of the French Revolution was a growth of nationalism among the European peoples subject to Turkish rule. The banner of revolt was raised in the Peloponnese in 1821, and the Greek insurgents were joined by many sympathizers, including the English poet Lord Byron. In 1827 a combined British, French and Russian naval force annihilated the Turkish fleet at Navarino. In 1832 the Great Powers established an independent state and chose Otto of Wittelsbach to be its first king (Table 107). The new Greece was of limited size, for its northern boundary ran from the Gulf of Arta to the Gulf of Volos. Otto was not a successful king; he brought numbers of Germans with him and tried to rule autocratically. The most memorable of his entourage was the Bavarian brewer Fuchs, whose name and products the Greeks have altered to Fix. In 1862 Otto abdicated; he was, as it happened, childless.

The Greeks wanted to have Alfred, Duke of Edinburgh, the son of Queen Victoria, but the Powers selected Prince William of Denmark, who became constitutional ruler of Greece as King George I of the Hellenes. Five of his descendants have since ruled. Great Britain handed over the Ionian Islands to inaugurate the new reign. The arms of Greece were a short cross, and the blue and white colours were copied from those of the Bavarian royal family, which can be seen on the small shield of Otto I

King George I of Greece (1845–1913), who founded the Greek royal family.

TABLE 107

GREECE
General survey

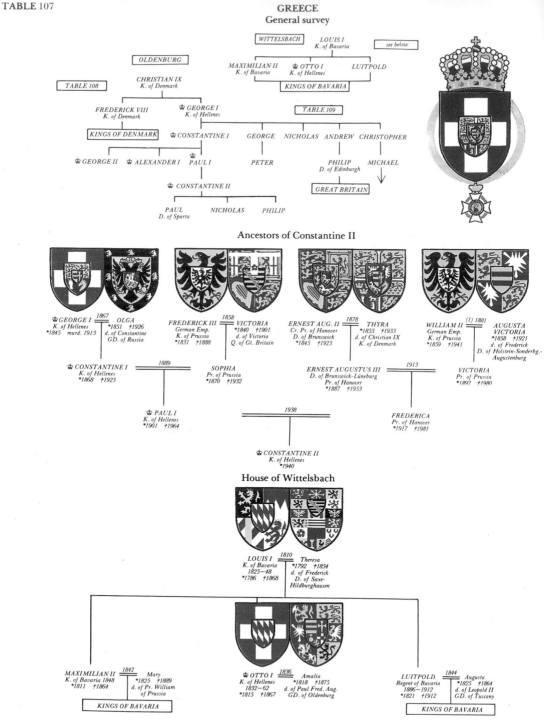

WITTELSBACH

LOUIS I
K. of Bavaria

see below

MAXIMILIAN II
K. of Bavaria

♔ OTTO I
K. of Hellenes

LUITPOLD

KINGS OF BAVARIA

OLDENBURG

CHRISTIAN IX
K. of Denmark

TABLE 108

FREDERICK VIII
K. of Denmark

♔ GEORGE I
K. of Hellenes

KINGS OF DENMARK

♔ CONSTANTINE I

GEORGE

NICHOLAS

ANDREW

CHRISTOPHER

TABLE 109

♔ GEORGE II

♔ ALEXANDER I

♔ PAUL I

PETER

PHILIP
D. of Edinburgh

MICHAEL

♔ CONSTANTINE II

GREAT BRITAIN

PAUL
D. of Sparta

NICHOLAS

PHILIP

Ancestors of Constantine II

♔ GEORGE I
K. of Hellenes
*1845 murd. 1913

—1867—

OLGA
*1851 †1926
d. of Constantine
GD. of Russia

FREDERICK III
German Emp.
K. of Prussia
*1831 †1888

—1858—

VICTORIA
*1840 †1901
d. of Victoria
Q. of Gt. Britain

ERNEST AUG. II
Cr. Pr. of Hanover
D. of Brunswick
*1845 †1923

—1878—

THYRA
*1853 †1933
d. of Christian IX
K. of Denmark

WILLIAM II
German Emp.
K. of Prussia
*1859 †1941

—(1) 1881—

AUGUSTA
VICTORIA
*1858 †1921
d. of Frederick
D. of Holstein-Sonderbg.-
Augustenburg

♔ CONSTANTINE I
K. of Hellenes
*1868 †1923

—1889—

SOPHIA
Pr. of Prussia
*1870 †1932

ERNEST AUGUSTUS III
D. of Brunswick-Lüneburg
Pr. of Hanover
*1887 †1953

—1913—

VICTORIA
Pr. of Prussia
*189? †1980

♔ PAUL I
K. of Hellenes
*1901 †1964

—1938—

FREDERICA
Pr. of Hanover
*1917 †1981

♔ CONSTANTINE II
K. of Hellenes
*1940

House of Wittelsbach

LOUIS I
K. of Bavaria
1825–48
*1786 †1868

—1810—

Theresa
*1792 †1854
d. of Frederick
D. of Saxe-
Hildburghausen

MAXIMILIAN II
K. of Bavaria 1848
*1811 †1864

—1842—

Mary
*1825 †1889
d. of Pr. William
of Prussia

KINGS OF BAVARIA

♔ OTTO I
K. of Hellenes
1832–62
*1815 †1867

—1836—

Amalia
*1818 †1875
d. of Paul Fred. Aug.
GD. of Oldenburg

LUITPOLD
Regent of Bavaria
1886–1912
*1821 †1912

—1844—

Augusta
*1825 †1864
d. of Leopold II
GD. of Tuscany

KINGS OF BAVARIA

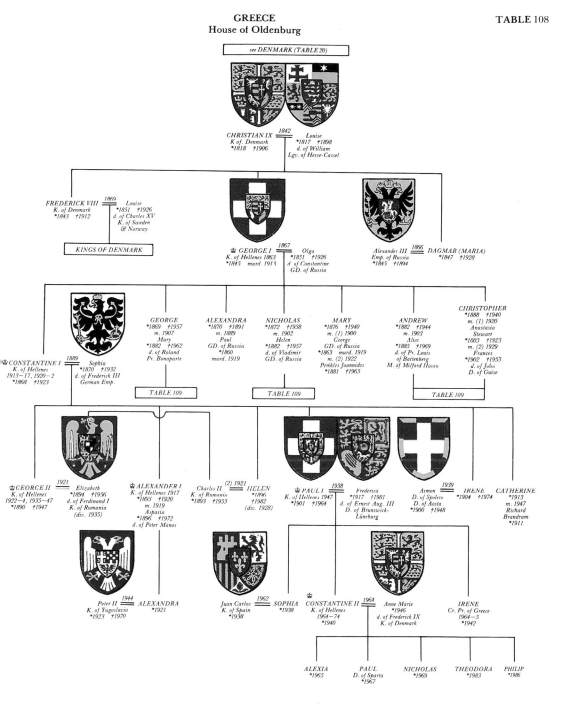

see DENMARK (TABLE 20)

CHRISTIAN IX — 1842 — *Louise*
K. of Denmark — *1817 †1898*
1818 †1906 — *d. of William*
Lgv. of Hesse-Cassel

FREDERICK VIII — 1869 — *Louise*
K. of Denmark — *1851 †1926*
1843 †1912 — *d. of Charles XV*
K. of Sweden & Norway

KINGS OF DENMARK

♔ **GEORGE I** — 1867 — *Olga*
K. of Hellenes 1863 — *1851 †1926*
1845 murd 1913 — *d. of Constantine GD. of Russia*

Alexander III — 1866 — **DAGMAR (MARIA)**
Emp. of Russia — *1847 †1928*
1845 †1894

♔ **CONSTANTINE I** — 1889 — *Sophia*
K. of Hellenes — *1870 †1932*
1913–17, 1920–2 — *d. of Frederick III*
1868 †1923 — *German Emp.*

GEORGE
1869 †1957
m. 1907
Mary
1882 †1962
d. of Roland
Pr. Bonaparte

ALEXANDRA
1870 †1891
m. 1889
Paul
GD. of Russia
1860
murd. 1919

NICHOLAS
1872 †1938
m. 1902
Helen
1882 †1957
d. of Vladimir
GD. of Russia

MARY
1876 †1940
m. (1) 1900
George
GD. of Russia
1863 murd. 1919
m. (2) 1922
Perikles Joannides
1881 †1965

ANDREW
1882 †1944
m. 1903
Alice
1885 †1969
d. of Pr. Louis
of Battenberg
M. of Milford Haven

CHRISTOPHER
1888 †1940
m. (1) 1920
Anastasia
Stewart
1003 †1923
m. (2) 1929
Frances
1902 †1953
d. of John
D. of Guise

TABLE 109

TABLE 109

TABLE 109

♔ **GEORGE II** — 1921 — *Elizabeth*
K. of Hellenes — *1894 †1956*
1922–4, 1935–47 — *d. of Ferdinand I*
1890 †1947 — *K. of Rumania*
(div. 1935)

♔ **ALEXANDER I**
K. of Hellenes 1917
1893 †1920
m. 1919
Aspasia
1896 †1972
d. of Peter Manos

Charles II — (2) 1921 — **HELEN**
K. of Rumania — *1896*
1893 †1953 — *1982*
(div. 1928)

♔ **PAUL I** — 1938 — *Frederica*
K. of Hellenes 1947 — *1917 †1981*
1901 †1964 — *d. of Ernest Aug. III*
D. of Brunswick-Lüneburg

Aimon — 1939 — **IRENE**
D. of Spoleto — *1904 †1974*
D. of Aosta
1900 †1948

CATHERINE
1913
m. 1947
Richard
Brandram
1911

Peter II — 1944 — **ALEXANDRA**
K. of Yugoslavia — *1921*
1923 †1970

Juan Carlos — 1962 — **SOPHIA**
K. of Spain — *1938*
1938

♔ **CONSTANTINE II** — 1964 — *Anne Marie*
K. of Hellenes — *1946*
1964–74 — *d. of Frederick IX*
1940 — *K. of Denmark*

IRENE
Cr. Pr. of Greece
1964–5
1942

ALEXIA
1965

PAUL
D. of Sparta
1967

NICHOLAS
1969

THEODORA
1983

PHILIP
1986

TABLE 109

GREECE
Collateral branches (sons of George I)

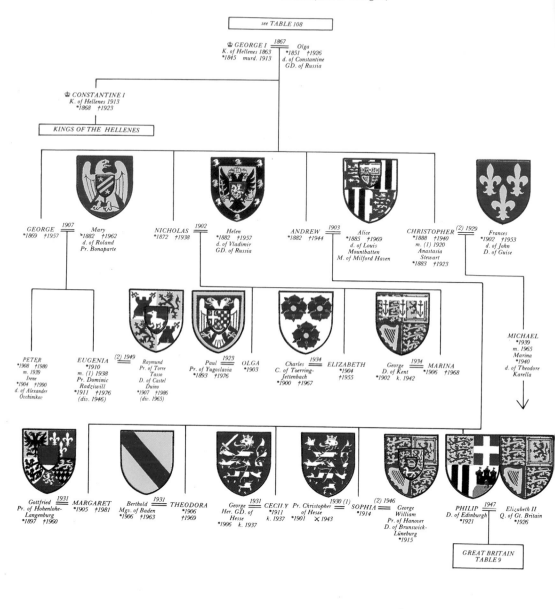

see TABLE 108

♔ GEORGE I — 1867 — Olga
K. of Hellenes 1863   *1851   †1926
*1845 murd. 1913   d. of Constantine
                           GD. of Russia

♔ CONSTANTINE I
K. of Hellenes 1913
*1868 †1923

KINGS OF THE HELLENES

GEORGE — 1907 — Mary   NICHOLAS — 1902 — Helen   ANDREW — 1903 — Alice   CHRISTOPHER — (2) 1929 — Frances
*1869 †1957   *1882 †1962   *1872 †1938   *1882 †1957   *1882 †1944   *1885 †1969   *1888 †1940   *1902 †1953
              d. of Roland   d. of Vladimir   d. of Louis   m. (1) 1920   d. of John
              Pr. Bonaparte   GD. of Russia   Mountbatten   Anastasia   D. of Guise
                                                                        M. of Milford Haven   Stewart
                                                                                       *1883 †1923

PETER   EUGENIA — (2) 1949 — Raymund   Paul — 1923 — OLGA   Charles — 1934 — ELIZABETH   George — 1934 — MARINA   MICHAEL
*1908 †1980 *1910   Pr. of Torre   Pr. of Yugoslavia *1903 C. of Toerring-   *1904   D. of Kent   *1906 †1968   *1939
m. 1939   m. (1) 1938   Tasso   *1893 †1976   Jettenbach   †1955   *1902 k. 1942   m. 1965
Irene   Pr. Dominic   D. of Castel   *1900 †1967   Marina
*1904 †1990 Radziwill   Duino   *1940
d. of Alexander *1911 †1976   *1907 †1986   d. of Theodore
Ovchinkov   (div. 1946)   (div. 1965)   Karella

Gottfried — 1931 — MARGARET   Berthold — 1931 — THEODORA   George — 1931 — CECILY   Pr. Christopher — 1930 (1) — SOPHIA — (2) 1946 — George   PHILIP — 1947 — Elizabeth II
Pr. of Hohenlohe-   *1905 †1981   Mgv. of Baden   *1906 †1969   Her. GD. of *1911   of Hesse   *1914   William   D. of Edinburgh   Q. of Gt. Britain
Langenburg   *1906 †1963   Hesse   k. 1937   *1901 ✕ 1943   Pr. of Hanover   *1921   *1926
*1897 †1960   *1906 k. 1937   D. of Brunswick-
                                                                                                                            Lüneburg
                                                                                                                            *1915

GREAT BRITAIN
TABLE 9

(Table 107). King George kept the cross but replaced the escutcheon of Wittelsbach with the blazon of the House of Denmark (Table 108). His long reign gave stability to Greece and witnessed a wide extension of her frontiers. In 1881 the Plain of Thessaly was added and in 1912–13 Greece, with her allies Serbia and Bulgaria, engaged in war with Turkey, triumphed and then fell out over the spoils. As a result Greece gained Crete and a large area of Macedonia including the important city and port of Salonika. Tragically, the venerable King was assassinated here by an idiot in the fiftieth year of his reign. It was the first of many misfortunes to his dynasty.

His son Constantine I had married a Prussian wife and been impressed by the glitter of German military might. The interests of his realm lay with the Allied Powers however; and in 1917 he left the country, nominating his second son Alexander as his successor. By the Treaty of Sèvres (1920) Greece was awarded almost all of Turkey in Europe (except Constantinople itself) and a considerable slice of Asia Minor round Smyrna. Unhappily in 1920 Alexander I was bitten by a pet monkey and died. In the election which followed the voters decided, against general expectation, in favour of King Constantine, who thus reigned again from 1920 to 1922, and excluded the distinguished statesman Venizelos. The victorious Allied Powers had not reckoned with the revival of Turkey under Mustafa Kemal; the Greeks were disastrously defeated in Asia Minor at the river Sakharia. In 1922 King Constantine left Greece a second time; on this occasion he abdicated in favour of his eldest son, and died soon after. The political scene was exceedingly disturbed and violent. The government, which was created after an uprising in Chios, actually executed five ministers and a general, blamed for the Sakharia disaster. At the end of 1923 King George II was advised to leave and in 1924 a plebiscite proclaimed Greece a republic. Grave social problems beset the new regime, since the small and barren state of Greece had to accept a large influx of refugees from Turkey and try to incorporate them into her meagre economy.

For eleven uneasy years the Republic endured, with a waxing revival of monarchic sentiment. At the end of 1935 another plebiscite restored King George II, who endeavoured to establish a constitutional monarchy. A sudden series of deaths among the better known politicians brought to power General Metaxas; and in 1936 he established a dictatorship. His authoritarian rule was resented, but he gave Greece heroic leadership when she was wantonly attacked by Italy in 1940. The Greeks held their own against the Fascist forces, but, even with British help, could not hold up the German attack in 1941 and the King and government went into exile. At the end of the war Greece was torn by civil war, launched by the Communists, but a plebiscite at the end of 1946 endorsed the return of George II. His Kingdom was augmented by the Dodecanese Islands, including Rhodes, which were ceded by Italy to Greece after the war. When he died, childless, in 1947 he was succeeded by King Paul, the third son of Constantine I to reign. Like his father, Paul had a German wife, Princess Frederica of Hanover.

On the death of King Paul in 1964, his son became Constantine II and married his distant cousin Princess Anne Mary of Denmark. As Table 107 demonstrates, the ancestry of the dethroned King is predominantly German, with a strong streak of Hohenzollern blood. The Order of the Redeemer beneath his shield was founded by Otto I in 1834 and adapted by George I in 1863. The difficult path of the Greek monarchy is not yet terminated. In 1967 elements of the army set up a military regime, the 'rule of the colonels'; at the end of that year the young King attempted a countermove which failed, and he was compelled to flee his realm. But though the increasingly harsh government of the officers crumbled into failure in 1974, the people of Greece voted at the end of that year against the monarchy. Accordingly the King and his heir, the Diadoch Paul, are still in exile. In the light of the many swings of opinion during this century, the idea of restoration cannot be eliminated but it would be a brave prophet who would predict the time and circumstances.

The younger descendants of King George I (Table 109) show a variety of alliances. One of the King's sons married a Bonaparte princess and another a Bourbon, an unusual combination. Two alliances linked Greece with England: Prince Nicholas was the father of Marina, Duchess of Kent, and Prince Andrew of the Duke of Edinburgh. The future sovereigns of the United Kingdom are, therefore, likely to stem back in the male line through George I of Greece to the royal House of Denmark.

INDEX

Figures in bold refer to Table numbers, all others to page numbers. Page numbers in italics refer to the black-and-white illustrations, which are either pictures of people or drawings of coats-of-arms at the head of each chapter. An asterisk indicates a heraldic term, which is usually explained on the first page referred to. Individuals are indexed under their family or country name, and a Table reference for an individual indicates that there is an illustration of the person's arms on that Table, although the person may also be found on other Tables referred to under the general, family or country heading.